# Business Marketing

## Connecting Strategy, Relationships, and Learning

**FOURTH EDITION**

**F. Robert Dwyer**
University of Cincinnati

**John F. Tanner, Jr.**
Baylor University

Boston   Burr Ridge, IL   Dubuque, IA   Madison, WI   New York   San Francisco   St. Louis
Bangkok   Bogotá   Caracas   Kuala Lumpur   Lisbon   London   Madrid   Mexico City
Milan   Montreal   New Delhi   Santiago   Seoul   Singapore   Sydney   Taipei   Toronto

**McGraw-Hill Irwin**

BUSINESS MARKETING: Connecting Strategy, Relationships, and Learning

Published by McGraw-Hill/Irwin, a business unit of The McGraw-Hill Companies, Inc., 1221 Avenue of the Americas, New York, NY, 10020. Copyright © 2009, 2006, 2002, 1999 by The McGraw-Hill Companies, Inc. All rights reserved. No part of this publication may be reproduced or distributed in any form or by any means, or stored in a database or retrieval system, without the prior written consent of The McGraw-Hill Companies, Inc., including, but not limited to, in any network or other electronic storage or transmission, or broadcast for distance learning.

Some ancillaries, including electronic and print components, may not be available to customers outside the United States.

This book is printed on acid-free paper.

3 4 5 6 7 8 9 0 QPD/QPD 0 9

ISBN 978-0-07-352990-5
MHID 0-07-352990-7

Editorial director:  *Brent Gordon*
Publisher:  *Paul Ducham*
Managing developmental editor:  *Laura Hurst Spell*
Editorial assistant:  *Sara Knox Hunter*
Associate marketing manager:  *Dean Karampelas*
Project manager:  *Dana M. Pauley*
Senior production supervisor:  *Debra R. Sylvester*
Design coordinator:  *Joanne Mennemeier*
Senior photo research coordinator:  *Jeremy Cheshareck*
Media project manager:  *Suresh Babu, Hurix Systems Pvt. Ltd.*
Cover design:  tbd
Typeface:  *10.75/12 Adobe Garamond*
Compositor:  *Aptara*
Printer:  *Quebecor World Dubuque Inc.*

**Library of Congress Cataloging-in-Publication Data**

Dwyer, F. Robert.
    Business marketing : connecting strategy, relationships, and learning / F. Robert Dwyer,
John F. Tanner, Jr. – 4th ed.
        p. cm.
    Includes index.
    ISBN-13: 978-0-07-352990-5 (alk. paper)
    ISBN-10: 0-07-352990-7 (alk. paper)
        1. Marketing. I. Tanner, John F. II. Title.
HF5415.D92 2009
658.8–dc22

                                                                                    2007049241

www.mhhe.com

# About the Authors

## F. Robert Dwyer

Dr. Dwyer received his MBA and PhD from the University of Minnesota and earned his bachelor's degree at Michigan State University. Prior to his academic career, he worked in a marketing position at Honeywell.

He is the Joseph S. Stern Professor of Marketing at the University of Cincinnati (UC) and currently serves as director of the Direct Marketing Policy Center. A member of the faculty at the University of Cincinnati since 1978, Dr. Dwyer also served on the faculty at Northwestern University's Kellogg Graduate School of Management and at the University of Arizona. His primary teaching areas include marketing channels, marketing strategy, and direct marketing. He brings a blend of rigor, interaction, relevance, and enthusiasm to the classroom that has resulted in two teaching awards at the University of Cincinnati. In 1991 he was named the Robert B. Clarke Direct Marketing Educator of the Year by the Direct Marketing Educational Foundation.

Professor Dwyer has published scores of articles in leading academic journals on the development and management of buyer–seller relationships. His most cited work is the *Journal of Marketing* article "Developing Buyer–Seller Relationships" which he wrote with business marketing expert Paul Schurr and noted Korean scholar Sejo Oh. He also boasts of his 1995 Best Article of the Year Award from the *Journal of Business-to-Business Marketing*, "Environment, Structure and Performance in Interfirm Exchange," co-authored with University of Kentucky professor Bob Dahlstrom (his former student) and gifted colleague Murali Chandrashekaran.

Dr. Dwyer serves on the editorial review boards of the *Journal of Interactive Marketing, Journal of Business & Industrial Marketing,* and *Journal of Business-to-Business Marketing,* among others. He has chaired the national conferences of the American Marketing Association and the Society of Franchising as well as the Direct Marketing Symposium, predecessor for today's Direct Marketing Educators' Conference.

Dedicated to the development of knowledge and the formation of human character even outside of the classroom, Dr. Dwyer is active in youth soccer, co-founder of the boys' club Millennium Falcon$_{24k}$, faculty advisor to several student groups, and co-founder and former board vice president of the private independent school Royalmout Academy. His consulting clients include many Cincinnati-area companies, and he has provided marketing and strategy training for executives at Lee Enterprises, Steelcraft, Hoxworth Blood Center, the Ssangyong Group, and other companies.

# John F. Tanner, Jr.

John F. "Jeff" Tanner Jr. is professor of marketing at Baylor University's Hankamer School of Business. Dr. Tanner spent eight years in marketing and sales with Rockwell International and Xerox Corporation. In 1988, Dr. Tanner earned his PhD from the University of Georgia and joined the faculty at Baylor University, where he serves as the research director of the Center for Professional Selling. He has taught marketing and sales to executives and business school students in France, Canada, Mexico, and India.

Dr. Tanner has received several awards for teaching and research, including the Business Deans Association Innovative Achievement Award. He is author or co-author of 11 books, including the best-selling textbook, *Selling: Building Partnerships* and his latest with George Dudley, *The Hard Truth about Soft Selling.* His books have been translated into several languages and distributed in over 30 countries. Dr. Tanner has published over 50 articles in trade publications such as *Business Marketing, Marketing Management,* and *Exhibitor Times* and over 50 research articles in academic journals such as the *Journal of Marketing, Journal of Business Research,* and *Journal of Personal Selling and Sales Management.* His research has won numerous awards, including Best Paper of the Year, 2000 from the *Journal of Personal Selling & Sales Management.*

Dr. Tanner and his wife have four children, and live on Jett Creek Farm in Central Texas, where they also raise horses.

# Dedication

*To Y.K.C., Kathy, Chris, Mike, Matt, Dan, and John*

*Bob Dwyer*

*To Karen, and my favorite "students," Emily, Ted, John, and Travis*

*Jeff Tanner*

# Contents in Brief

# Part 4

## *Managing Programs and Customers*

# Contents

# Part 3

## Business Marketing Programming

**Chapter 10**    **Creating Customer Dialogue**    **284**

# Part 4

## *Managing Programs and Customers*

# Preface

Welcome to the fourth edition of *Business Marketing: Connecting Strategy, Relationships, and Learning*. What makes this edition different, necessary?

For this edition, we had several goals:

- **Expand the coverage of services** and focus on the concept of "offerings" rather than product or services. This coverage is consistent with a service dominant logic of marketing.
- **Give students a glimpse of who does marketing** so they can see what their options are. One From the Field in each chapter is now a personal profile, written by a marketing practitioner about what he or she does. These boxes are also integrated into the chapter content in an effort to pique student curiosity and encourage reading of the sidebars.
- **Focus students on consideration of ethics;** we accomplished this objective by developing ethics-based discussion questions for each chapter, in addition to expanding coverage in the chapter. Each chapter also has at least one Business 2 Business box that considers ethics in relation to that chapter.
- **Incorporate more international or global examples and topics.** This text has always been well received in Europe and Asia; the requests for more global coverage come from U.S. users. We've accomplished this goal in two ways. First, one From the Field in each chapter has global examples or covers a topic of global importance. Second, we've expanded global examples within chapters.
- **Update pedagogical features** such as discussion questions, caselets, and cases. You will find at least several new discussion questions and a new caselet in each chapter.
- **New cases,** original to the text. In this edition there are six new cases, all original to this text. Cases are hard to come by, especially good ones. We hope you agree that these are the good ones!

Other changes to the book include:

Chapter 2—Stronger examples of relationships in business marketing, along with the latest research.

Chapter 3—Expanded coverage of supply chain management, including new topics such as strategic sourcing, and the impact of demand planning and the customer's customer on supply chain management. New trends in purchasing are also covered.

Chapter 4—Integrated individual buying theories for better understanding; included latest research on marketing to buying centers and how relationships form.

Chapter 5—Covers recent customer lifetime value methodology improvements, as well as updates segmentation approaches and tools to assess market potential.

Chapter 6—Provides a fresh look at forming a market orientation, including strategic perspectives derived from a customer "service logic."

Chapter 7—Recent research on marketing/finance interface, marketing/selling issues, and customer-centric culture is covered.

Chapter 8—Service dominant logic is covered; emphasis is on "offering" rather than product development. Customer relationship management's impact on new offering development is a focus, and the finances of new offering evaluation are clarified.

Chapter 9—Sharpens its focus on contemporary issues in channel management using construction and IT settings.

Chapter 10—Simplifies the approach to developing integrated marketing communications and gives increased emphasis to B2B brand building.

Chapter 11—Introduces topics such as event sponsorship, outdoor advertising effectiveness in B2B, and better coverage of media selection and creative development.

Chapter 12—Provides an updated view of online marketing, including SEM, e-mail within a permissions marketing context, and social media.

Chapter 13—Emphasis on sales as the position in which most students begin their B2B marketing career, along with discussion of the opportunity. Expanded coverage with strong examples of nonselling roles for salespeople, with special focus on customer knowledge responsibility. CLV-based segmentation strategy and effort allocation are also covered.

Chapter 14—Boosts its tutorial flavor on pricing tools and provides expanded coverage on negotiation.

Chapter 15—Greater focus on dashboards, as well as CLV-based metrics. Introduces concept of customer equity and ROMI (return on marketing investment).

Chapter 16—Incorporates recent research on CRM and streamlines coverage of several topics.

# Teaching Features

**Opening company profiles**—we've retained this popular feature; however, in addition to updating favorite company profiles like BASF, we've written new profiles for new companies in at least half the chapters. We've also purposely searched for services providers in order to strengthen the services flavor of this text. Companies profiled are:

| Chapter | Company | Comment |
| --- | --- | --- |
| 1 | BASF | Updated |
| 2 | Cessna | Updated |
| 3 | Ericsson | New |
| 4 | WebEx | New |
| 5 | FedEx | Updated |
| 6 | Dell | New |
| 7 | Eaton | New |
| 8 | EMC | New; shift from Chapter 13 |

| 9  | NEBS/Deluxe   | Updated |
|----|---------------|---------|
| 10 | Charrette     | Updated |
| 11 | Tektronix     | New     |
| 12 | ZoomInfo      | New     |
| 13 | HP            | New     |
| 14 | DuPont        | Updated |
| 15 | Rockwell      | New     |
| 16 | Plumtree/BEA  | Updated |

**Learning objectives**—each chapter opens with action-oriented learning objectives reflecting Bloom's taxonomy. An excellent Test Bank has been created based on these objectives; however, you can also use these to create your own essay questions.

**Personal profiles**—as mentioned earlier, we've created personal profiles (one From the Field in each chapter) that illustrate what people actually do in business marketing. Our thanks to the following individuals for providing their personal profile.

| Emily Tanner     | E-Rewards                    |
|------------------|------------------------------|
| Brad Bischof     | Stimulys Performance Marketing |
| Bobby Johnson    | Tymco                        |
| Jeff Pedowitz    | Eloqua                       |
| Kim Harris       | dunnhumby USA                |
| David Stein      | Convergys                    |
| David Dubroff    | Cypress Care                 |
| Tim Pavlovich    | Dell                         |
| Ed Jaroszewicz   | Ground Heaters               |
| Patty Bloomfield | Northlich                    |
| Paul Taroli      | CSC                          |
| Dave Allen       | Jaap-Orr                     |
| Kurt Knapton     | E-Rewards                    |
| Dan Ward         | Reynolds + Reynolds          |
| Bruce Culbert    | i-Symmetry                   |
| Bernie Joyce     | Harte-Hanks                  |

**Business 2 Business boxes**—each chapter has at least two of these boxes which are designed to encourage students to reflect on the chapter material. At least one contains consideration of ethical issues related to the chapter material. *We find students will read and consider these questions if you will point out that exam questions are often based on these features.*

**From the Field boxes**—two, including one personal profile, are found in each chapter. The second From the Field includes greater depth of issues around technology and global considerations. Many of these are original to this text, based on our own interviews of business marketing practitioners.

**Key terms** can be found at the end of each chapter. Each key term is in bold print in the chapter's sentence in which the definition is located. Further, each key term is also found in what is arguably the most comprehensive **Glossary** of any business marketing text. We've made a significant effort to include both academic terms and the jargon of the field.

**Discussion questions**—each chapter has at least 10, including two or more that focus on ethical considerations. We also attempt to integrate material across chapters in these questions.

**Caselets**—two or three follow each chapter; all are original to this book. These short cases are designed for homework or in-class use. The purpose is to provide opportunity for greater synthesis than in a discussion question without the depth of analysis of a full case. Some, though, do have data that must be analyzed.

**Additional readings** are provided for upper-level or graduate courses. These readings represent the most recent relevant research, and may also be used by students as a place to begin research on term papers.

**Comprehensive cases** are found at the end of the book. These full-length cases are designed to integrate material across several chapters. There are at least six new cases, three of which were written specifically for this book. Frankly, finding good, current business marketing cases is difficult, which is why we've written our own. We also encourage you to write cases and ask that you consider allowing us to incorporate them into future editions.

The *Instructor's Manual* contains several features that adopters will find useful as indicated below.

**Lecture notes**—we've included some ideas for class lectures based on our experience. We'd love to hear from you as to what works for you, so we can include that in future manuals (with credit of course!).

**Case teaching notes**—each professor teaches cases somewhat differently, but authors of cases have submitted teaching notes that can provide you with an idea as to how v students will respond to the case.

**Slides**—in the previous edition, John Thompson at TCU did a masterful job of creating slides that go beyond the exhibits in the book. This time around, though, we've also added more exhibits from the book so you will find more slides than ever before.

**Answers**—of course, we've got our answers to discussion questions, the B2B box features, caselets, and so forth.

**Test Bank**—this edition's Test Bank has been improved based on feedback provided directly from the people who use it in the classroom.

# Acknowledgments

Any textbook is a collaborative effort, just as teaching is. We appreciate all of you who have offered comments and support at conferences, by e-mail, or by telephone. We especially want to recognize the efforts of reviewers. Thanks to:

Andrew C. Gross, Cleveland State

Lee Richardson, University of Baltimore

Brian Rutherford, Purdue

And one reviewer who wished to remain anonymous.

Other faculty around the world have also given us cases and other material. These wonderful people put in a lot of time and effort into making these cases outstanding teaching tools. Susan Schertzer, for example, provided not only a case but also ideas that improved the text. In appreciation of their gifts to the book and to teaching of business marketing, we'd like to thank:

Raul Benavides, Baylor University

Roger Davis, Baylor University

David Eppright, University of West Florida

Mauricio Gonzalez, Tulane University

Ralph Oliva, Penn State University
Lou Pelton, University of North Texas
Constantine Polychroniou, University of Cincinnati
Salvador Trevino, ITESM, Mexico
Margit Weisgal, Sextant Communications
Jakki Mohr, University of Montana

The creative support and encouragement from the McGraw-Hill staff have been exemplary. We really appreciate the quality of work done by Laura Spell, Sara Hunter, Dana Pauley, Debra Sylvester, Joanne Mennemeier, and Jeremy Cheshareck.

A number of people assisted with manuscript preparation, including Ruth Pedersen, W. T. Tanner, Lisa Tyus, Adrienne Battles, J. R. Tanner, and Raul Benavides. In addition, we've received helpful comments from our students (and yours) who have used the text. They deserve our thanks, as do others who prefer to remain anonymous.

**Bob Dwyer**
bob.dwyer@uc.edu

**Jeff Tanner**
jeff_tanner@baylor.edu

# Business Marketing
## Connecting Strategy, Relationships, and Learning

# Part I

# Business Markets and Business Marketing

Congratulations! You have opened the book—really the door—to the dynamic world of business marketing. Get ready to explore a world that is brand new to most students.

We have organized *Business Marketing* into four parts. Briefly, Part 1 orients you to some of the unique phenomena and players in business markets. Part 2 delves into the world of strategic scanning, planning, and spanning in a business context in order to deliver superior value to customers. Part 3 covers the key areas of business marketing programming, from product development and channel management to the integration of advertising, trade shows, personal selling, Web sites, and more into a fitting communication strategy. Part 4 closes the book with critical concepts for evaluating and controlling marketing efforts and retaining customers.

Has Nestlé ever sent a specialist to your home to help you make the perfect iced tea for your weekend barbecue? In business markets, a seller's personnel sometimes work directly with the customer. They help the customer define specifications and test new products; plan delivery schedules; train production, sales, and service personnel; and, inevitably, "fight fires." In fact, exchange of personnel is just one means that buyer and seller in business markets *relate*. Part 1 provides the spectrum of buyer–seller relationships in business markets and addresses key motivations and challenges for their longevity.

Part 1 also distinguishes the business market from the more familiar consumer market in terms of its magnitude and volatility. More than a limited exposure to the varied relationships between organizations, we bet you have not purchased $40,000 of Steelcase furniture or invited participation by Service Master, Cintas, and other in a reverse auction for the opportunity to clean your apartment, nor have you received an invitation to stop by the Westvaco (envelopes) booth at the Promotion Management Association's Trade Show and Convention. Thus, Part 1 previews important distinctions on the concentration of participants, the types of products and customers, and formal and social dimensions of the purchasing process.

So let's get down to business. Part 1 introduces the fundamental character of business markets and the nature of decision making and purchasing by organizational customers—the very foundation for the strategic thinking we take up in Part 2.

# Chapter 1

## Introduction to Business Marketing

### BASF

For over a decade, BASF has advertised on TV that "We don't make the products you buy, we make them better." What is BASF? You may own a videotape or DVD made by BASF, but most of its products are not available directly to consumers. From its advertising campaigns, it appears that it doesn't exactly make anything (actually it makes chemicals), but it does make snowboards stronger, mattresses softer, boots drier, houses livelier, and carpets longer lasting. Can you go out and buy a BASF product to make your carpet longer lasting? No. So why does BASF continue to advertise on TV? Who is its audience?●

Its advertising is directed at the women and men who purchase products for their companies and to those people who design products such as snowboards, mattresses, and carpets. The purpose of the television ads is to create the image that BASF creates value in those products. BASF hopes that when its salespeople call on the buyers for snowboard, mattress, and carpet manufacturers, those buyers will recognize the BASF name, remember what BASF does, and let the salesperson in.●

BASF further supports its salespeople with a Web site, advertising in trade publications, and exhibits at trade shows that continue the same theme of making things better. All of these marketing efforts are aimed at reaching the persons responsible for deciding what the final product (be it a mattress, snowboard, or carpet) will be, how it will be designed to compete, and the bundle of benefits it will provide.●

The German company has annual revenues greater than 50 billion euros (or $74 billion), with 24 percent of its business in North America. Growth in North America accounts for most of the company's growth for the past few years. The company operates five divisions: oil and gas, plastics and fibers, chemicals, colorants and finishing products, and health and nutrition. As you can see, most of its products are intended for commercial users. ●

BASF says, "We don't make a lot of the products you buy; we make a lot of the products you buy *better*." ●

Visit BASF's home page: **www.basf.com.** ●

## LEARNING OBJECTIVES

As you can see from the BASF story, you've probably encountered business-to-business marketing (or just business marketing, for short) without actually realizing it. Students are more familiar with consumer marketing, because they are the targets of consumer marketing. But the opportunities for careers in marketing are particularly attractive for students who enter business marketing (the marketing of products and services to other businesses). In this chapter, we introduce business marketing.

*After reading this chapter, you should be able to*

- Define and explain the nature of business marketing.
- Illustrate the different types of business markets and how they differ from consumer markets.
- Discuss the nature of demand for business products and services.
- Explain the different approaches to business marketing, as typified in the relationships between buyers and sellers.

Business marketing is not the same as marketing to consumers. As you will see in this chapter, there are many differences that make business marketing unique and stimulating. At the same time, you will find what you learned in previous marketing courses to be helpful as you advance through this course.

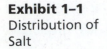

**Exhibit 1–1**
Distribution of
Salt

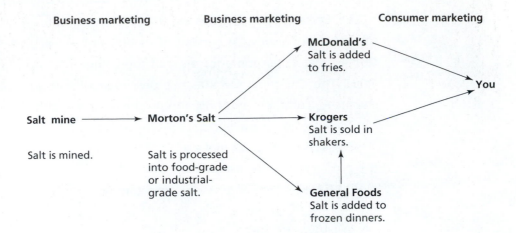

# THE IMPORTANCE OF BUSINESS MARKETS

How much salt does the average household in the United States use each year? Total food-grade salt sales for the United States are 1.33 million pounds annually. Consumption in the household, however, is 7 to 8 grams per day per person, which only equates to 824 thousand pounds. Why the difference? The consumption figure doesn't count the amount of salt that is in processed foods (such as frozen dinners) or foods we purchase in restaurants. Businesses purchase and use over 500,000 pounds of food-grade salt per year, or almost 40 percent of total salt sales, for such purposes as making pickles, breakfast cereals, and other food products.[1] Add to this amount the volume of industrial-grade salt (for such uses as chemical processes and salting frozen roads), and the industrial purchases of salt tower over consumer purchases.

To look at the magnitude of industrial purchases a little differently, consider that General Motors spends more than $58 billion per year on products and services—more than the gross national product of Portugal or Greece. General Motors employs over 1,350 purchasing agents, who *each* spend over $31 million annually! There are few consumers with that kind of spending power!

Most students, when they think of marketing, consider the marketing aimed at influencing their personal purchasing, which is marketing to consumers. Consumer purchases, however, represent a smaller dollar value than business purchases. Although marketing to consumers may be more obvious, more students will enter business marketing after graduation than consumer marketing.

**Business marketing** is marketing products or services to other companies, government bodies, institutions (such as hospitals), and other organizations. McDonald's and other companies buy products, such as salt, and services to use in the production of their product. Exhibit 1–1 illustrates a few of the possibilities for food-grade salt. Morton Salt also sells salt to food processors like General Foods (which use it in the food products they make) and to retailers (which sell salt to you). With the exception of the purchase you make, all of the buying and selling in the exhibit involves business marketing.

Business marketing also includes the marketing of products and services that facilitate their operations. For example, McDonald's purchases paper to run through its copiers. Copies facilitate McDonald's real business, which is making hamburgers and fries. Marketing to government agencies and institutions (which also buy salt for cafeterias and other such uses) such as your college or university is also business marketing.

# Why Study Business Marketing?

Business marketing is an exciting area of study. Students may be more familiar with consumer marketing; after all, everyone is a consumer. Business marketing, however, is new to most students. It is not the same as consumer marketing, and there are several compelling reasons for studying business marketing.

## Marketing Majors Begin in Business Marketing

Are you a marketing major? More marketing majors find jobs with businesses that sell products or services to other businesses rather than with businesses that sell to consumers. For that reason alone, it seems worthwhile to study business marketing. Recent college graduate, Emily Tanner, describes her start in business marketing in From the Field 1–1.

Indeed, the majority of business school graduates—whether in accounting, finance, logistics, management, production, real estate, or quantitative methods—will find themselves working at firms doing business with other organizations. Many companies have awakened to the fact that they must be market driven if they are to survive. Being market driven means that customer satisfaction and operational efficiency are the order of the day for every department and individual employee or associate. Market driven means that at many organizations, individuals with complementary expertise and skills work in teams to constantly strive to serve organizational customers better, to innovate, and to develop the means to approach new institutional markets. This book prepares you to make positive contributions to such teams in the business marketing environment.

## Magnitude of Business Marketing

One reason that more marketing majors begin their careers in business marketing than in consumer marketing is because of the magnitude of business marketing. Purchases by organizations such as companies, government agencies, and institutions account for more than half of the economic activity in industrialized countries such as the United States, Canada, and France, making business marketing an important activity. As mentioned earlier, few consumers have the purchasing power of an organization. Understanding how organizations buy is important to marketers who want to capitalize on the size of the business market.

## Business Marketing Is Unique

There would be no point in having a separate business marketing class if business marketing were the same as marketing to consumers. If one type of marketing fits all situations, then only one set of classes would be required. The way organizations buy is radically different from the way consumers purchase products and services, which results in different marketing requirements. Let's examine some ways in which business marketing is unique.

## 1–1

### FROM THE FIELD

## Starting a Career in Business Marketing

When I took Business Marketing at TCU my junior year, I really had no idea what I would do after I graduated. I just hoped my first job would be fun and exciting and present opportunities to develop a set of skills to use throughout my career. I got more than I could have ever hoped for. In the past two years since I graduated, I've been able to touch a number of different aspects of my company's marketing and sales initiatives, and have been able to really control my career path. The following is a look back at how I have arrived at where I am today.

The summer after I graduated, I obtained an internship at e-Rewards, Inc., an online market research company. The company was relatively small and growing, and due to that growth, the summer position presented me with many unique opportunities including assisting the EVP of Sales in developing sales performace tracking and forecasting. Upon completion of the internship, e-Rewards offered me a full-time position to support some of the day-to-day sales and marketing tasks of organization. In this role, I expanded my knowledge of the company and the overall market research industry by supporting the sales team in helping develop marketing brochures, advertising campaigns, and coordinating trade shows.

The company continued to grow rapidly, and after a year, we had hired seven people to support the sales and marketing function, creating a role known as Sales Support, which I managed as the team leader. In addition to coordinating marketing initiatives, we also wrote sales proposals and assisted sales managers and directors in calculating pricing for quote requests.

After a year in a half in my role leading the Sales Support team, I decided to pursue a role as a sales manager on the Healthcare Sales Team. I had developed a strong interest in the area and felt there was a lot of opportunity within the group. Healthcare market research was a new division in the company, and as e-Rewards had previously focused on other markets. I felt there was great growth potential in this niche market. In the first six months with the division, we had grown the team to four people and grown our customer base substantially. In this new role, I have also been presented with opportunities to represent the company at various conferences and trade shows, both domestically and internationally.

Looking back on the time since graduation, I can't imagine any other opportunity that could have been better. Business marketing companies may not be household words, but we do everything the consumer companies do and more. By choosing to start my career with an emerging organization like e-Rewards, I have been presented with the opportunity to contribute more to an organization in a shorter time than I would have anywhere else.

Emily Tanner, Sales Manager, Healthcare Solutions, e-Rewards.

## BUSINESS MARKETING VS. CONSUMER MARKETING

Business marketing differs in that channels of distribution are shorter and more direct, there is more emphasis on personal selling and negotiation, the Web is fully integrated, and complex buying processes result in unique promotional strategies. Relationships are also different between buyer and seller when both are organizations than when one is an individual consumer. Because relationships are so important (indeed, relationship marketing is a major theme of this book), we'll discuss it first. Exhibit 1–2 summarizes how business-to-business marketing differs from consumer marketing.

**Exhibit 1–2**
Business
Marketing Is
Unique

| How Business Marketing Differs | Example |
| --- | --- |
| Varying buyer–seller relationships | Relationships can be deep and involve several layers of the industry: BASF partners with Gaskell and GM, for example. |
| Shorter distribution channels | BASF sells fibers *direct* to DuPont for the manufacture of carpet and through distributors to smaller companies. |
| Greater emphasis on personal selling | BASF salespeople work directly with fire departments to sell the latest fire-fighting chemicals and ensure that they are used properly. |
| Greater Web integration | BASF uses its *cc-markets* Web site to create a communication space with special customers. |
| Unique promotional strategies | BASF exhibits at trade shows like Powder Coatings Europe, a show held every January in Amsterdam. |
| Consumption | Consumption of business products is by organizations who are then dependent on other markets, so how much carpet protectant BASF can sell to DuPont depends on how much carpet DuPont can sell. |
| Knowledge of customer's customer | BASF has to understand both consumers (of carpet, for example) and manufacturers like DuPont, not just consumers. |
| Marketing research | In smaller direct markets (such as carpet manufacturers), marketing research techniques tend toward qualitative. |

# Buyer–Seller Relationships

In consumer markets, there are few industries where close personal relationships exist between buyer and seller. Perhaps in those instances where personal selling is the most important element of the marketing mix and where customer service is also important, relationships between buyer and seller may exist. These situations, however, are rare.

In business marketing, situations where strong personal and business relationships grow between buyer and seller are not as rare. The strategic importance of many purchases is too great for companies to always shop around when making a purchase; they need to make absolutely sure that the product fits their needs and that it will be available when needed at the right cost. Therefore, many companies enter into long-term contracts, build relationships that enable buyers and sellers to plan jointly, and work to secure the future for both companies.

For example, BASF is a world leader in carpet fiber manufacturing. General Motors is constantly looking for ways to make cars and trucks less expensive to manufacture, as well as increasing the value delivered to consumers. BASF and GM work together with Gaskell plc. (a British carpet manufacturer) to improve the quality as well as the looks and life of automotive carpets. Note that the relationship extends from BASF to Gaskell to GM; a common element of business marketing is deep relationships between organizations at various levels of the industry. From the perspective of BASF, it makes sense to have a strong relationship with its customer, Gaskell. But it also makes sense for BASF to include Gaskell's customers so that they can all work together.

## 1–1

## BUSINESS 2 BUSINESS

### Fishing for Business

One company holds a series of fishing tournaments in which company employees are paired with customers and they compete for prizes. At first, the company was unsure of these tournaments' value. After all, not everyone likes to fish. Over time, however, it found friendships developing between employees and customers who ordinarily wouldn't have a chance to communicate, yet whose livelihoods depended heavily on each other. Not only has business grown as a result, both employees and customers are more satisfied with the company. Would it matter whether the fishing trip was an all-expenses paid holiday at a Caribbean isle or a cookout at a local lake? Just how important are social relationships in business?

## Shorter Distribution Channels

In most cases, distribution channels do not include anyone between the manufacturer and the customer who uses the product, or user. Many manufacturers sell directly to the user, which reflects a large difference between business marketing and consumer marketing. (Note that in some consumer situations, such as with Allstate Insurance or Burpee Seeds, there are direct channels, but companies with direct channels are much fewer there than in business marketing.) In situations where industrial distributors are used, there are still fewer steps between the consumer and manufacturer.

Shorter channels contribute to the closer relationship between manufacturer and buyer. Buyers can have more direct input into the product planning process. Direct relationships between various functional areas within both companies can result; for example, the accounts payable department of the buyer may talk directly with the billing department of the seller if problems arise.

## Emphasis on Personal Selling

Stronger relationships and shorter channels are two reasons why there is a greater emphasis on personal selling in business marketing. Salespeople are the members of the organization responsible for coordinating their company's efforts at satisfying their customers. That responsibility is greater when the organization is concerned about creating and maintaining partnerships with its customers.

Complex buying procedures involving many members of the buying organization also require personal selling. Only through personally getting to know each individual and coordinating the sales–purchase process can a business be successful. Multiple personal relationships can strengthen organizational relationships, and these relationships are the responsibility of the salesperson.

A customer's size and a direct channel also increase the importance of negotiation. Large orders sold directly by the manufacturer to the user or OEM (original equipment manufacturer) buyer increase the likelihood of negotiation because changes can be made to the product and price. There is greater flexibility in the seller's offering, increasing the potential for negotiating the final deal and adding to the importance of personal selling.

# Greater Web Integration

One unique aspect of business marketing is how the Web is used. The Web becomes the backbone of a supplier/customer communication network that enables customers to track shipment information, order products at prices and terms agreed to by the salesperson and buyer, and access other account information that helps manage the supply process. For example, if you visit the BASF Web site, you wouldn't know that they have special Web sites for customers. But if you visited Dell's site, you would see password-protected access for special customers. BASF has created special pages, in conjunction with customers, that are not linked to the general public site. Although the strategy for access differs between Dell and BASF, the general principle is the same. The Web is fully integrated into their customer relationship strategy. Contrast this form of integration with that of consumer marketing, in which the marketer does not involve the consumer in the creation and development of the site, and therefore the marketer must advertise to drive traffic to it.

# Unique Promotional Strategies

The complex buying process and inclusion of several people from different functional areas impact the business marketing promotional strategies, too. In a family, for example, the person who determines the budget is likely to be the person who makes the purchase and decides what is needed. When an organization makes a purchase, however, personnel from several different departments will together determine what the organization needs.

Each different department may have a separate set of needs and interests, which may influence how marketers promote their products. For example, BASF's carpet fiber may be advertised as a low-cost product to the finance department of carpet manufacturers. BASF's advertising to carpet manufacturers' marketing departments, however, would focus on how carpet companies' customers want longer-lasting carpet made with BASF's fiber.

Additionally, consumers can go to shopping malls for their purchases. Few business shopping malls exist, so trade shows or expositions are created. These shows last for a few days and bring together buyers from all over the world. As you can see, business marketers engage in many unique promotional activities that are different from what you see as a consumer.

As summarized in the Exhibit 1–2, business marketing is unique, with stronger buyer–seller relationships, shorter channels of distribution, a greater emphasis on personal selling, and unique promotional strategies. Another factor that makes business marketing different from marketing to consumers is that the buyers are different. In the next section, we explore the types of buyers for business products and services.

## *Consumption*

Because business markets consume products in the process of making other products, demand for business products is dependent ultimately on individual consumers. We talk more about the issue of demand later in this chapter, but the important point to recognize here is that the buyer is not the final consumer. If BASF sells carpet fibers to DuPont, who then make carpets for GM to put into cars, GM's customers (people like you) are the ones that ultimately judge the quality of the product.

But BASF can't just be concerned with how consumers appreciate how long a carpet lasts in a car. BASF also has to be concerned with how easy they make it for DuPont to include the fibers into their manufacturing process. DuPont also has to be concerned with how easy they make it for GM to install the carpets because the easier it is to install, the less it should cost. Consumption, then, is not only about how consumers use the product, but how organizations integrate the product into their processes.

### The Customer's Customer

From the preceding discussion of consumption should come the recognition that companies like BASF have to have some knowledge of their customer's customer. BASF can't just worry about their direct customers like DuPont. They also have to have an understanding of how GM manufactures cars and installs carpet, as well as how consumers use the carpet in the cars and how that differs from how they use it in their homes.

For example, Philip Buskens, head of procurement for BASF in Belgium, was working to develop fast-drying polymers that would go into epoxy-based paints. After a year of work, the product was still some time away from being ready for the market. But governments in the Middle East needed the product faster in order to seal underground water pipes more effectively. While the BASF product was sold to a paint company in Spain who then supplied the pipeline contractor in Egypt, it was the direct understanding of the Egyptian government's need that provided the momentum to pilot-test the product more quickly and produce several hundred tons in about half the time originally expected.[2]

### Marketing Research

There are 300 million consumers in the United States, and over a billion in India and another billion in China. But many business markets can be small. The auto industry, for example, has only a few manufacturers. The types of research used to understand consumer markets in the United States, India, or anywhere else in the world are likely to be very different from those in business markets. We devote a chapter to this topic later in the book; for now, the important aspect is to recognize that, like unique promotional strategies, marketing research reflects the nature of the business markets: small, compact, relational. For that reason, companies like BASF may rely on salespeople for marketing information (such as in the case of Philip Buskens' new polymer) and are more likely to use qualitative methods such as depth interviews or focus groups.

# BUSINESS MARKETS

There are numerous differences between purchasing by organizations and purchasing by consumers. Many of the differences are due to the fact that consumers purchase for personal consumption, and in most cases individuals within organizations do not, but instead purchase to satisfy needs of the organization. Other factors, too, influence the nature of business buying, making it different. These factors are the types of customers, the types of products they buy, the size and location of customers, the complex processes and rigorous standards of purchasing, the nature of business relationships, and the nature of demand. It is important to understand these differences so that you can appreciate the special challenges facing business marketers and so that you can better apply what you have already learned about marketing.

**Exhibit 1–3**
Types of
Customers

| Companies That Consume | Institutions |
|---|---|
| Original equipment manufacturers | Hospitals |
| Users | Schools, colleges, and universities |
| | |
| *Government Agencies* | *Resellers* |
| Country | Wholesalers |
| State or Province | Brokers |
| Local—county, parish, city | Industrial distributors |

# Types of Business Customers

There are four types of business customers, as illustrated in Exhibit 1–3: firms that consume the product or service (such as original equipment manufacturers), government agencies, institutions, and firms that purchase and resell the product. This book focuses on the first three—those organizations that purchase for consumption. We will discuss those firms that purchase and resell products, but we focus on industrial distributors that distribute products consumed by other organizations, rather than wholesalers and retailers of consumer products.

## Original Equipment Manufacturers

When a company purchases a product or service to be included in its own final product, the company is called an **original equipment manufacturer (OEM).** For example, General Motors may buy gauges for installation in the dashboards of its automobiles. In this instance, General Motors is an OEM.

## Users

Companies are also users of products. From the manufacturer's perspective, it is helpful to know if the customer uses the product or includes it in the manufacture of their product. So GM is also a user of products that help facilitate the operation of GM's business. When GM purchases paper from Boise Cascade, Boise Cascade considers GM a user. In this scenario, the **user** (GM) is the equivalent of the final consumer, though we typically think of a consumer as someone like you. This is important to recognize because products purchased for use within the organization may undergo a different form of scrutiny than those that go into the product. Moreover, users in organizations are more like consumers because satisfaction is determined through consumption. Yes, GM can be a user and an OEM, but to GM's vendor, GM is either a user or an OEM. We'll talk more about this when we discuss the different types of products; but for now, consider users as most similar to end consumers.

## Government Agencies

In the United States, the government is the largest single purchaser of products and services, buying more than $350 billion worth each year. The federal government is also the country's largest single landlord, renting and maintaining more property than any other individual organization. As such, the government buys and uses many products.

In this and other countries, the government may be the only customer for some products. In all countries, the government is probably the only buyer of tanks and other armored weapon systems. In the United States, companies can own their own telephone system for internal use. On the other hand, in some countries, all telephone systems must be leased from the government. The government, then, is the only customer for telephone switching equipment.

The purchasing processes used by the government can be frustrating and complex, particularly because the government seeks to accomplish social objectives through purchasing. Policies designed to encourage the growth of minority- or women-owned businesses as well as small businesses are examples of social objective policies that influence government purchasing. The government goes to great lengths to find and support these businesses. Once the qualifications for designation as minority- or women-owned or small business are met, however, such companies can grow significantly if they are successful in selling to the government.

The federal government is not the only government customer. State governments also purchase goods and services, as do local institutions. In addition to buying such products as copiers, buildings, and roads, they also buy salt, both for applying to roads and for use in jails, employee cafeterias, and other places!

## Institutions

Institutions include organizations such as schools (kindergarten through 12th-grade systems as well as colleges and universities), hospitals and nursing homes, churches, and charitable organizations. Some of these organizations may use purchasing procedures similar to those utilized by government agencies, whereas others may follow less standardized procedures. Hospitals, nursing homes, and psychiatric and substance abuse centers make purchases related to the medical services they provide and may use criteria similar to those used by OEMs in making these purchases. Churches purchase products and services for use to facilitate the services they provide, with criteria and buying processes that may vary widely from church to church. Because of the special purchasing needs of institutions, many firms have special divisions or sales forces for these markets. Xerox, for instance, offers educational and medical institutions the same prices as government agencies (the lowest that Xerox offers) and has special salespeople for institutional markets.

## Industrial Distributors

Industrial distributors are those organizations that supply industrial companies with products and services. For example, Brazos Valley Equipment supplies farmers and ranchers with John Deere tractors, harvesters, and other farm implements. Waco Hotel and Motel Supply provides central Texas hotels and motels with janitorial, office, pool, and restaurant supplies and just about anything else anyone needs to run a hotel or motel. C. M. Tanner Wholesale Grocery in Carrollton, Georgia, delivers produce, meats, and other groceries to institutions including several school districts. These distributors provide services similar to those delivered by wholesalers and retailers of consumer goods; they make large purchases of certain products and then sell smaller quantities of individual products—within a wide assortment of products—to industrial users or OEMs.

# Types of Products

Products are generally classified on the basis of the type of organization purchasing the products and for what purpose. Whether the product is part of the organization's final product or facilitates the organization's activities is the primary difference in determining product type. Because the buying organization has its own customers with their own demand for quality, doing a superior job of buying products that become part of the final product can be a competitive advantage. Therefore, understanding the types of products bought and sold in business markets is important.

Products used in the final product include raw and manufactured materials, component parts or OEM parts, and assemblies. **Raw materials,** or materials processed only to the point required for economic handling and distribution, are also sold to OEMs for use in the products they manufacture. Gold and silver, for example, are purchased by companies such as Nokia and Motorola for use in the manufacture of telecommunications equipment. Raw materials, such as iron, are often further processed into manufactured materials, such as steel. GM may buy sheet steel, which is called a **manufactured material** because the material, which has been transformed from the raw material, requires further processing before GM can use it; the sheets must be cut to the proper size and so forth. If BASF supplied its carpet treatment product to GM for application to carpets in cars and trucks, the BASF product would be considered a manufactured material.

**Component parts,** or **OEM parts,** are parts assembled into the final product without further transformation. In some instances, a company may purchase OEM parts and assemble these to make a component for installation into the final product by another company. The component may then be called a subassembly or assembly. For example, Gates Controls may purchase plastic casing (a component part) from Plastech and parts from Metric Devices and then assemble these into a tachometer that is sold to GM. GM would then put the tachometer into its cars or trucks. GM may refer to the part as an assembly.

Other products are facilitating products; they facilitate the company's achievement of its objectives, but are not part of the final product. Hand tools, such as sanders, routers, portable saws, and other light tools, are called **accessory equipment.** Office equipment, such as personal computers and desktop printers, would also fit in the accessory equipment category.

**Capital equipment,** also called installations, refers to large equipment used in the production process that requires significant financial investment. Capital equipment would include overhead cranes, blast furnaces, industrial robots, and other manufacturing equipment as well as forklifts, road graters, and other heavy construction machinery.

The difference between accessory and capital equipment is important when it comes to marketing the equipment to users. Capital equipment is much more expensive, and its purchase may involve more members of the organization than purchase of accessory equipment. Marketing requirements are different as more members of the organization must be reached by marketing efforts.

Products sold to users for use in the company's operations are often labeled **MRO** items **(maintenance, repair, and operations products).** Operating supplies would include the copier paper mentioned earlier. Another term is **facilitating supplies** or **facilitating services,** because they support company efforts but are not part of the final product. Banking services, marketing research services, advertising services, and transportation services also fall into this category.

Maintenance products or services include janitorial products, painting contractors who paint the buildings, plumbing services, and heating and air conditioning services. The term *repair products and services* usually refers to repair of the manufacturing equipment and tools rather than repair to the facility.

For example, GM purchases MRO items to maintain its plants and equipment. At the same time, GM buys OEM parts for use in its cars. GM will purchase both, but the classification system enables us to recognize the different decision processes used for each and the different marketing requirements brought about by those processes, which we will discuss in later chapters.

# Size and Location of Customers

Size and location of customers create unique challenges for business marketers that are not faced by those who market directly to consumers. As we indicated earlier, General Motors purchases $58 billion in products and services per year (Ford spends $90 billion). There are no individual consumers with that kind of purchasing power. *Business customers are larger than individual consumers,* so each business customer is more important to the financial success of the business marketer. At the same time, *there are fewer individual business customers.* For example, if a company's product is components used in new cars, there are only a few manufacturers to sell to. One dissatisfied customer can have a significant impact on the firm.

Business customers are also *more likely to be geographically concentrated.* Industries tend to arise around key resources. For example, steel manufacturing requires iron ore, limestone, energy, access to labor, and access to customers. Through the mid-20th century, the Great Lakes and major river systems enabled Chicago, Cleveland, and Pittsburgh to access ore from the Minnesota Iron Range; coal from the Dakotas, Kentucky, and Pennsylvania; and major steel markets in Detroit and the eastern seaboard. Breakthroughs in water transport and scale economies in production have now made steel an internationally traded commodity, but the early steel industry was located near those sources of supply.

For technology-driven companies, a key "raw material" is personnel, so some industries form around pockets of qualified personnel. For example, the "silicon prairie" (Richardson, Texas, a suburb of Dallas) is the U.S. home of many global telecommunications companies, including Nortel (formerly Northern Telecom) from Canada, Alcatel from France, and Ericsson from Sweden. New companies locate in the silicon prairie because of the availability of engineers with telecommunications experience.

Geographic concentration has an influence on marketing to these organizations. Firms that supply telecommunications companies also locate in the silicon prairie, which lowers their costs of serving these accounts. Whereas Coca-Cola has to be concerned with consumer access to Cokes in even remote parts of the country, electronics wholesalers may find most of their telecommunications market located in one metropolitan area.

At the same time that business markets tend to be geographically concentrated, they are also *globally oriented.* Because customers are fewer in number and tend to be larger and geographically concentrated in various parts of the globe, competition for business tends to be more global. Also, the large-scale operations and transportation systems that made steel an internationally traded commodity have made other markets more global. Cement is another example of an industry that was once regionally competitive. Constrained by rail and truck transportation, cement companies located near their major markets and competed in a limited geographic area. Today's specialized ships enable cheap water transport to complement production-scale economies. Cement companies are now more global, with CEMEX headquartered in Mexico being the world's largest producer.

Consider again the silicon prairie. Its importance at the advent of the handheld calculator was quite high, as Texas Instruments was a leader in developing both the silicon prairie and calculators. Initial product success hinged principally on the sophistication of the integrated circuitry. Now that the market has matured and circuitry is quite standard, efficient assembly is critical for success. Offshore assembly is now the norm; marketers of calculator parts may sell to assemblers in China one year, in Costa Rica the next.

Note that these generalizations about geographic concentration and global orientation do not hold for all business marketers. Xerox, for example, sells to all types of businesses and is less concerned with geographic concentration than with global orientation. Xerox must provide the same level of service for the products it sells in the most remote parts of the country as in urban centers. Xerox copiers can be found on U.S. Navy submarines, in oil fields, and on ranches and farms, as well as in offices of companies large and small. Although there are more copier users in New York City than in Bismarck, North Dakota, companies like Xerox face many of the same distribution and marketing challenges that consumer products companies must overcome.

# Purchasing Standards and Processes

Family decision making and consumer purchasing are different from organizational purchasing. Few consumers, for example, compare the cost of purchasing and leasing a new automobile on a spreadsheet under varying driving conditions. Few professional fleet managers, however, would buy a sedan because of how it looks. They would use stricter standards for judging a vendor, as well as somewhat different processes. While we discuss these distinctions in great detail in Chapters 3 and 4, buyers' strict standards and purchasing processes do separate business marketing from marketing to consumers.

## Strict Standards

When college roommates find that last week's reheated spaghetti tastes foul, they toss the stuff and call for a pizza. But if the food served to first-class passengers on Delta flight 34J to Salt Lake City is foul, no pizza can substitute. Frequent flyers are apt to fume. They may spend their company's travel budget on United next time. When a power company must brown out or purchase auxiliary power because a bad expansion joint has left a boiler out of commission, you can bet both the utility's purchasing agent and the vendor responsible for the bad expansion joint will get called on the carpet.

As you can see, business buyers have to apply strict performance standards to their purchases because their job is on the line, whereas Mom isn't likely to be fired if the kids don't like dinner. Professional purchasers and multiperson buying teams have formal responsibility for product and vendor evaluation. Inputs often must conform to design specifications, cost constraints, delivery windows, and the like.

## Purchasing Processes

The larger number of people involved in organizational purchasing contrasts sharply with typical household buying. Within families, purchasing roles are more flexible, often arising from implicit negotiation, expertise, and habit. Although in both cases, someone

Business marketers are more likely to conduct business globally and face global competition than are consumer marketers. This Web site helps buyers find suppliers anywhere in the world.

may purchase a product for use by someone else, the sheer size and complexity of organizations and the number of people involved often lead to a more complex purchasing process.

Furthermore, many organizational controls are in place to assist professional purchasers—and evaluate them. Comprehensive vendor scoring systems are commonplace. Quality inspection at origin, cost accounting systems, and cash flow management have only crude equivalents among consumers. For example, almost every home owner you know has probably complained about inadequate closet space. But do they calculate the "warehousing" costs of their golf clubs, camping gear, and heirlooms? Do they measure inventory carrying costs (e.g., spoilage, opportunity cost of money) on toilet paper or apples by the case? Even before you take up the chapters on purchasing and distribution, you can well anticipate these important distinctions in business purchasing.

## The Nature of Demand

Demand for business products does not always operate in the same fashion as demand for consumer goods. In part, the nature of demand in business markets is due to the types of products sold, varying for raw materials, component parts, and so forth. Understanding demand is important for business marketers because decisions concerning which markets to serve, what business to be in, and where to invest company resources are based on projections of demand. Two concepts, derived demand and joint demand, are useful in understanding how demand for business products can be determined.

**Exhibit 1–4**
Demand for BASF's carpet treatment is derived from demand for new homes. The homes need carpet, which needs treatment.

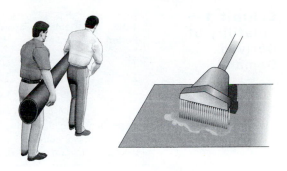

## Derived Demand

When business analysts and economists focus on consumer spending and consumer confidence, they are looking for indicators that affect the entire economy. Consumer and government spending ultimately drives all of the economy. Business marketers must recognize that the demand for their products and services is **derived demand;** that is, demand for their products and services is derived from the demand for their customers' products and services (whose demand may also be derived). Ultimately, most demand is derived from consumer demand, the exception being demand derived from government purchases such as arms sales.

In the salt example at the beginning of this chapter, it is easy to see how Morton Salt can predict salt sales based on the predictions of sales for institutional foods, meals purchased outside the home, and home purchases. The demand for salt is derived from the demand for, among other things, fast food. Similarly, as illustrated in Exhibit 1–4, the demand for BASF's carpet treatment product is derived from the demand for buildings, vehicles, and other products that use carpets as well as the demand for remodeling existing facilities and homes.

For suppliers to manufacturers of consumer products, the issue of derived demand may not be too great. In this situation, there is virtually a one-to-one relationship; for every consumer product purchased, there is a one-to-one relationship with the supplier of a component of that product. If we made bottle caps and sold them to Coca-Cola, for example, then the demand for bottle caps would be the equivalent of the unit demand for bottled Cokes.

As we move further away from the consumer market, however, derived demand can cause wide swings in demand, called **volatility.** For example, assume we make a machine that processes salt and makes it ready for human consumption. Morton Salt will decide how many of our machines to purchase derived from the need for salt. Morton has, let's say, 50 such machines. Assume that in a year of steady sales, Morton Salt will purchase 10 machines to replace those that are old and worn out. In year one, salt demand goes down 5 percent, and Morton Salt may decide that it can get by with purchasing only seven new machines. In year 2, demand goes up 10 percent. How many will Morton Salt now replace? If demand of 100 percent equals 50 machines, 95 percent demand equals approximately 47 machines, while 105 percent demand means roughly 52 machines (52.5 to be exact). Based on a replacement rate of 20 percent, as illustrated in Exhibit 1–5, demand for our machines went from 7 to 12 to 10. Demand for our machine went up almost 50 percent, then down 20 percent, as compared to the change in salt demand of 5 percent to 10 percent. Derived demand can cause wide swings, or volatility, in the demand for industrial products.

**Exhibit 1–5**
Volatility of
Derived
Demand

| Time Period | Demand for Salt | Machines Needed to Handle Demand | Worn-Out Machines | Machines Available | New Purchases |
|---|---|---|---|---|---|
| 1 | 100% | 50 | | | |
| 2 | 95 | 47 | 10 | 40 | 7 |
| 3 | 105 | 52 | 7 | 40 | 12 |
| 4 | 100 | 50 | 12 | 40 | 10 |

At the beginning of Period 1, 50 machines are required based on forecast of sales. At the end of the year, 10 are worn out but 7 are purchased because only 47 are needed. Over year 2, 7 machines wear out, but 52 are needed, so 12 are purchased.

Demand elasticity is also affected by derived demand. **Demand elasticity** is the percentage change in sales relative to the percentage change in price. In a consumer market, demand elasticity means that as price goes up, consumers will look for alternatives or do without, and sales will go down. Morton Salt may choose to do without our salt processing machines (elastic demand), but if the price of raw salt went up, Morton Salt would have little option but to pay the higher price. So for products without substitutes, there is **inelastic demand**—it is not affected greatly by price. Morton Salt cannot simply choose to do without salt, though you can if the price is too high.

On the other hand, there are many more substitutes for some industrial products than for consumer goods. When assembling a product, a manufacturer can choose between rivets, nuts and bolts, adhesives, and other forms of fasteners. When there are many substitutes and the choice of one or the other has no visible impact on the final product, demand will be more price elastic, or more affected by price.

Because of the importance of the concept of derived demand, business marketers are always paying close attention to consumer demand forecasts and reports. You may notice the importance paid by the news media to two types of consumer demand: that of new housing (often reported in terms of new housing starts) and that of new cars. The demand for so many industrial products and supplies is derived from the demand for housing and cars that they are important bellwethers of the economy as a whole. From the Field 1–2 describes the experiences of two very different companies as they deal with the consequences of derived demand.

# THE ENTIRE SYSTEM

So far in this chapter, we've used two companies as running examples: GM and BASF. Let's put it all together and examine the flow of goods and services that go into one car. Exhibit 1–6 illustrates this flow.

At the beginning are the suppliers of raw materials. The plastic, steel and other metals, rubber, and glass used in automobiles are manufactured materials derived from such raw materials as petroleum, iron ore, and sand. A mining company may sell the raw material to a mill that produces the manufactured material. The mill may then sell the material to a contract manufacturer, which creates the component part for GM. For example, sheet metal may be stamped into hoods for Chevy Monte Carlos.

Another company may supply gauges to GM. These gauges are assemblies composed of parts purchased from other manufacturers. BASF supplies manufactured materials,

## 1–2

### FROM THE FIELD
## The Reality of Derived Demand

Do you prefer diet drinks containing Splenda, the artificial sweetener? When you shop for a new computer, do you look to see if Intel processors are inside? If so, you are demonstrating derived demand, as the demand for Splenda and Intel is derived from your desire for a diet cola or new computer.

In fact, demand for Splenda has been so strong that the company that makes it, Tate & Lyle, had to halt taking on any new customers for nearly two years. Demand through its current customers grew so rapidly that all expansion plans were filled just by supplying current customers such as Coca-Cola (Splenda is in Diet Coke), Starbucks (used in low-calorie Frappuccinos), and Atkins Nutritionals (Splenda is in their low-carb diet foods).

The challenge for Intel has been somewhat different. Chinese Internet cafés contain some 11 million PCs—no small market. The average café has 100 computers—no small customer. If you are Ian Yang, and your job is to sell Intel computer chips in China, you can't ignore this market and the demand it creates for your products. Coming up with an answer for China's price sensitivity, though, took a while.

Stuck in a Beijing traffic jam, Yang, Minerva Yeung, and other Intel execs began to brainstorm. As the car crept along, they talked about the challenges facing Internet café owners. By the time they reached their destination, they had the beginnings of a new product line. The result was dramatic. China now accounts for 9 percent of Intel's worldwide sales.

Understanding the demand from which your products' or services' demand is derived is important to business marketers. These are just two success stories that began with a better understanding of derived demand.

Bruce Einhorn, "In China's Net Cafés, Intel Pours It On," *BusinessWeek* (November 6, 2006), p. 52; Elizabeth Esfahani, "What Works: Finding the Sweet Spot," *Business 2.0,* (November 2005), pp. 49–51.

such as a carpet treatment product to make the carpet last longer and a velour treatment product to make the seats last longer. GM assembles and paints the cars, using robots to spray each car with the correct amount of paint. The robots are capital equipment. Colors are chosen through marketing research, which determines which shades will sell best. That research is a facilitating service, as is the transportation of the cars to GM's customers.

Each purchase order is printed on a Xerox copier (accessory equipment). At the end of each day, all offices are cleaned by the personnel of local janitorial companies, an MRO service. All of this is necessary so that GM can serve its customers. GM's customers include government agencies, such as the armed services, which buy cars for staff transportation; institutions, such as universities, which purchase vans to transport students

**Exhibit 1–6**
The Entire System

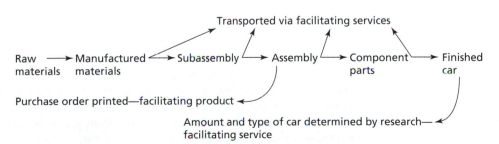

---

**1–2**

## BUSINESS 2 BUSINESS

### BASF and Derived Demand

Consider the demand for BASF's product for making fabrics brighter and longer lasting. From what products would demand be derived? Is this situation more or less volatile for carpet treatment products sold to consumers? Why? How would volatility influence the way you market these products?

---

on field and athletic trips; rental car companies; fleet users, such as BASF, whose salespeople drive company cars to visit their customers; and retail dealers, which resell their cars to you and other consumers. With all these customers to satisfy, it is no wonder that GM purchases over $50 billion each year in goods and services!

As you have seen, quite a few purchases must be made before GM can build a car, Shaw Industries can make a carpet, or McDonald's can salt your fries. Each of those purchases is part of a marketing process conducted by vendors such as BASF and Morton Salt. In this section, we examine the marketing process that is the subject of the rest of the book.

## Understanding the Market

Many organizations begin with a vision—the reason why the organization was created. Usually, that reason for being is based on some general need or set of needs that has been identified in the market, and the organization is created to satisfy that need. Simply recognizing the need, however, is not enough. Safer chemical processing was long recognized as a need but it wasn't until two chemical engineers at BASF developed such a process that chemicals could be mass-produced cheaply and safely. The means to fulfill the need must also exist. When the recognition of a need and the means to satisfy it come together, an organization or business can be created.

In recognition of the importance of understanding the market, the first part of the book is designed to give you an understanding of business marketing in general. The second part continues to build this understanding through a study of organizational buying behavior or why organizations buy. Based on this understanding, you can then appreciate how marketers evaluate markets, targeting only certain segments and creating offerings that meet the needs of those segments. These offerings constitute the marketing mix, which is the topic of the third part of the book, and the method by which marketing creates value.

## The Marketing Mix Creates Value

The marketing mix consists of the usual four Ps you probably learned in principles of marketing. The four Ps—product, place, price, and promotion—are based on the utilities, or general benefits, provided by marketing, which are having the product the buyer wants, where the buyer wants it, at the right price, and letting the buyer know about it.

The four Ps illustrate that marketing is a process of creating value. **Value** is equivalent to profit for the buyer; it is the perception of how much the buyer benefited beyond what was paid or invested in the product. A recent study of business buyers found that they break value down into three parts: value received from the product, value received from the services that the seller offers, and value received from the relationship with the seller.

For example, Dacin and Dacin is a manufacturer's agent who sells for various contract manufacturers. Lloyd Dacin was working with a client to develop a milk dispenser component of a milkshake machine. The client benefited from the product that was made by the company that Dacin represents, but the bigger benefits came from Lloyd Dacin's engineering services in designing the component. Through the relationship with Lloyd Dacin, the client was also able to meet another supplier who cut costs on another component by over 10 percent.

Dacin and Dacin enjoyed a significant competitive advantage over the other manufacturer's agents vying for that business. A **competitive advantage** is something that provides incremental value when compared to other offerings. The advantage can be gained through any of the three basic values of product, services, or relationship, either alone or in combination.

When BASF says that it doesn't make the carpet, it makes the carpet last longer, the company is describing the value it adds to the process of bringing you carpet. If it did not provide value, it would not be part of the process. Refer back to Exhibit 1–6 illustrating the complete system. That diagram illustrates what is called a **value chain,** or system of value creation. Each organization adds its value to whatever it is that the system is creating, in this case a mode of transportation.

Therefore, the third part of this book discusses the process of creating value. The section begins with a chapter covering the processes relating to developing an overall strategy and is followed by chapters concerning product development, channels of distribution, and integrated marketing communications. Two chapters examine portions of the communications mix, first advertising and trade shows, and then selling and sales management. A chapter on pricing rounds out this section.

## Marketing Is an Integrative Process

The final part of the book reflects the integrative nature of business marketing. You should already have glimpsed that a high degree of interaction and cooperation is needed among members of a value chain. Each member is both buyer and seller to other members of the chain, which often results in a different form of relationship between buyer and seller than in consumer markets.

Customer retention and relationship building are important elements of success in today's business marketing environment. For relationships to be strong, the entire organization must be dedicated to solving the needs and satisfying the wants of each business partner. Careful internal integration and coordination are needed in relationship-building strategies. This part of the book should integrate much of what you learned in the prior chapters.

## Summary

Business marketing is an important element in the economies of industrialized nations, accounting for more than half of the economy. Business marketing includes marketing to companies that buy products in order to make other products or to facilitate their companies' operations; marketing to government agencies, including state and local governments; marketing to institutions such as universities and hospitals; and marketing to resellers, including retailers and industrial distributors.

Most marketing majors will begin their career in business marketing. Understanding business marketing is also important because of the magnitude of business marketing and because it is different from marketing to consumers.

Business marketing differs from consumer marketing in the types of customers served, their relative sizes and locations, the nature of buyer–seller relationships, and the nature of business demand. Organizations that consume products as part of their normal operations include OEMs, which use products as part of their own products. They buy raw materials, manufactured materials, assemblies, and component parts, which all become part of their final product.

Users are those organizations that use a product in their operations but not as part of their own product. Users use accessory equipment, capital equipment, MRO items, facilitating services and supplies, and other products. The government is an important user of products and services. Governments work to achieve political and social objectives through set-asides, technology subsidies, target zone development policies, and more. Institutions such as universities, churches, and hospitals also use products and services.

Business marketers are more likely to find their buyers geographically concentrated, but are also more likely to serve global markets and face global competition. Business buyers are larger than individual consumers, giving each business buyer more power in relation to the seller.

At the same time, relationships between buyers and sellers tend to be stronger in business marketing. Although some business relationships are transactional, many companies seek partnership status with their customers.

Demand for business products operates differently than does consumer demand. Business product demand is derived from the demand for consumer products. As a result, business marketing demand can be quite volatile.

These factors make business marketing different from marketing to consumers. Channels of distribution are shorter, and there is a greater emphasis on personal selling. Relationships must be carefully managed. At the same time, unique promotion strategies such as trade shows are part of the business marketing mix.

## Key Terms

| | | |
|---|---|---|
| **accessory equipment** | **facilitating services** | **original equipment** |
| **business marketing** | (or **supplies**) | **manufacturer (OEM)** |
| **capital equipment** | **inelastic demand** | **raw materials** |
| **competitive advantage** | **maintenance, repair,** | **user** |
| **component parts** | **and operations** | **value** |
| **demand elasticity** | **products (MRO)** | **value chain** |
| **derived demand** | **manufactured material** | **volatility** |
| | **OEM parts** | |

## Discussion Questions

**1.** Identify three television advertisements you see regularly that appear to target a business market. What benefits are they trying to sell? How does their advertising differ from beer commercials, car commercials, and other consumer ads? Why do you think there is a difference?

2. Across the top of the page, list each type of product (such as an OEM product). Then list a product that would fit each category. Try to use products not mentioned as examples in the chapter. Use BASF as your buying company.

3. How can derived demand cause volatility when, at the same time, distribution channels are short and tend to be direct in business marketing?

4. What is the relationship between price and value? How does marketing provide value? What are the types of value that marketing provides?

5. You work for Black & Decker's DeWalt division. DeWalt makes professional-grade power tools like drills, circular saws, jigsaws, power hammers, and others. Both consumers and carpenters purchase these tools. What factors would influence demand among carpenters for power tools in general? What factors would influence carpenters to pick DeWalt over other power tool brands? What factors would influence consumers' demand for high-end power tools and how are those factors the same or different for professional carpenters?

6. How might Black & Decker promote DeWalt brand products differently for professional carpenters versus consumers? How might their promotion be the same?

7. How would Black & Decker's marketing of DeWalt brand tools be different for the following markets?
   a. The U.S. military for use in engineering divisions.
   b. School districts that still offer shop in high school.
   c. Furniture and cabinet-making manufacturers.

8. How does buying over the Web provide value that buying from a salesperson cannot? How does buying from a salesperson provide value that the Web cannot provide? When would each source (the Web or a salesperson) be more important to a company?

9. One business marketing student said, "All this stuff on relationships just means that it is who you know that counts. The good old boy network is what is important." Based on what you've read in this chapter, how would you respond to that statement? What value can be provided by good relationships?

# Cases

### Case 1.1   Friar Casing, LLC

When Tiffany Friar-Hakes graduated from college, she went to work for Coca-Cola, working on special event marketing. She could have taken an easier position in her father's company, but he wanted her to go out on her own and learn more about how business is done before joining the family firm. After five years, she thought it was time to return and her father agreed. But now, after six months, she was questioning her decision.

"Dad," she said, entering Mike Friar's office. "Sales have been stagnant for the last few years, at least five from what I can see. Yet we're paying our salespeople more now than we did then. Why is that?"

"Cost of living—they have to earn more just to stay even," he replied. "But I see your point. They aren't selling more."

"Well, what if we had our smaller customers order through the Web? Then the salespeople could have more time to find new customers." The company manufactures metal boxes, called cases, which other companies put their products in when those products have to be used in tough environments. For example, AirLink uses Friar cases to house high-tech communications equipment used by the military.

"I don't know—I think we'd have a riot on our hands if we tried to take customers away." He frowned as he contemplated the consequences.

"But our costs have risen and our sales haven't. I don't think we'll make money this year. If we don't find less expensive ways to sell, we'll be out of business before too long."

Her dad stared at her earnestly. "Look, this isn't Coca-Cola. We don't have their big budget for fancy marketing, and selling to people is a whole lot different than selling to companies."

1. What type of products does Friar make and sell? (Note: The type isn't "boxes" or "cases.")

2. What type of customers do they have?

3. What characteristics of the Friar Casing market are different from those faced by Coca-Cola, and how would that affect how Friar markets?

### Case 1.2   Dan Li Manufacturing

Dan "Gracie" Li, after a brief stint with Procter & Gamble (P&G) in the United States, returned to China and started her own manufacturing company. Her first customer was her old employer, who wanted lower-cost rubber and plastic products used in manufacturing machinery. Li began by doing the engineering design, then working with manufacturers in China to source the products.

Now she employs three design engineers and five procurement specialists, in addition to the usual office staff. Rather than design, she now focuses her attention almost exclusively on generating sales and running the overall company.

One challenge, though, is that these contract manufacturers want to do long production runs, whereas customers don't want to take delivery and store products. They want to receive the products as they need them. Li believes it may be time to get a warehouse in the United States so she is looking in the state of Washington.

"I think you'll find this space in Seattle to be your best bet," said Wes Tiffin, a real estate agent. "I realize a five-year lease may seem like a long time, but the price is right and it gives you room to grow in the future."

"I don't know, Wes," replied Li. "Two years ago, we sold twice what we sold last year. I think we can sell more if we can shorten delivery times by holding inventory in the states, but it worries me that sales jump around so much. This year could be three times last year but then next year could be down again. Can we get a short-term lease?"

1. What would cause such wide swings in Li's sales?

2. How can Li stabilize sales? What other aspects of the business are affected by these wide swings?

# Additional Readings

Carr, Jon C., and Tara Burnthorne Lopez. "Examining Market Orientation as Both Culture and Conduct: Modeling the Relationships between Market Orientation and Employee Responses." *Journal of Marketing Theory & Practice* 15 (2007), pp. 113–26.

Gebauer, Heiko, Chunzhi Wang, Bernold Beckenbauer, and Regine Krempl. "Business-to-Business Marketing as a Key Factor for Increasing Service Revenue in China." *Journal of Business & Industrial Marketing* 22 (2007), pp. 126–41.

Gupta, Manak, and C. Anthony DiBenedetto. "Optimal Pricing and Advertising Strategy for Introducing a New Business Product with Threat of Competitive Entry." *Industrial Marketing Management* 36, no. 4 (2001), pp. 540–53.

Jap, Sandy. "The Impact of Online Reverse Auction Design on Buyer-Supplier Relationships." *Journal of Marketing* 71, no. 1 (2007), pp. 146–59.

Johnson, Thomas E., and David Ford. "Customer Approaches to Product Development with Suppliers." *Industrial Marketing Management* 36 (2007), pp. 300–16.

Lynch, Joanne, and Leslie de Chernatony. "Winning Hearts and Minds: Business-to-Business Branding and the Role of the Salesperson." *Journal of Marketing Management* 23 (2007), pp. 123–34.

Merrilees, Bill, and Tino Fenech. "From Catalog to Web: B2B Multi-Channel Marketing Strategy." *Industrial Marketing Management* 36, no. 1 (2007), pp. 44–56.

Olson, Eric M., Stanley F. Slater, and G. Tomas M. Hult. "The Performance Implications of Fit among Business Strategy, Marketing Organization Structure, and Strategic Behavior." *Journal of Marketing* 69, no. 3 (2006), pp. 49–65.

Palmatier, Robert W., Lisa K. Scheer, and Jan-Benedict E. M. Steenkamp. "Customer Loyalty to Whom? Managing the Benefits and Risks of Salesperson-Owned Loyalty," *Journal of Marketing Research* 44 (2007), pp. 185–201.

Racela, Olimpia C., Chawit Chaikittisilpa, and Amonrat Thoumrungroje. "Market Orientation, International Business Relationships and Perceived Export Performance." *International Marketing Review* 24 (2007), pp. 144–61.

Schurr, Paul H. "Buyer–Seller Relationship Development Episodes: Theories and Methods." *Journal of Business & Industrial Marketing* 22 no. 3 (2007), pp. 161–74.

Sharma, Arun, and Anuj Mehrotra. "Choosing an Optimal Channel Mix in Multichannel Environments." *Industrial Marketing Management* 36, no. 1 (2007), pp. 21–38.

Tikkanen, Henrikki, Jaakko Kujala, and Karlos Artto. "The Marketing Strategy of a Project-based Firm: The Four Portfolios Framework." *Industrial Marketing Management* 36 no. 2 (2007), pp. 194–210.

# *Chapter* 2

# The Character of Business Marketing

**Chapter**

## CESSNA AIRCRAFT COMPANY

With a 57 percent share of the business jet market and sales at $2 billion, Cessna executives knew they'd have to be more efficient and quality conscious to thrive in the 21st century. When the Textron subsidiary launched its supply chain management initiative in 1997, Cessna had supplier on-time delivery running around 45 percent, supplier prices and costs escalating, extensive rework and redundant inspections making quality very costly, and top management raising questions about what should be made inside versus outside the company. ●

Hired to move the paper-clogged, transaction-oriented procurement function to an integrated process, Michael Katzorke, vice president of supply chain management, began to move the company out of its functional orientation to one that integrated three critical processes: new product development, strategic sourcing, and sustaining production. New product development required more supplier involvement in design and administration of specifications, as well as life-of-part contracting. Strategic sourcing implied specific sourcing plans for categories of inputs, long-term agreement negotiations that specified supplier integration into Cessna business processes, as well as supplier improvement processes. Sustaining production meant sharing production plans with suppliers, materials released against long-term agreements, and sustained efforts to purge waste. ●

Cessna uses full-time, cross-functional commodity teams to lead the transition. Each team has specialists from purchasing, manufacturing, engineering, quality, product design, product support, and finance working to improve supplier performance and meld them into Cessna's design and manufacturing process. For example, Cessna needed electronic data interchange (EDI) for just the rudiments of company-to-company integration, but EDI has been impeded in the past by financial and personnel constraints at small suppliers. Thus, Cessna developed a Web-enabled system that mimics EDI—avoiding time delays and the need to rekey (correct) data. ●

As Cessna untangled its legacy of vertical integration, management saw not only letdowns in areas of capacity planning and inventory management, but also hints of an identity crisis. One executive frankly confessed the need to rediscover core competencies: "It seemed we were just doing too much. We had no idea what our real costs were." As a result of this assessment, Cessna forged an outsourcing agreement with Alcoa for all coil, sheet, and plate aluminum that may one day establish a local Alcoa facility allowing electronic ordering and daily delivery. In another Cessna supplier agreement, Honeywell maintains a stockroom in-house and makes deliveries as needed on the production floor. Honeywell handles all ordering and scheduling and, along with other major suppliers, participates in the Cessna planning process for sales and operations. Using a large storyboard on the wall at Cessna headquarters, every associate knows his or her role in the supply chain management process. Foremost, the overall objective is to deliver value to the airplane customer.[1] ●

Visit the Cessna Web site at **www.cessna.textron.com.** ●

## LEARNING OBJECTIVES

This chapter aims to broaden your exposure to the realm of business marketing, introduce a bigger lineup of players in the field, and preview some of their roles for firms and the larger economy. We will emphasize the key marketing challenge of coordinating work that creates value. We begin with a brief review of the amazing performance of markets. For technically complex and specialized products, markets may need tweaking. Buyers and sellers complement their reliance on the price mechanism with a host of other means for coordinating action. As you might guess, the chapter discusses business relationships—long-run exchange between firms. We examine the motivations for relationships and how they develop. We also consider the special challenges of managing and sustaining business relationships. The closing section of the chapter underscores the connections each relationship has to a larger network of organizations. We want you to strive to examine any marketing problem within its broad context, the web of participants in value creation.

*After reading this chapter, you should be able to*

- Describe the effectiveness of price for coordinating business transactions to create value.
- Explain how value is determined in exchange.
- Identify conditions that impair the performance of pure markets to coordinate business exchange.
- Summarize the range of buyer and seller motivations to develop and maintain an exchange relationship.
- Describe a relationship development process for parties able to gradually deepen their interdependence.
- Identify three complementary mechanisms for coordinating business transactions.
- Describe the network of participants in the value chain.
- Illustrate the marketing efforts one firm might take with each member of the network.

# THE MAGIC OF MARKETS

A manufacturing firm often has a choice of whether to buy parts—standard switches or valves—on the open market or to make the parts in-house. Clearly, no firm does everything in-house. When you think about it, markets provide amazingly for most business needs. Consider that pencil on your desk. It probably sold for less than $.25 whether purchased singly or by the box. But where did it come from? Did the Regional Bureau of Pencils contract for all inputs and schedule productions for the holidays or back-to-school rush? No. Did you solicit bids for contract production of your pencil? Of course not. This handy tool of business came from the market.

## Markets Coordinate

Often taken for granted, markets provide a most amazing mechanism for meeting individual and organizational needs and allocating productive resources within a society. Office Depot knows that nearly every business needs pencils. Thus, it buys them by the gross from Dixon Ticonderoga or another supplier without a moment of thought about how a pencil might come into being. Similarly, anticipating summer orders from Office Depot, Dixon Ticonderoga orders more dowels and gum erasers, perhaps without any detailed knowledge of their origins. Let's look briefly at the work that almost magically gets done to yield a tool to sketch a budget, mark a board for cutting, or fill in bubbles on an answer sheet.

Detailed in a remarkable little story, "I Pencil: My Family Tree as Told to Leonard E. Read,"[2] pencil manufacturing involves the participation of scores of businesses, including thousands of individuals in many distinct steps. Indeed, the pencil boldly asserts in this story that "not a single person . . . knows how to make me." First, straight grain cedar is cut from forests in the Pacific northwest by loggers using saws, trucks, and other gear. Then it is cut into slats, and the material is transported to the pencil manufacturer. Here is added the lead center, really graphite, possibly mined in Ceylon. The eraser or "plug" is made by reacting Indonesian rape seed oil with sulfur chloride. And so it goes on.

No single person could measure up to this task of pencil making. Markets coordinate nearly all the work necessary to give you or the Boeing Corporation pencils that do their job. The following sections review the fundamental elements and mechanisms of markets. We briefly see how they work to improve productivity, quality, and living standards.

### Buyers Gauge Value

First of all, the buyer—you or Boeing—determined the value of the pencil when paying for it. Circumstances play a role in what buyers are willing to pay. Boeing's purchasing department may stock the supply cabinet with pencils ordered at $1.40 per box. Yet a forgetful industrial psychologist from Kansas City, staying in Minneapolis to give an assessment test to employees at Honeywell, might well pay $1 each for pencils from the hotel where she's staying. Nothing in the pencil has changed its worth. Clearly, the value of one pencil is less to a party who has several than to a party who has none. The buyer's circumstances play a great role in determining the value of any product or service.

### Sellers Opt In or Out

Of course, the seller has a role in valuation. If costs of delivering a pencil are higher than what potential users are willing to pay, why make or deliver them? As producers reduce the number of shifts or lines devoted to pencil production, in time pencil supplies will shrink. When buyers find that pencils are more difficult to come by, seller promotions and discounting will be less common and, in effect, buyers will tend to bid up the price. But notice that costs do not make for value. Would a handcrafted pencil made from hickory wood find buyers at $7.50 each? It seems doubtful. Would your bookstore sales clerk convince you that the $5 pencil was a real bargain because it cost $6 for UPS overnight delivery? Of course not.

Price coordinates the activities of the various businesses, from loggers to retail clerks. A boost in demand may tax current supplies. Price increases can slow purchases until new supplies arrive. Input prices will rise the same way, prompting input suppliers to hike the wages of loggers (to draw more to the forests) and graphite miners. On the other hand, a pencil glut will prompt deep discounting and eventually rollbacks in production and production capacity in various stages of manufacture. In this amazing system, prices serve as both signals and outcomes.

Marketers in this type of business environment must be attuned to changes in demand and sharpen their firm's attention to quality, particularly the quality aspects valued by end users. The system rewards efficient sellers with profits and penalizes flabby sellers with weak profits or even losses. Competitive intelligence and adaptability are advised too.

# BEYOND MARKET COORDINATION

Let's now consider situations where the market may fail. This sounds ominous, doesn't it? Actually, in today's world of commercial trading, the prevalence of transactional exchange—sometimes also called *spot markets* or *discrete markets*—is severely limited by technical complexity, exacting buyer standards, and a variety of dependencies between buyer and seller that arise from the exchange. In this complex and dynamic environment, price (the market) must be complemented with other mechanisms for coordinating work between two parties. Otherwise exchange will not take place, or exchange will prove unsatisfactory, even highly frustrating, for at least one of the parties. Some examples will clarify how markets can fail.

Countless products need mechanical fasteners in their assembly. Markets work extremely well for the provision of standard rivets, screws, staples, and bolts. Nearly 10,000 distributors carry the lines of scores of fastener producers in order to serve over 180,000 original equipment manufacturers. A manufacturing company using tens of thousands of standard fasteners will have its purchasing agents seek to obtain the best delivered price. Indeed, a handful of potential suppliers can vie for the order, and a savvy purchasing agent will often make each order a bidding contest. The low-price supplier in March has no advantage in April's reorder and may very well be replaced by a vendor with a price difference of just pennies per case.

As you can see, transactional exchange works quite well to keep suppliers on their toes, ever striving to offer the lowest price. Although there may be an adversarial character to the interaction (a consequence of short-run self-interest and the impersonal mechanism of the market), buyers benefit from low-cost inputs. And they don't have to needle underperforming suppliers to get proper service. Buyers work at arm's length from vendors and simply order from another source the next time around.

But transactional exchange has a limited range of effectiveness. Many products have a level of complexity and significance in the creation of value that are poorly served by transactional exchange. The purchasing agent seeking the lowest delivered price on standard fasteners might really do a disservice for the firm by not properly accounting for costs of defects, late delivery, inventory costs, ordering costs, and so on. In short, the benefits of transactional exchange might be improved by using additional means to coordinate activities between customers and suppliers. We can illustrate this more concretely with more examples. Obviously, some product designs—for functional or aesthetic reasons—require special fastening (e.g., tiny clips or large, lightweight, reverse-threaded bolts). Few distributors carry these items, at least not at inventory levels apt to satisfy start-up production levels. Possibly, the design calls for fasteners that do not yet exist.

# Supply Chain Management

If you are thinking that a company needing special fasteners ought to post its specifications on a Web site or take its distributor to lunch, you have a sense for **supply chain management,** proactively planning and coordinating the flow of products, services, and information among connected firms focusing on creating and delivering value to end users.[3] Vividly illustrated by Cessna's initiatives in the beginning of this chapter, supply chain management involves information sharing, joint planning, and coordination to improve business performance by eliminating waste, innovating, improving quality, and providing flexibility.

In the case of our OEM needing new fasteners, supply chain management can be used to coordinate work in situations where markets need a little push or lubrication. In theory, it gives attention to the entire value-added process.

In the last two decades, the strategic role of supply management (discussed in Chapter 3) has taken on new significance at many companies. Part of this interest stems from the global nature of competition in today's business markets. Indeed, companies formerly isolated from other players in the industry by cultural or geographic divides now find aggressive and creative rivals for market share. This has precipitated two related thrusts in business: (1) a press for accountability and effectiveness in marketing efforts (discussed in Part 2), and (2) an invigorated quest for operational efficiency, the elimination of any waste. *Often the profit impact from purchasing and logistical efficiencies outweighs that from market penetration.*

## *Efficiency Gains*

To illustrate, Exhibit 2–1 shows the impact on profits from two different business efforts. Case A shows a 10 percent sales increase over the base case as a result of a $200,000 promotional effort that hikes promotion expenses to $1.2 million. Because gross margin is 25% of sales, gross profits also surge 10 percent to $3.3 million. And deducting the program costs, net earnings before taxes show a 20 percent gain.

Case B shows the results of a $200,000 expenditure on supply management—especially collaboration in production planning and quality control. Later in the book we detail the purchasing and collaboration process, but for now let's presume that as a result of more frequent travel for meetings and software expenses to integrate the planning systems at its vendors, general and administration expenses rise to $1.7 million from the base case of $1.5 million, but supplier costs are trimmed, prices are reduced, defects are nearly eliminated, and the need for rework processes is all but forgotten. Consequently, costs of goods sold (COGS) are decreased by 10 percent from the base case. With sales unaffected, gross profits jump 30 percent from $3 million in the base case to $3.9 in

**Exhibit 2–1**
Profit Impact
from Marketing
and Supply
Management

| | Base Case | | Case A:<br>Marketing Impact | | Case B:<br>Supply<br>Management Impact | |
|---|---|---|---|---|---|---|
| *Income Statements* | | | | | | |
| | $ (000) | % | $ (000) | % | $ (000) | % |
| Net revenue | $12,000 | 100% | $13,200 | 100% | $12,000 | 100% |
| Cost of goods sold | $9,000 | 75% | $9,900 | 75% | $8,100 | 68% |
| Gross profit | $3,000 | 25% | $3,300 | 25% | $3,900 | 32% |
| Promotion | $1,000 | 8% | $1,200 | 9% | $1,000 | 8% |
| General and admin. | $1,500 | 13% | $1,500 | 11% | $1,700 | 14% |
| Net earnings | $500 | 4% | $600 | 5% | $1,200 | 10% |

Case B and net earnings climb to $1.2 million—a 140 percent bump from the base case and *twice* the impact of the promotion program. A 10 percent COGS savings can be tough to come by, but the payoffs of efficiency due to strategic purchasing management can be striking. Successful suppliers look beyond the receiving dock to recognize how they can support the efficiency and effectiveness goals of their customers.

In this vein, notice that Case B hints at a comprehensive approach to efficiency. That is, rather than simply negotiating for lower and lower prices on inputs, as we would see in transactional exchange, many buying firms—with the help of their suppliers—are looking at the bigger picture. It takes a bit of analysis to answer the questions: Is a $4.19 part a better buy than another at $4.65 if defects average 0.01 percent in the former and 0.0001 percent in the latter? What if the former comes in monthly shipments by rail car versus skids deployed on the shop floor as needed, just-in-time, for the latter? Clearly, acquisition costs don't tell the whole story on efficiency.

## Effectiveness Payoffs

We must emphasize that there is more to the story than efficiency. Savvy buyers are using their suppliers to make *market share gains*. A case in point is Brown–Forman Beverage Company's collaboration with Inland Container of Louisville, Kentucky, which makes corrugated containers.[4] Don Harris, Inland's account executive, spends three days a week in a Brown–Forman office. He gets involved in the design process from the idea stage. Recently, Harris helped design a packaging and shipping container for Tropical Freezes, a frozen drink sold at retail in pliable plastic pouches. Harris came up with a solution that protected the pouches from being crushed, made them in the optimum size, and made the product safe from accidental damage caused by retailers cutting open a case. Thus, Inland's role in making the product secure and convenient for retailers enhanced the product's strength in the market.

We illustrate the nature of business markets by taking the fastener case a little further. Consider a design calling for a brand new fastener, a tension-spring clip, for Hewlett-Packard's (HP's) new printer. HP must find a supplier with both interest in and capabilities for making the tiny parts. HP might send specifications to candidate suppliers and invite bids, but what assurance does it have that the low-priced supplier will be able to deliver reliably or provide zero defects? What assurances will suppliers need in order to invest in the capability to supply HP? Will HP be vulnerable to price gouging at

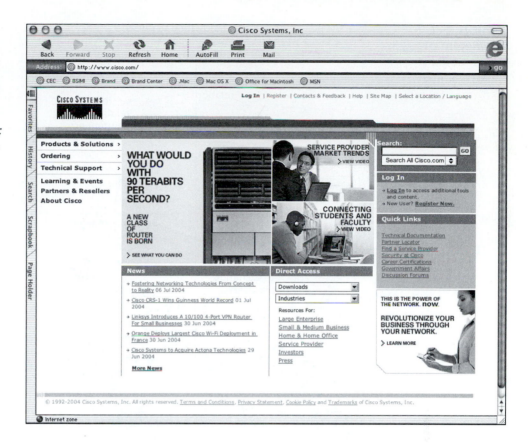

renewal time? These are just a few of the issues pertinent to buyers and sellers in business markets if they are interested in making a relationship work for an extended period.

# Relationship Management

Buyer interest in maintaining a high-performance relationship often has its counterpart on the supply side. That is, the supplier may be attracted by the promise of recurring purchases due to their volume and relative certainty. But the supplier has valid concerns about set-up, administrative costs, long-run payoffs, and vulnerability. Does it make sense to assign a team to prepare a bid? How much managerial attention will this customer require? Will the company need to dedicate personnel or production systems to this account? Can the company work with the other firm's people? How much training is involved? Will it compromise operations with current customers? What is the long-run promise of this particular account? In what competitive position does this put the company at renewal?

## A Map of Motives to Relate

Obviously, the stakes of both buyer and seller must be considered as factors of the exchange environment.[5] Exhibit 2–2 is a useful summary of our discussion to this point. It depicts each party's range of motivations for forging and sustaining a trading relationship. The horizontal axis represents the possibilities for a buyer. The buyer can

**Exhibit 2–2**
The Realm of
Buyer–Seller
Relationships

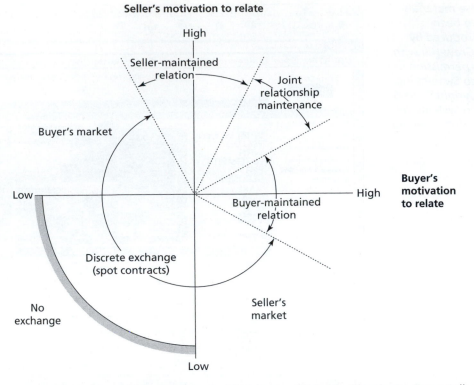

SOURCE: *Adapted from F. Robert Dwyer, Paul H. Schurr, and Sejo Oh, "Developing Buyer–Seller Relationships." Used with permission from the* Journal of Marketing, *published by the American Marketing Association, vol. 52 (April 1987), p. 15.*

be highly motivated to establish and maintain a relationship with a sole source supplier or a small set of vendors. For example, a large retail chain is looking to energy consultancy, eMotiv, to identify efficiencies in a panel of test stores, then devise systems for long-run energy management. Alternatively, the buyer may have little interest in a relationship or even a transaction—a commercial builder who makes a once-in-a-lifetime call upon a bee expert when a swarm at one job site slows springtime construction.

The vertical axis shows that a seller has a similar range of stakes in a relationship. This surprises some readers. Doesn't a selling firm want to do business or forge long-running relationships with all comers? The answer is no. Some business marketers choose not to sell to government agencies because the paperwork is too thick and the margins too thin. A business consultant in the Midwest declined business opportunities with a prospective client because the expected follow-up business was inadequate in light of the anticipated service burdens. Potential customers in a particular region or business sector may be bypassed to avoid head-to-head competition with a specific rival firm. Suffice it to say that sellers have motives to build and maintain relationships that vary from one prospect or customer to another.

## Spotting Transactional Exchange

Our discussion of pencils and standard fasteners in the opening section of the chapter actually previewed the lower left sector of Exhibit 2–2. What are essentially **transactional**

**relationships** or **spot exchanges,** money traded for easily measured commodities, include General Mills buying various wheat and other grains on commodities markets, a restaurant buyer at a cash-and-carry produce market, or a rail freight service offering standard boxcars to any shipper. Communication content is quite narrow between transacting parties, and their identity is hardly relevant. Trading terms are simple and clear. Performance is practically immediate.

Today's information technology has supported the creation of an important enterprise—market making. For example, FreeMarkets uses the Internet and its proprietary software to conduct online auctions for raw materials, commodities, and industrial parts. A successful auction sends business to the most-efficient suppliers and can yield purchasers savings upwards of 30 percent, compared to other purchasing approaches. But a successful auction demands a lot of front-end work. FreeMarkets consultants work closely with managers on the purchasing side in order to specify needs precisely and to accurately communicate them to potential suppliers (bidders) before each auction. Bidders, in turn, receive training in FreeMarkets' Bidware® software so they participate in the live auction.

Online auctions have their limits. Many products and services, like complex components, engineering services, or system installations, can't be fully specified. Perhaps their performance depends critically on a supplier's personal expertise and deft problem solving. Although market makers like FreeMarkets will strive to qualify supplier participants in the auctions, not all such factors are captured in the process. Indeed, Gene Richter, former chief of procurement officer for IBM, concedes that reverse auctions can work well between fully qualified suppliers—those meeting standards of delivery and quality. Practically, however, "suppliers are almost never equal in every aspect and an auction sends a dangerous message that the buyer only cares about price." Richter recommends picking the best source from the set of quotations—considering price, quality, delivery, technology—and then negotiating a better price, but a price yielding sufficient profits for the supplier to invest in new equipment, materials, and so forth. Richter's approach neatly moves us from a discussion of spot markets to a practical examination of relationships.[6]

## Unequal Interest in Relating

The upper right sector of Exhibit 2–2's relationship map captures our immediate discussion of relationships. Here, at least one party is motivated to build and keep a relationship.

In the upper sector we find seller-maintained relations—the situation typified by today's wireless communications industry. The value of any system depends on the depth and quality of ongoing support given by the vendor. Users are hardly locked in. For instance, if Verizon does not provide its users with high-quality reception, upgrades, and accurate billing, it risks losing accounts for good. Sellers in this sector of Exhibit 2–2 increasingly use a family of information technology tools for **Customer Relationship Management.** Typically dubbed **CRM** systems, these suites of software assist marketer efforts to: (1) collect and store accessible data on each account—the name and position of key personnel, purchase history, delivery specifications, sales calls, trade show interactions, e-mails, and other contacts, (2) evaluate customer, program, and product performance, and (3) support the development of customized services, communications, and more in order to maximize the long-run profitability of each account.

The right sector maps the realm of buyer-managed relationships. The chapter's opening vignette described the proactive management of the tiny suppliers to Cessna

Aircraft. In the field of professional services, we note how Procter & Gamble manages relationships with a network of marketing research suppliers, sometimes providing business to start-ups to change the unfavorable (to P&G) landscape of capable research vendors, or securing high levels of vendor service from branch offices in Cincinnati where P&G is headquartered. Similarly, Toyota shares its production schedules and orchestrates a giant network of suppliers in its Toyota City complex.

## Joint Interest in a Relationship

Between these two lopsided cases of seller-managed and buyer-managed relationships is an area where buyers and sellers have *mutual* stakes in a sustained trading relationship. A **strategic partnership** results when both parties have keen interests in maintaining an ongoing exchange. The strategic essence of the partnership rests on the significance of the resources and long-run consequences of the efforts. Thus, a three-year contract for a single supplier of lubricants to provide for all factory needs is apt to be regarded as less strategic than a joint R&D effort on new pollution controls.

Many of the strategic partnerships that characterize business markets have been sparked by the "quality revolution," a management process of renewed dedication to customer satisfaction and efficiency. Leaders in the quality movement—Xerox, Procter & Gamble, Dana Commercial Credit Corporation, and others—evidence an all-hands effort at continuous improvement in the systems of business: social (teamwork, creativity, motivation, etc.), technical (tool, machines, analytic techniques), and management (information flow, policies, adaptation of the other systems). Quite fittingly, suppliers have been brought into this process. From the Field 2–1 sketches supplier involvement at Palm.

## Key Managerial Implications of Relationships

Many companies have found it necessary to reduce the number of suppliers as they expand their involvement with source firms. When buyer and seller share forecasts and plans, they usually find they can reduce inventories. Buyer participation in the vendor's production setup and quality control processes eliminates the costly process of coping with defective inputs (rework, reorders, and scrap). This sort of managerial attention by the buyer could be spread too thin if given to several competing suppliers.

Reducing the number of suppliers, of course, reduces the number of competitive bidders and thereby dampens the power of the marketplace to affect prices. But often the parties can establish a commodity index or some standardized costing method to cope with this hazard. At the same time, when the buyer consolidates purchases, it often obtains a volume-justified price break from the supplier. Furthermore, with fewer suppliers, buyers often experience reduced variation on key part characteristics and service. This reduced variation enables higher uniformity and quality control in buyer operations.

On a related front, OEM buyers have worked with suppliers of component parts and materials to eliminate costly inventories and frequent handling costs by establishing just-in-time (JIT) relationships. Chapter 3 will address JIT as a purchasing strategy. Here we introduce its relationship character. A **JIT relationship** "requires the supplier to produce and deliver to the OEM precisely the necessary quantities at the necessary time, with the objective that products produced by the supplier conform to performance specification every time."[7] Unfortunately, some of the early JIT relationships were underachievers because buyers simply used their purchasing muscle to push inventories up the supply chain; no system efficiencies resulted. Others represented a simplistic attempt

## 2–1

### FROM THE FIELD
## Palm's Up!

You'll find lots of new handhelds in the $400–$500 price range. When Palm's Zire PDA was introduced in October 2002 for $99, it quickly became the fastest selling PDA in history. Credit Palm's strategic sourcing initiative for getting the Zire under $100.

Palm worked with original design manufacturers (ODMs) and its engineering and sourcing teams to hit cost targets for each component. The display target proved especially challenging, initially more than 50 percent above target. Looking at every specification and relying on input from four display vendors, it took less-expensive components, new processes, and a new Chinese manufacturer to trim the costs to target. An about-face from its past tendencies to "tell suppliers how to tie their shoes," Palm's reliance on vendor input has proved invaluable to its sourcing team—and its market position in the PDA arena.

Palm has sifted its suppliers and forged alliances with a select few. Texas Instruments, for example, is Palm's partner for supplying microprocessors. Calling the TI alliance one of the most complex, Palm senior VP for global operations sees "a lot of activities in marketing, co-marketing of products and funding of marketing. It also involves funding of new technology investments in hardware and software." Indeed, TI's willingness to invest in certain microprocessors gave it an edge over Intel and Motorola with Palm.

Jim Carbone, "Strategic Sourcing Is Palm's Pilot," *Purchasing* (April 17, 2003), pp. 32–36; http://www.palm.com/us/; Texas Instruments at http://www.ti.com/.

to mimic Japanese systems without thorough examination of the distance and climatic challenges posed for stockless throughput. Indeed, maybe the inefficiencies of a safety stock are more desirable than risking all-night truck driving on black ice or worse.

An assessment of JIT by suppliers to U.S. automakers showed evidence of missed opportunities. Fully 30 percent of the suppliers see JIT as merely an upstream shift of inventories, and only half the suppliers get stable delivery schedules from their customers.[8]

Clearly, the terms *relationship* and *strategic partnership* often convey trendy images or managerial intentions more than actions. In an in-depth interview with a marketing executive at a leading manufacturing company, one of the authors asked some of the standard questions used to assess a firm's intentions to forge relationships. The executive indicated his degree of agreement or disagreement to items such as "We expect our relationship with our supplier to last a long time" and "This company is (not) just another supplier." Intentions were good. Then the interview got to specific activities: Do you share market forecasts with your supplier? (No.) Do you involve this supplier in your production process? (No.) It went on like this. Good intentions and platitudes are not enough to make a relationship work.[9]

## DEVELOPING RELATIONSHIPS

Because we have already introduced the notion of motivations to sustain a relationship, we should elaborate on what it means when a relationship works. We can then consider the process by which relationships develop.

# High-Performance Criteria

As you might guess, managers want their relationships to be profitable. But the particular routes to profitability for trading partners don't strictly coincide with each other. Let's look at the preferences of sellers and buyers.

## Preferences of Sellers and Buyers

### Sellers

Sellers want substantial and reliable purchase volumes at adequate margins. And they want account management expenses, promotions, and other allocated costs to leave a large portion of the gross profit intact. A little cost accounting and historical comparison can reveal the profitability of newly established customer relationships. For example, a steel service center will strive to carry the specialty wires, I-beams, and alloys needed by manufacturers in its trade area. Its salespeople make regular calls and quotes, perhaps to attain a 40 percent share of State Fabricating's (SF's) purchases. If the steel service center can negotiate a contract supplying 80 percent of SF's needs at a price break of 10 percent, it can compute the incremental gross profit and add, say, 15 percent of the inventory reduction from knowing SF's production schedule and the cost of 10 sales calls per year. It would then deduct the equivalent of 25 percent of the full cost of an inside salesperson now dedicated to the SF account.

### Buyers

Buyers often turn to supply partnerships motivated by evident inefficiencies in the production process—costly safety stocks, high return rates, numerous reorders, or long lead times. These forces have prompted purchasing directors to seek suppliers that will work collaboratively to eliminate waste and improve system economies. In the beginning of such a relationship, any efficiency gains can be measured against historical data. Continuing our example from the previous paragraph, as State Fabricators moves to a JIT system from its steel supplier, the regional steel service center, SF can determine its own inventory reduction savings, productivity gains from decreased line shutdowns, and labor savings in its purchasing operation.

## Designing New Standards

After three or four years of JIT service from the steel supplier, the usefulness of historical data has waned for both parties. There is no obvious new performance yardstick. In this situation, partners rely on two broad types of assessments: internal and external.

### Internal Assessments

Some companies do periodic supplier evaluations, combining data on internal operations with assessments from their own managers on supplier professionalism, responsiveness, quality, technical capability, and vision. Hewlett-Packard, for example, evaluates its suppliers on technology, quality, responsiveness, delivery, and cost. The last two dimensions have gotten the focus of supplier attention since the ratings were instituted in 1985, largely because they are objectively measurable. That most suppliers have improved their on-time delivery by 20 to 30 percent, some even by 50 percent, supports the adage that what gets measured is what gets done. Cessna's supply chain initiative resulted in a scoring system for defects that considered not so much the

**Exhibit 2–3**
Sales Agent
Performance
for the Gamma
Corporation

| Agencies | No. of Reps | Estimated Market Size | Gamma Sales | Gamma % | Competitive Intensity Index[1] |
|---|---|---|---|---|---|
| Webster (Milwaukee–Madison) | 3 | $16,500 | $2,800 | 17% | 4 |
| Batham (Rochester) | 2 | $15,200 | $1,600 | 11 | 5 |
| Smalz (Phoenix) | 4 | $17,100 | $4,800 | 28 | 3 |
| Lincoln (Durham) | 3 | $16,800 | $2,320 | 14 | 3 |
| Maxington (Peoria) | 3 | $15,900 | $3,240 | 20 | 4 |
| Average | 3 | $16,300 | $2,952 | 18 | 4 |

[1] 5 = high, 1 = low.

cost of the part, but the cost to rectify given the stage of the assembly process. Thus, a defect discovered in final assembly is weighted 100 times higher than one detected at incoming inspection.

Likewise, sellers track key accounts against sales and profitability objectives, reorders, inventory and service burdens, and promise of future business. It is possible to do the cost accounting to result in a simplified income statement for each key account or group of accounts. Unisys, the $6 billion IT service and technology company, is even more diligent with its customer base. Once a year it conducts a 16-question, customer relationship survey to gauge customer satisfaction, loyalty, and advocacy—proven predictors of revenue growth.

**External Measures**
Sometimes a company can evaluate relationships on a relative basis against external norms provided by trade associations or consulting companies. Large firms may even produce their own profiles using supply relationships with various company operations. In this case each particular relationship can be compared to an external standard or profile derived from other relationships. It is not uncommon for electronics manufacturers to compare the performance of their independent sales agents across the country.

Although agencies are autonomous businesses and are paid a standard commission on sales, most participate in manufacturer training programs and may purchase demonstration equipment. Terminations and start-ups are far from costless. Cooperation between the manufacturer and agent enhances marketing effectiveness. Thus, comparing sales and market penetration rates between agents in similar markets helps the manufacturer to identify and analyze high-performance agency relationships.

We can see how external measures can be applied in an example. Exhibit 2–3 reveals that the Smalz agency in Phoenix is a high performer. Its market is less competitive than Batham's in Rochester, but the comparative data also reveal Batham's use of what appears to be an undersized sales force. Gamma might now effectively press Batham to add selling resources. Models such as these can be critical to the evaluation and direction of sustained business relationships.

## Higher Standards

When buyers or sellers in business markets are asked what makes a good relationship, they always punctuate with more than dollar signs. They want integrity, fairness, loyalty, flexibility, consideration in partner's strategy, partner's participation in their own strategies, and compliance with established administrative procedures. Most companies have internal value systems that support these behaviors in contractual relations. They stand behind the product and honor commitments. With perhaps millions of business transactions conducted each week, these nonlegal sanctions seem to work reasonably well. Sellers who shirk obligations, misrepresent their abilities, and issue empty promises stand to lose accounts. Their tarnished reputation limits their ability to gain new ones. Buyers who are rigid in their demands and foreclose supply partners from planning impair their own productivity. Good suppliers in some industries have chosen not to deal with such customers. Others simply pull back on their inputs to the relationship, performing at minimum levels to retain the account or milk it of its waning value.

So what's the relative importance of profits and propriety in business relationships? An executive who had terminated a well-known supplier summarized his decision: "It was not so much what they failed to do for us, but what they tried to do to us that led us to quit." Indeed, commercial trading cannot be sustained in the absence of virtue.

Fortunately, many forces in the business environment induce good conduct. The potential for repeat business and the reputational ripples through the market from each excellent—or awful—exchange provide simple but powerful sanctions for ethical behavior and cooperation in relationships. As this behavior is reinforced, reciprocated, reinforced again, and so on, businesses often deepen their relationship.

Hydrotech, a Cincinnati-based distributor of hydraulics, proved instrumental in machine tool development at Cincinnati Milacron in the late 1980s. Hydrotech developed expertise in new hydraulics from Europe and—based on deep knowledge of Milacron's product line—was able to help Milacron improve the hydraulic systems in its tools. Since then, Hydrotech's involvement in applications engineering at Milacron has expanded, particularly to its plastic molding machines, now the core business at Milacron. The next section explores a provocative model for the development of such buyer–seller relationships.

# A MODEL OF RELATIONSHIP DEVELOPMENT

We have found the metaphor of courtship and marriage to illuminate facets of business relationships. The language of business marketers reflects this. You may have heard them talk about "getting better acquainted," "courting a prospect," "setting up house with XYZ," or "tying the knot." Theodore Levitt has offered a concise and illustrative observation:

> The relationship between a seller and a buyer seldom ends when a sale is made. Increasingly, the relationship intensifies after the sale and helps determine the buyer's choice the next time around. Such dynamics are found particularly with services and products dealt in a stream of transactions between seller and buyer—financial services, consulting, general contracting, military and space equipment, and capital goods.
>
> The sale, then, merely consummates the courtship, at which point the marriage begins. . . . The quality of the marriage determines whether there will be continued or expanded business, or troubles and divorce.[10]

This section of the chapter develops the marriage metaphor using business examples to illustrate concepts and implications from research on interpersonal relationships. Exhibit 2–4 complements our discussion, showing buyer and seller in four stages of relationship development.

**Exhibit 2–4**
The Relationship Development Process

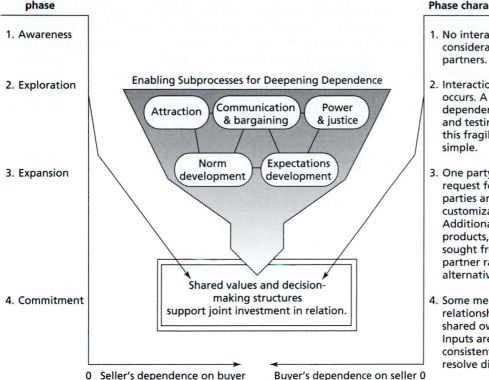

| Relationship phase | | Phase characteristics |
|---|---|---|
| 1. Awareness | | 1. No interaction. Unilateral considerations of potential partners. |
| 2. Exploration | Enabling Subprocesses for Deepening Dependence | 2. Interaction between the parties occurs. A gradual increase in dependence reflects probing and testing. Termination of this fragile association is simple. |

Attraction  Communication & bargaining  Power & justice

Norm development  Expectations development

3. Expansion — 3. One party has made a successful request for adjustment. Both parties are satisfied with some customization involved. Additional benefits from products, services, or terms are sought from the current partner rather than from an alternative partner.

Shared values and decision-making structures support joint investment in relation.

4. Commitment — 4. Some means of sustaining the relationship result: contracts, shared ownership, social ties. Inputs are significant and consistent. Partners adapt and resolve disputes internally.

0   Seller's dependence on buyer        Buyer's dependence on seller 0

SOURCE: *Adapted from F. Robert Dwyer, Paul H. Schurr, and Sejo Oh, "Developing Buyer–Seller Relationships." Used with permission from the* Journal of Marketing, *published by the American Marketing Association, vol. 52 (April 1987), p. 21.*

# Awareness

In the **awareness stage,** buyer and seller independently consider the other as an exchange partner. Supplier advertisements and trade show exhibits might be noticed by the prospective buyer. At the same time, the supplier may collect information about product specifications, buying process, and the like at the prospective customer. This stage may last indefinitely, or the parties may move to the next stage of the process by engaging each other in some form of interaction.

# Exploration

In the **exploration stage,** we find the parties probing and testing each other. The prospective buyer may attend a seminar given by the supplier. The supplier may make several sales calls. Even initial purchases can take place in this stage. They are part of a trial process. In the exploration phase, a relationship is very fragile. The parties have not significantly invested in the exchange. Neither party depends highly on the other. The association is easily terminated. But in this stage, the interplay of five enabling processes supports the developing relationship.

## *Attraction*

**Attraction** is the degree to which the interaction between buyer and seller yields them net payoffs in excess of some minimum level. The payoffs are tangible and intangible rewards from the association less economic and social costs. Practically, this can be illustrated by the buyer's purchasing director and a supplier's sales manager sharing college memories and striking a friendship at a Big Ten Alumni picnic in Atlanta. Atop these social rewards from the association the buyer looks for quality, technical know-how, a fair price, and logistical service. The supplier looks for steady orders at a fair margin plus a chance to satisfy additional needs within the buying organization. Both want minimal order costs, delays, and foul-ups.

In a fascinating case study in the automotive industry, business professors James Comer and B. J. Zirger (1995) detail the relationship development stages between an auto manufacturer, dubbed Zenith, and a supplier of vibration dampeners, labeled Alta.[11] Mechanical systems and road use in automobiles cause harmful vibrations that, unless dampened, cause mechanical stress and limit durability. Vibration dampers typically consist of a metal inner ring and outer rings separated by a ring made of a complex rubber compound. The product is not technically sophisticated, but a large number of variables in the design—width, thickness, metal and rubber composition, fit to other designs in the automobile—complicate product development.

The attraction between Zenith and Alta was triggered by the emergence of a new paradigm in the industry. Cost containment and reengineering in the late 1980s and early 1990s prompted automakers to examine long-standing supply relationships and explore value-added opportunities from engaging suppliers in product development. Suppliers, which had often dealt exclusively with a single automaker and simply priced dampers on the basis of blueprints received, began to send sales reps to engineers at prospect accounts. Their job was to find out what the prospective customer was working on and what problems it was facing, and then to develop credibility as a provider of solutions.

In the case study, Alta's salesperson responsible for new account development invited Zenith officials, primarily product engineers, to Alta's plant to demonstrate abilities, introduce the highly competent personnel, and ask for an opportunity to compete for an upcoming damper project. A few months later, Zenith had some problems with its current supplier's damper, and engineers suggested blueprints be sent to Alta for a bid. Alta received the prints and gave them number one priority by assigning topflight people to a bid management team.

## *Communication and Bargaining*

In the development of relationships, communication and bargaining enable the parties to rearrange the distribution of their obligations, rewards, and costs. Parties to most budding relationships hesitate to clearly state their needs, preferences, or goals. They talk around the issues or provide only vague hints of what they are after in the exchange. Not until they develop a level of comfort and familiarity do they begin to make disclosures. These disclosures will probably require **reciprocation**—a similar action returned by the other—if the association is to grow into a productive relationship.

Dramatic effects on a relationship happen when parties bargain. After all, for parties to "take the trouble, go to the bother, and expend the psychic and physical energies necessary to negotiate," the partners must see some potential for a rewarding association.[12] See if this principle applies to your own social relationships. Asking your third-time date to meet you promptly might be a bold request. It could fracture the fragile relationship or it could lead to an accommodation that signals your date's interest in sustaining the association too. Likewise, a buyer who asks for delivery between 3:00 and 3:30 A.M. from a supplier whose delivery runs begin at 4:00 A.M. risks forgoing service from this supplier. Should the supplier arrange to make 3:00 A.M. deliveries, the exchange relationship may start to crystalize or even expand.

In the case of vibration dampers, Alta used a multifunctional team to provide a set of cost estimates for the design provided by Zenith. Purchasing people at Alta contacted paint, material, and component suppliers, while manufacturing identified assembly time, tooling, scrap, and so on. Tech center personnel determined that more computer-controlled machining equipment would be needed for the job. After four weeks Alta sent Zenith a preliminary bid that met specifications for Zenith and profitability requirements at Alta. Moreover, Alta recommended some design changes to improve performance.

## Power and Justice

Adjustment in an exchange is a critical facet of relationship development. Concessions sought or granted in the bargaining process result from the just or unjust application of power. **Power**—an ability of one organization, Alpha, to get another organization, Beta, to do what it would not do otherwise—derives from Beta's dependence on Alpha for valued resources that are not easily obtained elsewhere. These valued resources can take many forms: status, economic rewards, expertise, and applied or ended punishments. **Justice**—the rendering of what is merited or due—results from the fair and respectful use of power. Evenhandedness and honesty characterize the just use of power. In contrast, the unjust application of power attempts to control another's actions against his will or without his understanding or in the absence of fault.

Akin to the significance of bargaining for marking progress, the successful (just) exercise of power sparks the transition from an exploratory relationship to one heading into the expansion phase. The premium dog food manufacturer IAMS enjoyed a strong market position among kennel owners. When it sought to penetrate the consumer market, it paid each kennel owner $5 per name for every new owner of a dog purchased from its kennel. Thus, instead of having to comply with some new requirement to obtain IAMS products or credit terms, kennels were delighted by the advent of a new profit center and a foundation for new kinds of cooperation with the IAMS company. It was the just application of power that established this basis for additional joint efforts between IAMS and kennel owners.

Zenith engineers reviewed Alta's bid for about three months before ultimately giving tentative acceptance. This meant that Zenith was willing to continue to work with Alta. Prices were in a reasonable range, and the redesign proposal was worthy of further examination and collaboration. This was a milestone in the developing relation, a platform for deeper cooperation.

## Norms Development

We forge business relationships to accomplish tasks and attain goals sought by each party. Simply put, there is work to be done. **Norms** are standards of behavior for the parties, the guidelines by which the parties interact. Some norms exist prior to and are brought to the exploratory phase. For example, buyer and sales rep share many elements when asked to outline a "script" for different types of sales calls.[13] Such scripts have less commonality when the parties come from different cultures or professions. As the parties interact, they customize their patterns of interaction. Practically, this means they may teach each other the language of their respective companies, meet with a negotiated frequency, communicate by mutually agreeable—even automated—channels, and begin to organize evaluation, planning, and decision-making tasks.

Zenith and Alta relied on common norms of exchange in their initial interactions. Professional courtesies, the language of automotive engineers, plant tour protocol, and the conveyance of blueprints inviting bids are general norms that enabled the two firms to begin to collaborate. The preliminary acceptance launches an opportunity for more customization of their patterns of interaction: frequency and locale of meetings, prototype development schedules, and product testing procedures.

### Expectations

As the parties interact and explore the potential for ongoing exchange, they develop expectations. Foremost among expectations is **trust,** "the belief that a party's word or promise is reliable and a party will fulfill his or her obligations in an exchange relationship."[14] The trusting party derives confidence from a belief that the other party is consistent, honest, fair, responsible, and helpful. These expectations can be shaped in part by the other party's image advertising and reputation in the industry.

Based on industry reputation and limited interaction, Alta expected Zenith to give it a fair opportunity for its business and it risked four weeks of team effort in the preparation of a serious bid. On the other end, Zenith regarded Alta as a credible potential supplier, sent its personnel to Alta's plant, and took a risk itself by disclosing its designs. Neither Zenith nor Alta saw large investments yet, only small exposures to risk for the promise of cooperation and higher payoffs. Positive outcomes from these occasions of vulnerability build trust.

We should look for direct experience to play a key role in the migration of the relationship past the exploration phase. The relationship must be solidified in the expansion phase, to be taken up next, and satisfy the critical prerequisites for the commitment phase!

# Expansion

In the **expansion stage** the association moves from one of testing and probing to one of enlarging rewards and the scope of exchange. Account development, cross-selling, and up-selling are manifestations of the expansion phase. Consider the experience of TMSS, a company providing consulting and administrative services in select fields. It is not uncommon for an advertising agency or financial service firm to use TMSS initially for mail, courier, and distribution services. Clients may then turn to TMSS for printing and reproduction services, later desktop publishing and creative services, and finally perhaps file and document management. As a client increasingly **outsources** or spins off internal functions to an outside provider, TMSS may realize a higher and higher proportion of its business from this particular client. Both firms find their dependence on the other has escalated. From the Field 2–2 illustrates today's collaboration in the automotive supply network.

The essence of the expansion phase is increasing dependence between the exchange partners. For Alta and Zenith the expansion is manifested in their interactions following their agreement on two critical documents: the "Presource Agreement" and a "Release

## 2–2

# FROM THE FIELD

## Technology & Trust for B2B Collaboration in Autos

"As soon as we think that we want to develop a new car, we bring in climate control, interior trim, chassis suppliers, and others, before we endorse a design," says Ford's vehicle line director for Lifestyle Vehicles, Nancy Gioia.

This level of collaboration between suppliers and OEMs aims for efficiency in product development, as well as low-cost production and ultimate consumer value. It takes not only a mindset that seeks to integrate processes in the supply network; it also takes technology to enable digital representation of the vehicle and seamless communication among firms involved.

For development of the new Thunderbird—from approval to showrooms in just 36 months—Ford engaged 52 suppliers to manufacture components and subsystems and participate in design and performance measures. Ford required all its vendors to work on the same software known as CP3, opened its internal design database to suppliers, and located many in its own offices.

As a key supplier in the increasingly collaborative automotive industry, Johnson Controls works both downstream and upstream. To build and deliver the cockpit module, seating systems, overhead consoles, and various electronic components for Chrysler's Jeep Liberty, Johnson Controls has just 200 minutes from order. And composed of audio systems, electrical controls, and instrument panel trim, the cockpit module by itself contains 11 major components! The components from 35-second tier suppliers must be integrated and delivered as one module.

Information technology and developing standards for the exchange of product engineering and manufacturing data support even deeper B2B collaboration in the auto industry. But technology won't go far in the absence of integrity. With over 50 percent of vehicle content outsourced, and approximately 80 percent engineered to order, we're looking at intellectual capital at risk. "You are basically sharing your family's famous secret sauce recipe. I have to trust you as a collaborative partner so that we can go to market together with a product plan, a product design, a bill of materials, etc.," sums up Johnson Controls' executive director, John Waraniak.

Laurie Toupin, "Needed: Suppliers Who Can Collaborate throughout the Supply Chain," *Supply Chain Automotive*, supplement to *Supply Chain Management Review* (July/August 2003), pp. 5–8; http://www.johnsoncontrols.com/; Automotive Industry Action Group at http://www.aiag.org/.

to Tool." The former precipitated the formation of a development team consisting of representatives from various areas of Alta's manufacturing, purchasing, and technical centers, along with fixed and floating representatives from Zenith's as well as Alta's suppliers. Weekly meetings alternated between Zenith's and Alta's facilities as the changes were made to damper designs as a result of ways that Alta and its suppliers knew to cut costs. Some of the lower-cost approaches involved redesign of other engine components. The ripple effect of such collaboration clearly reflected the growing interdependence of the two companies.

The "Release to Tool" agreement was a consequence of testing several hundred prototypes at Zenith's facility over the course of more than a year. But the words of the agreement—essentially a contract to purchase a specified quantity over a period of time at an agreed-upon price—were complemented by key bonding behaviors by each party. Zenith "desourced" its previous supplier of dampers for this application. Alta purchased special manufacturing equipment and made financial investment in prototypes beyond

Zenith's reimbursement schedule. *Both parties made concrete behavioral pledges to the relationship, in addition to reaching a verbal agreement.* They were nearing the commitment phase.

# Commitment

**Commitment** is a lasting desire to maintain or preserve a valuable, important relationship. In practice, the parties tend to fall short of this life cycle stage, despite their intentions. They may wrongly presume the progress in the prior stage has sufficient momentum for even greater levels of coordination and effectiveness or may underestimate the investment needed to make a relationship perform.[15] Indeed, this commitment phase is characterized by the parties' exchanging of significant resources. When the parties share a common belief in the effectiveness of future exchange in the commitment phase, they dedicate resources to maintain the relationship. Some buyers use a panel of suppliers to act as tribunals to arbitrate disputes. Buyer and seller may exchange employees in order to fully identify with the trading partner. Other means of cementing relations include the dedication of equipment and systems and even anniversary celebrations to reinforce the critical social bonds between the two companies. Commitment enables relationships to survive either party's foul-ups and environmental disturbances—blizzards, fires, truckers' strikes—that are neither party's fault.

Two months after reaching the "Release to Tool" agreement, Zenith hired a new purchasing director who was charged with instituting major cost reductions in parts purchasing. Alta renegotiated a new price schedule. Meanwhile, Alta's paint supplier caused several prototypes to fail corrosion tests. The relationship survived this breakdown because Alta secured a more capable paint supplier prior to the testing of production samples.

# Dissolution

In the early phases of relationship development, either partner can walk away from the exchange without trouble. Many do. But as mutual dependencies increase and the costs of switching to another exchange partner take on significance, ending a relationship can become a knotty problem. **Dissolution**—termination of an advanced relationship—can make assets dedicated to the relationship obsolete and require additional search, negotiation, and set-up costs for both parties. Indeed, it took more than a year for Alta and Zenith to forge a supply relationship. In some cases, costly litigation and emotional scars can add to the toll of termination.

What little research we have in this area suggests that dissolution is a counterpart to the process of relationship development.[16] Briefly, we know that parties remain in business relationships for two broad reasons: (1) they want to remain—the relationship is financially, strategically, or psychologically rewarding—or (2) they have to stay—exit is too costly, or no alternatives exist.

If a party wants to be in the relationship, it doesn't matter so much that it might have to be. Thus, the effects of a dissatisfying event depend on the overall attitude of the offended partner toward the relationship. If the attitude is favorable, episodes of dissatisfaction will be endured or redressed. When the partner has had to endure several letdowns, lingering dissatisfaction darkens the view of the future held by the "custodian" of the relationship, perhaps a sales manager or purchasing director. This person with day-to-day responsibility for the relationship sorts through the options, then makes a case to the firm's top management. For example, the marketing manager at a medical insurance company may note the sustained weak performance of a particular agency, despite a variety of assistances and slack for extenuating circumstances, and make a presentation to the home office to terminate.

Formal dialogue between the two firms may strive to address the status of the relationship. Likely, the insurance company will give 30 days' notice of termination of the agency. Cause may be given as substandard performance or policy breaches. Then in the aftermath, we can look for the dissemination of public accounts of a breakup and counterpart accounts for internal consumption only at the respective firms. Let's not expect company and agent always to tell the same story.

## Model Assessment

The marriage metaphor seems to apply to business relationships in many contexts. For situations that allow gradual testing and expanding reliance on a trading partner, the metaphor seems particularly useful. It focuses on mutual problem solving, the development of efficient routines, and the reinforcement of trusting behaviors. The perspective also lends its insights particularly to exchange relations between firms that have a key individual doing deals and renewal.

Because it does not recognize (1) the dynamics of decision making by the cross-functional work teams, which are becoming common at large firms, and (2) different levels of authority of relationship custodians across organizations, the marriage metaphor represents a gross simplification of the process. The model also is nearly silent on the effects of the larger exchange network on the relationship, such as Alta's suppliers or even their suppliers. We will amplify these in a later section. Likewise, because the model neglects the business equivalent of marriage without courtship, the next section will discuss alternative means of securing relationships.

# SAFEGUARDING RELATIONSHIPS

A variety of mechanisms can be used to cement strategic relationships. These mechanisms take on particular significance when there is no real chance to test the relationship. Indeed, some exchanges involve large-scale and long-run commitments. It may take 15 years to complete an oil field installation or start up a chemical plant. The Department of Defense has planned for 20-year horizons in the development of certain new weapons systems. When Apple brought Samsung in as a supplier of flash memory chips in its iPods, there may have been little opportunity for either partner to prove itself directly in the specific relationship prior to committing to substantial quantities at preset delivery schedules. Savvy business purchasers and marketers will set up terms and unique structures for the exchange to ensure its effectiveness over the long run.

## House Calls

Perhaps HP could send a couple of its managers—or an agent—to visit prospective suppliers. Do they have smooth-running shop floors? Is a supplier's personnel competent and dedicated to quality? Does it have access to the technology to do the job in the future? Activities such as these were part of the development of the Zenith–Alta relationship and are called **supplier verification.** They are formal efforts to obtain evidence of supplier capabilities and commitment. From a marketing perspective, it is important to

**2–1**

## BUSINESS 2 BUSINESS

### The Challenge of Cross-Cultural Partnerships

Many Western companies are trying to build business relationships in China. Although rigorous research has only just begun to study the process, we can identify a number of obstacles to the development of effective and lasting business partnerships. Perhaps due to the Confucian ethic stressing harmony in society and strong interpersonal bonds, business partnerships and joint ventures in China hinge on interpersonal relationships.

In initial interactions, managers from Chinese and Western cultures must first develop a level of trust that allows greater interdependence. How do business professionals overcome language barriers and a history of hundreds of years as adversaries? The Chinese culture exhibits a reliance on an extended family or in-group called *zijiren.* Western culture is more individualistic and measures time in shorter increments. Does it surprise you that some Western firms fracture relationships by prematurely pressing for written contracts? Would you expect some Chinese businesses to seek deals that in a demonstrable way "serve China"?[17]

recognize that the expertise, dedication to quality, professionalism, teamwork, and all-around customer focus of the supplier organization—not merely the sales rep—speak volumes to the prospective customer.

## Trading Places

Buyers and sellers may exchange personnel to provide assurances. Procter & Gamble engineers assist their suppliers with setup and testing of new production processes, such as cutting material for use in disposable diapers. Intel invited its furniture supplier to bring its expertise to reside in Intel's growing 1,600-person office in New Mexico. The supplier met with the building planners, Intel customers, and construction contractors, thereby reducing planning time. The furniture supplier then placed all orders, ensuring accuracy and tight coordination with its factory.[18] In this same way, HP could request its custom fastener supplier to come to its plant to become familiar with its workings and oversee the supply function.

## Managing Dependence

Alternatively, HP might set up two suppliers or do some of the manufacturing itself to avoid vulnerability to failures or "hold up" by the sole supplier. This is one example of a generic safeguarding strategy called **dependence balancing.**[19] In this approach a buyer reduces its dependence on the supplier by cultivating relationships with other exchange partners. You can easily see how the number one supplier might be motivated to give exceptional service if HP has a very attractive backup supplier. Recognize that this strategy may confound work flow by (1) introducing variation in delivery and parts performance and (2) stretching the supplier coordination and management resources across two partners. That is, the buyer may need to host two or more supplier teams in its product design efforts.

## Supplier Pledges

We saw this versatile strategy at work in the vibration dampers case when Zenith de-sourced its previous supplier. That bold move came after months of trust development with Alta at a time when it was important to signal its commitment. It also motivated Alta to reciprocate by investing in specialized machinery.[20]

Similar pledges could likewise be initiated by a supplier. Consider a supplier with a proprietary product. The supplier can empathize with a prospective buyer that is very reluctant to commit to any exclusive source, perhaps risking price gouging or restricted supply after production or marketing commitments that make switching impractical. As a pledge of good faith intentions to give good service and fair prices over the course of the relationship, the supplier could license its proprietary know-how to another company. This licensee would then be poised to serve the buyer in the event of performance breakdowns by the original source.[21]

## Contracts

The same effect, sustained commitment to the exchange, is sometimes achieved by inventive means of distributing the ownership of assets involved. For example, if HP wants a specially manufactured part that no other firm is known to need, prospective suppliers will require assurances that their investments in the ability to produce this product will pay out. Perhaps the parties could hammer out a complex contract with terms for long-run purchases at preset prices, with contingency clauses for every foreseeable circumstance—good and bad. But chances are good that the negotiators cannot anticipate every possible circumstance. Writing a rule now for how the parties will behave in the new environment four years from now could take more meetings than either firm wants to attend.

This problem of indefinite haggling can be solved by HP's ownership of the machinery to produce the part. HP can buy the machines to install in the supplier's plant, acquire and set up the supplier, or start up its own facility from scratch. Ownership of just the machines still leaves some control issues unsettled—issues such as training, maintenance, repair, and exclusivity. But these issues are not beyond the limits of contracts. **Relational contracts** are contracts that don't try to bring every future contingency up for consideration in the present, but establish means of continuous planning, adjusting, and resolving conflicts. Relational contracts can specify decision-making authority by issue (material standards, shutdowns, training, and maintenance) and establish procedures or structures for planning to ensure ongoing effective exchange.[22] Relational contracts play a key role in Cessna's supply chain management initiative.

## Ownership

**Vertical integration,** bringing a function or technology within the boundary of the firm, ensures continuity in the relationship because suppliers are now hierarchically connected employees. That is, employees work in an environment of formal rules, authority, reporting structures, and special responsibilities. Goals tend to be shared and, overall, control of activities is enhanced. Firms make a strategic choice to use distributors or their own sales force, outside research agencies or their own research department, third-party logistical services or their own traffic department, contract suppliers or inhouse manufacturing, and much more.

Coordination of selling, research, transportation, manufacturing, or other functions can be enhanced by a firm's own formal and informal communication systems, structured

---

**2–2**

## BUSINESS 2 BUSINESS
### Make-or-Buy Fuel Injectors?

AC Rochester develops and produces fuel injection and emissions systems. Product testing is quite extensive because fuel distribution systems play such a key role in a car's or truck's operation and because systems must perform in a wide range of situations. Indeed, the systems need to operate in both Alaska and Tucson, in both Denver and Miami. They need to perform using gasolines that conform to different standards across the country. Are you surprised to learn that AC Rochester is a division of General Motors? Assess the benefits this gives to GM. What other means besides outright corporate ownership could GM use to be assured of good fuel systems?

---

work roles, and decision-making processes. But there are real downsides to this solution to the safeguarding problem. Vertical integration swells fixed costs and may not well duplicate the motivation of owners of independent businesses. As Cessna discovered, integration also broadens the activities a firm tries to perform well and can dilute managerial focus. In short, it can't solve very many problems without seriously complicating the question, What business are we in? We will expand on this issue in Chapter 6.

## RELATIONSHIPS IN LARGER NETWORKS

We began this chapter with a quick review of the magnificent ability of markets to coordinate work. Then we focused on the special challenges of developing and safeguarding relationships, which are necessary for the exchange of complex, specialty, and risky products. This focus on buyer–seller relationships can be myopic, however, because the parties are not the only entities in the marketplace. They are connected in a network, a much larger and strategically significant *web* of organizations. We provided a preview of the significance of the network in our brief discussion of dependence balancing. In two examples, a party attempted to manage a focal relationship by purposely structuring another relationship. Håkan Håkansson, a leading expert in business networks from Sweden, paints the picture quite vividly. He reminds us that Swedish filmmakers like to make movies about marriage. The intrigue in these movies, however, invariably comes from introducing a third person. Intrigue in business relationships comes from new buyers (rivals to the incumbent), from new vendors, or from customers of the buyer or suppliers to the supplier. In any case, we agree with Håkansson that a triangle makes for drama.

But relevant business networks can be much larger than triangles. Rob Bestwick runs a public relations company with just four employees. His sustained growth is a result of a network of independent copywriters, designers, photographers, and other technical specialists that enable him to compete as a fleet-footed "virtual company."[23] In the automotive field again, Chrysler has reorganized its entire product development process around the concept of simultaneous engineering. In practice this involved six Mexican firms in the engine design for a new-generation vehicle.[24]

The Internet enables new types of B2B networks.

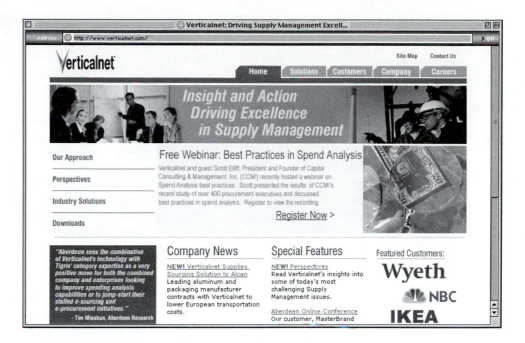

# SUMMARY OF TYPES OF BUSINESS RELATIONSHIPS

Markets are highly efficient mechanisms for the sale and purchase of commodities and general-use parts. Exemplified in cash-and-carry wholesaling, and online auctions, we've classified these exchanges as spot or transactional relationships. Self-interest motivates the exchange, and parties give little thought to future interaction.

At the other end of the business relationship continuum is the partnership, which many writers liken to a marriage. A partnership is a relationship characterized by mutual commitment, intense communication and collaboration, high trust, and common goals. With partnership status come opportunities to develop new business, a chance to gain access to valuable information, and many other benefits. Recall the partnership between Palm and Texas Instruments in From the Field 2–1.

Many marketing organizations aim to achieve partnership status with a range of customers. Likewise, many buying organizations look to form partnerships with a subset of suppliers. Obviously, a buyer–seller match in partnership motives yields a mutually maintained relationship whereas mismatches skew the relationship management responsibility to the party more interested in relating.

It should also be clear that business relationships can be distinguished on two other dimensions: the social dimension and the contractual/structural dimension. **Social relationship** is the term we use to describe a trading association supported principally by social bonds and habit. The "glue" holding together a social relationship includes interpersonal attraction and friendship between buyer and seller, similarity in background, a track record of successful cooperation, efficient communication, and general satisfaction. A transactional exchange could evolve into a social relationship as the parties forge customized routines, provide extraordinary performance, develop implicit and explicit understandings about needs and roles, trade favors, discover they both (dis)like fly fishing, French wines, the pope, Bob Marley . . . , and start liking each other.

The social bonds and the positively reinforced interactions that support the social relationships are important to most business relationships. Sometimes parties need more assurance than friendship—or prior to the possibility of developing social ties—that the relationship can be sustained. This includes assurances that the other party will stay motivated to perform up to established standards. These assurances usually involve some type of contract or "hostage" that constitutes a pledge for performance. Thus, such relationships are called **safeguarded relationships** because contracts or structural and technical ties bond the parties to the ongoing exchange. Contracts may have large penalties for termination and detailed procedures for resolving conflicts and adjusting to new working environments. For example, Unamin sells silica sand to Dow Corning, delivering 300 tons per day. The sand must meet very specific size and quality standards. If Unamin fails to deliver the right quality at the right time, the company must pay Dow Corning a substantial fee. Of course, Dow Corning has structurally tied its operations to Unamin and would also have to shut down the plant in the face of late deliveries and defects. The contractual provisions for the penalties, then, balance Dow Corning's implicit pledge in sole-sourcing silica and are a way of safeguarding by sharing risk.

**Corporate relationships** are exchanges safeguarded by ownership or vertical integration. A university assures itself of sustained access to printing services by having its own printing operation. A medical equipment manufacturer may acquire a wholesaler to provide the selling and distribution services. In each example the trading relation becomes circumscribed by an employment relationship. Generally, employees work with a set of explicit rules and under an authority structure that is difficult—but not impossible—to duplicate in contracts between independent organizations.

When grocery giant Kroger resolved to become more relevant to its customers and more efficient in its operations, in 2003 it formed a 50–50 joint venture with the British research and analytics firm, dunnhumby. The new entity, dunnhumby USA, seems like a fitting arrangement for tackling the immense volume of data generated by Kroger Plus Card-carrying customers, creating actionable market intelligence, and tracking short- and long-term results. Indeed, at the time of this edition, Kroger's same-store sales growth betters Wal-Mart's and other grocery rivals.[25]

The success of Cessna Aircraft depends on much more than its own humming production process. It critically rests on its selection of top-drawer suppliers, collaboration with key suppliers and their supplies in the development of high-performance components, and sound design and administration of the dealer network that serves its ultimate customers.

Many business marketers would point to some 15 years of supply chain management as our most significant breakthrough in network thinking. The market leadership of Grainger and Cisco can well be traced to strategic supply management that yields quality, speed, performance, and service levels that net out to superior value for their customers.

Historically, bringing elements of the value network together and into managerial focus has been no mean feat. It has happened only with the impetus of dynamic leadership and imagination. We see some of that in From the Field 2–3.

Today, global network convergence is one of the most useful Internet phenomena for business marketing. At VertMarkets.com, "hubs" or virtual market spaces for over 65 business-to-business product and service categories in eight distinct industries are just a few clicks away from any manager's desktop. Each hub is a nexus of trade groups, white papers, and product data for prospective buyers and the "storefronts" of sellers. Vendors pay VertMarkets a few thousand dollars a year to be in the network. In return they realize online sales revenue and high quality leads from as many 2 million registered users

## 2–3

### FROM THE FIELD

## Relationship Marketing . . .

My marketing career began straight out of college when Dun & Bradstreet recruited me for their Duns Market Identifiers division. Essentially, I began marketing "business information," previously used exclusively for credit purposes, to organizations to target, identify, evaluate, and prospect for new customers. This position gave me exposure to businesses in every industry and to each organization's unique marketing "challenges" and "pain points." The opportunity to learn about all kinds of businesses was fascinating!

With that initial experience working with businesses across many industries, I entered the Performance Marketing sector and began working with organizations to maximize their sales and profit performance. I designed and implemented Relationship Marketing initiatives utilizing incentives, rewards, and recognition programs aimed at organizations' three key audiences—their channel partners, employees, and customers.

Building and maintaining strong relationships is critical in the world of B2B. I was involved every day in identifying, measuring, and segmenting markets and then providing relevant messages to drive performance. This process was ongoing—not a one-time promotional campaign.

That said, providing consistent brand messaging, tracking key outcomes, and rewarding top performance takes many forms. It can involve sending 1,000 Honda Dealers to exotic destinations or distributing sales reps rewards as debit cards or gift certificates, cash, and other rewards. Loyal customers can earn points for purchases. Whatever the specific rewards and recognitions, building solid relationships and securing strong brand positions takes time and well-conceived relationship marketing strategies.

Brad Bischof
VP
Stimulys Performance Marketing, Dallas, TX

and 4 million page visits per month. Furthermore, the network is connected to other networks, because in the VertMarkets Supplier Syndication program, explains vice president, Tom Roberts, "syndication of our suppliers' data allows us to deliver more leads to each supplier, while providing industry marketplace users access to our depth of detailed product content across 68 industry marketplaces."[26] Even third-party industry marketplaces such as Office.com can incorporate supplier catalog data contained within VertMarkets' extensive supplier database.

If we back away a bit from the intimidating complexity of networks, we should be able to focus on the essential linkages for resources and skills in the creation of value. Consider George Washington Carver, a scientist most often celebrated for his development of scores of products made from peanuts. But Carver was not simply a productive laboratory dabbler. His efforts with "goobers" followed his vital research and demonstration projects involving crop rotation. His work at Tuskegee Institute was aimed at increasing cotton yields among Alabama's struggling small farmers. Planting peanuts restored nitrogen to the soil, enabling rich cotton harvests in subsequent seasons. Carver and the farmers seemingly had a productive relationship. But the farmers' success with peanuts glutted the market. Their bountiful harvests had no value. Thus, not until consumer preferences for peanut butter cookies built demand for peanut butter processors, which bid up the price of peanuts, did cotton growers benefit significantly from crop rotation. George Washington Carver's endeavor to develop markets for peanuts reflects his insight into the connectivity of any enterprise to the larger network creating value.

You know from Chapter 1 that today's business marketing is not just peanuts. Multiple firms interacting, or networking, with one another are using and discovering a host of mechanisms to coordinate their activities, of which price is but one. The concept of networks is not new. Indeed, in the long history of trade the prevalence of family enterprises, cartels, guilds, and conglomerate trading companies is undeniable. The scarcity of truly autonomous enterprises with strictly defined boundaries belies their dominance in formal economic models of the marketplace.

Unfortunately, the complexity of business networks and the infancy of scholarship in the field limit us to largely descriptive insights. Even the progress in supply chain management is confined largely to optimized linkages—two-firm interfaces—rather than systemwide flows. But Dave Wilson and Kristian Moller, top business scholars from the United States and Europe, respectively, contend, "Network thinking represents the most novel conceptualization about the nature of industrial markets and industries. . . . The emerging results suggest, however, that network concepts help to understand industrial markets in a more realistic fashion."[27]

## Summary

Markets represent a powerful system for coordinating exchange. They allow work to be divided among specialists and allow value to be determined by customers. But there are technical limits to the effectiveness of markets. Incomplete information about product performance, buyer or seller integrity, and hidden costs not well reflected in price limit the utility of market exchange. For complex products and uncertain transaction environments, buyers and sellers must find additional means—complementary to the price system—for coordinating their behavior.

In some environments, buyers and sellers can forge high-performance relationships by a process akin to courtship. It includes gradual probing, reinforced risk taking (trust), language and norm customization, and overall deepening of dependence. The request for adjustment and accommodation are key signals of the value of the association and allow expansion into other exchange activities. We used the running example of the new product development efforts for automotive vibration dampers to illustrate the processes of relationship development.

But some contexts simply do not allow parties to taper into a relationship. These must be set up in advance to safeguard each party's investment and ensure long-run performance. Supplier verification, exchange of personnel, and dependence balancing provide some assurances of continuity and performance. On another plane, the parties can strategically manage dependence through third-party relations. Relational contracts and vertical integration complete our illustration of the vast array of options.

Finally, we must not neglect to consider the nesting of each relationship in a larger business network. Each firm's connections to other players in the web of exchange relations will determine their competitive position to provide value.

## Key Terms

| | | |
|---|---|---|
| attraction | Customer Relationship | expansion stage |
| awareness stage | Management (CRM) | exploration stage |
| commitment | dependence balancing | just-in-time (JIT) |
| corporate relationship | dissolution | relationship |

| | | |
|---|---|---|
| **justice** | **safeguarded** | **supply chain** |
| **norms** | **relationship** | **management** |
| **outsource** | **social relationship** | **transactional** |
| **power** | **spot exchange** | **relationship** |
| **reciprocation** | **strategic partnership** | **trust** |
| **relational contract** | **supplier verification** | **vertical integration** |

# Discussion Questions

1. Evaluate the ability of spot markets to provide adequate resources for an organization seeking to purchase

   | | |
   |---|---|
   | O-rings | storage racks |
   | data entry services | project management software |
   | marketing research services | office furniture |
   | applications engineering | roofing |

2. Would a company marketing these products be interested in developing long-run relationships with any customer? Why?

3. Write a series of events that might well typify a developing relationship between an office furniture dealer and a growing investment company.

4. Is it possible to develop a corresponding series of events reflecting a relationship between this investment company and its phone system vendor?

5. The chapter mentioned that Samsung sells memory chips to Apple for its iPod Nano. At the same time Samsung sells its own MP3 players in competition with the Nano. On another front, Samsung sells flash memory used at Nokia, a Samsung competitor in telephones. Is it inevitable in B2B that some competitors will be customers? How does competition in certain markets between the parties affect their business relationships?

6. Marketing authors Robert Morgan and Shelby Hunt argue that trust and commitment are the central variables for understanding relationship marketing. Other scholars have suggested that power is the key variable. Explain which variable you believe is key.

7. A small group of parents in Kentucky formed a private, independent school. It opened recently in classrooms rented from an urban church with an oversized physical plant and a shrinking congregation. School officials forecast enrollment growing from about 40 in year one to about 120 over the next four years. Ample space for over 100 was available at the church, low-cost terms were agreed on, and an option to renew for up to four years at the same terms was signed. The pastor answered to the church council and recently wrote the school board president that because the school opened with 80 students instead of 40, the consistory wanted to double the rent. How do you respond? Could this relationship have been set up better?

8. Describe a situation in which an important business relationship developed because of other loosely connected business relationships involving the parties.

9. Many franchisers require their franchisees to follow strict operating procedures or face termination and forfeiture of large sums of money. In some circles this state of affairs prompts discussions of the abusive power of franchisors over their franchisees. But the chapter suggests these termination provisions might be considered for their use as a safeguard. Explain.

10. Explain the student recruitment imperatives for a top business school using a network perspective on value added.

**11.** Professor Susan Schertzer at Ohio Northern University studied over five years' worth of client satisfaction surveys derived from hundreds of marketing research projects. Time and again, the research supplier's reputation for quality emerged as a key predictor of the client's actual reuse of the agency—even stronger than interactions with the project manager and specific project outcomes. So might this indicate we have understated the role for branding in B2B relationships?

# Cases

## Case 2.1    Market Failure or Management Breakdown?

Many U.S. pets suffered illness and worse in 2007, seemingly, when tainted wheat gluten from China was used to make tons of dog and cat food. This appears to be a major supply chain failure in the B2B world. Beyond the harm to animals, this incident puts several brands in jeopardy, dents the credibility of regulators, and brings friction to international relations.

### What Happened?

Many facts have yet to become clear, but, according to U.S. regulators, it appears that Xuzhou Anying Biologic Technology Development (ZAB) is in the eye of the storm. It is accused of mixing melamine in wheat gluten. Melamine has no nutritional value but can elevate the apparent protein content of gluten. ZAB posted an offer to buy melamine scrap on its Web site in March 2007. It does not manufacture wheat gluten but purchased its products from 25 different manufacturers.

ZAB seemingly skirted Chinese inspections of food products by exporting through a textile company. Menu Foods, the first U.S. pet food maker to issue a recall of its products, obtained its gluten from ChemNutra, a Las Vegas pet food supplier. ChemNutra says it believed ZAB was the gluten manufacturer, but obtained its shipments from a third party—you guessed it—Suzhou Textiles Silk Light & Industrial Products.

Normally melamine is nontoxic, but scientists suspect the melamine scrap contained other poisons. The U.S. Food and Drug Administration currently has resources to inspect just 1% of food imports.

**1.** With just a small fraction of food imports inspected by the FDA, how is it that food supply episodes such as this seem rare?

**2.** Is this the gross underbelly of global sourcing?

**3.** Can the market fix this problem? In other words, what does this mean for ChemNutra's relationship with Menu Foods? And how should Menu Foods now manage its supply chain?

SOURCES: David Barboza, "Chinese Firm Dodged Inspection of Pet Food, U.S. say," *International Herald Tribune* (May 2, 2007) http://www.iht.com/articles/2007/05/02/africa/food.php; John Carey, ""How Safe Is the Food Supply?" *BusinessWeek* (May 21, 2007), pp. 40–42.

## Case 2.2    Just-in-Time JIT

You're the director of purchasing at a telecommunications company in Seattle and you've just gone to meet your sister-in-law for coffee at a little cafe off Rush Street. Earlier this week you arrived in Chicago to attend the National Association of Purchasing Managers Convention. As you waited in the cafe, you couldn't help but hear the conversation in the opposite booth. A group of three increasingly rowdy purchasing agents from different companies were clearly from the same convention.

One they called Xavier was from Tex Implements. He was warmed up and getting loud. "I just want to know how I'm supposed to get the best price from Prespec Spring, when I cannot even ask for a bid from anyone else."

"You think that's bad?" retorted a stocky guy called Hank, a streetwise purchasing manager at a Big Three auto company. "I got this dude from Magma in my department telling us how many hoses of which type we've got to get each month."

"We've got the same JIT II baloney. I call it 'JIP Too,'" said the woman in the teal suit.

You hoped you had done a better job getting the purchasing people at your firm committed to the concept of vendor consolidation, sole sourcing, and partnering, but the conversation prompted you to jot a few notes. At tomorrow's conference luncheon you were slated to accept an award for your company for purchasing excellence. You had been planning to make a few simple remarks off the cuff, but your napkin now has a short summary of the motivation and strategic payoff for this "new era in procurement."

## Additional Readings

Achrol, Ravi S., and Phillip Kotler. "Marketing in the Network Economy." *Journal of Marketing* 63 (Special Issue 1999), pp. 146–63.

Bowersox, Donald J., David J. Closs, and Theodore P. Stank. *21st Century Logistics: Making Supply Chain Integration a Reality.* Oak Brook, IL: Council of Logistics Management, 1999.

Dwyer, F. Robert, Paul H. Schurr, and Sejo Oh. "Developing Buyer–Seller Relationships." *Journal of Marketing* 52 (April 1987), pp. 11–27.

Gummesson, Evert. "Return on Relationships (ROR): The Value of Relationship Marketing and CRM in Business-to-Business Contexts." *Journal of Business & Industrial Marketing* 19, no. 2 (2004), pp. 136–48.

Gundlach, Gregory T., and Patrick Murphy. "Ethical and Legal Foundations of Relational Marketing Exchanges." *Journal of Marketing* 57 (October 1993), pp. 35–46.

Heide, Jan. "Plural Governance in Industrial Purchasing." *Journal of Marketing* 67 (October 2003), pp. 18–29.

Hutt, Thomas, and Thomas Speh. "Undergraduate Education: The Implications of Cross-Functional Relationships in Business Marketing—The Skills of High Performing Managers." *Journal of Business-to-Business Marketing* 14, no. 1 (2007), pp. 75–94.

Iyer, Gopalkrishnan R. "Internet-Enabled Linkages: Balancing Strategic Considerations with Operational Efficiencies in Business-to-Business Marketing." *Journal of Business-to-Business Marketing,* nos. 1/2 (2004), pp. 35–60.

Jap, Sandy D., and Erin Anderson. "Testing a Life-Cycle Theory of Cooperative Interorganizational Relationships: Movement across Stages and Performance." *Management Science* 53 (February 2007), pp. 260–275.

John, George, Allen M. Weiss, and Shantanu Dutta. "Marketing in Technology-Intensive Markets: Toward a Conceptual Framework." *Journal of Marketing* 63 (Special Issue 1999), pp. 78–92.

Kleinaltenkamp, Michael, and Michael Ehret, eds. "Relationship Theory and Business Markets." *Journal of Business & Industrial Marketing* 21, no. 2 (2006).

Moeller, Sabine, Martin Fassnacht, and Sonja Klose. "A Framework for Supplier Relationship Management (SRM)." *Journal of Business-to-Business Marketing* 13, no. 4 (2006), pp. 69–91.

Morgan, Robert, and Shelby Hunt. "The Commitment–Trust Theory of Relationship Marketing." *Journal of Marketing* 58 (July 1994), pp. 20–38.

Palmatier, Robert W., Rajiv P. Dant, Dhruv Grewal, and Kenneth R. Evans. "Factors Influencing the Effectiveness of Relationship Marketing: A Meta-Analysis." *Journal of Marketing* 70, (October 2006), pp. 136–153.

Purinton, Elizabeth F., Deborah E. Rosen, and James M. Curran. "Marketing Relationship Management: Antecedents to Survival and Dissolution." *Journal of Business-to-Business Marketing* 14, no. 2 (2007), pp. 75–105.

Jap, Sandy D. and Erin Anderson. "Testing a Life-Cycle Theory of Cooperative Interorganizational Relationships: Movement across Stages and Performance." Management Science 53 (February 2007), pp. 260–275.

Tompkins, James A. *No Boundaries: Moving beyond Supply Chain Management.* Raleigh, NC: Tompkins Press, 2000.

Wathne, Kenneth H., and Jan B. Heide. "Relationship Governance in a Supply Chain Network." *Journal of Marketing* 68 (January 2004), pp. 73–89.

Xie, Frank Tian and Wesley J. Johnston. "Strategic Alliances: Incorporating the Impact of E-Business Technological Innovations." *Journal of Business & Industrial Marketing* 19, no. 3 (2004), pp. 208–22.

"Best Practices: Dunnhumby Shops for Marketing Insight." http://wwwoptimisemag.com/article/showArticle.jhtml?articleID=197000211&pgno=3 (viewed June 7, 2007); http://www.dunnhumby.com/relevance/case_kroger.htm (viewed June 7, 2007); "Data-mining Central to Kroger Rebound Strategy." http://www.swlearnin.com/marketing/marketing_news/research_1106_001.html (viewed June 7, 2007).

# Chapter 3

## The Purchasing Function

**ERICSSON**

Ericsson, the $26 billion Swedish maker of telephones and telephone equipment, employs over 50,000 people worldwide. With a net profit margin of just over 15 percent, the company has enjoyed a surge in net profit from just two years ago, when net profit was languishing just above 12 percent. The difference? Cost control through a global purchasing initiative.●

At the heart of this initiative was standardizing on SAP's supplier relationship management (SRM) software. Over time, the various business units located around the world had developed a number of their own purchasing software solutions. In addition, they created their own networks of local suppliers. While Tomas Elken, who led the initiative at Ericsson, says that "This did not mean that we wanted to centralize all buying operations," an important goal was to standardize products and consolidate purchasing in order to reduce costs. Consolidation of purchases enables Ericsson to negotiate better prices, and "buying at retail prices is now a thing of the past."●

In addition, the software has automated many purchasing processes. The company identified that it cost about US$100 to process a purchase order before implementing the SAP SRM software—post-SRM implementation costs are now only $26. Given that the company issues some 200,000 purchase orders annually, the savings just in processing costs are well over $5 million alone. Other savings are also realized through shortening purchasing cycles, automating some purchasing and inventory management, and additional applications.●

Key to successful implementation is that over 30,000 employees use the system. "That's a large percentage," says Elken. But they aren't finished. While the system has been implemented in 30 countries, next is the United States, where additional savings await. ●

Sources: "Ericsson Case Study," SAP.com, 2007; Ericsson annual reports 2005–2007.

Visit the Ericsson Web site: **www.ericsson.com.** ●

## LEARNING OBJECTIVES

A key competitive advantage for Ericsson and for all other firms is an ability to control costs. One major input in their overall cost structure is their purchases. Therefore, attention to the purchasing function is important for firms trying to create or maintain a cost advantage or, at a minimum, a cost competitiveness. At the same time, marketers must understand the purchasing function in order to create effective marketing programs.

*After reading this chapter, you should be able to*

- Discuss how effective purchasing and materials management provide a competitive advantage.

- Illustrate strategies designed to provide the proper supply and tell why these strategies are used.

- Explain total cost of ownership, value analysis, and other forms of economic purchase evaluation.

- Describe the processes that purchasing uses to evaluate vendors and their offerings, as well as how the process varies depending on the organization's experience.

- Recognize the major ethical issues facing purchasing agents and how they respond to those issues.

- Understand differences in government purchasing and compare government needs in industrialized nations with those of developing countries.

The purchasing department has an important role to play in any organization. Controlling costs and managing cash flow are key issues that affect the ability of an organization to thrive. These issues are impacted by marketing programs, as you will see.

# THE IMPORTANCE OF PURCHASING

Purchasing is a strategic weapon. Companies like Ericsson that can source effectively can create a competitive advantage by building better value into their own products.[1] As you've already learned, value can be increased by delivering more benefits or by lowering costs; strategic purchasing can make contributions in both areas. In fact, strategic purchasing has become so important that many firms are adding chief procurement officer to their company officers.

Business marketers can also make contributions to the value delivered by their customers. Astute business marketers find ways to offer more benefits at the same cost or lower costs to benefit their strategic purchasing partners. In the next section, we examine the contribution purchasing makes to the firm so that we can understand how we, as business marketers, can support their contribution.

## Purchasing's Contribution to the Firm

As you've just read, a key contribution to the success of the firm is purchasing's ability to keep costs of supply down. That is not, however, the only contribution that purchasing makes. The three most important elements of the purchasing department's function are to:

- Provide appropriate levels of supply of the right product or service
- At the correct level of quality
- For the lowest total cost[2]

### *Providing Supply*

An important contribution of the purchasing department is to provide the right product or service in the correct amounts when needed. There are several important elements to recognize. First, purchasing has the responsibility to ensure that the right product or service is provided. For example, PPG Industries manufactures coatings, glass, and other products. Sand, a key component in glass, comes in many different grades depending on how much silica and other minerals are in the sand. Lower grades may cost less but require PPG to process the sand differently than higher-grade sand. If purchasing accepted a lower-grade sand, then manufacturing costs would increase and eat up any savings from lower prices. Worse still, the quality of glass might be compromised, resulting in unhappy customers. Purchasing must ensure that the right product or service is provided.

The other important element is availability. The product or service must be available at the right time. PPG sand buyer keeps a watchful eye on the prices of sand, ordering several months of production needs when the price is right. If the price isn't right, however, she sometimes has to buy anyway. Otherwise, all three plants would shut down, costing the company hundreds of thousands of dollars per week. If she buys too much, it costs more money due to higher carrying costs. Managing availability can be a delicate operation for the purchasing department.

One availability strategy is **just-in-time (JIT),** the concept of shipping products such that they arrive at the customer's location exactly when needed. As sketched in Chapter 2, this strategy reduces inventory carrying costs to next to nothing because little or no inventories of supplies are needed. Too often, though, suppliers bear the costs of carrying the inventory if the buyer and supplier don't share information and coordinate plans.

In order for suppliers to reduce their costs (for if the costs are simply shifted from buyer to supplier, the costs would be reflected in a higher price), they are turning to **concurrent manufacturing,** which means the suppliers schedule their own manufacturing based on the shipment needs of their customers. The ideal situation is that the part rolls off the supplier's manufacturing line and into the truck, and then it's shipped to the buyer's plant and rolled off the truck right into the manufacturing line. Concurrent manufacturing means that the supplier can also keep inventory costs down, because the supplier can engage its own suppliers in JIT systems. If the entire supply chain produces and ships based on demand, then inventories for the entire chain are kept to a minimum, reducing costs for the entire chain.

JIT and concurrent manufacturing are not just for suppliers of component parts. JIT is used in shipping supplies to hospitals, in shipping paper to offices for use in copiers, and in many other instances where the buyer is not a manufacturer using the product in the manufacturing process. For example, some plumbing supply manufacturers schedule their manufacturing based on sales of their products. When a plumber purchases a bathtub or sink from the plumbing supplies distributor, the distributor orders another. The manufacturer makes a small run of tubs or sinks, depending on the orders received.

A JIT supplier must quickly know when the customer needs a shipment. An important technological development that enabled many firms to use JIT was **electronic data interchange (EDI),** the use of electronic transmission of data between buyer and seller to order and maintain product inventory. EDI is not just ordering on the Web, but involves customer purchasing systems integrating with supplier software.

## The Correct Quality

A critical issue in purchasing today is ever increasing quality specifications from the customer because of the impact poor quality has on the firm. For example, PPG also makes paints and finishing products used on automobiles, farm and construction equipment, planes, ships, and other vehicles. If PPG sends Ford a lower-quality finishing product, then Ford may have to issue a recall to repaint cars. As Ford, Deere, Boeing, and other vehicle manufacturers improve their quality, so does PPG and other suppliers.

In some areas, though, higher quality can mean a higher cost for the product. In these instances, higher quality does not mean better quality. The finishing products used on aircraft, for example, may withstand heat and cold situations that automobiles never face. Therefore, PPG's automotive customers would not be willing to pay the extra it takes to have that quality because their customers—consumers—would not be willing to pay for it either. Choosing the right level of quality is an important element in the purchasing function, because quality impacts manufacturing and marketing in both cost and potential contribution.

Many companies recognize the importance of providing the right level of quality, and even work with suppliers of their suppliers to make sure that quality is high enough. Church & Dwight, makers of Arm & Hammer baking soda, buys little yellow boxes for the baking soda. Church & Dwight purchasing agents worked with cardboard makers that supply Church & Dwight's carton suppliers in order to know what quality of cardboard to specify so that bright yellow box would always look the same.[3]

## *The Lowest Total Cost*

As we said in Chapter 2, controlling the cost of supply can have a significant effect on a firm's profitability. As shown in Exhibit 3–1, suppose a firm's annual sales are $50 million, with a profit margin of 10 percent of sales, or $5 million. In general, companies spend more than half of their sales on purchased parts, materials, and services,[4] so this company would spend about $25 million per year. If the company was able to save 10 percent on its purchases, it would add $2.5 million to its profit, an increase to profit of 50 percent! The company would have to sell another $25 million to have the same effect on profit. Each dollar saved through careful purchasing can have a direct impact on the bottom line.

When Ericsson buys keypads, for example, it costs the same to deliver a truckload whether the truck is full or half empty. Preferably, the company can order and receive a day's requirements for keypads on the day the keypads will be turned into phones. But if the company carries inventory to protect against missed deliveries or to take advantage of temporarily low prices, then storage facilities have to be used to store the keypads. Building those warehousing facilities, maintaining them, carrying insurance on the warehouses, and other costs can eliminate any price savings.

The purchase price, therefore, is not the only cost that the purchasing department must contend with. Delivery, storage, service, and more can add costs. Several concepts are used by purchasing departments to examine and compare costs; these are the total cost of ownership, economic order quantity, and value analysis.

### Total Cost of Ownership

Many factors can influence the **total cost of ownership,** the total amount expended in order to own a product or use a service. If we are talking about a piece of equipment, total cost of ownership includes delivery and installation costs, service costs to maintain and repair the equipment, power costs to run the equipment, supply costs, and other operating costs over the life of the equipment. All of these costs must be added to the actual purchasing and financing prices in order to determine the total cost of owning that equipment.

Similarly, services have a total cost of ownership. We have to take into account supplies, inventory (in the case of services, what we are paying to have a trained person available, whether that person is our employee or a service provider's), delivery, and other costs of ownership. For example, if we do our own marketing research, we have to pay the research personnel each month, whether they are currently engaged in a research project or not. Many companies are outsourcing services so that they can reduce the total cost of ownership. Outsourcing, discussed in detail later in this chapter, means buying from another firm.

For raw materials and component parts, like the computer chips purchased by Ericsson, we have to account for delivery costs, inventory carrying costs, the impact of the product on manufacturing costs, and other costs. In all situations, we also have to include the costs associated with purchasing.

### Economic Order Quantity

A method of evaluating ordering and inventorying costs is to determine the economic order quantity. The **economic order quantity (EOQ)** is the quantity that minimizes both ordering and storing costs. Any more than that would raise costs and not be economical. Those costs would include paying for additional space for storage, additional insurance on the inventory, fire prevention costs, and the interest on the money that the firm would lose by having to pay early for supplies used later.

**Exhibit 3–1**
Saving Money Goes Directly to the Bottom Line!

| | Cut Purchases by 10% | Raise Sales by 10% |
|---|---|---|
| **Annual Sales** | $50 million | $55 million |
| **Profit Margin** | $5 million | $5.5 million |
| **Cut Purchase Costs—Savings** | $2.5 million | Don't cut purchases |
| **Total Profit** | $7.5 million | $5.5 million |

NOTE: Assuming that cost of goods sold represents 50 percent of sales revenue, cutting those costs by 10 percent has an effect five times that of increasing sales by 10 percent! That's why so many companies watch their purchasing expenses very carefully.

One strategic outcome of EOQ analysis that can occur is forward buying. **Forward buying** is buying in larger quantities than are currently needed because the discount is greater than the carrying costs. Although a seller may appreciate forward buying if it helps clear out inventories, forward buying is usually an unintended negative consequence of a poor pricing decision. Forward buying creates a spike in sales (see Exhibit 3–2), which can lead to stock-outs and damage to relationships with accounts that can't get orders filled. Buyers will buy a lot more than they immediately need in order to get the cheaper price, which can then cause the manufacturer to run out. Later, when prices return to normal, demand is low so the company begins to produce less, which can increase manufacturing costs per unit, cause plants to sit idle, and create other problems.

An effective response to the problem of forward buying is to separate the order quantity from the shipping quantity through an annual contract. We'll talk more about this in Chapter 14 on pricing, but the idea is that it costs less for a company when it can plan ahead and stabilize its manufacturing over the year. These savings can be passed along to the customer, which will agree to purchase the year's needs from the manufacturer but accept delivery throughout the year. This schedule allows the seller to lower the price but maintain margin because costs will be lower. JIT can represent one form of such a contract, but a JIT system doesn't have to be in place for annual contracts to be effective.

### Value Analysis

**Value analysis** is a method of comparing the benefit, function, and cost of materials, components, and work processes. A component part is a part of the finished product—for example, a gas tank on a lawn mower or keypad used on a telephone. Value analysis can be used to reduce costs or improve design. The value analysis concept was developed in the 1940s by General Electric and is often a part of the product design process. Value analysis, though, can be done afterward as well. For example, a PPG supplier suggested using one product that could do the job of two. The standardization meant a lower purchasing cost, because they could buy in bulk, also saving on inventory and other costs.

Complexity management is another method of controlling costs. **Complexity management** is the process of identifying links among components that raise costs if any changes are made. For example, Ford found that adding a new interior color meant having to purchase over 50 components in that new color. Such components might include interior lights, visors, coat hooks, lock buttons, and others. By simplifying the number of colors or by creating color schemes that allow for standardization of some components (all black door lock buttons, for example), Ford could reduce inventory costs, ordering costs, and other costs associated with greater complexity.

**Exhibit 3–2**
Forward buying in March and September causes spikes in sales, followed by low levels of sales as inventories smooth out.

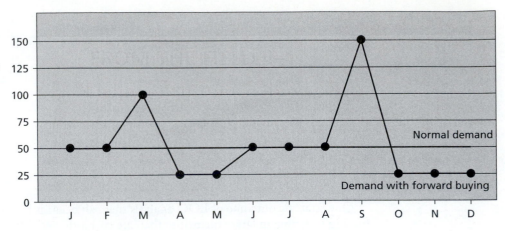

When conducting value analysis, the firm considers what, if any, alternatives exist. The key question is whether the firm can achieve the same or greater value for less cost. Sometimes, the vendor's salesperson can conduct a value analysis and suggest savings. For example, Emerson Electric had up to three labels on the back of their products. Their vendor, R. R. Donnelley, suggested combining the labels into one, saving Emerson Electric significant label costs but also saving Emerson manufacturing costs because only one label had to be applied. The value of the single label was greater than just the reduction in the cost of the labels themselves.

# PURCHASING PHILOSOPHY

In Chapter 2, you learned about the different types of relationships that are possible between buyer and seller. In this section, we will discuss a related topic, purchasing philosophies that buyers may use to guide their actions. This topic is related to the types of relationships because a company's philosophy toward purchasing will limit the types of relationships in which it can engage.

A traditional purchasing philosophy, the **adversarial purchasing philosophy,** is to have several vendors for each product. This philosophy was developed in order to increase competition for the buyer's business. Such competition is believed to lower prices while increasing the level of service and attention paid to the account. In one study, for example, having two sources reduced costs for some purchases.[5]

Buyers using an adversarial approach see the supplier as an enemy or at least as the opposition. The approach is based on caveat emptor (let the buyer beware) and assumes that the supplier will take the buyer for all there is, unless the buyer takes an adversarial position and fights for all it can get.

In the late 80s, the Total Quality Management movement influenced purchasing philosophy by creating an alternative to the adversarial approach that is still popular today. This alternative, called **partnership purchasing** or **preferred supplier systems,**[6] seeks to maximize the benefits of collaboration between the buyer and a few suppliers. Buyers operating under this philosophy seek out the best suppliers they can find and then work to develop close relationships, particularly in areas of strategic importance to the firm.

In general, partnering relationships are more likely to be established with vendors who provide one or more of the following:

- High purchase-volume materials, components, or products of strategic importance
- Specialized products requiring information and training for effective use
- Services that require specialized knowledge for cost reductions or performance
- Materials that no other supplier can provide[7]

These areas are usually those that contribute directly to the value provided by the buying firm in the supply chain, such as in the component parts of the finished product. Within the relationship, the two organizations work to increase value for both parties.

One frequent outcome is that fewer suppliers are needed. For example, Ericsson has eliminated about 90 percent of the vendors it used to do business with through its preferred supplier system. Ford announced recently that it intends to reduce the number of its vendors from 2,500 to 1,000 in order to have better relationships, lower cost, and greater joint commitment with suppliers. In both cases, preferred suppliers get first shot at any new business before nonpartners, make more profit than nonpartners, and provide Ericsson and Ford with higher quality than nonpartners could provide at a lower cost than nonpartners can charge.

**Single sourcing** occurs when a company selects one supplier to satisfy all needs in a given area. Some students confuse single sourcing with partnering, but single sourcing can occur in an adversarial setting and need not imply a long-term collaborative relationship. For example, a company may decide to buy all of its maintenance supplies from one vendor, but negotiate adversarially, trying to cut the best deal for itself without any thought of the consequences to the supplier. There is much more to partnering than single sourcing. Indeed, single sourcing without partnering can prove risky, for without the commitment of a partnership, the supplier will be free to operate adversarially too. Caveat emptor!

One difference between single sourcing and partnering is that buyers make investments related to the partner. These investments (which might mean the purchase of a computer compatible with the supplier's EDI system, for example) help bind the partners together.[8] In a single-sourcing situation without partnering, there are no such investments, and the buyer is free to look elsewhere when demands are not met.

Single sourcing can lead to higher costs, as the Department of Defense has learned. It has long used single sourcing based on the theory that (1) high investments are needed to build weapon systems for which there is only one customer and (2) companies willing to make such investments should be rewarded with all of the business. What the Department of Defense has learned through experimentation, though, is that costs are lower when two vendors are used instead of just one. Organizations that engage in single sourcing should not assume that costs will be lower and should balance any higher costs with other benefits that can be obtained.[9]

Purchasing is an important contributor to the profit potential of any organization. Purchasing contributes to the profitability of the firm by controlling acquisition costs, assisting in the control of manufacturing costs, and ultimately influencing marketing costs. Purchasing also contributes by making sure that the right product or service is available when needed, in the right quantity and at the right quality, all for the lowest total cost. In the next section, we explore the processes that purchasers go through when examining products.

## BUSINESS 2 BUSINESS
### When Relationships Change

In the past decade or so, many organizations have consolidated their purchases, reducing the number of suppliers, in order to (1) forge stronger ties and more collaborative relationships with a select few and (2) obtain significantly lower prices based on high-volume discounts. Over time, though, people move on but the companies continue. Consider this testimony about a key customer from a business marketer in the electric motors field. Are there ethical issues at work here? And what does this example have to say about matching corporate culture, changing business needs, and other factors influencing single sourcing relationships?

"Our dealings with this account have been both fruitful and difficult. The business volume is significant but it is labor intensive, and problematic to service this account. . . . My personal complaint is their tendency to say 'fix this problem or we will go elsewhere.' There are not that many other places for them to go. Other people in the purchasing department there were not as quick to respond this way as the current staff. Also, this account is not as significant as it once was, due to lost market share for them. Their corporate culture is still like it was when they were larger and more powerful."

# SUPPLIER EVALUATION

An important job of the purchasing agent is to evaluate potential suppliers and their offerings. The effects of purchasing on a firm's competitive ability are great, so companies pay close attention to how they evaluate suppliers. Marketers must also understand the process, for they are the ones being evaluated. Understanding the process is like understanding the rules of any game; if you don't know how to score, you are unlikely to win.

## Buy-Grid Model

The **buy-grid model** is a version of a theory developed as a general model of rational organizational decision making, explaining how companies make decisions about, for example, where to locate a plant or make a purchase. The buy-grid model has two parts: the buy-phase model and the buy-class.

You've probably seen the buy-phase model in a management class as the rational or extensive problem-solving model or in consumer behavior as a high-involvement model. This **buy-phase model** suggests that people go through a series of steps (or phases) when making a decision, beginning with problem recognition. They then search for alternatives, evaluate the alternatives, and select a solution, which is then implemented and evaluated. (See Exhibit 3–3.)

For example, when an organization needs new office space, crowded conditions help force recognition of the need. The next step is to define the type of product needed: Does the organization want to build a new office building, add on to an existing building, or simply find a larger place to rent or buy? As the organization continues to examine its needs, detailed specifications such as the size and number of offices are created. If the decision in the second step was to build, an architect would help create specifications by drawing plans. Then suppliers would be contacted, including those recommended by the architect. Step 5, acquisition and analysis of proposals, involves receiving and reviewing bids from each contractor. The architect and the executives would meet,

**Exhibit 3–3**
Steps in the
Buying Process
(Buy-Phase
Model)

*SOURCE: Barton A.
Weitz, Stephen B.
Castleberry, and John
F. Tanner, Jr., Selling:
Building Partnerships,
Sixth edition,
Burr Ridge, IL:
Irwin/McGraw-Hill,
2007.*

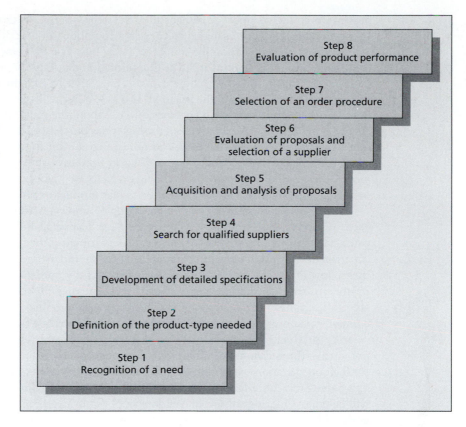

Step 8
Evaluation of product performance

Step 7
Selection of an order procedure

Step 6
Evaluation of proposals and
selection of a supplier

Step 5
Acquisition and analysis of proposals

Step 4
Search for qualified suppliers

Step 3
Development of detailed specifications

Step 2
Definition of the product-type needed

Step 1
Recognition of a need

evaluate the proposals, and select a contractor (step 6). Step 7 involves the creation of a contract specifying when the building will be completed, what it will look like, and when payments will be made. Evaluation begins as the project begins, but continues well after the organization moves in.

Many firms have well-established purchasing policies and procedures that formalize the steps of the model. In particular, government agencies establish and follow purchasing policies. For example, many state agencies are required to solicit bids from at least three vendors for any purchase over $10,000.

As observers of buying behavior quickly realized, many organizational purchase decisions do not involve that much work or include each and every step every time. A second element, the buy-class, was added to buy-phase, resulting in a grid. **Buy-class** refers to the type of buying decision, based on the experience of the buyer with a purchase of a particular product or service.

Organizational researchers realized that once a decision was made, products were bought automatically over and over; recognizing a problem might simply mean recognizing that the company is low in an item and needs to order more. The complete process was used only for **new buys,** products or services never purchased before. Automatic purchasing described what happened with **straight rebuys,** and only two steps were required. These steps are need recognition and placing an order. Note that straight rebuys do not imply a partnership or other strong relationship. Straight rebuys simply mean repurchasing regularly, which can be a function of a strong relationship, low price, e-procurement practices, or other factors.

At other times, however, a product or service would be bought again but not automatically. When a company was contemplating a rebuy but wanted to shop around, the process would include most or perhaps all of the steps—hence the term **modified rebuys.** In this instance, the process may involve need recognition, an evaluation of suppliers, and a decision—a process that can be similar to a new buy. The difference is not in the number of steps but in the amount and type of information that must be collected before a purchase can be made. Modified rebuys can also be similar to straight rebuys or new buys, depending on the specifics of the situation. In a new buy, the buyer has no experience with the product or service and must become educated about the product or service in order to make a purchase. In a modified rebuy, the buyer has purchased the product or service before. Therefore, the buyer will not spend time on education about the product itself, but about the various vendors and their offerings as the buyer shops around. The buy-grid model, therefore, describes how purchasing practices vary along a continuum depending on the buyer's experience in buying that particular product or service.

The personal computer industry is an example of how a market changes with experience. When the PCs were new, salespeople were needed to fully explain benefits and educate buyers. Buyers, particularly buyers in departments other than the data processing department, needed a lot of information in order to understand what PCs could do for them, how PCs work, and what was needed to be fully operational. Now PCs are sold in stores or through the Internet with little personal sales effort. Buyers are knowledgeable and can make their decisions without the marketer's help. In some organizations, computers are ordered through a Web site on a straight rebuy basis.

Some product decisions may never become true straight rebuys because of the importance of the decision. For example, fleet managers buy automobiles, trucks, and vans for their organizations each year. In some situations, they may simply pick up the phone and order a few more Ram vans or F-150 pickup trucks, but in most cases, more work will be done. Offerings of several vendors will be considered, and a contract will be negotiated because the size of the purchase is too great to do automatically. Modified rebuys are those situations where the same product or product type is being purchased that has been purchased before, but most of the decision steps are still taken.

Modified rebuys occur for several reasons, and we've already discussed the importance of the purchase. Other reasons include changing technology that improves product performance and requires reevaluation of vendors and their offerings, dissatisfaction with the performance of a supplier and/or the product, changing prices, or even a change in the personnel involved. Some organizations periodically review all vendors and regularly conduct value analyses, even though there may be no obvious problems.

Value analysis is one situation that can turn a straight rebuy into a modified rebuy. When a company is closely evaluating a particular part, one question that is asked is if the part is available elsewhere for less. As the answer is sought to this question, **out-suppliers** (those suppliers whose products are not considered in a straight rebuy) are given the opportunity to earn the business. **In-suppliers** (those suppliers whose products are ordered automatically in a straight rebuy) must prove value or create new value by redesigning their offering. Thus, the purchase moves from being a straight rebuy to a modified rebuy.

# Buy-Grid and Marketing Practice

The theory suggests that more information is needed by the buyer to make a new buy than when making a modified rebuy, and almost no information is needed for a straight rebuy. To use this model, a company would look at the degree to which a market is buying a product for the first time. If most of the market is buying the product for the first time, methods of communication such as personal selling may be used in order to

**Exhibit 3–4**
Marketing
Implications of
the Buy-Grid

| Buy-Phases | Marketing Element | |
|---|---|---|
| *New Task* | | |
| All steps of the buying process are taken, with emphasis on product definition and development of product specifications. | Advertising | Detailed, educational; must try to get users to try product, substitute for old method. |
| | Promotion | Use demonstrations at trade shows to show how it works. |
| | | Offer free trials or demonstrations at the customer's site. |
| | Selling | Heavy emphasis on understanding customers' needs and showing how new product satisfies needs better than old methods. |
| *Modified Rebuy* | | |
| Less emphasis is on product definition and more emphasis is on search and evaluation of suppliers. | Advertising | Use comparison advertising to show differences between your product and similar products. |
| | Promotion | Customer site demonstrations, hospitality events at trade shows. |
| | Selling | Protect relationship with current customers with plant tours, special trade-in pricing, and other offers. |
| | | Anticipate or respond quickly to changes in customer needs. |
| *Straight Rebuy* | | |
| Need recognition and purchase are the only steps used. | Advertising | Use reminder advertising. |
| | | Build image for company. |
| | Promotion | Hospitality events at trade shows. |
| | Selling | Any personal selling is designed to build relationships. |
| | | Automate the purchasing process, perhaps through EDI. |

provide the most information. Advertising would contain a lot of detailed copy that described the benefits and how the product worked. Over time, as the market grows more familiar with the product, less-educational methods of communicating may be used, such as catalogs. Exhibit 3–4 illustrates some of the marketing differences depending on the amount of the market's experience in buying the product.

Another marketing implication is that an in-supplier would like purchases of its products to be straight rebuys. Annual contracts are one method of creating straight rebuys. For example, Xerox offers its customers an annual supply contract. Each time a department is low in copier supplies, the purchasing department orders automatically from Xerox, perhaps using EDI. Out-suppliers would be locked out until the next time the contract comes up for review.

Research has found that marketers who can get involved early in the decision process are more likely to be successful.[10] In part, this higher probability of success is due to greater understanding of the buyer's needs, an opportunity to help shape those needs, and a better understanding of the process. The lower probability of success when starting later in the process is also due to the fact that buyers become committed to a course of action over the process of making the decision, and that course often leans towards alternatives presented early in the process.

**Exhibit 3–5**
Importance
Level of
Computer
Features

| Computer Feature | You | Another Buyer |
|---|---|---|
| Modem speed | 8 | 3 |
| Hard disk size | 6 | 9 |
| Screen size | 4 | 5 |
| Processor speed | 7 | 7 |

**Exhibit 3–6**
Computer
Ratings

| Computer Feature | You | | Another Buyer | |
| | HP | Dell | HP | Dell |
|---|---|---|---|---|
| Modem speed | 6 | 7 | 8 | 6 |
| Hard disk size | 9 | 4 | 7 | 9 |
| Screen size | 8 | 6 | 9 | 6 |
| Processor speed | 6 | 9 | 5 | 8 |

When buyers don't have experience, marketing strategies can provide buyers with the information they need to make a decision. Marketers consider how buyers use that information to be very important. In the next section, we examine how buyers compare vendors and products.

# Multiattribute Decision Making

In both new and modified rebuys, the vendor and product evaluation stages are important times for prospective vendors. One method used to explain the vendor and product evaluation stage of the buy-phase model is the multiattribute model. The **multiattribute model** is based on the idea that people compare products across attributes, or features, weighted by importance. Where this model fits the buy-grid model is in the evaluation-of-alternatives stage for new or modified rebuys; in the straight rebuy, there is no evaluation of alternatives, as the product or service is ordered automatically, perhaps using EDI.

For example, you may want high gas mileage, a comfortable interior, and a sporty exterior in a car (three needs). Although an aerodynamic design may improve gas mileage and provide for a sporty exterior, it does nothing for the inside! Therefore, there must be some method of accounting for a particular product's ability to solve all three needs.

Each need is more or less important than other needs, depending on the organization or individual making the purchase. For example, a company may be purchasing computers for salespeople to use (ignore for now that companies can buy computers made to order and assume they are comparing two off-the-shelf products). Hard disk size may be important to store the company's sales force automation software. A company purchasing notebook computers for salespeople to use may place the same emphasis on modem speed, but not care a great deal about processor speed. Each firm would place a different importance level on each attribute, as shown in Exhibit 3–5. On a scale of 1–10, with 10 being most important, one firm might rate modem speed an 8 whereas another rates it only a 3. This rating system is important, but isn't enough to determine which computer to purchase.

Each firm must also then rate each computer for each feature. For a Dell, you may rate it a 7 for modem speed and a 4 for disk size, whereas you give the HP a 6 and a 9. (See Exhibit 3–6.)

**Exhibit 3–7**
Computer
Scores

| Computer Feature | You | | | Another Buyer | | |
|---|---|---|---|---|---|---|
| | Importance Level | HP | Dell | Importance Level | HP | Dell |
| Modem speed | 8× | 6(48) | 7(56) | 3× | 8(24) | 6(18) |
| Hard disk size | 6× | 9(54) | 4(24) | 9× | 7(63) | 9(81) |
| Screen size | 4× | 8(32) | 6(24) | 5× | 9(45) | 6(30) |
| Processor speed | 7× | 7(49) | 8(56) | 7× | 5(35) | 8(56) |
| Total | | 183 | 160 | | 167 | 185 |

The next step is to multiply the weight by the rating and then sum the scores, as shown in Exhibit 3–7. So you would multiply 8 by 7 and 6 by 4 to obtain scores for the Dell, and then sum the products to arrive at the total. For the HP you would multiply 8 by 6 and 6 by 9, then add the products to arrive at the total for the HP. Based on these scores for the features, you would buy the HP. Even though the Dell outperformed the HP for your most important feature, the difference in hard disk size was so great that it outweighed the modem speed.

Mathematically, each product is given a score, which is the sum of the ratings times the weights. So when you multiply your importance weight of 8, times the rating of 6 for HP's modem speed, the score is 48. This score is added to the other scores for the HP, resulting in a total score of 183. You would choose the HP over the Dell because for you, the total score is 183 compared to 160. The other buyer would buy the Dell, because the total score was 185 to 167. You both arrived at different scores for two reasons: First, you value the features differently, and second, you rate the performance of each computer differently. Multiplied, then added together, these ratings result in a different decision.

We've asked our students if they actually calculate scores using ratings and weights. A few admit to this practice, but most believe that no one would be this formal. In organizations, however, you will find formal rating sheets used by purchasing departments to rate different suppliers and their offerings. Exhibit 3–8 is an example of a rating sheet used by DaimlerChrysler to evaluate potential suppliers.

A marketer would use this information by first determining what the most important attributes are, and then designing the product to rate the highest on those attributes. If you are a salesperson, however, and a particular buyer rated a competitor higher on an important attribute, you may work to change the importance of the attribute in the mind of the buyer if the product can't actually change.

Multiattribute models are not just for evaluating potential suppliers. Companies use multiattribute methods to analyze the performance of current vendors, too. Purchasing teams that include purchasing agents, engineers, manufacturing personnel, and other managers are used to develop the rating systems. Rockwell International's Defense Electronics Group was one of the pioneers of formal supplier rating systems with the development of its Supplier Rating and Incentive Program (SRIP). This system first identifies events, or problems with supplier service that require Rockwell personnel to take action. Examples of events are overshipments, undershipments, and rejection of products on receipt due to damage. Each event requires a Rockwell employee to take some action, such as seeing that overshipments are returned and a credit issued.

When the Rockwell employee has to take an action, a cost is involved for that employee's time. For example, Rockwell found that it cost $275 to return something to a

**Exhibit 3–8**
Sample Vendor
Analysis Form

| Supplier Name: _____ | | | Type of Product: _____ | | |
| --- | --- | --- | --- | --- | --- |
| Shipping Location: _____ | | | Annual Sales Dollars: _____ | | |

| | 5 Excellent | 4 Good | 3 Satisfactory | 2 Fair | 1 Poor | 0 N/A |
| --- | --- | --- | --- | --- | --- | --- |
| **Quality (45%)** | | | | | | |
| Defect rates | ____ | ____ | ____ | ____ | ____ | ____ |
| Quality of sample | ____ | ____ | ____ | ____ | ____ | ____ |
| Conformance with quality program | ____ | ____ | ____ | ____ | ____ | ____ |
| Responsiveness to quality problems | ____ | ____ | ____ | ____ | ____ | ____ |
| Overall quality | ____ | ____ | ____ | ____ | ____ | ____ |
| **Delivery (25%)** | | | | | | |
| Avoidance of late shipments | ____ | ____ | ____ | ____ | ____ | ____ |
| Ability to expand production capacity | ____ | ____ | ____ | ____ | ____ | ____ |
| Performance in sample delivery | ____ | ____ | ____ | ____ | ____ | ____ |
| Response to changes in order size | ____ | ____ | ____ | ____ | ____ | ____ |
| Overall delivery | ____ | ____ | ____ | ____ | ____ | ____ |
| **Price (20%)** | | | | | | |
| Price competitiveness | ____ | ____ | ____ | ____ | ____ | ____ |
| Payment terms | ____ | ____ | ____ | ____ | ____ | ____ |
| Absorption of costs | ____ | ____ | ____ | ____ | ____ | ____ |
| Submission of cost savings plans | ____ | ____ | ____ | ____ | ____ | ____ |
| Overall price | ____ | ____ | ____ | ____ | ____ | ____ |
| **Technology (10%)** | | | | | | |
| State-of-the-art components | ____ | ____ | ____ | ____ | ____ | ____ |
| Sharing research & development capability | ____ | ____ | ____ | ____ | ____ | ____ |
| Ability and willingness to help with design | ____ | ____ | ____ | ____ | ____ | ____ |
| Responsiveness to engineering problems | ____ | ____ | ____ | ____ | ____ | ____ |
| Overall technology | ____ | ____ | ____ | ____ | ____ | ____ |

| Buyer: _____ | Date: _____ |
| --- | --- |

Comments: _____

SOURCE: *DaimlerChrysler.*

supplier and $120 to follow up on a late shipment. These costs can be summed for each supplier, which Rockwell does on an annual basis to develop a Supplier Performance Index. The company can then analyze the quality of performance for each vendor. Rockwell's system has been adopted by such companies as Northrup, Motorola, and Honeywell.

Companies with high performance on SRIPs advertise their high ratings in order to attract more business. Buyers recognize that the quality of service is reflected in the total cost of ownership; poor quality does raise the cost of doing business. Companies that perform poorly will face difficulties no matter how well their products perform.

Buyers also evaluate suppliers for elevation to partner or preferred supplier status. The SRIP procedure is one method of evaluating suppliers, but it provides only supplier performance information. Other factors are important when deciding with whom the buyer wants to partner. When considering a candidate for preferred supplier status,

Bethlehem Steel uses six sets of criteria: capability, which includes an SRIP analysis; organizational motivation and quality of employees; financial health; corporate culture; willingness to commit to a partnership; and ethics. Using a multiattribute model, suppliers must pass minimum thresholds on each set of criteria and then reach an overall score before being offered preferred supplier status.[11]

Business marketers use the score sheets to create the right package of services to augment their core products. Not all buyers need the same level of service. The better that a marketer understands the buyer's requirements, the more likely that the total package of product and services, financial terms, ordering processes, and so forth will be what the buyer wants.

# TRENDS IN PURCHASING

Purchasing departments are very important to the success of an organization, as we saw earlier in this chapter. As companies select and implement various strategies, purchasing is always involved as resources are gathered to support those strategies. As a result, one trend is to increase the professionalism of the purchasing agent. Purchasing departments are not immune, however, to the influences of the economy. Therefore, trends caused by the economy as well as trends in organizational strategy influence the purchasing department.

These trends in purchasing reflect an overall trend toward strategic sourcing. **Strategic sourcing** is defined as the process of designing and managing supply networks to optimize operational and organization performance. A related concept is **supply chain management,** or the integration of supply processes from end user through original suppliers that provide products, services, and information that adds value for customers. From the Field 3–1 illustrates how three organization are responding to the challenges of strategic sourcing. As you can see, this concept of treating supply as a strategic component of how the firm provides value raises the importance of purchasing to more than just shopping and buying. Several factors and business trends are shaping the role of purchasing in organizations, such as increased involvement in demand planning, the importance of globalization, and others.[12]

# Demand Planning

**Demand planning** is a strategy of attempting to influence demand for products and services made by your company so that the supply chain can be managed most efficiently.[13] While demand planning is related to sales forecasting, or simply determining what the company will sell, demand planning ties those forecasts back into strategically managing the sourcing of services and products needed in order to supply the demand.

Jabil Circuit, for example, is a designer and manufacturer of electronic circuits that other manufacturers use in making their products. In fact, many of their customers actually make subassemblies that are then used in yet another company's products, such as cell phones, network routers, and others. Because Jabil is often three or four layers away from the final product, derived demand and the need for Jabil to manage some inventory for JIT delivery means that Jabil takes a risk with every product they make. Some of what they make may not ever be needed; alternatively, customers' needs may change rapidly requiring additional products on very short notice. Using demand planning enables Jabil to plan for various contingencies, improving their purchasing processes.

## 3–1

# FROM THE FIELD

## Strategic Sourcing the Globe

Strategic sourcing, early supplier involvement, and global sourcing aren't just terms in a textbook to Jim Scotti, vice president and chief procurement officer for Fluor Corporation (global construction contractor), Karen Weinstein-Millson, vice president of global sourcing for Boston Scientific (global medical device maker), or Marc Escande, vice president of global procurement for SNC-Lavelin (global construction company).

Scotti, for example, realized the importance of early supplier involvement when his company bid for a project in the Middle East. A major piece of equipment was bid by a supplier at a certain price with a 55-week delivery time. Three months later, Scotti got word that Fluor had won the project so he went back to the supplier and asked for another bid. This time, there was a substantial price increase and delivery was now 80 weeks. "A valuable lesson was learned. . . we must buy earlier in the process in today's market," he said. As he notes, "There's no reason to spend time and money bidding a project if you're not able to buy the materials and get them delivered in time to meet the schedule."

Weinstein-Millson agrees and has the targets to prove it. The sourcing organization at Boston Scientific plays a critical role in the company's overall strategy. Her department is expected to deliver 20 percent+ in cost reduction, quality and risk management, and growth/innovation. As she noted, 30 percent of Boston Scientific's new product ideas are to come from suppliers as part of the early supplier involvement program.

Escande has similar challenges, procuring for more than 1,000 projects a year around the world. Supplier relationship management and e-procurement are critical processes for, as Escande says, "I was able to tell one of our suppliers that we were spending several hundreds of millions of dollars with them on different projects. That gave us a big edge."

Early supplier involvement, supplier relationship management, global sourcing: All are part of strategic sourcing plans for Weinstein-Millson and Scotti and their procurement groups.

Sources: William Atkinson, "Boston Scientific Aligns Sourcing Organization with Corporate Goals," *Purchasing* 136, no. 7 (May 3, 2007), p. 17; John Yuva, "Procurement: Helping Fluor Accomplish Its EPC Mission," *Inside Supply Management* (January 17,) pp. 28–30; Paul E. Teague, "Change the Way You Source," *Purchasing* 136, no. 7, p. 49.

# Globalization

Globalization of sourcing has greatly influenced purchasing and will continue to do so. Just as an example, so much is now brought in from Asia Pacific through California ports that the ports are full. Companies are now searching for new ports. While that may seem like a small change, some of those ports may be in Canada or Mexico, adding additional issues in managing the logistics.[14] Thus, one aspect of globalization is sourcing in low-cost countries of supply and managing the logistics of getting the products here.

As an alternative to think about, recall Ericsson's need to standardize sourcing in business units operating in over 30+ countries. Since so many business companies operate in so many countries, or have customers who operate in many countries, globalization is not just a purchasing trend but an organizational trend with purchasing implications.[15]

# Increased Price Pressure

Managing costs is a major part of a purchasing professional's life, but with gas prices rising, the cost to produce and ship products has increased. Companies would like to increase prices but, at the same time, their customers are asking them to maintain prices because they have the same economic pressures from productivity gains, greater competition, and other factors. The only way to stay profitable, then, is to decrease costs.

Purchasing and supply professionals are considering every possible way to cut costs, including working with vendors to improve JIT systems, using RFID (radio frequency identification devices) to track the physical location of products and reduce shipping or storage costs, involving suppliers in product design to eliminate unnecessary costs, or consolidating purchases with fewer suppliers. For example, Ericsson reduced the costs of computers they buy by simply tracking how many were bought around the world from several dozen vendors and consolidating those purchases into one contract.

# Outsourcing

**Outsourcing** is the process of finding another organization to supply the buying organization with a product or service, usually one that was previously created in-house. Outsourcing is a strategic trend, caused in part by a trend in strategy where companies focus on their core businesses. For example, many firms outsource their advertising to advertising agencies because they believe the core competency of an outside agency is better than what they could do in-house. Note that outsourcing does not necessarily mean sending the job overseas; however, many companies have done just that in an effort to also reduce costs.

The Internet has made outsourcing, especially from companies in other countries, much easier.[16] The Internet enables easier communication between customers and vendors, as well as creates "marketplaces" where buyers can shop. For example, Planet Business is a Web site where companies can look for potential vendors by continent, or by country, while the Australia Business Marketplace is an Internet site devoted to Australian products only. In both cases, though, buyers can look for companies to send work to.

**Early supplier involvement (ESI)** is one outsourcing strategy whereby companies use suppliers to help design new products or processes. For example, everyone has heard of Intel and knows of their leadership position in the computer chip market. But few know that the reason for their success lies with their relationship with Applied Materials, the company that makes machines to manufacture computer chips. Most companies would design a new chip, then ask Applied Materials (or their competitor) to design the machine to make it. Intel asked Applied Materials to participate in the chip design process, designing the machines at the same time. As a result, Intel was able to bring products to market two years faster than anyone else and at a lower cost. By having suppliers working early in the process, both time and costs are reduced. We discuss this in greater detail in Chapter 8.

Outsourcing is one result of a make-or-buy decision. **Make-or-buy** is a comparison of the value created internally versus if created by someone else. Make-or-buy can include services such as training, but can also include component parts within the final product. For example, companies like Cisco, Hewlett-Packard, and others focus their efforts on design and marketing, rather than manufacturing. They assemble the final products, but the components that they once made are now made by contract manufacturers. These companies switched to contract manufacturers because there was greater value in doing so.

Outsourcing affects the purchasing department because it changes the way purchases are made. For example, outsourcing a subassembly may mean that fewer purchases are made, but the final purchase may require more input from the design department or a tighter communication link with manufacturing. As you can see from the examples, outsourcing can also have a major impact on the organization because important responsibilities are being moved outside the business. Companies that outsource poorly can be significantly hampered in their ability to compete.

Outsourcing has also meant continued growth in the services sector. Much of what is outsourced is services, such as marketing research, advertising and promotion services, training services, and other services that were formerly done by organizational employees, although more companies are also outsourcing production.

# Stronger Relationships with Sellers

As just pointed out, outsourcing means that important responsibilities are now being moved outside the organization. In addition, companies are trying to reduce the number of vendors and increase the amount of business with each vendor. These factors combine to increase the importance of strong relationships with suppliers. We've talked about this trend in the previous two chapters, but, as you can see, other trends influence the importance of relationships too.

Communication channels have changed greatly as a result of this trend. With direct communication, buyers can talk directly to key personnel and know that their needs will be met.[17] Buyers like Peak Electronics, for example, believe so strongly in the need for direct communication that they gave manufacturing line employees authority to contact suppliers directly and handle problems as they occur.[18] Smart marketers are finding ways to increase direct communication between their company and their partners.

Outsourcing can be part of supply chain management, but supply chain management also includes integrating such functions as logistics and marketing with outsourcing. Supply chain managent is often related to reducing the number of suppliers. As the number of suppliers shrinks but business with each one grows, supply chain management becomes more feasible.[19]

Supplier relationship management is another related concept. **Supplier relationship management (SRM),** such as initiated by Ericsson, involves the use of computer models to identify the most valuable suppliers and to identify purchasing opportunities. These opportunities may include consolidation of purchases to obtain bigger discounts or to automate supply chain functions. Kingfisher Asia Limited uses SRM software to track over 150 suppliers providing over 8,000 products to companies in Europe. For example, the software identified one supplier with delivery problems. While the prices were lower, poor delivery was erasing those price advantages and the company was able to take action to restore margins.[20] We'll discuss supplier relationship management and supply chain management in greater detail in Chapter 9, but for now, recognize that these processes require strong relationships between purchasing and sellers.

# Cross-Functional Teams

**Cross-functional sourcing teams** are purchasing teams that include members of various functional areas within the firm, and sometimes include personnel from suppliers and customers too. These teams are formed to develop cost-reduction strategies, create sourcing strategies, and handle other purchasing functions, many times in global servicing situations.[21] Cross-functional teams are designed to take advantage of the different types of expertise that reside in the various departments across the organization. Motorola, for example, combines cross-functional sourcing teams with early supplier involvement. Rita Lane, chief procurement officer, calls this process their Rapid Sourcing Initiative, because

**Exhibit 3–9**
Factors That
Lead to
Successful
Cross-
Functional
Purchasing
Teams

*Appropriate Leadership:* The nature of the purchase decision dictates who leads the team.

*Communication:* Face-to-face communication should be supported, but not dominated, by e-mail and teleconferences.

*Continuity:* Some purchasing areas require permanent cross-functional teams. One distributor of gas and welding equipment has a team that focuses on supplier relationships; this team includes a marketing manager to represent customers.

*Top-Level Commitment:* Management has to support the release of time for key individuals to participate.

*Embracing Diversity:* Successful teams not only have different functional areas represented, but also different races, backgrounds, and even corporate philosophies. Properly harnessed, the resulting tension can result in surprising creativity.

SOURCES: *"Cross-Functional Teams Flourish,"* Supplier Selection & Management Report *(March 2002), pp. 1, 12–13;* *"How Purchasing Can Build a Top-Notch Cross-Functional Team,"* Supplier Selection & Management Report *(March 2003), pp. 7, 11–12.*

the process enables them to develop new products and bring those products to market much more quickly than before. For example, Lonnie Bernardini, vice president for new product development, reports that over 1 million units of a new phone was designed, built, and shipped in under 30 days, a previously unheard-of rate of new product introduction. That kind of ability to respond quickly to market demand was only made possible by building teams that included supply management, marketing, and suppliers.[22] Exhibit 3–9 highlights the factors that lead to effective cross-functional teams.

From a marketing perspective, it is apparent that potential suppliers should seek to actively participate in their customers' cross-functional sourcing teams. For this to occur, salespeople must understand what cross-functional teams are, how to recognize such teams in their clients' organizations, and how they can participate. In addition, salespeople have to be given resources that allow others in their own organization to participate. Buyers need the expertise of the selling organization's engineers, finance personnel, and so forth in order to fully benefit from the seller's participation.

# Professionalism in Purchasing

Another trend is toward increasing the professionalism of the purchasing function. The Institute of Supply Management has contributed much to the development of professionalism by encouraging and providing certification for purchasing managers. Those who are certified as professional purchasing managers must pass a battery of tests that indicate knowledge of (and adherence to) the profession's code of ethics (which we will discuss later in this chapter) as well as procedures of purchasing. Because of the importance of purchasing to the bottom line, many companies are also encouraging their purchasing agents to seek certification.

In a survey of purchasing and corporate executives, the most important skills in purchasing and supply management can easily be seen as consequences of the increasing importance of supply management. As illustrated in Exhibit 3–10, negotiation, communication, and relationship building are very important skills. The survey also noted that if those skills were inadequate, serious consequences including dissatisfied company management, late deliveries, failure to understand and meet quality requirements, and unnecessary emergencies occurred, costing organizations lost productivity but also lost market share, dwindling profits, and other hazards.[23] For that reason, continued professional development is an important aspect of the professional supply manager.

**Exhibit 3–10**
Key Skills and
Training Areas
for Supply
Managers

| Skills | Training Areas |
|---|---|
| 1. Negotiation | 1. Negotiation |
| 2. Communication | 2. Contract management |
| 3. Analysis/Costing | 3. Leadership/Management |
| 4. Relationship building | 4. (Three way tie) Accounting, analysis, supplier relationship building |
| 5. Sourcing/Supplier selection | |

SOURCE: *Adapted from Charles Dominick, "The 2005 Purchasing Skills Report." White Paper published by Next Level Purchasing Inc., Moon Township PA, 2005.*

These trends, although discussed in the context of private industry, are also affecting the way the government buys. In the next section, we take a close look at government purchasing in order to successfully market to the world's largest buyer.

# PURCHASING IN GOVERNMENT

Government is the largest single buyer, the largest single employer, and the largest landlord. For example, the federal government buys about $500 million in desktop PCs each year; state local governments buy twice that![24] This kind of purchasing power makes selling to the government an important consideration for many businesses. The government, however, has a different agenda than private organizations, which influences the way the government makes purchases. For example, minority set-asides are programs designed to encourage the development and growth of minority-owned businesses. Reaching social and political goals, such as minority ownership of businesses, often influences government purchasing policies, which we will examine in this section.

## Political and Social Goals

All governments attempt to influence the achievement of political and social goals through purchasing. For example, the U.S. government encourages the development of minority-owned, women-owned, and small businesses through set-asides. The government also attempts to achieve social goals through compliance programs. **Compliance programs** are programs in which purchasers must be in compliance with federal guidelines in order to be eligible to supply the government. The government has used compliance programs to advance affirmative action programs for women, minorities, and the handicapped.

Minority subcontracting programs are another way that the government encourages the development of minority-owned businesses. **Minority subcontracting** programs require general contractors and other major suppliers to allocate a certain percentage of the total contract to minority-owned subcontractors. For example, a company building a research park for the EPA may have minority subcontractors to install the plumbing, lay the carpet, and perform other such jobs that are part of the overall contract.

## The Department of Defense

The Department of Defense is the largest single buying agency in the federal government, accounting for an estimated 80 percent of all government purchases.[25] Composed of the military branches (the Army, Air Force, and Navy), the Department of Defense also contains the

Purchasing agents now use the Web to shop and purchase everything, even complex machines.

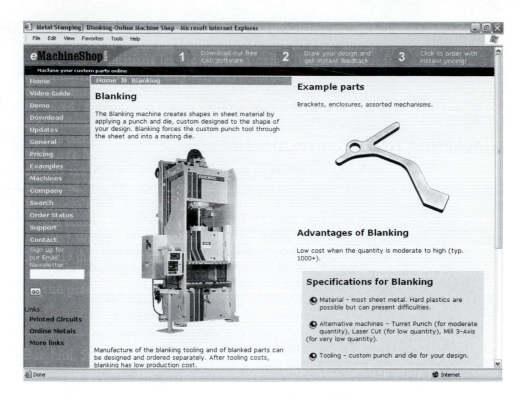

Defense Logistics Agency (DLA). The DLA purchases all of the facilitating services and products as well as MRO items. The purpose of the DLA is to secure volume discounts by buying for all of the military such items as copiers, office supplies, and office furniture.

As mentioned earlier, the Department of Defense developed many single-sourcing arrangements, in part because of the huge investment needed to develop weapon systems. Frequently, few vendors are even capable of bidding; for example, only Raytheon and General Dynamics entered the Sparrow air-to-air missile contract competition. The department, however, is now trying to develop additional vendors for many products, having found that multiple vendors can lower cost. In addition, due to its spreading purchases among suppliers, more suppliers learn how to do business with government, which further increases competition for government business. The increased competition should lead to lower prices and higher-quality products.

# Nondefense Buying

The rest of the government uses the General Services Administration in a fashion similar to the DLA; in fact, the DLA makes most of its purchases through the GSA. The GSA supplies government agencies with office space, facilitating services and products, and MRO items. The GSA and the DLA are the two most important agencies because of the volume of buying for which they are responsible.

The GSA negotiates the price to be charged the government, but in many cases, the GSA does not actually make the final purchase. Each agency can then make its own purchase directly, receiving the GSA price and using a GSA-approved vendor. (Many companies have copied this model of approving vendors at headquarters and allowing each division or local office to make the final purchase decision.) For example, the GSA has negotiated copier prices with several different manufacturers. The Federal Highway Department office in Fort Worth, Texas, can choose the copier it wants from any of those approved vendors and make the purchase themselves.

The GSA does not get involved in all of the nondefense buying, though. NASA, for example, buys space shuttles and space communication systems entirely on its own. The GSA does not have the expertise necessary to make those kind of purchases.

# Marketing to the Government

The size of the federal government of the United States, combined with the various social, political, and economic goals that influence government purchasing, makes selling to the government a complicated and arduous task, especially in comparison with selling to private industry. To assist potential vendors, the government has created booklets such as *How to Sell to the Air Force* and *Doing Business with the Federal Government.* Information on opportunities to sell to the government can also be found in the *Commerce Business Daily,* which is how Professional Restoration Inc. found the opportunity to build part of the Korean War Memorial in Washington, DC. In addition, government agencies have purchasing agents who seek out qualified vendors and are specialists in set-aside, compliance, or subcontracting programs. These agents are valuable sources of information for the vendor with little experience in marketing to the government.

As mentioned earlier, the GSA negotiates a price and, when successful, places that vendor on the approved vendor list. Each agency can then do business with that vendor. If you aren't on the list, then an agency cannot purchase from you. The first step, for many vendors, is to become an approved vendor. Then each agency has to be sold and marketed to as if it were a separate customer. For example, Digital Monitoring Product, Inc. (DMP), signed a contract with the GSA that allowed its dealers to offer products to the government at prenegotiated prices. More importantly, the agreement allowed DMP dealers to provide installation and maintenance services, important because many agencies no longer maintain their own technical staff. Dealers are listed in the GSA catalog, and agencies can call the dealers directly to place a purchase order or to order service.[26]

In major purchases, particularly when products are being built to specifications, pricing can be negotiated one of two ways. For example, when NASA negotiates to buy a new space shuttle from Rockwell International, NASA can negotiate a fixed price. A **fixed-price agreement** means that if it costs Rockwell more to build an item than it thought, Rockwell has to cover the higher costs. Or NASA can agree to a **cost-plus contract,** which means that NASA will reimburse Rockwell for all of its costs plus a certain percentage for Rockwell's profit.

Both cost-plus and fixed-price agreements are negotiated when selling to foreign governments too. In addition to the issues we've already discussed about how governments buy, marketers to other governments must consider the type of government and political system. In China, for example, one must understand not only the purchasing process of the agency making the purchase, but also the hierarchy and decision-making process of the local Communist Party office.

Selling to any government can be a difficult process made complex by the number of regulations involved. Selling to governments can take much longer than selling to corporations, require significantly more paperwork, and result in lower prices and margins. Still, the size of purchases made by governments makes them an attractive market for many business marketers. From the Field 3–2 illustrates how one marketing manager addresses the opportunity in selling to the government.

---

**3–2**

## FROM THE FIELD

## Patience, Patience, Patience!

If you have to have immediate gratification, selling to governments is not for you! When we sell to governments, it might take up to years to actually make a sale.

I work for Tymco International Ltd., a manufacturer of street sweepers. These products are also used at airports and for other special applications, and governments are a primary customer for us.

In a large city government, you have to sell to the user department, the department that manages the city's fleet of vehicles (which could include police cars, fire trucks, and street maintenance equipment in addition to sweepers), the public works management, a purchasing department, and even the city manager. In some cases, the specifications for a sweeper are written by someone who will never use it. Yet, each one of these groups within that government has to trust that we have the sweeper they need, and that we can take care of it.

We sell through a dealer network. That dealer's reputation is very important, but so is our reputation. Governments tend to avoid risk, so once they find a dealer they trust, they want to buy other products from that dealer. Our reputation with all of those areas is strong, which helps the dealer, too.

I direct regional sales managers who work with dealers, but I'm also responsible for advertising to each of those areas, developing trade show strategies and so forth. For example, we support the professional group the American Public Works Association (APWA) and are one of the sponsors of their trade show and conference,

but we also support trade shows aimed at purchasing professionals. We need to make sure that fleet management, public works, purchasing, and street maintenance professionals all learn about Tymco. At these trade shows, our engineers and company executives can meet with more current and prospective customers in one day than they could in a month.

One thing that has made life a little easier is that governments are getting away from buying the lowest-price product. Instead, they've begun considering the total cost of ownership and the value delivered. Bid processes are done on a point system where they evalute us so they can buy the best system for the money, not necessarily the lowest-cost products.

But I've learned that when I lose a sale, as much as I hate it, sometimes it works out better. Once they've experienced a product that isn't as good, or worked with someone who isn't as reliable, it makes us look that much better in the market.

Dealing with all of these areas is something I like. In the same day, I might meet with people who actually sweep the streets, fleet people, the city manager, and then appear before the city council that night. What I've learned through the years is that these are hard-working, underappreciated professionals—and they appreciate someone like me who works hard for them.

Bobby Johnson, Marketing Manager, Tymco International Ltd.

---

# ETHICS IN PURCHASING

Ethics in business are an important topic today. Issues such as price fixing, under-the-table kickbacks, and other shady practices continue to fill the media. Frequent cases, such as the CEO of a construction firm arrested for bribing government officials, create the perception that often sellers are unethical.

Ethics are of particular concern to purchasing management. The executive of the selling firm may offer a bribe, but it takes a recipient for the bribe to occur. Buyers are just as susceptible to the economic pressures facing salespeople that influence ethical behavior. In

**Exhibit 3–11**
Summary of
Institute for
Supply
Management's
Code of Ethics

1. Avoid the intent and appearance of unethical or compromising practice in relationships, actions, and communications.
2. Demonstrate loyalty to the employer by diligently following the lawful instructions of the employer, using reasonable care and only the authority granted.
3. Refrain from any private or professional business activity that would create a conflict between personal interests and the interests of the employer.
4. Refrain from soliciting or accepting money, loans, credits, or prejudicial discounts and the acceptance of gifts, entertainment, favors, or services from past or potential suppliers that might influence or appear to influence purchasing decisions.
5. Handle confidential or proprietary information belonging to employers or suppliers with due care and proper consideration of ethical and legal ramifications and government regulations.
6. Promote positive supplier relationships through courtesy and impartiality throughout all phases of the purchasing cycle.
7. Refrain from reciprocal agreements that restrain competition.
8. Know and obey the letter and spirit of laws governing the purchasing function, and remain alert to the legal ramifications of purchasing decisions.
9. Encourage all segments of society to participate by demonstrating support for small, disadvantaged, and minority-owned businesses.
10. Discourage purchasing's involvement in employer-sponsored programs of personal purchases that are not business related.
11. Enhance the proficiency and stature of the purchasing profession by acquiring and maintaining current technical knowledge and the highest standards of ethical behavior.
12. Conduct international purchasing in accordance with the laws, customs, and practices of foreign countries, consistent with U.S. laws, your organization's policies, and these Ethical Standards and Guidelines.

SOURCE: *Institute for Supply Management. Used with permission.*

this section, we will examine the key ethical issues facing purchasing and what companies are doing to encourage ethical behavior.

# What Are Ethics?

**Ethics** are moral codes of conduct, rules for how someone should operate that can be followed as situations demand. Codes of ethics such as the Institute for Supply Management's Code in Exhibit 3–11 are rules developed either by an industry association or by a company or some organization, but individuals also develop their own codes. Individual ethics can be developed through experience and through education. When conduct fails to meet the ethical needs of society, laws are passed; for example, the Robinson–Patman Act was passed because business failed to price products in a fair and ethical manner.

For ethical behavior to occur, the person must first recognize the ethical implications of the situation and then be motivated to act ethically. Knowledge of right and wrong is not enough; the individual must want to do what is right. Situational factors, such as the probability of getting caught, may influence some people's behavior, whereas others will always do what they think is right (or what is wrong, depending on their moral state) no matter what the situation.

# Ethical Issues Facing Purchasing

In purchasing, there are several key issues concerning ethics that revolve around the concept of fair competition. Fair competition means that any competitor has equal opportunity to sell to the buyer and equal access to information from the buyer. Actions

**Exhibit 3–12**
Purchasing
Agents List
Top Ethical
Problems That
They Face

| Issue | U.S. | Rank In Country | | |
| --- | --- | --- | --- | --- |
| | | Canada | U.K. | India |
| Showing partiality to firm preferred by upper management | 1 | 2 | 3 | 6 |
| Offering or soliciting payments or contributions for purpose of influencing government officials | 30 | 31 | 31 | 1 |
| Failure to provide products or services of highest quality in eyes of external customers (supply chain) | 11 | 14 | 2 | 3 |
| Offering or soliciting payments or contributions for purpose of influencing purchase decisions | 32 | 22 | 22 | 2 |
| Receiving gifts or entertainment that influences, or appears to influence, decisions | 7 | 5 | 7 | 4 |
| Allowing personalities to improperly influence decisions | 2 | 1 | 4 | 16 |
| Failure to provide prompt honest answers to customer inquiries | 3 | 4 | 4 | 10 |

SOURCES: *Robert Cooper, Gary Frank, and Robert Kemp, "A Multinational Comparison of Key Ethical Issues, Helps, and Challenges in the Purchasing and Supply Management Profession: The Key Implications for Business and the Professions,"* Journal of Business Ethics *23 (January 1, 2000), pp. 83–100; Robert Cooper, "The Ethical Environment Facing Purchasing and Supply Management Professionals: A Multinational Perspective,"* Business & Professional Ethics Journal *15, no. 3 (1997), pp. 65–89.*

such as bribery are unethical because they give one competitor an unfair advantage. Therefore, one issue facing purchasing is *equal access to the buying opportunity.*

Another basic issue is *responsibility to the buying organization,* the buyer's employer. For example, bribery may add to the cost of the product by raising the price, which is not the best thing for the buying organization. In addition, a buyer who has been bribed may not perform the buying duties completely, which means that the organization is not assured of getting the best solution for its needs.

These two dimensions of equal access and responsibility are the basic guidelines for evaluating ethical actions in purchasing. You can see, in Exhibit 3–12, how these two dimensions are expressed in the various issues faced by purchasing agents around the world. Let's now take a look at how these guidelines can be applied to purchasing situations.

## Receiving Gifts

Gifts of some type are accepted by an estimated 97 percent of all buyers, and gift giving has long been an accepted practice.[27] Most businesses believe that giving gifts is an effective activity that enhances their selling ability by strengthening relationships. Research, though, indicates that gift giving is not as effective as managers think and may cause problems for vendors.[28]

Expensive lunches, entertainment such as golf games and sporting events, and trips are also considered gifts. New federal ethics rules prohibit members of Congress from accepting free meals from lobbyists, as well as trips and other gifts. Some companies, such as IBM, do not allow their employees to accept anything from a vendor. Mead Paper, for example, has an annual golf tournament for its customers, but the IBM buyer cannot participate. By company policy, that buyer cannot accept so much as a cup of coffee from the Mead representative. Yet in other industries and companies, entertaining clients and prospective clients is accepted.

## Access to Information

Buyers have access to a lot of information. Having that information can be a competitive advantage. How that information is used can become an ethical issue. For example, suppose a purchasing agent is considering three vendors. If the agent tells one vendor the budget but doesn't tell the others, then the vendor with the budget information has an unfair advantage.

For example, it is quite common to have bids as part of purchase processes. In some cases, particularly with government entities, these bids are sealed and opened at the same time. An unethical act would be to open a bid early and give that information to another bidder in order to get a lower price. Although it may seem that getting a lower price is better for the government, as a society we've agreed to open competition, meaning that everyone has the same shot at getting the business.

A similar practice is called shill bidding. This practice involves getting bids from companies with no expectation of doing business with them, in order to drive down prices from the companies that you do want to do business with. An example is a reverse auction, common on the Web. In business marketing, reverse auctions occur when a buyer puts out a request for prices on the Web for a specific purchase. Suppliers bid on the business, lowering price until one bidder remains in the auction. At that point, the buyer is supposed to buy, but some don't. Instead they take the bid to their current supplier and expect the same price. In a recent survey of purchasing professionals, 41 percent believed this to be an unethical practice, 11 percent thought it was okay, and the rest chose not to answer the question.

Buyers and sellers sometimes work closely together in developing products. Sellers also give some buyers sneak previews of products. In these situations, buyers are often asked to sign **nondisclosure agreements,** which means that they will not share any information about the new products with anyone who has not also signed such an agreement. If a buyer were to offer this information in a trade to wrangle concessions from another vendor, the buyer could be sued. More importantly, the buyer would be guilty of unethical conduct.

## Encouraging Ethical Conduct

We've talked at length in this chapter about the importance of purchasing to the firm's success. Ethical conduct is a major contributor to effective purchasing; unethical purchasing can damage a firm because it will pay too much for lower-quality products. In addition, there is always the threat of legal action for unethical conduct.

Just as importantly, however, unethical conduct represents a breach of trust. Selling organizations have to trust their buyers on many levels, and trust is particularly important in building long-term partnerships. Without that trust, the buying organizations will not be privy to sneak previews of new products and will be unable to make fully informed decisions. Ethical sellers will look elsewhere to form strategic alliances, which will damage the competitive ability of the unethical firm.

The senior management of most companies wants their companies to operate ethically, but even if they did not care that much about ethics, it is good business practice. To encourage ethical behavior, many companies have developed specific and extensive policies concerning purchasing. These policies cover such things as when is it acceptable to receive a gift and how large a gift may be, issues concerning entertainment, and how a purchasing department will select products. For example, policies may dictate when sealed bids must be used, when the vendor with the lowest price has to be given the business, and other purchasing decisions.

Policies alone are not enough, however. Employees have to understand the policies and know how to apply them. For this reason, companies require their purchasing employees to undergo regular training about the policies.

Knowledge of the policies, however, is also not enough. Employees have to be motivated to follow the policies. Management can encourage employees to follow the policies by setting good examples and by punishing those who fail to follow the policies. When these two actions are viewed by purchasing employees, they know that the policies are real, and they will be motivated to act within the guidelines that management has set.

# Summary

Effective purchasing can be a source of competitive advantage for a company. Purchasing's responsibility is to provide an adequate supply of the right product or service at the best possible price. Purchasing's ability to effectively achieve this responsibility is affected, however, by manufacturing and marketing considerations. Reducing purchasing costs can have a negative impact on manufacturing and/or marketing, so purchasing must consider the needs of manufacturing and marketing when making decisions.

Many organizations are turning to just-in-time (JIT) systems, which means that they receive products and materials just in time to use them. JIT can reduce inventory carrying costs significantly. Suppliers are incorporating concurrent manufacturing as a way to supply the JIT needs of the customers without increasing their own inventory costs. Electronic data interchange (EDI) is electronic data transmission between the buyer and seller that is used to order products and can facilitate the implementation of a JIT system.

Purchasing the right quality of product or service is an important responsibility of the purchasing department. Quality is ultimately defined by the consumer; purchasing has to work closely with marketing and manufacturing to ensure that products of the proper quality are purchased.

Purchasing also has the responsibility to provide products and services at the lowest total cost. Lowest total cost, however, includes many elements beyond the initial purchase price. Purchasing departments, therefore, examine the total cost of ownership over the life of the product. Many companies are turning to outsourcing services as a method of reducing the total cost of ownership because of the high costs associated with retaining service personnel on staff.

To arrive at the lowest total cost, companies have tried to determine the economic ordering quantity. Forward buying is one practice that can result, having negative consequences for the supplier. Another practice is value analysis, which is a method of examining the total cost of ownership.

Traditionally, purchasing agents have had an adversarial philosophy toward their suppliers, but this is changing to a more collaborative and partnering philosophy. Preferred supplier systems are means that companies use to develop stronger relationships with their vendors. One outcome of the shift toward partnering is the growth in single sourcing, although single sourcing by itself does not necessarily mean a partnership.

Several steps are required to select vendors. The buy-phase model describes each step that organizations go through when making purchases for the first time (new buys). Modified rebuys may require fewer steps, and straight rebuys are often simply automatic purchasing when inventories are low. Out-suppliers encourage value analysis in an effort to move straight rebuys into the modified rebuy category, so that they will have a shot at the business.

To evaluate suppliers, companies compare and weigh benefits using a multiattribute process. This process requires purchasers to enumerate the desired benefits and rate the importance of each benefit. Then each vendor is evaluated and scored on each benefit. The rating of importance and the vendor's score are multiplied for each benefit, and then summed to arrive at a total score. The vendor with the highest score is the one whose product is selected. Companies such as Rockwell International use a formal process like this when evaluating current suppliers as well as potential suppliers.

Purchasing is an area where ethics are very important. Two basic dimensions guide ethical issues in purchasing: fair access and responsibility. Two activities are especially worrisome: gift giving plus information access and use.

Government purchasing represents a major economic influence in every country. Developing countries are especially concerned with making infrastructure purchases. Other countries may want to achieve social and economic goals through programs such as minority set-asides. For major purchases, a cost-plus or fixed-pricing agreement may be negotiated.

Understanding how purchasing operates is very important. The purchasing department is involved in over 40 percent of all purchases made by organizations and nearly all purchases involving MRO items and materials that go into the manufacturing process.

## Key Terms

adversarial purchasing
   philosophy
buy-class
buy-grid model
buy-phase model
complexity
   management
compliance program
concurrent
   manufacturing
cost-plus contract
cross-functional
   sourcing teams
demand planning
early supplier
   involvement (ESI)

economic order
   quantity (EOQ)
electronic data
   interchange (EDI)
ethics
fixed-price agreement
forward buying
in-supplier
just-in-time (JIT)
make-or-buy
minority subcontracting
modified rebuy
multiattribute model
new buy
nondisclosure
   agreements

outsourcing
out-supplier
partnership
   purchasing
preferred supplier
   systems
single sourcing
straight rebuy
strategic sourcing
supplier relationship
   management (SRM)
supply chain
   management
total cost of ownership
value analysis

# Discussion Questions

1. NASA has successfully landed several rovers on Mars, and accomplished several other feats as the space agency has been revitalized. What type of contract would you want to negotiate with NASA if you were to build a manned spacecraft to visit Mars, fixed-price or cost-plus? Why? Now assume you are negotiating the annual toilet paper contract with the Air Force. Which type of agreement would you want and why?

2. You were just told by one of your largest customers that they want to enter a single-sourcing agreement with your company. Your jubilation deteriorates quickly as you realize that they are now pushing for more concessions from your company. What are the factors, from the buyer's perspective, that would lead them to an adversarial single-sourcing relationship? What would you do to try to change that to a partnering relationship?

3. When does gift giving become unethical? Are there any times when a salesperson accepting a gift from a purchasing agent could be construed as unethical?

4. In this chapter, we discussed a number of trends and how they affect purchasing. Which trend do you think is most important? Why? Which is least important and why? What trends do you think we've overlooked?

5. Go back to the list of product types in Chapter 1. Which ones do you think are most likely to be purchased as straight rebuys and which are likely to be modified rebuys? Why?

6. Assume that you are the out-supplier for MRO items. How would you get that purchase changed from a straight rebuy to a modified rebuy? Would it make a difference to your ability to create a partnership if the purchase was made by the purchasing department or the maintenance department? Justify your answer.

7. Assume you are about to graduate and have received two job offers. One is in Boston, the other in Denver. Create a multiattribute matrix for this decision. Begin by listing all the factors that would influence your decision and the appropriate weights for each factor. Then rate the two cities and calculate the final score for each city. Do the final scores reflect what you would have picked anyway? If so, why? and if not; why not?

8. Read From the Field 3–1. What impact would the global sourcing strategies of Fluor and Boston Scientific have on your sales and marketing strategy if you supplied either company with components that become part of their products? How would your answer change if you sold them MRO products?

# Cases

## Case 3.1  Wipro's Guide to Outsourcing

Wipro is a company based in India that does information technology consulting and support, among other activities, for companies based all around the world. Recently, Vivek Ramamurthy was making a call on Ian McHaggle, chairman of McHaggle and Co. in Glasgow, Scotland. McHaggle has used Wipro's IT support and consulting for just over five years.

"I'd like you to consider moving the Wipro team that supports our activities to Glasgow," said McHaggle.

Ramamurthy thought for a moment. "Sir, that is about 100 employees."

McHaggle replied, "That's right. And I'd like you to rent the vacant office space in that building across from us. We feel like we need more on-site support and planning."

Ramamurthy told him Wipro would review the request and get back to him. But after thinking about it, Ramamurthy thought it would be less expensive to hire 100 Glasgow locals. When he approached McHaggle with that proposal, McHaggle nearly exploded.

"Ach, laddie, if I wanted it done with people from Glasgow, why would I come to you?" he said.

SOURCE: Case based on Jeet Thayil, "The Wipro Guide to Outsourcing," www.rediff.com, November 6, 2003.

**1.** What did McHaggle think he would get if Wipro followed his request as he had stated?

**2.** There is a tension in make-or-buy and outsourcing illustrated by this fictionalized account of a real situation. Describe the tension or conflict, and how you would reply to McHaggle.

### Case 3.2   Frenetic Inc.

Frenetic Inc. makes "green" energy products; that is, products that reduce energy consumption or generate energy via renewable sources such as wind and water power. Margaret Sebring was one of the first employees of the company in the early 90s, and is now the head of a 13-person procurement office. Her responsibilities include buying new equipment, most of which was purchased through Thomas Industries, a distributor.

Over the past two years, she has become more and more disenchanted with Thomas. Deliveries of two new pieces of plant equipment were late last year, causing significant problems in production. Then, just six months ago, the new materials handling unit required significant and frequent retooling during the first 90 days of use. Frenetic plant operators could not get the proper manuals shipped in order to figure out how to operate the new equipment. To make matters worse, invoices from Thomas were wrong, requiring careful backtracking by Margaret and her counterpart in Accounts Payable.

Just after Thanksgiving, she got a call from Mark Sawyer, the Thomas Industries salesperson who called on Frenetic. After some small talk, he got to the point of his call. "Maggie, I know you're working on budgets for next year, and I wondered where you stood on retooling the Hermosillo Mexico plant. Will that hit the budget next year?"

"Mark, that may not matter. Frankly, given the problems we've had this year, we're planning to really shop around for any further equipment purchases." She listened as Mark repeated the litany of excuses he used to explain the poor performance over the previous 18 months, and reiterated her position of shopping around before they concluded their call.

Margaret was working on the next year's budget about a week before Christmas when her assistant came into her office with the mail. On top was an envelope from Thomas Industries. She looked at it and thought, "Another Christmas card." Opening it up, the envelope did indeed contain a card proclaiming "Season's Greetings." Inside was a $100 gift card for Victoria's Secret.

Source: This case is based upon a true incident; however, the companies' and individuals' names have been changed.

**1.** Is there an ethical problem with Margaret's accepting the gift? Why or why not? What factors could influence your decision regarding the ethics of accepting the gift? Are there any other issues surrounding the gift other than ethics?

**2.** One problem that Margaret had was the lack of a formal supplier evaluation system. What components should such a system have? How would she measure

Thomas Industries' (and Sawyer's) performance on those components? Think as specifically as you can as to how you would measure a company's performance as a supplier.

## Additional Readings

Aaronson, Susan A. "Minding our Business: What the United States Government Has Done and Can Do to Ensure That U.S. Multinationals Act Responsibly in Foreign Markets." *Journal of Business Ethics* 59 (2005), pp. 175–98.

Berrios, Ruben. "Government Contracts and Contractor Behavior." *Journal of Business Ethics* 63, no. 2 (2006), pp. 119–31.

Emiliani, M. L., D. J. Stec, and L. P. Grasso. "Unintended Responses to a Traditional Purchasing Performance Metric." *Supply Chain Management* 10, nos. 3/4 (2005), pp. 150–56.

Freytag, Per V., and Ole S. Mikkelsen. "Sourcing from the Outside: Six Managerial Challenges." *Journal of Business and Industrial Marketing* 22, no. 3 (2007), pp.187–200.

Handfield, Robert B., and David L Baumer. "Managing Conflict of Interest Issues in Purchasing." *Journal of Supply Chain Management* 42, no. 3 (2006), pp. 41–50.

Hult, Tomas. "Global Supply Chain Management: An Integration of Scholarly Thoughts." *Industrial Marketing Management* 33 (2004), pp. 3–5. This is an introduction to a special issue on global supply chain management that includes nine more articles on the subject.

Rutherford, Brian N., James S. Boles, Hiram C. Barksdale, and Julie T. Johnson. "Single Source Supply versus Multiple Source Supply: A Study into the Relationship between Satisfaction and Propensity to Stay within a Service Setting." *Journal of Personal Selling & Sales Management* 26, no. 5 (2006), pp. 317–78.

# Chapter 4

## Organizational Buyer Behavior

### WEBEX

Webex is a brand name not familiar to most business students but it will be shortly after graduation. As the leading provider of virtual meeting tools, the company has grown tremendously, so it won't be long before graduating college students will experience their first Webex meeting. Recently acquired by Cisco for $3.2 billion, one key to the company's success is how they market to organizations. ●

"Our sales model is unique," says Dave Berman, vice president of worldwide sales. Because of the nature of the services Webex provides, many individuals in organizations will buy as they need it and do so on their own. As the number of Webex users grows in an organization, Berman's sales and marketing team is also talking to top level executives. "Eventually, we bring them both together to make a sale. It's a lot easier to sell when you show the C level (executives) how their people are already using your product." ●

Boeing, for example, had over 1 million virtual meetings using Webex services in one year. In fact, the company was so impressed with the productivity gains from virtual meetings, as well as measures regarding delivery, quality, support, and cost, that Boeing named Webex as Supplier of the Year for 2006. ●

What makes Webex so unique, in addition to quality product design, is how well the company understands how buyers within companies make decisions.

As Berman notes, the company sells to individual users as well as chief executives, and "we do vary the strategies. . . . If you're talking to VPs and above, you need to talk quantification—about productivity and revenue, not features and benefits." Webex is successful because the company understands organizational buying processes—how individuals make purchases within organizations. ●

Sources: Renee Houston Zemanski, "Identifying Decision Makers," *Selling Power* (November/ December 2006), p. 31; Colin Smith, "Webex Honored with Supplier of the Year Award from Boeing," http://www.webex.com/pr/pr90.html, April 20, 2007.

Visit the Webex Web site: **www.webex.com.** ●

## LEARNING OBJECTIVES

In order to develop profitable relationships with buyers, it helps to understand how they make decisions. This chapter describes the theories of how buyers in organizations buy products and services.

*After reading this chapter, you will be able to*

● Explain, using the most prominent theories of organizational buyer behavior, how individual needs may override or influence the rational decision-making process.

● Predict marketing action based on the choice of a particular buying theory.

● Describe the influence of risk on buyer behavior.

● Illustrate how these theories work in concert with partnering.

In the previous chapter, you learned about the influence of the purchasing department and the rational methods of making purchase decisions. You also learned about the importance to the buying organization of making sound economic decisions. In all organizations, however, it is people who make the final decisions—and they have their own agendas, quirks, likes, and dislikes. In this chapter, we explore the individual. You will find the theories presented here useful when making decisions about what products to market, how to set prices, what communication vehicles and sales approaches to employ, and other marketing decisions.

Chapter 3 focused on the professional procurement officer or supply chain manager. This professional works with professionals from many other areas in the organization, though, who also participate in purchasing decisions. While the last chapter dealt with formal purchasing strategies and processes, the reality is that many purchases are made or influenced by people who are not professional procurement specialists. If we want to market successfully to all of the people involved in making buying decisions, we need to understand them. That is why, in this chapter, we explore several organizational buying theories: that is, a group of theories designed to explain how people make decisions when buying for their organization.

There is a competitive advantage to be gained in selling the way buyers want to buy. For example, consider the Internet—with the exception of Internet services like those provided by Webex, all of the products sold on the Web existed before the Web. But the Web exists as a way to buy simply because buyers gain advantage in *how* they buy. If marketers can understand how and why buyers buy, then these same marketers can add more value in how they market. These theories help us understand the whys and hows.

We begin with the general and then move to the specific. The first theory, then, is buying determinants theory.

# BUYING DETERMINANTS THEORY

Buying determinants theory—a rather general theory of why buyers buy—can help us integrate buying theories. As you see in Exhibit 4–1, the theory describes behavior as due to the combined effects of four factors: environmental factors such as government regulations and technology; market factors, such as size and number of competitors; organizational factors, including company size, corporate culture, and policies; and individual factors, like age, experience, and education of any individual person involved in the decision.

In this and the two preceding chapters, we've already begun an examination of the buying determinants model, because we examine many of the individual and organizational factors that influence decision processes. One trap, though, that students may fall into is thinking that business marketing comes down to only personal selling, or the individual dealing with each individual decision process. The buying determinants model is useful because it offers a framework for combining buyers into groups and recognizing buying patterns, patterns that enable marketing managers to create marketing strategies.

## Environmental Factors

Environmental factors have a great impact on how decisions are made. **Environmental factors** are those characteristics of the world beyond the market level, and include the economy, technology, political factors, and social factors. As an economic example, one trend mentioned in the last chapter is globalization, a trend due to environmental factors such as free-trade policies and technology.

In some industries, technology is having a great impact. For example, computer technology is rapidly changing the publishing industry. In a few years, you may not buy textbooks for some classes but may purchase a CD instead. Look at this from your publisher's perspective: What could this mean in terms of the production equipment required? Similarly, this environmental factor will impact the market for printing presses.

The government's actions are also an important environmental factor. Trade treaties such as NAFTA and GATT may determine who your main competitors and customers

**Exhibit 4–1**
Buying
Determinants
Theory

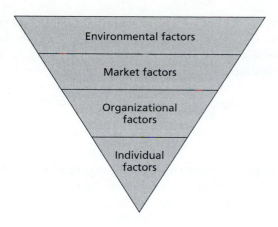

are. Turkey processor Cargill Foods, for example, found new markets in Mexico soon after the passage of NAFTA. Then the peso was devalued (due to economic factors) and Cargill could no longer make a profit in Mexico. The company temporarily slowed its marketing efforts in that country, but under the current economic conditions, the company has again increased exports to Mexico.

Cultural values also influence buyer behavior.[1] In Egypt, Islamic values of honor and family loyalty often guide buyer behavior; similarly, Indian values associated with family also influence how buyers choose vendors.[2] At the same time, ethical values in India are changing, and that influences how individual buyers make choices.

These environmental factors, in combination with market, organizational, and individual factors, greatly influence buying behavior. Marketers examine these factors in order to find patterns, which they can then exploit by adapting their marketing strategy. Based on how these marketing managers view their world and how it works, they develop strategies to take advantage of the opportunities provided in their markets. In the next chapter, you will see how marketers examine market and environmental factors in order to assess marketing opportunities as part of the strategic marketing process. The foundation for this process is a solid understanding of how buyers buy, which is the focus of the rest of this chapter.

# Market Factors

**Market factors** are the characteristics of the market that influence buyer behavior. Market factors include the number and relative size of competitors and the number and relative size of customers in a particular market. The number of competitors can be affected by the availability of substitutes. For example, Loctite Corporation makes glues and industrial adhesives. Screws, rivets, and other fasteners are competitive substitutes for Loctite's products in some markets. With so many substitutes in the market, competition can become quite heated. Buyers in such highly competitive markets may be wooed by so many suppliers that building relationships can be tough. On the other hand, vendors who can show creativity in solving problems over time can develop long-term relationships in such highly competitive markets.

The number of customers is also an important market factor. As discussed in Chapter 1, organizational markets are relatively small in terms of the number of customers.

Relative size of buyers can also make an impact on buying behavior. A buyer for GM can pull a lot more weight when purchasing auto body parts, for example, than can the owner of an independent body shop. Buying strategies, such as negotiating price, that are available to the GM buyer may not be available to the body shop owner.

In organizational markets, buyers may sometimes compete for sources of supply. Controlling supply costs or simply ensuring continuity of supply can be major competitive advantages. The number of buyers and their relative sizes can influence individual buyer behavior depending on the competition for better products and better terms.

# Organizational Factors

**Organizational factors** are characteristics of the organization that influence buying behavior. They include the size of the company, profitability, corporate culture, distribution of power, organizational policy, and other factors. For example, who participates in the selection of accounting services varies depending on large versus small buying companies. Small buying companies are less likely to have an audit committee, among other differences.

Organizational characteristics such as corporate experience can also influence purchase strategies. For example, companies with greater experience in importing and exporting are more likely to return to global markets. They have found mechanisms to overcome international trade barriers, for example. One recent study of buyers located in Cyprus found that experienced firms were only moderately affected by trade barriers and were able to source from virtually anywhere in the world, whereas less-experienced buying organizations sourced from a much smaller set of alternatives.[3]

Reward–measurement systems are another set of organizational factors that influence buyer behavior, as we discussed earlier. We also recognized organizational factors when we discussed the relative risk associated with a purchase and when we examined the role that the type of organization (such as government agency) could have on the purchase process.

# Individual Factors

**Individual factors** are demographic and psychographic factors (psychological factors) that influence an individual's buying behavior. These factors can include age, education, and title or organizational level of the buyer, or they can be psychological factors such as the propensity to take risks. One of the individual factors that has been found to influence buyer behavior is experience, or years in purchasing. Experience reduces risk because uncertainty can be more accurately evaluated.

You may have gotten the feeling in Chapter 3 that, without bribery, the best solution for the organization is always purchased. Organizational buyers, however, do not always seek to maximize the benefits for the organization; sometimes they seek to maximize benefits for themselves. In addition, relationships are between people, and buyers consider personal relationships skills as one important aspect of purchases.[4] After all, purchase decisions are not made by heartless, hyperrational machines. Purchase decisions are made by people, who act human with imperfections.

For the rest of this chapter, we examine the individual buyer, beginning with role theory.

# ROLE THEORY

Role theory has been applied to a number of social situations, such as families, friendships, and organizational buying. In general, **role theory** suggests that people behave within a set of norms or expectations of others due to the role in which they have been placed. For example, your instructor would act one way toward you because of the instructor role (and you would act in the student role). But if you also served on the city council with that instructor, your actions toward each other would be governed by another set of norms and expectations in your roles as council members.

When a person makes a purchase decision alone for an organization, the decision is said to be **autonomous.** When more than one person is involved, the group of participants in the company are called the **buying center** or **decision-making unit (DMU).** Role theory helps us to understand how those participants interact because it defines the roles people take when involved in purchases.

## Roles in the Buying Center

In organizational buying, several roles have been identified.[5] The **initiator** starts the purchase process by recognizing the need; at the other end of the process is the **decision maker,** the person who makes the final decision. (There could be several decision makers who may vote on the final decision; this is covered in greater detail later in this chapter.) The **controller** controls or sets the budget for the purchase.

The **purchasing agent** is the person who actually makes the purchase. If the decision maker tells a subordinate to order another box of copier paper, then the subordinate is the purchasing agent for that purchase. Often the person with the official purchasing agent title does much more than just order the product, but many students confuse the role with the title. The purchasing agent role can be filled by anyone in the organization, whereas the person filling the purchasing agent job may play several roles in a purchase.

**Influencers** are those individuals who seek to affect the decision maker's final decision through recommendations of which vendors to include or which products are best suited to solve the organization's needs. Influencers can also affect the evaluation of the organization's needs. Sometimes **users** are part of the buying center and try to influence the decision; sometimes, other influencers will represent the users' perspective.[6] Even when users don't participate, they influence the decision when decision makers consider the users' needs or ability to implement the decision.

**Gatekeepers** control information into and out of the buying group or between members of the group. Sometimes gatekeepers can actively influence a decision by determining what information is made available to the decision maker.[7] For example, in one study, an engineer was the primary contact with the vendors. The engineer controlled all of the information, deciding what to pass along to others in the decision. The result was that the engineer was able to slant perceptions of the vendors by choosing which information was passed along, and the final decision reflected his own personal preferences.[8] Secretaries can also be gatekeepers, as when they screen telephone calls for their boss. From the Field 4–1 illustrates Jeff Pedowitz's challenges when marketing Eloqua's services.

## Dimensions of Buying Centers

One misconception that students sometimes have is that a buying center means that a committee is formed, with individuals designated as a gatekeeper, influencer, or some other role. Cross-functional sourcing teams, discussed in Chapter 3, are formal examples of buying centers and are growing in use, but more often, the buying center is a changing, complex, and informal group.[9] Initiators, for example, may not be involved again once they've set the purchase in motion. Or initiators may also act as influencers and as gatekeepers. Influencers may seek to influence only which needs will be considered, only

---

| 4–1 |
| --- |

## FROM THE FIELD 4–1

### Helping Customers Buy

When I graduated from Penn State in marketing, I went straight into the restaurant business with my dad, as I had been in that business since I was 12 and it was what I knew. But I also had a passion for computers, so after a few years, I made the jump into technology.

What I learned running a chain of Subway franchises was how to market without a big budget. It takes a lot of creativity, creativity I still put into play. Now, I am vice president of professional services for Eloqua, a company that specializes in helping companies make their marketing more productive for their salespeople.

Most companies that buy our product and services do not start out the year planning to make this purchase. They have no budget for it. Because we are the market leader and do what few others can, our competition isn't another vendor but rather whether the company is going to pave the parking lot, expand the plant, build a new warehouse, or some other big project.

The average chief marketing officer (CMO) now has 23 months to make an impact or the company will find another CMO. The CMO understands very quickly how we can make their marketing more productive. But, since there is no budget and since it is a technology solution, we also have to help that CMO sell the head of IT, the chief financial officer, and the CEO. So we give that CMO the ammunition needed to convince those others that the return on an investment with Eloqua is better than expanding the plant. With our solution costing anywhere from $60,000 to $1 million per year, we have to demonstrate a real return on investment.

Getting the customer is only half the battle—since they can cancel at any time, we have to continue to sell, building relationships throughout the organization, and getting entrenched in all of their marketing activities so they can't live without us. If they don't use us, they don't renew. Our training and consulting services become just as important at retaining customers, helping them maximize their Eloqua investment, as these services are in selling customers. That's one area where my creativity comes in—the more productive I can help CMOs become, the more likely they are to stay with us.

Jeff Pedowitz, Vice President of Professional Services, Eloqua.

---

which vendors are considered, or only which product is selected, or all three elements of the decision.

## Time Dimensions

One characteristic of buying centers, then, is that members come and go. This characteristic is called **time fragmentation.** The more people are involved for only short periods of time in the process, the more fragmented the buying center is over time. If the same people are involved through the entire process, the buying center is not fragmented. Exhibit 4–2 illustrates how the decision to select a metal lathe might be time fragmented. As you can see, Bill and Dawanda participated in only three steps, Joe in five, Jackie in three, and Frank in three. Nobody participated in every step in this highly time-fragmented purchase.

Note, though, time fragmentation is not the same as the length of time for the decision to be made. The metal lathe purchase may have been accomplished in just a few days. Some decisions can take a long time without involving a high degree of time fragmentation if the same people stay involved.

**Exhibit 4–2**
An Example
of Time
Fragmentation
in Buying
Centers

Stage 1: *Need recognition*

Bill and Dawanda recognize a need for a new lathe.

Stage 2: *Definition of product type needed*

Joe, their supervisor, tells Purchasing to get a new metal lathe with a 5,000-RPM motor and computerized input.

Stage 3: *Development of detailed specifications*

Joe, Bill, and Dawanda meet with Jackie in Purchasing to develop detailed specifications.

Stage 4: *Search for suppliers*

Jackie and Frank in Finance visit a trade show and identify four potential suppliers.

Stage 5: *Acquisition and analysis of proposals*

Frank receives all proposals and evaluates financial aspects. He sends a copy to Joe for technical evaluation.

Stage 6: *Evaluation and selection of supplier*

Joe and Frank meet to select the supplier.

Stage 7: *Selection of an order procedure*

Joe sends a purchase order to Jackie. Jackie issues the PO to the vendor.

Stage 8: *Implementation and evaluation of performance*

Dawanda and Bill install the new lathe and try it out; they report to Joe that it works well.

Time fragmentation is important to understand for marketers. If a decision involves a number of people who move in and out over time, their influence is limited to only a few stages. The marketer must balance that influence with the cost of reaching those people. For example, if the marketing manager is involved only in determining what is needed, is it worth it to Webex to spend the money advertising in marketing magazines? Perhaps, particularly if Webex advertises why that marketing manager should request certain features.

Length of time is also an important consideration for the marketer. Shortening the decision cycle is always a goal for marketers because a shorter decision cycle means that salespeople can move on to other prospects and increase their overall sales performance. Length of time to make a decision can seriously impact marketing efforts.

Decision-making time is lengthened when buying centers are large and/or composed of many personnel who are inexperienced in making purchase decisions. Out-suppliers, those who are not established with the buyers, can actually benefit when decisions take longer and more information sources are utilized because they have the opportunity to plead their case. Shorter decision cycles tend to favor in-suppliers.

## *Vertical and Horizontal Dimensions*

Two other dimensions of buying centers are **vertical dimensions,** or how many layers of management are involved, and **horizontal dimensions,** or how many departments are involved. Both of these dimensions relate to the number of people involved and can be a function of how centralized the company is.[10] Decisions concerning component parts, for example, tend to be wide, involving members of the purchasing department, design engineers, manufacturing personnel, and upper management, as illustrated in Exhibit 4–3. Along the vertical dimension, that same decision may be considered tall if the vice president, many middle managers, and workers from the manufacturing line participate.

**Exhibit 4–3**
Vertical and
Horizontal
Dimensions of a
Buying Center
*SOURCE: John F. Tanner Jr., "Buying Center Formation Process," unpublished dissertation, University of Georgia (1988).*

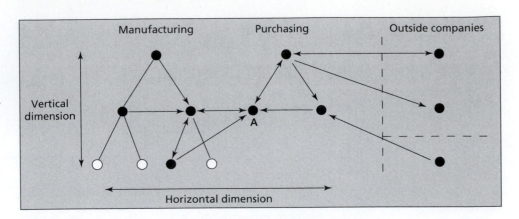

Wide buying centers present difficult challenges for marketers. Many different people must be reached in order to accomplish a sale. Advertising has to be placed in a wider variety of trade publications than when buying centers are narrow. For example, if the usual buying center for testing equipment included members from engineering, quality control and manufacturing, Tektronix would have to advertise in three different magazines, one for each area.

The vertical dimension alone is not as challenging. If all buying center participants are within the same department or functional area of the buying firm, they are likely to participate in the same media. These buyers would go to the same trade shows, read the same magazines, and so forth. The real challenge would be for the salesperson to uncover the true decision makers, for organizational position may not reflect who really will make this particular decision. For example, the salesperson would need to discover if the telecom manager makes the decision or simply rubber stamps the recommendation of a subordinate who investigated the various vendors' offerings.

A key challenge in highly fragmented buying centers is that needs and purchasing motivations vary greatly. For example, in a highly vertical buying center that may involve the chief executive officer all the way down to individuals in the manufacturing line, different benefits have different value. A willingness to handle sudden changes in delivery amounts, for example, may have great value to the factory manager but be of little importance to the CEO. That same CEO, however, may find the terms of payment to be much more important.

One way for marketers to understand the relationship between buying center position and benefits offered is to map the two. A benefit stack and a decision-maker stack can help the marketer understand the relationship between the vertical dimension of the buying center and who needs what, as illustrated in Exhibit 4–4.[11] However, a horizontal "stack" may also be needed to understand the needs of different buyers from different areas in the organization.

## Formalization Dimension

A related dimension is the degree of **formalization,** or the degree to which purchasing tasks and roles are defined by written documents describing procedures and policies. Formalization affects the latitude that a buying center member has in choosing how to go about making the purchase. Sometimes, formalization can lead to unproductive

**Exhibit 4–4**

Matching Benefits to Members of the Buying Center. One method of considering the vertical dimension of a buying center is to match the benefits offered to the various members of the buying center. Note that the importance of the individual in the decision is considered to be a function of that person's position in the organization. Good marketers verify that importance; sometimes a CEO may be involved, for example, but may not be the most important person in the decision.

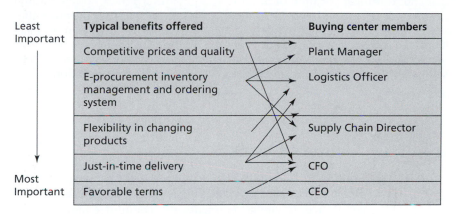

*Source: Adapted from Das Narayandas, "Building Loyalty in Business Markets,"* Harvard Business Review *83(9), September 2005, p. 134.*

behaviors, such as getting three bids because policy requires it, even though a vendor has already been selected. A buying center operating in a system without formal controls and policies, however, may change the process of making the decision many times, delaying the purchase and frustrating vendors. Formalized policies are most likely to influence the initiation and selection stages of the buying process, but not other stages such as searching for alternatives or evaluating alternative vendors.[12]

# Marketing to Buying Centers

Traditionally, it was thought that the best marketing strategy would be to determine who typically participated in the decision and then work to satisfy the needs of the participants.[13] In the purchase of component parts, for example, research has found that engineering, purchasing, and upper management each play roles. Engineers are concerned about products meeting performance specifications, whereas upper management worries about costs. A vendor would create marketing communication campaigns aimed at the engineers separate from those campaigns aimed at upper management. Features might be designed to the engineers' specifications, but within the budget set by upper management.

Recently, however, marketers have begun to recognize that it is important to influence who might participate in the buying center and to what extent.[14] For example, Premier Industrial sells MRO items that perform at a significantly higher level than most MRO products. They also charge a premium price. Unless the decision maker actually uses those items, the value may not be understood. Premier salespeople may try to encourage maintenance technicians to become **champions,** or **advocates;** that is, the Premier salespeople may try to get users to influence the decision in their favor.

# When Buying Centers Occur

In some organizations, buying centers occur because of organizational policy. For example, in government agencies, purchases over a set dollar amount are often reviewed by a committee. In city governments, this committee may be the city council or a finance committee, depending on the size of the purchase. Hospitals and other institutions also have committees that review purchases of certain types.

In situations not governed by policy, buying centers are more likely to occur when a lot of areas are affected, as illustrated in From the Field 4–2, or when risk associated with the decision is great. **Risk** is usually thought of in terms of the probability of an outcome and the importance or cost associated with the outcome.[15] For example, the risk of lung cancer for a nonsmoker is low, not because a nonsmoker with lung cancer is any less likely to die than a smoker with lung cancer but because the probability of getting lung cancer is less for the nonsmoker. A low-risk decision, therefore, is either one with a high probability of a positive outcome or one in which the outcome itself is relatively unimportant.

## Sources of Perceived Risk

Risk can come from any number of sources. There is **financial risk,** also called economic risk, associated with the cost of the new product and with the potential for lost revenue if the product breaks down or doesn't perform as advertised. **Performance risk** is the risk that the product will not perform as intended. Performance risk and financial risk can occur at the same time if the performance of the product is crucial to the financial performance of the firm. For example, if a piece of manufacturing equipment breaks down and the production line must stop, then sales may be lost. Both financial and performance risk would be realized in that situation. If a piece of equipment breaks down while under warranty and the breakdown doesn't slow down production, only performance risk would be realized, because there would be no financial loss. Performance and financial risks are highly correlated, for it is rare that a loss of performance would not have some financial impact.

Another form of risk is **social risk,** also called ego risk, or risk that the purchase will not meet the approval of an important reference group. The important reference group

## 4–2

# FROM THE FIELD 4–2
## Virtual Buying Centers

Deere and Company, the venerable farm equipment maker, has three plants that make machines to harvest hay: one in Iowa, one in France, and one in Germany. Hay harvesters may seem like an old-fashioned business to be in, but globally, the machines represent $2.5 billion annually. Marvin Wagner, an engineering manager for Deere, has spent the last four years trying to standardize Deere's hay products made at the various locations.

To accomplish this feat, he relies on suppliers that can supply all three facilities. Wagner reports that "I've worked with many sales representatives calling on the Ottumwa (Iowa) factory via teleconference with my colleagues in Arc-les-Gray (France)." He adds that it isn't unusual for the sales rep to also use Webex to show how a product works. "After the sales presentation, then our engineers at the three plants, the procurement specialists at our headquarters in Davenport, Iowa, and our supply chain professionals all have to meet to decide which one we'll standardize on." Sometimes, the decision can't be made until samples are shipped to each of the three plants for the engineers and manufacturing managers to try out.

"When I graduated from Texas A&M with a degree in engineering, I knew I'd play a role in purchasing products but I had no idea how large this role would become," says Wagner. "Or how global." The buying center rarely meets face-to-face, yet they are responsible for making decisions resulting in millions of dollars of profit for the company.

could be co-workers or it could be the buyer's immediate supervisor. Buyers concerned with social risk will carefully consider the desires of those they are trying to impress.

Organizational buyers reduce their perceptions of risk in three ways.[16] To reduce risk, buyers gather more information, remain loyal to present suppliers, and/or spread the risk, either to other members of the firm or among suppliers.

## *Using Information to Reduce Risk*

When collecting information, buyers seek help from a number of sources, as illustrated in Exhibit 4–5. Commercial sources are those sources controlled by the marketer, and include advertisements, brochures and other sales literature, personal selling efforts both at the customer's location and at trade shows, and product manuals. Noncommercial sources are sources outside the control of the marketer, and include word-of-mouth from colleagues within the organization, professional associates, and consultants as well as articles in trade publications.

Other research indicates that impersonal sources are more widely used early in the process, with personal sources growing in importance over the course of the decision. That research also indicates that noncommercial sources are relied on more heavily than are commercial sources and that buyers constantly review both types of sources, even when no purchase is imminent.[17]

Research indicates that salespeople can reduce risk through such efforts as demonstrations, samples, or free trials, and salespeople are often the most important source of information for buyers.[18] These efforts increase buyers' experience with the product, giving them the ability to more accurately evaluate product performance, which reduces their

**Exhibit 4–5**
Sources of
Information
*SOURCE: Adapted from Barton A. Weitz, Stephen B. Castleberry, and John F. Tanner, Jr., Selling: Building Partnerships, Sixth edition, Burr Ridge, IL: Irwin/McGraw-Hill, 2007.*

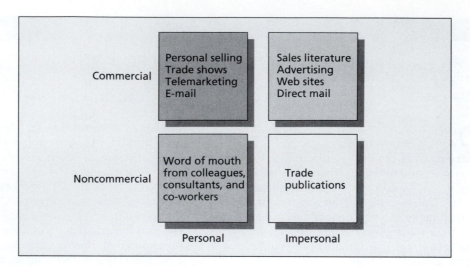

perceptions of risk. Demonstrations, samples, and trials are particularly useful when the issue is performance threshold because these marketing efforts prove performance.

Companies may also use advertising to educate buyers, providing information through details in advertising copy in order to reduce perceptions of risk. For example, Webex presented detailed advertising to help buyers make decisions concerning the use of an online business service. Case studies can also be used to prove performance and provide buyers with important information concerning product or service performance that can enhance their ability to make the decision.

Guarantees, are ways that marketers can reduce risk. Guarantees, though, are only as good as the reputation of the company that offers them. An unknown's guarantee may not mean much to a business buyer.

## Using Loyalty to Reduce Risk

Risk can both help and hinder the development of relationships. One purchasing strategy to reduce risk is to remain loyal to a known supplier—for example, to always buy from Webex. In essence, this strategy results in converting the decision into a straight rebuy, because other vendors are not considered. By converting decisions into straight rebuys, a poor decision is unlikely as long as the vendor continues to satisfy. With many firms downsizing, purchasing agents and other managers do not have the time they once had to evaluate all purchase decisions carefully. Therefore, they will only evaluate those decisions where the close examination of alternatives will result in benefits that outweigh the costs of looking. When a company routinizes a decision (makes it a straight rebuy), the opportunity is there for a vendor to build a relationship. Recognize, however, that the decision was made routine because the product being purchased is relatively unimportant, a factor not likely to contribute positively to the development of a partnership. Habit or lazy purchasing behavior is not the same as a partnership.

### The Importance of Trust
Loyalty is one way that buyers reduce risk, because loyalty implies trust. **Trust** is defined as the belief in the integrity, honesty, and reliability of another person, or in this case, of a supplier. Marketing organizations try to create trust through such things as warranties

and guarantees, but even that may not be enough. When buyers are seeking new suppliers, particularly through the Web, trust is an important issue.[19] Buyers examine suppliers' behaviors, such as how quickly phone calls or e-mails are returned and whether the little promises are kept, before deciding to trust the suppliers.

Dell, for example, has found that fewer than 30 percent of all customers who visit the Web site and then make a purchase actually order from the Web site. They visit the site, learn what they want to learn, then pick up the phone to ask questions of a live salesperson. A recent survey reports that organizational buyers find e-auctions don't work well except for commodity items. They fear that they can't trust suppliers they find over the Internet.[20] Buyers seek to find salespeople and companies they can trust as a way to reduce risk.

### Spreading the Risk

In contrast to the strategy of remaining loyal, buyers may consider many vendors when performance or economic risk is great and the benefits of looking around outweigh shopping costs. For example, the purchase of a telephone switching system can be a million-dollar decision. In a decision this big, most companies will shop around. Shopping around, though, is not just a risk reduction strategy—it can be used for other reasons. Shopping around is one way to spread risk when risk is large.

Similarly, buyers may elect to spread purchases among several vendors so that if one vendor does not live up to promises, others can take up the slack. Spreading purchases among several vendors reduces performance risk. For example, a company that purchases gas tanks from Plastech may also purchase identical tanks from two other vendors. If Plastech was unable to deliver one order, the buyer would simply pass it along to the next vendor. In most cases, neither this strategy nor the shopping around strategy of risk reduction promotes partnerships; however, recognize that a partnership is unlikely anyway if the buyer cannot depend on a vendor.

Finally, one way to reduce risk, especially social risk, is to have others involved in the buying process. For a self-oriented buyer, one defensive strategy is to increase the size of the buying center. Having others involved can also add to the total expertise of the buying center, reducing the risk of a poor purchase decision. Many government agencies, particularly cities where a city council must make the purchase decision, hire consultants in order to take advantage of their expertise and minimize the risk of making a poor choice. Consultants are often used in high technology decisions and other infrequently made decisions when the organization perceives a need for expertise it does not have.

Risk is an important individual variable that can influence the size of a buying center. Other factors can influence the behavior of individuals, as we will see.

# INDIVIDUAL BUYER THEORY

Role theory helps us understand the tasks set out for individuals in the buying center, but doesn't address individual differences in buying. For example, not all influencers act the same, nor do all users. For this reason, individual buying theories such as behavior choice theory were developed.

**Behavior choice theory** states that buyers go through a choice process to arrive at decisions of *how* they will buy, as opposed to the choice process of *what* will be bought modeled as part of the buy-brid. Behavior choice theory is illustrated in Exhibit 4–6. The first decision is to decide what type of situation they are in. For example, a buyer may believe that the purchase is an opportunity to show decision-making skills; as a management development opportunity, the purchase is more important than as an

**Exhibit 4–6**
Behavior Choice
Model

*SOURCE: Adapted
from John F. Tanner
Jr., "A Model of
Organizational Buyer
Behavior Choice,"*
Proceedings,
*Southern Marketing
Association (1987),
pp. 355–58.*

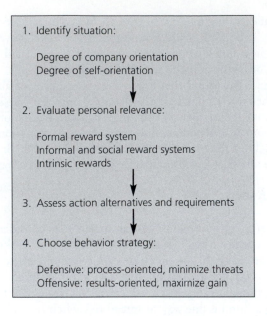

1. Identify situation:

   Degree of company orientation
   Degree of self-orientation

2. Evaluate personal relevance:

   Formal reward system
   Informal and social reward systems
   Intrinsic rewards

3. Assess action alternatives and requirements

4. Choose behavior strategy:

   Defensive: process-oriented, minimize threats
   Offensive: results-oriented, maximize gain

opportunity to obtain a particular product. The management development opportunity benefits the individual participating in the decision, whereas the product may benefit the company. This decision of the relative value of benefits and the type of situation leads to an orientation that influences the buyer's behavior throughout the rest of the purchase process.

The degree to which the individual works to achieve personal benefit is called **self-orientation** while the degree to which the individual works to achieve benefit for the company is **company orientation**. Self-orientation and company orientation operate independently so one purchase situation could result in both high self-orientation and high company orientation. For example, a buyer may work hard to review several vendors because the purchase decision is an opportunity to exhibit promotable managerial skills, and the buyer's self-orientation would be classified as high. At the same time, the service being purchased may be crucial to the company's performance, which may also motivate the buyer to review several alternatives. This latter motivation is an example of a high company orientation. In this example, the buyer is both highly self- and company oriented.

The second stage of the choice process is to evaluate personal relevance. In this stage, the buyer examines the reward structures, extrinsic and intrinsic, associated with the situation as defined in stage one. **Extrinsic rewards** are those given by the organization (salary, promotion, etc.) while **intrinsic rewards** are those that the buyers give themselves (feelings of satisfaction, for example). Thus, a buyer who defines the situation as an opportunity to purchase a product is going to engage reward structures associated with the product, such as satisfaction with the product. A buyer who sees the situation as an opportunity to show off decision-making skills, however, will engage reward structures that might include promotions, management recognition, and the like. Both reward structures are present but their importance, or **valence,** will vary from individual to individual depending on the strength of company and self-orientation, as well as other factors. For example, a buyer with a child about to enter college may find extrinsic rewards to be more important, as tuition payments are about to start.

In the third stage, the buyer assesses action alternatives and requirements. In this stage, the buyers look at the amount of control over the task: Do they have any choices in what they can and can't do? Company policies and procedures may limit their choice of buying activities; for example, company policy may require that they solicit at least three bids.

Further, in this stage, the individual considers such aspects as **instrumentality,** or the likelihood that if they successfully engage in certain actions, those actions will yield the rewards they want. For example, a purchase may be an opportunity to show off promotable skills and the promotion may be a worthwhile outcome but if reviewing three competitive vendors isn't likely to yield a favorable review, then the individual will seek other activities.

Each individual also evaluates **self-efficacy,** or the ability to carry out those tasks. A buyer who wants a promotion will avoid those activities which are too difficult, and would therefore result in poor evaluations. So a buyer who failed accounting would not try to calculate return on investment, for example!

The final stage of the model is the selection of a strategy. There are two types of strategies: **offensive strategies,** or strategies designed to maximize gain; and **defensive strategies,** or strategies designed to minimize loss.[21] Buying a market share leader, for example, could be a defensive choice because it is safe—no one was ever fired for choosing AT&T, for example. Other defensive strategies would include asking the boss to make the decision, getting as many people involved as possible in order to share the blame if things go wrong, and attention to the process rather than to the outcome. The latter strategy is useful because if the product doesn't work out, the buyer can say "Well, it is the vendor's fault; we did everything right in our selection process. We viewed 55 different models, evaluated 40 bids, and so forth. . . ."

Choosing an off-brand for service could be an offensive strategy, designed to maximize gain through saving the company the most money or making a name for oneself as an innovator. The selection of a strategy, either offensive or defensive, can relate to a single orientation or to both. For example, a buyer may want to get the company the best deal possible (high company orientation, offensive strategy) but at the same time minimize personal risk (high self-orientation, defensive strategy).

The process of purchasing, then, can be decided by the strategy of the buyer, not experience with the product, as suggested by the buy-grid. Experience with the product should influence the choice of a strategy; for example, an inexperienced buyer may be more likely to select a defensive strategy due to low self-efficacy. Other factors, such as reward/measurement systems, risk associated with the purchase, visibility of purchase participation, and management level of the individual, will also influence the selection of strategy.

Based on the strategy and action alternatives, the buyer selects a series of tasks. For example, when we mentioned viewing 55 models and evaluating 40 bids, we were discussing examples of tasks that may be selected to fit a defensive strategy. The actual purchase depends on the outcomes of those tasks.

# Comparing Behavior Choice and Multiattribute

How does the multiattribute model (from Chapter 3) compare with buyer behavior theory? First, buyer behavior theory recognizes intrinsic rewards such as feeling good about making the right decision or pride in making a contribution to the success of the organization, and that sometimes buyers may operate to attain intrinsic rewards exclusively. For example, a marketing manager who likes to get good deals would be more

**4–2**

## BUSINESS 2 BUSINESS

### Company or Self?

Organizations expect buyers to make decisions based on what benefits the organization the best, but as you've learned, an organizational buyer will also work to protect self-interests. How can an organization protect its interests when employees make decisions? How would you feel knowing that the building you're sitting in was designed by the lowest bidder, or built by a company that got the deal simply because it was a well-known company?

likely to do business with Eloqua. The multiattribute model does not allow for quantifying intrinsic rewards (which can't really be quantified anyway).

Second, behavior choice theory recognizes that extrinsic rewards are a function of the reward/measurement systems of the organization, and not a function of the product. In organizational buying situations, few buyers actually benefit directly from a purchase. At L.L. Bean, the catalog fashion retailer, the marketing manager who buys CRM software actually uses it. That marketing manager's performance is dependent upon how well that software is used to generate new business. At Thomasville (a furniture manufacturer), however, the buyer doesn't personally do anything with the wood that she buys to be turned into furniture. Her rewards are based on the evaluation of her performance as a buyer, not as a user of wood.

Recognize, too, that buyers may still use a multiattribute model when making a decision, even though they may be concerned with intrinsic rewards and the reward/-measurement system of the organization. Intrinsic rewards may be influenced by attributes of the vendor's offering; for example, that telecommunications buyer who likes to get a good deal will weigh price more heavily than other buyers. What buyer choice theory does mean is that the buy-grid (new buy or modified rebuy or straight rebuy) may not be as important as the reward structure, because effort is a function of probability and valence, not experience with the product.

Going back to our Eloqua and CRM software example, think about why Eloqua might advertise their software to marketing managers using fear appeals. By creating a fear of what will happen to those individuals if their CRM system goes down and customers can't call in or e-mail their orders or service requests, Eloqua could attempt to promote a defensive strategy. On the other hand, ads could encourage an offensive strategy by highlighting the outstanding performance and promotions that buyers receive.

## Integrating Behavior Choice and Buying Determinants

Recognize that the buying determinants and behavior choice theories interact at the organizational and individual levels, as illustrated in Exhibit 4–7. At the organizational level, the company's reward and promotion systems come into play, as do policies about who should participate in purchases that support vertical and horizontal dimensions of the buying center. Creation of cross-functional teams and a corporate culture of cooperation or competition will also influence buying.

**Exhibit 4–7**
Expanded Buying
Determinants
Theory

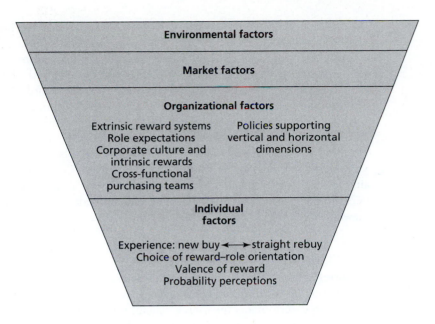

At the individual level, factors such as the buyer's experience and choice of reward and role orientation influence buyer behavior. Thus, the models integrate to provide a full picture of the factors that influence purchase choices.

# Marketing and Buyer Behavior Choice

Jeff Pedowitz (profiled in From the Field 4–1), faces difficult challenges when marketing Eloqua software. Not only do marketing managers who buy Eloqua have to learn how to use Eloqua software; they also have to learn more about the processes of marketing through technology as this is still cutting-edge territory. Self-efficacy perceptions can be very weak in this scenario, but extrinsic rewards will depend on how that marketing manager can grow the business. Growing the business should be the primary outcome of using Eloqua, which means the manager won't receive those extrinsic rewards when the purchase is made. Rather, those rewards are delayed until the buyer becomes proficient at using the software.

Marketers like Pedowitz can increase perceptions of self-efficacy by increasing the buyer's experience or knowledge. Pedowitz does this by holding a three-day conference for Eloqua customers. Here, they learn about how to use Eloqua more effectively; even prospective customers attend because the conference is more about the processes of technology-based marketing rather than which keys to push to make Eloqua work.

Demonstrations and free trials are ways that marketers increase self-efficacy. Also, advertising and other marketing communications that increase knowledge about products can increase a buyer's perception of self-efficacy. Self-efficacy is critical to securing the support of advocates. Buyers choose to do certain tasks (such as see demonstrations) based on the instrumentality associated with those tasks. How much and how well they do the tasks is a function of their motivation, which takes into account the valence for rewards associated with the purchase.

As marketers, if we understand the valence attached to the various rewards and how performance is measured, then we should be able to predict the amount of effort expended by the buyer on tasks such as information search, number of bids requested, and other purchase activities. We can also begin to understand what products might be purchased in which situations.

For example, in the CRM software industry, Eloqua is a minor player, having entered the market later than the dominant players like Oracle (with the Seibel product) and SAP. Buying Oracle is a safe decision; with their track record of service, market share, and product quality, anyone who recommends Oracle is not going out on a limb. If the buyers in a particular market have a high valence for security, Oracle might be selected. But if buyers in a market are rewarded for cutting costs or staying within certain budgets, Eloqua, Applicor, and other vendors may have a better chance. Similarly, SAP is viewed as a safe decision in Europe because SAP is a German company and dominates that market, while Oracle is perceived as more risky. You can see that this application is very similar to the multiattribute model in that valences and attribute ratings can be viewed in a similar fashion.

## Summary

Theories are a picture of how the world works. This chapter presented several theories of how buying works in organizations.

Buying determinants theory is a general theory of why buyers buy and incorporates the effects of environmental, market, and organizational factors on the individual. Buying determinants theory enables us to examine markets for patterns in buying behavior, which will be helpful to remember when we discuss market segmentation and strategy in the next chapter.

Role theory describes the roles that people can take on when more than one person is involved in the purchase. The group of people who participate is called the buying center, and they can be initiators of the purchase, influencers, the decision maker, the purchasing agent, a gatekeeper, controller, or any combination of these. Buying centers can be examined in terms of time fragmentation, of horizontal and vertical dimensions, and of governance, or how the centers make decisions.

Buying centers are often formed to minimize risk—either financial, performance, or social risk. Marketers can reduce perceptions of risk through guarantees, warranties, free trials, free samples, or demonstrations of the product. Marketers also attempt to reduce risk by educating buyers through advertising and other forms of promotion.

The final theory presented was buyer behavior choice theory. This theory states that buyers go through a series of steps in deciding what tasks they will perform. The steps are, first, determining the degree to which they should adopt a company orientation or a self-orientation and, second, determining whether to adopt a defensive or offensive strategy. Company orientation is the degree to which they attempt to satisfy company goals, whereas self-orientation reflects the degree to which they attempt to satisfy their own goals. An offensive strategy is one designed to maximize gain. A defensive strategy minimizes loss. Then they decide on which tasks to perform, which leads to the purchase of a product.

## Key Terms

| | | |
|---|---|---|
| advocate | company orientation | defensive strategy |
| autonomous | controller | environmental factors |
| behavior choice theory | decision maker | extrinsic rewards |
| buying center | decision-making unit | financial risk |
| champion | (DMU) | formalization |

| | | |
|---|---|---|
| **gatekeeper** | **offensive strategy** | **social risk** |
| **horizontal dimension** | **organizational factors** | **time fragmentation** |
| **individual factors** | **performance risk** | **trust** |
| **influencer** | **purchasing agent** | **user** |
| **initiator** | **risk** | **valence** |
| **instrumentality** | **role theory** | **vertical dimension** |
| **intrinsic rewards** | **self-efficacy** | |
| **market factors** | **self-orientation** | |

## Discussion Questions

1. Dean Rieck, president of Direct Creative, a firm that provides direct response advertising to B2B companies, says that business buyers act differently than consumers because they aren't spending their own money. While we're still dealing with people, what are the differences between individual consumers and business buyers, based on what you've read in Chapters 3 and 4?

2. A wood products manufacturing plant must buy cyclone separators, equipment that collects sawdust out of the air in the plant in order to provide a healthier work environment. What differences in criteria for evaluating proposals might be used by (a) the purchasing department, (b) the company treasurer, (c) the CEO, (d) the plant manager, and (e) the head of the legal department? Illustrate your answer by using the multiattribute matrix from Chapter 3.

3. Answer question 2 again, but this time, consider the roles that the different people would play in the decision process. Using the buy-phase model, when would each person in question 2 be involved? Create a chart like Exhibit 4–2 showing how each person participates in the purchase of logistics automation technology in the chapter.

4. Do you think that people tend to buy the same way, either offensively or defensively, over time? Or do people vary from situation to situation? If people vary, what causes that variance? If people don't vary, why?

5. How does a buying center differ from a cross-functional purchasing team (from Chapter 3)?

6. Based on your own awareness of current events, identify three environmental factors that are currently most likely to influence organizational buying. Relate these to the purchasing trends in Chapter 3.

7. In Chapter 2, you learned about how organizations create relationships; in Chapter 3, you learned about the professional purchasing agent and the importance of supply chain management. Integrate what you learned in the previous two chapters with the concepts in this chapter to create one chart that shows how the concepts relate.

## Cases

### Case 4.1   SRI International

Akshay Menon, head of SRI's Dallas operations, was reviewing proposals from three companies for a new scanner. The company had recently been awarded a contract to scan and electronically store the paper files of a large state government agency, and Menon knew he would have to add three to five new scanners. The contract called for the agency to begin shipping files in a week; Menon had to make a decision today.

Margie Cabellero, the production manager, had obtained three proposals at Menon's request, one for five moderate-speed scanners, one for three high-speed scanners, and one for three moderate-speed scanners and one high-speed scanner. She was pushing for five scanners, because she felt that more scanners meant greater protection in case one broke down. She also believed she had greater flexibility in assigning work if there were more scanners. Currently, her group operated 12 paper scanners, two microfiche scanners, and a microfilm scanner 24 hours per day.

George Whitaker, the chief financial officer, wanted Menon to buy three high-speed scanners. Whitaker thought that the higher cost would be offset by hiring fewer operators, and besides, the company was more likely to have trouble hiring and retaining operators than keeping the machines working. Further, when Whitaker factored in service costs, the higher-speed scanners were cheaper to operate. He recommended to Akshay that he buy the high-speed scanners and run only one shift on the new equipment for now.

Gloria Sigel, human resources manager, agreed that the local employment market made hiring more difficult. She really didn't care what was bought; she just knew that it was tough to hire new employees. She also told Menon the current operators thought that the high-speed scanners were too unreliable and that paper jams had to be cleared too often. Since their pay was tied to productivity, they didn't like working the high-speed scanners.

Menon wondered what he should do.

1. List the roles that each person plays in the buying center. Can you identify where Menon is in making a decision, and what he should do next? Other than Menon, who is most important and why?

2. Identify sources of risk for each member of the buying center. What are they risking? How important does that risk seem to be? How would you reduce that risk if you were a scanner salesperson?

3. Assume you market scanners, and this situation is pretty typical of what you find. How would this information influence your marketing activities? Be as specific as possible.

### Case 4.2    "I'm a Believer!"

Mark Shepherd, salesperson for Kone Elevator, reflected on his day. His company built a reputation as a low-cost provider of industrial elevators, but recently developed a new technology that deserved a premium price. The new system included many new features, of which a few were critically important. For example, the new system does not require a special housing on top of a building in which to place the motor that raises and lowers the elevator. An alternative is to tuck the motor to the side; either alternative adds significant costs to the design, costs equal to or greater than the elevator motor itself. A building with a large bank of elevators can have an entire floor dedicated just to the motors. Further, the new technology requires significantly less maintenance than most current systems, thereby reducing operating costs.

When selling the new system, Mark found it easy to convince architects. They could easily see the cost savings of not having to build an extra room on the roof for the elevator motor. Still, architects had to convince building owners and the general contractors who build the buildings that it was worth doing. Given that general contractors often got paid on a cost-plus basis, they were not always excited about cutting costs.

While leaving the 60-story office building of a major architect in downtown Toronto, Mark stopped to watch the technicians working on maintaining the elevator. Suddenly, one of the technicians let loose a loud oath. "What happened?" Mark asked. The technician's partner just laughed, and then began a long litany of complaints against the current elevator—an older Kone. "What if you had an elevator that ran like this?" he asked, showing the technician a cutaway drawing illustrating the new elevator mechanism.

The technician began to reach for the illustration, then realized he had grease all over his hands. Mark handed the brochure to him anyway. Within minutes, both technicians quickly saw the value of the new system. "This is what we need!" one of the technicians exclaimed. "You have a real winner there, pal!"

1. One of the challenges Mark faces is that there are three companies in the decision: the building owner, the general contractor, and the architect. What role does each play? What are the key benefits to each?

2. Only the technicians really understand the maintenance benefits of the new elevator. What can Mark, or his company, do to encourage these technicians to speak up and pass the word to the decision makers?

## Additional Readings

Borghini, Stefania, Francesco Golfetto, and Diego Rinallo. "Ongoing Search among Industrial Buyers." *Journal of Business Research* 59, nos. 10/11 (2006), pp. 1151–69.

Colgate, Mark, Vicky Thuy-Uyen Tong, Christina Kwai-Choi Lee, and John U. Farley. "Back from the Brink: Why Customers Stay." *Journal of Service Research* 9, no. 3 (2007), pp. 211–29.

Cooper, Marjorie, John F. Tanner, Jr., and Kirk Wakefield. "Industrial Buyers' Risk Aversion and Channel Selection." *Journal of Business Research* 59, no. 6 (2006), pp. 653–61.

Hackney, Ray, Steve Jones, Andrea Lösch. "Towards an E-Government Efficiency Agenda: The Impact of Information and Communication Behaviour on E-Reverse Auctions in Public Sector Procurement." *European Journal of Information Systems* 16 (2007), pp. 178–92.

Garrido-Samaniego, M. Jose, and Jesus Gutierrez-Cillan. "Determinants of Influence and Participation in the Buying Center: An Analysis of Spanish Industrial Companies." *Journal of Business & Industrial Marketing* 19, nos. 4/5 (2004), pp. 320–32.

Jacob, Frank, and Michael Ehret. "Self-Protection vs. Opportunity Seeking in Business Buying Behavior: An Experimental Study." *Journal of Business & Industrial Marketing* 21, no. 2 (2006), pp. 106–23.

Moschuris, Socrates J. "Triggering Make-Or-Buy Decisions: An Emprical Analysis." *Journal of Supply Chain Management* 43 (2007), pp. 40–9.

Park, Jeong Eun, and Michele D. Bunn. "Organizational Memory: A New Perspective on the Organizational Buying Process." *Journal of Business & Industrial Marketing* 18 (2003), pp. 237–57.

Supphellen, Magne, and Kjell Gronhaug. "The Role of Formal Authority in Buyer Evaluation of Business Research Suppliers: A Scandinavian Case." *Journal of Business-to-Business Marketing* 10, no. 2 (2003), pp. 53–77.

N ow you know that business markets are different from consumer markets in many regards: size and volatility, channels and sales complexity, and purchasing standards and processes. You also have a foundational understanding of how value creating activities are coordinated not just by markets but also by different types of relationships. The chapters in Part 2 take us to the business marketer's engine room. ●

Chapter 5 looks at opportunity and access to the rewards of more and better customers. The best business marketers recognize their advantageous position to serve and their potential rewards from delivering more value to current customers. We describe the structure and content of a customer database and illustrate its utility for mining opportunities and measuring the lifetime value of customers. With a lifetime value perspective, we can rightly regard the acquisition of new customers as a capital budgeting enterprise—an investment in a productive asset—rather than an expense. Of course, the development of new markets and the acquisition of new customers pivot on useful segmentation models. We review several approaches to segmentation in business markets and discuss the criteria for an effective segmentation scheme. ●

Chapter 6, an overview of strategic planning, is neither the first nor the last perspective you'll encounter that tackles the vexing problem of strategy formulation. Our emphasis in the chapter is on the definition of purpose and the match of distinctive competencies to opportunities. This matching process favors firms that act with a sophisticated understanding of the competitive forces in the product market. Furthermore, because the pace of technology and global nature of competition make almost any competitive advantage short lived, the only real strategic edge comes from an organization's ability to learn to disrupt the status quo and adapt. ●

Any business that takes its eye off customer satisfaction, quality, and routine review of its mission and strategy will also fail to finish the race. This is the stuff of Chapter 7. We chart the roles that marketing plays in a learning organization and the partnerships marketing personnel must forge with all functional areas. The skills for partnering are outlined in a manner that should enable you to contribute positively to the teamwork needed to deliver value efficiently and thereby satisfy and retain customers at a profit. ●

# Chapter 5

## Market Opportunities
### Current and Potential Customers

### FEDEX

Frederick Smith began Federal Express with a clever idea and a network of financial backers. He saw countless businesses needing rapid delivery of small repair parts, blueprints, and other documents. His plan was to use a fleet of planes to fly by night, out of sleepy airports, to a central hub in Memphis. There all parcels would be sorted and bundled for their destination, and flown out again to the still quiet airports. Then before lunchtime, snappy fleets of trucks would deliver components, perishables, documents, and more to the addressee. The concept was supported with award-winning advertising and a customer focus.●

What a stunning example of the impact of entrepreneurship! Although financial losses were substantial, it was critical to keep the system running while awaiting volume growth. But the growth did come. Many companies began using overnight air shipment in place of parts inventories warehoused in multiple locations throughout the country and beyond. But it was the document business that exploded.●

A few years later, however, there was more parity among the players in the overnight delivery business. Although all carriers faced the adverse impact of the fax machine on their document volume, perhaps none faced it more than Federal Express, the leader by far in next-day letters. New businesses beyond documents were needed.●

FedEx developed a new pricing schedule for heavy packages, hundred-weight rates, and it promoted the program especially to select customers known to ship heavy items. FedEx launched a similar program to its chemical and related customers to tout its ability to handle "dangerous goods." In a prize-winning program, FedEx used its own route personnel to deliver fresh baked coffee cakes to high-volume shippers to announce Saturday delivery. People in the office that Saturday shared the news of this service as they shared the goodies. To develop new customers, FedEx made a special pitch to catalog merchants, or (as its program dubbed them) "you who serve the mail order shopper." Today Lands' End, L.L. Bean, and more make FedEx delivery available to their customers for a small additional charge. A key benefit has been to enable last-minute shopping, effectively lengthening the Christmas season for catalogers. ●

But the acceleration of business globalization motivated FedEx to obtain authority to serve China in 1995, and acquire Tower Group International, a leading firm in the field of international logistics and trade information technology, in 2000. FedEx serves customers in over 200 countries today. In the meantime, FedEx acquired Caliber Systems in 1998 to enable it to provide an array of shipping services beyond express delivery. For example, it could handle less than a truckload and even small packages with ground-based delivery and provide airfreight forwarding regionally. ●

Closer to campus, FedEx/Kinko's originated from its 2004 purchase of the privately held Kinko's chain. This opportunity not only enhanced FedEx document management service, but gave the firm a huge boost in customer access through its 1,200 stores.[1] ●

Visit the FedEx Web site at **www.fedex.com.**●

## LEARNING OBJECTIVES

In this chapter you will learn to think creatively and boldly—like FedEx—about finding new opportunities. We will underscore the favorable circumstances and possibilities for gaining increased business from current customers. We also develop options for gaining new customers. Both arenas require formal evaluations of market potential and can be well served by marketing research. We aim to sharpen your perspective on opportunities and acquaint you with some of the key managerial tools.

*After reading this chapter, you should be able to*

● Seek to maximize the value of current customers.

● Outline the basic structure and capabilities of a customer database. Discuss the relative strengths and weaknesses of alternative means of customer research.

● Illustrate how suppliers and customers can collaborate to find opportunities.

- Segment business markets on the basis of industry codes, buying processes, benefits sought, media and memberships, and other criteria.
- Assess the utility of any market segmentation scheme.
- Apply basic models to evaluate the potential of market segments.

We don't promise to map every sector of market opportunities, nor do we review every known tool of market evaluation. But we give you what we hope is enough to jump-start your vigilance and imagination.

# FINDING OPPORTUNITIES

The word *opportunity* comes from the Latin *opportunitas,* meaning fitness or advantage. It represents a favorable circumstance, a propitious moment, or a promising course of events that bodes well for the attainment of a goal. Marketing opportunities derive from the "fitness" of a company to serve a specific market. They result from a seller's proximity, competencies, skills, and resources that can be brought to serve an identified customer or segment profitably. The seller's ability to provide value is its competitive advantage in that particular arena.

## Markets among Current Customers

Business managers have often noted the tendency of about 20 percent of customers to account for 80 percent of sales. A closer look at some companies shows even greater skewness—perhaps more than 75 percent of sales from fewer than 10 percent of accounts. Firms that sell to automobile companies or the military, of course, might not experience the 80–20 rule or 75–10 situation simply because there are only a handful of potential accounts. Both phenomena—the 80–20 distributions and firms selling to small numbers of customers—dramatize the importance of managing important groups of accounts if not individual account relationships in business markets.

### Best Customers

How much of its marketing budget should a firm allocate to efforts that serve its best customers? In the abstract, any firm should spend and spend until the payoffs from additional marketing efforts are no longer in excess of incremental expenditures. *Spending until marginal revenue equals marginal costs and marginal costs are rising* is the basic profit maximization approach many of you learned in economics class. In practice, this approach can be followed for narrow promotions and some specific marketing expenditures. For example, Federal Express promotions are usually measured against a control group of customers that matches the target group in every way but participation in the promotion. Thus, in the "Dangerous Goods" program that promoted FedEx's capability to ship toxic, caustic, and flammable materials, the additional daily volume over three months was twice as high in the promotion group as in the control group. This translated into over $20 in revenue per dollar of marketing expenditure. With variable costs per shipment so low in the overnight shipping business, this program certainly increases profits from one group of current customers. From this point FedEx could expand the program to other accounts, intensify the program with this same group of customers, or both.

Unfortunately, the payoffs from many other marketing expenditures are not so easily determined. A computer company's commitment to staff a 24-hour service line is justified not so much on the hard data showing the profitability of the service as it is on a commitment to market leadership (or catching up to competition) and need to signal commitment to customers. A credit card company hosts an annual weekend of recreation and entertainment for its best business customers. This extravagant "thank you" builds goodwill and channels of communication. The credit company hopes this translates into increased business or **account retention,** the percentage of accounts that continue doing business with the seller each year. But we can think of no practical way of gauging the effectiveness of the event on such criteria.

## Customer Maximization

Many companies find that it is much easier to get current customers to do more business than it is to get business from prospective customers. Many of those who have never transacted with the company know the company and its products, *but are just not interested.*

To illustrate, note that most metropolitan newspapers derive a significant portion of their advertising revenue from auto dealers in their readership area. Nevertheless, a number of new superdealers in the Midwest have elected to use *no newspaper advertising* in their promotion mix, relying instead on radio image advertising and highly targeted direct mail and telephone follow-up with referrals. How the local newspapers long to win over such accounts!

But that door seems effectively closed for now. Newspaper ad managers can use their time and talent more productively developing programs for the car dealers, real estate agencies, and department stores that are already buying ads. Indeed, Lee Enterprises in Davenport, Iowa, a media company publishing 56 newspapers, has expanded current client relationships by collaborating with its best advertisers on special events, preferred customer programs, and even the distribution of product samples.

## New Products

The same logic for increasing the volume of light and medium accounts applies to their potential for purchasing new products. Current customers know the company, its service standards, its dedication to quality, its technical capabilities, and more. With them the seller enjoys a level of credibility and trust that has yet to be measured and tested among noncustomers, even bright prospects. Thus, a marketing research company with a new forecasting technique or model is apt to develop and find keenest interest among its current clients. Similarly, FedEx tested a service for next-afternoon delivery—priced lower than its next-morning delivery service—paying particular attention to responses by its best customers in the test region.

## Network Payoffs

Account retention and penetration motivated our attention to current customers in the preceding discussion. But current customers can be strategic assets in other ways too. Foremost, every business must seek to understand fully its role in the value chain. By enabling one's customer to better satisfy its downstream customers, achieve market share growth, or compete in new markets, one's company stands to grow too.

For example, BOSE speaker design teams frequently help suppliers to meet their tough specifications and quality standards for new plastic and metal parts. Those suppliers who measure up not only reap more purchases from BOSE, but they are more competitive at other accounts as a result. Business 2 Business 5–1 recaps product development by a more complex network.

Certain customers may gain the company access to new accounts and markets. A consulting company that does an excellent job for one of the leading hospitals in St. Louis is apt to benefit greatly from the client's influence with hospital administrators in Kansas City, Chicago, Peoria, Evansville, and Louisville. Clearly, the value of a customer is more than its profit margin impact in the most recent accounting period.

## 5–1

# BUSINESS 2 BUSINESS
## Opportunities in the Network

Sweden's logging industry faces a significant problem: cutting frozen timber at the mill. One saw equipment manufacturer worked with several of its suppliers to develop a small prototype band saw. The product was tested successfully at a small mill. This drew the attention of the large, opinion-leading mill in the region where a new, bigger adaptation of the test saw was installed. Unfortunately, serious breakdowns resulted; weakness in the steel and welded seams were deemed the problem. Fortunately, the large mill forged a technical cooperation agreement with a blade manufacturer, and later brought in the steel supplier and welders. It took several years, but eventually the new processes were established and the saw equipment manufacturer found success.

The map of the key linkages in this value-creating process shows the importance of even remote participants in the network.

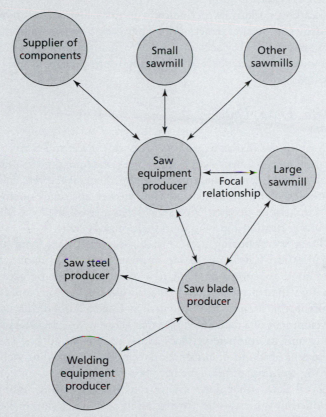

Source: Adapted from James Anderson, Hakan Hakansson, and Jan Johanson, "Dyadic Business Relationships within a Business Network Context." Used with permission from the *Journal of Marketing,* published by the American Marketing Association, vol. 58 (October 1994), pp. 1–15.

# Finding Opportunities with Customers

Opportunities to do additional business with current customers can be identified by informal and formal means. Feedback through the sales force and service and delivery personnel should be encouraged and rewarded. Their frequent contact with customers and empathic dialogue make them attuned to developing customer needs. **Empathic dialogue** is active listening and identification with customer concerns, resulting in customer-centered communication and problem solving. The Loctite Corporation developed an inexpensive dispensing system for liquid adhesives primarily as a result of the insistence by its sales force that it should fill a dire need among heretofore neglected prospects, small manufacturers who could use a lot of adhesive if they could get their hands on a reasonable dispensing system.

Marketing research companies and consulting firms frequently spark—and sometimes frame—their client's next project. IBM enjoys a productive working partnership with RealDanmark, one of Denmark's largest banks. Its assistance in the bank's application of IBM VisualAge Generator in a small intranet system to provide customer information to 50 end users prompted RealDanmark to adapt a family of add-on products called VA Assist Enterprise.[2]

Leading companies periodically profile their top accounts and formally develop strategies for greater penetration. They seek to understand the sales forecasts and business strategies of key accounts. They formally model the purchase process and identify the roles of key members of the buying team, perhaps as influencer, user, gatekeeper, or decider.

## Data, Data, Data

Some business marketers serve so many customers and execute so many transactions that account management—and other types of opportunities—are critically supported by sophisticated data management systems. Federal Express and UPS serve thousands of customers daily. Grainger and Dell answer customer queries and execute thousands of transactions on their Web sites. Even a small medical lab must efficiently manage customer relationships with hundreds of physicians.

**Data warehousing** uses centrally managed data from all functional areas of the organization (sales, purchasing, human resources, finance, accounts payable, etc.)—formatted to company standards—so that it may be accessed by authorized users through their personal computers for queries, custom reports, and analysis.[3] A major effort in the supply chain initiative at Cessna Aircraft discussed in Chapter 2 was the development of a data warehouse that allowed key executives to view price trends graphically and to compare vendors across criteria in ad hoc spreadsheets.[4] Indeed, with increasing amounts of information technology applied to Web sites and transaction processing, volumes of new data have become available. Complementary systems accessing archival data—that don't interfere with transactions, communications, and various production systems—are proving invaluable to decision makers.

To illustrate, please consider ScheduTrax, a fictitious software company selling desktop business software for scheduling and staffing. ScheduTrax has over 50,000 customers. An increasing number of companies are using part-time employees and trying to accommodate the flexible schedules their full-time people need to raise families, attend school, serve the community, or serve jail time. They use ScheduTrax programs to incorporate these complex constraints while scheduling staff, various operations, and service loads.

**5–1**

# FROM THE FIELD

## Market Research for Customer Loyalty

As I approached my degree in journalism, I realized I felt out of balance with my chosen career. Writing fulfilled my right brain, but my left brain longed for something more analytical. After a few years of working in journalism, going back to school to obtain my MBA provided a new and exciting career path. Market research became an outlet for my creative and analytical sides and deepened my sense of curiosity around how the art and the science of the world can merge.

My first job in market research was as a television advertising consultant. I was interested to learn that selling a product through advertising, which I thought was entirely driven by creativity and flair, was also driven by some basic foundational principles. Learning these principles and understanding their root in enabling customers to relate to a brand and product need was a key step forward in my career.

This experience was a perfect springboard for my next position in market research. Currently I work for a market research firm that is co-owned by a large grocery retailer. Our focus in everything we do is on creating a better shopping experience for our loyal customers. So many retailers are focused on winning their competitor's customers and overlooking those who are already walking through their door. Through understanding customer's behaviors and needs through their purchase data, retailers can create a differentiated and relevant experience that can drive true loyalty.

While I've learned so much from these experiences, I realize every day there is more to learn from our customers and our industry. Remaining eternally curious is the key, in my opinion, to a successful and satisfying career in market research.

Kim Harris, dunnhumby USA.

In the ScheduTrax database each customer comprises a record. Each record contains the following key elements:

User's name(s)

Company

Street address

City, state, and ZIP code

Latitude and longitude of business

Phone and fax numbers

Source code (origin of initial order)

Initial purchase date

Original purchase dollars

Purchase (upgrade) history

　　Transaction dates

　　Transaction amounts

　　Source code of transaction

　　Product type

**Exhibit 5–1**
ScheduTrax
Decile Report

| Decile | $ Spent | No. of Customers | Cum. No. of Customers | % of Customers | Cum. % of Customers | Average Purchases |
|--------|---------|------------------|-----------------------|----------------|---------------------|-------------------|
| 1 | 632,771 | 162 | 162 | 2% | 2% | $3,906 |
| 2 | 632,771 | 290 | 452 | 3 | 5 | 2,182 |
| 3 | 632,771 | 366 | 818 | 4 | 9 | 1,729 |
| 4 | 632,771 | 430 | 1,248 | 4 | 13 | 1,472 |
| 5 | 632,771 | 521 | 1,769 | 5 | 18 | 1,215 |
| 6 | 632,771 | 606 | 2,375 | 6 | 24 | 1,044 |
| 7 | 632,771 | 890 | 3,265 | 9 | 33 | 711 |
| 8 | 632,771 | 1,126 | 4,391 | 11 | 44 | 562 |
| 9 | 632,771 | 1,423 | 5,814 | 14 | 58 | 445 |
| 10 | 632,771 | 4,316 | 10,130 | 42 | 100 | 147 |
| Total | 6,327,710 | 10,130 | | 100 | | 625 |

Firm characteristics (industry, number of employees)

User demographics and lifestyles

Of course, the database requires both proper setup and ongoing maintenance to serve as a seed bed of market opportunities. Let's presume those challenges are addressed elsewhere in your business program and examine a couple of simple reports to illustrate opportunities among current customers.

Exhibit 5–1 is called a decile report. A **decile report** orders the firm's customers from best to worst, on the basis of purchase volume for the period, summarized by tenths. (Admittedly, we have heard executives give the same name—decile report—to tables summarizing purchase activity for 5ths or 20ths of the revenue base.) At the bottom of the left-hand column, Exhibit 5–1 reports that ScheduTrax has achieved a little over $6.3 million in sales. The bottom of the next column to the right indicates that the sales came from a little over 10,000 customers. Thus, average spending per customer, in the bottom right, is $625.

Each row in the report, however, helps the marketing manager break free of the tendency to think about the "average" customer. The customers are far from equal in the significance of their purchases! For example, ScheduTrax's weakest customers—in row 10—don't even spend a quarter of the average, and they represent 43 percent of the customer base! Now compare decile 10 against decile 1: A handful of best customers spend 26 times as much as the worst.

The decile report is simple, but quite helpful to the business marketer. How well do we know our best accounts? Which accounts get invited to the trade show reception? Which ones get a card and which ones get the two-pound box of chocolates with a card that says, "Thanks for your business" at the end of the year? FedEx often tests promotions to its best customers in a particular service category and then expands the program to successively less-important customers as long as returns are positive. Perhaps there are some accounts that have continued to get our marketing attention—mail and phone calls—that just don't seem worthwhile any more. We start to ask where else we can put such marketing effort to yield better payoffs.

Some of the preceding questions invite other questions. The very best accounts could be studied one by one. Exhibit 5–2 assembles the profiles of two specific customers to enable account strategies. Customer 2207 is relatively new and in the restaurant business. Customer 1761 is a retail auto parts chain and has been our customer since 1992.

**Exhibit 5–2**
ScheduTrax
Account
Profiles

| | | | |
|---|---|---|---|
| ACCOUNT NO. | 2207 | | |
| FIRM | Billy's Tavern | BUSINESS | Food Svc-Rtl |
| | 2295 Riverside | | |
| | Valdosta, GA | 31602 | |
| | 9125551234 | | |
| CONTACTS | Bradford, Jimmy | DEMO CODE | 2012 |
| | Manager | | |
| | | TRANSACTION SUMMARY | |
| ORIG DATE | 09/24/99 | LAST PURCH | 07/18/00 |
| ORIG $ | $159 | CUM $ | $3,882 |
| ORIG SOURCE | M63 | NO. TRANS | 13 |
| MODE | Phone | | |
| PMT | AmEx | | |
| ACCOUNT NO. | 1761 | | |
| FIRM | Midwest Auto Parts | BUSINESS | Auto parts-Rtl |
| | 27912 Telegraph Rd | | |
| | Detroit, MI | 48034 | |
| | 8105559999 | | |
| CONTACTS | Wolscheid, Emily | DEMO CODE | 4302 |
| | Office Manager | | |
| | | TRANSACTION SUMMARY | |
| ORIG DATE | 03/04/92 | LAST PURCH | 08/26/01 |
| ORIG $ | $139 | CUM $ | $4,891 |
| ORIG SOURCE | DM26 | NO. TRANS | 19 |
| MODE | Phone | | |
| PMT | PO, Amex | | |

These data support telephone and direct mail efforts at ScheduTrax. Marketing communications with 2207—and with those accounts in like circumstances—might convey special appreciation for adapting the software and provide application tips for food service firms—perhaps scheduling wait staff with high absentee rates. Customers akin to 1761 would receive affirmation of the long-running business relationship and might be sought as test sites for updates and new product prototypes. Indeed, the database can be mined for insights into user needs and motivations. Customers can be meaningfully grouped by size, industry, longevity, purchase volume, applications, and so on to enable a full range of marketing communications and customer service.

Individual customers in the second, third, and fourth deciles at ScheduTrax may not represent the sales volume to justify such close analytical attention, although firms with higher purchases per customer than ScheduTrax may, indeed, give close attention to key accounts in deciles 3 or 4 or elsewhere. Eventually, at some level of customer significance, we forsake individual account analysis to find significant patterns and groups of customers in these deciles.

Exhibit 5–3 profiles the groups of customers in deciles 2 through 4. Notice that 35 percent are in the retail business, including chains and independents. Among these purchasers of our scheduling software, only 15 percent have adopted Graph 1, the new companion software that gives (1) graphic display for departments or stores and (2) personal schedules addressable to each employee. The low adoption rate among retailers seems to be in sharp contrast to the nursing care segment, where 40 percent of the

**Exhibit 5–3**
ScheduTrax Profile of Customers in Deciles 2–4

| Type of Business | No. of Accts. | % of Deciles 2–4 | Last Year's Purchases | Cumulative Purchases | Adaptation of Companion Products | | | |
|---|---|---|---|---|---|---|---|---|
| | | | | | Graph1 | Pay1 | Pay2 | Phonlink |
| Education | 43 | 4% | $75,163 | $159,458 | 44% | 31% | 18% | 9% |
| Entertainment | 27 | 2 | 47,196 | 159,458 | 34 | 20 | 14 | 17 |
| Nursing care | 217 | 20 | 379,313 | 1,009,902 | 40 | 22 | 28 | 18 |
| Manufacturing | 72 | 7 | 125,855 | 372,069 | 33 | 19 | 22 | 11 |
| Professional serv. | 128 | 12 | 223,742 | 797,291 | 29 | 40 | 15 | 12 |
| Retail | 380 | 35 | 664,235 | 1,754,041 | 15 | 22 | 13 | 16 |
| Transportation | 104 | 10 | 181,791 | 584,680 | 48 | 20 | 28 | 20 |
| Other | 115 | 11 | 201,018 | 531,528 | 47 | 27 | 25 | 22 |
| Total | 1086 | 100 | 1,898,313 | 5,315,276 | 31 | 25 | 20 | 16 |

customers have bought Graph 1. Maybe we should think about putting together a promotion to these 323 customers—the 85 percent of 380 retail customers that do not have the Graph 1 software.

To go beyond standard decile reports or promotion program summaries, business marketing managers need a repertoire of data analysis tools. Evoking images of the quest for riches, the term **data mining** describes the process of using numerous query tools and exploratory techniques to extract information from a database or data warehouse. Some of this process can be automated, as in systems programmed to recognize purchase patterns at the account level or market level, defined, say, by industry or geography. Other tools are user controlled and may include creative, multivariate statistical approaches to reveal customer groups or predict behavior in a product market. Several large pharmaceutical companies use data mining to identify doctor prescription practices and even patient compliance rates in prescription refill patterns. The former may be used to direct sales efforts, whereas the latter are often used to structure self-help materials and education programs distributed through physicians' offices.

## Customer Research

Astute readers should be asking a key question here: Before running the promotion, why not talk to several current customers to learn their priorities and circumstances? Indeed! The database supports two different research approaches: focus groups and sample surveys.

### Focus Groups
**Focus groups** bring a small group of customers together to discuss a specific topic or issue. Our software company, ScheduTrax, might try to bring 6 to 12 customers together at a trade show or in three or four different cities where they conduct business. The meeting can be set up at a local hotel or conference facility or could be arranged to take place at the special facilities of a marketing research company. These might be quite elaborate. Most allow videotaping and direct observation through a one-way mirror.

This allows ScheduTrax representatives who watch the focus group to give the moderator some additional directions for the interview.

The moderator is an experienced professional, often with advanced behavioral science training. After providing a brief icebreaker and general introduction to the topic, the moderator generally tries to let the group carry on the conversation. His or her concentration should be on the discussion, along a general outline of topics needed to be covered in the discussion. Because the interview is taped, the moderator can let the group talk, with ample opportunity later to analyze comments and extract stimulating quotations.

No two focus groups are identical. Each has different participants, perhaps from different positions in diverse organizations, from different industries, and/or from different parts of the country. Depending on the nature of the topic and the diversity of the user segments, most companies conduct several focus groups, although the incremental value of each additional group interview will taper off after three or four, or maybe not until a half dozen.

The focus group is best used to generate ideas, gain insights into customer needs and constraints, and develop hypotheses about market opportunities. ScheduTrax might learn that department managers, who used to schedule dozens of part-time employees every two weeks, have split into at least two distinct groups: (1) those who have handed off this task to a staff person and (2) those who have used the software themselves to begin or expand their array of desktop personal productivity aids and decision support tools. Managers in the second group appear to represent an opportunity for ScheduTrax.

It is important to note that the focus group is not a fitting procedure for measuring market share potential or forecasting adoption rates. The focus group reveals a spectrum of customer motivations, suggests differences in usage patterns, provides close contact with actual customers, and thus stimulates thinking about new products and services and how better to market existing products. Focus groups do not provide quantitative results like percentages or sales estimates.

The popularity of focus group research rests on three major factors. First, it is supported by the efficient and accurate access to customers afforded by the database. Just imagine the daunting task of finding 10 moderate users in the automotive repair business in Jacksonville without using a customer database. Second, focus groups can be conducted quickly and relatively cheaply. Depending on the scale of compensation for participants, the amenities of the facility, and the moderator's fee, focus groups can cost between $1,200 and $8,000 each. Finally, focus groups almost always yield a surprising customer insight and some new ideas.

## Surveys

There are limits to what we can infer from behavioral information in the customer database. To illustrate, some percentage of current customers may be less than satisfied—even while they continue to purchase. A fraction of these may soon defect to a competitor unless given a chance to voice their dissatisfaction and receive seller's redress efforts. Meanwhile, focus group insights are typically exploratory. They seldom afford quantitative estimates of satisfaction or buying intentions, for example. The **sample survey**—a questionnaire administered to a representative group of a particular population—is a versatile approach to problems that involve asking people questions. But it too has limits, which is why companies often use many types of research.

Surveys can be administered to customers in four primary ways: (1) personal interview, (2) mail, (3) telephones, and (4) the Internet. Personal interviews allow good depth

**Exhibit 5-4**
Comparing
Focus Groups
and 1-on-1
Interviews

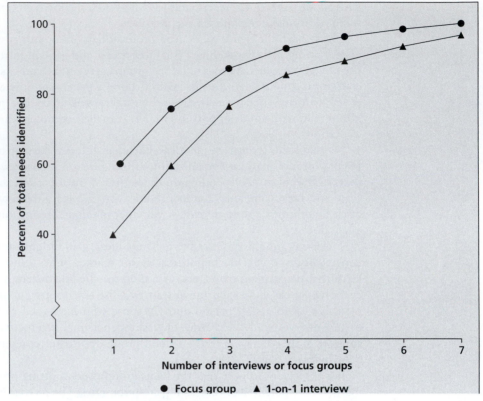

SOURCE: *See Abbie Griffin and John R. Hauser, "The Voice of the Customer,"* Marketing Science *12 (winter 1993), pp. 1–27.*

of questioning and probing. Answers can be clarified and feedback from product demonstrations or physical stimuli (e.g., a fabric or warning siren) can be ascertained. But the expense of sending interviewers to the field to secure elusive appointments and visit geographically dispersed customers is often prohibitive. Thus, a compromise approach may be some focus groups or an attempt to see customers one-on-one at a trade show. We should note here that for identifying unmet customer needs for guiding new product development, one-on-one interviews can be more economical than focus groups. Exhibit 5-4 shows a common pattern in the generation of needs: multiple focus groups are better than one-on-one interviews, but their advantage shrinks in the cumulative number of ideas as multiple interviews or focus groups are executed.

Questionnaires can be administered very efficiently by mail. But it is critical that the researcher design the survey with the nature of the current business relationship in mind. The recipient of the survey is a current customer, not a stranger. Thus, a number of imperatives govern the contact.

In most cases the researcher must acknowledge and affirm the relationship in the cover letter. Typically the survey aims to strengthen the relationship. Thus, affirmation of the relationship serves to motivate customers to reveal unmet needs and points of supplier weakness. Respondents should be given hope to realize greater satisfaction from within the current relationship, instead of seeking other sources. Even if the researcher's objective is to identify customers for disengagement, it is prudent to sever the exchange amicably, with minimal turmoil or stress.

Second, the survey must ask only questions that cannot be answered by information on the customer database. This is a matter of both credibility and courtesy. Out of respect for our customer's time and competing job demands, we should not ask survey participants to look up or compile information that we have in the database. In this same spirit, it must be clear to the survey respondent or informant whether the data are being compiled for statistical summaries or to augment the database.

No survey should be used to mask selling activities. **Sugging** is the unethical practice of using marketing research as a guise for selling. "Hi, this is Randy from Business Research Service. I'd like to ask you a few questions about office productivity. . . . Do you have a copy machine? . . . a fax? . . . laser printer? I'm going to switch you to Richard, who will tell you about the new all-in-one from Bosco." Sugging grossly misleads and "spoils" the marketplace for legitimate marketing research activities.

Finally, the questionnaire layout and length must reflect an overall appreciation for the respondent's time and effort. Ask the important matters first. Provide a postpaid return envelope. A fax number makes it easy for respondents to give quick returns and to ask questions of the researcher.

Unfortunately, many mail surveys age in a customer's in-basket for several weeks. Some surveys will never return, despite the best procedures: telephone prenotification, a postcard reminder, premiums or cash inducements, and sending duplicate surveys to nonrespondents. Some recipients simply can't or won't give the time to the task; others don't want to answer the questions; many simply forget.

Telephone and Internet surveys represent a partial solution. Indeed, the ScheduTrax company could send a questionnaire by e-mail to 2,000 customers in the nighttime. There might be 300 responses by lunchtime—and no data entry expense. Alternatively, two ScheduTrax staff members—or a couple of students from this class—could get on the phone this afternoon and have summary tables from 400 interviews by tomorrow. Both routes are supported by inexpensive software that processes online data or allows phone interviewers to follow a script on the computer screen, enter responses as they are given, conduct basic statistical analysis, and display results in report formats.

Telephone surveys have two key drawbacks. First, the telephone is a more intrusive medium than the mail. The interviewer may be interrupting a customer's schedule and may not receive enough of the customer's time to complete the survey. A key challenge will be to hold the respondent's interest through the entire set of questions that meet the information objectives of the researcher. It is wise to ask the most important questions up front.

Second, some businesspeople are very hard to reach by telephone. For example, pharmaceutical companies find it very difficult to survey physicians by telephone. When they are in the clinic, doctors are attending to patients, scribbling or dictating reports, and otherwise on the move. (Some drug companies have found that doctors are more responsive to mail surveys—that is, when they are printed on the back of $200 checks! Thus, the data come in as the checks are cashed.)

Online surveys are remarkably fast and cost effective. Their efficiency often leads users to seek huge samples. Their major disadvantage is that some populations are not well represented online. Machinists and the building trades are difficult to reach by e-mail or Web site. For ScheduTrax, the Internet is apt to be a very fitting survey medium because customers are computer users. Of course, recipient concerns about privacy and virus contagion will continue to bridle the utility of online surveys.

## Joint Development and Testing

Many products in business markets require ongoing adjustments and developments after the purchase. Computer/software and other installations require frequent vendor–customer

---

**5–2**

## FROM THE FIELD

### Supply-Side Opportunity

While the chapter material emphasizes the garden of opportunities in the firm's customer base, buyer–seller relationships provide opportunities for both parties. Alcoa's project leader for material handling systems, Ken Main, paints a critical role for their vendors:

> We accomplished a lot of our efforts from the design of this material handling system through what I call vendor integration meetings. These are held on a monthly basis starting in December, as we were selecting vendors and getting them on board. . . . We were depending upon our MAP (a material acquisition program at Alcoa) vendors to supply us with the utility that would allow us to send these defined message packets that we established. . . . All this was documented for our vendor use in what I call a vendor

integration document, which has become more or less the Bible by which we check and are doing our systems performance checking.[5]

Thus, formal interactions for material handling system development are important to purchasers as well as materials suppliers. Suppliers who participate in regular meetings with their customers the way Alcoa has invited its key vendors to do find themselves in a context to discover what strategic and operational issues keep their customers awake at night; what words, symbols, and communication channels are most reliable; what impediments prevent the full collaboration of a customer's personnel in the value creation process; and more.

---

interactions and joint activities to hone operations, adapt to new work requirements, and ensure the development of critical know-how for both organizations. For example, a vendor of pollution control devices called scrubbers will participate in the testing of its systems at an electric power company because both firms need the other's expertise and both recognize the emission control needs at multiple plants. This is discussed in greater detail in the product development coverage of Chapter 8.

### Customer Visits

If spending time at a customer's venue to test concepts and problem solve has value, it should come as no surprise that business marketers have been stepping up the frequency and complexity of customer visits. Hewlett–Packard is the oft-noted leader in design of and payoff from customers visits. Calling on a subset of key customers, using cross-functional teams, and following protocols that take the parties out of the conference rooms, a customer visitation program can be a powerful tool. Opportunities get spotted in operations, in the formal presentations of goals and plans, and—perhaps most uniquely—in the frank disclosures of customer's headaches and identification of problems.[6] From the Field 5–2 illustrates some of the parallel payoffs for customers.

## The Acquisition of New Customers

Now that we have emphasized and illustrated the ocean of business opportunities with current customers, we can take up the matter of new customer acquisition. Notice our terminology. Some texts talk about *getting* new accounts or *winning* customers, but these terms suggest the essence of conquest. We want to underscore the process as one of securing a vital strategic asset. When the potential exists for a long-run relationship with customers, their acquisition should be regarded as an investment.

**5–3**

## FROM THE FIELD
### ABCs of Customer Care in Steel Service

Asva Oy is the largest steel wholesaler in Finland, second largest in Scandinavia, and a business unit of the EUR 3 billion Rautaruukki Group. Offering customers steel, copper, and aluminum in various forms—sheets, coils, plates, bars—and performing many prefabricating services—cutting to shape, edging, slitting, and shot blasting, Asva can be a valuable partner with its manufacturing customers.

When the company charted its growth strategy in 2003—to forge deeper ties to customers through improved service, fabrication, engineering and customization—it needed an accounting system that would support the new knowledge-intensive initiative. Asva needed a handle on profitability by product and customer; it needed to know the true costs of metals and customer services as it priced the various custom processes. The strategy could not tolerate a "good relationship" that doesn't bring profits. But, unknowingly selling at a loss has

happened. Asva controller, Pirkka Kiema, explains, "(O)ne thinks that an X percent material margin can bear anything. Then, extra services are offered at a price which is too low, because one doesn't realize how much various stages of production add to the total cost."

Asva gets current and significant information about its product and customer profitability in a system involving SAS activity-based management. It enables Asva to find out how different processes applied to its products for customers affect the costs according to orders. Thus, Asva can see how these process operations affect its profitability on a per customer basis. In addition, Asva uses the activity-based costing model to produce information about the cost effects of customers' customization wishes, such as special assortments, delivery, machining, or recoiling.

AS Web site: http://www.sas.com/success/asvaoy.html; Asva Oy Web site: http://www.asva.fi/.

---

Most organizations make investment decisions on the basis of return on investment rates, net present value, or months (years) to reach break-even. When University Hospital buys a new magnetic resonance imaging (MRI) system, it estimates a multiyear stream of revenue from patients against the installation outlay and projected operating costs.

As we see in From the Field 5–3, an increasing number of companies have begun to formalize a similar approach to customer valuation. **Customer lifetime value (CLV)** is an estimate of the net present value of the stream of benefits from a customer, less the burdens of servicing the account or managing the relationship. For a basic illustration, consider a public accounting firm, which will often serve a client for many years. The revenue from this relationship represents the chief benefit stream. The burdens include the direct costs of audits and reports, plus the costs of maintaining the account—training, entertainment, periodic meetings, even the annual Thanksgiving turkey gift baskets to the client's personnel. With this CTV perspective, a client billed $30,000 per year can take on six-figure significance. Likewise, a small environmental engineering firm doing $50 of overnight shipping per week can represent $10,000 in net present value of FedEx.

Let's develop a greater understanding of the mechanics of CLV by returning to the ScheduTrax example. Exhibit 5–5 shows the purchase history of a group of customers at our software firm. Although some customers are one-shot buyers, the majority tend to purchase ancillary software products and upgrades over their lifetimes. Thus, the benefit stream from a new ScheduTrax customer goes beyond the initial software purchase.

To calculate lifetime value ScheduTrax uses a four-year horizon—after acquisition—and a 20 percent estimate for average direct costs. With customer mailing and quarterly

# Exhibit 5-5
ScheduTrax Customer Lifetime Value Analysis

| | | | | | Expected customer migrations following acquisition | | | |
|---|---|---|---|---|---|---|---|---|
| Yrs. since the Last Purchase | Purchase Probability | Expected $ Purchases | Account Service Costs | Acquisition Period | 1st Yr. after Acquisition | 2nd Yr. after Acquisition | 3rd Yr. after Acquisition | 4th Yr. after Acquisition |
| 0 | 0.60 | $90 | $20 | 100 customers | 60.0 | 36.0 / 16.0 / 52.0 | 31.2 / 9.6 / 4.8 / 45.6 | 27.4 / 8.3 / 2.9 / 1.9 / 40.5 |
| 1 | 0.40 | $60 | $10 | | 40.0 | 24.0 | 20.8 | 18.2 |
| 2 | 0.20 | $50 | $4 | | | 24.0 | 14.4 | 12.5 / 11.5 |
| 3 | 0.10 | $50 | $2 | | | | 19.2 | 17.3 |

## Profit forecasts

Acq +1   [60 buyers ($90)] × .8 gross profit − [100 accts × $20 service/acct] =   $2,320

Acq +2   [36 buyers ($90) + 16 buyers ($60)] .8 gr. profit − [60 accts × $20 + 40 accts × $10] =   $1,760

Acq +3   [31.2 buyers ($90) + 9.6 buyers ($60) + 4.8 buyers ($50)] .8 gr. profit − [52 accts × $20 + 24 × $10 + 24 × $4] =   $1,523

Acq +4   [27.4 buyers ($90) + 8.3 buyers ($60) + 2.9 buyers ($50) + 1.9 buyers ($50)] −
[45.6 × $20 + 20.8 × $10 + 14.4 × $4 + 19.2 × $2] =   $1,345

| Discounting profits: | NPV @ 10% | NPV @ 15% | NPV @ 20% |
|---|---|---|---|
| Acq +1 | $2,109 | $2,017 | $1,933 |
| Acq +2 | $1,455 | $1,331 | $1,222 |
| Acq +3 | $1,144 | $1,002 | $ 881 |
| Acq +4 | $ 919 | $ 769 | $ 649 |
| LTV/100 customers | $5,627 | $5,119 | $4,686 |

## 5–2

# BUSINESS 2 BUSINESS
## CLV for the Dreamliner?

Boeing's 787 should be undergoing flight tests as this book is coming off the presses. Belied by its familiar three-digit model designation, the 787 was made to best utilize Boeing's Sonic Cruiser technology that brought more fuel efficiency to flight around 2000, and represents a brand-new model for airliner design and assembly. First, the aircraft body is made from a carbon fiber composite material applied by computer-driven machinery to a mold, or mandrel, in a clean room. The mandrel is wrapped and moved to an oven to be cured under heat and pressure for 10 or more hours, then trimmed and drilled to make ready for assembly. The composite material is stronger and lighter than aluminum and will not corrode.

Assembly is truly global. Boeing's supply and design partners include Fuji Heavy Industries, Kawasaki and Mitsubishi in Japan, Alenia in Italy, Vought in Texas, Spirit in Wichita, as well as its own operations in Puget Sound, Washington. Mitsubishi built two plants for producing and assembling the composite wings. "We will succeed in making the world's first composite airplane in the spirit of working together," Mitsubishi's 787 program manager explained to the press at their factory tour in summer 2006.

What level of CLV analysis do you think went into Mitsubishi's decision to dedicate plants to the Dreamliner?

Sources: http://seattlepi.nwsourc.com/business/265465_japan27.html; http://www.designnews.com/article/CA6441528.html.

telephone contacts, annual account maintenance costs are expected to average about $20 to recent customers but are characteristically lower to "older" customer segments. That is, recent purchasers get more marketing attention from ScheduTrax.

Because most accounts are rather small and ScheduTrax wants to postpone decimals in the lifetime value calculations, it evaluates the CLV of 100 customers. The middle of Exhibit 5–5 maps the "migration" of 100 acquired accounts into different segments defined by the recency of their last purchase. Notice that over the first year some (60 percent) historically rebuy and remain "recent" buyers; the other 40 "age" into year-ago customers. Projecting the distribution of customers in the second year after acquisition involves calculating the expected purchasers from two segments: 60 recent buyers and 40 year-ago buyers. The former segment provides ScheduTrax 36 buyers (.6 × 60); the latter provides 16 buyers (.4 × 40). The 24 nonbuyers in the period from each of the two segments accordingly "age" into the next recency category. Accounting for buyers in the third year after acquisition involves estimates from three segments: recent buyers, year-ago buyers, and two-years-ago buyers. The process is repeated in the fourth year, when buyers come from four segments defined by years since last purchase.

The profit model in the bottom portion of Exhibit 5–5 reflects the historical pattern at ScheduTrax that customers who have not recently purchased show a lower probability of purchasing and a lower expected amount of purchase. The profit forecast reflects the gross profit from all groups of purchasers in each future period, less the service costs associated with the segment specific marketing program. At the bottom, cash flow is discounted at 10, 15, and 20 percent to highlight the sensitivity of the valuation to ScheduTrax's opportunity cost of money.

As you can see, CLV is a statistical estimate. It hinges on the relevance of historical data, the proximity of the horizon, the choice of a discount rate, and the accuracy of anticipated account maintenance charges. Furthermore, depending on the business

**Exhibit 5–6**
ScheduTrax Account Profiles with Penetration and Effort Scores

| Type of Business | No. of Accts. | % of Customers | Last Yr's Purchases | No. of Organizations in the Business | Market Penetration | Sought Mkt. Penetration | Effort Index |
|---|---|---|---|---|---|---|---|
| Education | 355 | 0.035% | $164,520 | 18,271 | 2% | 2% | 4 |
| Entertainment | 263 | 0.026 | 189,831 | 38,864 | 1 | 3 | 3 |
| Nursing care | 2,046 | 0.202 | 1,252,887 | 6,820 | 30 | 35 | 3 |
| Manufacturing | 739 | 0.073 | 455,595 | 431,278 | 0 | 2 | 4 |
| Professional serv. | 1,195 | 0.118 | 746,670 | 678,957 | 0 | 5 | 5 |
| Retail | 3,525 | 0.348 | 2,202,043 | 980,241 | 0 | 3 | 5 |
| Transportation | 1,043 | 0.103 | 651,754 | 13,289 | 8 | 6 | 3 |
| Other | 962 | 0.095 | 664,410 | | | | |
| Total | 10,130 | 1.000 | 6,327,710 | 2,167,720 | | | |

NOTE: Market penetration is ScheduTrax accounts/number of organizations. Sought mkt. penetration is ScheduTrax accounts/number of organizations in the business receiving marketing effort from ScheduTrax, reflecting other segmentation criteria (e.g., firm size) and $n$th name testing of certain segments.

context, it can be formulated different ways, perhaps utilizing expected longevity or defection rates. At no business is it a known constant, like the force of gravity on Earth's surface, 9.8 m/sec$^2$. Nevertheless, using the best available data in concert with one's explicit assumptions about buyer behaviors, CLV should be estimated and applied as a key yardstick for planning customer service strategies, assessing customer acquisition programs, and more. In the next section we will use the CLV calculations from Exhibit 5–5 as we explore a few of the more common means of acquiring new customers.

# The Search for Look-Alikes

The ScheduTrax customer mix we examined in Exhibit 5–3 showed a concentration of retail chains and nursing staffs. Maybe these two sectors represent our best growth opportunities. But let's not jump to this conclusion. Maybe this software has particular appeal in those sectors of the economy. Perhaps these are the markets in which ScheduTrax has concentrated its marketing effort. Perhaps the majority of businesses operate in these two sectors. Simply put, we need to augment information from the customer database with additional market data.

Exhibit 5–6 does just that. Market effort scores on the far right are the average of reports given by top management. Market size estimates come from a mailing list company that has compiled data from the Yellow Pages and other directories from across the country.

Now we can see that although ScheduTrax has a high number of retailers as customers, they represent just a small percentage of the market. ScheduTrax has attained only this modest level of penetration despite intense marketing effort. In contrast, hospital nursing directors are just 20 percent of the customers in deciles 2 to 4, but they have received just moderate marketing effort and represent a 30 percent penetration rate. Seemingly, ScheduTrax has a strong appeal in this market. Opportunity knocks!

Let's suppose the ScheduTrax marketing folks tell their advertising agency about their interest in developing the hospital market. Two weeks later the agency proposes a well-conceived program that integrates mail, telephone, and Web site demonstration for their top software product. Certainly, the proposed campaign is superior to anything ever done in this industry—it's creative, dramatic, and sensitive to market needs, the graphics are stunning, and it has a powerful close. ScheduTrax managers are now head scratching. Is it worth the agency's price tag, $45,000?

If we work the numbers a bit, we can see that ScheduTrax needs to get 375 orders of its introductory system to break even on this marketing program. That is, at a price of $150 and an 80 percent gross margin, the break-even volume is $45,000/$120 per order. In a target market of just 4,774 prospects (market size, less currently served ScheduTrax accounts), this represents a lofty response rate, 7.8 percent. No program at ScheduTrax has ever pulled more than a 5.4 percent order rate.

But isn't it shortsighted for ScheduTrax to require the acquisition program to produce what amounts to a one-year payback period? Indeed, the one-year break-even criterion smacks of conquest marketing. Schedu Trax is better advised to consider acquisition program costs against the expected CLV from new accounts. This new break-even number of customers is given by setting $45,000 = ($120 + LTV/acquired customer) × (no. of new accounts). Using the most conservative CLV estimate from Exhibit 5–5, we can solve for the break-even response rate.

At lifetime break-even:

$$\$45,000/(\$120 \text{ gr. Profit from initial purchase} + \$4,686 \text{ CLV}/100 \text{ customers}) = 267$$
$$267 \text{ customers to break even}/4,774 = 5.6\%$$

This break-even response rate is one-third smaller than the target for conquest marketing! Although still on the high end of the range of ScheduTrax experience, the strength of the agency proposal is apt to get it the go-ahead.

In summary, a firm's customers represent the intersection of its past marketing efforts and the competitive strengths of its offering to the target market. A business has an opportunity to acquire new customers that "look like" existing customers when the firm's offering represents a good match to their needs and the firm hasn't fully penetrated the segment. If the firm's market share in the segment is already high, the segment may be practically saturated. The search for opportunity might be better directed elsewhere.

## Finding and Developing New Markets

Our thirst for oil has brought us into some of the harshest environments on earth: the North Sea, the Arabian deserts, the Alaskan tundra, and the Andean jungles. In parallel, the quest for new business has brought companies to many vexing and precarious markets. What parts suppliers will serve the fledgling automotive industry in Vietnam? What broadcasting and telecommunications opportunities are unfolding in Russia?

Geographic expansion is a frequently used means of business growth. Of course, not every new territory is a strange new land. An industrial laundry service in Dearborn, Michigan, can open new plants in Lexington, Kentucky, and Knoxville, Tennessee, without coping with (entirely) new languages or currencies. Nevertheless, it may find unique competitive pressures and special customer needs in each new market.

Sometimes a business can transfer its experience in one industry to another. Sealed Air Corporation manufactures a variety of packaging materials, from Jiffy bags and foam to plastic bubble wraps. With slight production modification, the bubble wrap material can serve as solar blankets for swimming pools. CSI is an Ohio-based software firm that was built on the sales of its accounting software targeted to midsized construction companies. Later it was able to sustain its growth within the contractor segment by offering Project Management software. The result was sales success supporting operations in the field, as well as software solutions for back-office functions.

**Exhibit 5–7**
Secondary
Information
Sources

Just a few years ago a business marketer would call the public library to make sure the number one business reference librarian was on staff that day, and then plan to camp there most of the afternoon. Today, most of those eye-taxing microfilms and dusty bound onion-skin documents are available on the World Wide Web. Here are some key starting points for your specific subject searches:

1.   The University of Michigan Document Center is a compendium of statistical resources on the Web. Data on agriculture, business and industry, economics, energy, education, foreign governments, transportation and more are neatly indexed and available at **www.lib.umich.edu/libhome/Documents.center/index.html.**

2.   Thomas Register is a directory of businesses sorted primarily by industry and geography. The database can be searched to identify and access companies in a particular line of trade or region. For example, a search for companies that provide controls for oil field pumps reveals 19 companies, some of which have hyperlinks to online catalogs. Thomas Register maintains several specialty directories as well. Access this source at URL **www.thomasregister.com.**

3.   An excellent site for conducting company research is maintained by OhioLINK Small Grant Research Program.[7] It includes short tutorials and links to the Thomas Register, directories of private and public companies, Companies Online, Company Link, SEC documents, and much more. Visit **iws.ohiolink.edu/companies/indexcompanyresearch.htm.**

4.   North American Industrial Classification System Manual details the entire classification system and is available at **www.census.gov/epcd/www/naics.html.**

5.   A useful source for lists of prospects and credit reports is **www.dnb.com.** Dunn and Bradstreet is the foremost list compiler, with over 11 million U.S. companies and 115 million businesses worldwide.

Use your search engine to find a bevy of specialty resources. For example,

1.   To find architects in the southwest or contractors in New England, try Directory of Building Trades at **www.buildingtradesdir.com/.**

2.   To land conventions at your new conference center, try the Directory of Associations at Convention Central: **conventioncentral.com/.**

3.   **www.usadata.com** for business lists and sorts by SIC and geography.

## Roles for Marketing Research

Business marketing research has two broad purposes. First, as we have discussed, is the utility of marketing research for *customer management*—especially, grouping customers, seeking feedback, and analyzing needs. We do not think it possible to overemphasize this aim for managing customer lifetime value. A second and complementary role for research is to support the *acquisition of new customers.* To this end, we look to research for aid in the segmentation of markets, followed by the estimation of market segment size. Within each segment, the business marketer then strives to estimate and improve market share potential and track performance against this standard. Before moving deeper into this topic, let's briefly consider the differences between business and consumer markets.

   Marketing research in business marketing is vital and often highly sophisticated, but its scale and scope are a fraction of what one sees for consumer goods. In billion dollar consumer segments of a million or two home studies of brand perception, likeability of advertising, the preferred scent of the product, and such can pay for themselves with sales gains of less than a share point. In contrast, business markets often comprise just a few dozen customer firms—and they're evaluating complex products with more dimensions of performance than deodorants or yogurt. Furthermore, save for occasional surveys and hotline calls, consumers are largely mute about their needs. In business markets, buyers and sellers often have an ongoing, explicit dialogue to discover needs, frame solution proposals, and reveal dissatisfactions. Lacking relationships in certain segments, the business marketer has access to a wealth of secondary data. Indeed, in the interest of economic development, governments collect and disseminate data on populations, products, and industries. Exhibit 5–7 highlights some of the often-used public and commercial sources.

# MARKET SEGMENTATION

This is not your first marketing class. You know that market segmentation involves partitioning the general need for a solution to a class of problems into smaller clusters involving distinct markets. These clusters are composed of buyers or potential buyers that share similar traits, buying patterns, information needs, benefits sought, psychographic profiles, product experiences, industry participation, and the like. But the purpose is not to simply slice and dice, nor to produce snappy bubble charts or tables. The segments are meaningful to the extent they are differentially responsive to different marketing programs. And a business opportunity rests in segments where our firm has an ability to serve customers better than the rest at a profit.

We like the way English author Simon Majaro emphasizes this notion of fit in his definition of segmentation: "a strategy that enables the firm to maximize the results of a given marketing effort by exploiting clearly identified strengths in relation to a submarket which is either inadequately satisfied by other [suppliers] or where the firm is particularly well placed to do an effective job."[8] This perspective provides plenty of room for creative segmentation schemes and different segmentation tools. It also recognizes that not every product is a breakthrough and that the competitive arena is rarely docile. Let's illustrate some typical segmentation approaches in business markets and highlight the opportunities of "fit" they reveal.

## Industrial Classification Systems: SIC to NAICS

The **Standard Industrial Classification (SIC) codes** were developed by the U.S. government to collect and disseminate meaningful information on different sectors of the economy. Since the 1930s the SIC system has organized the nation's economy into 10 divisions. Within each division are two-digit designations of major groups of companies, categorized on the basis of their primary output. Each major group is composed of three-digit designated industry groups, which are composed of several specific industries designated by four-digit codes.

After decades of use by business marketers to classify customers and label target markets, SIC codes have now been replaced by a new system called **NAICS** (pronounced "knacks"), the **North American Industrial Classification System.** Although trade lingo, promotional literature, and company planning documents are sure to include some SIC holdover classification, NAICS establishes a common code between the United States, Canada, and Mexico. It is compatible with the United Nations' two-digit system of industry classification, ISIC, and has been designed to include industries in services and emerging technology fields.

NAICS is based on a six-digit hierarchical code, thus allowing for finer distinctions between industries than SIC does. This finer-grained approach begins at the first level. NAICS groups the economy into 20 major sectors. Newly created sectors including Education Services (61); Health Care and Social Assistance (62); Art, Entertainment, and Recreation (71); and Accommodation and Foodservices (72) were previously lumped into the SIC division called Service Industries. Exhibits 5–8 and 5–9 contrast and detail the new codes.

As a segmentation tool, NAICS and its predecessor SIC codes help the business marketer assess the size of a particular industry for which its product is thought to have particular relevance. For example, FedEx targeted companies in SIC 5961, "Nonstore

## Exhibit 5–8
NAICS Sectors and Their Corresponding SIC Divisions

| Code | NAICS Sectors | SIC Divisions Making the Largest Contributions |
|------|---------------|-----------------------------------------------|
| 11 | Agriculture, Forestry, Fishing, and Hunting | Agriculture, Forestry, and Fishing<br>Manufacturing |
| 21 | Mining | Mineral Industries |
| 22 | Utilities | Transportation, Communication, and Utilities |
| 23 | Construction | Construction Industries |
| 31–33 | Manufacturing | Manufacturing |
| 42 | Wholesale Trade | Wholesale Trade |
| 44–45 | Retail Trade | Retail Trade<br>Wholesale Trade |
| 48–49 | Transportation | Transportation, Communication, and Utilities |
| 51 | Information | Transportation, Communication, and Utilities<br>Manufacturing<br>Service Industries |
| 52 | Finance and Insurance | Finance, Insurance, and Real Estate |
| 53 | Real Estate and Rental and Leasing | Finance, Insurance, and Real Estate<br>Service Industries |
| 54 | Professional, Scientific, and Technical Services | Service Industries |
| 55 | Management of Companies and Enterprises | Financial, Insurance, and Real Estate auxiliary establishments in all industries |
| 56 | Administrative and Support, Waste Management, and Remediation Services | Service Industries<br>Transportation, Communication, and Utilities<br>Manufacturing<br>Construction Industries |
| 61 | Education Services | Service Industries |
| 62 | Health Care and Social Assistance | Service Industries |
| 71 | Arts, Entertainment, and Recreation | Service Industries<br>Retail Trade<br>Finance, Insurance, and Real Estate |
| 72 | Accommodation and Foodservices | Retail Trade<br>Service Industries |
| 81 | Other Services (except Public Administration) | Service Industries<br>Finance, Insurance, and Real Estate |
| 92 | Public Administration | Public Administration<br>Service Industries |

SOURCE: Paul Zeisset and Mark E. Wallace, "How NAICS Will Affect Data Users," U.S. Bureau of the Census, 1997.

retailers—catalog and mail-order houses," to generate leads where it might negotiate a contract for handling some or all of its package delivery. Similarly, if your company has developed an emergency safety bath for treating chemical accidents, it is useful to know how many chemical companies might need to be equipped with such a device. Alternatively, a producer of plastic diaphragm pumps may wish to craft different sales and advertising messages for different industries. It is likely that prospects in the chemical industry are seeking corrosion resistance whereas prospects in the pharmaceutical field will need information about purity and cleanliness.[9]

**Exhibit 5–9**
Examples of NAICS Hierarchy

| | Example 1 | | Example 2 | |
|---|---|---|---|---|
| NAICS Level | NAICS Code | Description | NAICS Code | Description |
| Sector | 31–33 | Manufacturing | 51 | Information |
| Subsector | 334 | Computer and electronic product manufacturing | 513 | Broadcasting and telecommunications |
| Industry group | 3346 | Manufacturing and reproduction of magnetic and optical media | 5133 | Telecommunications |
| Industry group | 33461 | Manufacturing and reproduction of magnetic and optical media | 51332 | Wireless telecommunications carriers, except satellite |
| U.S. industry | 334611 | Reproduction of software | 513321 | Paging |

SOURCE: Paul Zeisset and Mark E. Wallace, "How NAICS Will Affect Data Users," U.S. Bureau of the Census, 1997.

# Company Characteristics

Company sales, number of employees, number of locations, degree of vertical integration, and other fairly observable traits can be powerful segmentation variables. Because of differences in service needs, buying criteria, and expertise, many business marketers classify customers on the basis of size. Often the breakdown features Fortune 500 firms, other named accounts, midsized firms (say, those with $10 million to $90 million in sales), and small businesses. It is difficult for a business marketer to dominate across the size spectrum.

# Buying Processes

Business marketers often find it productive to sort prospective customers on the basis of how they buy. Is it a new task or a rebuy? Personnel from different functional areas may participate in the decision at some firms, whereas at others participation is limited. Some prospective accounts use a bidding process; others do not.

Some buyers work with a strict "purchasing mentality," meaning that they simply seek the lowest price on tightly defined products, such as corrugated boxes, printing, or bulk chemicals. Other buyers may rely on a buying center that takes a broader view of supply in the value creation process. Perhaps packaging is not just an afterthought, but a means of ensuring quality through storage and transport, an avenue for distinguishing the brand, and part of a process that offers opportunities for efficiency gains in the use of labor and working capital (especially inventory). For a supplier with excellent sourcing capabilities and efficient operations, the first type of buyer is its bread and butter. For a supplier with a distinguished sales force of packaging expertise, the latter type of account is its mainstay.

# Benefits Sought

Most business marketers find it difficult to be all things to all customers. When customers differ in the priorities they place on specific performance dimensions, marketers must be sure to properly match their offering to the segment seeking what their product does best. An electric motor company found its low-horsepower motors had special appeal for users in regions where electricity rates were high because they provided significant savings in operating costs. Users of motors in cheap-electricity settings put stock in other performance criteria, such as durability, torque, and ease of mounting, depending on their application.

A motor manufacturer that wants to serve several segments will need a carefully conceived positioning strategy. **Positioning** is a loosely used term that generally refers to marketing efforts to secure a valued categorization in the mind of a customer. Serving customers in a segment that values economy, the product perceived to have reliability and low operating costs will have a winning position. For the customer seeking performance in extreme heat situations, a seller must establish credibility as a provider of superior cooling or high stress tolerance. Because it strains credibility that a single product can be best across the diverse criteria of several segments, we typically see multiple product lines and distribution channels reflected in multiple positioning strategies.

A major manufacturer of large-scale electrical equipment (e.g., transformers) used a sample survey of potential customers—investor-owned electrical utilities, municipalities, rural electrification cooperatives, and industrial firms that generated or distributed electrical power—to identify customer characteristics, different levels of favorability toward the company ("switchability"), and preferences for product performance dimensions, as well as beliefs about the relative strength of the manufacturer on these dimensions. So electrical equipment buyers gave importance and performance ratings on criteria such as price, appearance of the product, availability of spare parts, ease of installation, energy loss, maintenance requirements, and so on. From statistical models based on the switchability and benefits-sought data, the manufacturer was able to segment the 7,000-customer market into 12 distinct segments. Targeting the "switchables" in each segment with unique direct mail messages—emphasizing the particular performance benefits and products the analysis identified as most important—the manufacturer achieved documented sales gains of 15 percent and more, compared to markets where the positioning strategy was not applied.[10]

Finally, as competing firms grow in their understanding of a market, each adapts what it regards as apt positioning strategies. Of course, what the customers perceive, believe, and retain becomes more important than the actual symbols, messages, and media used in the positioning campaigns. Now customer perceptions of the similarities in offerings start to take on special significance in the structure of the market. Perceptual maps represent a class of tools that help to reveal customers' mental picture of the marketplace. Typically beginning with customer survey data indicating attribute ratings or the degree to which pairs of products are regarded as similar, researchers apply a mathematical algorithm that puts the products in two- or three-dimensional space in a way that has similar products in close proximity. For example, Exhibit 5–10 shows the perceptions that MBA students have of four major computer brands on six online purchasing criteria: helpful and informative, order process efficiency and accuracy, reasonable prices, good after-sale service, rapid delivery, and technical performance of the products. The perceptual map clearly shows brand D as the leader in technical performance, but a laggard in value pricing, postsale service, and delivery time. Brand C offers me-too products at value prices, but is especially well regarded for its order process. With their emphasis on price and after-sale service, brands A and B are close rivals. Where do you think the largest market segments reside on this map? How could brand C hope to compete in engineering and design applications? Why might brand D have such a difficult time matching A and B's after-sale service stan-

**Exhibit 5–10**
Perceptual maps reveal opportunities in the dimensions customers use to discriminate among products and in the gaps and clusters of competing products.

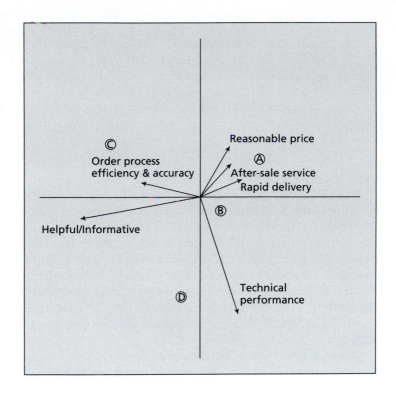

dards? And what brands (IBM, Dell, HP, and Toshiba) do you think correspond to their designates A, B, C, and D?

Marketing personnel often find value from perceptual maps because they can reveal (1) new dimensions on which customers seem to be discriminating among products, (2) clusters of competitors defined by customers, not by NAICS, and (3) opportunities for positioning products in new ways.

# Memberships and Media

Creative marketers have successfully served business market segments defined by membership in professional societies, trade associations, and even readership of a particular publication. If members of an association or professional group represent a population likely to have a significant number of potential buyers, it makes good sense to give them marketing attention.

Why not capitalize on what you know about association members in the design of your marketing program? Use the language of the particular group (e.g., Chem show attendees, Business/Professional Advertising Association members, pharmaceutical manufacturers) to convey your firm's understanding of their needs and to tout the benefits of your product measured against the member's priorities. Ads for a particular publication, direct mail copy for a specific association, and trade show materials for a defined group of attendees all reflect tailored marketing activities derived from segmentation based on memberships.

By now you should have a good sense for the assortment of variables that can be used effectively to segment business markets. We have not exhausted the possibilities. Certainly, geography, language, conformity to industry or government standards, affinity groups, usage of other products, or qualifying behaviors can be used as well. Even the simple classification of a professional title can be a powerful segmentation variable. FedEx would not send a Secretaries Day card to Joe Bagadonuts on the shipping dock, even though Joe—like many secretaries—makes the call to use FedEx.

We are certain to illustrate many of these segmentation possibilities in later chapters that discuss marketing program development and control. But before we leave the discussion of segmentation, let's take stock of the essence of a useful segmentation approach.

# SEGMENT CRITERIA

One's objective in this process is to define good market segments. Good markets are identifiable, accessible, and substantial. These criteria work well to discipline the tasks of gauging opportunities and directing marketing effort. **Identifiable** members of market segments can be enumerated and evaluated. Imagine a cardiologist who developed a healthy heart program for overworked and overweight executives. Is there a practical way to identify such individuals? The cardiologist might advertise her service and/or invite prospects to a power breakfast seminar or a free risk screening. Prospects might not be so willing to identify themselves, however, if the service were for coping with chemical addictions.

**Accessibility** means that members of a market can be reached or impacted by some directed marketing activity. American Express knew that to get companies to adopt its corporate card, an American Express sales rep had to get some time with the prospect firm's chief financial officer. Years of advertising, direct mail, and attempted sales calls still left 400 attractive but inaccessible accounts.

The ability to approach or address known prospective customers is necessary but not sufficient to make an opportunity. That market must be **substantial,** promising sufficient business to justify the efforts to serve it. Customer lifetime value is a useful criterion in an assessment of a target market. Unfortunately, a firm's history with its current customers may provide very little basis for estimating the CLV of customers from entirely new markets.

# MARKET ASSESSMENT TOOLS

Substantial markets can be revealed by a number of estimation techniques. One very powerful approach is the use of scenarios. **Scenarios** comprise a forecasting technique that requires managers to write explicit anticipated futures and articulate the chains of events that would need to occur to make the future happen. For example, Royal Dutch Shell tuned its supply strategy when its scenario process in 1973 found no compelling reasons for Arab states to increase their crude oil production.[11] Furthermore, one of this book's authors helped an environmental management company determine the market for certain types of training. The task involved getting accurate counts of employees in different industries who handled hazardous and toxic materials, plus an assessment of the likelihood of new government regulations that—by fiat or new economic sanctions—would impact the training demand.

A related approach involves hard thinking and analysis of how the product fits into the value-added process. This approach is sometimes called the **buildup approach** or **factoring.** Market estimates by this approach come from building up the materials or

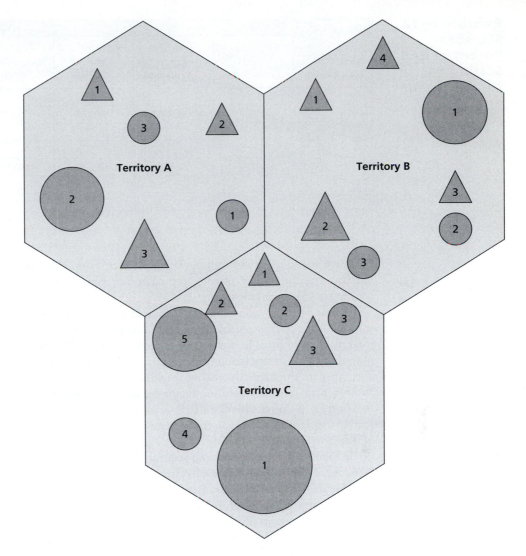

parts units needed in a specific application or from specific accounts. For example, potential demand for a surgical staple designed for closing Caesarian sections can be estimated from a count of the average number of staples needed to close a typical C-section, times the number of C-sections performed in different countries. Projections in each country are apt to show different trends, based on differences in hospital protocols, fertility patterns, and population distributions.

To illustrate how factoring can be combined with segmentation tools for market estimation, we outline a general approach for quota setting or marketing effort management. Exhibit 5–11 represents the sales territories for Tetragon, a fictitious regional media company in the Southwest. This analysis considers two classes of prospective advertising customers for its daily newspapers and TV stations—triangles and circles. You could regard them as specialty furniture stores and cosmetic surgery centers or fine-dining restaurants and optometry centers if you wish. We have limited the target segments to two for simplicity and drawn the size of each triangle or circle to be

**Exhibit 5–12**
Market
Potential and
Scaling Factor
for Newspaper
and TV
Advertising

| | A | B | C | D | E |
|---|---|---|---|---|---|
| Classification | Total Firms | Total Employees | Total Ad $ (000) | Scaling Factor (000) | Tetragon Market Share in Segments |
| △ | 1,235 | 2,395 | $6,370 | $2.66 | 11% |
| | | | | | |
| ○ | | | | | |
| | 376 | 12,854 | $7,510 | $0.58 | 7% |
| | | | | | |
| | | | | | |

proportional to its size in number of employees. From this figure it should not be too hard to envision other prospective customer types, perhaps represented by other geometric shapes or colors.

Exhibit 5–12 provides data and a foundational procedure for evaluating the opportunity in each territory. Using secondary data sources such as the census we can find the total number of firms in each category (column A) and the total number of people employed in the industry (column B). From a trade association or a sample survey, we can also estimate the total advertising spending by each category of business (column C). We can now calculate a scaling factor for ad spending per employee in each category (column D). Presume firm size affects adverting spending—or after empirical testing—the scaling factor allows Tetragon to estimate the advertising potential in prospective clients of different size.

In Exhibit 5-13 we apply the scaling factor to the prospective advertisers in each territory. That is, in Territory A, Triangle 1 has 20 employees (column B, data obtainable from Dun and Bradstreet (D&B) or infoUSA) and at the ad spending per employee rate determined from Exhibit 5–11 ($2,660 plugged into column C), Triangle 1 represents $53,000/year in potential revenue to Tetragon (column D). This potential can be compared to a "par" level of sales, determined by taking Tetragon's market share times the account potential (column E). We can now consider Tetragon's current ad sales to each account (column F) expressed as a percent of par (column G). Total potential and sales against par can be evaluated also. This type of analysis can help prioritize markets, guide the establishment of sales quotas, and support decisions to add or subtract marketing resources (e.g., direct mail or sales reps) in the territories. In this case, it looks like Territory C needs help, especially in cracking some of that potential to par in Triangle 3, and in penetrating Circle$_1$. Combined with mapping software and accounts defined in latitude and longitude, new territories can be defined as well.[12]

The same basic approach can be applied using survey responses from prospects (e.g., responses to "What volume of beer do you plan to brew in the coming years?" could help in estimating demand for water, yeast, and hops) or from members of the sales force (e.g., "What accounts are apt to replace their copiers in the next 12 months?")

Likewise, the volume of certain materials, logistical services, or MRO (maintenance, repair and operating) goods can be compared to finished products output in a

**Exhibit 5–13**
Tetragon Territory Analysis

| A | B | C | D | E | F | G |
|---|---|---|---|---|---|---|
| Accounts by Territory | Employees | Scaling Factor (000) | Potential (000) | Par Sales' (Ave. Share × Potential) | Tetragon Sales (000) | Penetration to Par |
| **Territory A** | | | | | | |
| Triangle 1 | 20 | $2.66 | $53 | $6 | $6.10 | 104% |
| Triangle 2 | 40 | $2.66 | $106 | $12 | $0.00 | 0% |
| Triangle 3 | 120 | $2.66 | $319 | $35 | $45.40 | 129% |
| Circle 1 | 10 | $0.58 | $6 | $0 | $0.00 | 0% |
| Circle 2 | 200 | $0.58 | $116 | $8 | $10.10 | 124% |
| Circle 3 | 40 | $0.58 | $23 | $2 | $1.40 | 86% |
| Total | | | $623 | $63 | $63.00 | 100% |
| **Territory B** | | | | | | |
| Triangle 1 | 50 | $2.66 | $133 | $15 | $8.40 | 57% |
| Triangle 2 | 140 | $2.66 | $372 | $41 | $6.70 | 16% |
| Triangle 3 | 80 | $2.66 | $213 | $23 | $0.00 | 0% |
| Triangle 4 | 30 | $2.66 | $80 | $9 | $0.00 | 0% |
| Circle 1 | 250 | $0.58 | $145 | $10 | $12.30 | 121% |
| Circle 2 | 40 | $0.58 | $23 | $2 | $0.00 | 0% |
| Circle 3 | 60 | $0.58 | $35 | $2 | $2.20 | 90% |
| Total | | | $1,001 | $102 | $29.60 | 29% |
| **Territory C** | | | | | | |
| Triangle 1 | 50 | $2.66 | $133 | $15 | $0.00 | 0% |
| Triangle 2 | 70 | $2.66 | $186 | $20 | $20.50 | 100% |
| Triangle 3 | 280 | $2.66 | $745 | $82 | $55.50 | 68% |
| Circle 1 | 600 | $0.58 | $348 | $24 | $0.00 | 0% |
| Circle 2 | 50 | $0.58 | $29 | $2 | $0.00 | 0% |
| Circle 3 | 30 | $0.58 | $17 | $1 | $0.40 | 33% |
| Circle 4 | 80 | $0.58 | $46 | $3 | $0.50 | 15% |
| Circle 5 | 120 | $0.58 | $70 | $5 | $5.90 | 121% |
| Total | | | $1,574 | $152 | $82.80 | 54% |

statistical series. A **statistical series** is an estimation technique that uses the correlation between demand and some other set of economic activities to yield a forecast. For example, Exhibit 5–14 plots a hypothetical relationship between gypsum sales and housing starts in a metro market. The top graph shows a fairly consistent trend in housing starts. The bottom graph shows a good, but not perfect, association between housing starts and drywall sales; their correlation is .93. To forecast sales, the linear relationship between housing starts and drywall sales can be applied in the bottom of the exhibit using projected housing starts for the next four years as the $x$ values.

**Exhibit 5–14**

Using a Statistical Series to Estimate the Drywall Market in S. Metro

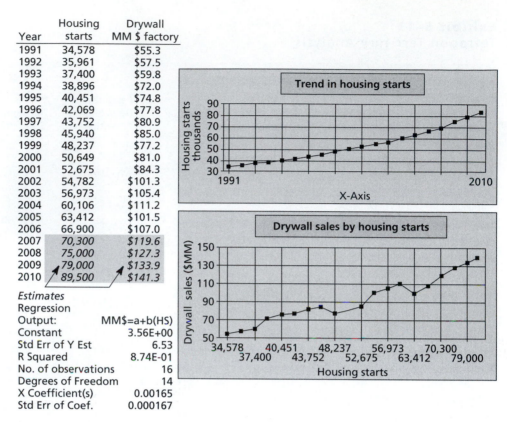

| Year | Housing starts | Drywall MM $ factory |
|------|------|------|
| 1991 | 34,578 | $55.3 |
| 1992 | 35,961 | $57.5 |
| 1993 | 37,400 | $59.8 |
| 1994 | 38,896 | $72.0 |
| 1995 | 40,451 | $74.8 |
| 1996 | 42,069 | $77.8 |
| 1997 | 43,752 | $80.9 |
| 1998 | 45,940 | $85.0 |
| 1999 | 48,237 | $77.2 |
| 2000 | 50,649 | $81.0 |
| 2001 | 52,675 | $84.3 |
| 2002 | 54,782 | $101.3 |
| 2003 | 56,973 | $105.4 |
| 2004 | 60,106 | $111.2 |
| 2005 | 63,412 | $101.5 |
| 2006 | 66,900 | $107.0 |
| 2007 | *70,300* | *$119.6* |
| 2008 | *75,000* | *$127.3* |
| 2009 | *79,000* | *$133.9* |
| 2010 | *89,500* | *$141.3* |

*Estimates*

| Regression Output: | MM\$=a+b(HS) |
|------|------|
| Constant | 3.56E+00 |
| Std Err of Y Est | 6.53 |
| R Squared | 8.74E-01 |
| No. of observations | 16 |
| Degrees of Freedom | 14 |
| X Coefficient(s) | 0.00165 |
| Std Err of Coef. | 0.000167 |

# MARKET SHARE ESTIMATION

The business marketer has segmented the market and gauged the size of particular segments. Now looms the sometimes daunting task of estimating share. What percentage of the market can our company obtain? One illuminating way to view this problem is to account for the handful of key impediments to buying the product in a share development tree. To begin, no one can buy a product about which they have no information. Logically, purchase requires that the buyer view the product favorably, regard the price as acceptable, and have some reasonable degree of access to the product. When we chart these dichotomous buying criteria in Exhibit 5–15 and plug in market research estimates for each criterion, we have a tree diagram. If we multiply the percentages in the darkened share development path, we get a market share index. Comparing that path to the bottom tree, indicating the desired level of response on each criterion, we establish some standards for performance evaluation and opportunity evaluation. Some marketers use the ratio of the *actual* market share index to the *potential* market share index to reveal a share development index—the extent to which actual share matches up to estimated potential. Of course, the gaps between actual and desired responses on each criterion have rich diagnostic value.[13]

The actual market share may differ from this market share index, but it is often quite close and the share development tree yields insights into lost market share opportunity. Furthermore, it allows us to assess the impact of changes on different marketing variables, perhaps to boost awareness via advertising or make the product more available through Internet distribution. This motivates our attention to the topics of strategic planning and marketing programming in the coming chapters.

**Exhibit 5–15**
Market Share Development Tree

| Communication Strategies | Product Management | Pricing | Distribution | | Market Share Index | |
|---|---|---|---|---|---|---|
| | | | | | | |
| *Current Levels* | | | | | | |
| | | | | | 0.400 | Unaware |
| Awareness? No = .40 | | | | | 0.390 | Aware but unattracted |
| Yes = .60 | Like product benefits? No = .65 | | | | 0.084 | Like but price too high |
| | Yes = .35 | Acceptable price? No = .4 | | | 0.038 | Like and accept but unavailable |
| | | Yes = .6 | Supplies available? | | 0.088 | Current share index |
| | | | Yes = .7 | | 1.000 | |
| Current Share Index = .60 × .35 × .60 × .70 = 0.088 | | | | | | |
| | | | | | | |
| *Desired Responses* | | | | | | |
| Awareness? No = .30 | | | | | 0.300 | |
| Yes = .70 | Like product benefits? No = .45 | | | | 0.315 | |
| | Yes = .55 | Acceptable price? No = .2 | | | 0.077 | |
| | | Yes = .8 | Supplies available? No = .1 | | 0.031 | |
| | | | Yes = .9 | | 0.278 | |
| | | | | | 1.000 | |
| Desired Share Index = .70 × .55 × .80 × .90 = .278 | | | | | | |
| | | | | | | |
| **Share Development Index** = | $\dfrac{0.088}{0.278}$ = 0.32 | | | | | |

# Summary

This chapter has emphasized the value of current customers as a treasure trove of opportunity. Because not all customers are created equal, it makes sense to develop distinct programs for different accounts and groups of customers. Best customers deserve special attention and marketing effort to retain and expand their purchase volume. Their familiarity with and trust of the company often make current customers a rich market for new products. And high-quality working relationships with select accounts often provide strategic connections to other opportunities in the business environment.

We highlighted the data warehouse in a brief overview of tools for finding opportunities among current accounts. The customer database is structured to support account management activities with best customers as well as targeted communications and programs for specific customer clusters. It also supports customer research by identifying potential focus group and sample survey participants.

Focus groups are a loosely structured interview of 6 to 12 individuals brought together at one location. A skilled moderator guides the participants in a rather free-flowing discussion of the specified topics. Often repeated in different locations with new participants, focus groups are an excellent means of exploring customer motivations and product-related behaviors, generating ideas, and provoking new questions about opportunities.

Surveys also belong in the customer research toolbox. The one-on-one field interview can be a rich source of information—even a strong rival to focus groups for finding customer needs. Mail surveys can be quite detailed and conducted at low cost. But even with all the tricks for garnering high response rates, responses may come slowly, or from the wrong informant, or never at all. The phone solves the turnaround problem, but often at a cost of frequent callbacks and shortened questionnaires.

The tools of customer research can be applied to the search for new markets, usually as complements to secondary market information from various trade and government sources. Unfortunately, prospective customers seldom participate to the same degree as current customers, making nonresponse a vexing issue for statistical estimation.

We affirmed the tendency of an increasing number of companies to treat customer acquisition as an investment. We have long given lip service to the notion that customers are a vital asset for the firm, but only recently have significant numbers of businesses begun to put a dollar value on the worth of the asset. Customer lifetime value (CLV) is a statistical estimate of the net present value of the cash flow from an account or group of accounts. CLV is not a hard number to be mechanically applied to the quest for new customers that look like current money-making accounts. CLV is better regarded as a perspective and tool involving significant judgment.

To evaluate opportunities to acquire new customers, it is critical to segment the market in a judicious manner that enables the matching of company strengths to unmet or underserved customer needs. Business markets can often be segmented meaningfully using industrial classification systems. SIC and the NAICS codes are hierarchically structured classifications of businesses based on their principal output, with 20 two-digit sectors plus four-digit industry groups and six-digit U.S. industries.

The chapter demonstrated how business markets can be segmented on the basis of organizational buying processes, benefits sought, and memberships. We highlighted the role of segmentation for positioning strategies and previewed the means of segmenting according to the prospective customer's location, language, personal characteristics, business behaviors, usage of other products, and more.

As we consider potential market segments, we should recognize that opportunity is related to three criteria: Members of the segment must be identifiable, accessible, and substantial. Segments can be substantiated by a variety of analytical tools. We highlighted the utility of scenarios, the buildup or factoring approach, and statistical series for segment evaluation.

## Key Terms

accessible (segment members)

account retention

buildup approach

customer lifetime value (CLV)

data mining

data warehousing

decile report

empathic dialogue

factoring

focus group

identifiable (segment members)

North American Industrial Classification System (NAICS)

positioning

sample surveys

scenarios

Standard Industrial Classification (SIC) codes

statistical series

substantial (segment potential)

sugging

## Discussion Questions

1. NCR's Teradata division is the market leader in data warehousing systems, with $1.5 billion in revenue in 2006 and annual sales gains of 7 to 9 percent predicted. Because many companies have determined that consolidating data into a large, single system can make them smarter and more nimble, prospects for Teradata, seem bright. But now HP has stepped up product development to challenge Teradata and in April 2007 introduced Neoview. At a price to HP customers of $.6 to

$15 million, Neoview uses an array of HP servers, storage devices, and software to provide on-demand number crunching for airlines, hotels, banks, and retail chains. To what extent does a rival's revenue growth represent an opportunity for one's own firm?

2. A small local graphics firm uses Quicksilver, a downtown courier service, to send art and proofs to clients, printers, and photographers in the conduct of its business. Sketch a framework for estimating the lifetime value of this account to Quicksilver.

3. Assess the utility of your university's information system to provide decile reports, decile profiles, and the like to support marketing efforts that maximize customer value and support the quest for look-alikes.

4. The university president has now indicated that all the student information management functions will be outsourced. How does a potential IT service firm differ from Quicksilver in its estimate of the CLV from its customer, the university?

5. The Holden brothers were experienced in travel and event promotions and explored the opportunity to sell promotional literature—especially maps—to chambers of commerce. They planned to sell advertisements in the literature to area businesses, including chamber members, returning a portion of the ad revenue to the chamber of commerce client organization. What would be some of the key impediments to testing this concept in two or three focus groups? What three objectives would motivate a telephone survey of chambers of commerce from the World Directory?

6. Write a scenario depicting the campus recruiting process by AT&T or Shell Oil company in the year 2010. Now, what enabling conditions must be met for this scenario to occur? What business opportunities become manifest to (a) campus career development and placement centers, (b) image makers, (c) resume consultants, and (d) multimedia conferencing?

7. Your company has just developed a polymer to extend the life of asphalt by 40 percent. The polymer is added in the manufacturing process and represents just .01 percent of the asphalt mass. Define the market opportunity for this product on the criteria of being identifiable, accessible, and substantial.

8. When a financial institution switches from one phone or computer system to another, the original supplier is rightly apt to regard the account as lost for good. Because the actual switch had to overcome significant costs—investments in equipment, habits, and the painful set-up period for the new systems—the original supplier is out in the cold, with little chance of ever returning to favor. For these types of accounts, lifetime value gets a highly deserved focus from vendors. It is an effective motivation for quality, logistical efficiency, and responsiveness because it is highly sensitive to the retention rate. Plot the eight-year CLV for an account that nets your firm $40,000 per year as its annual retention probability moves from 0.5 to 0.9.

9. You have invented and contracted the manufacture of a lightweight parts container that can be reused hundreds of times. Your research into global experiences with returnable parts containers indicates that government and industry in many countries are paying close attention to Germany, where returnable containers have been mandated. Meanwhile, voluntary use has expanded in tightly integrated firms where economic efficiency gains have been experienced. Develop a segmentation framework for your product.

10. What cautions would you issue to the expansion-minded distributor from Chicago thinking about planting a drywall warehouse in the market described in

Exhibit 5–14? He has used the exhibit's statistical model to predict sales (and make cash flow analysis) over the next 10 years.

11. Biomedical researchers at a Midwest medical school noted that jaundice is seen in approximately 60 percent of infants. Jaundice indicates an excessive accumulation of bilirubin, a breakdown product of hemoglobin, which can cause a neural dysfunction called kernicterus. To quickly diagnose this condition in neonates, the researchers developed the Belipen—a device utilizing spectrography and an ergonomic design that allows one-handed application of the test for belirubin. A key benefit from spectrography is for dark-skinned infants—a submarket in which belirubin cannot be measured by the common transcutaneous procedure. Is this an opportunity? How would you assess the potential of this device?

# Cases

### Case 5.1   Gleason Printing

Amy Morton is marketing manager at Gleason Printing. For nearly seven months she has been researching the printing needs at the Metro Alliance for Wellness, a consortium of hospitals and therapy centers in Uniopolis. Amy figures that, excluding forms and billing, Metro contracts for about $800,000 in commercial printing business each year. Granted, some of the jobs involve special imaging or sizing that doesn't match Gleason's printing capabilities. But there's about $600,000 in business that Gleason could do well. It's been rumored for some time that Metro is looking for a printing supplier to get involved in its internal operations, setting up a communications network for electronically transferring images and text—primarily for shared creative input and rough copy checking—that would enable even more rapid and efficient contact with its various stakeholders. Indeed, Metro's CEO often appears on the lecture circuit talking about harnessing technology, the efficacy of the "virtual organization," and the need for the modern enterprise to "negotiate favorable terms" with *all* its stakeholders.

Morton has also researched the systems and intranet parameters that Metro needs for this vision. Assuming Metro bought all the hardware, any printer in on the setup would have to invest approximately $400,000 in installation, training, and testing—and, frankly, the numbers could well be twice that estimate. Morton was grateful for Metro's enthusiastic response to her proposal for some "in-context research," which basically would be a chance to live with Metro systems and personnel to better understand the issues and activities at Metro. Still, she needs to review what might come from the research—she is just not sure if Gleason should seek the business.

### Case 5.2   Hi-Test Tests the Market

HiTest sells industrial safety glasses and goggles. Many companies make central purchases to provide their new hires with glasses. Employees who lose or break their glasses must repurchase from company supplies. HiTest has a professional sales force that has put the company in the number two position in this large company segment.

To improve its position among small firms—which don't have the purchasing power to justify a sales call—HiTest has begun a catalog operation. The table on page 153 summarizes its initial experiment in the business. HiTest rented business lists in what it thought were three promising market segments: SIC 7538 (auto repairs), 1541 (building construction), and 8071 (biological/pathological labs). Anxious to build its own house list with mail-responsive buyers, the management team wanted to test the clout of a first-time buyer incentive. They came up with a high-quality LED flashlight. With a retail value of about $30, in quantity HiTest purchased the lights for $7 each. Buyers could choose between two sizes—one for home, the other for auto—and received the light as a free gift with their initial order if it totaled $60 or more. (For $60 one might buy five low-priced glasses, or a top-of-the-line pair. Specialty goggles could run higher.) The results below show the total gross profit on purchases from resultant number of customers in each cell of the experiment.

| Gift with Order? | List (Segment) | | |
| --- | --- | --- | --- |
| | SIC 7538 Auto repair (*n* = 3,000/cell) | SIC 1541 Bldg. Construct. (*n* = 2,000/cell) | SIC 8071 Bio-Path Labs (*n* = 1,000/cell) |
| Yes ----> | $6,400/155 orders *154 flashlights* | $3,780/92 orders *92 flashlights* | $2,580/62 orders *61 flashlights* |
| No -----> | $1,625/61 orders | $ 850/30 orders | $930/31 orders |

1. Is the flashlight giveaway a winner?
2. What list performs best?
3. If HiTest can mail 40,000 catalogs next period, to whom should they be mailed, and what profit impact can HiTest expect if the catalog design, printing, and mailing cost $25,000?

# Additional Readings

Barclay, Donald W., and Michael J. Ryan. "Microsegmentation in Business Markets: Incorporating Buyer Characteristics and Decision-Oriented Determinants." *Journal of Business-to-Business Marketing* 2 (1996), pp. 3–35.

Blattberg, Robert C., Gary Getz, and Jacquelyn S. Thomas. *Customer Equity: Building and Managing Relationships as Valuable Assets.* Boston: Harvard Business School Press, 2001.

Data Warehouse Information Center, http://www.dwinfocenter.org/.

Deutskens, Elisabeth, Ad de Jong, and Ko de Ruyter. "Comparing the Generalizability of Online and Mail Surveys in Cross-National Service Quality Research." *Marketing Letters* 17, no. 2 (2006), pp. 119–36.

Dwyer, F. Robert. "Customer Lifetime Valuation to Support Marketing Decision Making." *Journal of Direct Marketing* 11 (Autumn 1997), pp. 6–13.

Gensch, Dennis H. "Targeting the Switchable Industrial Customer." *Marketing Science* 3 (Winter 1984), pp. 41–54.

Greenyer, Andrew. "Measurable Marketing: A Review of Developments in Marketing's Measurability." *Journal of Business and Industrial Marketing* 24, no. 4 (2006).

Gupta, Sunil, and Donald Lehmann. *Managing Customers as Investments.* Upper Saddle River, NJ: Wharton School Publishing, 2005.

Gupta, Sunil, Donald R. Lehmann, and Jennifer Ames Stuart. "Valuing Customers." *Journal of Marketing Research* 41 (February 2004), pp. 7–18.

Han, Jiawei, and Micheline Kamber. *Data Mining: Concepts and Techniques*. San Francisco: Morgan Kaufmann Publishers, 2000.

Hogan, John E., Katherine N. Lemon, and Libai Barak. "What Is the True Value of a Lost Customer?" *Journal of Service Research* 5 (February 2003), pp. 196–208.

Lockett, Andy, and Ian Blackman. "Conducting Marketing Research Using the Internet: The Case of Xenon Laboratories." *Journal of Business & Industrial Marketing* 19, no. 3 (2004), pp. 178–87.

McQuarrie, Edward F. "Taking a Road Trip: Customer Visits Help Companies Recharge Relationships and Pass Competitors." *Marketing Management* 3 (April 1995), pp. 8–21.

Rosenfield, James R. "My Life as a Customer, or Why 'CRM' Is the Biggest Hoax in Business." *Direct Marketing* (July 2001), pp. 16–22.

Roy, Abhijit, and Paul D. Berger. "Business-to-Business Approaches to Marketing to and through Associations: A Descriptive Analysis and Research Issues." *Journal of Business-to-Business Research* 12 no. 3 (2005).

Ulaga, Wolfgang, and Andreas Eggert. "Value-Based Differentiation in Business Relationships: Gaining and Sustaining Key Supplier Status." *Journal of Marketing* 70 (January 2006), pp. 1199–136.

Venkatesan, Rajkumar, and V. Kumar. "A Customer Lifetime Value Framework for Customer Selection and Resource Allocation Strategy." *Journal of Marketing* 68 (October 2004), pp. 106–125.

Witten, Ian H., and Eibe Frank. *Data Mining: Practical machine Learning Tools and techniques*. San Francisco: Morgan Kaufmann Publishers, 2005.

# Chapter 6

## Marketing Strategy

### DELL

Michael Dell was already taking apart computers when he was 15, but enrolled at the University of Texas with aspirations of becoming a doctor. Medical school was put on indefinite hold when Dell started "PCs Unlimited" in 1984 at the age of 19. With start-up funds totaling $1,000, he began assembling computers in a small apartment, using standard parts. Instead of selling through computer dealers—who really weren't too interested in adding a line of new PCs from this unknown brand—Dell used a variety of quick-print fliers and catalogs to sell directly to users at a very low cost. Furthermore, from phone and mail orders, Dell allowed customers to specify the particular features of their computer! ●

In 1988 the company name was changed to Dell Computer Corporation and an initial public offering raised $80 million. Dell continued to sell directly to users as the PC market began to mature and purchasers with more experience and sophistication began to upgrade. Dell now honed its ability to customize while pressing relentlessly for efficiency and low prices. In 1996 Dell began to harness—and develop—the role of the Internet as a marketing tool. Telephone sales were instrumental for initial orders from business, but most accounts migrated to purchase additional machines online. ●

This downstream strategy for efficient customer management using information technology had its counterpart upstream. Dell managed its supply chain to allow assembly with minimal inventory investment! While rivals were striving for efficient manufacturing at 10 to 15 inventory turns, Dell worked at 40! This meant Dell could give good value and react nimbly to changes in technology and market preferences. ●

Gateway was actually the first company to sell computers online, but founder Ted Waitt stumbled in the late 1990s by opening a chain of Gateway Country stores. With cow-spotted boxes and a heavy burden of overhead, Gateway slipped behind market leaders—Compaq, HP, and Dell. ●

As Dell's market share and operating margins continued to grow, IBM sold its PC business to Lenovo and HP acquired Compaq, in part, to regain leadership in share. Distracted by the challenge of merging two corporate cultures and slammed by a price war sparked by Dell's efficiency, HP's market leadership was short lived. With comparatively little spending in R&D and the field's low-cost position, Dell played the game only it could win. ●

Dell's position today is not so rosy. Its foray into printers has been lackluster, some customers report poor service, growth has stalled, and HP has closed the sales gap. Dell announced in May 2007 that it would sell computers bundled with accessories through Wal-Mart stores. "The Direct Model was a real revolution in the computer industry, but it's not a religion," Michael Dell explained to reporters in Toronto.[1] ●

## LEARNING OBJECTIVES

In this chapter, we want to examine how firms in business markets develop the vision and plans to make major initiatives with long-term impact. In the process, you will learn to think more strategically. In military jargon a strategy involves the science and art of conducting a campaign—achieving some end—on a broad scale. We distinguish strategy from tactics on the basis of scope, the magnitude of resources applied, and the duration of impact or consequences. Tactical decisions occupy the narrow, limited, and short-run poles of these dimensions.

In an important departure from the military metaphor, business strategy seldom concludes with a vanquished "enemy." In product markets around the world, new demands from users and adaptive competitors will continue to bring new strategic challenges. A goal in this chapter will be to offer ideas for enabling the organization to learn and adapt.

*After reading this chapter, you should be able to*

- Describe the key elements of a business strategy.
- Conduct a SWOT analysis of an organization with which you are familiar.
- Analyze the structure of competition, considering five forces.
- Give an example of the fleeting nature of competitive advantage.
- Outline firm characteristics that should enable learning and the creation of dynamic strategies.

# WHY A STRATEGY?

With just a small number of passengers and a worn-out cabin crew, the mischievous pilot came on the PA: "Ladies and gentlemen, this is your captain speaking. I have a bit of bad news for you tonight. Our navigation equipment and radio have cut out on us. We don't know where we are. On the brighter side, folks, we're making very good time."

It is easy for any organization to get so occupied with day-to-day operations that it buries its sense of identity and loses touch with where it is headed. Every member of the crew seems busy, but not even the pilot knows if the ship is on course. We suspect you have fallen into this trap more than once yourself. Perhaps your preoccupation with class assignments and midterms—not to mention your job or family pressures—have kept you from taking the school's career search workshop or charting your own plan to land a good entry-level position. Unless we give some time to reflecting on what we are about, what we want to achieve, and what matters on the way to those goals, we face a very good chance of sinking under the weight of urgent but increasingly unimportant activities. Furthermore, once we have settled and formally stated what we want to achieve and become, we need a plan to reach the desired ends.

# ELEMENTS OF BUSINESS STRATEGY

The word *strategy* has become commonplace. Straining the military metaphor reviewed in the opening of the chapter, you have probably heard the term used to describe plans to bring world peace, revitalize a downtown business district, halve the high school dropout rate, build a nest egg for retirement, plan a vacation, complete a major class assignment, or even get through Friday afternoon traffic. But we are talking about a *business strategy* in this chapter. We want to be sure we share the same understanding of what it actually is. A business strategy should develop or reiterate a formal mission statement—which we will discuss later in the chapter—and address four fundamental issues—which we take up now.[2]

## Product Markets

*What markets do we serve with what products?* To replay some of the essentials from Chapter 5, no company has the luxury of being able to serve every segment of potential customers. We have to consider how well equipped we are to serve different groups, relative to the strength of our competition in those segments. The breadth of our product line is motivated by the diversity of preferences in the market, but simultaneously constrained by production and operational economies, by managerial and marketing complexities, and by limited financial resources. In large part, the products we offer to particular markets define the focus and direction of our company.

The implications of market served are vivid in the airlines, where Southwest Air concentrates on low-price, no-frills flights between carefully selected pairs of cities. Meanwhile, USAirways and others emphasizing larger coverage via hub-and-spoke strategies have to emphasize service and connections.

Perhaps even more dramatic is the strategic significance of market selection in the computer field. For example, Cray Research, Inc., has concentrated on building supercomputers for research-intensive applications; NCR Corporation's Teradata division emphasizes parallel processing machines that can be bundled and used to manage large marketing and financial databases. Digital opted not to offer machines to the growing personal computer market in the 1980s. IBM offers a full line of computers, servers, and peripherals, but has achieved enviable growth and profitability in IT consulting and services.

**Exhibit 6–1**
Product
Market
Growth
Opportunities

|  | Present products | New products |
|---|---|---|
| **Present markets** | Market penetration | Product development |
| **New markets** | Market development | Diversification |

SOURCE: Reprinted from Igor Ansoff, *The New Corporate Strategy* (1988), p. 83, with the permission of the copyright © owner, John Wiley & Sons, Inc.

Exhibit 6–1 reveals another important and more dynamic way to consider the products and markets served. This graphic highlights the basic means by which an organization can grow. There are only four. A firm can seek greater **market penetration**—that is, endeavor to gain a larger share of the market in which it currently competes with its existing products. Hertz freshens its advertising and keeps its service levels high in an effort to raise its share of business car rental.

Alternatively, a firm may pursue **product development,** trying to serve customers in markets where it already has a presence with a new array of products. Corporate uniform leader, Cintas, has added entrance mats and janitorial supplies as cross-selling products to its uniform business over the years and has recently launched a new business called Xpect that delivers first aid kits, training, and safety services.

**Market development** is the counterpart: Current products are taken to new markets. Traditional clothing cataloger, Lands' End, received affirmation from the stock market in 2000 when it began to target business markets, thereby becoming a Cintas rival in corporate identity uniforms. Ground Heaters, now a Michigan-based subsidiary of Wagner (Germany), began offering its system of fluid-filled hoses, pumps, and blankets to eliminate frost and allow construction to continue during the winter. The system has found new applications around the world, especially for concrete curing in tilt-up warehouse construction.

Lastly, an enterprise may pursue **diversification,** an aim to serve new markets with new products, just as BBI added a management consulting service to its Burke Institute seminars and BASES new-product testing repertoire in order to broaden its account base as well as deepen its relationship with each client.

DuPont provides another clear example of diversification. Active in many product markets, DuPont competencies reside in research and managerial prowess. In 2006 the company organized nearly 100 business units into 11 industry groups. Three units yielded sales levels near the $6 billion level: Coatings and Color Technologies, Safety and Protection, and Agriculture and Nutrition. Importantly, at $1.1 billion Safety and Protection was more than twice as profitable as Agriculture and Nutrition.

# Relationships

Of course, strategic alliances and partnerships must be included as key facets of the product market selection component of strategy. We have already shown how new products can be developed effectively, with fast cycle times, in collaborations with customers and suppliers. Alliances for new product development enable the firm to access technology and other types of resources that would be quite difficult to acquire or grow entirely within a single firm. At the same time, large financial, physical, and personnel commitments—as well as the expected payoffs in market access or new products—heighten the significance of managing such relationships effectively.[3] We should note, too, the popular phenomenon of alliances with competitors. For Example, General

Motors has explored entering into alliances with Nissan and Renault for shared product development and manufacturing.[4] Certainly, competitors make promising partners because they know the stakes of new product development and share an understanding of the markets and the language of the industry. But a lack of trust and poor safeguards on proprietary knowledge often thwart the effectiveness of such alliances.

We know from our earlier chapters that partners can also play a strategic role in supply strategy, distribution functions, research and development, and more. Because firms must negotiate favorable terms of exchange with several varied partners, the portfolio of interfirm relationships takes on strategic importance.

# Resources

Financial and other resource considerations lead up to the next key question: *What level of investment in the product market?* We may be trying to convert the business to cash by selling off assets or selling the whole operation. Indeed, a family business with no off-spring willing to run it when Mom and Pop retire may follow this *divestment* strategy.

On the other hand, significant investment will be needed if the firm is seeking to enter and secure a footing in new markets or grow its share in a mature market. To make good on its promise to make "the fastest chips in the newest applications," Intel spent $22.1 billion on R&D from 2001 to 2005.

Between these poles a firm might make only the necessary investments to maintain the current position or investments—even forgoing maintenance—to bleed the life out of the firm. In your very neighborhood there is apt to be an aging urban school, a struggling printing business, or a small and dingy office supply store down the street from Staples. A "milking" strategy certainly has its place.

# Objectives and Plans

A business strategy also has to develop *the detailed aims and action plans for the functional areas.* A host of questions must be addressed in this portion of a strategy. Will special emphasis be given logistics for customer service or will the firm decentralize manufacturing to provide short supply linkages to key customers? Will the firm need a strong advertising campaign or will it need to support distributor activities that play key roles in product differentiation? How important is supply management, relative to other facets of the value creation process? How can the sales, service, and operations people at the branches be encouraged to work as a team?

In many markets, careful analytical attention and planning are given to the product line—its scope, composition by functional feature and durability, horizontal and vertical connectivity, price, and so on. A computer company must consider the relationship of each model to the others it markets. What is the positioning strategy for each model and the array of accessories and peripherals? Engineering, purchasing, manufacturing, and logistics must collaborate in the formulation of supporting goals and activities.

The growing interconnectivity in today's information environment has posed new challenges for computer makers. For the small and midsized firms that want network services, manufacturers are relying more heavily on their value-added resellers (VARs). But at least two distinct action plans are evident. The approach used by HP favors Internet and/or intranet technology to provide technical and strategic support to a broad base of VARs. The other approach, exemplified in moves by IBM and Apple, provides increased service (e.g., lead generation, training) and incentives for an elite group of VARs.[5]

Of course, the remainder of the marketing mix must also be tightly formulated. Advertising and distribution strategies must be worked out to support the intended positioning and product line strategies. The roles of the sales force with respect to each product and customer group (e.g., end user category or type of reseller) need to fit with the advertising and telephone marketing strategies. Also, pricing strategies need to be in harmony with the advertising, selling, distribution, and manufacturing strategies.

# Additional Facets of Strategy for a Stable of Businesses

Organizations that are composed of multiple businesses—GE, North American Rockwell, American Express, Grainger, and many others—have at least two other significant components to their strategy. They need to resolve the problem of how to allocate resources strategically to the different business units. They must also manage the mix of businesses to achieve positive outcomes from the intersecting operations, resources, and markets among the businesses.

## Resource Allocation

The assignments of key people, teams, and tasks to different facilities or plants need to be worked out. Financial resources—both internally generated funds and external capital—will seldom be sufficient to meet the requests of every line manager. "Projects" must be sorted and evaluated on different criteria in the firm: How risky is each of these endeavors? What return on investment will each yield? Is the venture consistent with the goals and aspirations of the company? Can the proposals develop new and relevant skill sets? Does the proposal access new and significant markets? Is the proposal so bold as to imagine we can change the rules of the game in our favor?[6]

Business managers make a strong pitch for their projects to their counterparts in other divisions as well as to corporate-level decision makers. In turn, the corporate-level executives decide to invest in the set of projects believed most likely to improve the financial, social, and market positions of the corporation.

## Synergy

To guide the resource allocation process, the multibusiness organization should have an explicit understanding of the synergies sought from its mix of businesses. **Synergy** means that the whole is greater than the sum of its parts. International Paper Company is really much more than a paper company. Its distribution business is called Xpedx, a $6.7 billion enterprise operating 250 warehouse and store locations plus a delivery fleet. As a result, International is well equipped to service retail customers, commercial printers and publishers, manufacturers, sanitary maintenance companies, quick printers, and more with dedicated stocking, just-in-time services, and technical support.

Synergy can also derive from systems and know-how. Omni Hotels operates several hotels, few of which share the same name. It may seem puzzling that it could run successful business and convention hotels, some airport hotels, and a handful of luxury hotels in the major cities, all under different names and different marketing strategies. But its success does not stem from economies in advertising or from an otherwise developed common brand. Rather, the management knows how to position properties in unique markets and deliver satisfying lodging experiences. In this case, clearly we cannot find the source of synergy without looking deeply at the company's culture and planning systems.[7]

We offer a word of caution about synergy. It can be elusive, surprising, and overpromised. For example, several companies have tried to acquire technical expertise thought to be essential to their future operations by acquiring marketing research or engineering firms. On paper, the plans have looked sound: Experts at making and selling will team up with experts at innovating, analyzing, or forecasting. The plan unravels, however, when the key scientists, analysts, or econometricians at the acquired firm get frustrated by the new ownership, reporting structure, or such. They then bolt to another firm or begin their own. Plans and incentives need to be well conceived, and implementation must be sound in order to realize potential synergies.

### Final Words on Business Strategy

A business strategy can exhibit different levels of detail and analysis and can focus on horizons 2 to 20 years out. Critical elements in any strategic plan include (1) product markets served, (2) resource commitments, and (3) objectives and plans for each functional area. Firms with multiple business units must include two additional elements in their strategies: the resource allocations to the different businesses and the synergies expected from the mix. Clearly, these are similar to the second and third elements in any strategy, performed at a higher level of aggregation of the product markets served.

# DEVELOPING STRATEGY

It may be several years before you make it to the top floor of corporate headquarters or take the helm of your family's business. In the meantime you should expect to contribute in several ways to your company's strategic planning process. In an entry-level sales position, you may find the firm using input from you and other field sales personnel for business forecasts. Your proposals for account and territory development might also be sought in the planning process. If your career progresses toward greater supervision of people and programs, perhaps including profit responsibility, your participation in the planning process will greatly expand. Until then, you will have a chance to hone comprehensive planning skills if you pursue entrepreneurial opportunities or take up community projects.

# The Process for Strategies

Exhibit 6–2 depicts three strategic planning models. Although the presentations differ, all three contain common elements—a process for reflecting on the purpose of the enterprise, a situation analysis that attends to both environmental and organizational elements, some more careful consideration of the competitive forces in specific markets, and the detailed objectives, budgets, and plans for strategy execution.

It is noteworthy that activities are not sequenced identically in the three models. That is a clue that each model is a gross simplification. As such, the summary diagram overstates the linearity of the process. Strategic planning is not a series of self-contained steps connected in a perfunctory way and guaranteed to yield action plans for profits. Indeed, many of the strategy process elements can be addressed simultaneously and iteratively between functions and levels in the organization. This section of the chapter will discuss the key elements of the strategy process, but we don't pretend that there is a formula or rigid mechanism for the process.

**Exhibit 6–2**
The Strategy
Process
Model 1

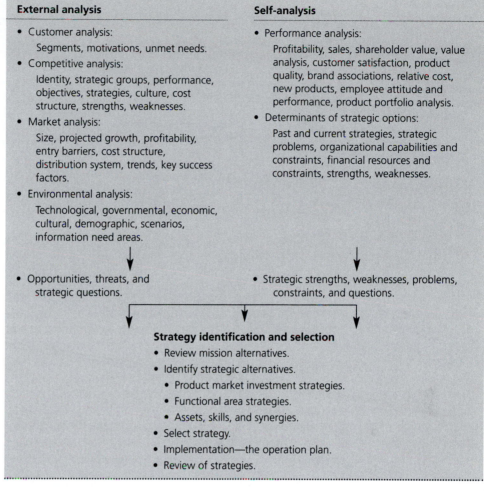

**External analysis**

- Customer analysis:
  Segments, motivations, unmet needs.
- Competitive analysis:
  Identity, strategic groups, performance, objectives, strategies, culture, cost structure, strengths, weaknesses.
- Market analysis:
  Size, projected growth, profitability, entry barriers, cost structure, distribution system, trends, key success factors.
- Environmental analysis:
  Technological, governmental, economic, cultural, demographic, scenarios, information need areas.

- Opportunities, threats, and strategic questions.

**Self-analysis**

- Performance analysis:
  Profitability, sales, shareholder value, value analysis, customer satisfaction, product quality, brand associations, relative cost, new products, employee attitude and performance, product portfolio analysis.
- Determinants of strategic options:
  Past and current strategies, strategic problems, organizational capabilities and constraints, financial resources and constraints, strengths, weaknesses.

- Strategic strengths, weaknesses, problems, constraints, and questions.

**Strategy identification and selection**
- Review mission alternatives.
- Identify strategic alternatives.
  - Product market investment strategies.
  - Functional area strategies.
  - Assets, skills, and synergies.
- Select strategy.
- Implementation—the operation plan.
- Review of strategies.

SOURCE: Model 1 reprinted from David Aaker, *Strategic Market Management* (1992), p. 23, with permission of the copyright © owner, John Wiley & Sons, Inc.

# Situation Analysis

Strategies are built on a solid foundational understanding of the organization's mission. The mission, in turn, derives from recognition of key capabilities, constraints, aspirations, resources, and constituencies in the task environment. This section will introduce some important perspectives for organizational and environmental analysis.

We have a number of tools available for situation analysis and goal setting. This section provides an overview of SWOT analysis, a powerful tool for internal and external strategic assessment. We spend a short time introducing the concept of organizational mission and its explicit sense of purpose. To bolster your own confidence and inspire creativity, we illustrate a number of devices for distilling details and conveying strategic insights. We then build up to a separate section that introduces a framework for evaluating the structure of competition.

**Exhibit 6–2**
Continued
Model 2

SOURCE: *Model 2 reprinted with permission from Donald Lehmann and Russell Winer,* Analysis for Marketing Planning, *Plano, TX: Business Publications, Inc. (1988), p. 8.*

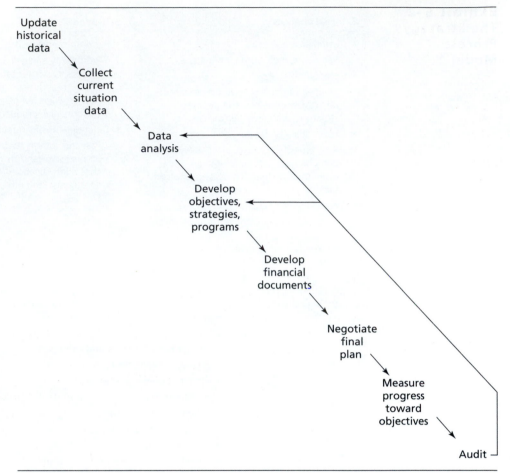

## SWOT Analysis

One of the most productive and memorable planning tools is a **SWOT analysis.** This is a self-assessment framework for examining our **S**trengths and **W**eaknesses, our **O**pportunities and **T**hreats. Strengths include the pockets of excellence *in the firm,* perhaps a strong sales office in Birmingham, a good supply relationship with XYZ, a good inventory system, or a solid financial position. Dell's world-class supply chain is clearly an enviable strength. Weaknesses are also characteristics of the firm itself and may include products with poor market positions, a lame channel of distribution overseas, a disadvantageous cost structure, or yesterday's technology. Aging assets, a locational disadvantage, or thinning talent in a key area represents weaknesses. In its efforts to stay lean and remain the cost leader, Dell has not invested aggressively in R&D, so its future growth avenues are foggy.

In this level of analysis, opportunities are favorable conditions in the firm's task environment. They can be recognized in access to growing markets, a market of escalating distribution service standards—standards we can meet—and new laws or regulations that might foreclose competitors. Threats are potential adverse conditions in the firm's environment. A margin squeeze from vigorous price competition and increasing input prices is a threat, as is a regulation that forecloses a particular input or distribution

**Exhibit 6–2**
Continued
Model 3

SOURCE: *Model 3 reprinted with the permission of the Free Press, a Division of Simon & Schuster, from Christopher Meyer,* Fast Cycle Time: How to Align Purpose, Strategy, and Structure for Speed *(1993), p. 92; copyright © 1993 by Christopher Meyer.*

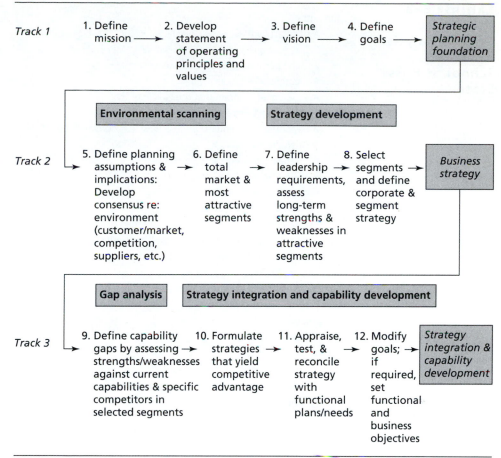

option. In the dean's office at your school, an analysis akin to the SWOT shown in Exhibit 6–3 may be one of the key working documents for goal setting and the revelation of distinctive competencies.

### King of SWOT

A good SWOT analysis has several distinguishing characteristics. First, it is *honest.* Despite its receiving three professional awards for design excellence, it would be wrong to consider your firm's design team a strength if consumer acceptance is low or there have been departures of key personnel. An honest label on the strength would be a "strong reputation among product design professionals."

Second, the analysis must be *broad* in focus. A distributor assessing trends for opportunities and threats should look at situations in markets outside its trade area. For example, T-Shirt City, a midwestern wholesaler of shirts and sportswear to the screen printers and embroidery business, has observed margins shrinking across the country, has witnessed consolidation at the manufacturing and wholesaling level, and has seen its thinning customer base replicated in other markets.

The anticipation of customer needs requires a close look at the competitive pressures faced by each customer or customer group. Similarly, the business environment of direct and indirect suppliers must be considered. We also recommend that SWOT analysis be conducted at different levels: key products, lines of business, divisions, and countries.

**Exhibit 6–3**
Composite SWOT Analysis of the B School at Bliss State

I. Strengths
  A. A solid faculty base, particularly new faculty
    1. Improving research and professional activity and reputation
    2. High percentage of excellent teachers
    3. A number of research stars
  B. An undergrad program that offers
    1. The co-op program
    2. Opportunity to enter *College of Business Administration* (CBA) as freshmen
    3. Identifiable majors
    4. Some excellent undergrads
    5. Extensive student involvement
  C. A strong evening MBA program
  D. Several strong PhD programs
  E. Several centers with unique niches and solid support
  F. A large reservoir of potential goodwill, presently untapped
  G. Increased visibility from basketball success
  H. Decision-making autonomy within university
  I. Adequate facilities—good physical plant
  J. Urban location
II. Weaknesses
  A. A faculty characterized by
    1. Apathy
    2. Low expectations: tenure, aspirations, amount of work
    3. Many faculty not doing research or doing research with little impact
    4. Low levels of externally supported research
    5. Several departments in disarray
    6. Poor interdepartmental relations
    7. Inconsistent departmental workloads
    8. Distribution of faculty across departments that doesn't match our mission
  B. An undergraduate program characterized by
    1. An "average" undergrad student body, with a very wide range of abilities
    2. An aging curriculum that is inefficient and too specialized
    3. Lack of solid undergraduate recruiting
    4. Students distracted by work demands
    5. Lack of student identification with CBA
  C. An MBA program featuring
    1. Excess capacity in daytime MBA
    2. A part-time MBA longer than many prospective students would prefer
    3. A me-too curriculum
    4. Delivery in only one location
  D. Strong student–community ties, reducing the possibility of broader placement, visibility
  E. Weak management development programs that are not supported by faculty
  F. Low level of alumni and community support, including external funding
  G. Reputation that hasn't kept up with improvements in CBA
  H. Lack of support (financial or otherwise) from central administration for CBA's goals. CBA is expected to be a cash generator for the university
  I. Inadequate centralized administrative services: student recruiting and placement, public relations, information systems

**Exhibit 6–3**
Continued

  J. Inflexibility created by the unionized environment

  K. Lack of galvanizing strategy

  L. Facility inadequacies: case classrooms, office space, technology

  M. Aesthetics of urban location

III. Opportunities

  A. Capitalizing on the strengths noted above, particularly by

   1. Expanding and promoting the co-op program

   2. Expanding the evening MBA program

   3. Encouraging high-impact faculty research

  B. "Fixing" certain weaknesses, particularly by

   1. Upgrading management development programs

   2. Making the MBA program more accessible (shorter, more locations, etc.)

   3. Improving community and business relations, including fund raising

   4. Revamping the BBA curriculum to teach more efficiently and effectively

   5. Changing the organizational structure and choosing more appropriate administrators

   6. Improving marketing efforts

   7. Increasing the amount of externally funded (contract) research

  C. Responding to new standards of accreditation

  D. Use of our urban location and improved business ties for teaching innovations, expanded placement, and research possibilities

  E. A large local market, particularly for evening MBA

  F. An untapped market for joint MBA programs with engineering, law, medicine

IV. Threats

  A. Declining interest in majoring in business (due to demographics and attitudes)

  B. Actions by competitors to enhance their programs

  C. Potential loss of strong faculty

  D. Lack of faculty optimism and enthusiasm

  E. Stable, if not declining, state support for higher education

  F. Dissatisfaction among businesses with the education business schools provide

  G. Increasing accountability

  H. Changed standards of accreditation

  I. Negative attitudes by central administrators, particularly concerning the importance of sponsored research as a basis for BSU resource allocation

  J. A tight job market

SOURCE: SWOT analysis used with the permission of the dean at "Bliss State."

  Third, a SWOT analysis should consider *multiple time horizons* and label features of each dimension as such. For example, a drought in the Grain Belt is an immediate threat to flour and cereal processors; its impact on costs and eventual market prices must be considered. Firms in this industry such as Peavy and Cargill should also look ahead to new transport systems that may make inputs accessible that are currently remote. Evidence of new dietary habits, signs of breakthroughs in grain preservatives, and emerging package recycling imperatives ought to be considered. Even the durability of current strengths must be factored into the analysis.

  Finally, because the SWOT analysis is built on *perceptions* of the firm and its environment, it is good to get the perceptions from several individuals or groups. Have purchasing, marketing, sales, human resources, and traffic departments each do SWOT analyses. This should broaden the scope of the analysis and capture strategic implications that stem from a variety of assumptions.

**Exhibit 6–4**
Mission
Statements

We aim to be a leading and flexible world manufacturer of audio acoustic products, meeting the needs of our customer, employees, and shareholders.

*Polish electronics manufacturer*

We aim to be the friendliest Saudi bank which best anticipates and responds to the needs of our customers, employees, and shareholders.

*leading Saudi Arabian bank*

Fast, flawless, and simple delivery of value as perceived by our customers such that Digital becomes the benchmark toward which others can strive.

*Digital South Pacific*

To improve the health status of the people we serve. We pursue our mission by providing a full range of health-related services, including prevention, wellness, and education. Care is provided with compassion consistent with the values of our organization: respect for all people, stewardship, delighting customers through commitment to quality, response to community needs, respect for our spiritual heritage, valuing differences.

*an alliance of hospitals in the Midwest*

Become the premier custom sales research company offering the highest-quality product, the most responsive client service, the most flexibility, and the fastest service in the industry.

*a national custom research corporation*

SOURCE: The first three mission statements are reprinted from *Practical Business Re-Engineering,* 2d ed., p. 47, by Nick Obolensky. Copyright © 1994 by Nick Obolensky. Used with permission. All rights reserved.

### SWOT Recap

It takes two mirrors to show how the back of your hair was cut. And most of us also run our fingers through it. A SWOT analysis works similarly. It begins with a good look at the enterprise—front, back, up close, down deep. And it takes stock of the firm's external environment. How has it changed in the last few periods? What do we anticipate in the time ahead? Is our firm poised for success in the current and anticipated environment? Are we ready to track the changing environment and maintain a leadership position therein? Or have we faced up to the reality of our problems? Perhaps the discomfort of the recent period can no longer be endured. Maybe top management is ready to lead the firm to make radical change. Whatever the case, an honest, broad, and timely examination from multiple perspectives is needed for reliable self-assessment via SWOT.

## *The Mission*

In the strategic process of self-analysis, a company will often pause to reconsider its **mission statement,** a formal expression of why the organization exists. This sense of purpose works well to frame key strategies and day-to-day decisions. It also helps with the enculturation process needed when new employees join the firm or two firms merge.

Developing a mission from scratch or reassessing a prior mission statement can be a useful strategic exercise. Broad company participation in the visioning process necessary to develop a mission often yields new insights, a renewed sense of purpose, and broad-based commitment.

Even without broad participation in its development, a mission statement serves to clarify the goals and values of the enterprise to all constituencies or stakeholders in the firm. Most organizations can place the majority of their stakeholders into one of four key categories: customers, suppliers, employees, and owners. Are the stakeholders recognized in the sample mission statements in Exhibit 6–4?

**6–1**

# BUSINESS 2 BUSINESS
## Your Mission

As a student in business marketing, you can benefit from having a mission statement. This is not a self-help seminar, but with just some rudimentary tools we can direct the effort and point to some key benefits. If you take some time over the next few days now to develop your personal mission statement, we think you will find a greater appreciation for the mission statement of a business organization. And we suspect you will produce a useful platform for finding personal success.

Management consultant Stephen Covey underscores our need to find balance and synergy in four principal spheres: physical, mental, spiritual, and social.[8] In each of these areas, list some of your strengths, shortcomings, and obstacles to overcoming the weaknesses. Where do you see your strengths in these areas overlapping? Identify some of the most important roles in your life (e.g., student, coach, employee, spouse, parent, son, or daughter). What will be your accomplishments when you look back at your life from ages 30, 50, and 70?

With the insights from these exercises, write a private mission statement. Covey argues effectively that a good mission statement is true to one's inner self, reflects use of unique talents to serve others, integrates the four needs spheres, is anchored in truth, deals with the significant roles in your life, and inspires. But mix in a good measure of humility in order to cope with setbacks, be robust to disturbances and sidetracks, and admit the possibility that you may indeed have another mission. The payoff is a clarity of focus—doing what's important, attending to the right factors in the strategic environment, and running ahead of the pack.

## Strategic Spectroscopy

A spectroscope is an optical instrument for forming and analyzing the spectrum emitted by an object or element. Physicists know that each element emits a different type of radiant energy. Each is distinguished by the different color bands on its spectrum. Although we know many managers who long for a marketing spectroscope, they accomplish the same objective by using a raft of tools that simplify and summarize the complex. We have already discussed some of the input data: customer surveys, industry studies, focus groups, and segmentation analyses. From here strategic planners need to grasp the big picture and trends. This need compels most managers to use graphics and charts in place of multiple, detailed tables. Managers and their analysts may move mountains of data, but now comes the time for visual tools that summarize the big picture.

Let's illustrate with a model that's been reinvented in many of our own student teams. Exhibit 6–5 derives from survey data asking customers (1) to rate the company's products on different functional attributes and (2) to indicate the degree to which each attribute is important. The graphic combines the data in a most illuminating way, reflecting an implicit management theory that the firm should do best what customers value most. In this sense, attributes below the diagonal represent underachievement; those above the diagonal represent overachievement. Why put company resources to tasks that are not important? The result is a Wants–Gets Grid, simple but demonstrably illuminating.

**Exhibit 6–5**
Wants–Gets Grid

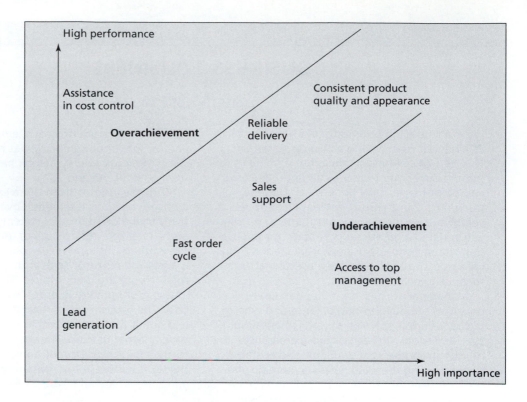

The same sort of creativity can be applied to summarizing segment data, market share information, or anticipated market evolution. Exhibit 6–6 illustrates the oft-used strategic planning graphics called the conceptual map. A **conceptual map** is a picture of abstract ideas, options, persons, or companies on two or three key variables. The perceptual maps we discussed in Chapter 5, made from the subjective perceptions of customers, are one type of conceptual map. The vice president of marketing can make effective use of a conceptual map showing the evolution of shrink wrap applications in industrial markets. Alternatively, an export manager can effectively convey shipment volumes and products to various country clusters by a conceptual map.

A conceptual map like the one in Exhibit 6–6 has been used in many businesses over the years. A graphic representation of competitors on key dimensions of customer value can convey a message more powerfully than a table of data. But it may not always rest on data. A conceptual map can be a useful summary of management perceptions and assumptions because it makes them explicit. The conceptual map is an effective internal communication device. One banking expert's insightful view of the nature of competition in commercial banking was represented in a "radar screen" that included some unconventional and potential competitors to commercial banks. In this vein, one bank executive recently remarked, "I used to track six banks. Now I have to track over 100 different financial service firms that are competing for my customers' accounts. Measuring where the money is going is getting tougher. Parsing through the data is getting harder and harder. It gives me a headache."[9]

The conceptual map is a headache remedy of sorts. It's a communication instrument and tool for understanding. It is a model, a gross simplification of the real situation. It helps us to get a handle on the complexity of the real thing without all the messy details.

**Exhibit 6–6**
Conceptual Map
of Competitive
Positions on Key
Attributes of
Service Quality

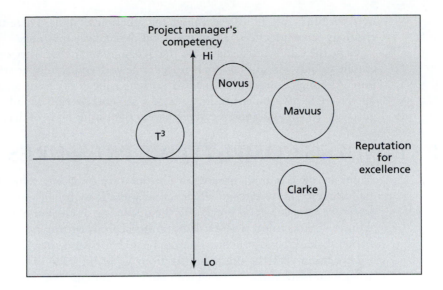

But if the model were as complicated as the real situation, it would no longer work as an analogy.

It can also be illuminating to examine the supply chain to identify key points of value added. Exhibit 6–7 compares the estimated value-added chain of two products from the same industry; share of market through channel 1 is climbing while share of market through channel 2 is waning. The numbers reflect use of average factory-direct costs in channel 1 as the base. Although manufacturers in channel 2 are a bit less efficient, they nab higher prices from their distributors, and distributors enjoy 30 percent margins in their sales to end users. But the real action seems to be happening "downstream" in channel 1. In channel 1, dealers earn 50 percent gross margins on a sales level that has grown much faster than channel 2's. The market seems to be shifting toward a preference for dealer services! When this type of analysis is combined with other data on the environment (segment trends, technology, market share histories), we can get deep insights into the evolution of the product market, the emerging value priorities. In the computer field, this evolution manifests a diminished value from chips and even sharper decline from hardware and peripherals. We note increasing value provided from operating systems, applications, and network functionality.

These three tools are merely representative of the grids, bubble charts, flow diagrams, and other graphics that can be used in the strategy process. We have underscored the

**Exhibit 6–7**
Value Chain
Analysis. Numbers
represent cost of
goods sold at
each level,
indexed to inputs
of manufacturers
in channel 1.

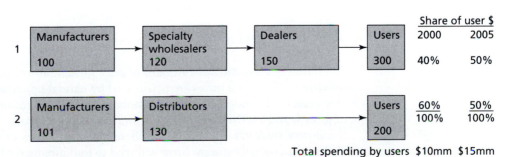

need for broad and multilevel inputs for situation analysis. These tools and your own creativity can work effectively to synthesize and convey meaning.

Now, the value-added chain and the dynamics of any industry can be more systematically studied within a comprehensive framework addressing the structure of competition. Although competitive analysis is technically a situation analysis tool, we take up the topic of competitive analysis in a separate section mainly for organizational purposes. As you will soon see, it contains a significant body of detailed material.

# UNDERSTANDING COMPETITIVE PRESSURES

Profits are the economic rewards to a business for providing value to customers better than the rest and running an efficient operation. If we briefly examine a few sources of profit, we can get a good preview to the upcoming discussion of the anatomy of competition. Competition is more than industrial rivals cutting prices in an effort to gain market share. It has a structure that can be described and analyzed.[10]

Let's begin with the profit impact from a gain in share of a growing market. The struggle for market share fits well with our commonsense notion of competition. But let us presume a gain of one share point brings a manufacturer a well-earned profit increase of $500,000. Is it likely we would regard some other means of earning an additional $500,000 as inferior? Would the dollars be less valuable if they came from, say, an ability to charge higher factory prices to dealers? Of course not. The dollars gained in net profits from share of market increases and from price increases are the same value.

In the same manner, as we showed in Chapter 2, profits can increase by using effective supply strategies, perhaps reducing spoilage, downtime, or ownership costs to achieve a $500,000 bump in profits. Finally, we might find $500,000 in new profits from regulations that foreclose a toxic substitute product from competing or beginning to compete for our accounts, thus relieving a degree of price pressure from our line.

# Five Forces

The preceding scenarios suggest that firms have improved profit capabilities to the extent that they can withstand price pressures in the business environment. If we pause to reconsider each scenario, we see that price pressures come from five distinct sectors. Depicted in Exhibit 6–8, the **five forces of competition** are:

1. Rivalry among firms in the industry
2. Powerful customers
3. Powerful suppliers
4. Threat of substitutes
5. Threat of potential entrants

## *Rivalry in the Industry*

Not all businesses face the same amount of price pressure from their competitors in the same business. Some industries are partitioned by natural boundaries or customer purchasing constraints. Indeed, Grainger's emphasis on MRO items reflects both the promise of growth and a relative weakness of competitors in the arena.

If industry rivals offer relatively undifferentiated products or if demand is significantly less than overall capacity, firms will tend to find intense rivalry. Price competition

**Exhibit 6–8**
Five Forces of
Competition

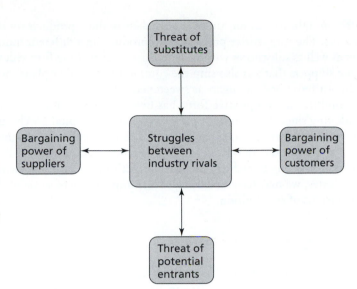

frequently intensifies in declining markets because firms try to grab market share to cover fixed expenses that can't be shrunk as rapidly as the market. T-shirt City is a wholesaler in such a situation of intense rivalry.

## Powerful Customers

Their abilities to contract for large purchases make large customers attractive to many business markets. The seller's risk is that large buyers may press hard for price concessions, effectively squeezing out profit opportunities. Another possibility is delayed payments or returned products, both of which can sink an undercapitalized firm.

## Powerful Suppliers

A manufacturer that relies heavily on a unique input for its product becomes vulnerable to price hikes or other means of "holdup" from the supplier. Of course, the unique input may provide a means of differentiation for the manufacturer. The "Intel inside" sticker on a desktop computer provides many buyers assurance of a top-quality processor, no matter what the brand name on the PC. The buying firm must carefully weigh the benefits from depending on a powerful source of supply and after looking hard at AMD's superior chip performance in 2004, Dell nearly left its partnership with Intel. A key question may be what the future supply situation and quality differences will look like. Perhaps there will be alternative suppliers when patent protection expires or when another source—maybe even one internal to the firm—has been brought up to speed.

## Threat of Substitutes

Industries are typically defined by their channel position and their output. Are they manufacturers or distributors? Do they sell chemicals or rolled wire? Notice that user considerations get no mention. But clearly, if a buyer regards the products from two different industries as substitutes, the makers of those products must be considered competitors. The competitive pressure from products in a different industry can affect prices just as well as substitutes within the industry. A trucking firm will vie for business from some shippers that can also ship the commodity by rail or plane. Soft-drink bottlers can use corn syrup or cane sugars as sweeteners.

Frankly, this competitive force has been the cornerstone of competitive analysis in marketing since the infancy of survey research. A hospital purchasing manager may not only compare prices and capabilities of different makers of diagnostic equipment; she may also examine the services of independent laboratories. But, while marketing research has long aimed to describe competition in terms of customer perceptions of substitutes, we may have underplayed the importance of some of these other structural dimensions of competition.

## *Threat of Potential Entrants*

Rapidly growing or profitable markets tend to attract new sellers. And newcomers can change the competitive landscape in several ways. First, new participants in the market increase the productive capacity serving the market; therefore the existing demand from customers has to cover more fixed costs. Second, a new rival will fight to increase market share, perhaps displacing incumbents in the assortments of resellers or underbidding the established firms. Third, new rivals can bring new or substantial resources to the fray. Resources might be a reputable brand name brought to a new arena (e.g., 3M in fertilizers) or could include technical expertise (Samsung in the Asian auto market) or financial muscle (Wal-Mart in food service).

In the competitive arena for flash memory chips—those used in cell phones and other portable devices—AMD enjoyed technology leadership and a price premium in 2004. Indeed, 50 percent of its sales came from flash memory chips, compared to 7 percent for rival Intel. Nevertheless, when Intel improved their flash memory chips and stepped up their marketing efforts in 2005, flash memory prices dropped 30 percent.[11]

# Barriers to Entry

A keen analysis of competitive forces will seek (1) to gauge the barriers to entry in the particular industry and (2) given a sense of what it takes to enter, to identify the significant potential entrants into a field. If barriers are high, incumbent sellers enjoy a shelter from competitive pressures. **Barriers to entry** are the obstacles a potential entrant must overcome in order to compete in a market. Essentially, they are like the prerequisites you need to satisfy before you can take a particular course; they are the capabilities or resources necessary to succeed in a market.

Antitrust lawyers and economists have identified six types of barriers to entry. We need to turn their motivation inside out, because we are looking at barriers to entry from the firm's perspective. That is, Department of Justice and FTC lawyers are concerned when barriers create a monopoly and thereby restrict output and choice, impairing the customer satisfaction focus of the market mechanism. However, business executives, from a strategic business perspective, know that better profit opportunities exist in markets insulated from new entrants. Furthermore, even as a potential entrant to a market, we should carefully size up the skills and resources needed to compete. Thus, we briefly review the barriers to entry in Exhibit 6–9.

**Exhibit 6–9**
Barriers to
Entry

| | |
|---|---|
| Product differentiation | If customers are loyal to brands because of effective advertising, customer service, or unique features, it will be expensive for a new firm to overcome that loyalty. |
| Economies of scale | Technical matters of production or distribution often demand that new players spend heavily to enter the industry on a large scale, or come in at a cost disadvantage. |
| Capital requirements | Consider the financial requirements to enter shipbuilding, mining, pharmaceuticals, or public accounting fields. One must cover the heavy equipment and fixed site requirements, plus finance inventories, R&D, start-up advertising, and sales. |
| Access to distribution channels | A new entrant to the business copier field will have to find and motivate dealers to add another model to their assortment or develop their own distribution and sales system. The former route is often confounded by exclusive dealing terms enjoyed by entrenched makes of copiers. |
| Cost disadvantages unrelated to size | This is a potpourri of possible advantages enjoyed by incumbents: a premium site, low occupancy costs (a paid-off mortgage), patent protection, lots of experience, access to inputs, etc. |
| Government policy | Licensing requirements, regulated distribution, and safety and pollution standards can limit or foreclose entry. |

# Barriers in Flux

In today's global business arena, dynamic and uncertain conditions describe most markets. For example, technology may radically affect the scale economies in an industry. In the marketing research field, powerful desktop computers and flexible software enable many small start-up companies to begin to offer marketing research *projects*. Meanwhile, capital requirements have escalated for firms participating in the new marketing research *systems* field. They need superpowered computers to clean and merge scanner data with information on geodemographics, promotions, and media activities as well as to develop, test, and apply new "products"—analytical models and report formats in tune with client needs. Analytical and customer service talent plus strong corporate reputations represent new barriers to entry.

Change can also affect other entry barriers. For several software companies the Internet has served as a distribution channel, enabling the description and delivery of demonstration and shareware products without the costly headaches of gaining access to and managing performance of a dealer network. Remember also that patents do expire and, prior to their expiration, many patented products have been displaced by innovations. Indeed, new circumstances and the transmission of knowledge enable new firms to leapfrog the reputation and experience edge held by incumbent firms. For decades, petroleum companies turned primarily to Red Adair to extinguish wellhead fires. When hundreds of wellhead fires were left by the Iraqis in Kuwait at the end of the Gulf War I, scores of newcomers and novel methods were enlisted in the firefight.

## Spotting and Defending against Potential Entrants

We can better scan the horizon for potential new entrants with an informed sense of the barriers to entry to our market. What businesses have the ability to complete the "package" of skills and resources to compete in our market? Have they given any signals of their intention to enter? Some of the signals we should look for include a potential entrant's discussions with or purchases from suppliers. Note also the skills of the people they have recently hired from our field or a related field. Perhaps they paint their growth strategies broadly in their annual reports and are lining up dealers or sales reps at trade shows, field testing products and systems, or inviting presentations from advertising agencies. In short, we should be very attentive to potential competitors and the signs they provide about their marketing objectives and strategies. We should prepare defensive strategies or position the firm in a manner that deters the entrant. Vigorous defense of a position discourages other potential entrants who observe the high stakes of entry.

# STRATEGIC IMPLICATIONS OF THE FIVE COMPETITIVE FORCES

If you know the nature of competitive challenges in your market, you should be sure your firm is adequately prepared to meet them. Every firm has both strengths and weaknesses, but it is how they match up against the competitive structure of the market that determines success.

Three broad types of action plans are implicated by competitive analysis. A firm will want to *choose its competitive battlegrounds judiciously.* If it is the low-cost producer, it might enjoy profitable business from a large, powerful buyer. A firm that is disadvantaged on the cost side should probably not pursue business from the powerful buyer, but compete in another customer sector where quick response and specialized technical service are critical. Solar Kids, a Cincinnati-based computer training company, faced up to the waning profit opportunities at elementary and high schools: lots of rivals, impoverished and slow-paying customers. It changed its name to Solar Comp and moved into corporate training, where competition pivots on expertise with the latest applications software and personal productivity tools. In 1998 DuPont set out to reduce its dependence on oil and gas products (spinning off Conoco) in order to be a strong player in the emerging biotech field. It has since forged several joint ventures to develop crop-protection products and soy-based consumer foods, and its Agriculture and Nutrition segment has become DuPont's most profitable business.

Innovative organizations will sometimes pursue a strategy designed to *change the competitive structure of the industry.* Advertising and a sophisticated means of programmed merchandising for resellers may transform a market characterized by small regional manufacturers into one dominated by a few national marketers. In markets where this has occurred (e.g., construction adhesives and sealants), the new competitive structure creates barriers to entry through new distribution requirements and product differentiation by branding.

The third strategic approach is to *anticipate and exploit change* in the competitive structure of the industry. Our challenge is to look carefully at each competitive force, understand its root causes, and forecast its impact on the profitability of an industry. Then, with insight and mobility superior to our competition, we try to secure a position to capitalize on the evolution of the field. In the opening vignette to this chapter, we profiled moves by Dell to capitalize on the new information technology and harness efficiency from sound supply chain management. The vignette ended, however, with Dell in the doldrums. It needs to find new avenues of growth.

# Cautions and Limitations

Despite the power of competitive analysis as a tool for situational insights and general options for broad strategic moves, it is not the do-it-all Swiss Army knife. Competitive analysis leaves plenty unsaid in terms of designing an organization structure and control system. Company culture, leadership, and learning are not in the lens of competitive analysis. These facets of business strategy are critical. We address them in the following section.

## Sustainable Advantage?

If we use the five-forces analysis to position our company in markets where barriers to entry protect us and where we can preserve good margins in our negotiations with customers and suppliers, we risk complacency and vulnerability to innovative competitors. Commenting on the types of situation analysis reviewed in this chapter, Columbia University professor Richard D'Aveni says they

> provide an invaluable set of tools for analyzing the competitive environment and position of a firm at any point in its evolution. They identify some of the key sources of advantage at a given point in time. As firms maneuver to create these advantages and erode the advantages of competitors, these static models provide important insights. However, they fail to recognize competitive advantage as a fluid and dynamic process. Advantages that worked in an industry's past only continue to work in a relatively static environment.[12]

Indeed, competitive advantage is fleeting, as is evident in the opening vignette. In the mid-1990s Gateway was displaced by Compaq as the number one seller of personal computers. After being surpassed by Dell, Compaq was purchased by Hewlett–Packard in 2000 to give H-P market share leadership until the top spot was regained by Dell again in 2004. In 2007, HP was closing in on Dell.

The speed and intensity of competition in an ever increasing number of business markets demand a strategic emphasis on a new set of organizational strengths.[13] Depicted in Exhibit 6–10, these strengths include

| | |
|---|---|
| Superior stakeholder satisfaction | We focus on customers, employees and associates, shareholders, and top management, in that order of priority. |
| Strategic soothsaying | We are looking for advantages in the future, anticipating customer needs, and building the strengths we will need for future success. |
| Positioning for speed | We need flexibility and adaptability to compete in a changing environment, especially to preempt the moves of other players. |
| Positioning for surprise | Disruption derives from the ability to move covertly and creatively in ways competitors don't anticipate. |
| Shifting the rules of competition | A true innovation practically destroys the previous business format. New distribution channels (machine tools) or process technology (printing) has the potential to shape new rules. |
| Signaling strategic intent | We want competitors to highly regard our commitment to defend positions or penetrate markets. This enhances the credibility of our threats |

**Exhibit 6–10**
The Ability to
Disrupt Markets

*SOURCE: Reprinted with the permission of the Free Press, a division of Simon & Schuster, from* Hypercompetition: Managing the Dynamics of Strategic Maneuvering *by Richard A. D'Aveni. Copyright © 1994 by Richard A. D'Aveni.*

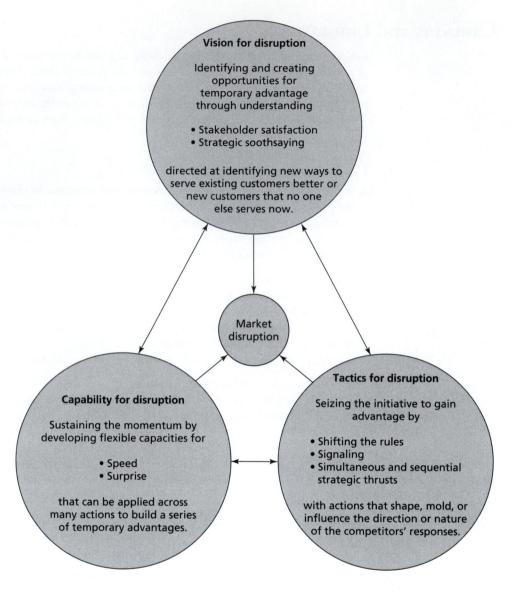

**Vision for disruption**

Identifying and creating opportunities for temporary advantage through understanding

• Stakeholder satisfaction
• Strategic soothsaying

directed at identifying new ways to serve existing customers better or new customers that no one else serves now.

Market disruption

**Capability for disruption**

Sustaining the momentum by developing flexible capacities for

• Speed
• Surprise

that can be applied across many actions to build a series of temporary advantages.

**Tactics for disruption**

Seizing the initiative to gain advantage by

• Shifting the rules
• Signaling
• Simultaneous and sequential strategic thrusts

with actions that shape, mold, or influence the direction or nature of the competitors' responses.

and diminishes the necessity that we will have to carry them out.

Simultaneous and sequential strategic thrusts

We must not get enamored with the competitive clout of a single strategic asset (e.g., deep pockets or product quality) because those can be easily predicted. Multiple assaults and the series of contingent moves ought to be formulated.

These New 7-Ss enable firms to "disrupt" the status quo in markets to achieve temporary advantages. If the advantage is regarded as short lived, the strategic aim will be to develop a follow-up disruption that yields another advantage. From the Field 6–1 profiles Komatsu's disruption strategy against Caterpillar.

## 6–1

# FROM THE FIELD
## Komatsu v. Caterpillar

Between 1981 and 1984 Caterpillar's share of the world's earth-moving equipment slipped from 50 to 43 percent. Japanese manufacturer Komatsu surged over this same period from 16 to 25 percent of the world market. Before this skirmish, Caterpillar seemed unbeatable as it followed a "Perpetual Motion Machine" for sustainable advantage: It provided dependable machines, strong service, and high world volume. The high volume yielded scale economies and enabled high R&D investments, which led to further quality enhancements, which commanded price premiums and high margins, thus a loyal dealer network. On it churned.

Intending to halt Cat's relentless machine, Komatsu devised a bevy of strategies to cripple each component. Under the company code name "Maru-C" (encircle Caterpillar), Komatsu moved aggressively in four key competitive arenas:

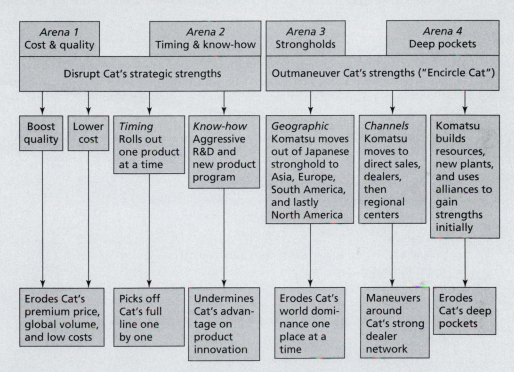

Komatsu: A Strategy of Disruption to Derail "The Perpetual Motion Machine"*

In 1985 Komatsu took a hard hit from a 20 percent devaluation of the yen against the dollar. With most of its production in Japan, Komatsu had to bump prices and relinquish price leadership to Cat.

Source: Reprinted with the permission of The Free Press, a division of Simon & Schuster, from *Hypercompetition: Managing the Dynamics of Strategic Maneuvering* by Richard A. D'Aveni. Copyright © 1994 by Richard A. D'Aveni.

\* Based on research by Chris Bartlett.

# THE ORGANIZATIONAL CONTEXT FOR COMPETING

Organizational and environmental analyses enable us to take stock of strengths, weaknesses, opportunities, and threats. A framework for competitive analysis helps us identify "fitting" positions for our business within the economic structure of a market. If we build from this static analysis to forecast cost and quality trends, the evolution of distinctive skills and know-how, the development of new barriers to entry, and the likely distribution of financial resources, we can begin to see what resources and skills we will need to protect our turf, minimize adverse impact, survive on carrion, or disrupt markets and achieve a series of temporary victories.

Indeed, organizations respond differently to their competitive environments according to their strategic personality or character. Organization researchers have verified four archetypes: **Prospectors, Defenders, Analyzers,** and **Reactors.** Exhibit 6–11 profiles each, showing still another tool for evaluating competitors. Notice that only Prospectors and, to a lesser degree, the Analyzers are inclined to define and disrupt the competitive arena to their advantage. What is it that drives these two types? What is the organizational engine that drives industry leaders? We argue that the firm's pervasive and deep-rooted market orientation is that engine.

## Market Orientation

Of course, industry competition motivates customer service, logistical efficiency, and the search for production economies. But as customer needs are changing, new market opportunities arise, and technology expands the realm of possibilities, success should favor

**Exhibit 6–11**
Organizational
Types

*Prospector*
Likes being first mover
Detects early signals of opportunity and moves on them
Competes in new markets or with new marketing methods
Operates in a broad domain of products and markets

*Defender*
Aims to find and secure stable product market positions
Offers limited range of products
Is not at the forefront of technology
Ignores dynamic events on the outside of its core area of operation
Defends market position with low price plus quality and service

*Analyzer*
A combination prospector–defender—less aggressive with innovation and change than prospector, but not so attached to stability and efficiency as defender
Very selective in developing products and pursuing opportunities
Seldom a first mover, but often a strong second or third, offering high quality and service

*Reactor*
Lacks a well-defined strategy
Product mix is inconsistent
Not a risk taker, not aggressive
Takes action generally under environmental pressures

SOURCE: Adapted from R. E. Miles and C. C. Snow, *Organizational Strategy and Process,* p. 29, copyright © 1979 by McGraw-Hill. Used with permission of McGraw-Hill.

the truly market-oriented enterprise. "A **market orientation** is (1) the systematic gathering of information on customers and competitors, both present and potential, (2) the systematic analysis of the information for the purpose of developing market knowledge, and (3) the systematic use of such knowledge to guide strategy recognition, understanding, creation, selection, implementation and modification."[14]

## Unique Character

The unfortunate state of affairs is that a market orientation is rare. Yet quite clearly, as the orientation develops in the culture of an organization, it becomes a significant resource for sustaining a competitive advantage. Compared to its internally focused competitors, a market-oriented company selects its target markets more wisely and offers a product mix better matched to customer preferences. Although it may face the same risks as any other firm when it comes to neglecting market intelligence or acting sluggishly in an environment requiring adaptation, its knowledge of customers and competitors is apt to overcome occasional errors. Superior self-knowledge will reveal the source of its competitive advantage and it will then be protected.

## Market Orientation Payoffs

Because many firms give lip service to being market oriented, the truly market-oriented firm may not be easily recognized by its inwardly focused competitors. And market orientation is not something one puts on like a new T-shirt. It requires supportive administrative and social systems, formal and tacit routines, and professional associates who incorporate the orientation into their entire work lives.

At least three payoffs point to a sustainable competitive advantage from a market orientation. First, a market-oriented firm should benefit from better marketing programs, efforts that fit the needs of customers. In general, it realizes efficiencies from precision targeting and avoids trouble because it is adaptable. Second, the market-oriented firm is difficult for competitors to spot easily. Because talk is cheap, lots of organizations say they have a sophisticated customer focus. But the truly market-oriented will only be revealed over long time periods. Thus, the market orientation has a stealth character. Finally, a market orientation is apt to be unique. It is typically a very distinctive skill because it is complex, intangible, and inimitable. Two competing distributors could match each other in offering bar-coded parts, overnight delivery, and Internet ordering. But matching on market orientation—values and systems for market knowledge and strategy development—is not as easy as buying a scanner, hiring more drivers, or contracting for Web site development.

## Forming a Market Orientation

Recently, marketing professors Stephen Vargo (University of Maryland) and Robert Lusch (Texas Christian University) sparked interesting discussion in the discipline of marketing by proposing a new "logic." Instead of thinking about marketing as the activities to facilitate the exchange of "goods" for the betterment of customers, they suggest a service-centered view because it brings into focus the firm's mission to provide superior value.[15] Indeed, an overemphasis on "goods"—the product—risks neglect of the very needs or wants it should be serving. A product focus can interfere with the true market orientation, as Ted Levitt warned in his classic article, "Marketing Myopia,"

**Exhibit 6–12**
Comparing the Logic of Marketing from a Product versus Service Orientation

| Thinking about marketing as primarily goods as the unit of exchange carries with it the following positions. | Thinking about marketing as services that create utility brings these activities into play. |
|---|---|
| 1. The purpose of economic activity is to make and distribute things that can be sold. | 1. Identify or develop core competences, the fundamental knowledge and skills of an economic entity that represent potential competitive advantage. |
| 2. To be sold, these things must be embedded with utility and valued during the production and distribution processes and must offer the customer superior value. | 2. Identify other potential customers that could benefit from these competences. |
| 3. The firm should set all decision variables at a level that enables it to maximize the profit for the sale of output. | 3. Cultivate relationships that involve the customers in developing customized, competitively compelling value propositions to meet specific needs. |
| 4. For both maximum production control and efficiency, the product should be standardized and produced away from the market. | 4. Gauge marketplace feedback by analyzing financial performance from exchange to learn how to improve the firm's offering to customers and improve firm performance |
| 5. The product can then be inventoried until it is demanded and then delivered to the customer at a profit. | |

SOURCE: Adapted from Stephen Vargo and Robert Lusch, "Evolving to a New Dominant Logic for Marketing," *Journal of Marketing* 68 (January 2004), pp. 1–17.

almost 50 years ago.[16] But Vargo and Lusch develop the idea more fully, as we summarize in Exhibit 6–12. We underscore the merits of their perspective for supporting a market orientation.

# ORGANIZATIONAL LEARNING AND MEMORY

So far in this chapter we have defined business strategy, identified key elements in a strategy (product market emphasis, objectives and plans, synergies, etc.), highlighted critical facets of the strategic planning process (SWOT, mission formulation, competitive analysis), and flagged the imperatives for sequential disruptions of market and a market orientation. Now we must emphasize the ability to learn and transfer knowledge as vital skills for both the development and execution of business strategies. Indeed, they represent the critical prerequisites for the judicious selection and development of other strategic resources and skill sets.

# What Is Learning?

You have been in college for some time now. One measure of its value so far might be to ask you to define learning. Students in our classes often give the following answers: "information," "facts and concepts you can use," "knowledge," "skill acquisition," "discovery," "to memorize." Although learning touches on all of these, we like the very concrete definition: "**Learning** occurs when we connect new information to what we already know. We're learning when we can say, 'Hey, that's just like ————.'"[17] The ancient Egyptians made awesome and lasting architectural structures knowing only that a triangle with sides measuring 3, 4, and 5 units produced a perpendicular. Later, in the 6th century B.C. the Greek mathematician Pythagoras gave his famous theorem. (The square

**Exhibit 6–13**
**Requisites for the Learning Organization**

SOURCE: *Adapted from Calhoun Wick and Lu Stanton Leon, "From Ideas to Action: Creating a Learning Organization,"* Human Resource Management 34, no. 2 (1995), pp. 299–311, *with permission of the copyright © owner John Wiley & Sons, Inc.*

of the hypotenuse is the sum of the squared adjacent sides, "just like the Egyptian's 5–4–3 triangle.") And sooner or later in statistics class you learn the concept of Euclidian distance, perhaps saying, "Oh, that's like the Pythagorean theorem!"

We can now define the **learning organization** as one that consistently creates and refines its capabilities by connecting new information and skills to known and remembered requisites for future success. Recognize implicit humility in this definition; it does not presume *all* success factors are known. It surely includes the endeavors by the organization to learn more about what are the requisites of future success.

## Managing Organizational Learning

Management scholars have only just begun to investigate how one creates and maintains a learning enterprise. One useful way to represent the process is the multiplicative model shown in Exhibit 6–13. A key feature of this type of model is that if any variable is zero, the product of the remaining variables is zero, in which case we do not have a learning organization.

### Visionary Leadership

Ronald Reagan was twice elected president in landslide proportions. Many pundits credit Reagan's success to his ability to communicate a clear vision for his administration: cut and simplify taxes, grow the economy, and rebuild the U.S. military. Hernan Cortes conquered the Aztec empire—some 200,000 warriors—with 508 soldiers, 16 horses, 10 bronze cannon, four falconets, and 13 muskets. Cortes attacked when retreat seemed proper, he praised the valor of his defeated opponents, and made peace with the Aztecs' enemies. His vision—in speech and action—to take the Gospel to the New World, find fame in this fantastic adventure, and claim wealth beyond compare motivated superb effort and loyalty in his men.[18]

POSCO, Korea's giant steel maker, is driven by the company motto of "3 Bests," meaning best quality, minimal pollution, and zero accidents. Boeing's vision directing effort on the new 777 was even simpler than POSCO's: "Working together to produce the preferred new airplane family."[19] Indeed, a vision should be simple and easily communicated throughout the business.

We are not out to replay our discussion of organizational mission in this section. The emphasis is on leadership. Organizational leaders determine whether the vision is concrete or wimpy. Cortes scuttled his ships after landing to end any doubt about commitment. GE's former CEO, Jack Welch, had to follow through with rewards and divestitures when he called for all GE products to be first or second in their markets.

High-profile CEOs are the subject of many articles and lore. But visionary leadership for the learning organization must extend throughout the organization: the executive committee, the senior partners, the regional heads, and department and branch managers. Especially in the nebulous assignment "to improve capabilities to attain success" every supervisor is a role model in character—prudent, just,

## 6–2

# FROM THE FIELD

## Goodness in Good Strategy

In 1985 General Dynamics, the second-largest U.S. defense contractor, was charged with improper expense billings to the government. Shortly thereafter, Secretary of the Navy, John Lehman, ordered the company "to establish and enforce a rigorous code of ethics for all General Dynamics officers and employees, with mandatory sanctions for violations."[20] To carry out the order General Dynamics created a company ethics office, the first of its kind in business.

More recently, at many companies compliance with laws and rules is not enough. They've sought a higher moral standard. The aim is an organizational culture built on core values and steadfast adherence to legal and ethical principles in everyday action. As much as a SWOT and competitive analysis, the moral principles of the firm are embodied in the strategic planning process. "This approach starts at the highest level of an organization, with the leaders in top management who buy into the core values, have aligned their personal values with company values, and serve as guardians of the process. When leaders are committed, and their behavior is consistent, employees become committed."[21]

Cintas, the leader in corporate identity uniforms, serving Delta Airlines, Wal-Mart, Hertz, and Avis, and with floor mats, first aid, and other services to the business market, recorded sales of nearly $3.4 billion in 2006. Touted by *Forbes* as one of America's Most Admired Companies, Cintas is the 1998 award winner for Strategy Excellence from Bain & Company, one of the world's leading consulting firms.

Cintas chairman, Richard Farmer, points to the company culture as the foundation for its planning excellence and its sustained superior performance. Cintas has a clear vision. Yes, it includes market-based goals: "To be well known as the obvious leader in the business," and "To have a uniform rental presence in every city in the United States and Canada." Yes, it seeks synergies: "To leverage our infrastructure to become a more valuable resource for our customers by providing additional products and services."

But the Cintas culture is knit by the visions of virtue also: "To be recognized as a company which insists upon absolute honesty and integrity in everything we do," and "To have a highly talented, diverse and motivated team of partners who are compatible with our culture and enjoy what they do."[22]

Everyone at Cintas is a partner. To see the Cintas Way that this vision is expected to be lived each day, visit www.cintas-corp.com/hr/cintasway.asp.

---

constant, and sober—as well as a potential champion of innovation, skill development, risk taking, and success sharing. From the Field 6–2 profiles the moral culture at Cintas. And From the Field 6–3 profiles an executive marketing strategist.

### Target and Trajectory

It takes resources and plans to create a learning enterprise. When a firm's leadership has determined to build a learning culture, a program and administrative structure must be designed. A timetable should be developed to specify when each enabling phase or critical event ought to take place. It took Xerox six years to move from its first "Leadership through Quality" initiatives to winning the Malcolm Baldrige National Quality Award. Even a firm with a rich tradition of managing intellectual and moral capital must attend to the maintenance of these strategic assets. What programs, tracking measures, and new hiring criteria should be applied or reviewed?

## 6–3

### FROM THE FIELD

## This Way to the Office of Marketing Strategist

My strategic planning career evolved out of a series of positions early in my career. In my first job as a member of technical staff at AT&T Bell Laboratories in the early 1980's, I was lucky to have the opportunity to work on a couple of "intrapreneurial" ventures. These new ventures were intended to commercialize some of the Labs' technological breakthroughs. Leveraging my masters in industrial and operations engineering with a specialty in operations research–which might be considered a technical business degree–I became a founding member of two startup companies within AT&T.

The first venture commercialized interactive video technologies, the second commercialized decision support systems built upon applications of a patented mathematical programming algorithm. This exposed me to the disciplines of product management, business development, and strategic planning. In addition to designing and developing software, I wrote proposals, negotiated contacts, managed client relationships. I then supervised a marketing-oriented group of operations research PhDs charged with developing several new business applications for the decision support systems division. These experiences served me well when I moved to a small systems integration company, Cincinnati Bell Information Systems (CBIS).

I was brought on board to help CBIS's federal systems integration unit expand into the commercial marketplace. I led the development and launch of an insurance systems integration business and manage several telecommunications billing products. Along the way, I played an increasing role assisting senior management in refining the long range growth strategy of the company. When Convergys was spun out of Cincinnati Bell Inc. (combining CBIS with its sister company, Matrixx Marketing), I was asked to head up marketing strategy in the core products and marketing division. A corporate restructuring lead me to the VP strategic planning role, where I monitored overall industry conditions and led planning operations across all divisions of Convergys.

As the head of strategic planning, I developed the annual five-year strategic plan intended to increase competitiveness, improve profitability and create shareholder value, including recommendations for new product investments, partnerships and potential acquisitions.

Skills required in strategic planning include analyzing market trends, identifying sources of sustainable competitive advantage, devising product and pricing strategies, developing business plans, negotiating alliances and supporting M&A activity.

David Stein VP Convergys Corporation – Cincinnati, OH

### Information and Value Systems

We have already discussed situation analysis, SWOT, competitive analysis, customer satisfaction studies, and more. The learning organization develops *systems* to gauge internal matters: efficiency, employee morale, and cross-functional knowledge. Unisys integrates several technologies to automate management and vendor reporting systems. Customer Relationship Management and sales force automation tools are used to plan and record customer contacts, process customer surveys, address "hot" problems and opportunities, and verify the progress on initiatives for improving customer loyalty.

Value systems encouraging honesty and information sharing and quashing the need to cover up errors with the need to fix problems are part of the equation. But sometimes not all the needed values are in place. In 2003 Dell CEO, Kevin Rollins, said in an interview, "There are some organizations where people think they're a hero if they invent a new thing. Being a hero at Dell means saving money."[23]

Other systems must focus on the external environment. Competitive intelligence can be gained by talking to distributors, monitoring advertising and trade shows, reading corporate annual reports, tracking dialogue on the Internet, and more. Recognize good ideas from customers, competitors, foreign markets, and elsewhere. David Luther, senior vice president of quality at Corning Inc., says, "It's absolutely crazy to reinvent something that somebody else has done."

### Creating and Striving

Vision, plans, and information are certain to be bland and feeble if not energized by creative effort. To create means to bring something into existence, to make something original. What does it take to be creative? Well, researchers in a variety of fields have told us that creative people tend to be or have:[24]

| | | | |
|---|---|---|---|
| Curious | Persistent | Imaginative | Visual thinker |
| Sense of humor | Motivated and energetic | Energetic | Unique |
| Independent | Eclectic taste | Hard-working | Confident |
| Observant | Avid reader | Ambitious | Able to see the big picture |

Thomas Edison claimed that creativity was 1 percent inspiration and 99 percent perspiration. That essence is reflected in the preceding traits and in our experience with effective managers. Creative professionals work hard. Their efforts are efficient in the sense that they don't try to force fit a tired solution to a new challenge and they often recognize the payoffs that can come from finding new ways to frame problems. They recognize that a crisis in sales force performance may be a training problem, a motivation problem, or even a selection problem. By examining the data from different perspectives, the creative manager tends to see the limits of existing routines and the need for new solutions at any level of operations or position in the value-added chain.

### Execution

Ariba is a key player in e-marketplace development for business. Its slogan, "making the net work for B2B," is lived in its competitive superiority in using its technology to host the critical mass of buyers and sellers; it serves both players. Buyers realize benefits from price exploration and procurement efficiencies. Sellers stand to acquire new customers and strengthen existing relationships with market-based performance measures.[25]

Learning organizations know the competitive advantage to be gained from execution. Lear Seating can deliver a car seat system ready for installation within two hours of the time it was ordered. Kuper Maintenance emphasizes fix-it-right the first time, knowing the nuisance and frustration that come from lingering problems at its customer's physical plants.

Quality execution takes practice. So learning organizations make or find practice fields. They simulate market situations in training sessions. They use customer quotations and other feedback to tune systems. They hone routines in low-risk environments, perhaps in isolated test environments or in cooperation with a key supplier or customer with a shared stake in the excellence of operations. For example, Microsoft may pilot test a new operating system or software application at organizations that are apt to find and stretch the limits of functionality. Not only are kinks ironed out, but "new wrinkles" may be added to enhance system performance.

---

**6–2**

## BUSINESS 2 BUSINESS

### Listen Up!

Learning organizations listen to their customers. An airline customer told the aeronautical engineer at Boeing that he wanted a jet with a fuselage that could change size. Regarding the request as a technical impossibility, the Boeing engineer delved a little further: "Why do you want such a plane?"

The customer explained, "We don't know 10 years from now what size plane we will need. If we had the flexibility to shrink or expand the size of the plane, it would help us meet future travel demands, even those we cannot anticipate."

Largely as a result of this exchange, Boeing reframed its notion of a plane's interior. It created a plane with quick-change seats and movable galleys—the flexible interior. The 777 can be outfitted for packing in vacation travelers or accommodating the need for room among business passengers traveling overnight.[26]

What business are you familiar with that really listens to its customers? Why do you say that? Who does the listening? How does listener input get translated into action?

---

# Summary

This chapter has pointed to the significant probability that you will give forecasting input to your company's strategic planning process. Although many planning models can be summarized in crisp flowcharts and path diagrams, appreciate the iterative and multiple-tasking character of planning in action.

You may also be asked to provide a SWOT analysis. Consider the various internal and external forces within your bailiwick and try to convey them to top management. Conceptual maps, value-added chains, and customer profiles will be helpful in this regard. These are just a small sample of singular situation analysis tools. Recognize that most students will plug into the planning process of their employer. For formulating a strategy for your own company or organization, we strongly recommend you use a variety of approaches. Of course, do not forget to spend time talking with and listening to members of your stakeholder groups—customers, suppliers, employees, owners—firsthand.

We spent several pages on the analysis of competition. The heat of competitive pressures comes not only from intense rivalry among firms in the same industry chasing the same group of customers, but also from negotiations with powerful customers and suppliers. We must also regard the full range of existing and potential alternatives to our products as competitors. For example, potential customers of our information technology consultancy can consider other consulting firms, outsource their operations, or develop an internal strategic support staff.

Potential entrants to a market represent a fifth competitive force. The chapter underscored the importance of choosing one's competitive arena judiciously. By developing strong service organizations or channel relations, a business may thwart potential entrants who don't have the time, resources, or know-how to serve customers that value these dimensions. Alternatively, a firm investing in high-efficiency, high-volume productive capacity needs to capitalize on this strength in securing large accounts, where few other players can hold their own in the slim-margin trade terms. In sum, stress the unique and inimitable.

Market-oriented firms recognize the fickleness of customers and the fleeting nature of any sort of competitive edge. They are not enamored with the product, but the value it contributes to customers, in conjunction with feedback and adaptation within a working relationship and a measure of coproduction of utility-providing service. Thus, getting and staying market oriented is a competitive advantage in its own right. The foundation for the market orientation, in turn, is an organization that learns. The learning organization has visionary leadership, thorough plans, and good control systems. The learning organization manifests persistence, creativity, and an ability to execute.

# Key Terms

| | | |
|---|---|---|
| analyzer | learning | prospector |
| barriers to entry | learning organization | reactor |
| conceptual map | market development | SWOT analysis |
| defender | market orientation | synergy |
| diversification | market penetration | |
| five forces of | mission statement | |
| competition | product development | |

# Discussion Questions

1. "Plans are nothing. Planning is everything." Can this be true?

2. The conduct of a SWOT analysis seems rather straightforward. But problems arise as both external and internal factors intersect. To illustrate, Sealed Air Corporation prided itself on its technical leadership and consultative sales force in the packaging field. Does this strength become a liability when effective, low-cost competitive offerings begin to flood the market? What would you say are the corporate strengths of, say, Microsoft, 3M, and United Parcel Service? Are there environments where these strengths become weaknesses?

3. "Analyzing a competitor's current strengths and weaknesses and playing strengths against weaknesses may work in the short term but is not an effective long-term strategy in a dynamic environment. . . . Consistently playing against the weaknesses of a competitor is both predictable and a strategy that ultimately builds its weaknesses into strengths. A tennis player who serves to his opponent's weak backhand will eventually force the opponent to develop a stronger backhand. Then the first player faces a rival with a strong forehand and a strong backhand."[27] Do you agree? Is there another strategy?

4. The Indian economy has grown in large part from the outsourcing of technical services by companies in the West. Indian companies such as Wipro, Genpact, and Infosys Technologies boast highly competent personnel and labor costs at 50 percent of their Western counterparts. The business shift has affected the revenue growth of EDS, Capgemini, and IBM. In contrast, Accenture has built a staff that includes 35,000 Indian employees, up from almost nothing at the beginning of this decade. By this move, Accenture could serve its accounts on "low-end jobs"

and blend services to optimize costs and service in more complex assignments, such as clinical research trials for pharmaceutical clients. Explain what has happened here in terms of the five forces model of competition.

5. Chapter 6 sketched the role of conceptual maps and other models to cope with the complexity of markets and business planning. A lesson on this point is the Battle of Midway, required reading in the U.S. Naval Academy. In the aftermath of the sea battle that changed the direction of the war in the Pacific, it seems that the Japanese overplanned and overrehearsed. They followed static assumptions and enjoyed an abundance of resources. Japanese Admiral Isoroku Yamamoto "succumbed to the temptation of taking on a broad set of objectives (capture Midway, attack the Aleutians, destroy the U.S. fleet). As underdogs with limited resources, the Americans were constrained to pursue a simpler, more straightforward mission: defend Midway Island. As a result, their strategic responsibilities were much different: to be alert to whatever opportunities might arise within the context of their single mission and to be sufficiently flexible to act on them."[28] Use Web and library sources to sketch a time line and simple set of maps to show the key events at Midway. (Try **www.geocities.com/Colosseum/Arena/2951/english.html.**) Contrast this with a corporate example (e.g., DuPont, HP vs. Dell, NCR, or AMD).

6. Interview two business executives—the higher their rank the better. Ask them for their company's mission. Then invite them to tell you how it came about and how it affects the direction and activities of the company.

7. Our experience indicates that few student organizations on a college campus can show a history of sustained effectiveness. Analyze this phenomenon by considering the impediments to organizational learning in this context. Can you identify exceptional organizations on your campus? How have they overcome the impediments to learning?

8. What are the key strategic decisions facing managers at 3m, Citi Corp, DuPont or Firestone/Bridgestone?

9. Managerial Performance, Inc. (MPI) is a small human resources consultancy in the South. President Sid Luster leads a staff of five consultants and a support staff in a four-year endeavor to double the firm's billings to $2 million. MPI specializes in motivation, personal development, and workplace morale, sometimes union avoidance. MPI would like to have ongoing relationships with its clients. Frustration has crept into the firm in year two as sales growth is only 8 percent per year. Analysis of the revenues shows 20 percent repeat clients. Of the 27 new clients served, 22 were procured by Sid. Many of these accounts want Sid to be project leader. Thus, while his professional staff dub Sid the "rainmaker," his business development initiatives are quite limited by the time he must give to ongoing projects. Recommend a strategy for MPI to attain its growth objectives.

10. Is it possible for organizational learning and memory to be liabilities in a fast-changing market?

11. A number of marketing executives and consultants have identified relationships as another key element in a strategic plan. At the corporate level of strategy, relationships are cast by the position of the firm in the value chain. At the business unit level, partner selection, timing, and management take on significance. Using our discussion of relationship development and structures from Chapter 2, identify two relationships in the business press, one that you regard as a B2B strategic home run and the other a strategic strikeout. Justify your answer.

# Cases

### Case 6.1    Power in Africa

AES is a 25-year-old Virginia-based electric utility that has helped drive energy sector growth on a global basis. In 2001 AES bought a 57 percent share in Cameroon's state power company. The state-run company was broke. It had neglected many of its power-producing assets—dams were cracking and poles rotting—and had been badly bled by the government and rogue employees who stole power and resold it to "special customers" or entire villages.

Things continued to go badly despite the new ownership until AES put Jean-David Bile in charge in February 2004. With a doctorate in economics, an undergraduate degree in engineering, and fluency in French, Bile began to turn things around. Days after he took charge he gathered employees and made a short statement: "If you guys have been stealing, taking bribes, stop it now . . . if I catch you you're finished." More than 50 people have been fired for wrongdoing and even tribal chieftains have pleaded for employees to be given a second chance. The answer: "No."

For trimming the bloated workforce by 25 percent, he offered, "negotiated departure agreements." He rationalized purchasing—shutting out cronies by using a bid system on many supplies and obtaining price concessions on service contracts. Interestingly, he outsourced the task of meter reading because he came to the conclusion that too many of the readers were in cahoots with customers.

Because Cameroon's power supply was almost entirely dependent on hydroelectricity, in 2004 AES constructed an 85 MW thermal power plant to provide a 20 percent boost in dry season–generating capacity. From a $340 million financing package to AES in 2006, the company expects to add 50 thousand new electricity connections per year through 2021, upgrading transmission, and distribution and generation facilities.

1. Does AES appear to be market oriented in Cameroon?
2. Are there "traps" from a goods-centered (power) orientation that might be avoided with a service-centered view?
3. How critical is leadership to the whole enterprise?

### Case 6.2    Petrex: Competition in Emerging Markets

The Petrex Corporation is an environmental services company that has been a leader in the field of chemical storage, disposal, and cleanup. Management at Petrex routinely monitors—and participates in—local, national, and international environmental policy forums. Recently there have been indications that the Environmental Protection Agency and Federal Emergency Management Agency will push to have regular filtration (every 24 to 36 months) of the diesel fuel that is stored in tanks for emergency power generation at nearly 12,000 hospitals and nursing care facilities.

The equipment to conduct these filtrations is widely available. Anyone with a small tanker truck can attach the filtration device and be in business within a few days. Thus, as demand for diesel fuel filtration may go from zero to nearly 5,000 jobs at $300 to $500 at the issuance of new regulations, start-up suppliers can appear just as quickly.

Petrex has tanker trucks it can retrofit and commit to this opportunity, but there have been heated debates in the company. Some argue that the potential sales numbers are too good to pass up and that Petrex is one of only two firms that could well participate as a nationwide supplier. Petrex already has waste disposal contracts with about 15 percent of the firms apt to be affected by new regulations. Others have cautioned that this is a new game—a mundane operation compared to the complexity and risk in most of its jobs. Also, the field is wide open to any local tanker jockey who wants to put down the $3,000 to outfit a truck.

Describe the competitive forces at play in this opportunity and justify a recommendation to Petrex.

# Additional

Covey, Stephen R., A. Roger Merrill, and Rebecca R. Merrill. *First Things First.* New York: Simon & Schuster, 1994.

D'Aveni, Richard. *Hypercompetition: Managing the Dynamics of Strategic Maneuvering.* New York: The Free Press, 1994.

Day, George S., John Deighton, Das Narayandas, Evert Gummesson, Shelby D. Hunt, C. K. Prahalad, Roland Rust, Steven M. Shugan. "Invited Commentaries on 'Evolving to a New Dominant Logic for Marketing.'" *Journal of Marketing* 68 (January 2004), pp. 18–27.

Fulmer, Robert M. "A Model for Changing the Way Organizations Learn." *Planning Review* (May–June 1994), pp. 20–24.

Gomes-Casseres, Benjamin. "Do You Really Have an Alliance Strategy?" *Strategy and Leadership* (September–October 1998), pp. 6–11.

Gummesson, Evert. *Total Relationship Marketing.* Boston: Butterworth Heinmann, 2002.

Hunt, Shelby, and Caroline Derozier. "The Normative Imperatives of Business and Marketing Strategy: Grounding Strategy in Resource-Advantage Theory." *Business & Industrial Marketing* 19, no. 1 (2004), pp. 5–22.

Kumar, Nirmalya. *Marketing as Strategy.* Boston: Harvard Business School Press, 2004.

Selden, Larry, and Geoffrey Colvin. *Angel Customers & Demon Customers.* New York: Penquin, 2003.

Slywotzky, Adrian J., and Fred Linthicum. "Capturing Value in Five Moves or Less: The New Game of Business." *Strategy & Leadership* 25 (January–February 1997), pp. 5–11.

Tzokas, Nicholaos, and Michael Saren. "Competitive Advantage, Knowledge, and Relationship Marketing: Where, When, and How? *Business & Industrial Marketing* 19, no. 2 (2004), pp. 124–35.

Wilson, Ian. "The New Rules: Ethics, Social Responsibility, and Strategy." *Strategy & Leadership* 28 (May–June 2000), pp. 12–16.

# Chapter 7

## Weaving Marketing into the Fabric of the Firm

### EATON

In just 10 years, Eaton Corporation has grown its aerospace operations 10-fold. Sustained growth of this sort doesn't happen by accident; for Eaton, the plan for growth included both acquisitions of other companies and growth through product development, service quality, and other factors. Now Eaton Aerospace accounts for nearly $1.5 billion in sales and will be well over $2 billion by 2010 (Eaton overall enjoys almost $13 billion in annual sales). ●

Eaton Aerospace manufactures component parts, subassemblies, and assemblies for aircraft as varied as the Airbus A380 (the world's largest plane seating over 600 passengers) to the Embraer Phenom100 (a small private jet), to the F-22 fighter plane. Two critical acquisitions for Eaton Aerospace were Perkin–Elmer's aerospace segments and Cobham plc's fluid and aero business, but the company also bought several other smaller parts makers since then. ●

Many companies have tried to grow through acquisitions only to encounter insurmountable obstacles when integrating the acquired company into operations. While any acquisition has its challenges, Eaton has been unique in bringing together its acquisitions in order to better serve its customers. "Eaton will have a much broader portfolio of components to offer an OEM," says Bradley J. Morton, president of Eaton Aerospace. "More importantly, we understand the components and can build that into a system or a subsystem. . . . We have engineers sitting side by side with Boeing engineers integrating the 787 fuel system into the wing, the fuselage, the tail section—all the way to the nacelle." ●

By remaining customer-focused, Eaton Aerospace has been able to integrate these different companies into one unit. Some of that integration has involved closing plants and moving some of the manufacturing to a plant in Tijuana, Mexico. The key, though, is the integration, not the location. That's why Eaton Aerospace has been able to win new jobs from companies like Sikorsky. Over the next four years, Sikorsky and Eaton engineers will work together to develop a new military heavy-lift helicopter. ●

Sources: Joseph C. Anselmo, "Market Focus," *Aviation Week & Space Technology* 164 (May 15, 2006) p. 10; Joseph C. Anselmo, "Buying In: Acquisition Binge Bolsters Eaton's Aerospace Business; Aerospace Acquisition Binge helps Eaton Evolve from Component Supplier to Systems Provider," *Aviation Week & Space Technology* 166 (April 2, 2007) p. 69; Joseph C. Anselmo, "Made in Mexico: Eaton Shifts Aerospace Jobs to Mexican Factory," *Aviation Week & Space Technology* 166 (April 2, 2007) p. 67; Anonymous, "Sikorsky Selects Eaton to Supply Hydraulic Power Generation System and Fluid Conveyance Package for New CH-53K Helicopter," http://www.eaton.com/EatonCom/OurCompany/NewsandEvents/CT_128486, accessed July 18, 2007.

## LEARNING OBJECTIVES

In forward-thinking companies like Eaton Aerospace, the marketing function has taken on increased significance in recent years. As companies recognize the importance of the customer, marketing's importance grows because of the responsibility for the customer. In this chapter, we examine the role of marketing in carrying the voice of the customer to the rest of the firm. In Chapter 6, we learned about strategic planning; in this chapter we learn how marketing builds internal partnerships in order to devise and implement the most effective strategic plan possible.

*After reading this chapter, you should be able to*

- Describe the role marketing plays in creating and maintaining a market-oriented culture.
- Describe the internal partnerships that marketing must develop.
- Illustrate the partnering process for various internal partnerships.
- List the skills that are needed by marketing managers to build internal partnerships.

The concepts of market orientation and learning organization were first introduced in Chapter 6. In this chapter, we explore how those concepts must be carried into every activity of the firm so that the value delivered by the value chain is maximized.

Visit Texas A&M and you'll find a military tradition; more Aggies have won the Congressional Medal of Honor than graduates of any of the service academies. Just 60 miles up the Brazos River is Baylor University, with its very different culture shaped by close ties with the Southern Baptist Church. What makes each university unique, including yours, is the unique culture, the values that began as reasons for starting each university, and the forces that have shaped that university's past and will shape its future.

**Organizational culture** is the collectively held values, ideology, and social processes embedded in a firm.[1] When we entitled this chapter "Weaving Marketing into the Fabric of the Firm," we meant that marketing should be such an integral part of that culture that marketing activities are not identifiable with just one department but are part and parcel of the activities of virtually every employee. Implementing the marketing strategy becomes the responsibility of everyone, not just the marketing or sales departments.

When marketing values are embedded into the culture of a firm, then marketing managers have one important additional responsibility: to carry the customer's voice to the rest of the firm. The medium by which this is accomplished is organizational learning; the result of such learning should be a reinforcement of the market orientation of the firm.

# MARKET-ORIENTED COMPANIES

Critical to the success of any company is understanding customers and acting on that understanding. Learning organizations, first introduced in the previous chapter, have created processes and methods for learning, especially about customers, as a way to gain competitive advantage. One could argue that a **market orientation** is a customer-centric form of a learning organization because a market orientation, also introduced in Chapter 6, is defined as superior skills of understanding and satisfying customers.[2] When a firm has a market orientation, it is more likely to be financially successful and superior in many areas of performance, such as product development.[3]

A market orientation is the principal *cultural* foundation of the learning organization.[4] By cultural foundation, we mean that a market orientation must exist in the culture of the organization, and that such an orientation should be part of the values and norms of the organization. A company needs a market orientation in order to learn successfully. Some companies have created a chief customer officer, equivalent to a chief financial officer or the like, but with the responsibility of creating a market-oriented organization.[5]

Working for a market-oriented company should be a goal of most business marketing students. Market-oriented companies understand the importance of marketing, which should create better opportunities for marketing majors. Just working in a market-oriented company is not enough, however. As you read this chapter, consider the importance of these topics to your career.

## How Market Orientation Impacts Performance

Market-driven companies, or those with a strong market orientation, are superior in two important ways. First, market-driven companies do a better job of **market sensing,** or anticipating market requirements ahead of competition. Market sensing is the gathering of information from the market. Market research, such as that discussed in Chapter 5, is one form of market sensing, but market sensing can be achieved through listening to the sales force, observing competition at trade shows, and developing stronger ties with innovative customers and suppliers.

**Exhibit 7–1**
Classifying
Capabilities

*SOURCE: George S. Day,
"Capabilities of
Market-Driven
Organizations,"
Journal of Marketing
58 (October, 1994),
pp. 37–52.*

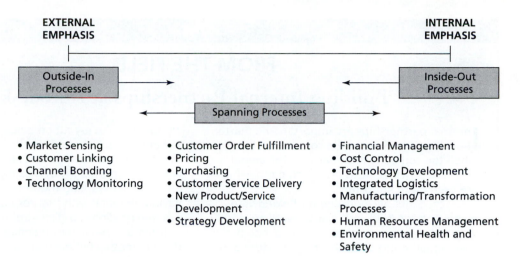

**EXTERNAL EMPHASIS** — Outside-In Processes

**INTERNAL EMPHASIS** — Inside-Out Processes

Spanning Processes

- Market Sensing
- Customer Linking
- Channel Bonding
- Technology Monitoring

- Customer Order Fulfillment
- Pricing
- Purchasing
- Customer Service Delivery
- New Product/Service Development
- Strategy Development

- Financial Management
- Cost Control
- Technology Development
- Integrated Logistics
- Manufacturing/Transformation Processes
- Human Resources Management
- Environmental Health and Safety

Similarly, the second important difference is that market-driven companies are able to develop stronger relationships with their customers and their channels of distribution. Stronger relationships include more direct lines of communication; instead of all communication going between a purchasing agent and a salesperson, interaction among engineers in all three firms (customer, manufacturer, and supplier) can occur. Stronger relationships can result in greater attention to the customer throughout the firm.

Research indicates several outcomes of market orientation. The most important is increased profit.[6] Market orientation improves profit through three primary ways: more innovative product development, better marketing communication, and lower cost.[7] The first two seem obvious—the better a company understands its customers, the better products and marketing strategies it should create. Lower costs then accrue by having a more efficient supply chain.

Further, a market orientation influences performance more strongly in economies or industries that are rapidly changing. Market orientation enables firms to adapt more quickly in turbulent industries, whereas such adaptation is less necessary in stable economies or industries.[8] Ashland, a manufacturer of chemicals, has maintained a market orientation in an environment that is rapidly changing due to government regulation and technology. As the government changes requirements for environmental protection reasons, new technologies have to replace old ones or the company will not have products it can sell. At the same time, staying close to customers in order to understand how they deal with changing regulations is also important. Ashland's market orientation enables them to pick the right new products and technologies that will really serve customers.

Companies that want to adopt a market orientation must have adequate **spanning processes,** processes that link internal processes with the customer. New product development is one such spanning process, as it links market requirements with internal processes such as manufacturing. All companies have new product development processes; the difference is how the process incorporates the voice of the customer. Exhibit 7–1 illustrates the relationship of internal processes with spanning processes to link with customer requirements. In this exhibit, internal processes such as financial management are shown to link with spanning processes, such as order fulfillment, which then impact customer linking processes or other external processes. For internal processes to contribute to the value delivered by the value chain, there must be adequate spanning processes.

**7–1**

## FROM THE FIELD

### Building Internal Partnerships at Autodesk

Internal partnerships are important, no matter how big or how small the company is. But when the company is global, as is the global software provider Autodesk, such partnerships are even more important.

Tracey Stout, vice president of worldwide marketing for Autodesk, began working closely with the chief financial officer to "define the role of marketing, the reporting structure and how to get our teams closely aligned." She notes that marketing investment decisions are made jointly, with reviews from senior executives across the organization. "One of the things that finance brings to the table is a real quantitative orientation to looking at marketing, as if it were less of a function and more of a business," says Stout.

For Autodesk, the problem wasn't only partnerships outside of marketing but between marketing and sales. Global sales organizations have salespeople scattered literally all over the globe. Mike Columbo, Autodesk's senior director of worldwide sales execution, said, "It took a while to get it right, but our divisions see how critical this is." Most companies would not task a person with the responsibility of making sure marketing and sales are working together, but at Autodesk, having someone with that responsibility makes sure the relationship stays strong.

Stout also has a person dedicated to managing the relationship between finance and marketing, someone from the finance department called a finance business partner. While this person reports to the CFO, she works directly with Stout and is firmly entrenched in understanding marketing challenges and opportunities. Concludes Stout, "More often than not, when (your partner) understands what you are trying to do from a business point of view, they are in a position to help you achieve those goals and not a barrier."

Sources: Kate Maddox, "CMOs, CFOs Work on ROI, Relationships," *BtoB* 91 (August 14, 2006), pp. 1–2; Christopher Hosford, "Aiming to Close a Perpetual Gap," *BtoB* 92 (June 4, 2007), p. 16.

## Internal Partnering to Create a Market Orientation

Yet internal and external processes are often in conflict, as different sets of objectives are sought. Internal partnering is one spanning process that, when done well, can result in managing such conflict so that it has a positive effect on the firm. **Internal partnering,** or creating partnering relationships with other functional areas (customers and suppliers within the firm), can also serve to carry market requirements to those managers in charge of internal processes. Internal partnering is a spanning process that creates a framework or environment for other spanning processes, such as postsale service, new product development, or market penetration and development processes. The result is a market orientation throughout the firm and not just in the marketing department. From the Field 7–1 illustrates the challenges at Autodesk in creating internal partnerships.

### Internal Partnering Carries the Voice of the Customer

Lenny Chesnal, chief marketing officer for Host.net, recognizes the importance of capturing the voice of the customer so that his company does what the customer wants—whether it is having the right product or being at the right trade show. As he says, "We have to capture what the client says, whether it is in meetings, telephone calls, surveys, or other customer touches. Then we have to get that information to the right people so the company can act."

In some organizations, it is the sales force that has the greatest contact with customers, and is therefore charged with capturing the voice of the customer. Alex BeMent, whose sales team at Worldwide Express sells overnight package delivery services for DHL, says, "A key competitive advantage we have is that we can take a client's needs and create a customized system. Our salespeople have to fully understand a client's billing and shipping needs so that our finance and order management personnel create the right solutions." He notes, too, that salespeople know that the data they collect on customers is then used to create new products by the marketing department, so the salespeople take care in recording information accurately.

Other parts of the marketing department also take on the voice of the customer; for example, when new products are being developed (as discussed in the next chapter), it is the responsibility of marketing research to speak for the customer. If that voice isn't heard, then the product may be built to suit only the company's needs.

The customer's voice must be carried to many parts of the firm—internal partnering is one mechanism for carrying that voice. Recognize, though, that it is the marketing manager's responsibility to build these partnerships. Although a customer focus should pervade the firm, rarely have we seen information systems, employment selection systems, personnel evaluation systems, or other systems that encourage other departments to take the initiative. In fact, it is more likely that just the opposite is true, that there are incentives not to listen to the customer. For example, it costs manufacturing managers to change production from one product to another, yet a marketing manager may need to be able to offer different products in order to meet the customer's objectives.

## Barriers to Internal Partnering

What are the barriers to internal partnering? One barrier is having too strong an internal focus in a department. The Total Quality Management (TQM) movement of the late 1980s decried the silo organizational structure that typified many organizations at that time (and still does). A silo is a large cylinder several stories high in which grain is stored; some companies consist of a number of silo departments, with high walls built around them and no ability or desire to go between the departments. Each department does its own thing without regard for other functions in the firm, with communication between departments kept to a minimum. TQM proponents fought silo management because they recognized the importance of communicating customer requirements across all parts of the firm in order to develop a market orientation.

In addition to silo organizational structures, interdepartmental rivalry can also serve as a barrier to internal partnering.[9] Rivalry has been found to lower the perceived value of knowledge transferred from one area—for example, marketing—to another, such as product development. Rivalry increases political pressure to even ignore information, no matter how vital it is to the success of a project. In a study of new product development, marketing's information about customer needs was ignored if rivalry with the product development team was high, even though all would agree that designing products to meet customer needs is an important objective of any research and development department.

**Exhibit 7–2**
Order Fulfillment
Process: An
Example of a
Critical Spanning
Capability
*SOURCE: George S. Day,
"Capabilities of
Market-Driven
Organizations,"
Journal of Marketing
58 (October 1994),
pp. 37–52.*

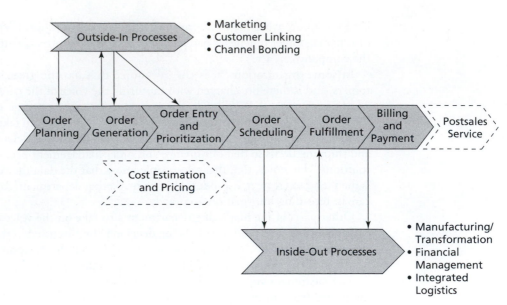

## *Internal versus External Partnering*

In Chapter 2, we discussed the importance of building a partnership with customers and, in several chapters, we've learned how to do that. We also learned in Chapter 3 that purchasing departments build partnerships with key suppliers because of the importance of managing costs and the contribution to innovation that such partnerships can bring. External partnerships, however, are just part of the story. One benefit of the TQM movement is that it forced companies to recognize that there are internal customers and suppliers, because each work process has inputs and outputs. Therefore, once marketing managers identify who supplies inputs for their work process and who uses their work outputs, they've recognized who the internal suppliers and customers are.

For example, when a salesperson takes an order from a customer, there is a piece of paper or an electronic record that spells out the terms of the agreement. The order contains vital information used by other departments; that information is input into their work processes, processes such as shipping the product, invoicing the customer, and recording the sale on an accounting ledger. The order is a product of the salesperson's work process (an output) and an input into other work processes, as illustrated in Exhibit 7–2. The salesperson, according to TQM, should view those other departments as customers.

Partnerships are characterized by open communication, trust, and commitment to the partner. Whether internal or external, partners are able to align their goals with the goals of the other. Internal partnering also requires open communication, trust, and commitment, but the alignment of goals is a little different. What happens when internal partnering is developed is that customer satisfaction becomes the **supragoal,** a goal against which other goals are aligned.

Further, internal partnering is like external partnering in that the same stages of awareness, exploration, expansion, and commitment characterize the creation of a partnership.[10] Many internal relationships never progress to the partnership level because in non-marketing-oriented companies, lip service to the same supragoal does not support such relationships. As we've said earlier, there can be conflicts between functional areas in an organization. What should also be recognized is that if profitability is the supragoal, customer satisfaction may, at times, become of little importance. In such situations, each functional area may be able to contribute to profitability in ways that can damage customer satisfaction or make internal partnerships possible.

For example, Ross Controls is a company that makes pneumatic valves. Not too many years ago, it was slowly and painfully going out of business as profit margins fell and market share shrank. The company tried to cut costs so that prices could be lowered without hurting margins; the manufacturing department worked to cut costs by standardizing products and parts as much as possible, and by making longer runs of each product. As a result, the company had large inventories of products that were not always in demand, while it was unable to deliver some products because they were not scheduled for production for several months. When the company decided to make customer satisfaction the supragoal and offer custom products with faster turnaround than competition, prices were raised but so were profits and sales. Now financially healthy, the company is receiving worldwide acclaim as a leader because of internal partnerships based on delivering customer satisfaction.[11]

In the next section, we'll examine those areas of the company with whom the marketing manager works, their internal processes, and their needs and motivations. Then we'll discuss how they partner with marketing to create a market orientation.

# Internal Partners

The business marketing manager interacts with many parts of the firm. Before we describe those areas, let's first define what we mean by a marketing manager. For the purposes of this discussion, a marketing manager is anyone on the marketing and sales management team, so we include marcomm (marketing communications) managers, sales managers, product managers, and others who serve as managers in the marketing function. Few of these managers will have all of the internal partnering responsibilities described here, but all of these responsibilities are part of one or more of those managers' duties.

Because partnering requires open communication, it promotes spanning processes and organizational learning. Marketing managers work with many areas of the firm, including manufacturing, shipping, finance, information systems, engineering, and (as you've probably guessed) just about every other area of the firm. In many cases, these areas work in the dark as far as customer requirements are concerned, particularly in silo organizations. They rely on the marketing manager to provide those customer requirements. The areas that marketing must partner with are illustrated in Exhibit 7–3. In forward-thinking companies, though, partnering across the organization opens up those silos. From the Field 7–1 illustrates how partnering works in one global organization, Autodesk.

## Manufacturing

Marketing has to work with manufacturing so that enough of the right products are made at the right time. There are three types of marketing–manufacturing situations that represent the range of customization: make to stock, make to order, and engineer to order.[12] In a **make-to-stock** situation, marketing supplies forecasts of demand and manufacturing makes enough to handle that demand. The company then draws on inventory to fill orders as they come in. There is no customization at all.

**Exhibit 7–3**
Marketing
Interfaces

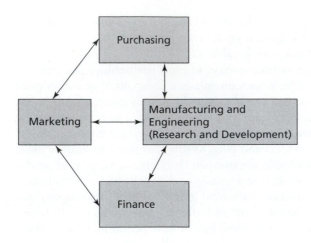

**Make to order** means that manufacturing or production begins making the product after receiving an order. Dell, for example, builds each computer by assembling the appropriate parts as called for on the customer's order. Customization, in this case, is handled by assembling stock parts into a custom-completed product, a process called mass customization. **Engineer to order** is complete customization, with the product designed from scratch to meet the customer's needs. In these situations, engineering is a key partner with manufacturing. (In Chapter 8, we'll talk about the engineering and research and development functions in more detail.)

In general, manufacturing is concerned with producing product at the lowest possible cost, so make to stock is the most desirable situation from manufacturing's situation. In most cases, this means that it wants long production runs, little customization, and low inventories of raw materials. Customers, however, want their order shipped immediately and custom made to their exact specifications—if not engineered to order, then at least made to order. Salespeople have to negotiate compromises between what customers want and manufacturing can deliver. Further, marketing managers must recognize manufacturing's responsibilities when making promotion plans, creating product line extensions, and making other marketing decisions.

Many companies are relying on technology to solve such problems. Software that informs salespeople of product availability, manufacturing schedules, and so on can solve some of the communication problems. That software, provided by companies like Siebel and Salesforce.com, can also provide forecasts from salespeople to manufacturing. But technology is only part of the total solution.

Marketers who have developed partnerships with manufacturing can coordinate promotion schedules to fit manufacturing schedules and vice versa. Further, the stronger the partnership, the greater the communication between marketing and manufacturing, which should result in greater success in a stronger market orientation in manufacturing.

## *Finance*

As we will discuss in Chapter 14, pricing is a marketing function, and several models are presented to aid in making pricing decisions. Yet determining prices is not done entirely by the marketing department; as Exhibit 7–1 showed earlier, pricing is a spanning process. It is the finance department's responsibility to manage the company's cash flow, which includes setting prices at a level that contributes to profit, whereas it is marketing's responsibility to reflect the value a product delivers in its price.

Finance departments allocate the company's money across investment decisions. Many of those decisions are marketing plans while others may be new manufacturing facilities, shipping facilities, and so forth. Recall in From the Field 7–1 how closely Tracey Stout works with the chief financial officer (CFO) in her company. Together, they make decisions about which marketing plans deserve investment; without such a partnership, it would be much more difficult for her to meet her goals.

## Purchasing

Purchasing plays an important role in the product development process. The function of purchasing is to watch the company's purchasing dollars by developing policies and procedures that carefully husband those dollars. Product development, however, needs purchasing's estimates of component costs and performance (or quality) ranges, as these ripple through the value chain. It is easier to evaluate a supplier on the basis of cost than quality; after all, quality is determined by the customer and is not always as easily quantified. Purchasing, therefore, relies on the marketing manager to present the customer's definition of quality in a way that enhances the purchasing process, whereas the product development part of marketing relies on purchasing to meet the customer's cost needs.

From this discussion of some of the departments with whom marketing managers work, you should have some idea of the needs of other departments. At the same time, recognize that those needs may be in conflict with the needs of the customer. Making the largest profit possible, for example, conflicts with the customer's need to save money. The marketing manager's responsibility is to see that the customer's needs are met in a way that enables the company to meet its overall goals. At the same time, however, the marketing manager has to recognize that unless a firm is market oriented, there may not be motivation for other managers to follow the marketing manager's recommendations.

# PARTNERSHIPS IN MARKETING

Partnerships must also be formed within the marketing department and the marketing function. In some organizations, a corporate marketing team works with divisional marketing teams. Such is the case at E-Rewards, which is owned by Brierly Group. When Emily Tanner (profiled in Chapter 1) was buying advertising and planning for trade shows to market E-Rewards, she coordinated her efforts with help from the Brierly marketing team. Jeff Pedowitz, on the other hand (profiled in Chapter 4), finds that most of his coordination efforts are between marketing and sales.

In some companies, marketing and sales are two peas in one pod; in other companies, marketing and sales aren't even in the same garden. Failure to align sales and marketing efforts can result in many negative consequences. In one study of over 1,500 executives, over 60 percent reported that failure to align properly meant selling price over value, a practice that significantly lowers profits. Thirty percent also said a lack of alignment leads to failure to meet sales quota.[13]

Salespeople say the problem is poor marketing materials, including out-of-date Web sites and poorly crafted sales brochures (called collateral). Judy Jones, marketing director for Unisys (a computer services company), says, "Ideally, you have to take a look at all of the great things that marketing is doing, and then examine if it is really what sales needs."[14] Andrea Wharton, trade show manager with the telecommunications equipment manufacturer Alcatel, says she spends a great deal of time with salespeople "understanding how they talk with customers so our trade show program can fit into that dialog." Her goal is to support what salespeople do, rather than create something flashy that might look good but not sell well.

When a firm selects a particular marketing strategy, there should be decisions made at every level of the organization to support that strategy. One outcome of poor relationships in the marketing department is that marketing strategies are not implemented consistently across all elements of the marketing mix. A recent study found that over 25 percent of implemented sales strategies conflict with the overall marketing strategy,[15] which indicates the serious extent of poor relationships between sales and marketing. Reasons for the strategy–implementation mismatch were poor communication, misleading information promulgated by one or more departments, distrust and resentment between departments, and other factors that represent the opposite of partnerships.

What happens when there is conflict in the marketing activities? There are few companies that will admit that they've had difficulties. One anonymous sales manager described a situation where a direct mail campaign was targeted to a small segment of the market not being called on by field salespeople. The campaign was so successful, however, that the marketing department sent direct mail offers to a much larger group and included 10 percent off the list price, a lower price than the field salespeople could offer. That larger group included many prospects of the field sales force, who lost sales to the direct mail offer, missing commissions and bonuses as well. To make matters worse, the field salespeople were expected to train the buyers on how to operate the equipment without any additional compensation.

A distributor for several electrical parts manufacturers reports that one manufacturer introduced a new product and shipped her an initial order. But she couldn't get brochures or any other written material for the product, nor was there any dealer training because those "weren't ready yet." Her sales rep had explained what it did and why she should carry it, but this was not enough information to really sell the product. Advertising in trade journals was focused on getting new dealers, not new customers. After two months of waiting, she sent it all back, and eventually canceled all of her business with that company. So as you can see, all elements of the marketing and sales plan must work together for a market opportunity to be fully captured.

# Integrating Marketing Efforts

As we've discussed, marketing strategy must reflect a coordinated effort of product performance and two-way communication. Within the communication process must be integration of marketing efforts and messages, as is discussed in Chapters 9 through 12. Further, what is communicated about the product must be accurate, or the position won't be supported. How can a company make certain that such integration occurs?

Several factors can encourage the appropriate level of integration within the marketing program. Clear strategic decisions, personnel stability, compensation systems that support the marketing strategy, and formal communication and organizational structures that encourage cross-functional interaction are among the more important.[16] David Dubroff, executive vice-president for Cypress Care, discusses the factors that make a customer-centric culture possible at Cypress Care in From the Field 7–2.

---

**7–2**

# FROM THE FIELD

## Customer Centricity at Cypress Care

Cypress Care helps companies contain costs in providing quality health care to our clients' injured workers. We consider this to be an important and noble service that requires a customer-centric culture because we are involved in improving the quality of someone's life. Our customer centricity starts at the top of the business. Any time you see successful cultures like ours, it comes from the leadership at the top. You can have subcultures, like these within the sales team or a product development team but customer centricity has to come from the top. In a small organization like ours, it is tied to our founder, our president, and our CEO. The three of them understand how being customer centric not only drives business results; it also means, at least in our business, higher-quality health care.

At Cypress Care, there is absolutely no tolerance for an operations versus sales mentality. This means for me, as executive vice president of sales and business development, that we have to acquire and service clients that are true to our core—we have to get the right kinds of clients so we can serve them appropriately. It's hard enough to sell clients, and harder sometimes to keep them because our competitors are always trying to take them away. This customer-centric culture means that we are able to exceed the customers' expectations, which then results in a partnership. They invest in us, as we invest in them.

Customers invest in us by not only paying us for services, but also by giving us their time. For example, I just returned from Austin, where I met with a client organization's CEO and seven of his team to review the business we've shared with them and plan ahead as to how we can deliver greater value to them in the coming year. We piloted a program with them that showed great results, and now we're rolling it out companywide with our other clients.

We continue to build this customer-centric culture by treating each other at Cypress Care as internal customers. I serve my CFO (chief financial officer) by bringing profitable customers. He serves me by working with me to develop the right kinds of incentive programs for my salespeople but also for the operations department and everyone in the organization. For example, our patient care providers (our operations people who serve customers) can earn a bonus if a customer simply writes a letter telling us how good they are.

We can't get the necessary market research, the effective trade show programs, the creative marketing collateral (brochures, Web sites, etc.) unless we have internal partnerships. And that means internal partnerships with finance (which pays for these activities), marketing, sales, and operations. In Cypress Care, everybody in the company truly understands how they are driving client satisfaction and improving the quality of life for our clients' injured workers.

Dave Dubroff, Executive Vice President, Cypress Care.

## Clear Strategic Decisions

In one study that examined mismatches between marketing and sales strategies, an issue that surfaced was a lack of decisiveness on the part of senior marketing executives. For example, two sales managers said that, although formal strategy indicated that a product would be on the market for the next few years, informal signals from marketing management indicated that the product might be withdrawn. As a result, the sales force was not putting any effort into those products. Sales and marketing strategies are neither immediate nor irreversible; if management waffles on strategic decisions, then marketing and sales investments could be wasted and relationships (both internal and external) damaged.

### Personnel Stability

Relationships take time to build. As mentioned earlier, internal relationships go through the same stages as external relationships. Moving people rapidly through the organization can mean that relationships between areas of the marketing department are never built. One manager in one study reported three marketing executives in five years; one salesperson told us he had three different sales managers in one year! While each successive manager had to try to quickly build rapport with each subordinate and superior, the whole sales team suffered because new relationships had to be built between each new manager and all of the other functional areas. When rapid personnel turnover occurs, the relationship cannot get past the exploration stage.

### Compensation

A key issue that creates ill will is the fact that different groups within marketing compete for the same budget. Fights over budgets can create bad feelings and damage relationships. Budgets, though, are not the only "money" issue that can damage or enhance relationships.

Many companies are evaluating and testing compensation plans that encourage teamwork. For example, marketing managers may find that their pay contains incentives based on sales or contribution margins. When that is the case, they are incented to work more closely with the sales force. Morehead Supply is one company that pays quarterly bonuses to all marketing personnel if sales targets are achieved. Unlike profit sharing plans that the company also uses, these bonuses are specifically designed to encourage teamwork within the marketing–sales interface.

Compensation can also help turn budgeting into teamwork. By using a joint compensation system, all of those competing for budget end up being paid based on the same performance. As a result, they are more determined than ever to see that the budget results in effective marketing. The issue, though, also affects how areas such as manufacturing, engineering, and other functional area bonuses are paid. When those areas are also compensated for customer satisfaction and teamwork, then those outcomes are more likely.

### Organizational Structure

Compensation plans, though, should be supported by the appropriate organizational structure. The structure of the organization can enhance or inhibit the ability to create internal partnerships. In the next section, we discuss different types of organizational structures, as well as the different groups within marketing between whom partnerships are created.

## Organizational Structure—Marketing Partners

Marketing is usually organized into four functional groups: sales, product development and management, marcomm, and marketing research. Sales may report to a marketing VP, along with the other areas of marketing, or may be entirely separate.

**Exhibit 7–4**
Functional
Organization

Organizing by marketing function is called a **functional structure.** Exhibit 7–4 presents an example.

When many markets are served, remaining in a functional structure can actually become dysfunctional. Allocating appropriate resources to each functional group and to each market becomes too challenging, and a market structure is created. The primary difference is that each market gets its own marketing department, which may be further organized using a functional structure.

An alternative is a matrix organization, in which the marketing function may serve multiple vertical or geographical markets. Many global companies, such as ABB, Honeywell, Measurex, and Valmet Automation, use a matrix approach to reduce marketing costs and to create opportunities to transfer learning across business units.[17] A centralized marketing department works with a decentralized sales structure, for example. However, creating coordinating devices and methods can still be very difficult.

Customer-focused teams are a sales-led example of organizing around the customer in a hybrid format. The functional groups still remain, but are also organized around specific customers or customer groups. Each group is represented on the team and each representative is charged with ensuring that his or her area supports the customer-focused marketing strategy.

## Structure and Formal Communication

The customer-focused team (CFT) formalizes communication between parts of the organization that should be communicating anyway. As a result, some level of communication is ensured. It is still up to the marketing manager to ensure that the communication is timely and accurate.

Organizational structure is important to understand because it defines much of communication. In a functionally structured organization, for example, communication usually flows up and down reporting lines, as illustrated in Exhibit 7–5. Cross-functional communication only occurs at points when the managers of functions report to the same person. Customer-focused teams and other types of cross-functional organization structures remove formal communication barriers and require communication at the point of need.

For example, under a formal communication structure, if a salesperson had a problem with shipping, then the problem would be reported to the sales manager, who might be able to call shipping or might have to report it to a regional level, depending on where a peer relationship existed. In the illustration in Exhibit 7–6, there is no equivalent of a district sales manager in the shipping department, so the information has to be passed along to the regional level. As you can imagine, the message gets garbled

**Exhibit 7–5**
Customer-
Focused Team
Structure

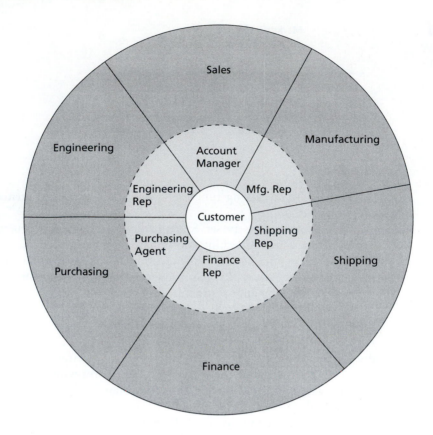

and delayed, which reduces customer satisfaction and also the job satisfaction of the salesperson who needs to get the problem resolved. In a CFT, the information goes straight from the customer to the responsible person in shipping or, at worst, through the account manager to the team member in shipping. The result is that the customer's needs can be assessed and satisfied.[18]

**Exhibit 7–6**
Communication
Example. In a
functional organi-
zation structure,
communications
have to wind their
way through the
chain of command,
increasing the
likelihood of mis-
communication
and lengthening
the time to get a
response.

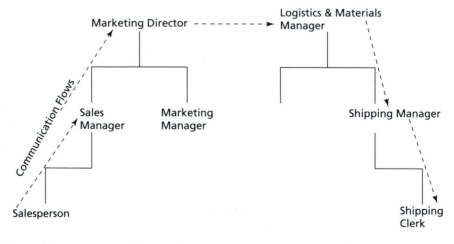

# MARKETING ORIENTATION AND ORGANIZATIONAL LEARNING

Organizational learning is an important element in the marketing success of any business marketer, and a market orientation is the principal cultural foundation for successful learning. As you read in the opening vignette, GE is committed to creating a culture with a "thirst to learn," a commitment that is paying off with superior performance. As defined in Chapter 6, a learning organization is one that consistently creates and refines its capabilities by connecting new information and skills to known requisites for future success. Where do these "known requisites" come from? From the customer. **Known requisites** are requirements for success that have been identified by the firm; thus, the market-oriented firm is able to generate customer requirements that are then part of the learning process.

## Organizational Learning and Competitive Advantage

At the most basic level, **organizational learning** is the process of developing new knowledge that has the potential to influence behavior.[19] Learning facilitates behavior change that leads to better performance. For example, GE marketers learned that products could be managed using portfolios similar to financial portfolios. The outcomes included the development of a portfolio method of product management discussed in the next chapter, as well as overall performance improvement in GE's sales and earnings. In fact, GE's approach made such good sense that it has been incorporated into numerous textbooks, including this one.

Many executives have said that the only truly sustainable competitive advantage is to be able to learn faster than competition, a contention supported by research.[20] In fact, one study showed that companies that exhibit greater organizational learning are more likely to offer innovative goods and services, grow more quickly, and remain more entrepreneurial. Such learning is a function of stronger knowledge management involving internal spanning processes; in other words, sharing what is learned across functional areas enables these companies to innovate and grow more quickly than companies that cannot share knowledge.

Note that this does not mean that all organizational learning is good. Organizations can learn the wrong things, such as concluding that the initial high sales of a new product were due to its features rather than to its low relative price and availability. As soon as even lower-priced models become available, that new product will fail.[21]

Further, companies can get caught in competency traps, which are a form of learning boundary. A **competency trap** is any skill or technology that a company sticks with due to comfort with the familiar, in spite of evidence that better alternatives may exist. A competency trap can be something like Dell's build-to-order competency; one criticism is that it makes customers wait for their PCs when other competitors are available for immediate pickup at a retail location.

Because learning is key to creating competitive advantage and bad learning can have serious negative consequences, it behooves all managers to study learning processes and tools. Perhaps, though, it is more important for marketing managers to understand organizational learning methods, as known requisites are derived from customer requirements.

**Exhibit 7–7**
How Marketing
Learns

| Information Acquisition | → | Information Dissemination | → | Shared Interpretation |
|---|---|---|---|---|
| Marketing research | | To | | Through |
| Sales and service feedback | | Marketing management | | Brainstorming |
| Environmental scanning | | Senior management | | Planning |
| Competitive intelligence | | Manufacturing | | Other processes |
| Other learning tools | | Engineering and R&D | | |
| | | Finance | | |

# How Marketing Learns

Business marketers learn through three processes: information acquisition, information dissemination, and shared interpretation, as seen in Exhibit 7–7. Marketing's role in acquiring information, via marketing research, feedback from the sales force, and other methods, is an important element in the acquisition of vital information for the rest of the firm. That information is then disseminated through interpersonal communication and reports created as a function of internal partnerships. Together, as internal partners create a shared interpretation of the information (in other words, decide what the data mean for the organization), they can create an effective strategy to take advantage of what has been learned.

Further, marketing acquires and disseminates information for its own use through competitive intelligence, environmental scanning, accounting systems, information systems, case studies, experiments, and benchmarking. What we will discuss now are tools of learning, tools that are used to create new knowledge or understanding from the information acquired and disseminated in a market-oriented learning organization. The tools we will discuss are cognitive mapping, experiments, learning laboratories, and tools for learning from others.

## Cognitive Mapping

**Cognitive mapping** is a learning tool that is used to explore mental structures of beliefs and assumptions. In one respect, cognitive mapping is used to draw one's theories; the map is a diagram of cause-and-effect streams. Research shows that cognitive mapping is also an effective group learning tool, particularly in marketing. Several studies show that cognitive mapping can aid in identifying market opportunities, developing strategy, and communicating strategy.[22]

Cognitive maps are useful for identifying the limits of one's understanding. Each link between a cause and its effects can be considered for what it really is—a tested conclusion or an untested assumption.

For example, suppose one assumption is that as price goes down, sales go up. Yet more than one marketer has found that if price goes too low, quality is questioned and sales decrease. In some cases, marketers have actually seen sales increase when prices increased. Suspending the assumption that as price goes down, sales go up, marketers can create new strategies that increase sales with higher prices.

Exhibit 7–8 illustrates how assumptions can lead to different conclusions. Assume FedEx Kinko's is trying to determine how many stores to place in a city. By beginning with a different observation and different assumptions, two opposite conclusions are reached.

**Exhibit 7–8**
Two Cognitive Maps

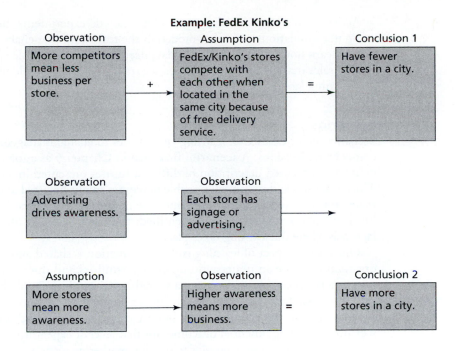

When a marketing team creates a cognitive map together, then a shared understanding is created. By stating beliefs and probing to uncover the assumptions that underlie those beliefs, each individual's cognitive map can be explored. Then the team's cognitive map can be created and tested.

## Experiments

Experiments are a form of marketing research that test cognitive maps. For example, FedEx Kinko's could test both maps by conducting experiments on the incremental impact to individual store and area sales when a new store is opened. Test markets are one form of experiment, as are rolling launches. Companies use a rolling launch when they introduce a new product to a limited market so that they can test the effectiveness of the marketing campaign and so that they can make sure that operational issues, such as the training of service personnel, are working appropriately. The product is then launched across the rest of the market in phases. Both test markets and rolling launches give the organization the opportunity to learn from market reaction to the product introduction.

## Learning Laboratories

**Learning laboratories** are environments set aside for learning. For example, companies such as Motorola and Johnson Controls have created special campuses for training and other learning experiences. Even corporate museums, such as Johnson's Global Controls Center, are being used as learning laboratories. Exhibits of products in use, company history, and other informational exhibits make up the museum, and the area is used for training, simulation of customer experiences with products, and other forms of learning.

Activities in a learning laboratory might include experiments, but can also include computer simulations and other models of the real world that enable managers to practice, to learn how to learn, or to simulate decision outcomes. Role playing, such as that used in sales training and customer service training, is an example of a learning activity in a learning laboratory.

### Scenarios

Scenarios are often used in learning laboratories to enable management to predict outcomes from decisions. A **scenario,** first used in Chapter 5 as a forecasting tool, can be defined as a focused description of different futures presented in a coherent manner.[23] Thus, for a single decision, all possible outcomes might be listed and probabilities estimated for the likelihood that each outcome might occur. Factors that affect the probability of each outcome are then identified; the recognition or identification of these factors is where the learning takes place.

One critical aspect of learning is that information is shared and managers across the organization share an understanding of opportunities and threats facing the organization. Scenarios can also help create a shared understanding simply by forcing the sharing of knowledge. For example, creating a budget for promotion activities can be accomplished using scenarios. Each budget alternative would be examined by creating scenarios regarding potential outcomes for that level of expenditure. Royal Dutch Shell is one company that uses scenarios to develop marketing plans and to create a shared understanding of what is expected to occur. As plans are launched and results come back in, the shared understanding enables staff to go to plan B or some other appropriate plan for that particular scenario.

### Case Studies

Case studies can also be used in learning laboratories to share learning throughout the company. The case study method can be used to search for causes when evaluating outcomes within a functional area. For example, when a company has a wildly successful new product, it should conduct a case study on how that new product was developed so that the process can be repeated. Similarly, if the product is a complete failure, examining how it was created can be used to avoid such problems. Product development areas in other divisions can use such cases to learn how to develop products more efficiently and with greater probability of success.

Satyam Computers, one of India's largest software engineering firms, recently used the case study method to first understand what occurred at a large Japanese account, then to transfer that understanding to other Satyam managers. Japan is an important market to Satyam for a number of reasons, of which the size of the market is only one. The company, however, experienced great resistance from the Japanese buyers, and even when Japanese companies bought from Satyam, the projects were only marginally profitable, if at all. This resistance and difficulty in earning a profit were attributed to cultural differences, and many marketing managers were calling for a pullout from Japan. The company brought in a team of consultants who worked with marketing managers who had Japanese accounts. A case was written, much like the cases you read at the end of this book, that illustrated the combined knowledge of the various managers. This case was then used to teach all of the marketing team how to do business in Japan. What the managers realized is that the cultural differences are fewer than they thought, and much of what they knew from dealing with European and American companies could apply.

---

**7–1**

## BUSINESS 2 BUSINESS

## Organizational Learning and GE

In the General Electric annual report, the executives wrote that they wanted to preserve big-company advantages while eliminating big-company drawbacks. What big-company drawbacks make it difficult for learning to occur? How do big companies do a better job of performing as learning organizations? Do you believe it is possible to develop "the soul . . . of a small company" in a company as large as GE?

---

### Strategic Planning

The strategic planning process itself can serve as a learning laboratory. A learning laboratory is an environment for learning; remember that strategic planning involves removing the planners from daily firefighting so that they can step back, consider the big picture, and make plans for the future. For generative learning to occur and to develop strategies that create systematic performance improvement, strategic planning must be done in an environment that allows for free thinking without fear of penalty. Activities such as brainstorming must be encouraged.

### Learning from Others

Learners learn from others and do not seek to reinvent the wheel each time a wheel is needed. Benchmarking is one method of learning from others and includes examining the processes of others in order to copy what can be used at home.

Learning from others can also include learning from partners in joint ventures or strategic alliances, from consultants, at seminars, and via other external sources.[24] Another form of learning from others is to be a learning customer. Virtually every large organization will purchase products from competitors in an effort to learn how to put its own product together in a more effective and economical fashion. Yet, learning from suppliers is also an important opportunity.

For example, John Paduch, vice president of sales for American Supply Co. of Gary, Indiana, saved one client over $1.5 million by showing how changing from stainless steel valves and pipes to cast iron would not reduce quality. That type of learning from value analysis (discussed in Chapter 3) is obvious. Less-obvious opportunities for learning are also available from partners. For example, Shell's ethics officer presented seminars to several of the company's big accounts regarding privacy laws. Shell isn't in the ethics business, but partners found the seminars valuable nonetheless.

### A Commitment to Learning

When an organization is committed to learning, it finds that learning can occur in many ways. For the marketing manager (you), commitment to learning must be personal and ongoing. Learning for an organization and the people that make up the organization is not simply about what needs to be done but also about how to do it. This means that you must be committed to continuing to develop your marketing skills, industry knowledge, and other facets of professional development long after graduation.

# THE LEARNING MARKET-ORIENTED INDIVIDUAL

## Important Internal Partnering Skills

Building partnerships has been a major theme of this book. In many respects, building partnerships with internal partners is no different than building relationships with customers. Several skills are useful in building internal partnerships, skills such as questioning and listening, negotiation, and financial and accounting skills. We'll discuss finance and accounting skills first, because they represent the language of business.

### Finance and Accounting Skills

When we consider the mind-set of those in the company who are not part of the marketing department, it is important to remember that almost everyone wants to do their job well. No one likes to fail. Engineers want to use their creativity to design successful products, finance managers want to beat the market by managing the company's investments well, and manufacturing managers want to operate a profitable, safe plant. In almost every situation, success is measured, at least partly, in terms of profit. The common denominator is the bottom line on the income statement.

Marketing managers who fail to understand finance and accounting fail to communicate well with other managers. They just don't understand the language. Understanding finance and accounting, though, is needed for more than just the sake of good communications; good business managers must understand these areas in order to make good decisions. Trelleborg is a London-based multinational group of companies that supplies manufacturers of railroad equipment and off-road vehicles (such as used in mining or construction) and shipbuilders. The $4 billion dollar company uses customer profitability analysis in order to allocate marketing and sales dollars to various accounts and market segments. Dollars are then allocated to grow those accounts and segments that are worth more to Trelleborg. Further, the profitability analysis is also used to project the profit potential of new accounts; accounts that do not fit strict criteria for potential profit are not accepted.[25] Those marketing managers have to understand accounting procedures in order to make wise investment decisions. We can't teach those procedures here, though. Our purpose is to sensitize aspiring business marketing managers to the importance of what they will learn in their finance and accounting classes.

### Questioning and Listening

Understanding needs of others is the first step to building a partnership. Understanding the profit needs and cost structures of the internal partner is an important part of understanding their needs, but more is also required. The marketing manager must understand the individual's wants and aspirations as well. This level of understanding requires questioning and listening skills, the same types of skills needed among salespeople.

**7–2**

# BUSINESS 2 BUSINESS
## Practice Partnering Skills Now

Consider student group projects. Do people want to work with you? How was your reputation created? What specific events contributed to that reputation? What can you learn from those experiences that could help you become a better internal partner?

## *Negotiation*

Understanding the needs of an internal partner, though, is not enough. That partner's needs must be aligned with the marketing department's needs, in terms of both the final outcome and the timing of the decision. **Negotiation** is a method of decision making that is used to resolve conflicts; it is important for the marketing manager to develop skills that enhance the use of this method.

Negotiation is a mutual problem-solving process rather than an argument. When managers use negotiation to build consensus through tactics such as brainstorming rather than bullying, internal partnerships can be developed.

### Create a Sense of Urgency
One reality that marketing managers face is that their sense of urgency, or need to get something done now because the customer is waiting for it, is not always shared by the internal partner. Without a shared sense of urgency, the other party may not participate fully in the negotiation, so good negotiators are adept at creating a sense of urgency. Appealing to supragoals is one method of creating a sense of urgency. If the customer's needs are of paramount interest (and not the needs of the marketer), then that can help to create that sense of urgency to get the job done.

### What Is Negotiated
Intraorganizational conflict, or conflict between two departments or functional areas, is well suited to negotiation. Other methods of handling internal conflict can be used, too, but negotiation is the most often used method. Because negotiation can be used as a decision-making process in any conflict, it is important to recognize that, although it is advisable to hold to one's goals, you should be open to multiple means of achieving those goals. With this recognition, nearly anything is negotiable, and the marketing manager creates a level of flexibility that opens new vistas for decisions—the opportunity is there for double-loop learning.

### Be Prepared
The first step in being prepared for negotiation is to have negotiation skills. There are many excellent books that can help you continue your learning of negotiation and conflict resolution. If your school's management department has a change management or conflict–negotiation course, you may want to take it. The second step is to recognize negotiation opportunities and plan accordingly. Because anything is negotiable,

negotiation can occur at any time. If the manager has not prepared to negotiate, a competitive negotiator can win at the manager's expense before the manager even recognizes that negotiation is occurring.

## Analytical Skills

A critical area of expertise that is in short supply is analytical skills. Many students enter marketing because they don't like the math required for finance or accounting only to find that jobs in marketing require an understanding of statistics. In fact, a recent study shows that the skills that have become the most important are analytical and measurement skills. These skills have become far more important than skills in promotion or branding. More importantly to students of business marketing, 83 percent of executives surveyed said they had difficulty finding people with those skills.[26] Thus, those who have mastered the analytical and measurement skills taught in marketing research classes and applied in this class should find themselves in high demand.

# Summary

Marketing is an important element in the learning organization, and should be an integral element in the culture of all business marketing organizations. Learning organizations use marketing to determine known requisites (the requirements for success). Two types of learning occur in organizations: single-loop (adaptive learning) and double-loop (generative learning). Both types of learning can provide companies with competitive advantages when companies learn faster than their competitors.

Marketers can learn a number of ways, including through experimentation, cognitive mapping, and learning laboratories. Even the process of strategic planning discussed in Chapter 6 provides an opportunity for organizational learning. But not just any learning is useful; companies also seek to create a market-oriented culture in order to learn what can provide competitive advantage.

Market-oriented companies do a better job of market sensing, or anticipating requirements (known requisites). They also build stronger spanning processes so that information from customers can get to the areas within the firm where it will do the most good. Internal partnering can strengthen spanning processes and communication, and is a strategy effected by salespeople and marketing managers. Marketing staff and salespeople want to partner with their peers in finance, manufacturing, and new product development.

Market-oriented companies also integrate their marketing activities better than do companies that are not market oriented. In the chapters ahead, we will discuss each of the marketing activities in greater detail, but it is important that you now understand how marketing efforts are integrated.

Marketing efforts are integrated when strategic decisions are clear and carry throughout all marketing activities. Further, internal relationships take time to build. For partnerships to develop, personnel stability is needed. Compensation plans should also take internal partnerships into account. Teams should be supported with team compensation and team organizational structures.

Professionals are also learning individuals. Business marketers must develop their finance and accounting skills in order to be successful businesspeople. Communication skills, such as questioning, listening, and negotiation, are also useful skills to learning professionals.

In the next set of chapters, we discuss various marketing activities such as product development and marketing communication. As you've learned in this chapter, though, these activities are not isolated accidents, but are part of an integrated marketing and corporate strategy.

# Key Terms

cognitive mapping
competency trap
engineer to order
functional structure
internal partner
known requisites

learning laboratories
make to order
make to stock
market orientation
market sensing
negotiation

organizational culture
organizational learning
scenario
spanning processes
supragoal

# Discussion Questions

1. "Internal partnering?" says one business student. "That is just manipulating people to do what you want." Do you agree? Why or why not?

2. What is the importance of market sensing, as compared to other marketing functions? What is the potential impact of a mistake in market sensing?

3. Create a cognitive map that illustrates the relationships of organizational learning, market sensing, marketing functions, strategy development and corporate planning, strategy implementation, and evaluation. You may need to bring in other concepts from this and earlier chapters.

4. Consider your relationships with others in an organization that is important to you, preferably one in which you hold an office or position of leadership. Select three people in three different relationship stages. How do you know those relationships are in different stages? Specifically identify differences between the relationships. What can you do to strengthen those relationships?

5. How does creating a chief marketing officer or chief customer officer help a company become more market oriented? What other actions could a company take to become more customer-centered?

6. Identify five negative consequences caused by poor relationships between (a) marketing and manufacturing, (b) marketing and finance, and (c) marcomm and sales.

7. The example of Dell's competency in build-to-order was given to illustrate a competency trap. Yet Dell is likely to consider this competency a competitive advantage. Discuss how a competitive advantage could become a disadvantage, and the implications this has for a company's leaders.

8. Individuals can also have competency traps. Identify examples of personal competency traps from any field (sports, politics, business). What are the implications for people who have a competency trap? How can such a situation be avoided?

9. Jack Welch, former CEO of GE, says it is important for companies to have enemies so that you can be at war. Explain how this statement relates to the concept of a supragoal.

10. How does a professional marketing manager choose what she should learn? Relate your answer to the methods and types of learning presented in the chapter.

# Cases

## Case 7.1   Mercator Corp.

Sally Flanagan was concerned. After six years with Mercator, she loved its culture of everyone calling on customers, trying to come up with new ways to serve them and, at the same time, competing among themselves to grow the business. New product development cycles were five weeks or less, compared to industry averages of six months. Mercator also enjoyed the highest customer satisfaction ratings in the industry and regularly won awards for innovation.

But a few months ago, Mercator was bought by a company 10 times its size. While the executives of the new company, Etron, promised that Mercator could continue to operate on its own, the weight of the large company seemed to be slowing Mercator down. In fact, executives stated both publicly and privately that Etron needed a culture like Mercator's and that's why the company was purchased.

Sally's responsibility is to grow electronic channel sales: that is, sales through the Web site and e-mail marketing plans, and to manage the company's social media such as customer service Web sites. As she lamented to her husband, "We now have to get approval for any expenditure over $10,000 from Etron's corporate marketing office. That takes six e-mails, five voice mails, two phone calls, and then two more!"

Worse yet, her boss, Maria Gutierrez, had to back out of a trade show commitment because she had to go to a meeting at Etron headquarters. As Maria told Sally, "I've not been able to talk to a customer in over a month. Used to be, I could ride along with a salesperson, go to a trade show, or sit in the call center and take calls for one day a week. Now all I do is sit in conference rooms and hear people talk about customers, yet none of them have actually spoken to one of our customers."

1. The culture has changed at Mercator due to being acquired. What are the implications of this culture change for Mercator?

2. How can Maria and Sally defend their market-oriented culture—how can they stay close to the customer and continue the innovation of Mercator?

3. Given that Etron executives publicly and privately stated that they needed more of a culture like Mercator's, what is causing Mercator's culture to be changed in the wrong way?

*Note: This case is based on an actual situation but the names have been changed.*

## Case 7.2   Morgan John, LLC.

Morgan John, LLC is a small firm that manufactures hoses for agricultural and manufacturing applications. Begun in 1961 by two fraternity brothers, David Morgan and Stanley John, the company grew to nearly $12 million in sales last year. Now the company employs eight manufacturing employees and four salespeople. David focuses on running the operations while Stan manages sales.

The hoses that Morgan John manufactures can be custom fit to a specific manufacturing application or off-the-shelf standard sizes for agricultural equipment and some types of manufacturing equipment. For example, it is common for hoses to have 2-inch and 3-inch diameters. For these sizes, Morgan John keeps a stock of plain hose (purchased from Asian suppliers), then cuts it to order and adds any bends or other special applications a customer needs.

Over coffee one morning, the two friends pondered their company's future. "You know, we only started this business because Stan stumbled across the equipment sitting in a warehouse when working a summer job," mused David. "We paid $100 for that equipment that the owner thought was junk."

"It was junk!" laughed Stan. He paused, then added, "Boy, the market has sure changed." The two men made the following observations:

- Agricultural equipment hoses are now almost entirely stock products, and are sold to agricultural implement dealers, who then sell them to farmers and ranchers.
- Manufacturing hoses are almost all make-to-order. The number of customers has gone down, as manufacturing has shifted overseas, but the number of orders per customer has shot up, as they utilize their plants more heavily to boost production.
- The number of inquiries regarding custom and made-to-order belts has increased from both sectors. David has argued for going into the business of belts, too, while Stan feels the company should wait as both David and Stan will be retiring soon. "Let our kids tackle the new business," he says.
- Many of the buyers that Stan and David worked with have retired, and most of the selling is now done by their kids, two each, who have found it hard to penetrate new accounts. First, the growth is in manufacturing but second, the need for quick turnaround when a hose breaks is so critical that companies are reluctant to try new vendors unless or until they have a bad experience.

1. Discuss the market-sensing abilities of this company. What mechanisms does it use, and how would these compare to the mechanisms used by a company like Halliburton, doing billions of dollars of business each year? How are the challenges different for this small company versus the larger companies?
2. Discuss the spanning processes of this company in comparison to large companies. What is different, and why? Which company has it easier in terms of spanning—Morgan John or Halliburton?
3. Should the company add custom belts? Why or why not? What organizational limitations might keep them from doing so?

# Additional Readings

Biemans, Wim G., and Maja Makovec Brencic. "Designing the Marketing–Sales Interface in B2B Firms." *European Journal of Marketing* 41 (2007), pp. 257–71.

Bowers, Michael R., and Charles L. Martin. "Trading Places Redux: Employees as Customers, Customers as Employees." *The Journal of Services Marketing* 21 (2007), pp. 88–102.

Campbell, Alexandra J. "Creating Customer Knowledge Competence: Managing Customer Relationship Management Programs Strategically." *Industrial Marketing Management* 32 (2003), pp. 375–83.

Chaston, Ian, Beryl Badger, and Eugene Sadler-Smith. "Organizational Learning: An Empirical Assessment of Process in Small UK Manufacturing Firms." *Journal of Small Business Management* 39, no. 2 (2001), pp. 139–51.

Coakes, Elayne, and Peter Smith. "Developing Communities of Innovation by Identifying Innovation Champions." *The Learning Organization* 14 (2007), pp. 74–87.

Deng, P-S, and E. G. Tsacle. "A Market-Based Computational Approach to Collaborative Organizational Learning." *Journal of the Operational Research Society* 54, no. 9 (2003), pp. 924–35.

Ellis, Paul D. "Distance, Dependence and Diversity of Markets: Effects on Market Orientation." *Journal of International Business Studies* 38 (May 2007), pp. 374–86.

Gebhardt, Gary F., Gregory S. Carpenter, and John F. Sherry, Jr. "Creating a Market Orientation: A Longitudinal, Multifirm, Grounded Analysis of Cultural Transformation." *Journal of Marketing* 70 (October 2006), pp. 1–18.

Im, Subin, and John P. Workman, Jr. "Market Orientation, Creativity, and New Product Performance in High-Technology Firms." *Journal of Marketing* 68 (April 2004), pp. 114–132.

Jayachandran, Satish, Kelly Hewett, and Peter Kaufman. "Customer Response Capability in a Sense-and-Respond Era: The Role of Customer Knowledge Process." *Journal of the Academy of Marketing Science* 32 (2004), pp. 219–34.

Keskin, Halit. "Market Orientation, Learning Orientation, and Innovation Capabilities in SMEs: An Extended Model." *European Journal of Innovation Management* 9 (2006), pp. 396–408.

Kirca, Ahmet H., Satish Jayachandran, William O. Bearden. "Market Orientation: A Meta-Analytic Review and Assessment of Its Antecedents and Impact on Performance." *Journal of Marketing* 69 (April 2005), pp. 24–41.

Luo, Xueming, Rebecca J Slotegraaf, and Xing Pan. "Cross-Functional 'Coopetition': The Simultaneous Role of Cooperation and Competition Within Firms." *Journal of Marketing* 70 (April 2006) pp. 67–80.

de Madariaga, J. Garcia, and C. Valor. "Stakeholders Management Systems: Empirical Insights from Relationship Marketing and Market Orientation Perspectives." *Journal of Business Ethics* 71 (April 2007), pp. 425–39.

Maltz, Elliot, William E. Souder, and Ajith Kumar. "Influencing R&D/Marketing Integration and the Use of Information by R&D Managers: Intended and Unintended Effects of Managerial Actions." *Journal of Business Research* 52 (2001), pp. 69–82.

le Meunier-FitzHugh, Ken, and Nigel F. Piercy. "Does Collaboration between Sales and Marketing Affect Business Perfomance?" *Journal of Personal Selling & Sales Management* 27 (Summer 2007), pp. 207–20.

Narver, John C., and Stanley Slater. "The Positive Effect of a Marketing Orientation on Business Profitability: A Balanced Replication." *Journal of Business Research* 48 (2000), pp. 69–73.

Nonaka, Ikujiro. "The Knowledge-Creating Company." *Harvard Business Review* 85 (July–August 2007), pp. 162–70.

Shaw, Vivenne, Christopher T. Shaw, and Margit Enke. "Conflict between Engineers and Marketers: The Experience of German Engineers." *Industrial Marketing Management* 32 (2003), pp. 489–99.

Weerawardena, Jay. "Exploring the Role of Market Learning Capability in Competitive Strategy." *European Journal of Marketing* 37, nos. 3/4 (2003), pp. 407–30.

Weinzimmer, Laurence G., Edward U. Bond III, Mark B. Houston, and Paul C. Nystrom. "Relating Marketing Expertise on the Top Management Team and Strategic Market Aggressiveness to Financial Performance and Shareholder Value." *Journal of Strategic Marketing* (June 2003), pp. 133–60.

# Part 3

# Business Marketing Programming

Part 3 prepares us to develop marketing programs that serve the customer and attain organizational objectives. Fittingly, Part 3 has seven chapters: four on marketing communications elements and one each on the management of product, channels, and price. ●

We start with what are generally the most strategic of the marketing variables. Chapter 8 looks at product development, including the role of suppliers and customers in the process. With large investments, long-run implications, and interactions with other marketing activities, product management across the life cycle is a critical strategic competency. ●

Chapter 9 deals with the management of interfirm relationships for the proper execution of channel functions—key tasks for providing apt service to target customers. Again, significant financial resources, a durable character of relations with channel partners, and connections to price, promotion, and other marketing variables make channels difficult to alter in the short run. Meanwhile the new information technologies have spawned new capabilities, expectations, and competitive environments. Careful forecasting of customer needs, planning, and relationships open to adjustment are key. ●

Chapter 10 previews an integrative approach to marketing communications strategy. It pivots on a Customer Relationship Management (CRM) perspective and the premise that individuals involved in the buying process—and members of other key constituencies—have different information needs and communication channel preferences. The communication vehicles covered in Chapter 11 (public relations, advertising, and trade shows), Chapter 12 (direct mail, telephone, and Internet), and Chapter 13 (personal selling) differ in their impact and cost efficiency for delivering the needed information to the targets. Thus, a marketing communications manager will play no favorites, but will blend the media synergistically to fit the message requirements of the product with the various needs of the target. ●

Finally, we take up pricing and negotiation in Chapter 14. We offer a comprehensive framework for pricing decisions that accounts for many factors—costs, demand, competitors, channel coordination, and regulations—and we speak to tactical issues in pricing. Brief coverage of price negotiation recognizes different strategies of bargaining and uses several principles of conflict management from Chapter 9 as a frame of reference. ●

# Chapter 8

## Developing and Managing Offerings
### What Do Customers Want?

### EMC

In the first edition of this textbook, we profiled EMC for its sales prowess. But in 2001, a company whose stock had appreciated some 83,000 percent suddenly posted its first loss. And in 2002, the information technology company's sales declined some $3.5 billion, a reduction of nearly 40 percent. Dave Donatelli, executive vice president, recalls, "The real challenge was deciding, Is this just a blip or is it really a fundamental change in the business?" ●

Deciding the change was fundamental, EMC had to reconsider its offerings. High-end hardware had accounted for three-fourths of company revenues; Joe Tucci, CEO, believed it was crucial for EMC to move into the middle and lower tiers of hardware offerings, as well as enhance software and service offerings. Gross margins had declined on hardware from 60 to 20 percent; software, however, enjoyed 85 percent margins while service margins were in the 30 percent range. ●

Importantly, though, EMC never stopped investing in research and development (R&D). EMC's investment in R&D is, as a percent of sales, one of the highest in information technology and twice that of IBM. EMC has taken this investment, resulting in a number of patented technologies, and partnered with other companies such as NEC in order to bring fully featured software to market. ●

Critics, especially competitors, charge that EMC is technology-oriented rather than customer-oriented. The result is too much focus on product rather

222

than benefit. But David Goulden, executive vicepresident of customer operations, responds that the goal was "to have a value proposition that went above where we were." Tucci also recognized that it was critical to help customers get the maximum value out of EMC offerings. The result is a doubling of revenue to nearly $12 billion in the past five years, so customers must agree. ●

Sources: Anonymous, "Decision Brief, EMC Turnaround," *Columbia Ideas at Work* (Summer 2006), pp. 12–14; Anonymous "NEC and EMC Announce Alliance Focused on IT Operations Management Software," JCN Newswire—Japan Corporate News Network (June 12, 2007); Joseph F. Kovar, "Name Drop-Reputation, History Gives Startup a Leg Up," *CRN* (June 11, 2007), p. 34.

## LEARNING OBJECTIVES

Is having the right product the most important factor in marketing strategy? Some would argue so, saying that without the right product, no one will buy twice. All of the rest of the marketing mix might get someone to buy once, but if the product is no good, no one will buy again. For companies that wish to compete effectively over the long term, developing products that deliver value is essential. Developing products that deliver value by serving organizational buyers' needs is best accomplished when strong relationships exist between manufacturer and buyer. Then those relationships serve to ensure that value really is delivered.

*After reading this chapter, you should be able to*

- Apply portfolio and product life cycle approaches to managing existing products.
- Identify the process of developing products internally.
- Discuss the importance of lead users to the product development process.
- Indicate what partnering, with both suppliers and customers, means to the product development process.

Satisfying customer needs is an important objective in product management. As you will see, however, successful product management depends on the successful integration of many areas. Pricing, promotion, selling, and manufacturing are just a few of the organization's strategic areas that must operate in concert with product management in order for the firm to enjoy success.

# WHAT IS AN OFFERING?

What is a product? To some, a product is a collection of **features,** or physical characteristics of the tangible item or service. For example, a computer may have a hard drive capable of storing 25 gigabytes of information. Storing 25 gigabytes is a physical characteristic, or feature, of the computer. Getting a haircut completed in less than 30 minutes is a feature of a service.

Other people might think of a product as a collection of **advantages,** or reasons for having those features. For example, a 25-gig hard drive may mean that users can store a lot of software on their computer. Getting a haircut in under 30 minutes means it can be done during a lunch hour, saving time.

What is important to a buyer is the **benefit,** or how the product or service satisfies a need. If you have all day to get a haircut, 30 minutes means nothing to you. It is more useful for you to think of a **product** as a bundle of benefits, a collection of solutions to needs and wants.

## Service-Dominant Logic

When the concept of a product is introduced, most students think of a tangible product. The reality is that, while the core product is important, it is the services that often separate one vendor from another. **Services** are defined as the application of specialized competences (skills and knowledge) through acts or processes for the benefit of another.[1] Services, it has been argued, are not separate or distinct from tangible products because what customers buy is an **offering,** the complete package or bundle of benefits that includes how easy the product is to buy, how it has to be paid for, services that help the buyer get full value from the product's use, and sometimes assistance in disposing of the residual product when finished with it. While product typically means the tangible part of the offering and service means the intangible, there are times when the terms are used interchangeably; a firm selling services may refer to a new service as a new product, for example. This language is common among banks, which refer to a type of commercial loan as a loan product though there is no tangible, manufactured product.

As an example of the importance of service to the overall offering, Tim Pavlovich may sell Dell products to be integrated into other manufacturers' products but what those OEMs are buying are not just Dell computers. They are also wanting Dell's engineering expertise to help design the best final product, Dell's inventory management expertise so that inventories can be kept to a minimum, Dell's financial strength so they can get good credit terms, and other services as part of Tim's offering.

Note that in business, many manufacturers partition their services into presales and postsales service. Presales would be those services that help the buyer make a decision and would include financial services such as credit terms, engineering services involved in designing the product into the customer's product, and other such services. Postsales services would include such services as customer support to ensure smooth installation or technical support or maintenance for full use of a product. From the buyer's perspective, though, these are all part of the offering. For example, in a study involving a major equipment manufacturer, customers considered technical service as part of the brand. When the manufacturer sent untrained and unprofessional technicians to fix equipment, the brand was damaged and customers indicated lower intentions to repurchase or recommend the manufacturer to others.[2]

**Exhibit 8–1**
**The Product Line and Technology Platform**
A product line is typically composed of several products based on the same technology platform. An example might be Honda's gasoline-powered cars; the internal combustion engine is the technology platform while the Civic is a product. Another technology platform, though, is Honda's hybrid engine technology.

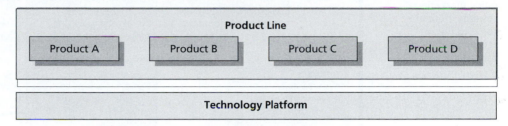

# MANAGING PRODUCTS AND SERVICES

Few companies exist on just one product or service. Most have several lines of products and services designed to work together to satisfy a broad range of needs and desires. An important element of business marketing is deciding which products to introduce or keep, which products to promote heavily, and which products to cut or market less vigorously. There are several different tools that managers use to manage their company's products, including the product development and life cycle, and product portfolio tools for the sake of brevity, we use product to refer to services, too.

Before we can discuss these tools, however, it is important to recognize that product management tools can be applied at different levels. There are four such levels: the product itself (e.g., Canon's imageRunner 1310 copier), the technology platform (e.g., Canon's digiting scanner), the product line (Canon's imageRunner line), and the product category (plain paper copiers). A **technology platform** is the core technology that is often the basis for a **product line,** or group of products,[3] as illustrated in Exhibit 8–1. A product line does not have to share the same platform, but sharing a platform is usually the case. Another example is Accenture's technology consulting services. The platform is technology consulting, but there are different areas such as ERP (enterprise resource planning), CRM (customer relationship management), and other specific "products" in which Accenture can apply its technology and process engineering skills. These definitions of platform, product line, product category, and product apply to services as well as tangible items, something to keep in mind as we discuss product management tools such as the product life cycle.

# Product Life Cycle

Products have been likened to living organisms. They are introduced to the market or have a birth. Then they grow (in sales), mature, and at some point, die out. This cycle of development, introduction, growth, maturity, and decline in sales, is called the **product life cycle (PLC)** (see Exhibit 8–2). The cycle can be applied to individual products or to product platforms or categories, with differing implications as we will discuss. For example, daisy wheel printing was a technology that used a wheel with a number of petals, like a daisy. Each petal contained a character, and the petal was struck against a ribbon in order to print the character. Quality of print was high, but speed was slow. This technology was introduced by a number of vendors, grew, matured, and then declined as it was replaced by newer technologies, such as ink jet and laser printing.

**Exhibit 8–2**
The Product
Life Cycle
The product life cycle has been used to guide marketing strategy. Here are some common recommendations for each stage.

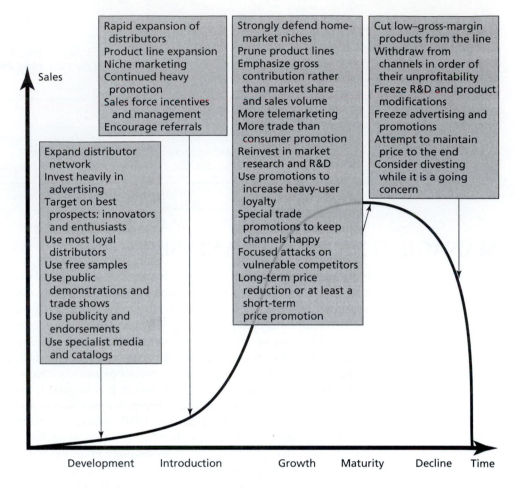

Sales

Expand distributor network
Invest heavily in advertising
Target on best prospects: innovators and enthusiasts
Use most loyal distributors
Use free samples
Use public demonstrations and trade shows
Use publicity and endorsements
Use specialist media and catalogs

Rapid expansion of distributors
Product line expansion
Niche marketing
Continued heavy promotion
Sales force incentives and management
Encourage referrals

Strongly defend home-market niches
Prune product lines
Emphasize gross contribution rather than market share and sales volume
More telemarketing
More trade than consumer promotion
Reinvest in market research and R&D
Use promotions to increase heavy-user loyalty
Special trade promotions to keep channels happy
Focused attacks on vulnerable competitors
Long-term price reduction or at least a short-term price promotion

Cut low–gross-margin products from the line
Withdraw from channels in order of their unprofitability
Freeze R&D and product modifications
Freeze advertising and promotions
Attempt to maintain price to the end
Consider divesting while it is a going concern

Development    Introduction    Growth    Maturity    Decline    Time

Within the life cycle of the daisy wheel technology, however, companies introduced new products at different times; some grew and matured, and others died fairly rapidly.

Products can have multiple lives. A product may fall out of favor in one market, but may find new life in another. When this occurs, the product begins a new life, with all of the same strategy issues that any new product faces.

Products may also die young. There is no guarantee that a product will live to maturity or even make it to the introduction stage. And unlike living organisms that have similar life cycles (for example, adolescence hits all of us at about the same period), products can go through the stages at very different rates. The PLC, though, does offer a useful tool for understanding product strategy.

# PLC and Product Strategy

Products have a **development stage,** that stage in the product's life when it is designed and readied for market. Some products are never brought to market simply because someone else gets there first or leapfrogs. A product is **leapfrogged** when a competitor brings out a product that is at least one step better technologically.

Leapfrogging can have serious consequences when it occurs so early in the life of a product, but leapfrogging can also occur in the development phase. Xerox had a word-processing software product that never made it to market because other products were coming out that were already better. Thus, you can see that a key stage in the life cycle is the development stage. If it takes too long to bring a product to market, the product may die before it has a chance. One major trend in product management is to shorten the product development stage in order to lengthen the overall life. We'll talk about how companies are doing that when we discuss product development strategies later in this chapter.

When the product is first introduced to the market and potential customers are learning what the product is and does, it is in the **introduction stage.** Sales are relatively low and profits are unlikely, as sales revenue is invested in creating awareness. If distributors or other intermediaries are needed, getting their agreement to carry the product can be difficult because there is not yet a well-defined market for the product.

For truly innovative products, this stage requires marketers to educate buyers (and channel members) as to the function of the product. **Primary demand,** or demand for that type of product, must be created. For example, ColorSpan introduced a new product that printed huge pictures. At first, buyers didn't know what to do with the pictures. Primary demand for large pictures had to be created before anyone would buy a ColorSpan product, so the company had to teach the market how to use large pictures. Creating primary demand and educating the market can require a tremendous communication investment in advertising, trade shows, free samples or trials, and other marketing elements. Copycat products also have an introduction stage, as do new products that are improvements over existing products. Copycats do not have to educate the market, but do have to announce their presence. Improvements require some education, but not as much as innovations do.

The second stage of the PLC is the **growth stage,** when sales and profits grow at a fast rate. Competition against an innovative product is most likely to enter the market in this stage, and vendors begin to differentiate their product in order to create **secondary demand,** or demand for a particular vendor's offering. Significant marketing investment may still be required in order to create a position for the product separate from others in the market.

The third stage is the **maturity stage,** when sales level off. Note that sales can level off for a product category, in which case that market is said to be mature. Profits are relatively high and marketing expenses should begin to decline. A new product or vendor, however, can enter the market and take away sales at the expense of competitors. For example, the basic cellular service market is a mature market, but new products are introduced regularly. Each product represents a slight improvement and, although none are truly innovative, each new cell phone service may go through all stages of the PLC.

In the maturity stage, product differentiation is even more important. With little or no product differentiation, price becomes more important, and companies try to reduce costs. Companies that want to differentiate rather than lower prices try to augment mature business products with more services or create images of differentiation through effective promotion. Research indicates that successful companies don't always reduce their marketing investment in mature products; rather, they change the nature of their marketing communication to emphasize their competitive advantages.[4]

The final stage is the **decline stage,** or that stage when sales decline and products are removed from the market. Marketing investment may be cut and managers look for ways to milk the last few dollars of profit before withdrawing the product. In some cases, marketers look for new markets or new applications and the life cycle starts all over again. We'll talk more about the decline stage later in this chapter.

# Product Portfolios

There are several types of product portfolios. Perhaps the most famous is the one developed by the Boston Consulting Group and called the BCG grid or matrix. **Product portfolio management** suggests managing all products simultaneously as you would a financial portfolio, balancing risk and return among all product investments. Most models involve a grid and suggest that product decisions should be based on where each individual product, product line, technology platform, or product category is along the combination of two dimensions.

The BCG grid is the simplest of the grid models, with dimensions of market share and market growth. This model has been criticized for being too simple and too similar to the product life cycle (which is also based on market growth).

In the upper left corner of the BCG matrix, products are considered **stars** because market growth is high in a market where we control a large amount of the total market. Stars create cash through high sales but require high levels of investment in order to maintain or increase market share in that growing market. The investment made is in the form of marketing and distribution, as stars require more advertising, more personal selling, and the development of appropriate distribution in order to gain market share.

The hope is to turn stars into **cash cows,** which have high market share and strength in a steady market and are those products that should contribute the most to the company's profit. This contribution is possible because it should not take as much investment to maintain market share in a stable market as it does in a growth market; economies of scale and return on the investment of marketing dollars made when the market was growing should pay off. For example, Pak-Sher is a company that manufactures flexible packaging used in the restaurant business. They developed the Sinewave system, a packaging system that helps keep food hot for to-go orders that is more effective than Styrofoam containers and also has a carrying handle. When the product was introduced, it took a strong (and expensive) sales effort for buyers to learn of the value it delivers. Now, the company does not have to educate the market, and they can enjoy the higher gross margins of this cash cow.

**Question marks** are those products in high-growth markets that currently have low market share and may not be too strong. If the product's position can be strengthened, then the potential is for the product to become a star and perhaps a cash cow when the market stabilizes. Question marks require a great deal of investment, using cash generated from cash cows, in order to be successful. Investment alone, though, is no guarantee of success. Success still requires wise investment into sound marketing strategy.

Products with low share in a poor market are called **dogs.** These products are usually thought to be in the decline stage of their life. Some products become dogs after beginning as question marks while others become dogs after a long life as cash cows. In most cases, dogs are not worth much investment and most companies want to withdraw dogs quickly from the market.

A more advanced model developed by General Electric is called the GE grid (as illustrated in Exhibit 8–3). It has **market attractiveness,** or a composite measure of the potential for sales and profits in a particular market segment, and **business strength,** or the strength of our offering relative to other companies' products, as its dimensions. Attractiveness determinants include market size, growth rate, competitive structure, industry profitability, and environmental (legal, social, etc.) factors. Determinants of strength can include our market share, our growth rate, the company's image, people resources, and other similar factors.

Exhibit 8–3 illustrates both grids; note that the GE grid is really just an expansion of the BCG matrix. A product that is sold in an attractive market and represents a strong product for the company (because of market share, growth rate, etc.) would be similar to a star in the BCG matrix. The advantage of the GE matrix, however, is that the dimensions are more comprehensive and detailed. For that reason, more effective decisions can be made.

Note that the PLC also involves two dimensions: time and sales. One property of time, however, is that you cannot go back. With product portfolios, products can move along both dimensions in either direction—if overmilked, a cash cow can become a dog,

**Exhibit 8–3**
Product Portfolio Matrices

whereas with the right opportunity and investment, a dog can become a cash cow, for example. One problem with the use of portfolio matrices is that decision makers assume that products follow a PLC beginning as question marks, moving to stars, then cash cows, then dogs. The reality is that movement can occur between any two quadrants. Although it is unlikely that a dog can become a cash cow, it can happen.

# Harvesting a Product

At some point, all good things must come to an end. So it is with a product's life. When the product no longer contributes to the firm's success, then it is time to stop production and turn resources to more profitable ventures.

## *When to Harvest a Product*

Products are not harvested or terminated just because they are unprofitable or because they are classified as dogs. Several considerations must be reviewed, of which cash use and contribution to profit are two. For example, a product may be profitable and selling at a reasonable rate, but if investment (or cash) can be diverted to an even more profitable product, the company may decide to harvest the first product. Or a product may not be profitable after overhead is allocated, but have a positive contribution margin otherwise. If the company were to stop selling that product, overhead would have to be reallocated elsewhere, perhaps making another product look unprofitable.

Customer demand should also be considered. Some products are useful because they mean that customers do not need multiple vendors. For example, Moore Wallace sells ribbons and ink cartridges for computer printers, including ribbons for the now unpopular daisy wheel printer. If Moore Wallace did not offer daisy wheel printer ribbons, customers would have to buy those ribbons from someone else. Customers who have some daisy wheel printers, as well as laser and ink jet printers, might decide to buy all of their printer supplies from a Moore Wallace competitor if they couldn't also get their daisy wheel supplies from Moore Wallace.

Note that the decision to harvest a product is not always technology driven nor does it occur at the end of a long life. IBM pulled its Stretch computer off the market shortly after it was launched, not because the technology had been replaced by newer technology or because the company had enjoyed a long product life cycle, but because IBM misestimated demand for the computer's features. That product failure, however, led to significant and important learning, which was then used in the creation of IBM's very successful System 360.

### Challenges to Harvesting

Products are managed by people, and sometimes people overinvest their egos in a particular product. This may make it difficult to halt producing a product, particularly if the product was designed by the owner, for example.

Similarly, a product may not be eliminated because of the jobs that might be lost. Every day we see fights in Congress over what plane the air force will build; many times, these fights may be about saving jobs (and votes) rather than what is best for the air force. Similar situations can occur in companies unwilling to lose good personnel. Political difficulties can make harvesting products a challenge.

# NEW PRODUCT DEVELOPMENT

New products are launched and old products withdrawn from the market at an increasingly rapid rate. Estimates are that more than one-third of new products ultimately fail.[5] Many companies such as 3M set corporate objectives that include sales or profits from products that don't exist yet. At the same time, new product development and the costs associated with launching a product are so great that a single product launch can mean the difference between profit and loss for many companies. As a result of the intense risk associated with new products, many marketing strategists believe that the key to success lies in solid planning.

## Risk and New Product Decisions

The most basic decision in product management is the go–no go decision. Do we launch (or continue developing) the product, or do we kill it now? There are two types of risk associated with this decision: investment risk and opportunity risk. **Investment risk** is the risk that we decide to go ahead with the product, it fails, and we lose some or all of our investment. **Opportunity risk** is the risk that we decide to kill a product and thereby lose all of the revenue we would have gained if it had been a success. In marketing research class, you probably learned about these types of risk as Type I and Type II errors involved in making decisions based on what we observe relative to our hypotheses. Keep this in mind, because for new products not yet launched, the go–no go decision is often based on marketing research. As a marketing manager, you need to recognize when you've set up the decision process in order to minimize either investment risk or opportunity risk.

Several factors will impact your decision. For example, the size of the investment relative to the fiscal health of the firm can determine your willingness to assume investment risk. A company with $2 million in annual revenue may not want to risk $1 million in new product development, whereas the potential loss of $1 million to DuPont may be minimal.

Another factor that impacts risk is the newness of the product. A product new to the company, but similar to others available in the market, is less risky in terms of market

---

**8–1**

## BUSINESS 2 BUSINESS
### Intel's Market Risks

Consider Intel, the manufacturer of computer chips. A constant flow of new products is needed but at the right speed. If Intel moves too quickly, software designers won't keep up and there won't be demand for the new chip. If Intel is too slow, then competitors that can move more quickly will capture market share.

What are Intel's risks when developing the next new PC chip? What risks face the company should the market move toward less-sophisticated computers designed more for Internet browsing than heavy-duty computing? How can Intel minimize those risks?

---

acceptance of features (which should reduce investment risk) than a product that is completely new to the world. The sales potential for a me-too product is less than for a completely new product too, so the opportunity risk is lower.

Based on consideration of the risks involved, decision rules are set that minimize either investment or opportunity risk. For example, suppose you believed that 5 percent market share was essential to the success of the product, so market research is conducted to estimate market share. If the answer was 4.8 percent, is that close enough to go ahead and launch? It depends. If investment risk is more important, you may decide that the risk of not reaching 5 percent is too great, and the answer is no. If opportunity risk is more important, then you may decide to continue with the product launch.

The process used to develop new products can reduce the risk. In the next section, we'll discuss product development processes that companies use to keep a constant flow of new products.

## New Product Development Process

The essential steps of an internal product development process are presented in Exhibit 8–4. We present a seven-step process; most experts agree that there are six steps, to which we have added an evaluation step. Kodak and Bombadier Aerospace both use a six-step process; General Electric added several steps to make it 10. Motorola and Lucas Industries, however, only have four and five steps, respectively.[6]

### Generating Ideas

As mentioned earlier, a key to the entire process is a constant flow of new ideas. New product ideas can come from many sources: suppliers, customers, salespeople, marketing research, and competitors, as well as others. The challenge is to get the ideas submitted; if employees don't know what to do with ideas (whether they got the idea from their own inspiration or it was given to them by someone like a supplier or customer), then the idea will never be considered.

Promoting a central location for submitting new product ideas is especially critical if there is no new product development department or otherwise obvious location. Employees must also believe that their ideas will be taken seriously, so following up with a phone call or letter to acknowledge receipt of the idea is important, as is letting the

**Exhibit 8–4**
The Product
Development
Process

*Idea generation.* In this step, the basic idea is created. The key here is to have a steady flow of new ideas.

*Screening and preliminary investigation.* In this stage, ideas are examined for fit with corporate objectives, current product offerings, and other factors to see if it is worthwhile to continue developing the ideas into products. Information is gathered to determine development costs and time, potential sales, and other factors that influence whether the process should continue.

*Specifying features.* Detailed specifications for the product are developed. These specifications should be centered around features that lead to desired benefits, as expressed by customers and channel members.

*Product development.* The purpose of this step is to develop and test a prototype of the product in the lab (called alpha testing), based on the specifications developed in the previous step.

*Beta testing.* Beta testing is field testing, or testing the product at the customer's location, to see if the product will work under real-world conditions.

*Launch.* Finally, the product is brought to market.

*Evaluation.* The product is evaluated and elements of the marketing program are adapted to fit changing market conditions.

originator know of the final decision.[7] Another element that can spur new product ideas is to recognize those individuals who contribute ideas that turn into successful products. Such recognition can include awards or cash bonuses.

CRM tools can also provide insight into new product ideas. Software that tracks individual customer preferences through transactions with customer service, salespeople, and even the Web site can be used to detect demand shifts, which can lead to new products. Union National Community Bank, for example, has seen revenues grow 11 percent, primarily from new products and services for commercial accounts. The ideas for these products came from analyzing data from the company's CRM system.[8]

### Lead Users

Many ideas start with customers: for example, the original designer of the printed circuit board was the U.S. Army's Signal Corps. The army needed a way to miniaturize communications equipment and seized on the idea of the printed circuit board, designed it, and produced the first one. It looked for potential suppliers; after all, the army is not in the business of printing circuit boards. In this instance, the army served as a *lead user,* or a user that develops its own solutions to problems using available technology in a new or innovative way. **Lead users** face needs that will be general in the marketplace, but they recognize these needs months or years before the market is aware, and/or they are able to generate solutions to needs independently of manufacturers.[9]

Companies that seek a product innovation position in the marketplace should look for lead users among their customers. Strategically, lead users are accounts for which partnering relationships should be developed. They possess important insight into the evolution of their needs and the needs of customers similar to them, as well as knowledge of how those needs can be met. Such knowledge can be invaluable when developing new products.

Lead users can be identified in a number of ways. Lead users can be found participating at the conferences of trade associations. These conferences often include seminars concerning the most pressing problems facing a particular industry. Because lead users are those users that have found solutions to problems before others in their industry, you may find them presenting their solutions at conferences.

Lead users can simply be the source of new product ideas, or they can work with product designers. For example, Diamond Shamrock has a vice president of future systems, whose department is charged with planning for technology five years and further into the future. Software engineers from several vendors meet regularly with this person and his department at Diamond Shamrock, codeveloping computing and communication platforms. Diamond Shamrock benefits because it plans computer purchases more wisely. The vendors gain valuable expertise that results in more marketable products.

Business marketers have to develop mechanisms to link lead users to product designers. 3M uses structured cross-functional teams who work with lead users. As Mary Sonnack, a 3M division scientist who works with lead users notes, routine users can only provide incremental product improvements. For truly innovative products, she looks far afield. For example, when her group explored the need for germ-killing surgical draping cloth, she worked with a veterinarian whose patients never bathe, U.S. military surgical teams in Bosnia, and an expert at decontaminating flooded hospitals.[10] In fact, 3M has found that lead user–generated new products enjoy sales eight times those generated internally.

Keep in mind that the channel of distribution may separate the user from the manufacturer. Product development processes should also include distributors, either as suppliers or as customers, when they are part of the marketing channel. Often, a distributor can represent many suppliers or many customers, bringing additional valuable expertise to the process.

## Screening and Preliminary Investigation

Screening involves examining new product ideas to see if they are worth investing any time at all. Screening is a first look at the following factors, in order of importance:

- Consistency with corporate objectives
- Ability to serve customers' needs
- Market potential
- Competitive advantage gained with the product
- Ability to manufacture and service the product

Some companies are using expert systems, or computer modeling programs, to screen new products.[11] Nortel, the Canada-based global telecommunications giant, developed a four-step process to screen new ideas, a process it terms *Galileo*. The Galileo process uses a computer support program that uses questions and templates, a rating system, and a generic evaluation model to help managers evaluate new ideas. The purpose is to determine if a new product idea is worth spending money to develop further.[12]

If the answer is yes, then the product concept is worth pursuing and a more detailed examination of the factors that will contribute to the product's success is undertaken. When screening, we examined the product concept for potential success. Now we consider such questions as which market segments will be interested, why they will be interested, and how the competition will react. An important aspect is understanding demand for the product or service. As you may recall from Chapter 5, demand analysis is difficult when a product already exists and has been marketed; the challenge is even greater when attempting to determine demand for a product that is not yet on the market. Customers may not understand what it does or how they will use it, so they may not be able to tell you. But some estimate of demand is necessary to determine if the product is worthwhile. Keep in mind that the product can still be killed at any time. The data that we obtain are then fed into the next stage, when the product is designed in terms of what it will do.

**Exhibit 8–5**

**Four Phases of the Quality Function Deployment Process**

SOURCE: *Adapted from Linda S. Morris and John S. Morris, "Introducing Quality Function Deployment in the Marketing Classroom,"* Journal of Marketing Education *21 (August 1999), pp. 131–37.*

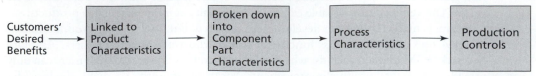

Keep in mind, too, the investment and opportunity risks and sources of those risks. The newer the product to the market, the more you may want to spend in time and resources on research. For an innovation, it is often important to spend more on planning, in order to get the product developed right, than on later stages in the process. If you introduce the product and it isn't exactly right, a competitor will copy and improve on your idea, stealing your market.

## Specify Features

Based on your research in the preliminary investigation, it is now time to begin specifying features. This stage is when you begin to decide just what the physical characteristics, or features, of the product or service will be. At this time, you should also begin working with suppliers. Companies can shave a great deal of time off the product development cycle if they will follow the example of the Japanese and solicit assistance from suppliers as early as possible. When suppliers are involved early, product planning can benefit from their insight. They are also more aware of the cost parameters associated with the product that will influence the product. If suppliers are brought into the loop later, then the product design may not meet cost requirements, causing the need for redesign and an addition of months to the development cycle.

### Quality Function Deployment

The value chain represents how suppliers and customers work together to create value through new products and augmented services. Many companies now incorporate **Quality Function Deployment (QFD)** to link customer needs to product attributes.[13] QFD is a process to describe how benefits are linked to product, component part, and process characteristics, as well as production controls. Each of these steps is represented in Exhibit 8–5.

The first step links what the customer wants to what the product should have. This step results in a matrix very similar to the multiattribute matrix presented in Chapter 3. Along the vertical axis are listed the customer's requirements, or what the customer wants. Across the horizontal axis are product features. Through the use of marketing research, the attributes are identified, the weights are determined, and the trade-offs between various desired benefits and product characteristics can be understood.

For example, Cordis (a division of Johnson & Johnson that makes cardiac care products like angioplasty balloons and stents) conducted in-depth interviews with cardiologists and nurses. From these interviews, they first identified the processes that customers were actually using when installing Cordis products. Then they identified what customers wanted and why. From these interviews, the company was able to identify the key features and the benefits that would be received. More importantly, the company

**Exhibit 8–6**
Design
Considerations
in Computer
Printer

| Benefits | Average Importance | Toning System | Paper Feeder | On-Board Software |
|---|---|---|---|---|
| Cost under $500 | 10 | − | | |
| Quality of print | 9 | | + | |
| Speed | 8 | | + | |
| Noise | 6 | − | | |
| Printer size | 5 | − | | |
| Number of fonts | 4 | | | + |
| Type sizes | 4 | | | + |
| Cartridge life | 4 | − | | |

was able to introduce 12 new products in the space of one year and grow its market share from 1 to 10 percent.[14]

Exhibit 8–6 illustrates an example of desired benefits and the importance weights associated with each benefit for a computer printer. We also see that some product characteristics enhance the delivery of certain benefits, whereas other characteristics detract from those same benefits. As illustrated in the exhibit, a better toning system may improve quality of print, but lowers the life of the toning cartridge and makes reaching the price objective difficult.

Products, including competitors' products, current product offerings, and the proposed new product, can then be assessed as to how they perform. Comparisons can be made across the products that help companies understand how to market the new product. The final product features matrix is illustrated in Exhibit 8–7.

The second step of QFD, parts step, is completed with the aid of suppliers. In this step, the product developers are considering such issues as make versus buy the part and whether any improvements can be made to specific parts. The process step examines the manufacturing process, linking with the parts step. Finally, the production controls step plans production of the product and implements the processes for monitoring the actual production process. Although we focus on the product characteristics because of the link with the customer, business marketers must recognize that many of the savings that enable the product characteristic goals to be met that were identified in that first step are the result of what happens in the other steps as the product is developed.

One company, Eicher Motors, makes heavy commercial vehicles between 2 tons gross vehicle weight (GVW) and 12 tons GVW. This company, located in Greater Kailash, India, has demonstrated a reduction in development time of one-half to one-third by using QFD. The company has also improved customer acceptance of new products. One example is the market for hauling chickens. Chickens are typically hauled at night, when it is cooler, because chicken mortality is a major problem when they are trucked. Eicher Motors learned that buyers were willing to pay for drivers' comfort, because they found that drivers who stop less have fewer chickens die in transit. Chicken trucks have more driver comfort features than do other trucks.[15]

## Develop Product

Once the features are specified, the actual product is designed and prototypes are developed for lab testing. One strategy to speed up the development process is to divide the product into component modules, which can then be designed concurrently. More

New Printer Design

**WHATS vs. HOWS**

| | | |
|---|---|---|
| Strong | ● | 9.0 |
| Moderate | ○ | 3.0 |
| Weak | ▽ | 1.0 |

**Customer Requirements (Whats)**

| Product Features | Toning | Paper feed | On-board software | Customer importance | Our current product | Competitor's product ranking | Product plan (future product) | Improvement factor | Absolute weight | Demanded weight (%) | Max = 70.0 / Demanded weight (%) / Min = 5.0 |
|---|---|---|---|---|---|---|---|---|---|---|---|
| Print quality | ● | | ○ | 4.0 | 2.0 | 4.0 | 5.0 | 2.50 | 10.00 | 46.88 | |
| Speed | | ● | | 5.0 | 3.0 | 5.0 | 5.0 | 1.67 | 8.33 | 39.06 | |
| Noise | ▽ | | ● | 3.0 | 4.0 | 4.0 | 4.0 | 1.00 | 3.00 | 14.06 | |
| Total of columns | 435.94 | 351.56 | 267.19 | | | | | | | | |
| Percent importance of the HOW | 41.33 | 33.33 | 25.33 | | | | | | | | |
| Max = 70.0 / Percent importance of the HOW / Min = 5.0 | | | | | | | | | | | |

## Exhibit 8–7
### An example of QFD

Quality Function Deployment links *what* the customer wants (customer requirements) to *how* the product will deliver. Designers can then use market research information to see how the current product and proposed product compare to competitive products so that appropriate trade-offs can be made in product design.

---

**8–1**

# FROM THE FIELD
## Services Make the Supplier

I've been an account executive at Dell for three years; prior to that I was with Carleton-Bates, a company that supplied electronic components to manufacturers. I still sell to manufacturers, now with companies that embed computers into their products, products such as medical test machines, kiosks (like how you can check in at the airport), ATM machines, and other such products.

We have to use a strategic approach, starting with my customer's design engineers and marketing managers. We need to understand what they are trying to do with their products, what benefits they are trying to provide their customers, and then we match that to what we have to offer. Half the time we spend convincing them that they don't want to build their own computer; the other half is convincing them that Dell is the right supplier.

For my customer's marketing manager, we can sometimes leverage the Dell name. They can gain a marketing advantage by proclaiming that their system is powered by Dell.

For my customer's design engineer, we also encourage them to do what they do best, which is usually writing software or designing the overall system. Our engineers also work with

their engineers, which means our design engineers work with their design engineers, then our factory engineers work with their factory engineers so that after the design, it is built into the factory operations properly.

Another aspect is that we provide service after the sale. So we also work with their service personnel. We ask, "What happens if the computer breaks down after you've sold it to your customer?" They can leverage our global service structure to improve their recovery time. If a doctor can't take X-rays when a hard-drive goes down, and we can get that doctor up and running in under four hours because we have a service person already nearby with parts, then my customer wins and my customer's customer wins.

I may have 25 people from 25 different areas work with one customer. We can have the design engineers, the factory engineers, the systems consultant, the finance person, the service person, etc. What's fun is that it is more than selling a computer; I and my team become a part of their product design process. Once I'm engaged in all of those parts of my customer's business, I become a real strategic partner.

Tim Pavlovich—Account Executive, Dell Inc.

---

designers may be needed, but the additional cost is made up in the speed in which the product is brought to market.

Manufacturing should be involved in this process because how the product is designed will impact how it is manufactured; sometimes, simple changes in product design can have a major impact on product cost. Many companies are also bringing in suppliers at this stage in order to take advantage of their expertise. For example, Ci-Dell Plastics eliminated a step in the manufacturing process for one of its customers by molding a hole in a plastic part. Previously, the customer was drilling the hole. Saving that step cost Ci-Dell nothing but saved the customer several thousand dollars per year.

Using supplier expertise can also reduce the cost of designing. Instead of needing, say, 30 in-house designers, five teams of four in-house designers plus two supplier's designers per team are used. The speed of design is much quicker, while at the same time, the suppliers can participate intelligently to keep later production costs low.

**Early supplier involvement (ESI)** is the concept of involving suppliers early in the product design process. Because of ESI, purchasing agents are also becoming more involved in the product development process, since an important element of the design process is to find vendors who can make the components. For example, when Applied

Materials developed the Producer S line of silicon wafer manufacturing equipment (sold to companies like Intel and used in making computer chips), a goal was to make the equipment smaller. Computer chips are made in a "cleanroom," a room that must be free of dust and other potential contaminants. To make the equipment smaller means that customers can make more chips in the same cleanroom, which means significant savings in capital expenditures. Applied Materials involved suppliers early in the process and, with their design help, achieved a 29 percent reduction in the size of equipment.

The design process involves creating prototypes, or versions of the product that are then tested to make sure they meet performance specifications. For example, a software company would test a word processing program to make sure that it works with Lexmark Optra Et Printers or HP Laserjets.

Outsourcing product development is increasing. Xerox, for example, outsourced the software development for a new line of digital copiers to a company in India and another in California. Procter & Gamble now expects to source half of its new products from outside the company. In some instances, only design is outsourced; features are fully specified to the designer. In other cases, the product may be completely outsourced with only the most general of specifications given to the designer. Research shows that the greater the creativity needed on the part of the designer, the more that the buyer needs to specify the requirements up front and then let the designer work without close control. Too much supervision during the process can stifle the designer's creative process.[16]

## Beta Testing

But will the product work the way customers want it to in real-world conditions? That is the objective of beta testing. **Beta testing,** or **field testing,** is testing the product by letting customers use it in real-world conditions. Beta testing is most often used in high-tech industries, whereas field testing is traditionally used in manufacturing industries. Not all companies beta test, because competitors can get an early peek at the product, the test can delay the launch of the product, and a weak product can significantly damage relationships with customers who use it. Beta testing does make sense when the product represents a new platform, rather than a product extension, because the likelihood of unforeseen problems is greater.

The rush to get products out can cause companies to skip the beta testing stage. Among the countless examples of companies that rushed products out too quickly are Intel with its Pentium processor (although Intel recovered very well) and Xerox with its 3300 copier (which jammed and caught fire often).

When companies do decide to beta test, key questions to answer include how long the test should last. In most cases, the beta test is really designed to see if the product delivers the benefits in the minds of customers for whom it was designed. The beta test is not usually a test of how well the product works—finding out that the copier catches on fire is not the kind of result you would usually expect from a beta test and should be caught in a lab test. What you are really trying to answer is questions like whether customers like the speed of the copier and how the document feeder works.

## Launch

Finally, the product is launched in the market. Companies must develop a launch strategy based on the innovativeness of the product, service needs related to the product, and other factors.

The innovativeness of the product, or the degree to which the product represents a new technology or new way of solving buyer needs, influences how the product is launched. Potential customers must be educated about the innovation and shown how it will solve their needs. Products that are not innovative, that represent add-ons or extensions of an existing technology or copies of competitive products, do not require the same education-focused launch.

Service needs related to the product also influence how the product is launched. The greater the need for accompanying service, the more training of support personnel is required before the product can be launched. IBM, for example, cannot launch a line of servers until there are enough trained technicians to support the product. For this reason, some technology-based companies will conduct a **rolling launch,** or launch the product in certain areas, rolling to new areas as support personnel are trained and ready.

We will discuss promotion and service issues, and other details of marketing products at the appropriate points in the book. For now, recognize that launching with a big splash isn't always the best strategy, and that the launch strategy is influenced by a number of factors such as the innovativeness of the product and service-support issues.

## Evaluate

The decision to go or halt a new product is not made once; rather, it may be a single decision made repeatedly. Companies may need to evaluate the potential for a new product after each step.

Research indicates that those involved in the development of a new product develop a bias toward the product that may color their ability to judge the potential success of the product. This overly positive bias can cloud the decision. To avoid such a bias, companies should consider two approaches.

The first is to have someone objective and outside the development process evaluate the product's performance. It may require a different person or team for each stage of the process. The second is to put into place objective measures of performance. For example, requiring a new product to reach a certain return on investment or yield a certain **payback,** or the amount of time it takes to cover the investment costs, can quantify the success of a new product and eliminate bias.[17] As an example of payback, if it costs EMC $5 million to create a new product that generates $2 million in profit the first year, the company is looking at a payback of greater than two years, usually considered too long. Most companies prefer a payback on new products of under a year, but it depends on the anticipated product life cycle. The longer the cycle, the longer the payback.

In addition to evaluating the product, the development process must also be evaluated so that it can continually be improved. Three factors guide the evaluation of the product development process. First, what was the time to market, from conceptualization to launch? Many companies set time targets for bringing new products to market so we must first examine if we met those targets. These targets reflect the competitive nature of new product development. There is a significant market share advantage to be gained by being the first in the market, called the **first-mover advantage,** although being first is no guarantee of success.[18] Companies can also gain just by looking like they were first or by introducing a product soon after the original product was introduced by a competitor, but introducing it with a bigger and more effective launch. Time in the development process is an important element in being able to capture a first-mover advantage.

The second factor evaluated is the cost of development. Development costs can be significant, and once money has been invested in a product, it is considered a **sunk,** or irretrievable, **cost.** The company hopes, of course, to recoup that cost by selling the product. The point here is not whether the product is profitable, but whether the process brought a finished product to the market within the budget. The company will also evaluate the success of the product, but what we are focusing on now is the evaluation of the new product development process, so the focus is on whether the process stayed within the budget.

Finally, were we able to create the desired competitive advantage? In other words, did the new product development process result in a product that has a sustainable competitive advantage relative to other products that are available? If so, the opportunity for rewards are great, which can offset long, costly development cycles. If not, then the company will have difficulty covering those costs. One method of increasing the likelihood of creating a competitive advantage incorporates the value chain concept first introduced in Chapter 2.

# SUCCESS OR FAILURE?

The ability to develop successful new products is necessary for a company to thrive over the long term. Yet, nearly one in three new products will fail, and research finds that having customers involved does not necessarily improve your odds.[19] Although this failure rate is significantly lower than that for consumer products, the company with an expensive failure on its hands is just as unhappy. In this section, we discuss some of the factors that have been found to be related to a particular product's success or failure.

## Components of Success

In general, there are five key components for success. (See Exhibit 8–8.) First, the company has close ties to a well-defined market, so it is able to anticipate customer needs, creating a product advantage. For example, HARD Manufacturing makes an $11,000 crib, which happens to be the best-selling crib on the market. The market is hospitals, and the crib was designed by the nurses and doctors who use the cribs daily with patients. The design includes such features as technology that takes the baby's vital signs without having to take the baby out of the crib. These advantages saved patients' lives, so nurses began quickly calling other nurses to pass along the product advantages and recommend the product.[20] No wonder, then, that product advantage is a dominant factor in success, according to research.[21]

A related factor that influences success is the degree of market orientation. When there is integration and market orientation, customer insight is more readily accessible to product designers. One concern is that customers often don't know what they want

**Exhibit 8–8**
Factors
Influencing
New Product
Success

- Close ties to a well-defined market that lead to a product advantage
- Highly integrated and market-oriented company
- Competitive advantages in technology and production
- Strong marketing proficiency
- Strong financial support

or can only think in terms of what they have which can lead to incremental product development rather than real innovation. Yet, research shows that being close to the customer and market oriented can lead to innovative product design.[22]

Another element is that the company has a strong marketing proficiency. The final element is that the new product launch is adequately financed and takes advantage of the marketing proficiency. In addition, it helps to choose a market with a high growth rate. These factors aid success because even a superior mousetrap must be marketed well.

# Accelerating the Development Process

Several case studies indicate that one important element in successful new product development is finding ways to bring products to the market more quickly. Accelerating the development process can significantly improve an organization's chances to achieve a first-mover advantage, an advantage that can be retained for many years. Four strategies have been found to significantly shorten the process: Streamline each stage of development, develop products in parallel, launch products simultaneously in world markets, and use upgrades strategically.[23]

## *Streamline Each Stage*

Streamlining each stage means being as efficient as possible in each stage of the design process. Streamlining can mean, for example, screening each new product idea within 24 hours of receipt at the central location designated for new ideas, rather than at a quarterly idea review meeting. Streamlining can also include simplifying the process, sometimes as easily as by reducing the number of people who have to approve designs before work can proceed.[24]

Product life-cycle management (PLM) software is one tool companies are turning to in order to streamline product design. PLM software is used by HB Fuller (a chemicals company) to create an automatic communication system so that, as products are designed, Fuller's engineers and suppliers are notified of changes as they occur. Further, the system allows for cross-product comparison so that components can be used in more than one product, reducing design and supply costs. Says Mark Brewer, vice president of global information technology for HB Fuller, the system will shorten the time it takes to "run the marketing challenges and product rationalization through R&D, manufacturing, and sourcing."[25]

## *Develop Products in Parallel*

Breaking a product into modules and developing it in parallel means that more designers can work on the product simultaneously, accelerating the design process substantially.[26] The high level of communication between each team of designers required by QFD improves the likelihood that the modules can be assembled without fear of a lack of fit. Without that communication, new product development might be like building a railroad by starting from both ends and working toward the middle, only to have both lines miss by a couple of miles.

Hitachi uses several software and other types of design firms to design portions of products. Satyam Computers in India, for example, will develop software that controls the electronics of Hitachi products while another vendor creates the circuitry. Instead of

**8–2**

## BUSINESS 2 BUSINESS
### Building Relationships with Lead Users

Earlier in this chapter, you read about the army's role in the development of printed circuit boards. Suppose you are a salesperson for TI, a semiconductor manufacturer, and your customer is the U.S. Army's Signal Corps, a lead user. Whom would you want in your company to begin building relationships with people in the customer's organization in order to take advantage of their innovative abilities? Is that ethical? How would you begin? What would you hope to offer those people in the signal corps so they would want to work with your personnel, and how would you convince your company's engineers that they should work with the Signal Corps?

developing one module at a time, simultaneous development in parallel results in significantly faster product development.

Recognize, too, that it takes a lot of time to create the processes that support a new product. Companies have to devise marketing communications plans, develop brochures and advertising, create training packages, and the like. Often, these ancillary processes and products are designed concurrently with the design of the new product in order to minimize total development time.

### Launch Products Worldwide

Earlier we noted that some companies engage in a rolling launch in order to train service personnel and minimize the impact of the investment required to support a launch. On the other hand, rolling launches give competitors the opportunity to capture markets with copycat products. When possible, a global launch means faster sales acceleration, which leads to a faster return on the new product investment. This return can then be used to support further product development. From the Field 8–2 illustrates how global launches can be managed.

### Use Upgrades Strategically

Siebel Systems is a company that introduced its first products at 80 percent functionality, meaning that the products met at least 80 percent of the customer's needs. The company believed it was important to enjoy the first-mover advantage; therefore, getting the product to market quickly was more important than getting it 100 percent right. While competitors could try to copy what Siebel had already introduced, Siebel was working on perfecting the last 20 percent, which meant that it could be a step ahead of competitors. Competitors who wanted to leapfrog Siebel had to learn what Siebel already knew about customer requirements, then design a product, a difficult feat.

Many companies can launch a product much more quickly that meets the most important need than if they try to fine-tune the product to meet every need. By launching quickly a product meeting the most important need, they gain the first-mover advantage. By then upgrading regularly, they can maintain that advantage. The key is to

---

**8–2**

## FROM THE FIELD
### Launching around the World

When launching new products into global markets, reaching as many buyers as possible as quickly as possible is critical to success. For SAS, the statistical software maker, the launch strategy for SAS*9 was to involve as many local SAS offices as possible. Throughout the launch day, in country after country, SAS sales offices hosted customers, journalists, and analysts to view a Webcast in which SAS CEO Jim Goodnight and other executives introduced the new product. Then local salespeople provided demonstrations and let customers take a brief test-drive.

Dow Corning took a different tack, though, when introducing its new silicone acrylate copolymers. The chemical is used for personal care products like cosmetics, helping provide greater consistency for gels, waxes, and other such bases for consumer products like deodorant, hair products, and cosmetics. Dow Corning launched these new ingredients at the In-Cosmetics trade show in Barcelona, Spain.

Why the different approaches? Because both reached buyers where they are. Most cosmetic and personal care manufacturers have someone attend In-Cosmetics, and many will send a complete team of product designers who are looking for new ingredients. SAS, on the other hand, had to reach customers scattered in many different industries. One trade show would not reach them all.

All new product launches need to reach buyers quickly. Global launches are no different; it is just that buyers can be much more difficult to locate. Yet fast reach is what product launches are all about.

Anonymous, "The Launch Heard 'Round the World," SAS.com (second quarter, 2004), p. 33; Doris de Guzman, "C&T: On the Winding R&D Road," *Chemical Marketing Reporter* 269 (May 22–28, 2006), p. 19.

---

incorporate planned upgrades in the product strategy from the beginning; otherwise, you may get leapfrogged.

## Keys to Innovation

Innovation can mean many things, such as innovative marketing strategy, innovative corporate structure, or innovative manufacturing processes. In this chapter, our context is new product development, which is dependent on creativity leading to innovation, or the creation of market-changing products. Some companies are better at innovating than others.

In a study focusing on flexible manufacturing equipment, innovative companies were found to have a corporate culture that supported innovation. This culture is dominated by a desire for the firm to grow, to improve, and to take advantage of all possible opportunities. Innovative firms tend to focus on opportunity risk while noninnovative firms focus on investment risk.[27]

Several studies have consistently found several factors to contribute to the likelihood of success. One factor is vision, or the degree to which the development team shares a vision of what the new development project is supposed to accomplish. Another factor is a structured new product development process, such as we've discussed in this chapter. Finally, having a long-term perspective is another important characteristic.[28] In many ways, these factors may be characteristics of an innovative culture. What is consistent about these studies, though, is that attention to the basics is important for new product success. As Peter Drucker once wrote, "When all is said and done, what innovation requires is hard, focused, purposeful work."[29]

## Challenges to New Product Success

A number of research studies have examined new product or service successes versus failures. Most of the failures can be attributed to the inability to meet one of the criteria for success. Thus, most products that fail do so because the firm does not have a market orientation throughout, or there is poor coordination, or the firm does not have or does not use a technological advantage. These factors contribute to a product that does not provide value.

Another key factor in product failure is poor marketing, either through failing to launch the product with adequate or appropriate support, or by pricing the product inappropriately.[30] Again, the marketing department plays a key role in determining the success of a new product or service and, ultimately, the success of the firm. Citibank, for example, created a card that allowed merchants to track consumer spending by household. Opting to launch the product nationally rather than rolling it out in a phased launch, the company spent $100 million on the launch. When the market failed to materialize, Citibank pulled the product. Worse, the company sold off the assets of the program rather than trying again. The problem turned out to be a marketing failure, rather than a lack of demand, something that Citibank's competitors overcame.[31]

One difficulty with new services is getting potential users to understand what the products or, services do, what benefits they provide. Employee Resource Management (ERM), a South Carolina company that transfers client company employees to its own payroll and then leases the employees back to the company, relieves its clients of many of the problems associated with human resource management. The problem is that ERM solves so many of the clients' problems and makes human resource management look easy that once the problems are fixed, clients think ERM isn't needed anymore. ERM management has to constantly educate the customer, so that the client continues to recognize the value ERM provides.[32] This education can be difficult because potential users can't touch or see the product because it is intangible.

## Summary

The first step in product management is to understand that a product is viewed by the customer in terms of what the product does, not what it is. A product, therefore, is a bundle of benefits, or a bundle of need satisfiers. Companies that can exceed expectations by adding desired services or augmenting the core product can achieve a significant competitive advantage.

Products have a life cycle consisting of five steps: development, introduction, growth, maturity, and decline. The technology platform's life cycle can be separate from the life cycle of the product itself. A technology platform's life should be longer, but leapfrogging can quickly end a platform's usefulness.

As products go through the life cycle, marketing emphases will change. For example, early in the life of a technology, the issue is simply creating primary demand. During maturity, however, a company wants to maintain the product's position or increase it relative to competitors.

Product portfolio management is a set of management tools that recognizes that companies manage many products in the same manner as they do financial investments. Products can be classified as dogs, stars, question marks, and cash cows. Marketing efforts, or investments, will change, depending on the product's classification.

Products must also be withdrawn from the market at the appropriate time. Companies have to consider not only each product's profit and loss statement, but also the impact that the product has on the sales of other company products. Sometimes, a money loser has to be kept in order to round out a product line, maintain a foothold in a market, or for other strategic reasons.

New product development processes are more important than ever due to shorter average life cycles. At each step of the process, management must make the decision to continue or kill the product. Influencing the decision are the risks—both investment and opportunity risk.

Internally developed products begin as an idea that must be screened to determine if it is worth further development. Features are specified and then a prototype is created. A small run of the product is manufactured and beta, or field, tested. Then the product is launched and evaluated.

An important element to successful business marketing is to develop products with customers. Through understanding the value chain and using Quality Function Deployment, an internal development process can include customers and suppliers. The resulting product should have greater value (and greater likelihood for success) than one generated entirely internally.

Lead users can lead product development. Lead users recognize needs months or years before the rest of the market recognizes those needs, and they generate their own solutions. Smart business marketers identify lead users and build them into the new product development process.

In general, five factors are key to success. The first three relate to the company's ability to identify needs and satisfy them: close ties to the market, highly integrated and market-oriented organization, and competitive technology and production advantages. The second two relate to the company's ability to market products: strong marketing proficiency and the resources necessary to launch the product.

Shorter average life cycles, though, mean that successful companies must also develop new products more quickly than ever before. Therefore, companies are trying to streamline each stage of the process, developing products in parallel and launching globally in order to preempt launches by competitors. Innovative companies are finding ways to create new products quickly, and an important element in their success is their corporate culture of innovation. Barriers to new product success usually relate to a failure to secure one of the five keys to success.

New products are the essence of growth for most companies. Managing products well and creating processes for continuous product development are important aspects of business marketing, particularly in today's market of short product life cycles.

# Key Terms

| | | |
|---|---|---|
| advantage | early supplier | leapfrogged |
| benefit |    involvement (ESI) | market attractiveness |
| beta testing | feature | maturity stage |
| business strength | field testing | offering |
| cash cow | first-mover advantage | opportunity risk |
| decline stage | growth stage | payback |
| development | introduction stage | primary demand |
|    stage | investment risk | product |
| dog | lead user | product life cycle (PLC) |

| product line | question mark | services |
|---|---|---|
| product portfolio management | rolling launch | star |
| Quality Function Deployment (QFD) | secondary demand | sunk cost |
| | | technology platform |

# Discussion Questions

1. Consider the cellular phone for a moment. In one column, make a list of all of the benefits that you derive from a cell phone. In a second column, list the features that provide these benefits. What is the offering? What is the product and what are the services?

2. A big issue for salespeople who work on straight commission is this: On what products will they place their emphasis during a sales call? For these salespeople, time with the customer is their most important resource, so they have to choose how to use that time. Draw a blank product portfolio matrix and decide how much time should be spent on products within each square, assuming equal numbers of products in each of the quadrants. What are your reasons for each decision?

3. Alfonso Wee is a senior business manager with BASF, the chemical company profiled in Chapter 1. He recalls developing a new polyurethane product that eliminated the need for Freon 11, an ozone-depleting chemical, in spite of warnings that customers didn't care about a safer environment and wouldn't want to take a risk on something new. Now everyone is aware of global warming, but how would you market such an innovation with no direct benefit if it were priced about the same as the old product? (Source: Alfonso Wee, **www.my-basf-story.com,** accessed May 24, 2007.)

4. Some authors have combined the life cycle and portfolio matrices into one model. How would you do that? What are some limitations of the model?

5. The chief engineer for Portland Purifiers, a maker of industrial water filters with annual sales of $5 million, has an idea for a new product that would represent a major (and patentable) improvement over current market offerings. She estimates that the development of the product will cost half a million dollars, including tooling the manufacturing line. The last product launch cost about $200,000 in marketing and promotion costs. She thinks the product would sell for about $50,000 and should sell 75 units in year 1, 140 in year 2, and then level out at 200 per year. Contribution margin is 40 percent. Should the company continue with this project? What do you need to know about the company in order to understand its decision to go or not go ahead? What is the payback period?

6. What criteria would you use to determine which customers would make good beta test sites? Would you want to choose lead users? Why or why not?

7. Larger companies seem to have difficulty innovating. Why is that? What are some examples of large companies that have brought out what you would consider to be innovative products, and how did they do that? (Note, go online and read what they did.)

8. Shred-All is a security company that takes company documents (on paper, disk, or any other media) and destroys them. Shred-All had a difficult time when the service was launched because companies failed to recognize a need for the service. Describe the investments Shred-All needed to make to prepare to launch the company so that

you can understand the "inventory" that it had to manage. Then discuss how you would overcome barriers to success if you were Shred-All's management. Finally, how would you educate potential customers so they understood the need for your service?

9. In this chapter, we noted the importance of an integrated market orientation to new offering success. In the previous chapter, we discussed how you build a market-oriented organization. What is central to both a market-oriented culture and successful new product development? What does a service dominant logic have to do with both a market-oriented culture and new product development?

10. What are the potential ethical issues in obtaining innovations from customers? For example, if a salesperson sees a customer using the product in a new way or with some modification, are there any ethical issues in copying the new application or modification?

# Cases

## Case 8.1   Majestic Mattress

Majestic Mattress sells mattresses and other bedding products to institutions such as hospitals, hotels, and universities (for dormitories). Monica Ramirez, president of Majestic, had just returned to her office from the annual Hospitality Squared convention, a trade show for the hotel industry, where she spent an enlightening evening with a representative from the company's former top account. She called in Monty Rupp, vice president of manufacturing, to discuss what she learned.

"Monty, we're having some problems," she opened the conversation, pointing to a chair for Monty to sit. "Patel tells us that he's switching to a no-turn single unit for their Comfotels." Comfotel is the lowest-priced hotel in the Patel chain, and a no-turn single unit is a mattress that goes on a plywood frame, not needing a box spring. No-turn means that it doesn't have to be turned over regularly to maintain its comfort and shape.

Monty grimaced in reply. "Who came up with that?"

"He didn't tell me," she said. "But I'm afraid that we're going to lose our box spring and mattress sales in his higher-level hotels if we aren't careful. One problem is he says that when they don't use fitted sheets, the sheets won't stay on the mattress because our cover is too slick. He has some other concerns too. I want you to call on him right away and see what you can find out."

1. What should Monty do when he calls on Mr. Patel?

2. The issue seems to be innovative products being delivered by someone else. How can Monica create a system to encourage new product ideas?

3. Majestic Mattress salespeople are not company employees but independent manufacturers' reps. They also sell furniture, linens, and other related products to the same customers but for other manufacturers. How, then, can Monica identify and develop relationships directly with customers to develop lead users? Are lead users appropriate in this instance? Why or why not?

4. What new markets can she consider to extend the life of her current products? What can she do to identify those markets?

## Case 8.2   The Right Offering?

Virtua offers a closed-loop lead management software tool. What this tool does is help marketing managers capture information about prospective clients and track these sales opportunities until they either close into business or decide to buy something else or nothing at all. More important, the software also includes a number of marketing tools such as e-mail marketing campaign software, Web site chat, and other tools that can engage potential clients.

Ted Edwards' challenges in marketing Virtua's products center around several issues. First, customers don't really understand the benefits. Unless they are in trouble, they tend to be complacent and believe that what they are doing is working fine. And if they are in trouble, they can't afford Virtua. Second, customers who do understand the benefits, at least conceptually, may buy but not fully utilize Virtua's applications. As a result, the returns are not as high as hoped and the customer's belief is that the product was a failure. Negative word-of-mouth then occurs, making it harder to make the next sale.

Some customers, though, are much farther ahead of others. They understand what Virtua can do, and they are really good at using it. Ted has written several case studies highlighting their effectiveness, which salespeople use when selling. Ted believes that education is the problem, but he has no budget for any significant free training nor do all customers need it.

**1.** What options does Ted have to help customers fully utilize Virtua's offerings?

**2.** What options does he have to help prospects understand the value that Virtua offers?

*Note: This case is based on a real company but the name has been changed. However, your instructor can tell you who it is and you can visit their Web site to see how they've handled it.*

# Additional Readings

Biyalogorsky, Eyal, William Boulding, and Richard Staelin. "Stuck in the Past: Why Managers Persist with New Product Failures." *Journal of Marketing* 70 (April 2006), pp. 108–21.

Brockman, Beverly K., and Robert M. Morgan. "The Moderating Effect of Organizational Cohesiveness in Knowledge Use and New Product Development." *Journal of the Academy of Marketing Science* 34 (Summer 2006), pp. 295–307.

Carson, Stephen J. "When to Give Up Control of Outsourced New Product Development." *Journal of Marketing* 71 (January 2007) pp. 49–66.

Chan, Lai-Kow, and Ming-Lu Wu. "Quality Function Deployment: A Comprehensive Review of Its Concepts and Methods." *Quality Engineering* 15, no. 1 (2002), pp. 23–36.

Forlani, David, and Orville C. Walker Jr. "Valenced Attributions and Risk in New-Product Decisions: How Why Indicates What's Next." *Psychology & Marketing* 20, no. 5 (2003), pp. 395–433.

Garver, Michael. "Best Practices in Identifying Customer-Driven Improvement Opportunities." *Industrial Marketing Management* 32 (2003), pp. 455–66.

Homburg, Christian, Martin Fassnacht, and Christof Guenther. "The Role of Soft Factors in Implementing a Service-Oriented Strategy in Industrial Marketing Companies." *Journal of Business-to-Business Marketing* 10, no. 2 (2003), pp. 23–49.

Im, Subin, and John P. Workman, Jr. "Market Orientation, Creativity, and New Product Performance in High-Technology Firms." *Journal of Marketing* 68 (April 2004), pp. 114–32.

Johnson, Thomas E., and David Ford. "Customer Approaches to Product Development with Suppliers." *Industrial Marketing Management* 36 (April 2007), pp. 300–13.

Lilien, Gary, Pamela Morrison, Kathleen Searls, Mary Sonnack, and Eric Von Hippel. "Performance Assessment of the Lead-User Idea-Generation Process for New Product Development." *Management Science* 48 (August 2002), pp. 1042–60.

de Luca, Luigi M., and Kwaku Atuahene-Gima. "Market Knowledge Dimensions and Cross-Functional Collaboration: Examining the Different Routes to Product Innovation Performance." *Journal of Marketing* 71 (January 2007) pp. 95–112.

Nordberg, Markus, Alexandra Campbell, and Alain Verbeke. "Using Customer Relationships to Acquire Technological Innovation: A Value-Chain Analysis of Supplier Contracts with Scientific Institutions." *Journal of Business Research* 56 (2003), pp. 711–19.

Prins, Remco, and Peter C. Verhoef. "Marketing Communication Drivers of Adoption Timing of a New E-Service among Existing Customers." *Journal of Marketing* 71 (April 2007) pp. 169–83.

Robinson, William T., and Sungwook Min. "Is First to Market First to Fail? Empirical Evidence for Industrial Goods Businesses." *Journal of Marketing Research* 39 (February 2002), pp. 120–29.

Walter, Achim. "Relationship-Specific Factors Influencing Supplier Involvement in Customer New Product Development." *Journal of Business Research* 56 (2003), pp. 721–33.

# Chapter 9

## Business Marketing Channels
### Partnerships for Customer Service

### NEBS KNOWS: HYBRID CHANNELS SERVE DISTINCT SEGMENTS

New England Business Systems (NEBS) is a $550 million company serving 3.1 million small business customers in the United States, Canada, U.K., and France. Its broad assortment of products includes business forms, greeting cards, packing and shipping supplies, personalized apparel, advertising specialties, and a variety of management tools. Direct mail was the primary channel at the company's founding in 1952, but soon NEBS became one of the first direct marketers to offer toll-free customer service numbers and specialized product catalogs including 40 separate lines of business.●

Today NEBS serves its customers with a portfolio of channels, including direct mail, telephone sales, a direct sales force, dealers, and the Internet. A number of factors drive the channel strategy. For one, customers often have a channel preference. NEBS has found that customers generally prefer to be reached by a channel that matches the means by which the customer initially contacted NEBS. Customers who place their initial order electronically typically want to be dealt with electronically.●

In addition, the channels can be used synergistically across the sales cycle. For example, NEBS knows that when trying to educate the customer and not necessarily make a sale, outbound telephone is highly effective. Furthermore, NEBS's database of customer purchasing behavior is analyzed to reveal patterns. For example after a customer buys a particular product, based on profiling done in the customer database, NEBS knows the customer is likely to buy related products and will promote them most effectively through the mail.●

Each channel broadens NEBS's ability to serve its different market segments. Notably, its Web site allows delivery of Web-based services, including small business planning tools, a resource library, Web hosting, a business plan template, and WYSIWYG (what you see is what you get) design of customized products. It also has opened bridges for new Internet partnerships. Deluxe Corporation acquired NEBS in June 2004 to advance its mission to be a leading resource to small businesses and home offices. Today it serves more than 6 million customers and contributes favorably to the Deluxe strategy to cross-sell its check printing and related products to small businesses and benefit from referrals from its relationships with financial institution clients.●

Susan Nawrocki, vice president of marketing, attributes recent growth at NEBS from Web site initiatives and selling to best customers the way they prefer to be reached. "Obviously, the result of everything we do is to sell product," Nawrocki says. "But we understand it's not that simple, especially since the marketplace is so competitive. We're always looking for value-added things."[1]●

Visit the NEBS Web site at **http://www.nebs.com.**●

## LEARNING OBJECTIVES

**Marketing channels** are systems organized to deliver products and related services. They save buyers the costs of searching and waiting. Because of the breadth of tasks needed to be done, most channels are composed of multiple businesses. To be effective, these firms typically work as partners to coordinate their activities to serve ultimate customers and to remain competitive as a "team."

We begin the chapter with an orientation to the reasons for channels and an introduction to some of the types of businesses involved. We then provide a model for channel design and take up the key issues of channel management.

*After reading this chapter, you should be able to*

● Describe the functions of a marketing channel.

● Classify the various intermediaries used in business marketing.

● Analyze customer needs for channel service outputs.

● Design a channel system that can (1) provide customers with the services they want and (2) attain a competitive advantage.

● Discuss the challenges of managing channel relationships and coordinating activities across organizational boundaries.

● Frame a basic make–buy analysis involving different distribution system functions.

**251**

# WHAT IS THE MARKETING CHANNEL?

Business marketing channels are systems designed to close numerous gaps between the manufacture and use of products. Some of the gaps are between places. For example, coal is efficiently mined in enormous quantities in China and the Dakotas. But it must first be graded and transported before it can be used at the university or metropolitan power plant. Coal is hardly a commodity one might ship by overnight air. Thus—to close another type of gap, a time gap—the power plant's supply depends on accurate information about coal in transit by rail and barge, plus probably occasional truck deliveries from a local depot. The marketing channel functions to sort the output, break bulk, and deliver.

These physical distribution tasks are not the only ones performed by a channel system. A builder who picks up attic fans at a Home Depot not only enjoys the convenience of a local supply source, but might also get a tip or two on installation from the floor personnel at the outlet, have to pay for the goods only in the next 30 days, and grab some shingles and flashing in the same trip. In this instance, the dealer—a channel partner of the fan manufacturer—provides sales help, financing, and an assortment of other products. We are apt to find several builders using Home Depot to the same ends.

So notice in the top portion of Exhibit 9–1 that five builders transact directly with six material suppliers. Each channel is very short. No **channel intermediaries**—organizations that facilitate the transfer of title between the producer and user of a product—are involved in the supplier-to-builder channel. But the whole system requires 30 (5 × 6) transactions. The bottom of Exhibit 9–1 shows a longer channel. Between supplier and builder we find a distributor carrying the lines from all six material suppliers and serving all five builders. Notice that in this longer channel only 11 (5 + 6) transactions are needed to serve the builders—and the suppliers.

So let's forget—for the time being—the superior services the Home Depot might provide over direct-from-factory orders (e.g., sales help and an assortment of materials). We've shown that adding an intermediary can reduce the number of transactions in a system. Channels can affect the efficiency of buying and selling.

## Channel and Supply Chain Management

When the players are mapped out so neatly as in Exhibit 9–1, it's plain to see the overlap of supply chain management and channel management. Each builder sees a supply chain and is looking for manufacturer and distributor help in the management of building inputs. Each manufacturer looks at the distributor as a customer, a channel partner, who must then market to builders. (Builders, of course, have customers too, and manufacturers have a chain of suppliers.) Thus, perspectives and goals differ at each organizational level, but the interfirm system is the same regardless of one's position amidst upstream or downstream phenomena. Especially in the last decade, the overall goal of a competitive edge in system efficiency and customer value—in a global marketplace—has prompted new means of coordinating the parties.

### Channel Outputs and Costs

When we consider channel costs, we must really look deeper into what is getting done by the channel and what other means we might have of achieving the same end. Any marketing channel exists to provide specific service outcomes that are valued by

**Exhibit 9–1**
Trading Efficiency from an Intermediary

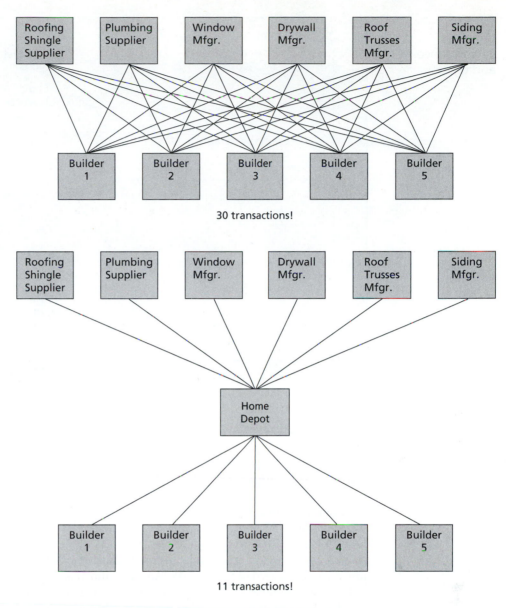

30 transactions!

11 transactions!

the supplier and the buyer. Exhibit 9–2 formalizes the chapter's opening discussion. The horizontal axis is an abstraction representing a combination of channel service outputs: fitting quantities are available, convenient selection and order are the rule, and we see rapid delivery, wide assortment, installation or application assistance, and so on.[2]

None of these services can be provided without cost. You know that oil by the tanker costs less than oil by the drum or liter; 20 distribution centers cost more to operate than 10; overnight delivery costs more than second-day; it takes a huge showroom or catalog to display office supplies or building products, but only a kiosk or trifold brochure to peddle business forms or insulation batts; and distributor service and support require higher prices (margins) than self-serve alternatives. Thus, Exhibit 9–2 shows channel costs rising with the provision of increased levels of service.

**Exhibit 9–2**
Channel
Performance
and Costs

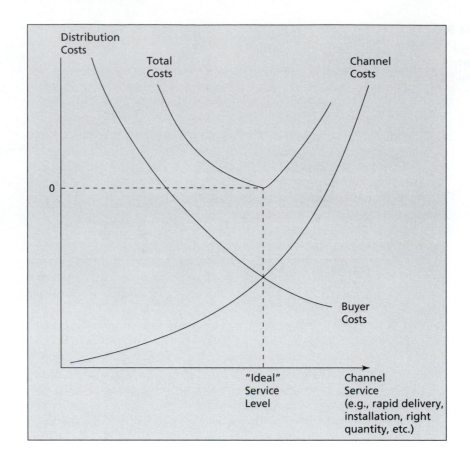

## Buyer Effort and Costs

But as these channel service outputs increase, the work required by a buyer—and the associated cost of this work—decreases. For example, a law office that can purchase letterhead in lots of 2,000 instead of 10 reams has less office clutter and saves on inventory investment. More of these savings accrue if the printer can replenish the stationery in just 72 hours instead of three weeks. An environmental engineer who can take the hazardous waste seminar locally saves the cost of airfare to the national training center. A purchasing agent who can get all the factory's lubricating oils from a single supplier saves on the costs of searching for and haggling with numerous vendors of specialty lubricants. Finally, a sales office that gets dealer installation assistance and training on the new copier saves on its own start-up efforts and avoids downtime resulting from misuse of the machine. In sum, many functions in the conduct of business—and their associated costs—can be shifted between buyers and members of the channel.

## A Best Channel Structure?

Economic pressures on the exchange network tend to move the channel to the structure that yields minimum total costs, point zero in Exhibit 9–2's curve representing the sum of buyer's costs and the costs of the commercial channel. Inefficient intermediaries will find their business going elsewhere, perhaps to more competitive intermediaries, but also perhaps to their suppliers, or their customers, who decide they can do certain functions for themselves.

Of course, habits, vested interests, and social and political ties can impede the evolution to this minimum-cost "ideal." For example, a company trying to use its website to sell routine supplies and its sales force to sell more complex products may nevertheless have to "buy peace" with its reps by providing them a small commission on the online orders in the territory.

Noncompetitive markets can likewise thwart more efficient systems for a time. For example, many municipalities have found that they can save money by outsourcing water and wastewater management to independent companies in the chemical process industry.[3] In essence, a water management company is an intermediary in a new, more efficient channel system. But more than economics determines the channel structure for any municipality. Outsourcing is dubbed "privatization" in government. Regardless of its true economic merits or, in other cases, demerits, use of such an intermediary often serves as a political lever for elected officials, strikes fear in the hearts of municipal employees, and mobilizes union opposition.

Part of the evolutionary equation must be the cooperative spirit between channel participants. As we have discussed in prior chapters, when buyers and seller collaborate, they often find ways to coordinate activities to eliminate waste or gain impact. For example, Covenant Transport is a transportation company that uses electronic communications and the Internet to allow its customers to track the location of orders 24 hours a day. Certainly this innovation affects needed inventories at both customer and shipper locations.

In this vein, let's not presume there is a single and permanent "best channel." Because of technology, experience, innovation, regulation, and the variability of costs of different system inputs (e.g., jet fuel or telecommunications), the minimum-cost channel and the ideal service level are moving targets.

### Channel Member Profits

In a competitive environment channel, members receive compensation that corresponds to the value they add to the product. For example, a small manufacturer of computer peripherals needs a dealer network not only to inventory and display its line, but also to demonstrate its products and ensure proper use with different operating systems. Dealer compensation in the form of margins may be more than 50 percent for such a role in differentiating the product in the value-added chain. In contrast, dealers simply taking orders for stock office or medical supplies play a much smaller role in the value-added chain; their margins will be quite thin.

Similarly, we see the market rewarding unique excellence. The hydraulics distributor, Hydrotech, with the distinct capability to provide applications engineering assistance to its OEM account, Milacron, is highly sought and valued as a channel partner—by both suppliers and customers. Such uniquely skilled intermediaries are apt to preserve their margins and enjoy market leadership without resorting to the deep discounts offered by distributors who lack the expertise or credibility.

## TYPES OF CHANNEL INTERMEDIARIES

To this point we have provided a justification for channels of distribution in general. We have referred to different types of channel members, but have not provided formal introductions. This section briefly reviews a number of the major types of organizations in business-to-business marketing. Actually, there are more types than we can afford to cover here. Simply keep in mind that several industries feature unique channel institutions that combine attributes of the forms we review next.

# The Ownership Distinction

We distinguish two major classes of business marketing intermediaries on the basis of whether or not they own the goods they sell. **Merchant wholesalers** are intermediaries who take title to the merchandise. Sometimes called **industrial distributors,** merchant wholesalers include a number of subtypes, which differ in the functions they perform. **Agents** and brokers represent the other class of intermediaries; they do not buy or own the goods they sell.

Why is product ownership such a key distinction? Product ownership brings with it a substantial business commitment. It involves cash or financing to purchase, requires proper storage and handling, and always includes risk of spoilage, theft, or obsolescence. Consider a small distributor doing $10 million in sales with 20 percent gross profit. Stocking an inventory sufficient to turn over four times per year requires an inventory investment alone of $2 million. Add to that the racks and bins, forklifts, systems, security, and more to see that the *ownership* commitment is substantial.

A third class of intermediaries consists of **manufacturers' sales branches and offices.** These are wholesaling operations that a manufacturer owns and operates. For example, ABB (Asea Brown Boveri), the $28 billion power and automation technology group headquartered in Zurich, Switzerland, has over 60 sales offices throughout the United States.

Any such subsidiary may have a measure of autonomy within the corporation, but its ownership by the manufacturing organization distinguishes sales branches and offices from the independent merchant wholesalers and agencies introduced above. Later in the chapter we will revisit some of the concepts from Chapter 2 and elsewhere in the text regarding the strategic costs and benefits of vertical integration, particularly the distribution functions.

# Other Distinguishing Functions: Merchant Wholesalers

## *Full Service*

Some merchant wholesalers, called **full-function wholesalers,** provide a broad array of services for their suppliers and customers. Exhibit 9–3 highlights the range of functions a full-service distributor is apt to provide. In essence, with a little foresight and candor from the buyer, the distributor can serve as an extension of its purchasing department. Similarly, good product training and marketing support from the manufacturer can enable the distributor to be an effective partner in the execution of sales and service functions. A good distributor partner enjoys a strong reputation in the regional industry or product area. Inventory levels should be sufficient to provide ready supply to users. Its sales force is knowledgeable and gives adequate attention to current customers and the tasks of developing new accounts. The distributor also provides market intelligence and new product ideas to both its suppliers and customers.[4]

In several product categories the distinction between wholesaler and retailer is blurred. Computer dealers, office supplies resellers such as Office Max and Staples, and warehouse clubs such as Sams sell to households. But they sell substantial volume to what some call the soho segment—the small office and home office—as well as to schools, restaurants, event marketers, and other organizations.

**Exhibit 9–3**
Functions
Performed by
Distributors

SOURCE: *Adapted with
permission from Bert
Rosenbloom,*
Marketing Functions
and the Wholesaler–
Distributor: Achieving
Excellence in
Distribution, *Washington, DC:
Distribution Research
and Education
Foundation, 1987.*

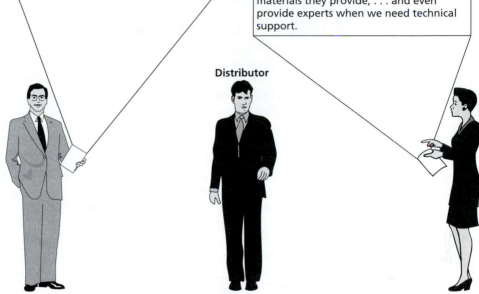

As a Manufacturer, I look to my distributor to give us a presence in the local market, . . . to call on customers and prospects—even small ones, . . . to have our product in stock when customers order, . . . to get the right orders and payment, . . . to help customers define their needs and solve special problems as they come up, . . . and to keep us abreast of market trends and looming issues in the business.

As a User, we count on the distributor to make sure the product we order in the morning is there by early afternoon, . . . and to carry the full range of related products in his assortment, . . . to allow us to purchase items as needed—instead of a whole pallet or truckload, . . . to let us pay in one monthly bill or finance the purchases, . . . to give us good service such as helping us determine needs and sort out options when we're in a pickle, . . . to set up our equipment to use the parts and materials they provide, . . . and even provide experts when we need technical support.

**Distributor**

## Selective Service

Many channels consist of **limited-function wholesalers.** These firms don't provide the full spectrum of services listed in Exhibit 9–3. For example, **single-line wholesalers** don't carry an assortment of items, perhaps just seed corn or certain chemicals. This concept can be carried further to **specialty wholesalers,** firms carrying a very narrow line and supporting that with technical expertise and consultative selling. An example is High Ocean Products Co., a Redmond, Washington, distributor of sea-frozen, sashimi-grade fish.

Merchant wholesalers also include **cash-and-carry distributors,** firms that provide no buyer financing or delivery. Many cities have downtown produce markets with several cash-and-carry wholesalers serving restaurants or other institutions. A **drop shipper** or **desk jobber** buys products from a supplier but never takes physical possession; instead they are delivered directly to the user. Bulky products such as coal and gypsum board are often drop shipped.

If one can job (wholesale) from a desk, one ought to be able to job from a truck. A **truck jobber** carries all its inventory on a truck and services customers on a frequent basis or route. The Snap-on-Tools distributor calling on service stations and garages is a truck jobber. This can be an effective means of reaching a market of small customers constrained by high search costs.

Finally, we should recognize the role of catalog wholesalers. Although almost any distributor will have a catalog to serve as a reference and ordering tool for customers, the **catalog wholesaler** relies exclusively on mail, phone, Internet, and fax orders from its catalog and Web site, but does not have a field sales force. Selling through catalog wholesalers such as Quill (for business products) or American Scientific Surplus, a supplier wants a high level of market penetration, its products prominently featured in the catalog, and Web pages, and wholesaler inventories sufficient to fill orders promptly.

### Management Issues with Using Merchant Wholesalers

Key management challenges for manufacturers using distributors—full service or otherwise—include sustaining distributor sales support for the line. A distributor with 200 reps calling on 10,000 hospitals and medical labs can't possibly satisfy every supplier's wish for a high percentage of its overall selling effort. When distributors carry strong competing makes or private-label merchandise, the problem becomes even tougher. High margins on top-quality products, fitting trade promotions, advertising, and the manufacturer's own selling activities will be required to motivate distributor efforts.

Manufacturers also complain about distributor shortcomings in market development. They point to a short-run orientation and a tendency merely to take orders on stock items instead of calling on *new* accounts and demonstrating *new* products. This difficulty can be a manifestation of a deeper problem, lack of manufacturer–distributor trust in the relationship. Perhaps distributors have seen the manufacturer terminate other wholesalers when markets grew big enough to support its internal sales force. Sometimes selling effort is discouraged by too much competition from other distributors in the region selling the same line. Maybe the technical specialists or other missionary sales work evidenced by the manufacturer is thought to be a prelude to designating large customers as its "house accounts" no longer serviced by the distributor.[5] In these cases the manufacturer should work primarily to restore trust with channel partners before tinkering with incentives or channel system redesign.

Many wholesale businesses are small, family-run operations. Frequently, the success of the enterprise is attributable to one person. What is the state of this person's health? Is he or she ready to retire or step out of day-to-day operations? Can the manufacturer see or assist the distributor in planning management succession? If we do not see a certain depth of leadership and continuity, suppliers and customers alike should hedge against breakdown of the current arrangement by cultivating other channel options.

## Agent Intermediaries

Among the channel institutions not taking title, **manufacturers' agents** sell the lines of noncompeting principals for a commission. A **principal** is the manufacturer or other person or firm that contracts for the services of the agent in its own behalf. Their job is to promote the line, develop new accounts, and take orders. When a manufacturer of radio receivers uses manufacturers' agents to sell its products, it avoids the overhead associated with its own sales force. Also, the commission compensation of an agent makes selling a variable cost. Agents typically bring knowledge of the regional market, established client relationships, and a modest assortment and affiliation advantage from the other *noncompeting* lines. They are a rich source of information on innovations in

---

**9–1**

# FROM THE FIELD

## Joseph: Iron Man or Super Broker?

The David J. Joseph Company is one of the world's first and largest scrap metals brokers. The $5 billion company headquartered in Cincinnati, Ohio, trades in ferrous metals around the world. The company builds, refurbishes, leases, and sells railroad boxcars; and it has a network of 35 scrap processing centers that include 11 automobile shredders capable of processing over 1 million cars a year. These activities are highly synergistic with its brokerage business. Joseph Company's professional brokers use sophisticated electronic communications and a network of supply and demand contacts to spot and act on opportunities around the world.

As summarized from the company Web page (**www.djj.com**):

The Joseph Company offers overseas buyers and sellers an insider's view and expert's perspective of the U.S. market. At the same time, it offers domestic customers access to an in-depth knowledge of overseas markets that can enhance their own operations.

Their goal is to benefit both metals producers and metals buyers alike, creating long-term partners.

---

the industry for customers and often can be counted upon to go the extra mile to solve problems such as scarce supply situations or adaptations to new uses.

Agent commissions vary by industry. Agents representing automotive OEMs earn about 5 percent commissions. Electronic products agents can earn between 7 and 12 percent. They often work under contracts requiring only 30 or 60 days' termination notice. This means that the contracts themselves provide little assurance of longevity. More important are performance and *strong working relationships*—with principals and agency customers. When these characteristics bond the parties, both principal and agent may be motivated to invest in training, materials, and other productive assets of the relationship.[6] Dow Corning has used manufacturers' agents for over 20 years, bringing them closer to the company by providing voice mail boxes, software tools, and training.

## Brokers

**Brokers** bring buyers and sellers together, typically in environments where buyers and sellers lack the information needed to connect with one another. For example, scrap metal and used machinery can originate from any of thousands of businesses. But who are the likely buyers and where are they? Brokers succeed by maintaining information on demand and supply situations. They can be engaged by either buyer or seller and receive a commission from the engaging party. Brokers often attend to an array of details associated with the execution of the exchange, perhaps negotiating the purchase, setting up delivery, and tracking. From the Field 9–1 profiles the Joseph Company, one of the top brokers in the world in ferrous metals.

Exhibit 9–4 summarizes the functions performed by the channel institutions we have just introduced. We have also included types of intermediaries that we have not discussed in the chapter. For purposes of this chapter, their role is sufficiently outlined in the table. Use it for reference when analyzing cases or considering channel design problems beyond those taken up in the next section.

**Exhibit 9–4**
The Functions of Different Types of Channel Intermediaries

| | Holds Inventory | Holds Title | Promotes | Provides Negotiator | Provides Credit |
|---|---|---|---|---|---|
| Merchant wholesalers | ● | ● | ● | ● | ● |
| Full-function or service wholesalers; | | | | | |
| Limited-function wholesalers | | | | | |
|   Drop shipper (desk jobber) | ○ | ● | ◐ | ● | ● |
|   Cash-and-carry wholesalers | ● | ● | ◐ | ● | ○ |
|   Wagon (truck) jobbing | ◐ | ◐ | ◐ | ● | ◐ |
|   Rack jobbers (service merchandise) | ● | ● | ● | ● | ● |
|   Wholesaler-sponsored (voluntary) chains | ● | ● | ● | ● | ● |
| Retailer cooperative | ● | ● | ● | ● | ● |
| Agents and brokers | | | | | |
|   Brokers | ○ | ○ | ● | ◐ | ○ |
|   Manufacturers' agents | ○ | ○ | ● | ○ | ○ |
|   Selling agents | ○ | ○ | ● | ● | ○ |
| Commission merchants | ● | ○ | ● | ● | ● |

● = High levels of involvement in this function.
◐ = Only some modest involvement in this function.
○ = Does not perform this function.

# MARKETING CHANNEL DESIGN

Marketing channel design is certainly a fitting topic to take up after a discussion of marketing strategy. Remember that strategy involves a commitment of *significant resources* in a *coordinated* manner for outcomes over a *long period*. By this measure, most channel decisions are essentially strategic: inventories, sales forces, technology investments, distributor support programs, and other channel activities involve large financial outlays. Hundreds and perhaps thousands of people—very likely housed in two or more distinct organizations—need to coordinate their activities. Furthermore, the whole structure is difficult to reconfigure or dismantle because implicit and explicit coordination processes, customized work habits, and special equipment *get dedicated* to making the system work.

The channel design process consists of four primary steps: (1) identify and anticipate end user needs for an array of channel services, (2) create a vision of an ideal channel that could provide customers with those services, (3) evaluate current channels and all practicable options against this ideal system, and (4) implement the best practicable

**Exhibit 9–5**
A Model for Channel Design

*SOURCE: Adapted with permission from the MAC Group, now known as Gemini Consulting, Inc.,* The Planning Forum: Differentiation through Channel Strategy: Concepts and Practice, *May 1, 1990.*

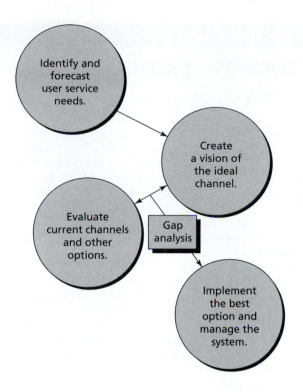

option and setup for ongoing channel management. Exhibit 9–5 shows these steps. Let's take up each in detail.[7]

# Identify and Anticipate User Needs

You have a good sense of the menu of channel services from this chapter's opening discussion of the purposes of channels. In the planning process, we need to go beyond the abstract notion that customers want convenience and quick delivery. We need to attend to different needs that exist across different segments. Air-conditioning systems for schools and government offices don't require the same emergency service and component replacement standards as systems for hospitals, theaters, or large computer installations. Small bakeries have different delivery and assortment needs than a microbrewery, and both differ from their large-scale counterparts.

Within each segment, we must try to identify the entire array of services sought. To say that customers are seeking "convenient delivery" or "set-up assistance" does not lend enough detail to the planning effort. We need to be more explicit: Convenience comes from delivery before business hours, within a two-hour window, using returnable cartons. We need to dig deep to learn that "setup assistance" for one segment means delivery of tubing in machine-feeding bins to the work stations on the factory floor; for another it means resetting the tube bender–beader to the new product.

In short, the channel service outputs we described in just a half-dozen dimensions at the start of the chapter get sliced into perhaps a score or more benefits.

# Create a Vision of the Ideal Channel

The channel system that yields the service outputs identified in the first phase may very well not exist. When Milacron developed low-cost plastic injection molding machines, it knew that the product's low-price position and scattered target market precluded use

---

**9–1**

# BUSINESS 2 BUSINESS

## Got a Match?

A key to channel profitability is a three-way match among product categories, customer types, and service levels. In principle, best customers purchasing profitable products should get blue ribbon channels services. Transactional customers who occasionally order low-margin products should get minimal service, or perhaps be charged for services. Indeed, it makes sense to make a grid with categories of customer quality across the top, and three-to-five product profitability categories down the side. Each cell can then be considered for a fitting service level.

A manufacturer of light commercial air-conditioning systems found over 80 percent of its units were sold in the replacement market—nearly all of which sold on the hottest days of the year, when the replaced units broke down. When the breakdown occurred at a retail business, immediate availability and installation was needed. Price was not a pressing concern.

In light of this, the manufacturer consolidated its product line to offer more flexible "base" models, which could be modified by sheet metal workers to fit the installation. A reworked distribution channel increased the number of full-service wholesalers and added public warehouses for seasonal demands. With the exception of the full product line available from just two sites, all locations carried just a small number of units. These basic units—with sheet metal modifications—could serve 98 percent of replacement demand! Overall supply chain costs increased by over 20 percent, but so did market share. Profits doubled.

Source: Robert Sabath and Judith M. Whipple, "Integrating Supply Chain Management to Improve Profitability," *Explores* 4 (Summer 2007), pp. 3–15.

---

of its own sales force. It needed an outside sales force. But which one? No distributors had ever carried such a product and there was doubt that an agency could be adequately supported logistically from factory inventory to provide the needed delivery time and availability.

Thus, the ideal channel featured a low-cost sales force, equipped with product knowledge and motivated to assist with machine setup, installation, and some training. The machine itself supported easy entry into the plastics business and its low cost made it affordable to small firms, even start-up companies. Thus, potential customers were numerous, and actual prospects difficult to identify. The ideal channel would need to generate and qualify leads efficiently to allow the sales force to follow up efficiently. Many customers would want financing and rapid delivery once they made the purchase decision. Parts and supplies would need to be readily available. Postsale service could be a little slower than instantaneous.

## Assess Options

We have profiled a number of types of channel intermediaries, firms that specialize in several channel functions. In this stage of the planning process we want to consider the adequacy of these different business types and our prospects for finding a place in their product line. Examine the viability of a system using full-service wholesalers. Compare that to a hybrid system using limited-function wholesalers and manufacturer-performed functions. Frequently, a manufacturer will increase its participation in different channel functions—lead generations, presale service, expedited shipments, after-sale service, and training—and wonder if its "full-function" wholesalers are rightly labeled.

**Exhibit 9–6**
The Economics
of Direct and
Indirect
Distribution

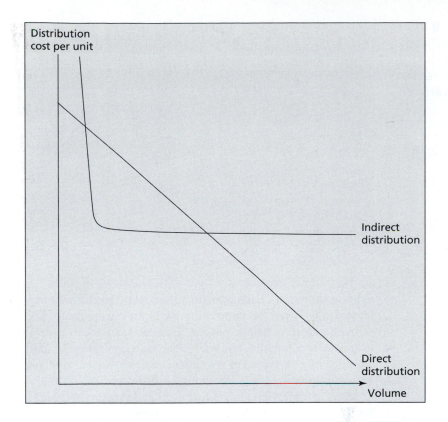

Can we use combinations of intermediaries to achieve the majority of the sought outputs? Consider an electronics components manufacturer that uses its own sales force for market development activities such as trade shows, seminars, and low-key visits to purchasing managers. Agents are relied on to sell and get major orders. Most shipments are made from the factory. Federal Express and a single inventory in Memphis are used for urgent small orders. Smaller accounts are served by AVNET, a leading electronic components distributor and e-commerce pioneer.

Sometimes different structures are required in different parts of the country. That is, in medical and electrical products we find two or three national distribution organizations available. Still, other distributor firms compete quite effectively with the nationals within geographic regions or within certain customer groups. In this situation, the alternative channel structures involve not merely different business types but different specific companies.

Face it; some options we might consider are simply beyond company capabilities. Examine the graph in Exhibit 9–6. It shows that sales and distribution costs per unit using intermediaries are consistent over a large range of volumes. But at very low start-up volumes, the curve elbows upward as the manufacturer faces stiff resistance from distributors and must provide all sorts of inducements—high margins, promotion allowances, and good credit terms.

Distributor interest in a new product from a small company may be negligible until the start-up firm has done some channel activities itself to "buy" channel support or demonstrate demand for the product. Even if intensive personal selling is involved, the start-up firm simply lacks resources to initiate a national sales force. Instead, the firm might sell on consignment, focus on a regional market, or use direct response advertising and a strong telephone marketing staff to demonstrate demand (i.e., push out to the

**Exhibit 9–7**
Gap Analysis:
Channel
Options versus
Ideal Channel

| Channel Service Output | Company Sales and Distribution Centers | Distributors and Small Company Service Staff |
|---|---|---|
| Product knowledge of sales force | 2 | 6 |
| Customer relationship of sales force | 5 | 3 |
| Assortment match | 6 | 3 |
| Inventory investment | 7 | 2 |
| Inventory controls | 2 | 5 |
| Delivery cost | 5 | 3 |
| Delivery reliability | 3 | 3 |
| Product setup | 1 | 5 |
| Customer training | 1 | 4 |
| Emergency service response | 2 | 5 |
| **Total gap score** | 34 | 39 |

Key: 0 = match to ideal; 10 = gross mismatch to ideal.

right on the graph). Early participants in the personal computer field, such as Apple and Hyundai, followed this approach prior to generating dealer interest.

In the channel design process, each alternative can be evaluated against the ideal structure. It is rare that any alternative matches up to the ideal because each option is bounded by constraints in resources and know-how as well as coordination difficulties and incompleteness in performance evaluation.

Many managers have found that overall assessments of channel options are enabled by a feature-by-feature comparison. **Gap analysis** is a set of tools for comparing performance outcomes or expectations on specific criteria. Exhibit 9–7 shows a gap analysis for two channel options against the ideal. It relies on a mix of objective measures as well as scaled subjective inputs from managers. The decision maker can follow a weighted or unweighted point system to tally an overall gap score. Coca-Cola Foods used this approach to change its channel from a hybrid of brokers and its own sales organization, to one that used brokers exclusively and compensated them on a detailed performance-based commission structure.

In contrast, the analysis in Exhibit 9–7 favors the company sales force over the use of distributors. Although this means significant inventory investment and a lot of relationship building, the payoffs appear in distinctive customer service on such dimensions as product setup, customer training, and emergency service. Thus, this analysis can sometimes lead to a channel structure that is shorter than the existing channel, eliminating an intermediary. Especially when margins are high and intermediary performance is suspect, any manufacturing organization is apt to consider eliminating the distributor or agent.

Heed our warning: Eliminating an intermediary does not eliminate the need for performing the channel functions. Firms that try to vertically integrate the functions of an intermediary often underestimate the full scope of functions or neglect a number of costs of doing business.

# Implement and Manage

Channel structure or strategy selection must include consideration of how to set it in place and how to make it work. Although the complexity and scope of channel structure change urge one to move carefully and methodically, competitive realities and vulnerability to opportunism in any adjustment period call for swift execution. We take up these two challenges next. From the Field 9–2 previews the challenges of changing channels.

**9–2**

# FROM THE FIELD

## Sun's Service Network No Longer Heliocentric

With $13 billion in sales and offices in 170 countries, Sun Microsystems looks to its service arm to handle critical field functions—installation, integration, education, repair, and maintenance. It's a huge operation that generates $3.7 billion in annual revenue and receives 150,000 orders for parts each quarter in the Americas.

For nearly 10 years Sun has outsourced many facets of the service and repair operation to repair companies, transportation companies, and warehouse management firms. This service channel helped Sun focus on its core business while developing a new strong competency in channel management. But it came at a high cost, the high cost of coordinating. Each time a transaction occurred, say, a part moved from a warehouse to a service provider or back to a stocking bin, it had to be recorded and audited by Enterprise Services. It was a hub-and-spoke configuration that involved 70 vendors, each with systems not fully compatible with all the others; Enterprise Services coordinated communications and resolved each bit of incompatible information. Overall, the system failed to capture the synergies and efficiencies possible. In the face of increasing customer service expectations, it just wasn't up to the task.

Sun retooled this service channel by taking itself out of the middle and consolidating its network of service providers. These members comprise the Alliance Council. Members use Sun hardware, software, and networking configuration to interact seamlessly. Sun links all providers in the channel to make visible the entire value chain. For example, repair companies receive advance notice before receiving parts so they can operate more like manufacturing operations than firefighters. Similarly, warehousing has become information management. System tracking and standards make management an exception-based process. Sun still maintains purchase order commitments, financial valuation, and disaster recovery within Sun, but inventory flows, parts call assignments, delivery reporting, and the like are "fluid" processes maintained by Sun's service channel partners.

Sun counts the payoffs on several dimensions. Customer service has been significantly enhanced. Sun's service network not only gives complete solutions to customers, but the business is scalable and flexible. Inventory investment and carrying costs—and the paperwork—have been trimmed.[8] In April 2006, Sun was ranked number one compared to Dell, HP, IBM, and Microsoft for technical support personnel, quality of service, service plan features and deliverables, and clarity of service plan offerings in a market study by TNS Prognostics.[9]

## Tough Competitors

What can a competitor do to disrupt the channel implementation process of its rival? If the strategy calls for enlisting distributors, competitors may try to "load up" distributors with inventory so they see no need to carry a new line. Many distributors pledge not to carry competing lines in exchange for a manufacturer's pledge to restrict product distribution through other distributorships.[10] In the face of a potential entrant in the channel, they can use some heavy-handedness with distributors, making broad interpretations of their exclusivity contracts and contending the new product is competitive with their lines.

Sometimes the competing incumbent supplier will challenge the adequacy of a distributor's or agent's selling effort, requesting more people in the field or the promotion of fewer products to the target market. In the face of pressure from an important supplier, a reseller or agent will show some reluctance to carry the new items.

### Saboteurs

The channel intermediaries themselves can thwart even the best channel strategy. How much selling effort would you give if you got word that your principal was terminating your agency in favor of a company sales force in three months? Would a terminated distributor work hard to get equipment repaired or defects replaced? Will payment for final shipments be made promptly and completely? In the local market, performance breakdowns will tend to be attributed to the manufacturer. As the battle for accounts now rages between the distributor and the brand, situations can get ugly.

### Speed and Redundancy

Of course, channel redesign can feature disintegration, in which performed functions are spun off to intermediaries. Then the opportunity to reassign personnel may soften the shock on individuals from the change, but in harsh competitive environments, there may be no place to move personnel internally. Like the bitter intermediaries described, disgruntled employees can jeopardize account relationships and operations.

Thus, channel structural change must be communicated carefully and executed swiftly. Because contractual obligations may require 30 to 60 days' notice for termination, it may be wise to operate parallel channels—redundant operations—during the wind-down period. This affords a measure of slack for learning new routines and serves as a buffer against some types of opportunism. Redundant systems also provide a backup for current accounts that should not suffer through the transition.

# CHANNEL MANAGEMENT: THE POLITICS OF DISTRIBUTION

The justification and planning sections of this chapter have emphasized the economic function of marketing channels. This matches the text's perspective on value creation and provides a very useful normative framework. But let's not pretend that market share, efficiency, and return on investment are the only goals motivating functional arrangements and activities in channels. The interfirm relationships we find in marketing channels exhibit political as well as economic phenomena.

Your understanding of the value-added chain makes our discussion of interfirm partnerships for achieving channel services quite plain. This section delves deeper into some of the *behavioral* factors that interact with margins, performance standards, purchase terms, multipage sales contracts, and other *economic* factors. Because trading between firms inescapably involves human beings who have limited mental capacity, incomplete data, different goals, and feelings, it is critical to address some of the key behavioral dimensions of channel management.

## Relational Exchanges

Organizations exchange because it is beneficial to do so. These are voluntary associations, at least at the beginning. Each firm expects to be better off by trading some of its resources for the resources of another. A distributor carries a line of products it thinks will sell in the industries it serves in its market area; the supplier concedes the distributor's margin as payment for the distribution functions performed. Mutual gain is expected from the exchange.

But exchange between channel members has a little different character than, say, a contractor hired to paint a couple of offices or other *transactional* exchanges we illustrated in Chapter 2. It will take both distributor and supplier several months or longer to ascertain accurately the benefits of their exchange. And what looks okay after six months may sour in the next for any number of reasons. With the investments each party makes in the exchange—inventories, delivery systems, product knowledge, selling approaches, systems integration, brand image—not to mention sticky termination provisions in sales contracts, channel associations are seldom transactional. Channel members generally exchange in an outgoing relationship.

Channel members will need to make adjustments to their relationship because they depend on each other in dynamic environments over time. New demands may arise at the distributor level, perhaps affecting inventory costs or selling efficiency. New competition from online competitors may motivate discounting, which shrinks the margins that were allotted to compensate for the long selling cycle. At the supplier end, new profit requirements from the division may demand a cut in print advertising, an activity regarded as an important source of leads by distributors. Perhaps the supplier is broadening its product line and sees strategic payoffs from more in-house selling activities.

# Conflict and Its Types

**Conflict** is felt or enacted tension between parties—in this situation, channel members. The source of this tension can reside in the different goals of the members, preferences for different roles or activities, and sometimes in different perceptions of the task environment.

### Goal Conflict
Most agency relationships have a degree of inherent goal conflict in that manufacturers push for higher and higher sales, whereas agents must be concerned with profit—that is, sales (commissions) less expenses. Even on this goal, agents are not apt to seek some hypothetical maximum profit, but some satisfactory level that affords their sought lifestyle. In manufacturer–distributor relationships we often see different growth aims. Manufacturers generally are more aggressive, caring particularly more about their product category than the distributor's overall growth.

### Means Conflict
Conflict over how things get done arises when channel members dispute how the EDI system will be implemented, who will solve a customer complaint, who will prospect and cultivate accounts and who will close, who will service mail-order customers, what accounts will be house accounts, and how much inventory is appropriate. This is a big arena for conflict. Often the activities have different costs for the parties, but simply compensating the more efficient member to do the task is difficult when performance is costly to measure. How does the other party know when the tasks are done and whether they're done well?[11]

### Conflicting Views
The problem of monitoring performance leads well into the third source of conflict: different perceptions and theories. For example, sometimes distributors won't follow up on leads generated by manufacturer advertising because they believe the leads are lousy. And as leads

---

### 9–3

# FROM THE FIELD
## Finger Pointing and Ego Stroking

In the mid-1990s, Lexo, a five-year-old software development company, wanted to build on its regional success and serve the national market. To establish a nationwide dealer network it enlisted two master dealers (MDs)—one for the East Coast, the other, GrayShow, for the rest of the country. Both MDs were also among Lexo's small (three-firm) dealer network. All dealers were granted exclusive territories and 60 percent margins; MDs were granted a commission on dealer sales.

GrayShow added a half dozen dealers by the late 1990s when Lexo's rival had serious pricing and performance difficulties and many of its dealers defected. Lexo's revenues grew and both MDs were highly involved with Lexo's marketing program development. GrayShow even developed demo discs and brochures for which it was reimbursed by Lexo.

Although GrayShow was a superior dealer, as an MD its dealers underperformed on quota (a penetration percent of estimated market potential) compared to the East Coast dealers. Because MD GrayShow declined the provision of dealer support on the new software, Lexo took up the responsibility and requested and received a return of a portion of paid commissions. Lexo urged GrayShow to hire a person dedicated to dealer recruitment and development, but GrayShow declined.

In 2005 Lexo hired its first national marketing director—to the delight of most dealers—and terminated GrayShow's Master Dealership. As a dealer GrayShow dropped Lexo from its line of products and sued Lexo, claiming its work was highly valuable to Lexo's success and merited GrayShow status as business owner. Lexo's countersuit claims GrayShow was a party to a pay-for-performance agreement, did no investment in the enterprise, and was dismissed for poor performance. Despite years of exchange and days of federal mediation, the parties cannot see eye-to-eye and legal bills continue to mount.

Note: Company names and certain facts have been changed to disguise this ongoing conflict.

---

sit too long or receive halfhearted follow-up, sure enough, the leads play out as poorly as the distributor expected. Different views of reality also clash over how much inventory is appropriate, how many sales calls a certain customer type should receive, how many items in the line will be carried, and whether sales are down because of market softening or flagging effort in manufacturer advertising. Or is it poor intermediary selling effort?

## Conflict Consequences

First, we should recognize that the total elimination of conflict chokes a relationship. Any partnership with vitality has conflict. But will conflict prove destructive, or will conflict have some valued function? The managerial challenge for channel members is to enable conflict to be addressed positively and to harvest constructive outcomes. If disparate goals are not reconciled, at least one party will go unsatisfied and perhaps the relationship will fail. If parties work at cross-purposes or redundantly, the system will get trounced by a competitive channel. If the parties do their work according to different views of the world, coordination will be impossible, and critical functions may go undone as we see in From the Field 9–3. Again, the relentless tide of competition will swamp such a poorly coordinated channel.

## *Responses to Conflict*

Channel members can have five primary reactions to conflict: exit, voice, loyalty, aggression, and neglect.[12]

### "I'm Out of Here!"

**Exit** means leaving a relationship. This is a bold move and is perhaps difficult to see as a positive approach to conflict. But recognize that exit ends what may have been a prolonged period of squabbling. It also signals important limits: "You can't push us any further" and "We have an option." Although the focal relationship terminates, the abandoned party sometimes processes the signal and makes adjustments in its relationships with other channel partners.

### "What I Really Need Is . . . "

**Voice** involves some means of articulating dissatisfaction. A leader in a negotiation seminar once described a conflict between two roommates. They were cooking late one night and each used a recipe that called for an orange. With only one orange in the house and the nearby stores closed, the cooks argued over who needed it more and who had eaten the second to last piece of fruit. Alas, they halved the orange and each halved the recipe. One roommate then squeezed the juice of half an orange into the bowl; the other grated the peel.

Sadly, the parties had argued over means and never clearly voiced their respective goals. Had they done so, it would not have taken much problem solving at all to find a solution satisfactory to both parties.

Not every conflict problem has such an obvious win–win solution, but many do when they are accurately and fully framed and creativity is applied. We advise conflicting parties to hold fast to their goals. Be clear about what they want from the relationship. Compromising on one's objectives takes no creativity. Put imagination to the task of finding a means that meets the goals of both parties. Usually, the pie is bigger than first thought.

*Voice is a critical process for uncovering the origin of the conflict.* Consider the conflict situation described earlier involving a distributor's low regard for manufacturer-generated leads. It seems highly unlikely that the manufacturer aims to generate weak leads, although there may be a misplaced emphasis on getting large numbers of leads. The distributor, meanwhile, has no interest in doing all lead generation itself. It makes good sense for the manufacturer to manage the brand Web site and do the national print advertising needed. The conflict resides not in goals, nor significantly in preferred activities. This seems to be a conflict resulting from both parties working with tainted or incomplete information.

Remember from Chapter 2 that an exchange partner requesting adjustment—an act of voice—implicitly signals that there is potential benefit from staying in this relationship. There is a measure of confidence that the request will be entertained by the other party. Thus, there is hope that the other sees longer-term payoffs from the relationship too.

### "Aye, Captain."

**Loyalty** is steadfast perseverance in the face of conflict's felt tension or abuse. Suppose you exhibit loyalty in a conflict situation. You see conflict of interests, inappropriate roles, or wrong-headed perceptions, but you hold onto hope that the other will (1) eventually come around or (2) prove you wrong. More typical of alumni patience with a new football coach or a spouse's steadfastness in a rocky marriage, loyalty in business marketing channels characterizes struggling new-channel relationships, nonprofit partnerships, and channel members tied by family bonds.

## 9–2

# BUSINESS 2 BUSINESS
## Voice Supports Problem Solving

The conflict of lead quality is common in the business marketing channels. One tack taken by some manufacturers is to make joint calls on a sample of leads. Another is to give distributors five business days to follow up before passing the lead to an internal sales force. A more integrative approach is to enlist a third organization, a telephone service bureau, to receive the inbound calls generated by advertising, qualify leads on the spot, and electronically distribute them to regional distribution sales offices within 24 hours, at a price to distributors of $4 each. Ads that generate an abundance of nonqualifiers tend to be rooted out by the expense of fielding all the 800-number calls. Distributors generally are less inclined to let purchased leads languish, and the $4 fee partially offsets the service bureau costs. See how accurate representation of the problem and creativity are so critical to the conflict management process.

Dr. John Graham is a marketing professor who has conducted conflict resolution workshops around the world. He has frequently used the following game to see if exchange partners can solve problems together.[13] One person or team is asked to play the role of buyer, another plays seller. The parties have only their own profit table and make offers and counteroffers for three different products as they try to discover what is important to the other party and then come to terms of agreement that are profitable for the whole transaction. Each is out to make the most it can, regardless of what the other earns. Payoffs from each price for the two players are shown in the accompanying table. Can you see a win-win solution to this particular exchange?

### Payoff Matrices for Negotiation Game

| | Buyer Profits | | | Seller Profits | | |
|---|---|---|---|---|---|---|
| Prices | Product 1 | Product 2 | Product 3 | Product 1 | Product 2 | Product 3 |
| A | 40 | 24 | 16 | 0 | 0 | 0 |
| B | 35 | 21 | 14 | 2 | 3 | 5 |
| C | 30 | 18 | 12 | 4 | 6 | 10 |
| D | 25 | 15 | 10 | 6 | 9 | 15 |
| E | 20 | 12 | 8 | 8 | 12 | 20 |
| F | 15 | 9 | 6 | 10 | 15 | 25 |
| G | 10 | 6 | 4 | 12 | 18 | 30 |
| H | 5 | 3 | 2 | 14 | 21 | 35 |
| I | 0 | 0 | 0 | 16 | 24 | 40 |

HINT: Buyer and seller have complementary priorities on which to make concessions. Buyer wants the A-level prices on Product 1; Seller wants I-level prices on Product 3. E seems fair for Product 2. Profits work out to 52 for each at these terms.

### "You Dirty @!"

**Aggression** includes open or covert actions intended to injure the conflict party. Yes, this includes hurtful words and shoving on the golf course or in the office. More common are retaliatory business practices that accelerate a downward trust spiral. Regis Blahut, a manufacturer's agent in Wexford, Pennsylvania, notes that one of his "principals had some internal problems which resulted in new management and a total misunderstanding of what a sales rep does for a living. As a result, a significant commission due is in jeopardy."[14] Delayed shipments or payments are just an example. Other aggressive behaviors include tardiness in communications, empty promises, bait-and-switch, violating assigned territories, or simply going through the motions in assorted channel roles.

Sadly, aggression tends to add fuel to the sparks of conflict. As trust deteriorates and negative sentiments harden, it becomes quite difficult to restore the relationship to gain some value from the conflict situation. Acrimonious terminations, tarnished reputations, and costly litigation that often drags on for years are the sorry fruits of this strategy when played to the hilt.

### "Ho-Hum."

**Neglect** means to leave the conflict untreated, perhaps allowing the relationship to atrophy or fade in significance. A distributor often does 70 percent of its business with less than 15 percent of its suppliers. If one of its suppliers of the remaining 30 percent is unreliable in delivery or order fill rates, how much effort should the distributor give to straightening out the situation? No redress in this situation is not really loyalty or perseverance; it's a case of minimal interest in the conflict. Akin to the early stages of the relationship development process reviewed in Chapter 2, the parties in this situation are not deeply dependent on each other—at least the distributor has little stake in this supplier. If performance slides further, the distributor can cut back on selling effort or inventory, or even replace with another supplier. If things improve, perhaps the supplier's share of the distributor's business will climb too. In neither case have we seen proactive effort by the distributor.

## Structures for High Performance and Conflict Management

Rather than relying on ad hoc activities to address conflict—and other operational or strategic matters—participants in some channels establish formal mechanisms.

### Private Referee

A manufacturer may enlist managers from a subset of its distributors to serve on a distributor council or planning panel. The distributor council then is a forum for all distributors to air complaints, underscore competitive threats, identify opportunities for better coordination, and give input on channel strategy for better customer service or service of new markets. Dayco Corporation in Dayton, Ohio, uses its distributor advisory council to provide suggestions for new channel policies and programs.[15] Large distributors set up similar panels of suppliers.

### Third-Party Solutions

So that channel members in dispute can avoid the costly and highly uncertain route of litigation, some channel relationships and trade associations have established third-party systems for conflict resolution. Akin to a corporation's internal grievance procedure for employees, distribution channel members can agree to seek a mediated resolution before an industry referee. For example, the retired founder of Businessland computer stores, once the largest company-owned chain of PC dealers, was enlisted to mediate a dispute between the chain and one of its key suppliers.[16] Other arrangements can provide for arbitration.

### Empathic Mechanisms

Three other approaches deserve mention here. Some organizations assign the task of managing channel member relations to a particular manager. This person's title could be dealer advocate, ombudsman, or director of trade (supplier) relations. In essence, they are diplomats, contacts for channel members with problems, firefighters, and initiators of policy changes.

Channel members can attain better understanding of each others' managerial challenges and find forums for constructive dialogue by joining each other's trade association. Chemical manufacturers, for example, will attend meetings of the National Association of Chemical Distributors (NACD). Many distributors will participate in the manufacturers' meetings.

Finally, consider the utility of exchanging personnel. By bringing reps to the factory for several days, or sending production people into the field with sales reps, better empathy results and shared perceptions of the value-added process result. If longer periods of exchange are feasible (say, a distribution executive in residence at the supplier for six months or more), the implicit reasons for a supplier's routines become verified or tuned, and new understandings of the other's operating environment enable joint problem solving for distribution channel competitiveness.

## Some Final Words on Conflict

We view the marketing channel as a set of interdependent institutions performing functions necessary to provide customers with valued services and time and space utility. Because the goals, skills, expectations, and perceptions of the firms in a channel are different, the potential for conflict is ever present. But this stress over what to aim for, who does what, and in what vision of reality is a double-edged sword. If properly managed, it can lead to more efficient operations, identify opportunities for growth, enable marketing innovations, and prompt the whole channel system to improve its competitiveness. Accordingly, we discussed several means for gleaning the positive outcomes from conflict.

Not all system improvements benefit every member of the channel. And even if a particular change might actually bring mutual gains, it is often the case that at least one participant doesn't see it that way. In addition, some conflicts hinge on the distribution of system payoffs (or losses). This reality prompts us to attend to another critical facet of the politics of distribution: power.

# Power in the Channel

In Chapter 2 we briefly introduced the concept of power between organizational buyers and sellers. Again, **power** is a property of a relationship deriving from one member's dependence on another for valued resources—resources that are not readily available elsewhere. It is a potential to get another to do something that he or she would not otherwise do. Because each party is somewhat unique in skills, resources, and connectivity to other candidates for exchange, seldom is power distributed equally in a relationship.

Some inevitable power inequalities in channels are quite subtle or shifting, especially in light of changing technology and markets. For all practical purposes, such relationships can be regarded as balanced. Nevertheless, many channel relationships reflect unbalanced dependence or asymmetrical power distributions. Consider a billion-dollar distribution company and its hundreds of small suppliers, a large manufacturer and its agents doing $150,000 in commission, and finally, a large OEM and its MRO supplies provider.

You should not be surprised: Power too cuts both ways. Lord Acton cautioned that "absolute power corrupts absolutely," and we have the historical evidence of the abuses of mercantilist monopolies, Nazi genocide, and Tiananmen Square to support him. In marketing channels we want to examine how a powerful firm might judiciously use its resources—not to exploit—but to *lead* the interfirm system, effectively coordinating the behaviors required to deliver value to customers.

## Sources of Power

In an exchange relationship one party can depend on the other for a variety of resources: discounts, selling assistance, promotional ideas, affiliation, access to new markets. We want to take a portion of this section to identify some of the key resources and those too often neglected.

### Carrots and Sticks

Probably the most common means of coordinating channel behavior involves the use of rewards and punishments. **Reward power** is the ability to provide payoffs to a party for specified behaviors or outcomes. A principal may promise an expense-paid trip to Hawaii to any agent selling $.5 million in a quarter. A distributor might be given 12 cases for the price of 10 for ordering during a particular period or participating in a supplier promotion.

**Coercive power** is the ability of one channel member to mediate punishments to get another to do what it otherwise would not do. A supplier may threaten to set up another sales or distribution relationship or terminate a distributor—as in From the Field 9–3—if the quality of selling effort is not up to standards. Likewise, a distributor can punish a supplier by delaying payments, withholding sales efforts, trimming inventories, and terminating also.

Rewards and punishments are a very direct means of changing another's behavior. They work by altering the outcomes of the particular action. Neither approach affects the other's motivation for the behavior itself. That is, rewards and coercion don't compel others to comply for the rightness of the act. But sometimes if a channel member can witness other positive outcomes of compliance, it will begin to internalize the behavior.

Punishments tend to move the channel members apart, fracturing their sense of solidarity and possibly alienating the punished party. We can expect a member to mask noncompliance in the face of punishments. Therefore, a coercive channel member must also implement a monitoring system. But policing and other detection systems similarly risk alienation. Intentions to maintain a working relationship should bridle a member's application of coercive power.

People generally seek rewards and enjoy "prizes" significantly more than avoiding punishments. Auditing behavior too is a little easier with rewards because channel members staking claim to rewards will tend to document their own compliance. Nevertheless, even the use of reward power can be overdone. Relationships can get muddled when members do every little thing in order to claim the goodies. A sense of pressure mounts as one works without a grasp of the real reasons for performing the channel functions. Think about it: We want our agents making monthly calls on "A" accounts because they agree with us on the service level needed with these particular customers—not simply because they earn more chances to golf at the Greenbrier!

### Persuasion

The ability to get a channel partner to change behavior by bringing it to the point where it sees the merit in the activity is a type of power too. This ability stems from three key power bases: information power, expert power, and referent power. **Information power** resides in a channel member's reliance on facts and figures, models, and insights from its partner. A manufacturer that invests in a market-tracking system that can provide product category forecasts for different regional wholesalers will possess information power over the buying and inventory activities of its wholesalers. Agents have information power over their principals in areas of customer buying cycles and the competitive products they are considering. From the Field 9–4 reveals the measure of success that can result when channel participants exchange information and respect each other in their areas of expertise.

### Image

Information power can be well complemented by expert power. A source's **expert power** is the ability to gain a target firm's compliance based on that target's regard for the source as knowledgeable. The target doesn't need to read the source's analysis or follow the logic. It's the source's *reputation* as an expert in the eyes of the target that brings behavioral change. Because a key requirement for the use of information power is gaining the target firm's attention to the information, expert power seems to work well in concert with data and models.

Another power base that rests in the perception of the target firm is **referent power,** the potential to influence another based on the other's desire to identify with or be like the source firm. The firm with referent power in some relationships will be able to change its partner's behaviors by modeling those behaviors or making simple requests. A manufacturer's reception for its agents at a trade show builds rapport and identification. When training sessions occur and new planning systems are introduced, any agents' tendency to emulate the manufacturer enables channel coordination.

### Authority

The last dimension of channel power we need to discuss is called legitimate power. This is not to imply any illegitimacy in previous dimensions. This basis of power stems from one of two roots: tradition or contract. In **traditional legitimate power,** the source is able to direct the behavior of the target because cultural norms support the source. A supplier can rightly ask that distributors properly handle paints or adhesives that would not perform properly if frozen or overheated. The culture maintains the value that customers deserve a product that performs up to promises. Other examples of the power of tradition are resellers' final say on prices to customers and a host of operating issues (business hours, employee qualifications). **Legal legitimate power** is explicit authority over certain behaviors granted to the source in a sales agreement or contract. For example, a distributor may agree not to carry competing lines and to recognize the penalty of termination for a breach. Similarly, a manufacturer may promise service within a specified period of time when distributors call for it.

## 9–4

# FROM THE FIELD

## Ground Heaters and Channel Partners Revolutionize Construction

After spending many years in well-established, highly recognized brand name companies, I had the opportunity to be involved with a start-up company called Ground Heaters, Inc. (GHI), which manufactures revolutionary hydronic heat products that allow construction contractors to effectively control their construction environment during cold winter months. Although we had some early success selling to end users, it became apparent that this was not going to sustain long-term growth objectives. Despite our knowledge and passion that reflected the benefits of Ground Heater products to end users, we lacked local knowledge of the multiple business communities around North America. Combining our strength of product support and application knowledge with a local channel partner who not only had an established business relationship but understood the construction customer needs became the basis for GHI's aggressive marketing and channel development.

During the late 1990s, the construction industry embraced rental equipment as a strategy to minimize capital investment. Contractors often rented equipment that had a "limited need" or an "unexpected need." As an unknown and seasonal product, Ground Heaters became the perfect rental equipment. GHI, therefore, focused its channel development to some of the largest, most successful rental companies and equipment distributors in North America. These include:

1. Consolidators—National Rental Accounts, such as United Rentals, Rental Service Corporation, Hertz Equipment Rental.

2. Integrated dealers—Dealers affiliated with large construction equipment, such as Cat Rental Stores and Volvo Rents.
3. Other dealers—Mainly independent dealers who have local or regional areas of service, specializing in niche products, such as concrete equipment or heat equipment.
4. Independent rental—Local, regional independent dealers that focus on construction rental equipment and generate most of their revenue from those rental activities.
5. Hardware dealers—National small equipment and supply stores, such as True Value.

I particularly enjoyed demonstrating huge savings to construction contractors and higher than normal ROI to distribution partners and enabling Ground Heaters products to grow at a 30 percent annual rate over a seven-year period. A major component of that growth was a "pull strategy" to develop demand within the immature construction heating market. We established a field sales force structure that included metro job site specialists focused on end users, district managers focused on channel development, and regional product specialists creating application awareness.

A key to our success has been treating everyone in the channel as a customer and providing creative solutions fitting their respective businesses, helping them succeed.

Ed Jaroszewicz, VP Sales, Ground Heaters, Inc.

Unlike traditional legitimate power, legal legitimate power is often obtained in a trade for some other resource. Holiday Inn franchisees agree to change the sheets and clean rooms according to franchisor-established standards because it pays to be a Holiday Inn. They would never agree to follow the 200-page book of standards for the Tanner and Dwyer Lodge. They want the green and orange sign in front and they need the national reservation system. Simply put, the Holiday Inn franchisees trade some of their freedom—meaning they grant the franchisor legitimate authority over some matters—in order to gain anticipated rewards.

*Final Words on Power*

Channel systems are often composed of multiple organizations holding different stakes in the success of the system. Without leadership, the organizations may work at cross-purposes and operate in a manner devoid of customer focus and efficiency. Channel leadership is the judicious use of power to coordinate channel member behaviors. A member's power stems from another's dependence on the member for scarce resources. We have described and weighed the merits of using different power resources: rewards and punishments, information, expertise, identification, and legitimacy. These resources can be applied to effect specific behaviors by channel partners. Power can also be used to effect more permanent properties of the channel relationship such as contractual provisions and even ownership.

# RELATIONSHIP FORMS IN CHANNELS

This section elaborates on the idea that channel members can apply their power not only to specific behaviors, but to the establishment of enduring *structures* for exchange. As a result, channel members interact to coordinate their work in four classes of exchange systems or vertical marketing systems. Here we rely on some of the notions from Chapter 2 to detail alternative contractual and ownership structures of marketing channels. We discuss four classes of channel systems: transactional, administered, contractual, and corporate.

## Transactional Channels

In transactional channels the members trade at arm's length. Each firm operates on its own, with no significant coordination with its channel partners. An insurance company planning its company picnic may buy 500 #10 duro bags from a cash-and-carry wholesaler. A church group staging a community Thanksgiving dinner might buy 300 pounds of potatoes from the riverside produce market. As you can see, finding channels that exemplify no relationship characteristics is quite difficult. This form is rare. We use the description largely as an endpoint in the classification scheme.

## Administered Channels

Members of **administered channels** recognize their participation in a larger system, but they interact without a formal chain of command or a set of rules. Coordination results from an ad hoc division of labor and informal leadership. The leader has no legal legitimate base of power, but mobilizes social and economic resources to coordinate behaviors for competitiveness. The use of promotional allowances and discounts to load resellers or blitz a market area is quite common but doesn't represent the systematic approach to lead or administer the entire channel. In contrast, Cardinal Health administers hospital supplies channels by analyzing hospital needs, trimming the variety of items ordered, and planning just-in-time deliveries. With its now spun-off Sabre system, American Airlines was first to provide a computer reservation system to agents. Many credit this program for American's leadership in U.S. air travel. Sealed Air coordinates its distributor efforts in stocking and selling various packaging materials using programmed sales aids and stocking guidelines.

## Contractual Channels

**Contractual channels** are tightly coordinated by formal procedures and pledges of ongoing exchange. Nonrefundable fees and 5- to 10-year agreements are common devices to ensure longevity. We mentioned the Holiday Inn franchise system earlier in the chapter. Other franchising operations in business markets include ServiceMaster in the field of building maintenance and custodial services, Insty-prints in printing services, Manpower in employment services, and Avis in rental cars.

More narrow in scope than these franchisor–franchisee systems are *authorized* wholesalers and dealers. Under these systems, resellers are allowed to promote that they are authorized by the manufacturer to carry a particular line. In return, the resellers agree to meet specified service standards.[17] An authorized Apple dealer must stock a range of Apple products and software, attend training programs, use promotional material from Apple, and provide information about market conditions.

# Corporate Channels

It is difficult to imagine total integration of all channel functions: delivery, selling, promoting, customer feedback, inventory, ordering, service, and so on. In **corporate channels,** what we tend to see are high degrees of vertical integration in the sales and distribution functions. A firm that uses its own sales force, its own fleet of trucks, from its own distribution centers is highly integrated, even though it may use UPS for next-day shipping of orders taken at night at the telephone service bureau it uses in off-hours.

Ownership provides a significant measure of control over channel functions because one's own employees are generally more inclined to take direction than are associates of an independent organization. It can safeguard investments that have no use outside of the relationship. For example, if we spend heavily to develop a brand image, but buyers of the product rely on personal sales reps for information about the product, we will want to be sure we can control the selling process. Corporate ownership provides a number of coordination advantages that arise from employees working in close proximity, using common communication standards, and following explicit procedures.[18]

Of course "owning" a channel function does not guarantee that you can perform it well or economically because of scale. Intermediaries specialize in certain functions. Therefore, intermediaries can often perform activities cheaper and better than a vertically integrated firm.

Thus, to close the chapter on a note similar to its launch, if we are a manufacturing firm unhappy with the support we are getting from our distributors, we must look very carefully at the costs and likely effectiveness of performing distributor functions ourselves. Based on the dispersal of accounts and the selling tasks, how many calls per day can our own reps make? How many calls per year are demanded by the market? How many reps will it take? Can we deliver products by UPS from a central inventory? Does the "recaptured" distributor margin allow us to internalize? Do we have the investment capital and do we really want to be in this business?

Exhibit 9–8 details this type of analysis for a manufacturer currently using distributors. With distributor margins averaging 35 percent, we know that the factory sales of $26 million must be 65 percent of distributor sales. Thus, total distributor sales volume is about $40 million, and margin is about $14 million. Looking at the estimated costs of performing the distributor functions—selling, sales management, inventory, and accounts receivable—we sort start-up from annual costs. Then we can evaluate the magnitude of savings, if any, against the investment needed.

Of course, the analysis is just as informative for the evaluation of a corporate sales and distribution system. Like Sun Microsystems in From the Field 9–2, the make–buy analysis can point the way to disintegration and a focus on a narrower set of competencies as well.

## Exhibit 9–8
### Analysis for Integrating the Distributor Functions

*The Setting:* A manufacturer doing factory sales of $26 million sells exclusively through distributors who earn an average margin of 35 percent, unless they discount radically from manufacturer's list price. Distributors call on 5,000 customers an average of six times per year and finance receivables for 30 days. Inventories turn about four times per year and overall are four times the current factory inventories of about $1 million. Customers pay no explicit delivery charges now, but the manufacturer's accounting people estimate that UPS and other delivery modes can be achieved from central stores at about 10 percent of prices to users.

#### Estimating Revenues

The manufacturer selling direct—all other things equal—stands to realize total distributor revenue. Thus, its current sales of $26 million represent just 65 percent of distributor revenue. The distributors' 35 percent margin is missing here. Thus total sales to end users are $26 million/.65 = $40 million, and incremental gross margin for the manufacturer is the $40 − $26 = $14 million currently earned by distributors.

Can the manufacturer perform the channel functions for less than what it "pays" distributors, $14 million?

#### Converting Functions to Costs

There may be a host of incidental costs and benefits from internalizing the wholesaling functions, but now that we've shown that the manufacturer "pays" the distributor about $14 million in margin, let's focus on the costs of performing these marketing functions. We'll estimate two types of costs: (1) those one-time costs associated with start-up, and (2) the annual expenses apt to recur, all else being equal.

Selling costs:  5,000 customers × 6 calls/yr. = 30,000 calls per year. A company salesperson working 250 days per year, making four calls per day can make 1,000 calls per year. → Thirty salespeople are needed in the field. Add four sales managers. Plan (est.) to pay $58,000 per year plus another 50 percent for expenses each. Managers will cost $100,000 plus 100 percent in office and clerical. Total selling cost: $3.41 million. Cash needed for payroll and expenses → (say) $.5 million

Inventory:  Inventory investment increases from $1 million to $4 million = $3 million

Estimate inventory carrying costs (Interest, spoilage, etc.) @ 20 percent = $.6 million

Financing sales:  Estimate 1/12 of sales at 10 percent. With manufacturer selling to end users, sales—all things equal—are $40 million at distributor prices. Thus, the balance sheet will require $40/12 = $3.33 million in accounts receivable. There is an interest or opportunity cost of carrying these receivables of $3.33 × .1 = $.333 million.

| Start-up costs: | | Annual expenses | |
|---|---|---|---|
| Cash for selling expenses | $.50 million | Selling | $3.41 million |
| Inventory | 3.00 | Inventory | .60 |
| Receivables | 3.33 | Receivables | .33 |
| Total investment needed | $6.83 million | Total yearly costs | $4.34 million |

| | |
|---|---|
| Compare current distributor margin | $14.00 million |
| To new expenses | $4.34 million |
| Savings | $9.66 million/yr. ⟶ |

on an investment of $6.8 million, this is a very nice return. It would be so even if distributor discounts cut their margin in half!

# Summary

Marketing channels are multifirm systems at work in the flow of products from producer to user. Their purpose is to deliver needed services, spatial convenience, and time utility to customers. They represent a highly strategic decision arena in that they are expensive to establish, costly to coordinate, and difficult to adapt to new environments.

Practically no firm can perform all the complex functions of sorting, assorting, transacting, risking, delivering, promoting, and servicing involved in providing sought channel outputs. Firms specialize in these functions and realize profits by performing them better and more efficiently than manufacturers, buyers, or others in the channel.

Many different kinds of intermediaries operate in business markets. We make a major distinction between merchants—who take ownership of products—and agents—who do not. Ownership brings substantial investment and risk. Other subclasses of intermediaries can be distinguished on the basis of their performance of several channel functions.

The emphasis on channel functions and institutional structure should not lead us to neglect their social and political dimensions. Because channel members have different goals, different preferences for routines, and different views of the world, but still must depend on each other, the potential for conflict is ever present. Conflict can tear a system apart or prompt members to reassess motives, innovate, buttress, and survive.

The major responses to conflict by individual channel members include exit, voice, loyalty, aggression, and neglect. At the industry, trade group, and relationship levels, conflict resolution mechanisms can be established to improve system competitiveness and to resolve disputes fairly and efficiently, but avoiding the uncertainty, acrimony, and glacial pace of court action.

The interdependence of channel members means that power is a character of their relationships. Power can be used to exploit or coordinate. We defined and illustrated how six bases of power can be used to coordinate channel behaviors, or structure the exchange for the potential to coordinate behaviors.

Finally, the chapter reviewed four basic structures by which channel members exchange. In rare cases, exchange is characterized by arm's-length, transactional dealings. Even between independent organizations there is a measure of informal administration and coordination. Contractual arrangements provide for legitimate power to coordinate channel activities and are exemplified in licensing and franchising relationships.

Corporate systems benefit from employee commitment, communication efficiency, and tighter administrative control, but require significant financial resources, technical know-how, and motivational mechanisms. We provided a framework for examining the economics of making or buying channel functions.

## Key Terms

| | | |
|---|---|---|
| administered channels | exit | merchant wholesaler |
| agent | expert power | neglect |
| aggression | full-function wholesaler | power |
| broker | gap analysis | principal |
| cash-and-carry distributor | industrial distributor | referent power |
| catalog wholesaler | information power | reward power |
| channel intermediary | legal legitimate power | single-line wholesaler |
| coercive power | limited-function wholesaler | specialty wholesaler |
| conflict | loyalty | traditional legitimate power |
| contractual channels | manufacturer's agent | truck jobber |
| corporate channels | manufacturer's sales branch or office | voice |
| desk jobber | marketing channel | |
| drop shipper | | |

# Discussion Questions

1. Against the reputation and operational efficiency of Dell, how has CDW Computer Centers continued to thrive? As a reseller in the technology field in a flat economy, it has enjoyed back-to-back sales records, surpassing $6.8 billion in 2006. What are the channel services it provides to its target segments in superior fashion? Visit **www.cdw.com.**

2. Most steel is ordered and shipped directly from the steel mill. Still, a significant percentage of steel is sold through steel service centers, wholesalers that carry a wide assortment of specialty steels, bars, I-beams, wire, sheet steel, and so on. Identify the likely channel service outputs sought by two or three of the following businesses: small steel fabricators, rail car manufacturing, commercial construction, tool manufacturing, saw blade manufacturers, and environmental engineering. What channel structure do you expect for each?

3. With the great diversity of market segments, many manufacturers actually use multiple channels: direct sales, distributors, dealer networks, catalogs, and perhaps some private brands for other manufacturers or resellers. What is the potential for conflict in such a system? Can it be managed in the way territories are configured or margins structured?

4. The World Wide Web has enabled electronic markets. The new marketplace has been especially important for recyclable materials. Surf the cyberwaves for brokers or cooperative exchanges (such as the Chicago Board of Trade at **http://cbot-recycle.com**) in the area of wood by-product, crumb rubber, plastics, or scrap metal. Prepare a short summary of the operation.

5. Many OEMs have enlisted distributor participation in their supply chain initiatives. Often the talk about collaboration and stripping out waste is heady and bold. When it's all said and done, many distributors complain that buyers did little to shave costs on the supply side and used SCM to squeeze better prices on the buy side. As a manager for a large industrial distributor, what would you do to make sure the promise of collaboration is fulfilled with your large OEM customers?

6. Electronics distributors are now charging customers on a fee-for-service basis for information they often can use in product design. For example, they can tell design engineers what products and components have been "end-of-lifed" and, therefore, won't be available after X months of production. What other opportunities exist in today's B2B channels for distributors to secure fee-for-service opportunities?

7. In 2006 Ground Heaters was acquired by one of North America's largest light construction equipment manufacturers, largely for the distribution channels it had developed. But drills, saws, and jackhammers have been around a long time and don't need the same market development effort as GHI; the equipment brand carries a lot of clout in the marketplace. What channel management challenges do you anticipate from this company's product mix?

8. Sharp's LCD projectors have been among the industry leaders for almost 15 years now. With almost all manufacturers selling through indirect channels, Sharp knows it must work hard to support its efforts. Of course, product training, market development allowances, communication and reporting tools, and tech tips are important. Another key assistance is lead generation. How would you generate leads for Sharp projectors and convey the leads to dealers promptly?

9. Chapter 6 related Dell's decision in May 2007 to sell computer products through Wal-Mart. In what way might synergies with the direct channel result from this move? What channel management challenges does it bring?

**10.** What type of channel relationship structure will enable the most and richest communication between members? Why?

# Cases

## Case 9.1   Steel Service Center

Years ago, metals were distributed mostly by small companies. They typically processed and shipped small quantities to small metalworking shops. Today metal service centers play a key role in the supply chain. They stamp, cut, and otherwise transform plate steel, coiled metals, bars, and other semifinished metal products into other forms that metalworking companies can use in further processing or assembly.

These days, few so-called metal distributors simply warehouse metal. As manufacturers continue to curtail in-house production and administrative functions, the service centers are evolving from simple distributors to complex providers of processing and information technologies. In many ways, this evolution reflects the trend toward outsourcing: As producers concentrate on making metal, and steel customers concentrate on making their own products, each side is willing to outsource more tasks to the metal service providers.

As we note the changing service standards in the field—metals with greater strength, more complex shapes, and other attributes; JIT deliveries; and materials management services—it's important for manufacturers, top service centers (such as Reyerson Tull, Thyssen, and Russel Metal), and customers in construction, automotive, machinery, and other fields to anticipate the needs for the future.[19]

Based on globalization trends, technological advances, and economic policy, what are some of the key avenues for growth we might see in metal distribution in the next five years?

## Case 9.2   RFID: ru g2g?

Compliance. That's what Wal-Mart and the Department of Defense are looking for from suppliers they have mandated to tag products with tiny radio transponders. Based on a technology called RFID—radio frequency identification—small chips or tags store a unique product identifier. Unlike barcodes, the RFID tag can be read from great distances and without line-of-sight readers. RFID receivers interface with software that sifts data for relevance and routes it to the appropriate enterprise applications systems—logistics, product management, maintenance, and so on.

Thus, a manufacturer of aeronautical parts will tag the parts or box of goods with a tiny chip and antenna which sends a signal to a reader, which displays the Electronic Product Code and other information such as date and origin of manufacture. These data are used by other Department of Defense contractors, accounting, and inventory managers for planning and decision making.

International Paper Company, the $25 billion forest products company headquartered in Stamford, Connecticut, has developed one of the first RFID systems at its Texarkana mill and warehouse. Forklift-mounted RFID receivers and related technology allow International Paper to track inventory to within 6 inches. Other companies have since come to review the IP experience in Texarkana to apply in their own distribution center or factory.

Indeed, RFID has drawn keen interest and pilot projects in the automobile industry and other retailers. Experts point out that the technology is still in development and many shortcomings limit wide-scale applications, but the next decade should be interesting. Imagine a channels environment where resellers cannot mask their inventory levels, or might be able to trim them to bare bones levels, knowing that replenishment is 30 miles away in a truck.

What are some other benefits promised by RFID? What about risks, too?

To learn more about RFID, visit AMR Research for cases and reports. Search RFID at http://www.amrresearch.com/. Also visit the worldwide EPC standards organization, EPCglobal at http://www.epcglobalinc.org/. Opposition to RFID is summarized well on a Web page for C.A.S.P.I.A.N. (Consumers Against Supermarket Privacy Invasion and Numbering) at http://www.nocards.com/AutoID/overview.shtml.

# Additional Readings

Abrahamsson, Mats, and Staffan Brege. "Dynamic Effectiveness: Improved Industrial Distribution from Interaction between Marketing and Logistics Strategies." *Journal of Marketing Channels* 12, no. 2 (2004), pp. 83–112.

Achieving Supply Chain Excellence through Technology, www.ascet.com.

Anderson, Erin, George Day, and V. Kasturi Rangan. "Strategic Channel Design." *Sloan Management Review* 38 (Summer 1997), pp. 59–69.

Canning, Louise. "Rethinking Market Connections: Mobile Phone Recovery, Reuse, and Recycling in the UK." *Journal of Business & Industrial Marketing* 21, no. 5 (2006), pp. 320–29.

Eyuboglu, Nermin, and Sertan Kabadayi. "Dealer-Manufacturer Alienation in a Multiple Channel System: The Moderating Effect of Structural Variables." *Journal of Marketing Channels* 12, no. 3 (2005), pp. 5–26.

Gundlach, Gregory T., Yemisi A. Bolumole, Reham A Eltantawy, and Robert Frankel. "The Changing Landscape of Supply Chain Management, Marketing Channels of Distribution, Logistics and Purchasing." *Journal of Business & Industrial Marketing* 21, no 7 (2006), pp. 428–38.

Jap, Sandy. "An Exploratory Study of the Introduction of Online Reverse Auctions." *Journal of Marketing* 67 (July 2003), pp. 96–107.

Marchetti, Maichele. "When Channel Conflict Is Good." *Sales and Marketing Management* (April 2000), p. 13.

McMurray, Scott. "Return of the Middleman." *Business 2.0* 4 (March 2003), pp. 53–54.

Mentzer, John T., and Mark A. Moon. "Understanding Demand." *Supply Chain Management Review* 8 (May/June 2004), pp. 38–45.

Miller-Holodnicki, Madeleine, and John A. Caltagirone. "RFID—Supply Chain Savior . . . or Totalitarian Tracking Tool?" *CLM Logistics Comment* 38 (March–April 2004), pp. 1+.

Rangan, V. Kasturi, Melvyn A. J. Menezes, and E. P. Meyer. "Channel Selection for New Industrial Products: A Framework, Method and Application." *Journal of Marketing* 56 (July 1992), pp. 68–81.

*RFID Journal,* http://www.rfidjournal.com/.

Rutner, Stephen, Matthew A. Waller, and John T. Mentzer. "A Practical Look at RFID." *Supply Chain Management Review* 8 (January/February 2004), pp. 36–41.

Sabath, Robert E., and John Fontanella. "The Unfulfilled Promise of Supply Chain Collaboration." *Supply Chain Management Review* 6 (July/August 2002), pp. 24–29.

Srivastava, Joydeep, Dipankar Chakravarti, and Amnon Rapoport. "Price and Margin Negotiation in Marketing Channels: An Experimental Study of Sequential Bargaining under One-Sided Uncertainty and Opportunity Cost of Delay." *Marketing Science* 19 (Spring 2000), pp. 163–84.

Stern, Louis, Adel El-Ansary, and Anne Caughlin. *Marketing Channels.* Upper Saddle River, NJ: Prentice Hall, 2006.

Wathne, Kenneth H., and Jan B. Heide. "Relationship Governance in a Supply Chain Network." *Journal of Marketing* 68 (January 2004), pp. 73–89.

# Chapter 10

## Creating Customer Dialogue

### CHARRETTE.COM

Charrette Corp., Woburn, Massachusetts, is a 40-year-old company that makes and sells design products to engineers, architects, and Web designers. Like many B2B companies, Charrette built a Web site and hoped that buyers would find it. In the first 18 months of the Web site, the company increased regular customers in its database by some 67 percent.●

But just having a Web site was not enough. The company realized that there was power in the information it held on its 100,000 regular accounts. To unleash that power, the company began using its database to create groups of similar customers. To be sure, the company had always known that architects need some different products than do Web designers. With additional knowledge about customers, though, the company was able to divide architects into smaller groups. By understanding their customers a little more clearly, the company was able to create communications that reach customers more effectively.●

One such campaign was the Brooklyn Bridge campaign. A campaign that featured the Brooklyn Bridge and its designer, John Augustus Roebling, the company combined direct mail, e-mail, and print advertising, along with a drawing for specialty advertising products. The call to action was to visit the Web site, and some customers got only direct mail, some e-mail, and some a combination. While at the Web site, customers can order products, check on shipments, view their account balance, and monitor other information.●

Charrette's Brooklyn Bridge campaign has proven very successful, so successful that the company plans to continue the theme in future communications. As the company has learned, effective customer communications begin with understanding the customer. ●

Visit **www.charrette.com.** ●

## LEARNING OBJECTIVES

To many people, marketing is all about communications. Certainly, communication by marketers is the most obvious activity. What may not be as obvious is that marketing communications has evolved into much more than simply broadcasting persuasive messages. Marketing communications is now a dialogue that is actively managed, a part of customer relationship management. In this chapter, we integrate the discussion on relationships with communications, setting the framework for a closer examination of such activities as advertising, trade shows, and e-mail in later chapters.

*After reading this chapter, you should be able to*

- Understand the process of customer relationship management.
- Relate various marketing activities to that process.
- Understand how strategy varies depending on the application of buying theory.

Thoreau once remarked, "Build a better mousetrap and the world will beat a path to your door." If that were true, marketing communications would not be necessary. Managing customer relationships through intentional dialogue is an essential business process.

Creating a dialogue with customers is an important part of building an effective relationship. Consider the importance of good communication in relationships you share with your friends, roommate, and family members. With customers, the importance of good communication is no different—it has to be two-way communication.

In this chapter, we focus on that portion of business marketing that involves dialogue with the customer through marketing communications. Customer relationship management, or CRM, though, is more than just talking; it is interacting. It involves how the customer chooses to interact and buy from the organization, and it involves listening to and learning from the customer.

As you saw in Chapter 8, listening to customers and involving them in the design and development of products is one important way to increase value. Our emphasis in this chapter is on creating value in the communication process itself. In later chapters in this section, we'll discuss specific channels of communication, but in this chapter we'll focus on the more strategic issues. First, we'll discuss the **customer relationship management (CRM)** process because it provides us the strategic framework for understanding how to create customer dialogue.

# THE CUSTOMER RELATIONSHIP MANAGEMENT PROCESS

The CRM process involves four steps, as illustrated in Exhibit 10–1. These steps are to segment and profile the market, design communication strategy, implement, and evaluate.

The first is to segment and profile the market. We create segments by grouping similar customers together, and segments are created by marketers for many different reasons. For example, when we employ QFD as discussed in Chapter 8, we create a segment in the market. Then we design a product to meet that segment's needs. But even in that segment, there are subsegments, buyers who respond and want to interact with us in different ways. Some want to order over the Web whereas others have a high need for the added value of a salesperson. So when a company segments for CRM purposes, the segmentation is based on how the customer wants to interact, rather than on what needs the product should meet.

For example, Charrette segmented based on whether customers like direct mail or e-mail. How did Charrette know what customers like? By tracking their response to earlier communications and by asking. Charrette maintains a database of over 100,000 customers that includes information like what they have responded to in the past.

In Chapter 5, we also discussed segmentation using the decile strategy and determining customer value. Such segmentation strategies often form the basis of the customer relationship management process, too.

In the second step, a communication strategy is designed. Typically, the strategy involves multiple channels of communication, channels such as direct mail, e-mail, print advertising, trade shows, and even field sales efforts. Recall that the Charrette campaign involved several different channels of communication. We'll discuss these in greater detail in this chapter. Strategy also involves what offers are made. For example, Charrette could offer different percentage discounts based on the customer's value segment and previous purchasing preferences.

The third step is to implement the strategy. In the Charrette example, a campaign was used. A campaign has a definite start and stop date. The mailers are sent out, the advertising runs, and so forth. Strategy, though, is broader than just one campaign. A CRM strategy would also include providing customer service personnel with

**Exhibit 10–1**
Customer
Relationship
Management
Process

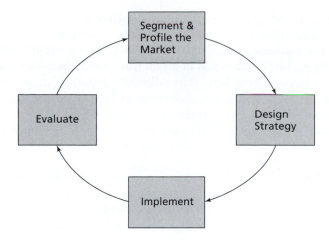

segment information on each customer, along with the appropriate level of service for that customer. If a customer called with a complaint, for example, the customer service rep would know if this was a gold or platinum customer and would respond accordingly.

Evaluation in CRM is continuous. Yes, certain campaigns may have discrete endings, and a formal report giving a wrap-up assessment is in order. But today's CRM systems afford dashboard reports on key metrics—orders, sales, returns, inquiries, Web site visits. Managers also get on-demand or periodic customer reports, highlighting positive departures from forecast and flashing alerts to complaints or waning purchases at key accounts.

In the next section, we will focus on the communication element in the CRM process. The integrated marketing communication strategy is an important part of the overall CRM process.

# INTEGRATED MARKETING COMMUNICATION STRATEGY

Developing an integrated communications strategy is really a part of the strategic planning process discussed in Chapter 6. Here we are focusing on a portion of the overall strategy: How will we communicate with our (prospective) customers? This communication should be two way, so we should also ask, "How does our customer want to communicate with us?" Rather than being a strategy that we launch and then sit back, watch, and hope it works, communication strategy involves making adjustments as we go. As measures are taken and feedback is received, changes are made, communication improved, and relationships strengthened.

## Integrated Marketing Communications

**Integrated marketing communications (IMC)** is strategic, two-way communication targeted to specific customers and their needs, all coordinated through a variety of media.[1] Business marketers are more likely to capitalize on the power of integrated marketing communications than consumer marketers.[2] Coordination is a powerful element of an integrated communications strategy. Still, many companies find integration difficult due to turf battles and a reluctance to invest in the needed databases.[3] Indeed, the marketing planning at one agency was thwarted by the client's CEO who wanted to see his company's ad in his morning newspaper—no matter the media preferences in emerging markets. When different departments are responsible for different elements in the communications strategy (say, an advertising department, a direct response or direct mail department, and a trade show and events department), each is reluctant to give up control over its respective area and will fight each other for a piece of the marketing budget. A result is that the communication strategy is fragmented, rather than integrated.

What happens when interaction with the customer is fragmented? The customer gets annoyed because different parts of the company don't know what the others are saying. Customers feel like they are talking to many different companies instead of one, which is not the way to build a relationship. Let's look now at each element of the definition of integrated marketing communication.

## Integrated Marketing Communication Meets Customer Needs

With laserlike precision, integrated marketing communication aims to *meet the information needs* of the buyer, result in the desired position, and secure the appropriate action at the right time. In any target market, the business marketer faces buyers and potential buyers across a spectrum of "readiness." Some are unaware that a commercial solution to their problem exists. Some are aware of some options, but not the marketer's brand. Some have become aware of the marketer's products, but are having difficulty evaluating them. And the business marketer has current customers, too: some are in a fragile association with the marketer, others are doing reliable repeat business, and a few of those are even recommending the marketer to others. Obviously, not every member of the target market has the same information needs, and their needs are changing in response to the business environment and the marketer's portfolio of communications. Furthermore, a single communication mix element—advertising, personal selling, trade shows, etc.—may be incapable of delivering the variety of messages needed across this spectrum and the buying cycle.

Thus, through thematic unity and coordinated execution—with the aim of retaining and maximizing the value of acquired customers—it is imperative to integrate marketing communications. If IMC does not provide value to the buyer, then the buyer will not participate in the dialogue. IMC seeks the answer to the question "What does the buyer want or need to know in order to make the next decision?" That decision may be to visit the booth at a trade show or to place an order or to elevate the vendor to preferred account status. In any event, if IMC does not meet the information needs of the buyer, there is no reason for that buyer to interact with the marketing communication.

## Integrated Marketing Communication Is Strategic

Integrated marketing communication is *strategic* in that the content and delivery of all messages are the result of an overall plan. The result is that messages across all communication channels work together to create the appropriate position and result in the right action. Delivery of messages is synchronized so that synergy can be reached. For example, remember how Charrette timed magazine ads to support the e-mail and direct mail campaigns?

**Exhibit 10–2**
IMC Strategic
Planning
Process

1.  Set communication goals.
    Who is the audience?
    What do you want them to do with the information?
2.  Determine roles for each communication element.
3.  Create messages.
4.  Place messages in appropriate media.
5.  Measure results.
6.  Make adjustments in messages and/or media.

## Integrated Marketing Communication Is Two Way

IMC is a two-way dialogue. Without feedback, marketers may never really know if anyone is listening. Feedback is shared within the organization for learning purposes, so that the strategy can be adapted to fit customer needs and provide value. Although a single point of communication may be one way (for example, an advertisement in a magazine), the point here is that any communication such as an advertisement should be part of and reflect a dialogue with customers. Charrette chose a Web site interaction format, but could also have used a call center.

# The IMC Planning Process

The integrated marketing communications planning process, illustrated in Exhibit 10–2, begins with setting goals, creating the overall message, and then determining how the various communication mix elements will be used. The next step is selecting specific media or channels of communication, creating the specific messages for those channels, and implementing them. Based on results, media and messages are altered and adapted in order to achieve the strategic goals. In this chapter, we will focus on the first three steps, as the other steps will vary greatly from advertising to personal selling to other elements. Those issues—placement, measurement, and adjustment—will be handled in greater detail in Chapters 11 through 13, where we will also discuss message creation in greater detail.

# Setting Goals

First of all, we should set communication goals based on the strategic marketing goals. For example, assume we are going to introduce a new product through selective distribution among leading pump and valve distributors, and we set a year 2 goal of 20 percent market share for this product. Our communication goals would be derived from the market share and channel penetration goals. These are just two marketing goals that would influence communication goals. Total sales goals, account penetration goals, and others should influence the selection of communication goals.

Marketing goals help communications planners determine the audience for marketing communications. Therefore, the goal-setting process for communications planning includes determining the audience and deciding what the marketer wants the audience to get out of the communication.

**Exhibit 10–3**
Hierarchy of
Effects

## Who Is the Audience?

Our target audience depends a great deal on how the market has been defined, as well as how the buying center operates. Assume for the moment that your company sells plastic components made to custom specifications. The market is any manufacturer that uses plastic components. From Chapter 4, though, we know that members of several different functional areas may be involved in the purchase of component parts. Engineering, purchasing, manufacturing, and upper management may all play a role in the purchase. We really have four audiences, not one.

Further, marketing objectives may involve multiple market segments. For example, the plastics components manufacturer may sell plastic components to computer manufacturers, stereo and consumer electronics manufacturers, and aircraft manufacturers. Each of these market segments represents a different audience.

## What Should the Communication Say and Do?

When the marketer asks the question "What should the communication say and do?" the answer lies in what the audience is intended to do with the information. When education and persuasion are involved, the hierarchy-of-effects model can be quite helpful.

## Hierarchy of Effects

The **hierarchy-of-effects model** is used by many companies when planning communication campaigns because it describes the mental stages through which the target must progress prior to reasoned action. These stages are Awareness, Interest, Desire, and Action (AIDA), as illustrated in Exhibit 10–3; the pyramid shape is chosen in order to reflect the reality that not everyone who is aware becomes interested, nor does every interested person desire the product and then take action.

**Awareness** is created when potential buyers become acquainted with the product or brand. **Interest** is the next step and reflects the buyer's desire to learn more about what (e.g., product, brand, company) is being discussed. **Desire** is the recognition by the buyer that when the needs occur, that is the brand or product to buy (or the company to visit at the trade show, or the home page to visit, etc.). **Action** is the desired behavior that we want from the audience.

Hierarchy-of-effects models such as AIDA help B2B marketers recognize and classify the different goals to pursue. Two dichotomies should be evident. First, we can distinguish *strategic* from *tactical* goals. On another plane, we can distinguish goals aimed at changing minds (e.g., corporate images or beliefs about the specific product) from goals seeking action (e.g., repeat purchase, or a call to set an appointment). We call the poles in this second dichotomy *positioning* and *action* goals. Exhibit 10–4 illustrates and previews the brief discussion of each type of goal on the next page.

**Exhibit 10–4**
Goal Grid

|  | Positioning | Action |
|---|---|---|
| Strategic | Intel takes you where you want to go with your computing | Market share<br>Total sales<br>New account sales |
| Tactical | Remember Intel theme after leaving trade show | Number of visitors to booth who attend video presentation |

One of Dow Corning's award-winning ads, designed to launch the new division and its brand name, Xiameter.

### Building the Brand and Other Strategic Goals

**Strategic goals** are what you want the overall strategy (in this case, the communications strategy) to accomplish. For example, a communication strategy to launch a new product will involve press releases, interviews, sales force training and incentives, advertising, and more, over several months. Strategic goals would be set to drive the planning of messages and media selection.

We are hard pressed to conceive of a more important strategic goal than building the brand. Sure, buyers in business markets strive for cool-headed, objective purchasing—only price and performance matter. Furthermore, the complexity of many systems and services tax the utility of a clever tag line; intimacy derives from face-to-face interactions. And for some markets that are comprised of just a handful of customers, why bother?

But think of some of the B2B brands we have mentioned in this book—Caterpillar, IBM, UPS, SAP and DuPont. Each conveys a bundle of images and assurances to a harried decision maker. Caterpillar's reputation for service may not win the purchase contract, but it certainly brings its offerings into the buying center's set of options to consider. IBM's professionalism, process expertise, and leadership likewise earn a seat at the table when a potential client seeks to outsource high-volume transaction processing.

In business markets, brands tend to be built upon experience and long-run consistency, more than clever advertising and a single campaign. Thus, every customer contact is a brand-building enterprise. An unkempt sales representative or disorganization at the trade show can undo a slick, compelling ad in a flight magazine. Getting your promotional calendar into the buyer's conference room is not the end of branding. It's about getting what your company stands for—qualities such as reliability, value, trust, collaborative, thorough, innovative, finisher, and connected—into the minds of participants in the buying center, and other relevant publics. Thus, no communication program—or other market behavior—should bring harm to the brand. Indeed, the brand not only serves as an information processing heuristic for buyers; it can serve as a safeguard in the exchange, the seller's pledge to be honored.

With this orientation, every communication program should be seen as a brand-building opportunity, reinforcing what the brand is to be known for or judiciously extending the brand promise. Akin to the process of product positioning, to be discussed below, brand building is the process of creating that personality or set of association for the brand. From the Field 10–1 describes how Dow Corning created and launched a new global brand.

### Tactical Goals

As mentioned earlier, **tactical goals** are desired outcomes for specific communications. For example, tactical goals include the sought number of qualified leads who respond to an ad in a magazine, or the number of prospects generated at a trade show. As you may recall from the previous chapter, leads are potential buyers; the more a lead is *qualified,* the higher the probability of purchasing, but in general, less is known about leads than about prospects. A **prospect** is someone for whom we know needs, budget, and time frame for purchase. Tactical goals may include both lead generation and prospect generation or other goals. Note that these goals require a dialogue, or two-way communication, for without a dialogue, we would not know if the person was a prospect.

### Positioning

As discussed in Chapter 6, a product's **position,** or place in the mind of the buyer, is determined by the buyer's evaluation of the product along every dimension relative to all other offerings. Then, depending on the application and other situational issues, the buyer selects a product.

**10–1**

# FROM THE FIELD
## Creating a Global B2B Brand

Most students have probably heard of Dow Corning, or at least they think they have. Dow Corning is actually a company jointly owned by Dow Chemical and Corning Glass, both of which make consumer products. Dow Corning, on the other hand, makes no consumer products. Instead, this company was formed over 60 years ago to exploit the potential of silicones.

As the market for silicone technology matured, many customers did not perceive any value in Dow Corning's premium-priced services and products. In order to take advantage of a lower-cost segment without detracting from the value of the Dow Corning brand, the company created a no-frills division to offer lower-cost, lower-service commodities. This new division, however, needed a brand of its own.

Once the needs of this lower-cost segment were understood, the company began developing a list of brand values, including a central idea or theme that would unite all brand actions and expressions. This theme, the attendant values, and the positioning strategy were the basis for a visual and verbal identity that was then executed across all communication channels. Of key importance was to differentiate the brand from Dow Corning so that the new brand would

be "more than silicones but a new business model," rather than, say, Dow Corning Lite or Dow Corning Cheap. At the same time, Dow Corning planned to give the new brand instant credibility by endorsing it.

After creating a list of possible names, the company had to make sure the new name would work anywhere in the world. Native speakers in key markets conducted a check to make sure the names created the right impression. Lack of Web site availability eliminated 30 names, while legal screenings eliminated over 110 names.

The winner was Xiameter. Follow-up measures indicate that the brand is creating the reputation that was desired. In addition, the endorsement by Dow Corning is giving the brand credibility without compromising existing Dow Corning offerings. Dow Corning has even won several awards for its advertising and promotion campaigns involving Xiameter. While the process was a complex task, it appears that Xiameter was a resounding success.

Randall Rozin and Liz Magnusson, Processes and Methodologies for Creating a Global Business-to-Business Brand, *Journal of Brand Management* 10 (February 2003), pp.185–208; "Xiameter Advertisements Wins Design Award," *Advertising* (May 10, 2004), p. 1.

A key goal for our communication strategy is the position we desire to achieve. A position is not just a communication goal, however; we must also design a product that has the attributes we say it has, offer it at the appropriate price, and so forth. If we want to communicate that our processor is faster, we must first build a faster processor. There would never be any repeat business if we created a position for which we could not deliver.

Keep in mind that positioning goals can be set for individual products and for companies. For example, you've probably seen computer commercials for many brands on TV that end with the Intel Inside symbol and jingle. Those commercials support the importance of the Intel brand processor as the right choice.

It is unlikely that one message will completely communicate a position, or that the position will be permanently retained by the audience. For that reason, communication often has tactical goals. For example, in order to occupy a position in the mind of a buyer, the buyer has to associate certain characteristics with the product. If speed is one characteristic, then Intel might measure buyers' perceptions of speed after they've received

---

### 10–1

## BUSINESS 2 BUSINESS
## Road Trip for Face Time

Hewlett-Packard Software had a story to tell—updates on various services and HP products—but it wanted to listen too. It wanted true engagement with its best customers and prospects. So a team of 10 HP execs and staff booked facilities in six cities, including at Soldier Field in Chicago and NBC Studios in New York, for breakfast meetings with 10 to 30 CIOs and CTOs. Throughout the tour, HP Senior VP world-

wide marketing, David Gee, maintained a blog, highlighting the activities and key topics at each venue. Photo galleries were later posted on the Web and clips were posted on YouTube.

What would be the key takeaways for CIO participants and HP executives from this tour?

Source: Renee Knight, "HP Hits the Road to Meet Its Customer," *B2B* (April 2, 2007), p. 3+; http://www.outcomescio-tour.com/.

---

a communication. Or Charrette might ask buyers if they recall the Charrette image (it was a Brooklyn Bridge image) or logo. Tactical positioning goals are desired outcomes relating to specific communications messages that contribute to the achievement of the strategic positioning goal.

### Action Goals

Some communications aim to motivate the receiver to take an action. It may be that the desired action is to visit a booth at the show or, in Charrette's case, visit the Web site. **Action goals** are set for those communications that are intended to cause the receiver to do something.

Examples of action goals in business marketing are

- Secure 300 visitors to a trade show booth who bring coupons from a direct mail campaign
- Generate 100 inquiries from an ad in a trade publication
- Book 22 appointments for field salespeople by a telemarketing program
- Receive 1,200 orders from a catalog mailing
- Obtain 900 surveys completed and returned

All of these goals reflect desired actions to be taken by the receivers. Note that sales are one action goal and that other actions may also be appropriate—including giving feedback.

The choice of an action goal depends on what you want the communication to do within your understanding of the buying process. For example, Intel introduced a new processor at the Consumer Electronics Show with a preshow mail campaign, a strong at-show attraction involving a number of Intel software partners, and the theme of "Intel Takes You There." Each visitor to the Intel booth received a passport, which they took to the booths of Intel's partners. After hearing each presentation, the passport was stamped. When attendees brought it back to the Intel booth, they turned it in to claim a prize. Information about each attendee was then entered from the passport into Intel's database to support future marketing efforts. Intel's Consumer Electronics Show strategy was based on its knowledge of chip procurment as a multiperson buying center involving thorough consideration on many criteria, as you can see in Exhibit 10–5.

**Exhibit 10–5**
The Buying
Process for
Computer
Processors

*Awareness:* Buyers become aware through articles in trade publications that Intel is introducing the processor.

*Interest:* Buyers become interested in seeing the processor when they receive an invitation to visit the Intel booth at the Consumer Electronics Show.

*Desire:* Buyers desire the processor after they visit the Intel booth and see the video, and then visit software vendors' booths and see how the Chip makes the software faster. Desire is further enhanced by television commercials.

*Action:* Buyers who indicated that a decision is approaching receive a letter shortly after the show with a special offer. Action is taken when the salesperson calls to visit the buyer.

## Challenges in Goal Setting

Two special difficulties arise in this process of goal setting. First, communication goals don't automatically harmonize. For example, the communication efforts seeking buyer action—trade show visits, request for a demonstration—can achieve excellent tactical results while giving little or no regard for the company's long-run positioning aims. Goals need to be integrated. Second, especially for attainment of positioning and strategic goals, fitting measures of effectiveness are not always obvious. The specification of success measures warrants creativity and consideration.

### Integrating Marketing Communication Goals

Suppose a company's advertising discussed its service quality, its employees' commitment to excellence, and the investments management has made in upgrading every area of the firm. What would a buyer's reaction be if the talk at the trade show booth centered on how cheap the company's products were? Conflicting messages would be sent, creating confusion or disbelief in the mind of the buyer.

Although such extreme conflict is rare, much more common is the creation of separate messages for each channel without regard for what is expressed through other channels. For example, an advertising campaign could focus on a particular service, but that service may not be supported by the right people at the trade show. Or, in the same scenario, salespeople could be pushing another service at the expense of selling the advertised service. Integrated communications are designed to support the same overall objectives.

Integrated goals that successfully position a product or company in the buyer's mind can also predispose that buyer to react appropriately to communication designed to create action. For example, advertising can create an image for a company that opens doors for its salespeople; a direct mail and advertising campaign can lead buyers to stop at a booth they see at a trade show. Integrating communication creates synergy, a synergy that begins by integrating the communication goals across media.

### Setting Measurable Goals

As you probably know from other marketing classes, effective marketing goals are measurable. The process of setting measurable communication goals can actually cause problems because the tendency is to set goals that can be easily measured, rather than devising measures to fit the goals. When you first read it, 8,000 visitors to Intel's booth probably seems like a reasonable goal; however, traffic alone at the Intel booth did not contribute to the creation of their desired position. They rightly believed that unless a prospective buyer participated in the intended communication, then no contribution to the desired position occurred. Specifically, a visitor wasn't a visitor at Intel's booth unless the person had seen Intel's video, been qualified as a potential buyer, received a passport, and then used it to visit Intel's partners. Visitors were counted on the basis of returned passports, which meant that the buyer had participated in the complete set of communications. Set the objective on the basis of what you want to do; then develop an appropriate measure; don't do something just because it is measurable.

# Roles for Each Communication Element

The marketing communication (marcomm) manager has an ever growing toolkit to pursue IMC goals. We take a brief look at the strengths and weaknesses of the communication elements in order to develop an appreciation of what role they can play in our IMC plans.

## Advertising

Advertising is nonpersonal, one-way communication; although a buyer can respond to advertising by calling or faxing a response card, the message is not altered as a result of feedback. Business advertising is found in **trade publications,** or magazines written for a specific profession, industry, or trade. *Marketing Educator* is a trade publication that your professor probably receives.

Business advertising is also found on the Web, television (remember the BASF ads!), radio, billboards, and other media. Strengths of advertising include the low cost per contact, an ability to reach inaccessible or unknown buying influences, and the ability to reach large numbers of potential buyers.

Advertising is used for many reasons, but because of the strengths just listed, advertising is often used for one of several related purposes. As illustrated in Exhibit 10–6, the roles of advertising are related and begin with a base of creating awareness and strengthening a company's position or image. Prospects are more likely to let salespeople into their offices when the salespeople represent known companies—and it is advertising that makes the companies known. The second role, then, is to create a favorable climate for salespeople. Even better is to have a prospect call and ask for a salesperson to visit. This is the third role of advertising—generating leads. In some instances, customers will order directly from the advertising, so the final purpose of advertising is to generate sales.

## Direct Marketing

**Direct marketing** uses advertising media to obtain a measurable action outcome. The effort's origin or outcome (or both) connects to a marketing database. The role of direct marketing is to generate sales—especially from current customers—followed by generating leads (or some other action, such as visiting a Web site or trade show booth), and so forth. Direct marketing communication can be delivered by mail, fax, or Internet, and includes catalogs. By selecting a particular trade publication or other medium, business marketers hope their advertising reaches prospects. With direct marketing, however, marketers should know more about the people with whom they are communicating than when advertising otherwise.

Direct marketing is also used for obtaining feedback from potential and current customers. We discussed surveys in Chapter 5, but it is important that you remember the need for two-way communication and feedback from potential and current customers.

**Exhibit 10–6**
Roles of
Advertising

Direct response communication is an opportunity to receive feedback. We aren't suggesting that **sugging,** or selling under the guise of doing research, is appropriate; it isn't. Sugging is considered unethical because the basic premise ("talk to us, customer; all we want is information") is a lie. What we are saying is that market surveys are one form of direct response communication.

## Public Relations

**Public relations (PR)** is the management function that focuses on the relationships and communications with individuals and groups in order to create mutual goodwill.[4] PR is not just crisis management, like Intel had to do with the Pentium processor when the public discovered that it had a bug. PR is also creating good relationships with the media so that it is easier to get good news presented, as well as creating good relationships with other important constituencies.

PR plays a supportive role in most cases and is used to inform audiences about the company and its products. PR, in the form of news stories or blogs, can have a lot of impact because the content is actually written or appears to be written by someone other than a company employee or agent. Thus, the audience tends to give the message greater credence. But compared to advertising, PR doesn't offer marketers the same degree of control over what is said, where it is said, and to whom, which can negatively impact the power of PR.

## Internet

We can hardly imagine an IMC plan today that excludes Internet communications. Of course, e-mail can support existing customer relationships and spur traffic to Web pages—although its impact is on the wane. The Internet especially empowers buyers in their searches for and access to information. Because it tends to put the marketing company in the response mode, Web sites must be designed to anticipate the information needs and functionality preferences of customers and potential customers. With potential customers searching for information and solutions, astute business marketers find ways to make themselves found. In **search engine marketing (SEM)** the marketer may bid on key search terms and thereby have its firm name appear when a potential customer searches using that term. The bid level is what the marketer offers to pay per click on its site when sought this way. A midwest software company bid up to $8 for the key words, "accounting software," but it bailed out a short time later after learning the lead conversion to sales rate did not support the $8 price per lead.

Alternatively, firms can try **search engine optimization (SEM),** an effort to manage the key word content of their Web pages and the number of external links to their site on other sites in order to come up on the first page of searches. Leading agencies have staff specialists who strive to be abreast of the latest criteria and algorithms used by the major search engines. They can then help their clients design their Web sites and suggest bloggers and other sites in the market space from which it would be advantageous to be linked.

## Trade Shows

**Trade shows** are temporary exhibitions of products and services. The first trade shows were open-air markets set up at fairs and festivals. Trade shows can contribute to both positioning and action goals. For example, recent studies indicate that 20 percent of all show attendees actually buy something at the show and 76 percent will ultimately purchase something they saw at the show.

Trade shows offer the advantage of personal interaction, which gives the seller the opportunity to observe nonverbal communication as well as listen to verbal communication. Products can be demonstrated, particularly products that would be impossible to take to a customer or expensive to demonstrate otherwise. Trade shows can be very cost effective, bringing many buyers together with a sales staff, buyers who often have not had any prior contact with the selling firm.[5]

## Telemarketing

**Telemarketing,** conducted by call centers, is the systematic and continuous program of personally communicating with (potential) customers via telephone and/or other electronic media. Telemarketing is a type of direct marketing that often gets special discussion and budget attention from marcomm managers. **Inbound telemarketing** is electronic communication initiated by the customer; **outbound telemarketing** is initiated by the marketer. Inbound can be used to take orders and for customer service. Outbound can be used to set appointments for field salespeople, invite prospects to visit the trade show booth, renew memberships, and other actions. Telemarketing does include feedback, and messages can be immediately altered due to feedback.

## Personal Selling

At the most basic level, **personal selling** is interpersonal communication in which one person attempts to secure a purchase from another person. Personal selling can be accomplished using different methods, which we will discuss in Chapter 13. The advantages of personal selling are that communication can be adapted to fit the needs and personality of the buyer, the offer can be changed to fit the buyer's requirements, and the sale can be completed. Disadvantages revolve around the cost of personal selling; maintaining a sales force is expensive, requiring investments in management structures, training, and other items. On a cost-per-contact basis, selling is very expensive compared with other forms of communication. On the other hand, the quality of a sales contact should be substantially higher than advertising, for example.

Typically, goals for personal selling should reflect buyer actions. A successful sales call is one that advances the buyer to the next stage of the buying process. Salespeople can make other types of calls, such as training calls, service calls, and calls that strengthen the relationship. Different communication objectives would be set for each type of call, reflecting the nature of the desired communication.

## Marketing Research

Marketing research is not usually included in the same conversation as selling or advertising, but marketing research is part of the overall communications mix. Marketing research can communicate to the customer that the organization is committed to the customer. Feedback is an important element in successful communication, and research is one avenue for feedback.

Another form of marketing research, though, is capturing information from the customer during the interaction. For example, when a customer visits a Web site, the company can track how the customer uses the Web site. That provides information as to what is helpful and what isn't. Similarly, Charrette tested different mailing lists when it launched its Brooklyn Bridge campaign. When customers responded, the company was able to determine which list was more effective. These forms of marketing research are an important element in customer relationship management because, many times, the way the customer communicates is by taking, or failing to take, action.

## Other Touchpoints

Every time a customer interacts with a firm, either with a person or with the company's technology through a Web site or automated telephone response system, that interaction is considered a **touchpoint.** Some of these touchpoints include service calls made by field technicians, telephone calls from the customer to shipping or billing, or simply checks made on the status of an order on the Web. Touchpoints can be used to collect information from the customer if the company has a system for gathering and sharing that information. For example, a customer service representative can ask a few questions to gauge the customer's satisfaction or intentions to repurchase, which can then be used to trigger other communications. Belgacom, the telecommunications company headquartered in Belgium, created such a system which the company credits as an important element in its growth to becoming the leading supplier of telecom connections in Europe. Because customer communications should be a dialogue, companies like Belgacom must find ways to gather and record data at every touchpoint.

Further, these touchpoints are important opportunities to reinforce the brand position. For example, a high-quality, premium-value company should have high value, premium service. Touchpoints that provide less will create confusion and dissatisfaction in the customer's mind. From the Field 10–2 profiles a soldier in the "battle for the mind."

# Create Messages

The IMC plan requires that each message delivered through each medium will achieve tactical positioning, and action goals that support strategic positioning and action goals. Now that you have an understanding of the advantages and disadvantages of

---

**10–2**

# FROM THE FIELD

## Branding and Positioning in Business Markets

I started my advertising career at Leo Burnett in Chicago after graduating from The Kellogg School at Northwestern with an MBA in marketing and finance. Over the course of my 21 years at Burnett, I was fortunate to work on many icon brands, including Kellogg's, Kraft, Oldmobile, Disney, Crayola, and Sara Lee. On all these brands, the consistent challenge was to identify a core bulls-eye target; uncover insights about their lives and their beliefs , attitudes, and behaviors for the specific category; create the connection between target and brand; and develop ideas that were meaningful, relevant, and engaging.

When I started working on the Arthur Andersen account back in the late 1990s, I figured out pretty quickly that many of the same challenges were as relevant in the B to B space. But much of the advertising targeted to C-level executives was dry, boring, chock full of a lot  of copy . . . almost like a  brochure disguised as a print ad. Because the target was CEOs and CFOs, and they're "serious" businesspeople, the advertising had to be serious, straightforward, and lacking any emotion. The reality is that C-level executives are exposed to Nike, Coke, Budweiser advertising and can (and will) respond to brands as emotionally as other audiences. So the adver-

tising we developed for Arthur Andersen (before the company imploded!) was written from the POV of the CEO and tried to capture some of the joys, struggles, and challenges they faced in running their companies. We used storytelling to connect to them . . . it was received extremely successfully and clearly communicated that Arthur Andersen understood their needs and had solutions to address them.

Similarly, work I've done in the insurance category, with agents as the primary target, has to connect on both an emotional and informational level. The agents need to *feel* that the company understands them and is positioning itself to meet agent needs. With the advent of the Internet, advertising can work to create that emotional connection and send them to a Web site to satisfy those informational needs.

More and more kinds of companies, like financial and professional services institutions and technical and commercial products companies, are realizing that they are "brands" and need to create positionings in their respective categories that are differentiating, motivating, and meaningful to the constituencies they serve in order to survive and thrive.

Patty Bloomfield, VP Account Director, Northlich, Cincinnati, OH.

---

each element, as well as the types of goals typically set for each element, the next step in developing a communication strategy is to orchestrate their respective contributions.

In order to create specific messages, it is important to recall what the communications plan is trying to achieve. At the same time, however, the marketer must also understand what buyers already think and do, what information buyers need, and what competitive actions are currently (or could be) undertaken.

### What Do Buyers Currently Think and Do?

Marketers need to recognize that buyers enter the market with preconceived ideas based on experience, education, competitors' communication, and other factors. Marketing communication never starts with a completely blank slate. Recognizing what buyers already think and how they purchase should significantly influence the design of any communication strategy.

For example, using the Buyer Behavior Choice model might enable the marketer to recognize that buyers see the purchase of plastic components as a minor task with little self-relevance. If so, there is little reason for buyers to shop around. Communication strategies might center on creating a position that it is easier to purchase from the marketer's company.

A marketer who subscribes to the reward–measurement theory would examine the reward–measurement systems for members of the buying center in an effort to predict buyer behavior. If purchasing agents were rewarded for reducing costs, then resulting communication strategies may focus on the firm's low-cost components.

### What Information Do They Need?

Communication, particularly marketing communication, must serve the buyer. If marketing communication only serves the need of the marketer, the buyer will ignore it. When developing marketing communication strategy, it is important to consider the information needs of the buyer. If the product is a new buy, for example, the buyer needs information that will help in understanding what the product does. Conversely, if the decision is a straight rebuy, a buyer may only need to know where or how to buy it. Research has determined that buyers attend trade shows, for example, with three sets of information needs:

- They need to find vendors for a particular product.
- They need to explore different possible solutions to a problem they are facing.
- They need to stay abreast of the latest technology in their field.[6]

Successful trade show marketers attempt to deal with each set of needs for their visitors. A visitor whose information needs are satisfied is more likely to continue a relationship with the vendor who filled those needs.

### What Are the Competitors' Actions?

At the same time that a marketer is trying to create a position in the mind of the buyer, so are all of the marketers' competitors. Sometimes the desired positions are very similar, creating the likelihood of confusion for the buyer.

Additionally, competitors are unlikely to allow a company to achieve a desirous position without challenge. Marketers must consider what competitors are doing as well as how they are likely to respond. For example, each time Intel introduces a chip and creates a communication strategy, Motorola and Cyrix are also changing their communications strategy to counterattack.

# Strategies for Customer Retention and Acquisition

Strategies can be classified on the basis of what the company is attempting to achieve. Although there are classification schemes for overall marketing strategies that you read in Chapter 5, to some degree, all communication strategies can be divided into either customer acquisition or customer retention strategies.

## *Customer Relationship Communication*

As you know, a key theme of this book is that customer retention and growth through current customers is an important, if not the most important, element in a business marketing strategy. As we discussed in Chapter 3, one impact of downsizing is that fewer people are available to make purchase decisions. One result of that fact and the drive to

**Exhibit 10–7**
Imperatives for
Communicating
with Customers

1. **Communicate proactively.** Don't presume that all customers are satisfied and will repurchase automatically. Competitors are ravenous for your customers. Your customers with whom you have partnered need direct lines of communication between functional areas in both firms. Formal meetings should be set for specific intervals and communication structures (closed Web sites, computer-to-computer linkages, RFID) should be considered. When the customer association is not a strategic partnership, proactive communication is nevertheless critical. Identify every opportunity—even invoices, technician visits, and product delivery—for tactical communications to support the strategic aims of the IMC plan.

2. **Make dialogue easy.** You're in big trouble if your customers can access your competitor easier than your firm. Provide customers a toll-free number to call with issues and complaints. Then empower customer service personnel to respond. Likewise make ordering easy, perhaps automatic when customer inventiories trigger replenishment.

3. **Make it easy to respond to the customer.** Many firms, such as Vulcan Binder & Cover, are empowering every employee to receive information from customers and to act on issues, even when outside the employee's usual area of responsibility. Likewise, strengthen internal communication channels in your company so teamwork might flourish. For example a delivery person may come upon information that represents a new selling opportunity, but it can only come to fruition if he knows the sales rep for the account and can talk to her. Finally, marketers can be well served by access to the company's customer database when customer interaction occurs. For example, when a Dell customer calls with a technical or transactional question, the Dell associate with a screen full of account history, market sector, systems used, and more can be knowledgeable and responsive.

improve quality is that stronger relationships are needed with vendors. In addition, for some products of little strategic value, companies may buy repeatedly from the same vendor simply because the costs of shopping around (particularly in terms of time) do not outweigh expected benefits. Customer relationship communication will be important to vendors in both situations.

Several communication mechanisms are used to strengthen customer relationships and meet growth objectives. These mechanisms take advantage of the customer's need to minimize costs associated with purchasing, in terms of both shopping behaviors and actual costs of processing purchases. Lowering costs raises the value. Several principles are at work in designing communication elements to achieve customer retention and growth (that is, growth within current accounts) objectives. These principles include communicating proactively, making it easy for customers to communicate, and making it easy for the company to respond. They are detailed in Exhibit 10–7.

## Customer Acquisition Communication

Customer acquisition communication must follow the same principles of proactive communication, making communication easy and making it simple to respond. Customer acquisition communication, however, must also convince the buyer to receive and process the communication. In a customer retention situation, there is a natural communication link already established; that is not always the case with customer acquisition.

To overcome a prospect's reluctance to process information, some acquisition efforts will skirt the hierarchy of effects and go right after the action using **direct influence.** They apply a number of social influence tactics that seek certain behaviors but have little to do with changing attitudes toward the product or company. They use appeals based on human tendencies to respond almost automatically to influence attempts based on scarcity ("while supplies last"), reciprocity ("order today and we'll also provide the travel alarm and free shipping"), and authority ("3 out of 4 doctors recommend"), among others. For harried buyers in a message-cluttered environment the marcomm

**10–3**

## FROM THE FIELD

## Who Needs People?

With the Internet, who needs salespeople? Oracle, maker of enterprise software to manage virtually every activity in the organization, has shifted to 100 percent online ordering. Yet this software giant has the world's fourth-largest sales force (nearly 16,000 people worldwide) who build relationships with customers. What has been eliminated is not salespeople but their paperwork.

That's not to say that the Internet isn't an important marketing tool. Oracle adds online seminars, a TV-style E-Business Network, and Web-based public relations to its field sales mix. The E-Business Network is a 24/7 e-cast that includes shows such as *Geek of the Week*. Customers gain affinity for Oracle with this constant interaction.

Public relations is also important. Oracle has a sizable PR staff who write constant releases. Some are sent as e-mail to readers who have signed up to receive the releases, whereas others are read at Yahoo! or in trade magazines. The online versions drive traffic to the Web site (www.oracle.com), which then creates leads for field salespeople. Then, if the customer wants a demo, the salesperson refers the customer back to Oracle.com, where they sign up for an online demo given by a product specialist.

Are relationships lost in all this technology? Oracle's CEO, Larry Ellison, doesn't think so. When it all works together, the relationship with the customer is managed efficiently *and* effectively. Oracle's goal is to be number one in every market in which it operates, and with a careful blend of people and technology, it is getting the job done.

Andy Cohen, "The Traits of Great Sales Forces," Sales & Marketing Management (October 2000), pp. 67–72; "America's Largest Sales Forces," Selling Power (September 2000), pp. 67–103; Michelle Marchetti, "Master of the (Online) Universe?" Sales & Marketing Management (June 2000), pp. 52–60.

manager applies these tactics believing that buyer action (trial) can be an effective precursor to attitudes and the attainment of positioning goals (liking and loyalty).

## BUDGETING FOR COMMUNICATIONS

Traditionally, the advertising budget was also the marketing communications budget. Salespeople did not require a budget because they were paid straight commission and they paid their own expenses or, if they were paid a salary, the sales budget was calculated separately. Other elements of communication were treated as afterthoughts and given only a small percentage of the total budget. When business marketers discussed their marketing communications budget, they meant their advertising budget.

With the advent of CRM and recognition of the power of all of the forms of communication (like Oracle in From the Field 10–3), new organization structures and strategic budgeting processes have been developed. Many methods exist to determine the communications budget and allocation among elements; the choice may depend more on the sophistication of the marketer than any other factor. Exhibit 10–8 illustrates how business marketers, on average, allocate their marketing budget. Before we examine how companies budget, though, it is important to recognize why companies budget.

## Benefits of Budgeting

As anyone who has watched the federal government try to determine its budget knows, budgeting can result in disharmony, fighting, and even long-term feuds. Yet without budgets, spending can spiral out of control. For organizations, including the government,

**Exhibit 10–8**
Where Marketing
Dollars Are Spent
SOURCE: *Adapted from
Kate Maddox, "New
Marketing Index to
Benchmark
Spending,"* B-to-B,
*March 8, 2004,
pp. 13–14.*

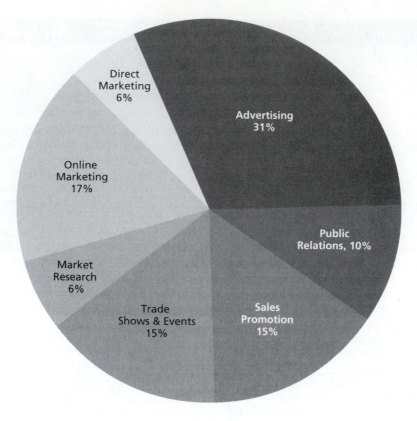

such a lack of control can be devastating. Yes, there will always be someone who uses the budgeting process to feather a nest, but budgets and the budgeting process have several benefits, including planning, coordination, and control.

## Planning

Budgets should be part of the planning process. When decision makers recognize their budget constraints, they can evaluate alternatives in a realistic fashion. Far too often, budgets are set and then planning takes place. When planning occurs after the budgeting process, some tasks may be underfunded, whereas other areas may enjoy a surplus. So that each task can be properly funded, budgeting should be part of the planning process.

## Coordination

Budgets should be part of the integration of communication. When resources are allocated among various forms of communication, the integrated marketing communications concept demands that all communication methods work together to create synergy. If coordination is attempted after budgets are determined, then integration may not occur because funds may not be available. For example, suppose Intel's trade show manager wanted the sales force to supply 12 salespeople to work the Comdex trade show. Sales would have to fly 12 salespeople to Las Vegas for a week. Whose budget will pay for the travel? If the trade show budget can't cover it and the sales manager

---

**10–2**

## BUSINESS 2 BUSINESS
### Turf Battles

Earlier in the chapter, we mentioned turf battles as an obstacle to integrating communications. How can the budgeting process cause or reduce turf battles? Among whom would those battles occur? Review the opening vignette about Charrette, Xiameter and Dow Corning in

From the Field 10–1, and From the Field 10–3 about Oracle, as you think about who would be involved in a turf battle. As you read the following section, think about how these methods can contribute to increasing or lessening turf tension.

---

had already allocated travel funds for other events, Intel's booth at Comdex may go understaffed. Good budgeting processes cause stronger coordination and support IMC; postbudgeting integration, or trying to integrate after the budget is set, is difficult.

### Control

Budgets provide boundaries on what can and cannot be done, thereby framing decisions for marcomm managers. As we will see below, the very process of budgeting can provide another type of control, a discipline for planning, forcing attention to the resources needed to execute a strategy or maintain a marketing process.

## Methods of Budgeting

Some methods of budgeting lend themselves to better planning and stronger integration. **Breakdown budgeting** methods, though, begin with the manager setting a total communications budget, then allocating (breaking down) the budget to the various forms of communication. Unfortunately, we lose many of the planning and coordination benefits of budgeting when we attempt to integrate communications after the overall budget has been specified. As a rule, we don't recommend breakdown methods, but their use in business continues as a result of myopia, inertia, and occasional exigencies.

### Breakdown Budgeting Methods

Our chief rap against breakdown methods rests on their perverse logic that past or expected sales determine the amount to be spent. And you thought marketing communications were supposed to affect sales! (They are! So don't change your mind on this.)

Consider the all-you-can-afford method. Here the marketer examines the organization's projected cash flow—primarily from sales—and allocates as much as possible to communications. Cash-strapped, start-up enterprises tend to follow an all-you-can-afford approach. Indeed, not long ago, the author of a marketing text received an e-mail from his publisher saying that sales of the new book were better than forecast: *they could now afford to do some advertising.*

Although this may seem like a very naive method of allocating funds, keep in mind that the method is an implicit element of every method. No manager is going to allocate

**Exhibit 10–9**
Breakdown
Methods of
Budgeting for
Communications

| Method | How It Works | Why It Is Less Desirable |
|---|---|---|
| All you can afford | The decision maker examines cash flow and sets the budget based on cost targets. | Budget is based on cash flow, which is based on sales. But if more sales could occur, then more could be "afforded." |
| Percentage of sales | Sales are forecasted and then a percentage of that forecasted sales is allocated to marcomm. | Same problem as with all-you-can-afford method. Also, in many cases, the percentage is equal to the industry average or historical amounts, neither of which is related to the company's goals |
| Competitive parity | Dollars are allocated to match one or more competitors' spending. | This type of budgeting assumes that competitors' sales are due to their communications, and that they are using dollars efficiently. It also assumes that our company wants to sell similar amounts and does not consider our competitive position. |
| Share of market— share of voice | Budget is some percentage of the total industry's marcomm expenditures. | Similar problems as with competitive parity, particularly if budget is set as a percentage of last year's industry expenditures. It assumes that industry figures are accurate and that the desired share of voice will result in the desired level of sales. |

more than the company can afford! The problem arises when the all-you-can-afford method is the only method used. There is no strategy to determine how much you should communicate, and the potential effects of communication are not fully considered. For example, the decision maker doesn't consider that more communication might mean greater sales, which means that the company could afford more communication.

Many business marketers rely on a percent-of-sales approach. As benchmarks for budgeting, one can examine the selling expenses percent or the advertising to sales (A/S) ratio in an industry. Ad spending rates across industries vary significantly: 0.5 percent of sales in construction machinery and equipment, 1.9 percent in chemicals and allied products, and 9.7 percent in manifold business forms.

The percent-of-sales approach is simple to apply, and spending near the industry average may tend to nurture stability among rivals; but it ignores the different market positions rivals occupy. For example a 10 percent boost in advertising by UPS might boost brand recall from 95 to 96 percent because it's near the saturation level. A 10 percent increase by the upstart DJ Express may be too tiny to have a measurable impact. Meanwhile, at DHL, the 10 percent increase in advertising may bring a 5 percent gain in recall. Like many customer response variables, recall may respond to marketing expenditures in an S-shaped function, so the same percent-of-sales does not befit all competing firms. Exhibit 10–9 gives a brief summary and assessment of these and two additional breakdown methods.

## Setting Budgets to Reach Strategic Objectives

The best method for budgeting in order to reach strategic objectives is the objective-and-task method. The **objective-and-task method,** also known as the **budget buildup method,** requires the decision maker to set the budget after determining the

**Exhibit 10–10**
Budget Buildup versus Breakdown

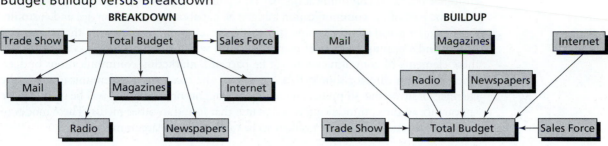

communication strategy. The method has three steps: defining objectives, determining strategy, and estimating cost. Of course, the decision maker will balance what can be afforded with what is desired. As the communications strategy is implemented and results become available, changes can be made to enhance efficiency and effectiveness.

One distinction that sets the objective-and-task method apart is that strategy precedes budgeting. With all other methods, communications strategy cannot be determined until the budget is known. The advantages for the marketer using the objective-and-task method are several: First, the budgeting process is less of a hindrance than in other situations. Effectiveness of a particular strategy can be examined—not just efficiency or cost. Second, the method is strategy driven and learning based. If tasks are based on objectives, and budgets are based on tasks, then the decision maker had better know with a reasonable degree of certainty that the tasks, or strategy, will achieve the objectives. The marketing communications manager justifies a budget based on performance, which requires learning which tasks work when and why. The objective-and-task method may require more sophistication on the part of the marketing decision maker, but should be the most effective when learning takes place.

## Allocating among Communication Elements

For most budget-setting methods, once a total communication budget is set, each form of communication will require a budget. If the objective-and-task method is used, however, each form of communication already has a budget, which is why that method is also called the budget buildup method. As objectives are set, tactics involving various elements and media are created, along with a budget for each tactic and medium. These are then added together to create the final budget. Thus, objective and task should lead to highly integrated communications. Exhibit 10–10 illustrates the difference between budget buildup and other methods.

How the budget is allocated among the various elements is a measure of the degree of integration in the firm's communications. We can illustrate this idea with the all-you-can-afford method. If that method is used to determine the total budget, then the marcomm (marketing communications) director says, "We can afford only this amount on advertising, this amount on trade shows, and this amount on direct mail." Then the manager of each takes that budget amount and tries to develop a strategy. Any integration in communication is likely to be a function of sharing budget dollars to cut costs; for example, the trade show manager asks the advertising manager to mention in upcoming ads that the company will exhibit at the Widget Show. Yet allocation of budget can be accomplished using the objective-and-task method within limits established by an all-you-can-afford total.

On the other hand, customer-acquisition communication may be fully integrated, yet customer-retention communication may be separated. For example, should marketing research be part of the communication budget? What about customer service and customer satisfaction measurement systems (these involve communication with the customer)? Billing and shipping are part of communication with customers, but it is unlikely that these elements of communication will be part of a marketing communications budget. The marcomm director should have input into the creation of communication via the channels of invoicing, shipping, and others so that corporate graphics will be used and the appearance of the communication will match that found in other media. These modes of communication, however, are unlikely to be found in the marcomm budget.

## Summary

Business marketing communications should be integrated. IMC is strategic in that content and delivery are part of an overall marketing plan. IMC is also two-way communication, incorporating learning from customers into the design and execution of marketing communications. Customer needs can be met, which increases customer participation in the marketing communications dialogue.

The hierarchy-of-effects model profiles the stages that buyers progress through when interacting with marketing communications. Using this model, marketers set two levels of goals for their marketing communications: strategic and tactical. Strategic goals are the goals for the entire marketing communications plan, whereas tactical goals are those outcomes desired of specific communications. In addition, marketers set two types of goals: action and positioning goals. Action goals are those desired actions we want buyers to take, whereas positioning goals involve the attitudes and beliefs we want the buyers to have about us and our products. Positioning goals reflect the ratings we want our offerings to have in the customer's multiattribute evaluation of the options.

There are many challenges when setting goals. Such challenges include integrating goals across the various forms of marketing communications and setting goals for performance that can be measured. The challenge with setting measurable goals is to make sure that what is measured will lead to desired outcomes such as increases in sales. Often, what is easiest to measure is the least important.

Several forms of communication channels or promotional elements can be used to communicate with the market including the Internet, advertising, direct marketing, trade shows, telemarketing, public relations, personal selling, and marketing research. Choosing a promotional element for a particular message depends on a number of factors. Marketers should also consider such questions as Who is the audience? What do they currently think and do? And, What do they need to know when selecting a medium? Current customers, for example, already like our product, whereas acquiring new customers may require first creating a liking for the product.

Budgeting (another important decision set) can be accomplished by breakdown or buildup methods. Buildup methods are recommended because the dollar amounts allocated to various media are based on strategic objectives and are therefore more likely to result in achieving those objectives.

## Key Terms

| | | |
|---|---|---|
| **action** | **breakdown budgeting** | **customer relationship** |
| **action goals** | **budget buildup** | **management (CRM)** |
| **awareness** | **method** | **desire** |

| | | |
|---|---|---|
| direct influence | objective-and-task | search engine |
| direct marketing | method | optimization (SEO) |
| hierarchy-of-effects | outbound telemarketing | strategic goals |
| model | personal selling | sugging |
| inbound telemarketing | position | tactical goals |
| integrated marketing | prospect | telemarketing |
| communications | public relations (PR) | touchpoints |
| (IMC) | search engine marketing | trade publications |
| interest | (SEM) | trade shows |

# Discussion Questions

1. Microsoft Corp. introduced Office 2007 in the spring of that year. The marketing communication program for the launch began in 12 countries and included print and outdoor ads, as well as a "digital hallway" at JFK airport in New York that allows people to try the product in kiosks. Rachel Bondi, senior director of brand and ad strategy at Microsoft, said 60 percent of the budget went to online expenditures, including an April 19 "takeover" of the MSN homepage enabling a trial of a new Office 2007 feature. The plan emphasized building traffic to the Web site, watching a demo online, downloading a free 60-day trial, and watching a series of online videos. Interestingly, the previous Office campaign in 2005 had just 30 percent of expenditures online. Do you agree with the online emphasis for Office 2007? Source: Kate Maddox, "Microsoft Puts Emphasis Online," *B2B* (May 7, 2007), p. 14; **http://office.microsoft.com/en-us/suites/HA101656501033.aspx.**

2. Misrepresentation occurs when, as a result of deceptive marketing communications, a customer believes a product will do something that it doesn't. Assuming no intent on the part of the seller to deceive, what could cause a buyer to hold incorrect expectations as a result of marketing communications?

3. Should all marketing research be part of an integrated marketing communications plan? Why or why not? If only some marketing research should be part of the plan, which part? Why?

4. Assume your company sells first-aid—CPR training and supply products to companies. They are required by OSHA to have someone trained and to have the proper supplies on hand. Assuming that most buyers are defensive (to minimize the threat of an OSHA fine), what would your strategic communication goals be? What would your primary message be? Relate your strategic goals and message to positioning goals.

5. Why has American business historically focused on customer acquisition strategies? How has that influenced marketing communication and the public's perception of marketing communication?

6. The field sales force is still the largest part of the marketing communications budget, but other areas are growing. Why?

7. How the budget is allocated may be the most telling sign of the degree of integration for a company's marketing communication. Why is that?

8. In a previous chapter, we discussed investment risk (the possibility of losing one's investment) and opportunity risk (the possibility of missing out on an opportunity). Discuss how these types of risk may influence the choice of a budgeting procedure.

9. Financial service companies represent substantial sales opportunities for some well-poised companies. For example, Sarbanes–Oxley and the Patriot Act have brought demands on financial institutions for storing and securing information, while protecting earnings. What would be the key elements of an IMC plan by IBM to reach the sophisticated, elusive, and keen-witted executives, at, say, the top 50 commercial banks, who stand to benefit from your new data encryption and warehousing service? Would it change much if the supplier were an Ivy League university IT lab spin-off?

10. Does changing to integrated marketing communications require organizational structure changes?

11. "Touchpoints aren't about selling," gripes one customer service manager. "We shouldn't pump our customers for information." How would you respond?

12. In the past decade, many businesses have funded their CRM expenditures by trimming the sales force and decreasing expenditures in print media. What type of budgeting does this represent? As a sales representative for a trade publication visiting a longtime advertiser in your magazine, outline why such an approach for budgeting for its CRM initiative is very dangerous.

# Cases

### Case 10.1   Budget Time

The conference room was filled with the friendly buzz of chatter between colleagues when Marisa Hernandez entered. As she sat, she noticed that she was the last of the marketing staff to arrive for the budget meeting.

"OK, now that Marisa is here, we can get started," smiled Tom Davis, director of marketing. "The purpose of this meeting is to review the budgets you have all submitted and then chop off 15 percent." This remark was met with nervous laughter, as Tom smiled ruefully. "Sorry, gang, but it's true. If we can't improve our profitability by another 5 percent, it seems that our parent company will sell us off after this year. So top management has asked everyone to reduce their costs by 15 percent without losing sight of their sales goals."

Marisa groaned. She was relatively new and was responsible for managing trade shows and other special events, but she had been there long enough to know that the company had been wasting its trade show money in the past. With a little rearranging of the show schedule and the increase in budget she had asked for to build a new booth, she felt sure that she could increase the number and quality of leads enough to handle the 12 percent increase in sales that management had already asked for. Cutting 15 percent of the budget, though, eliminated the new booth.

Tom passed out copies of the summary budgets of each department. "Whoa; here's the culprit right here," exclaimed Shelly Tap, national sales manager. She slammed the copies to the table, saying, "Our trade show budget request is 30 percent higher than last year." Turning to Marisa, she said, "I can't cut our budget 15 percent and expect to reach the sales target, but if you cut yours to 5 percent less than last year's, that'll equal 5 percent of my budget."

"But if I can upgrade the quality of leads you get, as well as the quantity, you can still achieve your sales targets," replied Marisa, trying to hide her irritation. For some reason, she didn't hit it off with Shelly.

"Oh, sure. Everyone knows that trade shows are just a wild party. We haven't closed a lead from one in years." Shelly, along with all of the other staff, laughed. "Look, Tom, let's put our money where the results are, and that's in sales."

"Yeah, Tom, and you know how important advertising is to our image," added Brian Black, director of advertising. "We can't possibly cut 15 percent."

At this point, Marisa began to worry about keeping her job.

1. What type of information does Marisa need to justify her proposed budget? Where would she go to get that information?

2. Similarly, how would any other marketing managers justify their budget requests?

3. What type of budgeting does it seem the company does now? What should the company do? What challenges will Tom face in implementing a different budgeting process? How should Tom go about that implementation?

### Case 10.2   Kmotiv: IMC for SBC?

Carolina Baretto had just returned to campus from the Mother's Day weekend when the call came. It was the head of client services, Bud Franklin, offering her an entry position on his team with a competitive salary, plus 5 percent commission. Kmotiv is a growing marketing agency specializing in serving companies in the building trades. Carolina was delighted to land this job. In the semester-long internship at Kmotiv, she so impressed the founder and president, Chas Franklin, with her resourcefulness and attention to detail he dubbed her head of the "Department of Class."

Two months have now passed since Carolina graduated from Landgrant State with a degree in marketing and supporting course work in information systems. She was one of two newcomers to Kmotiv in the training program, and enjoyed both the client interaction and excellent mentoring from the Franklins. Chas was the visionary and time and again he painted the picture for Carolina. He saw the early promise of CRM a decade ago, and left an executive position at a major ad agency to build the IT platform to allow his new company to manage customer databases for its clients. He called it Kmotiv because he thought the term simply conveyed the dynamic capabilities so necessary in the new marketing environment. "Motiv" spoke to the firm's ability to reach a target market in the right medium with compelling copy and art that delivered a message. The "K" component of the name was taken from "kinetic" and it represented the energy in motion. "We're not just here to build awareness, sprinkle happy thoughts," he told Carolina when he stopped by one afternoon as she proofread some copy. "This is about getting our client's prospects to show up at the trade show, or pick up the phone, or log on and reorder. ACT! Once that behavior becomes part of the customer database, we want to maximize it—upsell, cross-sell, referrals. Retain that customer. We help our clients to be proactive in customer retention. It's all about ACTION."

All of Carolina's training and wits were being tapped next Wednesday over lunch with Earl Crossworth. Kmotiv's client services people had been pursuing the architectural firm, Schniky, Bilge and Crossworth (SBC), for years. SBC had enjoyed a decade of 15 percent average annual growth as a result of a strong and spreading reputation for school design. The firm had a lackluster Web site and for years its only advertising has been a quarterly ad on the back of *New School* magazine. In his own frustration with SBC, Bud once said the whole firm was "nearsighted from too much time at the drafting table." Crossworth tended to dub it "professionalism" rather than myopia. "Our concepts, renderings, and the completed structures themselves are worth more than all the ads in the industry," he once told the local paper.

Carolina happened to achieve this breakthrough appointment after some careful research sparked by her reading of a brief article that described an SBC project that had soured in Memphis. Ongoing investigations have yet to determine whether design flaws or contractor negligence caused the foundation to collapse in the renovation of a historic urban school. Two workers were seriously injured in the collapse. When she called Crossworth to ask for the appointment, he confided,

*I take about two calls a day from school superintendents or board members. About half are former clients, the others from schools where we have proposals in the works. I think I put their mind at ease about the tragedy in Memphis, but I worry about some of our contacts that haven't called. Frankly, I sometimes wonder if we haven't become too dependent on academic projects.*

Carolina didn't intend to linger on the negative over lunch. She saw this as an opportunity to sow a customer orientation at SBC. She estimated that nearly 65 percent of its business each year was with school districts or universities for whom it had designed previous school buildings. She planned to print a few screen captures of the Web sites of SBC's top rivals. She wondered what else she should bring up or show briefly over lunch in order to get Crossworth to invite Kmotiv to make a formal presentation next month. If Carolina could lead the team from Kmotiv to win this account, she'd not only make the Franklin brothers proud; she would have a strong business base for years to come, and those pesky college loans might soon go away.

Carolina wanted Bud to come too, but he just rolled his eyes at the suggestion and said, "I've already had my cracks at SBC; I'd be a liability." Help Carolina prepare a one-page agenda for introducing IMC to Crossworth over lunch.

# Additional Readings

*B2B's Interactive Marketing Guide.* "Taking It to the Next Level: B2B's Panel of Experts Agrees that Engaging Customers Online Is No Longer a Value-added Proposition but Is Essential for Success." (2007), pp. 4–9.

Cano, Cynthia Rodriquez, James S. Boles, and Cynthia J. Bean. "Communication Media Preferences in Business-to-Business Transactions: An Examination of the Purchase Process." *Journal of Personal Selling & Sales Management* 15 (summer 2005), pp. 283–294.

Christopher, Martin, Adrian Payne, and David Ballantyne. *Relationship Marketing: Creating Stakeholder Value.* Oxford: Butterworth Heinemann, 2002.

CRM Today, http://www.crm2day.com/relationship_marketing/.

Gosselin, Derrick P., and Guy A. Bauwen. "Strategic Account Management: Customer Value Creation through Customer Alignment." *Journal of Business & Industrial Marketing* 21, no. 6 (2006), pp. 376–85.

Gronroos, C. "The Relationship Marketing Process: Communication, Interaction, Dialogue, Value." *Journal of Business & Industrial Marketing* 19, no. 2 (2004), pp. 99–113.

Gummeson, E. "Return on Relationships (ROR): The Value of Relationship Marketing and CRM in Business-to-Business Contexts." *Journal of Business & Industrial Marketing* 19, no. 2 (2004), pp. 136–48.

Jensen, Morten Bach. "Characteristics of B2B Adoption and Planning of Online Marketing Communications." *Journal of Targeting, Measurement and Analysis for Marketing* 14, no. 4 (2006), pp. 357–68.

Kotler, Phillip, and Waldemar Pfoertsch. *B2B Brand Management.* New York: Springer, 2006.

Lamons, Bob. *The Case for B2B Branding: Pulling Away from the Business-to-Business Pack.* Boston: South-Western Publishing, 2005.

Pickton, D., and B. Hartley. "Measuring Integration: An Assessment of the Quality of Integrated Marketing Communications." *International Journal of Advertising* 17, no. 4 (1998), pp. 447–66.

Samaniego, M. José Garrido, Ana M. Gutiérrez Arranz, and Rebeca San José Cabezudo. "Determinant of Internet Use in the Purchasing Process." *Journal of Business & Industrial Marketing* 21, no. 3 (2006), pp. 164–74.

Tzokas, N., and M. Saren. "Competitive Advantage, Knowledge and Relationship Marketing: Where, What, and How?" *Journal of Business & Industrial Marketing* 19, no. 2 (2004), pp. 124–35.

# Chapter 11

## Communicating via Advertising, Trade Shows, and PR

**BENDIX**

Advertising, trade shows, and other forms of promotion are often used to trumpet new products. In business marketing, though, a product is only part of an offering. Other important elements are aspects such as how dependable the company is, how innovative it is, and other factors that can have a positive effect on the buyer's experience.●

That's why winning the Frost & Sullivan Customer Value Leadership Award was so important to Bendix Commercial Vehicles. The award was given because of the company's advances in heavy truck safety-enhancement technology—something that spreads across product platforms. For example, advanced technologies were put into the company's antilock braking systems, improving the safety capability of that platform. In addition, the company released new training software, at no charge, designed to help technicians maintain equipment more safely. The company also launched adaptive cruise control, a system that combines braking, throttle reduction, and an engine retarder to safely slow heavy trucks in tight traffic.●

The award was announced at the Mid-America Trucking Show, a trade show that is known as the industry's premier showcase for new products. Frost & Sullivan and Bendix held a joint press conference to announce the award, which was then reported in several trade magazines. In addition, Bendix included mention of the award in advertising after the show.●

314

Consistent with building a reputation for safety and innovation, the company also sponsors the annual competition for the best truck technician. The competition is based on technical competency, as well as contributions to the industry. While some companies may sponsor NASCAR, Bendix sees this type of sponsorship as more consistent with the reputation the company wants to enjoy in the market. ●

Bendix expects sales to slow for all truck manufacturers and those that supply manufacturers in the near future. With a reputation for leadership in innovation and safety, though, the company expects to increase its market share in spite of the industry downturn. ●

Sources: Bruce Adams, "Growing the Business," *Fleet Equipment* 33 (April 2007), pp. 56–57; Tom Gelinas, "Safety with a Payback," *Fleet Equipment* 33 (May 2007), p. 4; Jim Mele, "Talk of the Show," *Fleet Owner* 102 (May 2007), pp. 40–53.

## LEARNING OBJECTIVES

As you learned in the previous chapter, communication involves dialogue. It is not just one-way communication. In this chapter, we will examine specific communication tools and venues, some of which look like one-way communication. As you will see, however, astute business marketers are finding ways to make these methods part of an overall dialogue.

*After reading this chapter, you should be able to*

- Set goals for advertising.
- Develop advertising strategies to achieve those goals.
- Compare and contrast the types of advertising commonly used.
- Illustrate how subscription to a particular buying theory influences advertising strategy.
- Describe principles of sound public relations.
- Set goals for trade shows, and develop a trade show strategy.
- Illustrate the complete marketing mix of the trade show experience.

As you learned in the previous chapter, effective marketing communications not only sell the product; they also help the buyer set expectations for product performance. These expectations are then the basis for determining product satisfaction. In this chapter, we will learn how to communicate and build desire for the product, while also setting the proper expectations, through methods of communication to the larger market.

# ADVERTISING TO BUSINESS

The biggest part of the marketing communication budget (not counting the cost of a sales force) is devoted to advertising. Advertising by businesses can serve many objectives but the primary objective is to talk to large groups. Those groups can be potential investors in the company, influencers of government regulation, and even buyers. Yet we discussed, in earlier chapters, how business markets are smaller than consumer markets in terms of the number of buyers, how important the personal relationship between buyer and seller is, and other factors that might lead students to believe that advertising is relatively unimportant. Why, then, is advertising so much a part of the budget?

# Why Advertise?

John Wannamaker, a British executive, once said, "I know half of my advertising works; I just don't know which half." That somewhat facetious comment reflects the fact that we can't always see when advertising works. The action a buyer takes may have been influenced by advertising seen long before the action. Advertising, though, is important in business marketing because it does work—advertising does influence action.

As we discussed in Chapter 10, advertising influences action by creating awareness and strengthening attitudes, and advertising can also lead directly to action. As we discuss these benefits of advertising in greater detail, keep in mind that business marketers use advertising to communicate to any large group, not just potential customers. Advertising can be used to create favorable attitudes in financial markets, among potential suppliers, with government officials, and with other important groups.

## Advertising Creates Awareness

Before a product is positioned in the mind of a buyer, the buyer must be aware of the product. Products of which the buyer is aware are part of the **evoked set.** The process is one of the buyer becoming aware of the product, developing an attitude about the product (the attitude represents the position), and then acting. Advertising, because of its ability to reach so many prospective buyers, can create awareness.

For example, when ColorSpan launched Displaymaker, a large graphic printer, ColorSpan was an unknown company to most of the potential buyers for DisplayMaker. ColorSpan had to first make the market aware of both ColorSpan and DisplayMaker. Not only did neither the company nor the product hold a place in the mind of the buyer; the product platform (in this case, large graphic printers) was unknown to the market. ColorSpan had to build awareness for several things, not just the product name.

## Advertising Strengthens Attitudes

Once awareness is obtained, advertising can influence the creation of attitudes. A company's position is similar to the buyer's attitude toward the product, with one exception. A position is the summation of beliefs held about the product, but the attitude also includes how strongly the beliefs are held. A weak attitude can be easily influenced by information from either advertising or other sources. Advertising can strengthen beliefs about a product (thereby strengthening the position) or weaken beliefs held about a competitive product.

### *Advertising Leads to Action*

As described in Chapter 3, buying is the result of a series of decisions. Although it is rare that an industrial buyer will purchase only as a result of seeing an advertisement, a number of actions can be taken as a result of seeing an ad. Prospects may send in cards asking for more literature, may visit the trade show booth, may visit a Web site, or may call an 800 number. It is not uncommon to see ads that say "Visit us at www . . . or at the Mega Trade Show!" Advertising can move prospects more quickly through the decision process when it leads to action, and the desired action may vary from ad to ad.

### *Advertising Influences Financial Performance*

Advertising has been shown in several studies to influence the financial performance of companies. Several studies, for example, found that investment in advertising has a positive effect on business performance;[1] however, the effect is not universal. Another study found that standardizing advertising messages across countries led to stronger financial performance, for example.[2] While Wannamaker, quoted earlier this chapter, may not have been able to pick a specific element in his advertising that influenced firm performance, research has since made significant strides in understanding what drives financial results.

## Advertising Strategy

Advertising strategy consists of two elements: the creative plan and the media plan. Essentially, the **creative plan** is determining what the content of the message will be (encoding), whereas the **media plan** is choosing the channel of communication. Both plans should result from objectives set for the advertising communication. From the Field 11–1 illustrates how Paul Taroli integrates marketing and promotion strategy.

### *Determining Advertising Objectives*

Advertising objectives include performance objectives (what the advertising should do) and the audience (with whom the firm wishes to communicate). Setting objectives is important in order to evaluate the success of the advertising and to learn what works and what doesn't, particularly as one can't always observe an immediate change in sales due to an advertising campaign.

As we discussed in the previous chapter, marketing communications objectives include both position and action goals. In Exhibit 11–1, we list a number of such objectives (and measures of performance) that are commonly used for advertising.

At the same time, objectives should state the intended audience. For example, if Bendix is promoting new braking technology for heavy trucks, the audience could be engineers who design new models, fleet managers who purchase finished trucks, or technicians who maintain trucks. Given that Bendix is positioning itself as the safety and innovation leader, drivers may also be an important audience as they will demand safer vehicles. And, since heavy trucks are capital equipment, the chief financial officer may also be involved in purchases so that could be another audience. One campaign may include messages targeted to all of these audiences or may focus on one specific audience; the objectives should state which audience.

---

**11–1**

## FROM THE FIELD

## Integrating Offerings with Marketing Communications

As director of marketing for a business services company, part of my responsibility is to figure out what five or six market factors will drive our business and then leverage those factors. Our company has three divisions: a global outsourcing division, a division that integrates software into business processes, and the consulting organization. I'm responsible for the marketing for the consulting organization. That means I'm involved in pricing, product development, and promotion strategy.

We have 15 geographic markets and each geographic market, run by a geographic marketing director (GMD), has several vertical sales forces. For example, in New York, one vertical is fashion/retailing; in Denver, a sales force calls on the defense and aerospace vertical market.

One member of my team gathers two critical pieces of data each year: GMDs' perspectives on what's hot and what's not for the next year and their three-year strategy. We then cross that with our solutions and offerings—our products. If strategies and our solutions and offerings don't line up, then we have a problem. Either our products aren't right or the GMDs' strategies aren't. It is then my responsibility to bring our strategies and our offerings back into alignment.

Then we plan our marketing strategy. People buy services from smart people, so a key part of our strategy is to put as many of our people out as speakers at conferences and trade shows as we can. Two members of my team plan and implement all of those events. Another member of the team handles major events, events where we may spend well over $100,000 to exhibit and speak. We also commission research on important business trends and issues so that when our people speak they have something to say. These research reports also help position us as thought leaders.

Another strategy is to comarket with our partners. For example, we work with companies like Oracle (a leading business software provider) to advertise together, stretching our advertising dollars. Then we'll also participate in Oracle Open World, a trade show for Oracle's customers.

We also run our own events, of which the most important is the Executive Exchange. We spend about $1.5 million on the Executive Exchange. Three times a year, we'll bring chief executives together to hear featured speakers like Steve Forbes, John Ashcroft, and other business celebrities. For us, the benefit is in building relationships with these chief executives. We learn from them what they are most interested in, what they need the most help with, and other information that we can then use to create the right services. Plus, they get to know us and realize that they can rely on us to do what they need.

Paul Taroli, Senior Partner and Marketing Director, CSC.

---

### Determining the Creative Plan

The creative plan begins with the creative strategy statement, which is a summary of the strategy objectives. If the desired position for Bendix is based on building its reputation for safety and innovation, then the creative strategy may be "To strengthen our position as the leading innovator that makes better safety features standard."

From the creative strategy statement, an appeal would be developed. The appeal can be based on rational motives (such as showing increased profit) or emotional motives (how the decision maker might spend the extra profit). For example, United Van Lines' corporate moving division's ad has "Dependabity" as its headline, followed by a list of reasons to choose United. This rational appeal is very different from Group 1 Software's emotional appeal, "Do you know which of your leads will turn into sales?" Exhibit 11–2 illustrates how one company included both types of appeals in one ad on the Web. Then marketing

**Exhibit 11–1**
Examples of
Advertising
Objectives

### Positioning Objectives

- Develop the brand. (Conduct surveys to determine brand's personality among the audience members.)
- Create a favorable climate for personal sales calls. (Examine sales call reports regarding the ability to see new accounts of other hard-to-reach accounts.)
- Support other communication channels. (Observe results of other channels.)
- Stimulate derived demand. (Observe sales of product later in the value chain.)
- Project a financially healthy image. (Examine reports by financial analysts.)
- Support distributors or other resellers. (Count the number of distributors who feature our product in their advertising or promotion.)
- Create favorable image among difficult-to-reach influencers. (Conduct surveys of attitudes among those individuals.)

### Action Objectives

- Generate leads for field or telemarketing salespeople. (Count leads.)
- Increase attendance at a trade show. (Compare the number of visitors at the booth this year and last year.)
- Increase distribution of catalogs. (Sum the number of telephone calls asking for the catalog.)
- Secure investment in company through sale of stock or other methods. (Observe stock sales.)
- Generate sales. (Observe sales.)

**Exhibit 11–2**
Appeal Ad
Example.
This Web site
presents both an
emotional appeal
(avoid pitfalls) and
a rational appeal
(accurate data—
effective
communications).

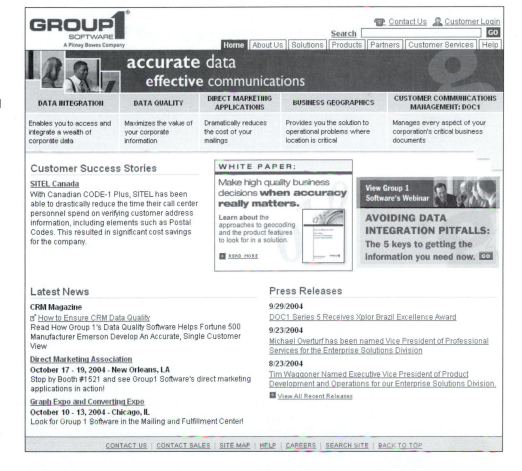

**Exhibit 11–3**
Avoiding
Common B2B
Advertising
Mistakes
According to
a survey of
marketing
professionals,
business advertising
frequently makes
one or more
mistakes. Here are
the mistakes listed
by respondents,
from the most
frequent to the
least, along with
ideas for avoiding
those mistakes.

| Typical Ads Have | What Should Be Done |
|---|---|
| Too much information | Highlight one important benefit—from the customer's perspective |
| Failed to address audience's needs, concerns, questions, or problems | Focus on the problem being solved |
| Too much corporate "chest-pounding" | Avoid over-sensationalizing company capabilities |
| Lack human interest, emotion, or passion | What are the people benefits, not just the business benefits? Tell a story. |
| Too safe—no creative risk | Invoke creativity—get out of the office and into the minds of the buyer |
| Lack visual interest | Place products and benefits in unusual or unrelated contexts |
| Lack of continuity across campaigns or even within a campaign | Create a positioning and branding strategy, then use that to drive creative strategy |

SOURCE: Based on Kate Maddox, "Marketing Messages Missing the Mark," *BtoB* (January 14, 2003), pp. 3–4.

managers would decide copy, theme, colors, headlines, and other creative elements. Every element of the advertisement would then contribute to achieving the creative objectives.

When developing a creative plan, the marketer implicitly bases that plan on a theory of how the buyer buys. For example, if the marketer believes that most buyers in the target audience are offensive (that is, they want to maximize gain as opposed to minimizing loss), then the ads may be like IBM's e-business ads that ran in *Economic Times,* a European and Asian business daily. These ads presented success stories of how IBM's servers enabled e-business and made someone a hero. Similarly, Intel ran a series of ads in *Economic Times* that were focused on defensive buyers. These ads focused on Intel's reliability, raising the fear of what could happen with less-reliable processors.

As you can see in Exhibit 11–3, business marketers typically fail to create exciting and engaging advertising. In fact, in a study conducted by Mobium of business professionals, 74 percent said business advertising typically has too much information and fails to connect with buyers. Exhibit 11–3 presents the results of the study, along with ideas to avoid creating "typical" advertising.

## Media Selection

BASF, featured in an earlier chapter, uses a lot of television advertising compared to the average business marketing firm. Other forms of media include radio, outdoor advertising (billboards, signs on buses, etc.), as well as magazines and the Internet. Choosing the particular form of media is a function of cost and access. In other words, what does it cost to access the market? Another consideration is the quality of the message possible. Print ads are not the same as television ads, for example, and each medium has its communication advantages and disadvantages.

### Magazines
Most business marketers rely on **trade publications,** or magazines written for a particular trade, profession, or industry. Popular business press, such as *BusinessWeek* and *The Wall Street Journal,* are also important. One particular form of popular press with business advertisers is in-flight magazines, such as American Airlines' *American Way* magazine. Business advertisers favor these magazines because the readership includes a high percentage of business travelers.

## 11–1

## BUSINESS 2 BUSINESS

When Bendix announced the Customer Value Leadership award, the award represented several important new technologies. Because these technologies were so new, some potential buyers did not believe that the new systems were that effective. The award provided objective third-party verification that the systems are effective in making trucks safer. But other awards, most notably Good Housekeeping's Seal of Approval in the consumer market, can be purchased. How does an ethical business marketer leverage an honest award without raising cynicism among buyers? Even purchased "awards" are subject to some level of scrutiny as the givers of the award crave credibility, so should a business marketer participate in such a program?

As with most forms of marketing communication, marketers want to know that their advertising dollars are being spent on communicating with their desired market. For that reason, magazines with **controlled circulation** (distribution only to qualified readers) have been developed. The magazines are distributed free to qualified readers, and *qualified* usually means that the readers play at least an influential role in the buying process. Because the magazine does not allow subscriptions to anyone who does not meet the purchasing criteria and because the magazine focuses on a particular profession or industry, advertising can be efficient because few readers will be nonbuyers for advertised products. Still, because these are nonpaid subscriptions, some advertisers wonder if these magazines are read. The readership of trade magazines, whether circulation is controlled or open, is verified by an independent company; the verification is called a **circulation audit.** Circulation audits tell marketers who gets the magazine; therefore, the marketers can determine if their ads are reaching the right buyers.

Audience quality is the most important variable to consider when selecting a publication. Audience quality is high when the readership of the magazine is composed of important decision makers and key influencers for the advertised product. Some trade magazines, however, are more like new product brochures with very little editorial content or articles. Buyers are likely only to scan these types of magazines, whereas magazines with strong editorial content are likely to be read more carefully. Ads in magazines with well-written articles relevant to your audience can have greater impact because the buyer spends more time with the magazine.

Overlap between trade publications should be considered when selecting magazines. For example, the trade show industry is served by *Trade Show and Exhibit Manager, Exhibitor Times, The Exhibitor,* and *Trade Show Week.* One study by Cahners Publishing Company found that, in general, advertising in three magazines reaches only 2 percent more of the audience than advertising in two magazines, because most professionals read more than one magazine. **Reach** is the total number of buyers that see an ad. If Freeman Exhibit Company, for example, advertises in those magazines plus general marketing magazines like *Potentials in Marketing,* then overlap may waste advertising dollars by duplicating reach.

At the same time, however, overlap can help companies achieve the frequency of readership. **Frequency** is the number of times a potential buyer is exposed to an ad. Again, the choice of media should reflect overlap but be based on goals for frequency as well as reach.

**Cost per thousand (CPM)** readers is a critical variable in selecting trade publications and can be calculated by dividing the cost of an ad's space by the number of readers (in thousands). For example, it may cost $600 to place an ad in *Potentials in Marketing.* If the readership includes a potential 2,000 buyers for the product advertised, then the CPM is $300 (or $600/2). Although the publisher will quickly give CPM for the overall readership, it is important to recognize that not all readers are in the target audience. An astute marcomm manager will calculate CPM on the basis of the total number of prospects in the total audience.

### Broadcast Media

Television and radio are forms of broadcast media, and the audience is audited. In most cases, though, the audits do not determine the position or industry of a listener or viewer, so many members of the audience may not be part of the desired market. Therefore, there is more waste, or advertising that reaches unintended audiences, because only a small portion of the audience represents potential prospects. Sometimes, however, products have an appeal wide enough to warrant television and radio. Office products, for example, are not limited to a particular industry or profession. Southwest Airlines' "You Are Now Free to Move About the Country" campaign is designed to attract business travelers who must travel frequently and within a budget. In cases such as office products and airline travel, broadcast advertising (both TV and radio) can be useful in building sales.

Companies also use broadcast media to build company images or to position a company. The BASF ads mentioned in Chapter 1 are a good example of corporate advertising that positions the company.

Television provides an advantage that the previously discussed advertising media cannot match. Television combines both sound and visuals, including full motion. Ads on TV can have more impact or involve the prospect more fully than ads in other media. On the other hand, the audience watching a particular TV show may not have enough prospects in it to justify the expense, and some argue that TV watchers are less involved than magazine readers.

Radio can also deliver the frequency and reach of TV and at a much more affordable rate. By advertising during commute time, radio advertisers believe that they are reaching their audience of business decision makers. The medium also allows for a high degree of creativity. With short production times, ads can be easily and inexpensively altered should the need arise. One difficulty with radio, however, is that it is difficult to purchase national coverage. Radio is used most often to encourage action within a local market and can also be used to support TV advertising. For example, Southwest Airlines also has a radio version of their "Free to Move" campaign.

## Outdoor Media

Outdoor media are any signage that advertises a business, and can include rented locations such as billboards, the sides of buses, street furniture (like a bus stop), and others. Outdoor media can also include signs on the company's delivery trucks. Research shows that business marketers use outdoor media to reach concentrations of buyers, such as visitors to a trade show. For example, billboards between the Dallas Convention Center and the convention hotels advertised the Canon line of digital equipment at a recent office equipment show. Recall also that there are industries concentrated in specific areas, and there are industrial parks where outdoor advertising may be effective.

Outdoor advertising is not used a great deal in business marketing; however, when concentrations of buyers exist, it can be quite effective.[3] Outdoor advertising can also be used to create derived demand; for example, outside an Owens Corning glass plant was a billboard that beer is better in a bottle, perhaps a reminder to the plant employees!

## Electronic Media

Electronic media include the Internet and World Wide Web. Home pages serve as a form of advertising that the audience seeks. The effectiveness of home pages is often measured in "hits" (the number of times someone looked at the page), yet many service providers, which provide advertisers with space for home pages, also audit the readership of those home pages so that advertisers know who hit the page. Creative home pages are often hit by other people who have to make their own home pages, by competitors, by the curious, and by accident, which means that some hits aren't worth counting. Additionally, even though someone may hit a site repeatedly, it is difficult to determine new hits from repeats without an audit service.

Another limitation is that anyone can put just about anything on the Web. Credibility of messages is somewhat suspect to many potential buyers.

Many advantages exist, however, for Web advertising. First, it can be *interactive*. The person has to choose to enter a company's home page so there is more active participation than when reading a magazine, and the ad is next to the text of an article. Readers then select the additional information they want, clicking only on what interests them. They choose the advertising they want, making readership more valuable because they already have an interest. Click-through is another measurement, and it is a measure of how deep into a Web site the visitor goes.

In addition, the Web can be more *responsive*. Because visitors can choose from a wide array of information, they can get their answers more quickly, especially with search capabilities. Many sites also offer the opportunity to chat with a representative by simply clicking on an icon. Other sites may only offer e-mail contact methods but even these are seen by visitors as opportunities to communicate with the vendor. Any communication from buyers can also be captured and analyzed for any patterns, such as growing interest in a particular offering or signaling the possibility for a potential offering.

Such was the case for the Faucet Outlet, a discount plumbing supply house. Initially, the company relied on catalogs mailed to plumbers, builders, and other plumbing supplies buyers. In just a year, however, sales taken from browsers of the company's online catalog represent 5 percent of the company's total business, and that amount is growing rapidly.

One problem with the Net is that searching for vendors can be difficult. IBEX, the International Business Exchange launched by the U.S. Chamber of Commerce, is one virtual marketplace designed to overcome that limitation. Companies that have IBEX software can enter offers to buy or sell, which are then matched. Through secure electronic mail, negotiation can take place between matches, anonymously if preferred. Once an agreement is reached, IBEX also offers both parties the ability to review each other's profiles, an important consideration when extending credit or depending on a vendor to supply a crucial product. Because IBEX is not an Internet service but a private network, users expect IBEX to provide greater security for transactions—still a major concern for transactions conducted over the Net.

Banner advertising on the Net can also attract attention. Banners are those small advertisements that you see when you use a search engine like Yahoo or Lycos. Some experts have begun to question the effectiveness of banner advertising, as click-through rates have declined to only 1 percent. However, brand awareness increases an average of 6 percent for those companies that use banner ads, so any evaluation should be based on the appropriate objective.[4]

## Directories

Industrial buyers sometimes use directories to locate potential suppliers. Unlike consumers who can just open a phone book, organizational buyers cannot always find

## Exhibit 11–4
### Advertising Measures

| Measure | How It Is Calculated | How It Is Used |
|---|---|---|
| Recall | Surveys of magazine readers (or television viewers) asking which ads they remember seeing. | Did the ad attract attention? Was it remembered? Assumption is that if the ad is remembered, it was effective. |
| Inquiries | Sum of bingo cards, faxbacks, or calls to the 800 number in an ad. | Did the ad cause readers to take action? Were the people who responded really interested in buying the product? |
| Position | Preadvertisement and postadvertisement surveys of attitudes toward a product. | Did the ad change the market's attitudes toward our product? Is the attitude now what we want it to be relative to attitudes about our competitors' products? |
| Reach | Using circulation or readership audits, the number of readers among the target market is calculated. | Does this magazine reach our desired audience? Used to assess media choices, rather than the effectiveness of a particular advertisement. |
| CPM (cost per thousand) | Divide cost by readership, expressed in thousands. | How does the reach of this magazine compare to the reach of a similar magazine, relative to how much each charges? Again, used to assess media choice. |

suppliers in the Yellow Pages. Specialized directories, though, can serve the same purpose. Many trade publications include an annual directory of companies for a particular industry. There are also directories in which companies buy space. As in the phone book, companies are listed but can also purchase ads. Most directories are now electronic, available on the Web rather than published. For example, Manufacturers' News Inc. publishes a number of directories, available in book format or on a CD or as a database (see **www.mnstore.com**).

### *Measuring Advertising Performance*

Advertising performance is like all other forms of marketing performance; to evaluate whether advertising worked, the advertising manager must compare results with objectives. The real challenge, though, is to create measures that can enable that type of analysis. For example, if the objective was to change a position, then postadvertising surveys determining the relative position of the advertised product should be developed. (Refer back to Exhibit 11–1 for a list of objectives and measures.) All too often, though, objectives are set around what can be measured, such as the number of inquiries or CPM, which may not reflect the original objectives.

Another factor of concern to marcomm managers is the need to determine the efficiency of advertising. Efficiency is usually determined by comparing inputs with outputs or, in this case, advertising dollars are compared with results. Efficiency is relative, not absolute, meaning that we must compare a new advertising campaign against an old one or compare two new campaigns in test markets to learn which campaign is more efficient. Exhibit 11–4 lists different measures commonly used to measure advertising results.

# PUBLIC RELATIONS

**Public relations** is the management function that focuses on the relationships and communications with individuals and groups in order to create mutual goodwill.[5] Some people define public relations (PR) as the quality of relationships with the various

# Public Affairs

Many people contact companies for many different reasons. Schoolchildren may write to learn more about business, a local government official may ask about a company policy, a local journalist calls with questions about employment figures, or a charity calls asking for a donation. All of these inquiries must be handled, and it is usually through a public affairs office. **Public affairs** is the part of PR that deals with community groups. In addition to the inbound examples just mentioned, there are two types of public affairs: lobbying and community involvement.

### Lobbying

**Lobbying** is any attempt to persuade a government official or governing body to adopt policies, procedures, or legislation in favor of the lobbying group or organization. Lobbying is an important activity and can affect the outcomes of planned mergers and acquisitions, product introductions and recalls, marketing communication activities, and other activities of the firm. While we were writing this chapter, the government announced new regulations concerning oil exploration. You can imagine that many environmental groups actively lobbied against the new regulations but oil companies were lobbying for them.

### Community Involvement

A form of public relations is a company's community involvement. Such involvement can range from sponsoring a children's soccer team to underwriting the costs of charity events to loaning an executive to run a charitable organization. Many companies use their PR department to create relationships with organizations that can benefit from the companies' participation. The PR departments then secure participation from employees.

# TRADE SHOW MARKETING

The trade show, or exhibition, industry is an exciting one because of the complexity of trade show plans, the excitement of traveling to exotic locales, and the pressure of managing the details necessary to pull a show together. In this section, we will examine trade shows primarily from the perspective of the exhibit manager. We'll also introduce the various service providers in this industry and discuss how trade show strategy is developed.

# The Importance of Trade Shows

Trade shows rank second only to advertising in terms of the marketing communication budget (taking out personal selling). For that reason only, trade shows are important. The biggest reasons that shows are important are that buyers depend more on trade shows, trade shows can provide an opportunity for dialogue, and trade shows reach buyers that salespeople have not. Lest you think, though, that shows are only about meeting potentially new customers, shows are important because of the opportunity to strengthen customer relationships. Relationships with the trade press can also be developed at shows.

# Setting Trade Show Goals

Seeing current customers, creating new customers, and strengthening relationships with the press—all are important functions of trade shows. Goals can and should be set for each function, yet most companies focus only on the acquisition of new customers. New customer goals include the number of leads, the number of sales, and the number of visitors to the booth; 3M Medical Imaging Systems, a company that manufactures X-ray and other medical imaging equipment, uses all three. It also sets goals for current customers, including the number of current customers who attend a function or visit the booth. 3M Medical Imaging salespeople are encouraged to set goals for each of their accounts who may attend. An example of such a goal might be to introduce a decision maker to a key executive in order to strengthen the relationship.

Companies should also consider press goals, or goals for meeting members of the media. 3M Medical Systems sets goals including the number of interviews given, number of people who attend press conferences, and number of media packets distributed. It also sets goals for the amount of press actually generated at a show and evaluates its ability to actually get its story in print after the show is over.

Setting goals depends on the overall marketing strategy. For example, when 3M Medical Imaging Systems introduced a new product, press goals included the number of mentions of the product in the trade media. The highest-priority lead goal was the number of leads for that product. Then, based on these goals, the strategy for the show is determined.

Once goals are set, the next step is to select shows. Show selection is like media selection in advertising; many of the same issues such as reach have to be considered.

# Show Selection

One of the primary responsibilities of an exhibit manager is selecting shows in which to exhibit. Factors that affect the decision include the expected audience at the show, the type of show, and the cost of exhibiting. Selecting a show is basically a process of comparing the number of potential prospects at the show with the cost of exhibiting. As in advertising, choice may be made on the basis of cost per exposure.

Two measurements can be useful in predicting the number of prospects at a show: net buying influences and total buying plans. **Net buying influences** is the percentage of show audience that has influence in the buying process for the specific product exhibited. A trade show audience may include students, job seekers, competitors, members of the press, and other nonbuyers, as you can see in Exhibit 11–6. Additionally, not every buyer in the audience buys for every exhibited product category.

**Total buying plans** is the percentage of the audience planning to buy exhibited products within the next 12 months. Both figures, total buying plans and net buying influences, are often available from show management for the most recent show and can be used to predict audience quality for the next show.

Other reasons for choosing a show may include the amount of press that participate and whether competition is there. Sometimes, not exhibiting may send negative signals to a market so companies can get locked into exhibiting at some shows just to show that their business is healthy. In addition, buyers go to shows because of the opportunity to examine a large number of vendors' offerings in one convenient place. The more competitors present, the more buyers who will attend.[6] Going where competitors go can be wise.

Choice may also be made on the basis of show type. There are several types of shows in which to exhibit: trade association conventions versus for-profit shows, regional versus national and global shows, and horizontal versus vertical shows.

**Exhibit 11–6**
Percentage of Attendees by Role in Buying
Twenty-nine percent of first-time trade show attendees and 40 percent of repeat attendees have final say in the purchase of products exhibited, whereas 22 percent and 15 percent, respectively, have no role in purchase.
*SOURCE: Center for Exhibition Industry Research, "Power of Trade Shows."*

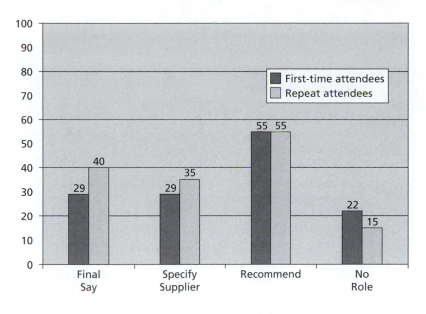

## Association-Sponsored versus For-Profit

Association-sponsored shows are exhibitions that occur as a sideline to a convention and conference of a trader or professional association. For example, the California Dental Association has an annual convention that includes seminars on the latest dental practices plus an exhibition of dental equipment. Sometimes, companies exhibit at association shows in order to support the organization.

Some shows are created and run by for-profit companies. For example, the American Contract Manufacturers' Shows (Amcon) is a company that produces exhibitions for contract manufacturers. Seminars occur in conjunction with the show, but the primary focus is on the exhibition.

The exhibition portion of an association conference can be a big moneymaker for the association. Attendance at the conference may be higher than at a for-profit show, but actual attendance through the exhibits can be low if attendees come only for the seminars. On the other hand, many marketers also seek to present at the seminars, thus increasing their visibility.

## Regional versus National or Global

Amcon shows are regional, which means that several versions of the show are held in various locations around the country. The California Dental Association is another regional show. Regional shows attract both regional exhibitors and regional attendees. Regional shows are usually the least expensive to participate in because they are smaller shows. Many exhibitors may not have a booth but simply use a table to display their offerings.

An interesting trend is that *regional* does not mean *domestic;* with NAFTA, some regional shows are international, drawing visitors from either Canada or Mexico, depending on the show's location. Shows that move from location to location each year and serve regions near a border are including Mexican or Canadian cities in their site selection. CeBIT Hanover Fair is the world's largest telecommunications show and brings visitors and exhibitors from all over the world to Hanover, Germany. Choosing a regional, national, or global show depends on one's market and marketing strategy.

**Exhibit 11–7**
Leading Trade
Shows in the
United States
by Industry
Classification

| | Number of Shows | Number of Attendees |
|---|---|---|
| Gifts and merchandising | 29 | 725,300 |
| Manufacturing and engineering | 29 | 633,720 |
| Computer and electronics | 20 | 828,540 |
| Jewelry and apparel | 18 | 270,700 |
| Sports and recreation | 17 | 347,980 |
| Hospitality and service | 14 | 254,410 |
| Food and beverage | 13 | 252,690 |
| Medical and related fields | 11 | 139,950 |
| Housewares—home and office | 8 | 135,175 |
| Broadcast and communications | 7 | 120,900 |
| Print—publishing and paper | 7 | 88,630 |
| Automotive and trucking | 6 | 122,450 |

SOURCE: Center for Exhibition Industry Research, "A Guide to the U.S. Exposition Industry."

### Vertical versus Horizontal

A **vertical show** is one that focuses on one industry or profession. Certainly, both Amcon and the California Dental Association meetings are vertical. Business expos sponsored by chambers of commerce or by the U.S. Department of Commerce to spur local and interregional business are examples of **horizontal shows,** or shows that include many industries and professions. For example, CinterMex, the convention center in Monterrey, Mexico, hosts an annual horizontal show designed to increase trade between Monterrey and Texas. The trend, though, is to vertical shows that narrowly define their target market. The narrower the audience, the more efficient trade show dollars can be because, with proper show selection, a larger percentage of the audience is more likely to be prospects. As you can see in Exhibit 11–7, the top 10 types of shows are vertical shows.

# Show Marketing Strategy

Once a show is selected, marketing for the show involves three sets of activities:[7]

- Preshow promotion
- Show management
- Postshow follow-up

   The challenge facing the exhibit manager is that a complete marketing plan is required just for the trade show! Considering the attendee's show experience as the product, the exhibit manager is responsible for designing a product, promoting that product, and then following up with the customer.

## Preshow Promotion

Preshow promotion activities include direct mail and advertising as well as invitations from salespeople. Telemarketing is also done but to a lesser degree. Preshow advertising promoting booth attendance, if done at all, usually consists of a sunburst saying "Visit Us at Booth #215 at *(name of show)*" added to current advertising.

There are two schools of thought concerning direct mail (including e-mail), which is the most popular form of preshow promotion. One school of thought is to mail to all preregistered attendees (or to all preregistered attendees who meet certain criteria). The objective here is to increase share of attendance or to increase the percentage of attendees visiting the booth.

Another school of thought is to e-mail all potential attendees from the company's own database and invite them to attend. Many shows may attract as much as 60 to 70 percent of the audience from the region, even though shows are global. When that is the case, a regional campaign may be more effective. This is the strategy that Paul Taroli and his team at CSC use.

On the other hand, research indicates that invitations from exhibiting companies are a primary reason that buyers attend.[8] Alcatel, the French telecom company, combines blanket direct mail with special invitations by salespeople. Salespeople call or hand deliver invitations to prospects to encourage them to attend. The risk is that a prospect may visit a competitor's booth; on the other hand, if a competitor invites the prospect, the prospect may never visit the Alcatel booth. Alcatel uses invitations to increase the motivation to attend and to help build stronger relationships.

## The Show Experience

Strategy for the show experience usually involves three elements: the attention getter, the message, and the close. Careful consideration of all three elements can not only increase the likelihood of success for the show, but also increase the synergy of the show with other messages in other media.

### The Attention Getter

The attention getter influences attendees to enter the booth. Invitations and offers for free gifts may encourage some attendees to stop by, but others either won't receive the invitation or will throw it away. As people wander the aisles of the trade show floor, booth design should include attention-getting elements that will entice visitors off the aisle and into the booth.

At the same time, however, some attention getters can bring everybody into the booth, whether you want them or not. Magic acts, free pictures with a movie star, comedy routines—all are used as attention getters. Express Personnel, for example, used a NASCAR simulation at one show, generating $1.2 million in new sales.[9] If the audience contains a high proportion of prospects, then these types of attention getters can be worthwhile. At times, however, such attention getters can work too well, resulting in wasted time for booth staff who have to deal with unwanted visitors. The challenge, then, is to attract attention but only the attention of the desired audience.

One strategy is to hook an attendee's attention and then move the desired attendee into another area of the booth for the appropriate interaction. Visitors who do not qualify as prospects are then free to leave as soon as the show is over. For example, Freeman Exhibit Co. recently used a mind reader as the attention getter. His show focused on Freeman capabilities. When the show was finished, sales staff met with interested visitors and then invited them to other areas of the booth for one-on-one conversations.

### The Message

Constructing the message is an important element in trade show strategy. Two considerations influence the construction of the show message. First, what are the positioning objectives for the products and services being offered; and, second, what are the action objectives? Any message must be consistent and integrated with messages sent via other channels.

Most of the message is delivered by the booth staff. Selecting staff appropriately is a delicate decision. Because the show experience is in person and results in sales leads, salespeople should want to participate. Salespeople, though, often dislike being away from their sales territory and may resist fulfilling their trade show responsibility. Technical staff, such as product development engineers, can provide visitors with the technical information they desire. Technical staff, though, may need supplemental training to prepare for the selling environment of a show. Top management is also needed.

### The Close

Because the show experience is face to face, it should end with some indication of an agreement concerning what should happen next. Asking for this agreement is the close. The close may be a request to have a salesperson call, to send information, or whatever else is appropriate for the situation. If the visitor is ready to move to the next step in the purchase process, then the staff member in the booth should note that information so that the appropriate follow-up can occur. The staff member, however, will never realize what follow-up is appropriate unless the visitor is asked. Exhibit managers should always specify how to close to staff members and how to record the information for postshow follow-up.

## Postshow Follow-up

Postshow follow-up is a critical element in the trade show marketing mix. In industries such as fashion, toys, and hardware, retailers place orders at the show. At most business marketing shows, however, few sales are made at the show, at least in the United States. (In Europe, more companies are likely to purchase at the show.) Getting the sales force to follow up on leads generated at the show is an important function.

### Lead Follow-up

After the conversation at the booth, booth staff enter information into the CRM system or into a contact management system provided by the show's organizer. At most shows, visitors have a name badge that can be swiped through a card reader which then downloads the visitor's name and contact information. The booth staff then add additional information such as the prospect's interest, needs, budget, and other data gathered during the visit. At the end of the show (or in some cases, at the end of each day), the data are then downloaded into the company's own CRM system, such as Applicor or Siebel, and the salesperson is immediately notified. Not only does the salesperson get the lead, but also all of the notes form the conversation, and can then follow up with sales calls.

Exhibit Surveys Inc. finds that up to 80 percent of the trade show visitors make a purchase soon after the show, usually within 30 days and that these visitors had not previously been contacted by a salesperson. That's why it is so important for salespeople to follow up immediately. In addition, most CRM systems like Siebel or Eloqua track the sale too. This information can then be used to measure how effective shows are.

### Communication

Shows are a venue in which a great deal of useful market information is available. Getting that information shared is an important element in a learning organization if learning is to result from the show. Information about new competitive products and programs (such as discount programs or joint marketing efforts like the Intel software partnerships) can be learned at shows. While at Rockwell, one of your authors had the job of going to competitors' booths and collecting brochures, as well as taking notes during competitors' presentations. This information was later used by the sales force in order to learn and understand competitors' strategies, as well as by the marketing staff.

In addition to competitive information, customer information is available. The seminar agenda can provide insight into key issues that your customers are facing. For example, if several seminars are presented on the subject of government regulation, then you can be sure that government regulation is an important issue for your customers. Companies that can respond, perhaps by helping customers comply with those regulations, will increase their market share.

Visitors to the booth respond to new products and programs. Learning organizations can take this feedback and use it to adjust marketing programs or new product introductions. For example, prospects may suggest minor changes to the product. If there is a mechanism for capturing that information and passing it along to the appropriate product developers, then important changes can occur. Otherwise, the information is lost and the company has missed a useful learning opportunity.

Postshow follow-up is an important activity but can often get lost in the rush to get ready for the next show. Yet it is really in the follow-up that the potential of trade shows is realized. Effective trade show marketers are effective because they don't allow their success at the show to wither and die for lack of follow-up.

# Other Events

Trade shows are not the only events that companies use to create an environment conducive for building stronger relationships or showing offerings. For example, as Paul Taroli mentioned in the From the Field, his company hosts the Executive Exchange, an event just for CSC customers. Richard Langlotz, of Konica Minolta, hosts a Technology Showcase once a quarter. Local former and current athletes and celebrities such as Roger Staubach (Dallas Cowboys) and Mark Texiera (Texas Rangers) will speak and sign autographs, but the focus is on introducing buyers to the latest products.

Another form of promotion is the event sponsorship. For example, Caterpillar has sponsored PGA (professional golf) events. Sponsors are able to bring customers or prospects, entertain them in a VIP tent, and spend time getting to know them. The benefits of sponsorship, though, can extend beyond entertaining customers. Research indicates that brand messages can be communicated to those potential buyers who attend, and any positive connotations associated with the event itself can also transfer to the sponsor.[10] For example, a golf fan that also works in chemicals may transfer positive connotations to BASF should BASF sponsor the U.S. Open, even though that buyer may not meet with BASF representatives at the event.

## Using Specialty Advertising

**Specialty advertising** is the use of products to advertise another product or company— for example, putting a company's name on pens and pencils, and then giving those away. Specialty advertising, also called premiums, freebies, and giveaways, is an important part of the trade show marketing mix, which is why we are discussing it now, but can be used with field sales or given through direct mail.

With **Split premiums,** which are becoming popular, half of the freebie is mailed to the prospect; the other half is given to the prospect after listening to the sales pitch at the booth. For example, a company might send one cufflink or earring in the mail, with the second available at the booth. Other popular forms of specialty advertising include premiums involving sports stars and other celebrities. For example, a common tactic is to have a professional baseball player sign baseballs that are given to attendees.

Another popular form of premium is something that will be used regularly, because any premium used regularly by the recipient has greater value to both the recipient and marketing company. The recipient appreciates the gift more, creating greater goodwill. The recipient also sees the marketing message more, increasing the value to the marketer.

Keep in mind that specialty advertising can be used in a number of ways, not just at trade shows. Specialty advertising can include logo-embossed merchandise given by salespeople to prospects, included in direct response mailings, or distributed through other methods. Specialty advertising is, however, very popular in trade show marketing because of its ability to lure potential buyers to the booth.

## Measuring Exhibit Performance

As we said earlier about advertising performance, the marcomm manager must develop measures that enable comparisons between objectives and results. (Exhibit 11–8 lists trade show measures.) Most companies want to generate qualified sales leads at a show, but just counting the number of people who stop by, for example, doesn't result in a useful measure of performance. Companies should measure such things as the number of A leads as a percentage of the total audience. This measure is called **attraction efficiency** and tells how well a company did in getting people to its booth.

Another method of determining the return on a show is to estimate sales made as a result of show activities. Peterson Manufacturing, for example, estimates the number of sales that will be made by keeping track of prior shows' performance. The firm has learned that, for it, about 30 percent of qualified leads from a show will result in a certain level of sales over the next two years, which it can use immediately after a show to determine if the show was profitable.

**Exhibit 11–8**
Measures of Trade Show Performance

| Measure | How It Is Calculated | How It Is Used |
|---|---|---|
| Traffic counts | At various times of the day the number of visitors in the booth is counted, then multiplied by a factor of time available to determine total visitors. Simpler methods are to estimate the number of visitors based on the total number of brochures given out, business cards collected, etc. | Did our exhibit program bring people into our booth? Some companies will also count the number of people in the aisles in order to see how well the booth pulled people in. (What percentage of aisle traffic actually entered the booth?) |
| Direct mail redemption | The booth staff counts the number of direct mail pieces redeemed (turned in) at the booth. | If preshow invitations or split premiums were mailed to attract visitors, the redemption rates tell us how effective the preshow promotion went. |
| Attraction efficiency | Divide the number of qualified prospects by the total attendees who meet the same profile. (That number is available from show management.) | This number tells us how well our exhibit program did in attracting the right audience. |
| Total press coverage | Number of interviews, given number of attendees at press conferences, press visitors to the booth. | Although we can't measure PR effects until the press writes articles on our company, this can tell us if we attracted their attention at the show. |
| Anecdotes | The exhibit manager collects stories regarding which buyers came to the booth and what happened during their visit. | In some markets, a single sale can offset the cost of the exhibit program. Anecdotes provide exhibit managers with tangible evidence of exhibit success, examples that can flesh out what can be earned through other measures. |
| Recall | Postshow surveys by independent auditors ask attendees which booths they remember visiting. | Like recall measures in advertising, recall measures examine how memorable the booth experience was. |

# Summary

In this chapter, we've presented three methods of communicating with large audiences: advertising, public relations, and trade shows. Advertising is used to create awareness of the company and the product, to strengthen attitudes toward the company or product, and to lead buyers to act. Advertising strategy begins with setting specific communication objectives. Objectives can be related to the desired position or an action by the buyer.

At the same time, the objectives should include a description of the intended audience. Such a description makes media selection easier, and also helps the creator of the advertising to craft a relevant appeal. This appeal is further based on the creative strategy statement. Business marketers tend to rely more heavily on rational appeals, but emotional appeals are also used.

Media selection is the next step. Choices include trade publications (some of which have controlled circulation), electronic media such as the Internet, and broadcast media. Bingo cards, faxback, and e-mail provide the audience with an opportunity to communicate with the advertiser.

Public relations is also an important element in the total communications plan. Publicity and press agentry are two forms of public relations. Public affairs, including lobbying, is another important form of public relations.

Trade shows are an important element of the communications mix, combining the mass audience of advertising with personal communication. Shows are important to buyers, too, because buyers use shows to shop for suppliers. Like other forms of marketing communications, it is important to set specific and measurable goals for a show program. Show selection is based on the number of buying center participants among the audience, based on information collected by the show manager. There are many choices of shows, such as those reaching a national or global audience or an audience within one industry.

Trade show programs consist of preshow activities designed to build traffic to the booth, activities in the booth, and postshow follow-up. Specialty advertising is a common part of the trade show program and can be used to build traffic to the booth, as well as increase memorability of the company.

Business marketers are growing more sophisticated in their advertising, PR, and trade shows efforts. Further, these are areas of marketing with increasing opportunities for college marketing graduates, perhaps more so than with consumer marketers. As with direct marketing, the subject of the next chapter, the future looks especially bright for students interested in mass communication areas of business marketing.

# Key Terms

| | | |
|---|---|---|
| attraction efficiency | lobbying | public relations |
| circulation audit | media kit | publicity |
| controlled circulation | media plan | reach |
| CPM (cost per thousand) | net buying influences | specialty advertising |
| creative plan | news release | split premiums |
| evoked set | press agentry | total buying plans |
| frequency | press kit | trade publications |
| horizontal shows | press release | vertical shows |
| | public affairs | |

# Discussion Questions

1. Advertising and other forms of marketing communication are often accused of misleading buyers. Yet buyers use advertising, trade shows, and other such marketing to reduce risk. How can advertising and trade shows reduce buyer risk? Why does this apparent conflict exist, and what can marketers do to assure buyers that their marketing communications can be trusted?

2. There is a quote in the chapter: "I know half of my advertising works; I just don't know which half." What makes it so difficult to know whether advertising is working? Is this statement true about PR and trade shows, too?

3. "Sales are the lifeblood of this company. Any marketing communication that doesn't directly contribute to creating sales is wasted money." If you were the marketing communications manager, how would you justify advertising, PR, and trade shows to the VP of sales who made this comment?

4. What is the relationship of positioning statements and corporate strategy? Write out a separate positioning statement for FedEx, UPS, and the U.S. Postal Service with respect to corporate rapid delivery services. Base each statement on what you believe to be competitive advantages for each. Why is each one different from the others? How are these differences communicated in their advertising?

5. Schuster Electronics must sell to a buying center composed of design engineers, finance managers, purchasing agents, and others. How is it that an ad aimed at design engineers may upset finance managers and yet be ignored by purchasing agents?

6. A marcomm director has to choose three magazines in which to advertise. Assume they have equivalent editorial content. Given the following information about the magazines, which three should be chosen and why? Calculate CPM as part of your answer.

| | % of Readership | | | | Total Readers | Cost |
|---|---|---|---|---|---|---|
| | Users | Influencers | Decision Makers | Controllers | | |
| Magazine A | 15% | 18% | 8% | 5% | 30,000 | $780 |
| Magazine B | 22 | 32 | 12 | 0 | 17,500 | 550 |
| Magazine C | 16 | 12 | 12 | 3 | 19,000 | 550 |
| Magazine D | 8 | 5 | 23 | 14 | 11,000 | 400 |
| Magazine E | 18 | 21 | 9 | 4 | 33,000 | 800 |

7. How might advertising, PR, and trade shows change over the course of a product's life cycle? What is the role of branding over a life cycle?

8. What roles do advertising, PR, and trade shows play over the customer cycle of acquisition, retention, and growth?

9. Several examples were presented regarding business marketers' use of buying theories (see Chapter 4) in the design of their advertising. Assume you are marketing communications director for FedEx. Identify who (by title) you think would be involved in deciding shipping contracts, and create advertising messages for each member of the buying center using buying theories. Identify which theory you are using and how.

10. One of the advertising examples in the chapter discusses the use of fear appeals. Fear-based commercials have been criticized as unethical when aimed at consumers because these commercials can raise anxiety that consumers cannot easily alleviate; besides consumers did not give permission to be made to feel afraid. Should the standards regarding ethics for advertising be the same for business-to-business advertising? Why or why not?

# Cases

## Case 11.1   Vivaldi's New Maestro Software

Jill Vivaldi was excited about the focus group results. After six months of product development, it seemed clear that the market liked the functionality of her company's new line of software that was designed to help companies manage their suppliers. The software identified and compared all vendors with whom a company does business, enabling the company to combine orders and obtain larger quantity discounts. It also helped buyers manage bid processes, reverse auctions, and other electronic methods of purchasing as well as identified "rogue" purchases, or those purchases that were made by lower-level managers from companies that were not on the approved vendor list or for whom there was no existing contract.

Picking a name was one of the objectives for the focus groups, and the resulting name was a good one, thought Jill. Maestro would work well with Vivaldi Software.

The next challenge was to come up with a marketing communication plan to launch the new product. Preliminary research indicated that the buying center would be composed of the purchasing department (that would be the primary users), the information technology (IT) department (that would install and support the new software), and the chief financial officer (CFO). The CFO would have to provide budget dollars for the purchase, as well as evaluate the return on investment. Jill's biggest concern was that the software represents a very new concept for purchasing departments, many of whom were not well automated.

1. Create a one-sentence positioning statement for Maestro, as well as a slogan. Create a print ad based on the positioning statement and using the slogan. What other potential executions (versions) could be created? How would you alter the ad for different members of the buying center?

2. Jill is focusing on advertising. How could she use trade shows instead of or, in addition to, advertising?

3. How should she measure results for her advertising and any trade show efforts? Be specific.

### Case 11.2   SMH Corporation

Superior Materials Handling Corporation (SMH) manufactures and sells equipment used in moving products through manufacturing and warehousing facilities. Conveyor belts, roller systems, and other such products comprise the SMH product line.

But as Bart Nesbit, chief customer officer, has recognized, global competition has cut the margins on products off the shelf. The only offerings with good margins are those that require significant engineering and custom manufacturing. As he said to Ann Cartwright, marketing communications director, "We've got to move upmarket. We have to sell the standard systems, but to make our profit numbers, we've got to sell the custom-build and engineering services."

Ann agreed, "But our brand has stood for quality manufacturing, not engineering. Not that we couldn't do the engineering; it's just that with a slogan like 'Made to Last—Made by Superior,' it just doesn't get across the idea of our services."

"That may be," Bart nodded, "so you'll have to come up with some ideas on how to make this change."

As Ann thought about it, she knew that architects who specialize in industrial design were a critical element. They may not make the decision, but their clients should also be SMH clients. Also important were the contractors who built the warehouses and plants. Ultimately, though, it was usually a CEO, CFO, and the chief manufacturing officer or supply chain manager who made the final decision as to which engineering services would be used. And, since many custom jobs didn't involve architects or contractors as these jobs are designed into existing spaces, those other buyers were probably the most important anyway.

1. Should Ann create an offering with a completely different brand? If so, why, and what should it look like? If not, why not?

2. What role(s) should advertising, PR, and trade shows play in launching the new offering? Would those roles be different if the new offering were a new brand or an extension of the old brand?

   What information would you like to have to help make the decision and how would you get it?

# Additional Readings

Andersen, Poul Houman. "Relationship Marketing and Brand Involvement of Professionals through Web-Enhanced Brand Communities: The Case of Coloplast." *Industrial Marketing Management* 34 (January 2005), pp. 39–52.

Bendixen, Mike, Kalala A. Bukasa, and Russell Abratt. "Brand Equity in the B2B Market." *Industrial Marketing Management* 33 (2004), pp. 371–80.

Berthon, Pierre, Michael Ewing, Leyland Pitt, and Peter Naude. "Understanding B2B and the Web: The Acceleration of Coordination and Motivation." *Industrial Marketing Management* 32 (2003), pp. 553–61.

Borghini, Stefania, Francesca Golfetto, and Diego Rinallo. "Ongoing Search among Industrial Buyers." *Journal of Business Research* 59 (October 2006) pp. 1151–64.

Grove, Stephen J., Les Carlson, and Michael J. Dorsch. "Comparing the Application of Integrated Marketing Communication (IMC) in Magazine Ads across Product Type and Time." *Journal of Advertising* 36 (Spring 2007), pp. 37–54.

Gupta, Manak C., and C. Anthony Di Benedetto. "Optimal Pricing and Advertising Strategy for Introducing a New Business Product with Threat of Competitive Entry." *Industrial Marketing Management* 36 (May 2007), pp. 540–53.

Hellman, Karl. "Strategy-Driven B2B Promotions." *Journal of Business & Industrial Marketing* 20 (2005), pp. 4–11.

Ling-yee, Li. "Marketing Resources and Performance of Exhibitor Firms in Trade Shows: A Contingent Resource Perspective." *Industrial Marketing Management* 36 (April 2007), pp. 360–76.

MacDonald, Jason B., and Kirk Smith. "The Effects of Technology-Mediated Communication on Industrial Buyer Behavior." *Industrial Marketing Management* 33 (2004), pp. 107–16.

Naik, P. A., and K. Raman. "Understanding the Impact of Synergy in Multimedia Communications." *Journal of Marketing Research* 40 (October 2003) pp. 375–89.

Pitta, Dennis A., Margit Weisgal, and Peter Lynagh. "Integrating Exhibit Marketing into Integrated Marketing Communications." *Journal of Consumer Marketing* 23 (2006), pp. 156–66.

Smith, Timothy, Kazuyo Hama, and Paul Smith. "The Effect of Successful Trade Show Attendance on Future Show Interest: Japanese Attendee Perspectives of Domestic and Off-Shore International Events." *Journal of Business & Industrial Marketing* 18 (2003), pp. 403–18.

Stafford, Marla Royne. "International Services Advertising (ISA): Defining the Domain and Reviewing the Literature." *Journal of Advertising* 34 (Spring 2005) pp. 65–86.

# *Chapter 12*

## The One-to-One Media

### ZOOMINFO

ZoomInfo is a business information search engine that develops and maintains profiles on 36 million people and nearly 4 million companies. About 70 percent of its customers are corporate recruiters looking for managerial, creative, and technical talent in ZoomInfo's database. Still, some HR departments haven't yet learned to use Internet solutions.●

ZoomInfo has taken up the challenge of overcoming HR routines and aversion to change by striving to convince recruiters to request a demonstration and free trial of PowerSearch, its primary search engine. The marketing message emphasizes how PowerSearch can quickly help them find candidates that are in their own networks.●

ZoomInfo has created a great deal of content for its Webinars, case studies, white papers, and customer testimonials in its efforts to educate prospective buyers and bring them to the close. To get prospects to its Web site, ZoomInfo has utilized both direct mail and e-mail. In a recent test, e-mail beat direct mail hands down. The mail program used a clever "ransom note" concept, including a crumpled letter; the e-mail featured a simple cartoon image and subject copy: "Too many clowns wasting your time?"●

ZoomInfo credited the availability of good e-mail lists and the ability to link to its site in the e-mail copy to its superiority over the mail. Indeed, it can be hard to get people to type in a URL to visit a Web site. As a result of ongoing tests and adaptations in its programs in 2006, ZoomInfo tripled the number of leads for its sales team from 2005. While sales more than doubled, actual media costs declined. VP Russell Glass noted, '"We have made a few mistakes on messages and collateral, as well as media, but overall we find it is tough to make a big mistake when the approach is to test first and then blow out the campaign when you know how it works.'"[1] ●

Visit the ZoomInfo Web site at **www.zoominfo.com/** ●

## LEARNING OBJECTIVES

This chapter is a bridge between advertising and personal selling. The media we will emphasize—mail, phone, e-mail, and other electronic forms—don't provide face-to-face contact. But they were developed to enable one person to communicate with another. We dub the chapter one-to-one media because it will greatly aid your understanding and, eventually, your effectiveness in the field, if you regard these marketing communication forms as dialogue. In essence they are closer to personal selling than mass communication in the communication mix.

*After reading this chapter, you should be able to*

● Map the range of utility for direct mail, telephone, and e-mail in modern business marketing.

● Frame the decision of whether to use a telemarketing service bureau or develop an inside telemarketing operation.

● Discuss a number of the synergies from combining media efforts in marketing communication programs.

● Select an evaluation process befitting the communication objectives of the program.

# DIRECT MARKETING

Direct mail, telephone marketing, Web sites, fax programs, e-mail listservs, and the like often fall under "direct marketing" in meeting topics and budget headings. The Direct Marketing Association has tried to tackle the task of defining **direct marketing:**

*An interactive form of marketing using one or more advertising media to effect a measurable response and/or transaction at any location, with this activity stored on database.*[2]

## Four Essentials in the Definition

The definition is not perfect. For purposes of this chapter's discussion, four key elements can be teased out of the definition.[3] First, *it is marketing,* not something else. (Don't laugh. One company's sales force denigrated a niche rival for years for exclusively selling by catalog and a dedicated telephone sales staff. They ate a little crow when they started their own catalog program and inside telemarketing unit to serve small and remote accounts.) We will firmly establish the need for direct marketing activities in the modern business marketer's tool kit.

Second, *it precludes face-to-face interaction.* Personal selling and trade show education and hospitality are out, although they could be supported well by direct marketing activities. In practice we always include the telephone and the online channels as "advertising media."

Third, *the definition implies uniqueness in seeking a "measurable response."* From Chapter 10 you already know that advertising, personal selling, and trade shows can generate responses. But remember that personal selling and trade shows were disqualified on the basis of their face-to-face character. That leaves advertising still up for discussion. The responses sought by direct marketing are *readily observable actions* that can happen almost anywhere in the marketplace. That means that only some of the responses sought in advertising count as measurable. Leads generated from a chemical company's ad in a trade magazine or clicks on its banner ads at the chemical online site are readily observable actions, easily measured responses. The same company might tout its prowess for innovation and quality in other ads. Its sought response is awareness, excitement, or attitude formation—and these are not readily observable actions. We can only gauge knowledge, attitudes, and emotional responses with paper-and-pencil instruments, physiological measures (e.g., pupil dilation or galvanic skin response), and telephone surveys.

*Database* represents the fourth essential component of the definition. We know of no business that dials or mails randomly to potential customers—anonymous spammers excepted. Whether aiming to acquire new customers or deepen the relationship with current customers, mail, e-mail, and telephone programs are built on a database. At a minimum, the database is a list containing company names, addresses, and phone numbers. Often the database contains industry codes, personnel at key positions (VP purchasing, president), firm size, and purchase history as discussed in Chapter 5. On its own files any firm should record each type of customer contact, whereas external databases purchased or rented for particular campaigns should be evaluated for their performance. Of course, respondents are added to the company database.

## Definitional Gaps

Direct marketing is ever changing and its trade association definition is usually trying to catch up with these changes. As the emphasis on buyer-seller relationships has crystallized over the years, professionals who regard themselves as direct marketers began to forsake the request for a response occasionally. Indeed, chatty newsletters, specialty magazines, birthday greetings, and invented occasions to say "thanks for your business" have become part of the direct marketing repertoire. The practice is less common via telephone, but many organizations find it another useful way for personnel other than salespeople to stay in touch with customers.

Thus, it seems difficult to identify a use of the phone, e-mail, or mail that is not regarded as direct marketing. Personal selling is always excluded from the picture. But a broadcast and print advertisement can be regarded as direct marketing if it enables an easily observable behavioral response, such as a request for information or a direct order.

The next section of the chapter provides a brief overview of lists. The two following sections treat the unique facets of direct mail and telephone marketing and their frequent use in concert. We examine the range of communication goals pursued online and conclude with a discussion of procedures for integrating programs in the one-to-one media.

# LISTS

Outbound telemarketing, e-mail, and direct mail require a list. Lists can be generated from internal databases, such as the company's customer files, also called the *house list*. Lists can also be rented or purchased from external sources. For example, show management can provide exhibitors a list of preregistered attendees for a trade show. An insurance company trying to line up additional agents to carry its line may rent names of independent agents in the markets it wishes to develop. In addition, trade publications are popular sources of lists.

Not all external lists are created equal. We can distinguish two broad classes of lists on the basis of their origins: compiled lists and response lists, basically the house files (customers and inquirers) of other companies.

## Compiled Lists

Some business lists, called **compiled lists,** are assembled by companies that comb directories and public records and even make physical observations. For example, American Business Information, Inc., collects data from Yellow Pages, Business White Pages, annual reports, and SEC information in concert with government data, business magazines, professional directories, and more. Over 14 million phone calls are made to update and verify the accuracy of records on 10 million businesses, 160,000 firms with 100 or more employees, hundreds of thousands of physicians, and 1.5 million professionals (accountants, architects, dentists, attorneys, etc.).

The names from compiled lists generally can be rented for one-time-only use for $70 to $120 per thousand, with $10 to $20 per thousand charges for submarket selections or conveyance on special digital or hard copy formats, and perhaps a $350 or 5,000-name minimum order. Reuse of the names constitutes theft and can be detected by a list provider from a few bogus names seeded into the list for such control purposes.

## Response Lists

Who would you guess is the best prospect to enroll in a correspondence course in how to teach computer graphics: Margaret Smith, drawn from a compiled list of fine arts teachers in secondary schools, or Leonard Brown, a paid subscriber to *PC Graphics* magazine, or Julio Guerra, a six-months-ago buyer of educational software from CDW's Mac Warehouse catalog? Direct-mail professionals would bet on Julio, the recent catalog

**Exhibit 12–1**
Listing Some
Lists

Nielson Business Media offers a number of databases comprised of subscribers to Nielson publications and attendees at its trade shows. They are available for business marketing through its brokers, Edith Roman for postal information or e-POSTDIRECT for e-mail information. They include:

**Continuing Education Solutions**

| | | |
|---|---|---|
| 1.4 mm postal addresses | 1.2 mm subscribers with phones | .6 mm e-mail addresses |

**Office Management Solutions**

| | | |
|---|---|---|
| 1.4 mm postal addresses | .9 mm subscribers with phones | .6 mm e-mail addresses |

**Wireless Solutions**

| | | |
|---|---|---|
| 1.3 mm postal addresses | 1.1 mm subscribers with phones | .4 mm e-mail addresses |

SOURCE: Company advertisement, *DM News* (June 18, 2007), p. 9.

buyer, because he is *mail-responsive.* If we are asking potential customers to order by mail or online, we will generally find that those with prior buying experience with the medium are most responsive. Lists of another company's previous mail or telephone purchasers or inquirers are called **response lists.**

# Renting and Using Lists

Marketers typically obtain lists from compilers or brokers. List brokers are professionals serving both list owner and marketer. List owners pay brokers a commission (usually 20 percent of the basic rental price) for "merchandising" the list—fitting it with an assortment of other lists, matching it to marketer needs, and executing the exchange. Marketers rely on broker knowledge of their business and their insight into the character of different lists. Any broker can provide at least 95 percent of all the lists available, but usually a marketer relies on and enjoys a close working relationship with just one or two.[4] Exhibit 12–1 highlights some lists from Nielson Business media.

Compilers invest heavily in the collection and verification of data in the public or commercial domain, and then generate revenue in the rental and resale of those data. Compiled lists offer an opportunity to saturate a niche or larger market segment. But don't assume complete accuracy or coverage! In times of corporate restructuring, relocating, and so on, a portion of almost every database is obsolete within weeks of its entry. List users should ask compilers about deliverability guarantees and measures to verify and update data. Some trade publishers, such as Virgo Publishing, **telequalify** their subscription list, which means that they call each subscriber to verify that person's title, level of purchasing influence, and type of products purchased. Telequalified lists cost more, but there is less wastage due to mail going to people who never buy the offered product or to people who have moved or changed jobs. Some lists grow stale at a rate of up to 2 percent per month, so a year-old list can yield less than 80 percent coverage.

Business marketers sometimes complain that they get minimal service from their compiler or list broker. In part this stems from their relatively small impact on broker or compiler revenue. Your firm's interest in renting a list of 10,000 electrical supply wholesalers may be dwarfed by the broker's consumer goods clients renting names by the millions. Many business marketers enlist a direct-mail or telemarketing consultant in this environment.

# ONE-TO-ONE MARKETING PROGRAMS

The mail and the telephone account for the vast majority of spending in the world of one-to-one marketing. One study pegs business-to-business spending on direct-mail and telephone marketing at $47.8 billion. In the field of online marketing, the numbers are not so well established, but a recent survey of 343 marketing executives by *BtoB* Magazine indicated they expected 2007 online spending to increase by over 30 percent from a 2006 level already more than half their advertising budget.[5] The next sections discuss the management of mail, telephone, and Internet marketing efforts.

# Direct Mail

Direct-mail spending in business marketing has flattened of late, but still dwarfs any other communication vehicle—except the personal selling and the telephone—because it can provide business marketers with a number of benefits. Direct mail excels at delivering a personalized message at a precise point in time to a well-defined audience. The cost per contact is greater than print advertising and e-mail but typically less than the telephone. Direct mail is almost always much lower than the $350 personal sales call. Indeed, from a comparative cost of one or more personal sales calls, some boldly creative and extravagant direct-mail programs are executed.

Direct mail probably leads all other media options in terms of versatility. Your mailbox at home may be stuffed with promotions to apply for the American Express card, order your class ring at the campus bookstore, and renew your membership in Gold's Gym. Although these examples hint at the range of communication objectives supported by direct mail, the staggering array of business-to-business direct mail is largely hidden. A few categorized examples reveal the multipurpose utility of direct mail.

## *Communication Goals*

### Create Goodwill

For the basic positioning goal of "please, like us" direct mail is used to send gifts, greetings, thanks, and even apologies. The goal is *goodwill*. A midwestern builder got into hot water with area real estate agencies when one of its now dismissed marketing employees sold a few homes directly, enabling the buyer to avoid the agent's commission, but really free riding on some of the agents' marketing effort. To repair damaged credibility and re-enlist agent support, the builder used private couriers to deliver 2-pound boxes of fresh-made, premium chocolates, a letter of apology, and a humble plea for "another chance." Of course, the message and the candy were shared throughout the offices. The builder enjoyed record showings that spring.

### Develop Familiarity and Interest

The theory motivating a mailer's interest in response lists can similarly anchor the communication objective to *establish mail responsiveness* and perhaps build or identify *interest in the general product category.* We have already noted that compiled lists often contain names of individuals with an aversion to direct response. It may prove useful to execute a low-cost mail program that weeds out such nonprospects and that allows costlier programs to be applied to a better prospect pool. For example, the 3M Corporation sells overhead projectors through the mail. To establish mail responsiveness it first offered prospective buyers a Wharton School white paper on the effectiveness of overhead projectors in professional presentations. Those who ordered this free publication were then targets of mail promotions selling projection equipment.[6]

The use of the mail in a complex multistep selling process also involves the *generation of inquiries and leads.* This approach is common when we need to better qualify our target before mailing an expensive literature packet, a costly catalog, or a demonstration system.

There are two types of lead strategies: loose and tight. **Loose lead strategies** attempt to generate as many leads as possible, relying on a qualifying process to sort out good leads from bad. Markets with high turnover among buyers or many members in the buying center, new products, and forays into new markets are situations that call for casting the widest net possible.

**Tight lead strategies** seek to generate response from individuals who are already highly qualified. Obviously, the response generated from a tight lead strategy should be closer to the actual sale, if not the sale itself, than a loose lead strategy. Loose lead strategies look for anyone remotely interested; tight lead strategies look for buyers. Stable markets, limited selling capacity, and high-cost-per-sales-call situations require tight lead strategies.

A lead strategy will affect list choice and may also affect the choice of direct response medium. A tight lead strategy may combine direct mail with telemarketing aimed at a focused list, whereas a loose lead strategy may combine advertising with direct mail. Additionally, the type of lead strategy will also influence the message content, for more should be known about the members of a list used for a tight lead strategy. Thus, the message can be aligned more closely to the prospects' needs.

### Provide Demonstrations

Under the right conditions the mail can, indeed, *provide a product demonstration.* Video demonstrations can be provided for less than $5. We know of a hospital garment manufacturer that sent hospital buyers a small box containing water, a jar, two small squares of fabric, and instructions for a test comparing the migrations or "wicking" tendencies of the two fabrics. (Spreading fluids can transmit germs.) Interestingly, the program was designed to look not too slick—two colors, plain box, crooked label—like a resourceful salesperson put the simple program together.

### Influence the Channel

Naturally, the mail can be used to *sell to dealers or other influencers.* Pharmaceutical companies are major users of mail to this end. If doctors, dentists, or veterinarians will accept and distribute drug samples, they are highly likely to write prescriptions for the same. (We've never visited a doctor who gave us a four-day supply of a drug sample and then wrote a script for a different drug to take us to the end of the treatment regimen.) In a dramatically successful dealer recruitment program, a former corporate sales rep sent personalized video presentations to 100 of his successful friends in the field, inviting them to join his new financial services company as agents. From the Field 12–1 reveals the needs for direct mail in food service.

### Direct Order

Finally, direct-mail efforts can seek purchases. Catalogs represent a significant source of revenue for computer accessories, office furniture and supplies, books, and MRO items.

Other communications through the mail may solicit registrations at a professional conference, new subscriptions to a market scanning service, or the latest desktop project management software. Within an established business relationship, the mail allows efficient and pinpoint targeting of communications for renewals, product upgrades, and changes in operations. When these communications have primarily a goodwill objective, we cycle right back to consider the "please, like us" capability of the mail.

## 12–1

# FROM THE FIELD

## Feeding Frenzy?

Consumers in the United States spend about 48 percent of their food budget away from home. With almost a million restaurants and food service outlets and total sales of over half a trillion dollars, food service draws the attention of many business marketers. Restaurants need architectural services, decorating expertise, plates and flatware of the durable or disposable or recyclable kind, seasonings and entrées, exterminators, and security. Leading firms such as Tyson and Kikkoman cultivate personal relationships with 1–2,000 decision makers at the top 100 food service companies, but that leaves a lot of others whose volume may not justify a sales call. And in contrast to other markets such as the home office market, education, or financial services, in most commercial kitchens you won't see the staff on the Internet. Direct-mail and telephone support of good service will continue to be the keys to success. [7]

## Limitations of Direct Mail

Direct mail can work very well when all of the elements work together to secure the sale. Although response rates may vary from less than 1 percent to 10 percent or greater, the value of each response can outweigh the cost and make direct mail very profitable. Still, it can take several weeks to design and execute a mail campaign. Nondelivery may shrink coverage by 10 to 20 percent. The recipient's crowded mailbox

FedEx uses a powerful headline in a letter's usual location for the inside address.
Courtesy Federal Express.

Federal Express will carry an unlimited number of your 2 day boxes.

And each box can weigh up to 150 pounds.

Please return the enclosed card for a STANDARD AIR™ Coupon worth up to $11.50.

We were going over our records recently and were pleased to see that you're a regular user of our Priority 1® overnight service.  I'd like to say thanks very much for your confidence and we look forward to more of your time-sensitive shipments in the months ahead.

At the same time, I thought I'd write and remind you of another opportunity you have to count on Federal Express.

Those records we were going over also show that you do not currently use our economical, 1 to 2 day STANDARD AIR service. Now, I don't know why this is ... but if it's because you're giving your less urgent boxes to UPS or the Post Office*, I hope you'll give our STANDARD AIR a try.

Just return the enclosed postage-paid card and you'll receive a Coupon worth up to $11.50.  It's our way of letting you see exactly how our 1 to 2 day service compares to the competition.

For example, just ask yourself these questions about UPS and the Post Office:

    Do you get on-call pick-ups?
    Do you get pick-up on Saturday?
    Do you get discounts?

*U.S. Postal Service

---

### 12–1

## BUSINESS 2 BUSINESS

## Impact from a New Dimension

Each year awards are given to the best art directors, copywriters, and electronic directors for their creative solutions to direct marketing problems. The Caples Awards are named in honor of direct marketing pioneer John Caples. One recent Caples winner in the business-to-business category was the creative staff at Catalyst Direct, Inc., not for a program they did for one of their clients, but for a self-promotion intended to bring in new clients.

The promotion mailed Soufflé à l'Orange to direct marketing managers at Fortune 1000 firms with the goal of getting past corporate gatekeepers and generating immediate interest in the Rochester, New York, agency. The

supporting copy and foldout poster delivered the message: While everyone has the same recipe, not everyone gets the same results. By calling an 800 number, prospects were put in touch with the "master chefs" at Catalyst.[8]

When one needs to reach identifiable prospects with a high-impact message, the mail is a powerful tool. Dimensionals help to survive corporate mailroom filters on promotional mail and creatively support the message.

Think of a dramatic mail package that your dean might send to 50 CEOs in your college community to entice them to come to next year's case competition, a professionally executed showcase of undergraduate business talent.

---

or overflowing in-basket may interfere with prompt attention and void any urgency in the copy.

## Telemarketing

Telemarketing was defined in Chapter 10 as the systematic and continuous program of personally communicating with (potential) customers via telephone. An important point to note in that definition is that telemarketing is both systematic and continuous. *Systematic* means that the campaign is designed to cover a market segment thoroughly and completely. *Continuous* suggests that telemarketing is not a random event, but part of a specific strategy of communicating with customers. Telephone programs can be designed, tested, and implemented in as little as a few days. Thus, a learning organization may use the telephone both in its ongoing operations plus in rapid deployment fashion in times of opportunity.

Telemarketing generally triggers recollection of the credit card protection service pitch that came at supper time. But the world of business telemarketing is much different and much larger than that. There are two types of telemarketing: outbound and inbound. **Outbound telemarketing** means that the contract is generated by the marketer; **inbound telemarketing** is just the opposite, with contact initiated by the potential customer or actual customer.

### *Telephone Versatility*

By now you should be aware of other objectives the telephone might pursue besides sales. Indeed, there are several purposes or strategies to telemarketing. These include account management, field support, prospector, and customer service strategies.

## Account Management

Many companies use telemarketing to serve accounts in a more efficient manner than could be accomplished with a field salesperson. For example, Shell Oil assigned its smaller dealers to a telemarketing sales force. These dealers were not buying enough to cover the cost of field sales calls. After one year of telemarketing account management, the dealers reported higher satisfaction levels because they felt they were getting more attention from their telemarketing rep than they used to get from a field salesperson. Average sales per dealer were also increased substantially.

A firm in the Midwest uses telephone marketing almost exclusively to sell computer software—some costing as much as $100,000. It employs this approach to serve accounts across the world. A central databank of product information and account records can be readily accessed by its technically skilled salespeople. With more efficiency than a rep in the field could offer, accounts receive technical support via phone, fax, and e-mail and get products by overnight courier. When used properly, telemarketing account management improves customer satisfaction and increases sales.

## Field Support

In some cases, covering accounts with just a single salesperson is too difficult, yet the account requires personal visits in the field. For example, Schuster Electronics, an industrial electronics distributor in Cincinnati, found that its field salespeople were having difficulty maintaining contact with all of the members of the buying centers. Field visits were necessary, however, in order to work with engineers who design products using Schuster components. The company teamed each field salesperson with a telemarketing rep. Now, when the field rep visits an account, she doesn't have to try to see everyone or drop everything to handle a problem. The telemarketing rep can take care of many problems quicker and more effectively, while also handling follow-up calls on any new members of the buying center. One result has been that, whereas the company used to lose about 12 percent of its customers each year, now the company retains 98 percent of its customers.

Field support means that the telemarketing rep supports the efforts of an account manager who makes personal visits to the account's location. As in the case of Schuster, most successful firms in this type of selling team their field reps with individual telemarketers, so the result is similar to account management, but responsibility for the account is shared. In most cases, the final decision for account strategy rests with the field rep, not the telemarketer, but compensation for both is derived from combined performance.

## Prospector

Similar to support activities, **prospector** telemarketing combines telemarketing with field efforts. The primary difference is that once a prospect is identified, the account is turned over to the field force. The telemarketer does not make any further calls on the account. In some cases, a telemarketer may work with an individual rep, but more likely, the telemarketer supports the efforts of several reps.

One company that found this method useful is Global Shop Solutions, a manufacturing software company in Houston. After trade shows, the company had so many leads that had to be called that the field reps were swamped. Telemarketers called the leads, qualifying prospects over the phone and setting appointments for the field rep with those prospects who were going to make a decision soon. The company further expanded its telemarketing efforts by purchasing lists of decision makers for manufacturing software. Results were so positive that the company doubled its field sales force in order to handle the increased opportunity.

Another use of prospectors is to call **dormant accounts,** or those accounts that have stopped buying. Goodall Rubber, for example, uses telemarketing to reactivate accounts. Reactivated accounts are then turned over to field reps. Additionally, the company can gather useful information about why companies stopped buying from Goodall.

### Customer Service

Most students think of customer service telemarketing as strictly inbound, such as the 800 numbers that you call if you need help with your downloaded software. Burlington Northern/Santa Fe Railroad uses customer reps in its inbound call center to track any caller's order and tell where the shipment is and when it should arrive at the destination. In business marketing, customer service can include both outbound and inbound calls. For example, customer service telemarketing can include follow-up telephone calls to ensure that field service was satisfactory.

## Outside Service or In-House Telemarketing

Everyone has used the telephone for some commercial purposes or to coordinate activities. We've scheduled meetings, landed jobs, sold raffle tickets, and confirmed reservations. Indeed, we use this business tool every day. So why should we bring in outside professionals to assist with telemarketing? When this line of thinking is combined with the prevalence of underutilized staff and phone lines at an organization, in-house telemarketing operations often spring up in a makeshift workspace. This is an accidental commitment to in-house telemarketing.

We would like you to consider the make-or-buy decision more strategically, certainly within your integrated marketing communications strategy, but also as part of your firm's mission and distinctive skill sets. Nearly 1,500 businesses provide telephone marketing services. Some have capabilities limited to lead generation and messaging. Others bring broad experience and capabilities to the tasks of strategic planning, program design, and implementation in coordination with other marketing efforts. A number of offshore agencies offer professionalism and cost advantages. What factors should one consider in choosing in-house or outside-vendor telemarketing services?

### In-House Advantages

Four factors tend to favor in-house operations. The major strength of a good in-house telemarketing operation is *control*. Representatives can be intensively trained and more knowledgeable about company products and programs than an outside agency. Proximity allows closer performance evaluation, even though most telemarketing activities at outside service bureaus are highly auditable—clients can observe operations, listen to calls, and review computer-generated reports of connect rates, duration, and more.

A second and related strength is *access to the company database*. Although electronic data interchange (EDI) has become increasingly used between marketing companies, resellers, and fulfillment agencies, organizational boundaries still make for distortions and delays in the transfer and dissemination of information. A central database is usually more accessible and current for employees than outside vendors.

Third, special motivation programs and the sustained company culture may be able to *secure a high level of commitment* to a well-integrated operation that is unmatchable by an outside agency. But several professionals caution that this benefit may be an illusion. Jim McAllister, formerly at Matrixx Marketing, observed, "Often, the telemarketing program has a champion who starts the in-house program with fanfare and company support and commitment. Once the champion leaves, the program is usually inherited by a subordinate without sufficient rank, or it's attached to another department head's function. . . . At this point the program stops evolving and it becomes static. It can't find a voice, can't command the resources in terms of personnel or systems. This lack of stature and status within the corporation prevents it from playing its proper role."[9]

Companies that attempt in-house telemarketing stand to attain one more key benefit: *they learn.* The individuals involved develop a unique set of skills and build experience in an area of growing importance to the company. As efficiency and effective performance improve, these skills increase in value and may be applied elsewhere in the firm.

### Vendor Advantages

Outside specialists can be enlisted by any enterprise. Competition among telemarketing service bureaus—especially in developing economies in India, the Philippines, Poland, and Tunisia—and the relatively measurable tasks we give to telemarketing make outside vendors attractive candidates as partners in integrated marketing programs. Let's highlight a few of the potential advantages of outsourcing most telemarketing services.

First, an outside company *skirts the investments* needed to do telemarketing. It avoids the need to purchase switching equipment, computers that distribute calls and generate productivity reports, ergonomic furniture, screens and script servers, headsets, trained heads, and more. An outside vendor has already made these capital investments and spreads the overhead costs across a broad base of clients.

Careful vendor evaluations should reveal *a high level of expertise* at a growing number of telemarketing agencies. Look at the experience base of an established agency and at its team of experts. They are apt to be economically priced, experienced, trained, motivated to serve clients, and ready to go now. Is it reasonable to expect to be able to staff quickly an in-house operation with the same professionalism and expertise? Many firms find the talent pool quite shallow and the time needed to "grow" talent too scarce.

Let's elaborate on the timing issue to recognize the *nimbleness* provided by an outside vendor. Compared to starting an in-house operation, a telemarketing agency can put its people and systems to work on a program much faster. Quick start-up is often a competitive imperative for rapidly changing markets and technologies. Global markets and escalating customer service standards require 24-hour telephone access. A service bureau has staff and systems in place to provide such access. At the same time, when change dictates program termination, it is easier to shut down an agency operation than an in-house unit.

As you can see, strong arguments can be made for both telemarketing options: in-house and outside agency. In general, a firm's initial ventures into telemarketing seem best supported by outside vendors. Experience and broader programs can bring more operations in-house, but this evolution may flow out of a strong working relationship between the marketer and the telemarketing service firm.

## Limitations of Telemarketing

The telephone's strength is also—in a sense—its weakness. It may be great to get a call from your cousin in Germany on your birthday. It's helpful when the bookstore calls to say your order is in. But when you're studying for a critical exam, you don't want to receive a phone solicitation for a political candidate. The telephone is intrusive. Give consideration to the time and duration of business calls. Respect your customer's requests not to be called.

Although telemarketing is used to sell everything from 25-cent supplies to $10 million airplanes, telemarketing does have its limitations. For example, the products that Schuster Electronics sells require face-to-face visits so that design engineers and salespeople can work together. Some products are too complex for selling over the phone, for buyers cannot visualize the benefits without seeing demonstrations. Similarly, the buyers' needs may be so complex as to require personal visits in order to define and understand them. Although telemarketing can't be used to demonstrate products or get orders in such cases, we shouldn't neglect the clout of telephone marketing to take requests for additional information, identify decision makers and purchase cycles, qualify leads, schedule personal sales calls, issue appointment reminders, follow up on recent installations, and more.

Both sets of limitations identified in this section—intrusiveness and incompleteness—suggest the inadequacy of the telephone as a stand-alone medium. Indeed, a theme of these communication chapters is that there probably is no such thing as a stand-alone medium. Each medium has certain strengths and undeniable weaknesses. The challenge is to use the different media in concert. The weaknesses of one medium are compensated for by the strengths of the others. The next section briefly surveys the complementarity of the one-to-one media.

## e-Mail Effectiveness

Tad X is an executive in the financial services field who returned from vacation to find some 300 e-mails in his INBOX. With a click-pull-DELETE they were gone in two seconds. Sure, this was a rash behavior, a postvacation funk. But what did Tad really risk? Thinking about that gives us some sense for the utility of e-mail marketing.

### Ubiquity Breeds Defenses

E-mail is inexpensive and fast and with many members of the buying center using online services, market coverage is quite good. But the indiscriminant use of e-mail—SPAM—has prompted defenses such as blockers and junk mailboxes. Companies following best practices tend to use e-mail on a permission basis. When a preexisting or current business relationship has been established by personal or online contact—a purchase, membership application, request for information—the user should be offered an opportunity to opt out, not be included in subsequent communications. Alternatively, when a user may elect to receive newsletters or commercial messages by checking the opt-in box, sometimes the marketing organization will send a follow-up e-mail notifying the user of their opt-in decision, and perhaps requiring another reply or click before being added to the list.

Most marketers do not want to communicate to individuals who don't want to hear from them, so getting explicit permission to communicate is more than courtesy; it boosts effectiveness, too. But how long does this permission last? If an HR manager requested a white paper on online recruiting from ZoomInfo in 2006, and granted permission for subsequent promotional e-mails, should ZoomInfo presume permission in perpetuity or should it monitor responses and quit after long periods of inactivity. It may be prudent to use another medium to get consent renewed or reaffirmed.

## 12–2

# BUSINESS 2 BUSINESS
## Social Engineering?

Engineers in the United States are getting pitched to use more sustainable systems and ecofriendly designs, incorporate new software and communications features into automobiles and manufacturing equipment, and advance quality in every subprocess in the value chain. In the United States, they tend to read heavily, attend trade shows, and rely on Webinars to learn about new products. They want data from their peers, not marketing hype. They tend to lag behind their technical counterparts in IT in the use of podcasts and blogs.

But today China graduates more electronics engineers than the rest of the world combined.

Their average age is under 30—compared to about 45 in the United States—and their involvement in online social networking is phenomenal. What role would the social media (e.g., MySpace, [rather, in China see: http://home.xiaonei.com/Home.do], blogs, Flickr, YouTube) in your marketing program have in offering an executive MBA program to Chinese electronics engineers?

Source: Roger Slavens "Connecting with Engineers," *BtoB's Vertical Insight: A Guide to Marketing to Vertical Industries* (June 25,2007), p. 13. See also http://socialmediareport. wordpress.com/.

### Tethers to Something Bigger

E-mail communication typically transpires within an established relationship—strengthening the association, maximizing value-added opportunities, improving coordination, and mobilizing resources. It also tends to be the most effective medium for driving traffic to a Web site, as ZoomInfo learned in its tests against creative direct e-mail programs. E-mails work well to remind of appointments, call out the need to renew, notify of shipment, and convey greetings and relationship milestones. In collaborative relationships they can carry attachments involving market analysis and forecasts, schedules, specifications, and more. A digitized message has durability in machine memory and is easily transmitted across other networks.

Thus, while our own company's e-mail will focus on current customers, our e-mail and Web site content can support proclivities among current customers—and the social networks of prospective customers—to be ambassadors for the brand. Screen Machine Industries, Inc., is delighted when a current crusher customer sends an e-mail to a friend — a noncustomer—containing a link to their YouTube demonstration of the Spyder 516T.[10] Business-to-Business 12–2 highlights the intriguing possibilities of reaching young engineers in China.

# The Synergy of One-to-One Media

Direct mail is probably peerless when measured on the criteria of personalization, amplification of benefits, and forcefulness of the call to action. Dimensionals can be used to get past office personnel who filter obvious promotional mail from their supervisor's in-basket. Moreover, a dimensional can effectively support the printed copy and will sometimes be retained as a reminder of the sender and the message—a personalized coffee mug or a Tonka truck with seller's logo. Relevant, urgent, and creative as these may be, they still fall short in their capacity to allow dialogue.

**Exhibit 12–2**
Synergy
between
Mail and
Telemarketing

| | A: Traditional Budget Application | | B: Synergistic Budget Application | |
|---|---|---|---|---|
| | Budget | No. of Leads | Budget | No. of Leads |
| Advertising | $175K | 438 | $25K | 375 |
| Direct mail | 75K | 812 | 63K | 750 |
| Telemarketing | — | | 162K | 2,625 |
| Total | $250K | 1,250 | $250K | 3,750 |

SOURCE: Experimental results presented in Ernan Roman, *Integrated Direct Marketing,* Lincolnwood, IL: NTC Business Books, 1995.

In contrast, dialogue is the telephone's unique advantage in the mix. Of course, the telephone might match the mail in terms of urgency and call-to-action effectiveness, and it can be highly personalized too, but it can come in "cold" and fall short of vividness and detail—a key strength of the mail.

## Lifting Response Rates

With careful planning, training, timing, and execution, the mail and telephone can be integrated into a highly effective program. A direct-mail piece might net us a 2 percent response rate. By introducing the availability of a toll-free call in the mail copy and adding 800 telephone service, potential customers can ask their questions at their convenience with no cost to them. They find value in the ability to initiate this contact and put the seller in a reactive or adaptive mode. It is not uncommon to see overall response rate increases of 50 to 100 percent, to 3 or 4 percent overall.

If we add carefully timed outbound calls (or e-mail) to the program, we may well find another 100 to 700 percent lift in response, compared to the base case of mail only. The outbound call or e-mail has been previewed by the mail package; it reminds the recipient of the prior communication. It allows for interaction in the case of phone and an easy reply or click in the case of e-mail.

## A Test for Synergy

The effectiveness of this approach is illustrated in a controlled test of two marketing programs directed at 25,000 small- to medium-sized businesses.[11] Test A featured heavy advertising in national publications and selected local radio. The mail part of the program included a prenotification postcard followed two weeks later by the direct-mail package. The program in Test B focused advertising on business decision makers. One week following the initial ad, the direct-mail phase began. Then, within 24 to 72 hours of receipt of the letter, outbound telemarketing was applied. Exhibit 12–2 summarizes the media mixes and outcomes.

Although Test B lacked the program visibility of A in the national publications, especially before the company sales force, it clearly bettered A in lead generations. On a cost per lead basis, the score was $200 to $67. But let's not forget the internal efforts to support sales force follow-up and belief in the quality of the leads from Test A. We will examine the quality of sales leads and follow-up in the next chapter.

### *About the Timing*

Many students and professionals are surprised that another communication should follow so soon after the mail effort. They contend that calling or e-mailing prospects a day or two after they have received the direct mail hardly gives them a chance to respond; many recipients would have responded by mail. Hence, this is pushy and wasteful, they conclude.

But think about this for a few moments. We'll take up the waste issue first. Imagine a mailing to 1,000 potential customers can reap a 1.5 percent response rate if we allow three weeks of measurement. If we call two days after the mail is delivered, only, say, .5 percent would have placed their order. That means 1 percent of the calls are "wasted" on eventual mail customers. But the cost of 10 calls in a program to reach 995 is barely significant.

Let's regard the cost of 10 "wasted" calls as a surcharge we pay to call potential customers when the impact of the direct-mail package is fresh. Call recipients remember the questions that were left unanswered in the mail, or are reminded of the need to act now, or are directed to additional benefits. The combined impact of the two media more than pays for the "wasted" calls. We have found similar payoff from promt e-mail follow-up.

Similar synergies can be realized when the promotion mix includes other media and communication channels. For example, as Chapter 11 describes, many trade show managers use direct mail and e-mail to build traffic to their booth. Likewise, inbound telemarketing may rely on the print ads in trade magazines to generate telephone calls.

# WORLD-CLASS MARKETING ON THE WWW

"Direct mail on steroids" is how the Internet and e-commerce have been described in some trade circles. Indeed, the Web enables interactivity beyond the scale long harnessed in direct mail and telephone marketing. It opens the door to new levels of connectedness to customers. From the Field 12–2 recaps an integrated marketing communication program using the Internet for customer education.

# Web Site Goals

If you think back to some of the Web sites you've visited on your own or by our direction in the prior chapters, you might be able to discern a spectrum of objectives. On the one hand, some are passive public relations stations, perhaps showcasing a mission statement, a company history, and some electronic brochures. Others clearly aim at generating orders, if not online, at least through the dealer network described on the hyperlinked pages, the 800 number by the company logo, or the e-mail address at the bottom of every page. Successful firms on the Web have used cyberspace to achieve three broad types of objectives: channel management, customer service, and back-office efficiency.[12]

### *Web Transactions*

The first objective, effective channel management, includes employing Web sites to satisfy transaction and presale channel preferences of existing customers, target new users, deliver information-based products (such as software and digitized photos and documents), and

---

### 12–2

## FROM THE FIELD

## Pass & Seymour Plug into New Markets: A Tale about PlugTail

A leading manufacturer of electrical and network wiring devices, Pass & Seymour put an innovative twist on the ubiquitous receptacle—like the one your desk lamp may be plugged into right now. But unlike conventional wiring devices that require workers to install receptacles using the usual hot, neutral, and grounded "pigtails" sticking out of the wall box, the Pass & Seymour PlugTail™ provides a factory-terminated connector with leads that allow fast and consistent installation and lifelong reliability.

Initially introduced for its productivity value at installation, the PlugTail soon found new applications with unanticipated appeal. For example hospitals and other health care facilities tend to replace receptacles periodically because when critical electrical equipment gets plugged in, it needs to stay plugged in.

To offer the PlugTail to this replacement market in the health care field, Pass & Seymour worked with its agency to develop an integrated marketing communications program. It used print ads in health care publications to generate awareness and interest and leads, online marketing for more education and demonstration, direct mail to generate leads, and industry events and product give-a-ways to allow trial. As a result the health care segment represents 40 percent of PlugTail sales. Education and retail represent new market efforts.

Kate Maddox, "New Markets, New Tactics," *B toB's Vertical Insight: A Guide to Marketing in Vertical Industries* (June 25, 2007), pp. 4–5; http://www.passandseymour.com/news/view.cfm?id=179.

---

effectively develop deeper relationships with customers. Grainger, Cisco, and Dell exemplify leading firms using the Web for effective channel management.

## Service 24/7

FedEx provides a compelling example of how the Web can be used in effective customer service, the second key goal. Around 1990 FedEx started giving key customers a $4,000 computer and software to enable them to communicate efficiently, manage logistical operations, and check the shipping status of packages. The Internet allowed FedEx to provide the same service to a wider array of customers and give them something of value. Indeed, FedEx built its highly touted Web site not for just PR impact and brochureware. It had to enable customers and prospective customers to do work, create value. It has! The FedEx Web site has enabled over 170,000 software downloads and receives over 3 million hits per month.[13]

To recognize and manage customer relationships at their Web site, a number of business marketers are using agent software. **Agent software** or **bots** are terms used to describe programs that collect data on product preferences, purchase history, firmographics, and demographics in order to automatically profile customers and call up custom pages, tailored to the interests and needs of the customer. Profiles now can be on the supplier's server, but as a result of standardization in the industry, profiles tend to reside on the user's browser. Thus, a profiled small manufacturer, frequently buying specialty steels, can visit a supplier's site and view a custom screen featuring information on new materials, availability, notice of a new white paper on specialty fabrication, and a calendar of Web seminars germane to the business.

## 12–3

# BUSINESS 2 BUSINESS
## Bolster the Brand and Boost Buyers with Blogs

In their quest to bring classroom science to life, since 1995 many teachers have looked to the Steve Spangler Science catalog and, since 2003, SteveSpanglerScience.com. There they can find educational toys and demonstration tools, such as the Baby Diaper Secret Science Fair Kit, or a dazzling classroom aid containing 1 pound of a polymer good for making 8 gallons of "Instant Snow." Not long ago, with the intention of boosting sales, Steve Spangler launched his blog. Spangler is a science teacher and carries loads of credibility when he discusses one of the lessons or catalog products "objectively." We like his coverage of the new Guinness world record for 850 simultaneous Mentos-in-the-2- liter-of-soda-geysers, using, of course, 850 Mentos Geyser Tube Toys available in his catalog! Apparently, Steve's blog has the right content and tone; nearly 3,000 people link to the site— including many journalists!

In the B2B space, Steve Spangler has a growing company. Dell's blog (direct2dell.com) was criticized as too promotional when it began in 2006, but Dell made adjustments and maintains the blog. Extended Stay Hotels seems to be courting the trust of business travelers with its blog, roadwarriortips.com.[14] What are the potential benefits and risks of blogging in the B2B market space?

### Back-Office Economies

Electronic ordering, order checking, and shipping eliminate unnecessary human interactions, avoid human error, and make redundant data entry a thing of the past. In this vein the FedEx Web site has cut in half 1-800 calls and automated processes that would have required FedEx to hire nearly 20,000 more employees.[15]

### Web Site Synergy in Integrated Marketing Communications

The leverage of Web sites on the effectiveness in other media—and vice versa—is only beginning to be explored. We note that most business advertisers put a tag with their Web address on their ads, but little integration is evident; we usually cannot discern any "teamwork" between the media. Remarkably, many Web sites have no phone number and no address! This neglects the diversity of communication channel preferences in the market—address and phone are just as easy to include on a Web page as the URL on the ad.

Clearly, the opportunities for integrated media abound. Dell Computer ads, Master Food Services ads, and others direct the reader to visit the company Web site. In these examples, the Web site serves as a problem-solving and selling center. As prospects visit a site and become known customers, they may be contacted and served by other one-to-one media. For example, customers who have not visited a firm's Web site for some time can be called or e-mailed an invitation to visit again. Technically complex products can be profiled in direct-mail catalogs and highly targeted trade magazines— but the details can await the reader's visit to the Web site and perhaps an eventual sales call.

## 12–3

# FROM THE FIELD
## Creativity That Hits the Target

I entered the field from the graphic design arena with a degree from the Columbus College of Art and Design and years of experience working as a corporate art director, agency art director, and creative director/vice president. Clients have been both consumer and B2B with the majority being B2B for the past decade.

This has been an excellent career for me. I enjoy going into new businesses, learning about them, their product/services and customers. What differentiates their product/services, from their competitors? What are the benefits to the customer? Who is the customer and what influences them to respond in the way we want them to respond? What vehicle will carry the right message and deliver it to the right consumer? I enjoy the challenge of staying within the boundaries of what research shows but being creative in the execution.

For example: One of our clients produces infrared imaging equipment and their clients are the military units of the United States and other countries. They wanted a unique item to give away at trade shows that distinguished the brand and provided a lasting connection.

Their product is high-tech and excellent. They can sight the enemy clearer, at a greater distance than their competitors and through a multitude of atmospheric conditions.

Their clients respond to military imagery. Detail oriented, they like a lot of information about the product.

We produced a business-card-sized CD, designed to resemble a dog tag, complete with drilling a hole and hanging it on ball chain. It contains all of their data sheets on pdf files, videos of their equipment in the field, a link to their Web site, test results, other equipment details, and company information. It has been extremely effective. The prospective clients get all the information they need in a high-tech format. They also hang them around their necks at the trade show, creating a buzz about our client. While not inexpensive, they are so successful that the client has reordered them for several years.

The challenge to being creative in the B2B business is that a lot of our clients are engineers. Rightfully so, they love their product and want to tell the world all about it—every little detail! Convincing them that in marketing *less* really can be *more* is sometimes difficult.

Dave Allen, Creative Director/Vice President, Jaap-Orr, Cincinnati, Ohio.

---

Avnet Electronics has pioneered the use of seminars on the Web. Thus, with no immediate selling objective, the site strengthens relationships with customers when used to train and educate customers in the capabilities of new products or the implications of new regulations. For selling and order placement, other media or other pages on the Web site may well lead to a trade show or dealer network. In short, for maximum marketing impact, the Web site should benefit from top management support and integration with other elements of the communications program.

Despite its power and unfolding potential, the Internet is not a stand-alone medium. User preferences for different communication channels will persist and some communication objectives—such as drawing new customers or negotiating a custom service—will require other media and personal selling. Astute business marketers such as Dave Allen, profiled in From the Field 12–3, will orchestrate the role of the Web site among roles of other media to fittingly attend to different segments, with varying degrees of product understanding and buying readiness as well as different information requirements.

# Summary

Mail and the telephone were invented to allow one person to communicate with a specific other person. Both media can be engaged to achieve particular communication objectives across a spectrum ranging from awareness and liking to "give us the money now." As the primary media of direct marketing, mail and telephone marketing often are regarded as synonymous with direct marketing.

Precision targeting is enabled by in-house databases or outside lists. External lists represent the house lists of other companies or data compiled by firms from public records and directories. Usually, lists are rented for one-time-only use, but many compiled lists can be purchased or obtained on a subscription basis for multiple use.

Telephone marketing consists of both inbound and outbound calling and can be performed by an external agency or a company unit. The in-house unit maximizes control and has full access of the internal database. It also enables the company to develop experience and skills in a growing business activity. But an outside vendor brings trained people and all the systems to the task, eliminating most of the needed capital investment. The outside vendor can set up and shut down quickly. We recommend that a business marketer forge a close working relationship with an outside vendor to develop telemarketing experience, then see if it makes sense to invest in the training, hardware, and systems for an internal telemarketing unit.

Telephone marketing can also be used for a wide array of communication objectives, spanning prospecting, lead development and qualification, sales support, order taking, customer service, and even consultative selling.

E-mail is a powerful relationship management tool. Used on a permission basis it allows for reminder messages, promotional communications, educational content, links to more information, and a host of means for coordinating interfirm value-added processes. That content is digitized means potential for storage/retrieval as well and transmission within other electronic social networks. Social media are increasingly utilized within certain business markets.

Many firms are realizing synergies from integrated marketing programs that combine the personal intimacy and detail of the mail with the interactivity and urgency of the telephone. Generally it is highly effective—and not at all wasteful—to closely sequence mail and telephone contacts because overlap is small and the repetition of messages by a different medium reinforces those messages.

Companies have used their Web sites to bolster company image and develop brands, but increasingly we see Web sites designed to manage channels of communication with new and current customers, open new channels, solidify existing channels of distribution, and develop stronger relationships with customers. We also see Web commerce providing significant economies in customer service and logistical functions via more accuracy and speed in ordering, delivery, and inventory management.

The evolution and design of virtual communities on the Internet provide an opportunity for business marketers to find their own role therein as organizers, sponsors, teachers, and advertisers. Finally, e-mail spending is expected to grow in the next five years as it proves itself as a powerful medium for communicating and expanding relationships with current customers.

# Key Terms

| | | |
|---|---|---|
| agent software | dormant account | prospector |
| bots | inbound telemarketing | response list |
| compiled list | loose lead strategy | telequalify |
| direct marketing | outbound telemarketing | tight lead strategy |

# Discussion Questions

1. Copywriter Robert Bly urges common sense in e-mail practice: (a) The "From" line must indicate a known and trusted source, (b) the subject line conveys the message payload and it ought to be refreshed periodically, and (c) start with the reader's needs and problems before spewing information about the service or product. Print two promotional e-mails to youself or a business marketing professional and measure them with Bly's criteria.

2. Precision Valve Corp. was about to initiate a new program directed to municipal water utilities. With 12,000 utilities in its target market, some debate among the managers developed over whether the safety or economy should be stressed in the program. Using 400 labels printed in zip code order, Precision Valve sent letters emphasizing safety to the first half and emphasizing economy to the second 200 utilities.

    Is this a good experiment? Does it allow Precision Valve to attribute differences in response rate to the appeal in the letter?

    It's not unusual for companies to test program A against B by mailing program A in March and program B in April. Is this a good experiment? To what else can we attribute differences between the two programs? Would it be better to mail A and B at the same time to a sample of prospects (randomly assigned), one half to each of the two programs?

3. What are the pros and cons of a proposed national B2B Do Not Call List?

4. With estimates of billions of wire hangers bound for landfills each year, isn't it about time someone invented Eco-Hangers, a product made entirely of recycled paper? Furthermore, the Eco-Hanger is a marketing medium as well. In June 2007, Staples used Eco-Hangers printed with its name at select dry cleaners in test cities throughout the United States to distribute $10 coupons. Do you think this is a good medium for brand development—as the hanger is seen in closets for months—and action? For more information visit: **http://www.hangernetwork. com.**

5. Advertisers often use a cost per thousand (CPM) measure as a standard for first-cut comparisons across different media. CPM numbers might run $45 for a jazzy color ad in a trade magazine, $450 for a direct-mail program, and $4,500 for a telephone effort. Briefly outline why mail and phone costs are often justified, despite the apparent advantage of the print medium.

6. In this same vein, we know that the average personal sales call in business marketing runs about $350. Identify three communication tasks each for mail, e-mail, and telephone marketing that stand to improve the productivity of a company's sales calls.

7. Much of our understanding of experimental design comes from agriculture, where different seeds, fertilizers, pesticides, and the like were tested in different soils or elevations for their effects on yield (bu./acre), harvest quality, and—when possible—profit per acre. Sketch the essentials of a marketing experiment to test two different copy strategies, two different price terms, and the order of the planned mail and telephone contacts for offering a training program targeted to 28,000 real estate appraisers in the United States. Identify and make the case for at least two useful dependent variables.

8. "Response rate tests are a trap. Sure, they allow you to hone your current program—always trying to beat the 'control' letter or top the proven script. But if

you're not careful, all your efforts are tactical and no effort is expended on strategic market development or programs with longer-run payout." Comment.

9. Convince an industrial distributor why it should enclose a business letter to its accounts with the trifold brochure introducing its new lines. (The cost of the brochure is subsidized by the new suppliers.)

10. Privacy is a major issue in all the one-to-one media. Although the popular press spotlights abuses in consumer markets, the possibility of increased governmental regulation is very real and likely to impact business-to-business marketing as well. Is permission marketing the answer? Does a manager really know what range of activities for which permission has been granted? Are bots a threat to privacy? Is company privacy the same as individual employee privacy?

# Cases

## Case 12.1    Direct Marketing the NanoV

NanoViz is a new company started by Billie Jean Hudak and Martin Wilkomen, two former tech heads, to develop and market small projection equipment for computer-driven presentations. For example, the current product line features four models ranging in price from $1,399 to $1,899. The firm's leading seller, the NanoV, sells for $1,599 and allows a presenter (a salesperson, professor, seminar leader, etc.) to connect the sandwich-sized projector to the video-out port on almost any DVD or notebook computer. Clear images are then projected on an ordinary screen or—in a pinch—even a wall. One leading computer magazine recently reviewed the NanoV in its new products feature, calling it "the next best thing to buying a cinema."

Hudak and Wilkomen don't want to sell through intermediaries, having been burned in their earlier days by a large department store that reneged on a large order of another home entertainment product. The partners have asked you to pick up the pieces of the marketing plan begun by Billie's father, just before he had a near-fatal heart attack.

NanoViz is working with little cash right now. Over 90 percent of its $500,000 in assets is tied up in parts (30 percent) and finished goods inventory (70 percent). Product costs run about $330 at the bottom end of the line to about $810 at the top end. Direct costs on the NanoV are $759. About $40,000 is on hand now for marketing, but crisp and early sales could fund substantially more marketing activities.

The following costs illustrate a number of the media options available (M = 1,000; MM = 1 million):

| | |
|---|---|
| Four-color ad in *PC Tec* magazine (circ. = 1.1 MM) | $14,000 |
| Black-and-white ad | 8,000 |
| Four-color ad in *Sales & Marketing Tips* mag. (circ. = 2.6 MM) | 18,000 |
| Black-and-white ad in *Wall Street Today* (circ. 21 MM per column inch) | 600 |
| Mailing lists: "Big Business" (n = 125,407) | $80/M |
| University info Technology directors (n = 27 M) | $70/M |
| *Razor Image* catalog six-mo. hot list (n = 49,379) | $90/M |
| Trade show exhibit and receptions/demo | $5K to 15,000 |
| Web site development: $5M–$25M; $10,000/mo. for upkeep | |
| Postal charges as low as $.30 | |
| Telephone service bureau: outbound calls @ $2.50 ea.; inbound calls @ $5.50 ea. | |

Outline communication objectives against targets, appeals, media, and expenditures over the coming year.

## Case 12.2

### Response Reality versus Clive: Worldviews Collide

At last month's meeting of the Three Rivers Ad Club a "shouting match" erupted between two executives at rival advertising agencies. Tad Snell, data-savvy exec from the new Response Reality agency got an earful from Gene Meeker from the Clive Agency: "You preyed on those cats at Willkommen (a regional hotel management firm and subsidiary in a diversified company headquartered in Munich). You know their current pressures from corporate for bottom-line improvements, so you pitched them a mechanistic program for cross-selling. You grabbed *our* account so your formula-driven copywriters could go at it again—squeezing more dollars from current customers."

"That's almost true, Gene, but we didn't have to do much persuading. Willkommen came looking for marketing ROI! They had had enough of your endless image building and the giant ego of your art director."

"But were you up front with them, Snell? Did you come clean and say you didn't know the difference between a brand promise and a Band-Aid?"

"I told them they had to stop the bleeding—retain customers—before they spend one more nickel in your fantastic quest for OZ."

Blah, blah blah.

What's going on here?

## Additional Readings

Deutskens, Elisabeth, Ad de Jong, and Ko de Ruyter. "Comparing the Generalizability of Online and Mail Surveys in Cross-National Service Quality Research." *Marketing Letters* 17, no. 2 (2006), pp. 119–36.

Geller, Lois K. *Response: The Complete Guide to Profitable Direct Marketing.* New York: Oxford University Press, 2002.

Humby, Clive, and Terry Hunt with Tim Phillips. *Scoring Points.* London: Kogan Page, 2003.

Hursh, Patricia. "Dating Tips for B2B Marketers." *Search Engine Land,* http://searchengineland.com/070620-094530.php.

Newell, Frederick. *Loyalty.com: Customer Relationship Management in the New Era of Internet Marketing.* Boston: McGraw-Hill Professional Publishing, 2000.

Picarille, Lisa. "Communication Translates to Profits." *Customer Relationship Management* (December 2002), pp. 46–47.

Pyke, David F. "Matching B2B e-Commerce to Supply Chain Strategy." *Supply Chain Management Review: Special Global Supplement* (July–August 2000), pp. 16–19.

Rayport, Jeffrey F., and Bernard J. Jaworski. *e-Commerce.* Boston: McGraw-Hill/Irwin, 2000.

Roman, Ernan. *Integrated Direct Marketing.* Lincolnwood, IL: NTC Business Books, 1995.

Schlosser, Ann E., Tiffany Barnett White, and Susan M. Lloyd. "Converting Web Site Visitors into Buyers: How Web Site Investment Increases Consumer Trusting Beliefs and Online Purchase Intentions." *Journal of Marketing* 70 (April 2006), pp. 133–48.

Scott, David Meerman. *The New Rules of Marketing & PR.* Summerset, NJ: Wiley, 2007.

Segal, Richard A., Jr. "The Buzz in B-to-B." *The Interactive Future: Advertising Age Special Issue* (2000), pp. 100–103.

Stone, Bob, and John Wyman. *Successful Telemarketing.* Lincolnwood, IL: NTC Business Books, 1992.

Thomas, Brian, and Matthew Housden. *Direct Marketing Practice.* Oxford: Butterworth Heinemann, 2002.

"Using Social Media Marketing to Get More Visitors to Your Site," http://ypnblog.com/blog/2007/06/26/smm-in-depth/.

# Chapter 13

## Sales and Sales Management

**HP**

When Mark Hurd took over the reins of HP as CEO, the company had a strong retail presence but the commercial division responsible for sales to businesses was pulling the entire company down. And since commercial customers accounted for 70 percent of HP's revenue, fixing the problem was pretty important. In an effort to find the right fix, he started with customers. They complained mightily that they didn't know whom to contact, that prices were different for the same products depending on whom they called, and that the offerings from HP were not competitive.●

From the sales force's perspective, though, the situation seemed just as grim. Salespeople averaged 30 percent of their time with customers; the rest was spent trying to negotiate the labyrinth that was HP. Salespeople reported it took two weeks or more to get a demonstration product installed at a customer's location. Managers said it took months to get permission to hire a new salesperson. HP required four sign-offs on a proposal while competitors required three; the loss in time waiting for approval was costing HP business and making customers angry. These were just some of the challenges that HP salespeople were working against.●

Hurd took immediate action, cutting layers of management. Further, he standardized the CRM software, giving him direct visibility into every account. He also rode with salespeople to call on their customers. Salespeople's time with customers increased to 40 percent and approval time decreased to days.●

What do customers say? Keith Morrrow, chief information officer of 7-Eleven Inc., says his HP sales rep calls on him all the time, and with better offerings. James Farris, senior technology officer for Staples, says he sees his HP rep now twice as often, also resulting in better offerings. ●

The financial results are strong, too. HP is now the largest technology company in revenue, more than IBM, Microsoft, or Google. With Hurd's leadership, salespeople can deliver more value to their customers, returning more value back to HP and its shareholders. ●

Sources: Louise Lee, "HP Sees a Gold Mine in Data Mining," *BusinessWeek* (April 30, 2007), p. 71; Pui-Wing Tam, "Rewiring Hewlett-Packard; Before Attempting to Fix H-P, Hurd Had to Understand It; Using Workers as Consultants," *The Wall Street Journal* (Eastern edition; July 20, 2005) p. B.1; Pui-Wing Tam, "System Reboot—Hurd's Big Challenge at H-P: Overhauling Corporate Sales; Years of Acquisitions Led to a Bloated Bureaucracy; Improving Client Relations; Mr. Ditucci Gets the Contract," *The Wall Street Journal* (Eastern edition; April 3, 2006), p. A.1.

## LEARNING OBJECTIVES

Most companies spend more on selling than on any other element in their marketing budget. They spend so much because personal selling is an effective way to transact business.

In this chapter, we focus on the strategic nature of managing sales. As business marketers, it is important to recognize the many different options from which to choose within the sales function.

*After reading this chapter, you should be able to*

- Identify sales' strategic communication role.
- Select the types of selling used for different types of relationships.
- Outline the sales strategy associated with each type of selling.
- Compare and contrast organizational structures used to manage sales.
- Illustrate when to use different control and compensation programs.
- Discuss how sales force performance is evaluated.

Professional salespeople are an important element in business. When managed properly, they can contribute to the firm's success, as well as the value produced by the entire value chain.

# THE NATURE OF PROFESSIONAL SELLING

A major premise of this book is that sound business marketing creates value. Yet the public perception of selling is that salespeople don't deliver value. The perception is that salespeople are out to get the sale, no matter what—and if the product is really a good one, salespeople and selling really aren't needed.

This perception that salespeople are unethical or unnecessary is unfortunate, for a primary role of professional salespeople is to create value. Most salespeople believe strongly in the efficacy of their product. When this belief is combined with genuine concern for the customer, salespeople are free to create value.

The misperception that sales is unethical is also unfortunate because most marketing students will start out in sales. Those students who hold that misperception are less likely to look for entry-level sales positions and less likely to stay in those positions if they do enter sales. Students who embrace sales as a professional opportunity, whether to start a career or build a career, are far more likely to have multiple job offers when they graduate. In fact, Manpower (a company that specializes in finding people jobs) reports that salespeople are in far greater demand than any other job type, with more open jobs than in teaching, nursing, or engineering.[1]

## Salespeople Create Value

A doctor with a patient who doesn't respond to traditional treatment is frustrated and unable to come up with a solution. The pharmaceutical salesperson describes a new therapy involving an old drug—the doctor tries it and the patient recovers.

A furniture manufacturer wants to expand but doesn't have the money. Salespeople (called loan officers) from two banks compete for the loan—the local bank wins because the salesperson identifies a free-enterprise zone where the company can expand and save money on taxes. The company builds a new plant and employs 200 more people.

A small manufacturer of trusses (components used in construction) has an old computer that seems to break down two or three times a month—always during payroll. Payroll checks are late and employees are grumbling. They wonder if the company has the money to pay them so they look for new jobs. A salesperson shows how replacing two peripherals can keep the old computer operational for at least a year, until the company has the money to buy a new one. Payroll checks are cut on time and key personnel stay with the company.

Although these stories may seem melodramatic, they illustrate the way that salespeople deliver value. Salespeople add value by identifying customer needs and devising or delivering a solution for those needs. Salespeople are able to adapt (change) how an offering is presented or even to adapt the offering itself so that it meets the needs of the buyer. Adaptation is something that other forms of marketing communication can't do. Such adaptation powers professional selling, because customers often don't know what they need or how to configure a solution for their needs. For example, how many new plants has the furniture manufacturer's management financed? The current management had never built a new plant before. The loan officers, though, had financed several. Similarly, the truss manufacturer's management were experts in building trusses, not computers. Professional salespeople create value by adapting to fit the needs of the buyer.

## Professional Salespeople Are Ethical

As stated earlier, many students believe salespeople will do whatever it takes to get a sale. For example, in a study comparing the perceptions of sales managers and students, students believed salespeople to be less ethical than did sales managers. So those with more direct experience with business salespeople were more likely to report that salespeople have high ethics.[2]

What these findings probably mean is that students expect business to have its dirty dealing, manipulating, and so forth. Salespeople, however, have found that they can be successful and be ethical; in fact, to succeed it is necessary to be ethical. The nature of professional selling in the business-to-business environment supports and encourages ethical behavior. Taking a sales job in the business marketing environment does not mean that a compromise of personal values will be necessary to be successful. Perhaps to understand this more clearly, it is necessary to understand the role of the sales force in the organization.

# SALES' ROLE IN THE ORGANIZATION

From an integrated marketing communications perspective, salespeople bring the dialogue to life. How they go about their job of selling? Offering must be consistent with the positioning strategy and messages sent through other channels.

One startling statistic in the profile on HP at the start of this chapter is that HP salespeople were spending only 30 percent of their time actually calling on customers. Yet that statistic is not that startling—it has long been estimated that salespeople can only spend about a third of their time with customers. The remainder of their time is spent coordinating resources within their own firm so that customers' needs are met, learning about new offerings and other training and other activities. Salespeople also gather important customer and competitor information that executives need for developing strategy. As such, salespeople are a critical lynchpin to the market for market-oriented learning organizations.

# Managing Relationships

In many cases, salespeople have the field responsibility of deciding which accounts to work with and which accounts to bypass. Other elements in the marketing communication mix do not have the same level of individual dialogue that enables the selling organization to adapt in the same manner as salespeople. Further, the sales force has the responsibility for determining specific account strategy, particularly with respect to how the relationship will be managed. Sales is also responsible for implementing the account strategy and ensuring customer satisfaction.

## Creating Customers for Life

Customer relationships should be managed such that the sales force achieves sales targets. Business is not about making friends, but making customers, preferably for life. For example, an office equipment and supply company can reasonably expect a small law firm to buy $83,800 in office equipment and supplies (not counting computers) over a 20-year period. If that office supply salesperson looks only for a copier sale and doesn't recognize the long-term value of the account, the additional revenue could be lost.[3]

## Customer Service

Serving the needs of customers can include training on how to use the product or service effectively, handling customer complaints, and taking care of customer needs. For example, Megan Derrick at Konica Minolta sells copiers. Her customer service activities include training new customers on how to properly use their new copier, taking toner and paper if they run out, and handling the occasional customer complaint. Her reputation for service has enabled her to build a loyal and growing customer base.

Serving the customer well is important to all companies. One study found that 65 percent of the average company's business comes from current customers. Another study found the cost of acquiring a new customer to be five times that of keeping an old customer.[4] These figures point out the importance of taking care of the customer in any reasonable manner.

### Coordinating Corporate Resources

Salespeople have the responsibility for making sure that the customer is satisfied, but often that satisfaction depends on someone else in the organization doing what should be done (as we discussed in Chapter 7). Salespeople depend on and interact with personnel from manufacturing, shipping, sales administration, credit, and billing, among others. For example, a salesperson may take an order and promise delivery in three months. Achieving that three-month target may mean that manufacturing has to schedule production of the order, shipping has to make sure a truck is available, and the credit department has to approve the customer's credit. If there's a breakdown in any one of those areas, the customer may not get the product when needed. It is the salesperson who coordinates with each of these departments to see that the product is delivered to the customer on time.

Technology plays an important role in sharing information. Contact management systems such as ACT! and similar software programs track sales efforts in each account. This information is then available to upper management in as much, or as little, detail as they want. The information can be summarized; for example, management can pull up reports and see how many prospects there are for a certain product and what the dominant buying need is. Thus, the dialogue with the customer gets shared with management as the rep goes about the business of talking with customers and recording the results of the conversation. From the Field 13–1 describes the challenges of managing sales knowledge globally.

# Gathering Information

Successful learning organizations gather, share, and act on information. Boundary spanning positions (those that cross beyond the organization's boundaries) are important information-gathering and sharing positions. Sales and purchasing can be the two most important boundary spanning positions because of the type of information they gather. (We discussed the information gathered by purchasing in Chapter 3.) Sales' responsibility is to engage the customer in dialogue, or two-way communication to achieve mutual interests. Salespeople also gather information concerning competitors and market factors. Salespeople who only *tell* miss a great opportunity: the opportunity to listen.

### Customer Dialogue

While the salesperson is only one communication channel (others include advertising and trade shows), salespeople are in the unique position of holding in-depth conversations with customers. Salespeople are also able to act on that information in a way that brings additional value to the customer.

For example, David Lowit represents i-Symmetry, a company that provides information technology (IT) professionals to companies for short or long-term projects or even

**13–1**

# FROM THE FIELD
## Managing Sales Knowledge Globally

Companies like John Deere are standardizing their products around the globe. Ford has announced that it is cutting the number of its vendors in half, meaning that companies that serve Ford's plants in England and Mexico must also serve Ford plants in Asia and the United States. But, in 2006, if you asked a Siemens salesperson if the company had done anything in the agricultural implement or automotive industry, you may have received a blank stare. And Siemens salespeople weren't the only ones having difficulty.

A recent study of sales executives in France, Mexico, and the United States pointed out that salespeople have to know more than ever. One sales executive was quoted in the study as saying, "Our salespeople used to have to know about two dozen offerings; now it is over two hundred." Such complexity is a challenge, particularly when salespeople are trying to sell to customers with locations around the world. Such buyers may not care what was done in

India, for example, until they know if it will also work in France.

Siemens addressed this growing complexity and global sales challenge by creating a Web-based knowledge management system. Think of a database of case studies, sales proposals, contact information for referrals (along with notes about what they will say), and other information about market segments, customers, and individual deals, and you begin to get close to what they developed. More important, given the global nature of Siemens's customers, the knowledge management system provided global salespeople with local contacts for referrals, case studies, and the like—the information they needed to prove their case.

John F. Tanner, Jr., Jorge Wise, Christophe Fournier, Sandrine Hollet, and F. Juliet Poujol, "Executives' Perspectives of the Changing Role of the Sales Profession: Views from France, the United States, and Mexico," *Journal of Business and Industrial Marketing* (Forthcoming); Michele Marchetti, "Are Your Salespeople Fit for Battle?" *Sales & Marketing Management* (March 2007), p. 12.

permanent placement. He has to clearly understand what the customer's requirements are or the wrong skills are brought to the customer and the result is a poorly completed or late project and an unhappy customer. At the same time, though, he also has to convince the buyer that i-Symmetry's team of IT professionals is the best one for the job.

The information that Lowit gathers, though, is also important for his company. By compiling this information over time, i-Symmetry's executives can determine patterns in customer requirements that may signal changes in market demand. Those changes then require that i-Symmetry find the right IT professionals so that they will be available as projects are won. Misreading those trends means that there is staff sitting around, collecting paychecks but not working while projects are lost due to inadequate resources.

## Competitive Information

In addition to gathering information from the customer, the salesperson is gathering information about competitors and market forces such as the economy. Although there are other channels of getting this type of information, salespeople can provide decision makers with timely and necessary information about a number of market factors.

For example, the first time management may hear of a new product is when a customer tells a salesperson about the competitor's proposal. It's more likely that pricing information, competitors' sales strategies, and similar information will be encountered first by salespeople than by any other source.

To summarize, the sales force is an important element in a firm's marketing mix because salespeople manage customer relationships to build sales, manage customer satisfaction by coordinating corporate resources, and gather key customer and market information. Other elements of the marketing mix may also perform some of these activities, but none do all of these activities all of the time and with the efficacy of the sales force.

# SALES STRATEGIES AND CUSTOMER RELATIONSHIPS

The sales force, including sales management, has the responsibility for developing and implementing account sales and relationships strategies. Yet, as we know from Chapter 2, not all accounts want, or are entitled to, the same level of relationship or service. In this section, we will review the types of customer relationships and then discuss the types of selling strategies appropriate for each one.

# Types of Customer Relationships and Selling Strategies

In Chapter 2, you discovered a model that indicated two dimensions were important in determining the type of relationship. Each dimension represented the degree of commitment and motivational investment to the relationship, one dimension for the seller and the other for the buyer. In Chapter 3, you learned that buyers are more likely to want a strategic partnership when the product or service supplied is a key element in their ability to create value. Sellers, on the other hand, want strategic partnerships with buyers who are lead users (Chapter 8), represent a large amount of (potential) revenue, and/or provide status. (For example, consultants often list the names of their largest clients in order to gain credibility with the rest of the market.)

When there is little product and service differentiation, there is little need to partner from the buyer's prespective. Similarly, when needs are the same across all customers, buying processes are virtually identical, and all customers are relatively the same size, there is little need to partner from the seller's perspective.

In each case, there is a different type of strategy that can be implemented. There are four basic sales strategies that illustrate the potential range of possible strategies: script-based selling, needs satisfaction selling, consultative selling, and strategic partnering, as illustrated in Exhibit 13–1.

## *Script-Based Selling*

In situations where customer needs do not vary much from one customer to another, script-based selling can be very effective. The product should be relatively simple and easy to understand. Also called canned selling, **script-based selling** involves using scripts or memorized sales pitches from which the salesperson does not deviate. The method is used by Premier Industrial, a company that manufactures and markets over 5,000 maintenance, repair, and operations (MRO) items. For example, it markets a solder that is much stronger than the solder sold in a hardware store. (Solder is used to weld two pieces together that have to carry electric current, such as welding a wire to a contact on an electric motor.) The strength is evident in a simple demonstration during which the salesperson solders two ends of a paper clip together

**Exhibit 13–1**
Selling
Strategies

*Script-Based Selling*
Customer needs are similar.                    Use same presentation from customer to customer.

*Needs Satisfaction Selling*
Customer needs vary among              Use questioning techniques to identify needs.
  a set of common needs.                  Present specifics about product to satisfy important needs.

*Consultative Selling*
Customer needs vary, with unique      Use questioning techniques to identify needs.
  needs from buyer to buyer.            Create or assemble a custom solution to fit needs.

*Strategic Partner Selling*
Buyer and seller cocreate needs and jointly develop solutions.

and asks the buyer to pull the two ends apart. The conversation may go something like this:

Premier salesperson: Do you ever solder anything on the equipment you maintain?
Maintenance manager: Of course.

Premier salesperson: Most guys I talk to resent having to solder the same thing over and over because the solder won't hold. [Buyer nods head to indicate yes.] If I can borrow a paper clip from you, I'll show you that won't ever be a problem for you again. [Salesperson bends wire into a circle and solders it together.] Now pull that apart. [Buyer tries and fails.] Isn't that the kind of solder you need?

Maintenance manager: Yeah! That stuff's great!

Premier salesperson: How many spools will you need?

Many people may believe scripted selling to be outdated and obsolete, but Premier is enjoying an enviable growth rate well in excess of 15 percent per year. Scripted selling is popular in telemarketing and in selling MRO items and other supplies.

## Needs Satisfaction Selling

A more advanced method of selling is **needs satisfaction selling,** or a process of selling that involves identifying the buyer's needs and tailoring the sales pitch to fit those needs. Thus, needs satisfaction selling involves two components: identifying the needs and making the presentation.

Needs satisfaction selling works best when there is variance in needs across buyers and choices have to be made among products, as opposed to custom-made solutions. For example, a Canon copier representative and a buyer may engage in a dialogue like the following:

Seller: How many copies do you make each month?

Buyer: Oh, about 2,000.

Seller: And what do you usually copy?

Buyer: We copy a lot of forms. Every time a customer comes in, we fill out the paperwork, then make a copy of it for our file. So it is probably three to five originals, with just one copy of each page.

Seller: So you need something with a fast first copy speed because a customer is standing there waiting for it?

Buyer: Yes! There's nothing I hate more than waiting for the copier to warm up.

Seller: And probably, if you could have a document feeder so you could just stack the originals on top and it would feed each one in as needed, that would speed things up, too?

In this example, the seller has identified two needs, one for fast first copy speed and another for a document handler. Copiers without these features would not be considered. But a copier with a running speed of 90 copies per minute would not be necessary, as the buyer never makes that many at one time.

## Consultative Selling

Consultative selling is very similar to needs satisfaction selling, but differs to a matter of degree. When a seller uses consultative selling, the solution choices are not simply a matter of choosing from an array of finished products. When truly using **consultative selling,** the seller is bringing specialized expertise into a complex problem in order to create a somewhat customized solution.

For example, the materials handling industry manufactures and installs customized equipment for moving products through manufacturing processes. Using belts, rails, wheels, hooks, motors, and so forth, products in the process of being manufactured are moved from one machine to the next. The assembly of standard materials handling parts into a customized system is an outcome of consultative selling.

In consultative selling, the salesperson is a consultant. More of the knowledge lies with the salesperson than with the customer in comparison to needs satisfaction selling. Still, there is not the commitment by the customer that exists when a partnership is created.

## Strategic Partner Selling

Partnering as a sales strategy goes beyond consultative selling. In **strategic partner selling,** both parties share expertise and resources to create customized solutions, and there is a commitment to joint planning for mutual benefit. As a sales strategy, partnership selling requires a commitment of resources well beyond that of just the salesperson and customer support staff. A company must also commit resources in all other areas of the firm in order to support the most effective creation of value possible, which is why some refer to it as enterprise selling. Further, the result should be a maximization of revenue for all areas of the company.

Partnering is more than just selling strategies aimed at increasing revenue within the account. In the next section, we will discuss selling strategies across the partnering cycle that are designed to lead to long-term commitment.

# Selling across the Stages of the Partnership

In Chapter 2, you learned the stages of a strategic partnership, from awareness to dissolution. Here, we focus on the three middle stages—exploration, expansion, and commitment—because these stages separate discrete transactions and functional relationships (which stop at exploration) from strategic partnerships, as illustrated in

**Exhibit 13–2**
Stages in Relationship Building
SOURCE: *Barton A. Weitz, Stephen B. Castleberry, and John F. Tanner, Jr.,* Selling: Building Partnerships, *6th edition,
Burr Ridge, IL: Irwin/McGraw-Hill, 2007.*

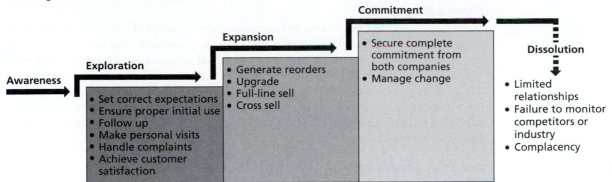

Exhibit 13–2. Recall, too, the crucial role that trust plays in building a strategic partnership. In this section, we will discuss the selling strategies used in each stage that are designed to create trust.

## *Exploration*

In the exploration stage, the relationship is defined through the development of expectations for each party. Each party, buyer and seller, explores what the other party has to offer. The buyer tests the seller's product, how the seller responds to special requests, and other similar actions after the initial sale. At the same time, trust and personal relationships are developed.

Beginning the relationship properly is important for the relationship to flourish over time. Keep in mind that the customer is excited about receiving the benefits of the product as promised by the salesperson. If the customer's initial experience is poor, it may be extremely difficult to overcome. Beginning the relationship properly requires the salesperson to set the proper expectations, monitor order processing and delivery, ensure proper use of the product, and assist in servicing the customer.

### Set Proper Expectations
As discussed in previous chapters, customer satisfaction begins with setting the proper expectations. No marketing communications should inflate the buyer's hopes unreasonably. Long-term relationships are begun by making honest presentations of the product's capabilities and eliminating any misconceptions before the order is placed.

### Monitor Order Processing and Delivery
Many people may work on an order before it reaches the customer, but it is the salesperson who is ultimately responsible for making sure that the product reaches the customer at the appropriate time. Business marketing is not like retailing in which the customer chooses a product in stock and takes it to the checkout counter; rather, the order is placed and the product shipped at the appropriate time. Because products may not be immediately available from another vendor should delivery fall through, customers rely on companies to meet their delivery promises. Imagine what would happen, for example, if a Thomasville furniture plant couldn't get any raw lumber. The plant would shut down.

Internet-based inventory management systems have taken the salesperson out of the order-delivery loop in many cases, but in most instances, the salesperson is still responsible for making sure the company lives up to the delivery commitment.

### Ensure Proper Use

Some buyers may not know how to operate the basic features of a product. If the product is not operating at maximum efficiency, the customer is losing value. Many firms have staffed a customer service department or tasked their technical support group with training customers, but it is still the salesperson's responsibility to make sure that the customer is getting full value. In England, for example, Thermofrost representatives train users in proper maintenance of their display and storage coolers. Proper maintenance not only increases the life of the coolers but also lowers electricity and repair costs associated with running the coolers.

### Assist in Servicing

Although complaints signal customer dissatisfaction, their absence doesn't always mean that the customer is happy. They may speak out only when grossly dissatisfied, or the purchasing agent may not be aware of any problems until users become furious. When salespeople assist technical support and customer service personnel in servicing the accounts, salespeople can learn why problems arise. Then they can address similar situations in other accounts before the problems grow into complaints.

Complaints can arise at any stage of the partnership, but when complaints arise during the exploration stage, the salesperson has the opportunity to prove commitment to the account. When customers sense that commitment, either through the handling of a complaint or through other forms of special attention, they may be ready to move into the expansion stage.

## Expansion

When a salesperson does a good job of establishing the relationship by ensuring a sucessful initial experience, the opportunity is there for additional sales. Trust is developing, allowing the salesperson to focus on identifying additional needs and recommending solutions. Note that the following strategies for increasing sales are sometimes used in direct response situations, particularly telemarketing.

### Generating Repeat Sales

In some situations, the most appropriate strategy is to generate repeat orders, particularly for supply items and other operating expenditures. For example, Morton provides salt and other cooking ingredients to food manufacturers like General Mills. The best strategy for a Morton's salesperson may be to ensure that General Mills continues to buy from Morton.

Generating repeat sales requires recognizing buying cycles and being present at buying time. Salespeople should also continue offering special assistance through value analysis. For example, Marvin Wagner, engineer for John Deere, meets with suppliers annually to review their performance. Those who have documented cost savings or additional value due to revenue growth and other benefits will be the ones that get the opportunity for repeat sales in the coming year.

### Upgrading

**Upgrading,** or **upselling,** is similar to generating reorders in that the same general needs are met, except upgrading involves convincing the buyer to use a higher-quality or newer product. The buyer selects the upgrade because it meets needs better than did the old product.

Upgrading is crucial to high-tech companies. For example, HP relies heavily on customers upgrading to newer products. Otherwise, customers might turn to IBM and HP would lose significant account share.

### Full-Line Selling

Parker-Hannifin (or simply Parker) manufactures and sells a line of industrial valves. These valves come in different sizes and are designed to turn off and turn on the pipelines for different types of materials—some toxic and others harmless. Depending on the materials that go through the valves, different materials are needed to make the valves. Suppose a buyer manufactures a line of oil storage tanks for use in oil fields, refineries, gas stations, and other situations. If the company bought one type of valve from Parker and other valves from other manufacturers, the Parker rep may try to convince the buyer to buy all of its valves from Parker. Selling the entire line of associated products is called **full-line selling.** Many companies try to get their foot in the door with any sale, hoping to then blossom into full-line selling once the initial product has proven its value.

Full-line selling is not the same as full-line forcing, a practice used when a company has one top-selling product that it sells through distributors. Full-line forcing occurs when the company forces distributors to carry the full line in order to be able to sell the top seller. Full-line selling is a sales strategy that involves leveraging the relationship in order to sell the entire line of products.

### Cross Selling

Similar to full-line selling, **cross selling** is selling additional products but these products may not be related. For example, the Parker salesperson may also try to sell meters and gauges along with the valves. Cross selling works best when the salesperson can leverage the relationship with the buyer. Trust in the salesperson and the selling organization already exists; therefore, the sale should not be as difficult if the proper needs exist.

If the buying center changes greatly, cross selling becomes more like the initial sale. For example, if Parker also has materials handling equipment, that equipment may be purchased by an entirely different set of people. For them, Parker has no reputation or relationship.

## Commitment

When the buyer–seller relationship has reached the commitment stage, there is a stated or implied pledge to continue the relationship. Formally, this pledge may begin with the seller being designated a preferred supplier. Although **preferred supplier status** may mean different things in different companies, in general it means that the supplier is assured a large percentage of the buyer's business and will get the first opportunity to earn any new business.[5] For example, at Motorola, only preferred suppliers are eligible to bid on new programs. Thus, *preferred supplier* is a buyer's term for partner.

To become a preferred supplier for PPG, a maker of paints and glass products used in automobiles and other products, a supplier must pass several criteria, some of which are listed in Exhibit 13–3. Research finds that many buyers examine the suppliers on criteria

**Exhibit 13–3**
Examples of
Supplier
Criteria to Sell
to PPG

SOURCE: Adapted from
www.ppg.com/$ave/
measurement_grid,
November 21, 2000.

---

*Hard Savings*

Payment terms, such as cash discounts
Improve process
 Cycle time reduction (shorter-order/delivery cycles, for example)
Inventory management
 Vendor inventory management
Quality and innovation
 Variability reduction—no defects, and no adjustments needed to make products fit the applications
supply chain management
 Optimum packaging—light packaging that reduces shipping costs while still protecting the product

*Soft Savings*

Commercial
 Minority-owned vendors
Global initiatives
 New markets—provide access to new markets, either by partnering into new markets or by
 adjusting products to fit needs of new markets
Improve process
 Improve safety or environmental procedures
Quality and innovation
 Training
Supply chain management
 Bar coding—can reduce the time employees take to process a shipment

Source: http://www.ppg.com/crp_purchasing/$ave/measurement_grid.htm, accessed July 10, 2007.

---

similar to those used by PPG. Although the salesperson may not be able to manage corporate culture, the salesperson can utilize appropriate selling strategies to lead the customer to the commitment stage.

### Securing Commitment

Commitment in a partnership should permeate both organizations. The salesperson must secure commitment not only from the customer, but also from the rest of his own company. Senior management must be convinced of the benefits of partnering with the account so that the appropriate investments will be made. Additionally, the salesperson has to see that others in the organization are empowered to serve the needs of this customer. For example, if a customer has a problem with the billing process, the billing department should work directly with the customer to resolve the issue and design a more appropriate process. For other accounts, the billing department would probably be unwilling to make changes to the process.

### Building Communication

For the billing department to handle a request for a new billing procedure, direct communication must occur between the department and the customer. Once in the commitment phase, the salesperson must take on a much stronger coordinative role and build direct lines of communication between the two organizations. In the previous stages, communication between the two organizations was really just between the purchasing agent or decision maker and the salesperson. Now, as illustrated in Exhibit 13–4, communication lines should be direct so that problems and opportunities can be identified and resolved as quickly and efficiently as possible. These direct communication lines are part of the commitment necessary to building partnerships.

## 13–1

# BUSINESS 2 BUSINESS
## Customer Power

Some customers try to take advantage of salespeople with special requests such as asking the rep to perform routine maintenance for free, or for free trials or samples. A customer may ask for free service in order to keep the account, or for a free trial with a big purchase as bait. How do you recognize which requests represent legitimate needs and are made in the context of good faith partnering and which requests represent an unfair use of the customer's power? What should a salesperson do to curb unfair and unnecessary requests?

As you have seen, the sales force plays an important role in the business marketing organization. How the sales force accomplishes that role is dependent on a number of factors, and one result is the choice of the most appropriate selling strategy. Selling strategy also affects the structure and practice of sales force management, which is the focus of the rest of this chapter.

**Exhibit 13–4**

Communication in the Partnership

*SOURCE: Barton A. Weitz, Stephen B. Castleberry, and John F. Tanner, Jr., Selling: Building Partnerships, 6th edition, Burr Ridge, IL: Irwin/McGraw-Hill, 2007.*

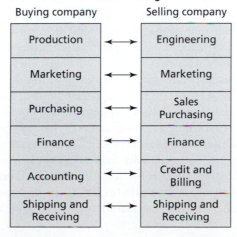

**Before Partnering**

| Buying company | | Selling company |
|---|---|---|
| Production | | Engineering |
| Marketing | | Marketing |
| Purchasing Department | | Sales |
| Finance | | Finance |
| Accounting | | Credit and Billing |
| Shipping and Receiving | | Shipping and Receiving |

Purchasing agent → ← Salesperson

**After Partnering**

| Buying company | | Selling company |
|---|---|---|
| Production | ↔ | Engineering |
| Marketing | ↔ | Marketing |
| Purchasing | ↔ | Sales Purchasing |
| Finance | ↔ | Finance |
| Accounting | ↔ | Credit and Billing |
| Shipping and Receiving | ↔ | Shipping and Receiving |

# ORGANIZING THE SALES FORCE

The sales function may be organized in many ways, depending somewhat on the choice of sales strategy as discussed earlier in this chapter. No matter how the sales force is organized, though, there is usually a sales executive in charge.

## The Sales Executive

Depending on the size of the organization, the chief executive officer may fulfill the responsibilities and duties of the sales executive, or the marketing executive and sales executive duties may be combined into one position, or the sales executive position may be a stand-alone function. Irrespective of whether the person handles only sales duties or has other responsibilities as well, the sales executive is responsible for decisions such as the choice of sales strategy, the number and location of salespeople, the setting of sales quotas and designing of compensation plans, and sales forecasting. We've already discussed the choice of a sales strategy so we will focus now on the other responsibilities. From the Field 13–2 profiles one such executive, Kurt Knapton, of eRewards.

## Size and Organization of the Sales Force

The sales executive determines how many salespeople are needed to achieve the company's sales and customer satisfaction targets. In addition, the executive must determine the type of salespeople needed. For example, the sales executive is the person who decides if a global account management team is needed or if local salespeople can handle all accounts. This decision, as well as other decisions concerning such factors as location and field management structure, is based on the executive's determination of the customer satisfaction level necessary to achieve sales targets.

There are many types of salespeople, including telemarketing representatives, field salespeople, product specialists, and account specialists. Sometimes there is overlap in responsibilities, such as when a telemarketer supports a field salesperson—both have responsibility for the same account. Usually, however, there are different responsibilities assigned to different types of salespeople, and companies often have more than one type.

### *Geographic Salespeople*

Most sales departments are organized geographically at some level. The most basic sales force structure is to give each salesperson all accounts within a specified geographic area—here we have the **geographic salesperson.** Companies often combine geographic territories into branch or zone offices, which are further combined to create regions. Konica Minolta Business Systems, for example, operates a geographic sales force. One rep may have responsibility for all businesses within three zip codes whereas a rep working in a downtown area may have responsibility for all businesses within three square blocks, depending on the number of businesses within each geographic area. The company attempts to balance the sales potential of each territory by determining how many businesses should be in a territory, and then dividing a city into areas that fall near the desired number of businesses. Geographic salespeople are used when all products serve the same general types of buyers.

Geographic reps are usually **field salespeople** (also called **outside salespeople**); that is, they call on accounts at the accounts' locations. **Inside salespeople** can also be found in business markets; these salespeople sell at the company's location. A telemarketer account manager is such a person. Inside salespeople also handle any walk-up business.

## 13–2

# FROM THE FIELD

## Self-Taught Sales Lessons from the Edge

With a degree in management from Baylor University and an MBA from the Tuck School of Business at Dartmouth, I fancied myself a business generalist. In fact, I spent nearly 10 years in the management consulting industry as a generalist at Accenture and Booz Allen Hamilton solving a wide variety of business problems for clients across a number of different industries: manufacturing, finance, energy, defense, insurance, etc. The last thing I was looking for was a career in sales. I always thought of sales as something you were "born to do" and you had to have that innate "gift of gab" to be successful. I was a consultant, a problem solver, good at analyzing data, making decisions, and leading others—I did not see a sales role in the cards for me.

With a growing family and a desire to travel less, I joined a start-up company during the "Internet boom." All was going well until the infamous dot.com "bubble burst" and Internet start-ups began failing right and left. The start-up company I joined was eRewards, Inc., headquartered in Dallas, Texas. The business model was sound—involving online market research and advertising effectiveness testing—but, as times became tough, it was clear that our sales were not covering our costs. If our company did not ramp up sales quickly, then we would likely become a dot.com casualty. At that moment, I decided to become a salesman.

I started cold-calling prospective market research clients, and I found out that they would not buy from us because we lacked credibility. So we applied for and were accepted in 2001 into a leading market research association, CASRO, which was intrigued with our unique use of the Internet to field market research studies. I started attending CASRO research conferences where I could shake hands with prospective clients and learn more about their "pain points." In short, I started listening and learning. My first sales lesson—*listen carefully to what your customer is saying.* As a result, eRewards adapted its approach to focus on an underserved segment of the online research market, business executive research. My second sales lesson—*you will be more successful selling a differentiated product than a commodity.* Next, as sales began to climb, I found myself recruiting additional salespeople to keep the success going. I evolved into a sales management role and spent my time motivating others to stretch to reach sales targets. I discovered that managing the sales function was very rewarding, and six years and over 30 salespeople later we have been able to retain over 95 percent of our sales force. My third sales lesson—*loyalty is a two-way street: If you treat salespeople fairly and provide them with opportunity, they will be loyal in return.*

Currently, I am chief revenue officer at eRewards which now has over 225 employees and continues to grow. My last sales lesson? *Success in sales does not depend on a silver tongue as much as two key traits: a desire to hear and serve your customer, and the tenacity and determination to never give up.*

Kurt Knapton, Executive Vice President, Chief Revenue Officer, eRewards, Inc.

Square D, a supplier of electrical components, has inside salespeople who help electricians select the right parts and close the sale.

When only a geographic structure is used, the organizational structure is likely to be line-and-staff. A **line-and-staff organization** is one in which those who conduct the primary tasks of the department (in this case, sales) are part of the line—their managers are called line managers—and all support personnel are staff. Authority and responsibility move up and down the organizational line, not across. A salesperson's responsibility for an account comes from the branch sales manager, who received that responsibility from the regional manager, who got it from the sales executive.

Companies may also organize their salespeople by account, and there are several ways to do this. In each method, the **account salesperson** has responsibility for specified accounts, rather than a geographic area. One method is to specify new account responsibility to one group of salespeople and current account responsibility to another group. For example, an RCA radio communications division uses field salespeople to develop new accounts and a telemarketing sales force to maintain accounts. Each telemarketer has a list of specified accounts and only that telemarketer works with those customers.

Similar customers often have similar needs, whereas different types of customers may have very different needs for the same product. In such cases, salespeople may specialize on one type of account. For example, Lanier has salespeople who only call on medical accounts. Similarly, Xerox has account salespeople who specialize in serving the education market, the legal market, or government accounts. These situations require special customer or market knowledge to be successful.

Companies also divide their accounts on the basis of size. Large customers, sometimes called **key accounts,** may have a salesperson assigned only to their account. The salesperson is called a **strategic account manager (SAM).** These salespeople work with geographic salespeople to handle local needs, but all account planning, pricing, and even product development are managed by the SAM. R. R. Donnelley has been a leader in using SAMs. Previously, for example, a local (French) R. R. Donnelley salesperson would sell to the American Express office in Paris, the Tokyo rep would call on the Asian office, and so forth. Each rep may have used a different strategy, different pricing, and so forth. Now American Express has a centralized purchasing office but needs global implementation; the R. R. Donnelley SAM calls on the central office but works with the Tokyo and Paris reps (and others) to make sure that local services are implemented properly.

Sometimes, a company may determine that a key account is a house account. A **house account** is handled by a sales executive and the company does not pay anyone commission on sales from the account. General Dynamics asked its suppliers to engage in this strategy and cut prices by an amount equivalent to the commission, but abandoned the strategy when it realized that service was also reduced. House accounts are generally not a good idea and should be served by an account manager.

## Product Specialists

When companies have diverse products using different technology platforms, their salespeople will specialize by product category. The need for technology expertise is too great for any one salesperson to understand, so the sales force is organized by product. HP, for example, has separate sales forces selling computers, electronic test equipment, components, medical test equipment, and analytical test equipment. Each sales force is geographically organized, and some may have account managers as well.

Product specialists must sometimes coordinate their activities with salespeople from other divisions. For example, an HP test instrument salesperson may have an account that also purchases electronic components. Sharing that information with the representative from the component division can help build a relationship that pays off with leads for test instruments.

## Sales Teams

In some industries, companies used product specialists to call on the same accounts, even the same buyers within each account. The buyers, however, grew tired of being

**Exhibit 13–5**

Sales Teams May Be Formed for Multilevel Selling

*SOURCE: Barton A. Weitz, Stephen B. Castleberry, and John F. Tanner, Jr., Selling: Building Partnerships, 6th edition, Burr Ridge, IL: Irwin/McGraw-Hill, 2007.*

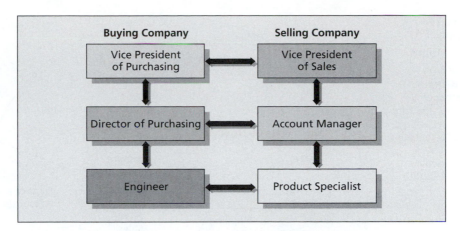

**Exhibit 13–6**

Matrix Team Selling Organization

In team selling, product specialists work with account managers. Account managers have total account responsibility, but product specialists are responsible for sales and service of only a limited portion of the product line, and may work with several account managers.

*SOURCE: Barton A. Weitz, Stephen B. Castleberry, and John F. Tanner, Jr., Selling: Building Partnerships, 6th edition, Burr Ridge, IL: Irwin/ McGraw-Hill, 2007.*

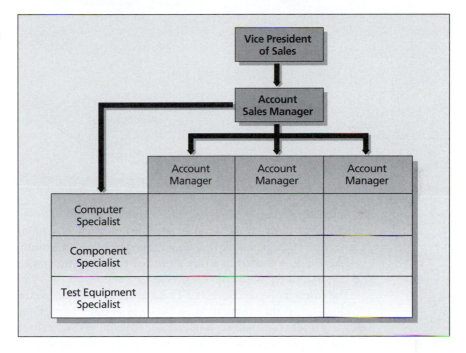

called on by five, six, or even more salespeople from the same company, especially when it was obvious that there was no coordination within the organization. In response, companies began developing sales teams, headed by an account manager. In **team selling,** a group of salespeople handle a single account. Each salesperson brings a different area of expertise or handles different responsibilities.

One type of team is the field salesperson and telemarketing support rep whom we've already discussed. Another type of team is used in **multilevel selling,** in which members of a selling organization at various levels call on their counterparts in the buying organization. The vice president of sales, for example, may visit the vice president of purchasing, as illustrated in Exhibit 13–5.

The most common form of team, though, may be one composed of product specialists and coordinated by account managers and organized using a matrix. As you can see in Exhibit 13–6, the **matrix sales team** may have each product specialist working with

**Exhibit 13–7**
Customer-Focused Team Structure

SOURCE: *Barton A. Weitz, Stephen B. Castleberry, and John F. Tanner, Jr., Selling: Building Partnerships, 6th edition, Burr Ridge, IL: Irwin/McGraw-Hill, 2007.*

three or more account managers. The account managers have total account responsibility and bring in the proper product specialist only when needed. Consultative and needs satisfaction strategies work well under this type of organization, especially when specialized expertise is needed to satisfy customer requirements but there is too much expertise required to reside in any one person.

The customer-focused team (CFT) is a structure that assigns customer responsibility to individuals across the organization, in sales and in other areas. Pioneered by NCR and Allegiance (a health care industry supplier), the structure resembles a wheel, with the customer as the hub. (See Exhibit 13–7.) In addition to product specialists, the account manager can draw on the expertise of a specific credit manager, a specific billing person, someone in manufacturing, and so forth. Each of these individuals has responsibility for coordinating the efforts of her individual functional areas in order to achieve the account strategy. Further, they are part of the account strategy development process and are headed up by the account manager.

Note that these individuals will also have line managers. There is still someone in charge of all manufacturing. The innovation lies in the fact that there is someone in manufacturing (and each other area) responsible for developing account goals and strategies and seeing that those strategies are implemented and account goals are met. All of the company's resources can be more effectively directed toward the needs of the account, so when relationships are important, customer-focused teams are an excellent method of organizing.

Team sales organizations raise issues of how to compensate for performance. In a customer-focused structure, bonuses are often shared among team members based on the performance of the company with that customer. The sales specialist may still receive a commission, but some incentive pay is offered to members of the team if it hits its goals.

## Sales Force Size

The sales executive may select one or more of the preceding types of salespeople and structures, based on the relationship quality, the complexity or variety of products, market size, and other factors. The sales executive is also responsible for determining how many of each type should be employed. The objective is to achieve the sales potential by providing each company that wants to buy the opportunity to buy.

One approach to determining the optimum number of salespeople involves an analysis of the salesperson's **workload,** or all of the activities that a salesperson must do to cover a territory. For example, a salesperson may be able to make six sales calls each day, but when training, sales meetings, and customer service responsibilities are thrown in, only four days per week are available for making sales calls. In the average month, the salesperson could make only 96 sales calls (6 calls $\times$ 4 days $\times$ 4 weeks). Keep in mind, too, that the more successful a salesperson is, the more time will be needed for customer service.

The next step is to allocate accounts such that all accounts will be called on with the desired frequency. For example, using the previous figures and assuming that there are 96,000 customers that you want called on at least once per month, then you need 1,000 salespeople. The desired number of calls per account will depend on a number of factors, including

- Sales strategy selected.
- Type of salesperson (geographic, account specialist, etc.).
- Nature of sales job.
- Nature of the product. More complex products require more calls.
- Stage of market development. A company entering a market has few customer service requirements and can use large territories.
- Competitive intensity. As intensity grows, so may the number of sales calls.

One method of allocating sales calls is based on a combination of the company's relative strength (either in the market or in an account) and the customer or market lifetime value.  Customer lifetime value has been discussed throughout this book, and a market lifetime value is simply a sum of those customers' lifetime values in a given market or market segment.  Simply put, the greater the lifetime value, the greater the resources likely to be allocated to that segment.

At the same time, however, relative market strength indicates the company's current position in the market and where it desires to be.  If the relative position is low but the company desires a stronger position in the market, compared to competitors, more resources are required. Thus, more salespeople may be added in order to make more calls and therefore strengthen the company's relative position for those segments with high lifetime value.[6] (See Exhibit 13–8.)

# Outsourcing the Sales Force

Not every business marketer that uses field or telemarketing salespeople uses its own employees. Manufacturers' reps, distributors, and telemarketing service bureaus can fill the requirement for salespeople without the fixed costs of hiring your own. Some companies even hire temporary sales forces for special needs, such as new product launches.[7]

**Exhibit 13–8**
Sales Resource
Allocation

SOURCES: Raymond LaForge and Dave Cravens, "Steps in Selling Effort Deployment," *Industrial Marketing Management* (1982), pp. 187–98. René Darmon, "Joint Assessment of Optional Sales Force Sizes and Sales Call Guidelines," *Canadian Journal of Administrative Science* 22 (2005), pp. 206–19.

|  |  | **Market Lifetime Value** | |
|---|---|---|---|
|  |  | Low | High |
| **Relative Market Strength** | Strong | Relatively fewer resources should be allocated here | Maintain sufficient resources to continue to reap the sales potential and strong position |
|  | Weak | Assign to alternative method of communicating, such as telemarketing | Direct more sales resources here |

## Advantages

There are advantages to outsourcing sales beyond just the costs issue. For example, manufacturers' reps and distributors are already in the field and already have relationships established with customers. When selected appropriately, they already have relationships with the customers you seek. Companies that are looking to enter a new market, particularly a foreign market, will use local distributors or manufacturers' reps in order to quickly penetrate the market through those established relationships.

Costs, as mentioned earlier, are variable, meaning that there are no selling costs to the manufacturer until the product is sold. There is no draw, only commission (or a profit margin earned by the distributor), and all selling expenses, such as travel or entertainment, are paid for by the distributor or rep. Therefore, less up-front investment is needed.

## Disadvantages

There is one major drawback to using distributors and reps—a loss of control. In most cases, the manufacturer's product is just one of many being sold. There is no guarantee that the product will even be discussed in sales calls. Nor is there any guarantee that the product will be sold in the manner desired by the manufacturer. Some manufacturers that sell through distributors or reps invest in training and merchandising materials in order to increase the likelihood that the reps will focus on their product. A common complaint, however, among distributors and reps is that the manufacturers do a poor job in supporting them with selling materials and training. It seems that most companies that use reps and distributors simply give them the product and a commission or a suggested profit margin.

Often, it is up to the salesperson to decide how much resources will be put into specific accounts. These decisions, though, are usually guided by strategies developed by the sales executive. In the next section, we'll examine how sales executives direct the activities of the sales force through several different methods.

# DIRECTING THE SALES FORCE

Once the sales force is in place, there remains the question of directing their activities. Part of the sales executive's responsibility is to ensure that the salespeople are working to achieve the company's sales and customer service objectives. Field salespeople are scattered over a wide area and operate without benefit of direct supervision. The sales executive faces the unique challenge of designing control systems that encourage each field sales manager and salesperson to maximize individual results through effective self-control. These control strategies often include quotas and compensation plans.

# Quotas

**Quotas** are a useful control mechanism, as they represent a quantitative minimum level of acceptable performance for a specific time period. Two types of quotas are used: activity quotas and performance quotas. **Activity quotas** specify the number and type of activities that salespeople should do; for example, a new business call quota would specify the number of noncustomers representing potential new business that should be visited in a period of time. Activity quotas are especially useful in situations where the sales cycle is long and sales are few, because activities can be monitored more frequently than sales. For example, some medical equipment sales cycles are longer than a year, and a rep may sell only one or two units per quarter. Having a monthly sales target would be inappropriate, but requiring a minimum number of sales calls is reasonable. Here management assumes that if the salesperson makes the calls, the sale will occur. Activity quotas can be specified for many types of sales activities, such as number of current customer calls, demonstrations, proposal presentations, and other activities.

**Performance,** or **outcome, quotas** specify levels of performance, such as revenue, gross margin, or unit sales in a period of time. Often, sales quotas are simply a breakdown of the company's sales forecast. Other types of quotas, such as gross margin quotas, can be used to encourage salespeople to sell profitable products, not just the products that may be the easiest to sell. Companies may convert gross margin to points and then allow salespeople to achieve their quota by whatever mix of products they choose. For example, suppose an office equipment company enjoys a 30 percent profit margin on copiers but only 20 percent on faxes. Copiers may be worth three points each whereas faxes are worth two. If the salesperson's quota is 12 points, quota can be achieved by selling four copiers, six faxes, or some combination.

Good quota systems are fair, recognizing the potential in a sales territory as well as the constraints. For example, someone who has to call on accounts scattered across Montana, Idaho, and Wyoming can't make the same number of calls each day that a rep in Chicago can. Good systems are also attainable, yet challenging. Quotas should set standards that encourage salespeople to stretch and improve their performance, yet represent reasonable performance standards. Quotas that are perceived to be unreasonable may be ignored or, worse yet, may demoralize the sales force.

A quota plan should also be complete, yet easy to understand. A complete quota system is one that covers all important criteria on which salespeople are judged. Yet the quota system has to be understandable, or salespeople will ignore it. The flexibility to handle unforeseen events (such as labor and transportation strikes, fire, and floods) is another characteristic of a sound quota plan. Sound quota plans motivate salespeople by providing goals and feedback on their performance relative to management expectations.

# Compensation

The salesperson's compensation is usually tied to how well he or she achieves quota. When designed well, the compensation plan satisfies the needs of both the company and the salesperson. The salesperson needs an equitable, stable compensation system, but the company needs a system that encourages profitable sales and customer satisfaction.

Sound compensation programs

- Base rewards on results and efforts
- Provide equal rewards for equal performance
- Provide competitive rewards
- Are easy to understand and implement

Salespeople who perceive the reward structure to be unfair will be demotivated. Similarly, if they can't understand the system, then the system will have no impact on their activities or performance. And, if they can get more money elsewhere for the same work, management can wave goodbye, for they will go where the money is.

## Types of Sales Compensation

Sales executives can choose to pay salespeople a straight salary, a straight commission plan, a combination of the two, and perhaps a bonus. Most firms pay a salary and a commission (a combination plan), with fewer than 4 percent paying only commission and about 5 percent paying only salary. Combination plans are used because most companies want a balance between "nonselling" activities such as taking care of customers (compensated for with salary) and sales activities (compensated by commission). Some salary provides salespeople with the security of knowing that they will receive a certain amount each month, which is another reason why some companies use salary as part of the compensation plan. Xerox, for example, uses combination plans, varying the percentage of total compensation allotted to salary based on how much customer care is involved. Jobs with little customer care and mostly customer acquisition pay about 60 percent salary and the balance is commission, whereas major account managers with lots of customer retention and customer care activities are paid about 80 percent salary.

### Straight Salary
Under the **straight salary** plan, a salesperson is paid a fixed amount of money for work during a specified time. A quota system may be used to determine annual salary raises, but otherwise pay does not vary. Straight salary is best used when sales cycles are long, when a team of people is involved and individual results are difficult to measure, or when other aspects of the marketing mix (such as advertising) are important to closing the sale (such as may be the case for inside salespeople). Salary is also useful when the position requires more customer service activities than selling activities.

### Straight Commission
A **straight commission** plan pays a certain amount for each sale, but there is no salary. The **commission base,** or the item from which the commission is determined, is usually unit sales, dollar sales, or gross margin. The **commission rate** is the amount paid per base item sold, and is usually a percentage (such as 10 percent of sales revenue or gross margin) or a fixed amount (such as $50 per sale). Using the preceding copier example, Exhibit 13–9 compares straight salary with two commission plans: one paying 10 percent of sales revenue and a point plan paying $100 per point.

A draw is usually paid as part of a straight commission plan; a **draw** is a loan paid to the salesperson to provide stable cash flow; it's then repaid from commission. For example, the company could agree to pay the salesperson $2,500 per month. If the salesperson

**Exhibit 13–9**
How Different Types of Compensation Plans Pay

SOURCE: *Barton A. Weitz, Stephen B. Castleberry, and John F. Tanner, Jr.,* Selling: Building Partnerships, *6th edition, Burr Ridge, IL, Irwin/McGraw-Hill, 2007.*

| Month | Sales Revenue | Amount Paid to Salesperson | | | |
| | | Straight Salary | Straight Commission* | Combination† | Point Plan |
|---|---|---|---|---|---|
| January | $50,000<br>6 copiers<br>10 faxes | $3,500 | $5,000 | $2,500 (salary)<br>3,000 (commission)<br>4,500 (total) | $3,800 |
| February | $60,000<br>6 copiers<br>15 faxes | 3,500 | 6,000 | 2,500 (salary)<br>3,600 (commission)<br>5,100 (total) | 4,800 |
| March | $20,000<br>2 copiers<br>5 faxes | 3,500 | 2,000 | 2,500 (salary)<br>1,200 (commission)<br>2,700 (total) | 1,600 |

*Commission plan pays 10% of sales revenue.
†Commission portion pays 6% of sales revenue.
NOTE: Copiers are worth three points, faxes worth two and each point is worth $100 in commission. Also, the commission rates are used for example purposes only, to illustrate how compensation schemes work. Point plans, for example, do not necessarily always yield the lowest compensation.

**Exhibit 13–10**
An Example of a Draw Compensation Plan

| Month | Draw | Commission Earned | Payment to Salesperson | Balance Owed to Company |
|---|---|---|---|---|
| January | $2,500 | $0 | $2,500 | $2,500 |
| February | 2,500 | 1,500 | 2,500 | 3,500 |
| March | 2,500 | 6,000 | 2,500 | 0 |

earns less than $2,500, the balance is carried over to the next month. An example of how this works is presented in Exhibit 13–10.

Straight commission ties pay directly to performance, but does little to engender company loyalty. Salespeople on straight commission are far less likely to do activities that they don't see tied directly to making a sale, activities such as paperwork, sales forecasts, and even customer service. Cargo Heavy Duty Inc. experimented with a straight commission plan, but found that customer service suffered, as did company loyalty among salespeople.

Companies engaged in transactional sales strategies and markets find straight commission to work very well. Premier Industrial, for example, pays a straight commission.

## Bonus

Bonuses resemble commissions, but a **bonus** is a lump sum payment for meeting a minimum standard of performance within a given period of time. The amount depends on total performance, not an individual sale. Bonuses motivate salespeople to overachieve quotas and can be used in conjunction with either commission or salary or a combination plan. A salesperson who has made quota with three months left in the year can be motivated to sell even more if a bonus is worthwhile. Cargo Heavy Duty uses bonuses to motivate balanced performance. Salespeople can earn bonuses based on customer satisfaction ratings, total sales revenue, and revenue growth over the previous year. Thus, Cargo Heavy Duty uses bonuses to encourage salespeople to take care of customers while also growing the business.

### Combination Plans

As stated earlier, most companies pay some combination of commission and/or bonus and a salary under a **combination plan.** Such plans are also called salary plus plans, because they pay salary plus a commission or plus a bonus. The salary portion can engender loyalty to the company and represent pay for activities that benefit the company more than the salesperson, whereas the commission or bonus portion can motivate the salesperson. Research by the Dartnell Corporation indicates that although the number of combination plans is holding steady, the percentage of total compensation that is derived from commission or bonus has doubled over the past years, from almost 20 percent to almost 40 percent.

The primary disadvantage of combination plans is that they can become very complex. Confused salespeople may unknowingly engage in inappropriate activity; sales management may even design the program such that salespeople emphasize the wrong products.

Note, though, that we are not talking about selling something to someone who has no need. Although commission and bonus plans can encourage that type of behavior, let's first assume that our salespeople are ethical. If a salesperson is paid the same for faxes and copiers, then most likely, the rep would sell more of the easier one to sell. The company, however, would benefit if more copiers were sold because the gross margin is higher. Compensation plans affect the choice of where salespeople place thier effort; good compensation plans encourage effort in the right activities.

Salary plus bonus plans are used when management wants long-term customer relationships and when teams are used. Long sales cycles also make bonuses effective. Salary plus commission encourages salespeople to increase revenue in order to get the commission, but also encourages nonselling activities that are paid for with the salary.

Companies sometimes cap earnings for their salespeople. A **cap** is a limit to how much a salesperson can make, no matter what the amount of sales. Caps can be unethical if salespeople are unaware of them. For example, one company paid a 10 percent commission. A salesperson who closed an $11 million sale, though, was only paid $100,000 because of the company's hidden cap. Caps are not particularly smart—if they're hidden, morale for the entire sales force is damaged when the cap comes to light. When not hidden, caps limit sales productivity.

## Motivating Performance

Compensation plans are an important element in focusing a salesperson's motivation. There are other important tools that companies use, too. Motivating salespeople is an important task, especially in situations where salespeople spend more time acquiring accounts and are likely to encounter a great deal of rejection.

**Exhibit 13–11**
**Five Steps
to Evaluate
Sales Force
Performance**

- Review objectives.
- Gather appropriate performance data.
- Evaluate influence of uncontrollable factors.
- Identify problems or opportunities.
- Develop and implement strategy to resolve problems and take advantage of opportunities.

In addition to compensation, companies also use contests. There are different types of contests, including contests that everyone can win by reaching a certain level of performance and contests that determine "a champion," or one winner. Most companies run an annual contest where everyone can win, and the prize is usually an exotic trip.

Some salespeople thrive on recognition, such as "Salesperson of the Month" awards. Recognition is an important outcome of effective contests, but recognition can occur outside of a contest, too. For example, Konica Minolta posts the top salespeople's names each month, and management sends out an e-mail blast to the entire sales force when a salesperson closes a big sale. Similarly, Axxis Dental posts letters from customers in company headquarters when a salesperson is noted for excellent customer service.

Motivation plans are an important element in directing the sales force. Compensation plans and quotas can also be useful motivation tools.

# EVALUATING PERFORMANCE

Sales executives aren't the only executives constantly evaluating the performance of their sales force. Every executive in the firm is interested in sales performance. Sales executives, however, are interested in more than total sales revenue; sales executives have to be concerned with sales productivity as well. In this section, we will discuss the various methods of evaluating sales performance following a five-step method.

## Five Steps to Evaluating Sales Force Performance

As illustrated in Exhibit 13–11, the first step in any evaluation is to review the objectives for the activity being evaluated. Although setting objectives is part of every planning process, results should be compared with what was desired so that overall objectives can be realized. For example, if the company set a target of a 20 percent increase in revenue and a market share target of 10 percent, management would be less thrilled with a 25 percent revenue increase if market share was only 8 percent. Management would realize that the market grew faster than 25 percent and the company must have missed out on some sales.

The second step is to gather the appropriate performance data. In a sales setting, this means observing both performance and activity (both outcomes and effort). The third step is to evaluate the influence of any uncontrollable factors. The sales force can hardly be blamed for poor performance if the company was late in introducing new products; similarly, the sales force should not rejoice overly in any sales increases if they're due to the sudden bankruptcy of a key competitor. The economy, the weather, and other uncontrollable factors can influence sales performance. Identifying the impact of those factors enables sales executives to focus on how well the sales strategy is being implemented.

Based on these three steps, the company can then identify any problems or opportunities, which is the fourth step. These problems and opportunities are then fed into the strategic planning process, and/or tactical actions are taken to minimize problems and take advantage of activities for the final step of the process.

# Measures of Performance

Sales performance is measured in two ways. Outcome measures record performance concerning important results such as sales volume, total revenue, total profit contribution, number of new customers, and increase in sales from old customers. These numbers can be compared to performance or outcome quotas to determine if goals were met. These numbers alone, however, can be misleading. External factors, new products, and other issues can make performance look stellar or terrible in spite of anything the salesperson does.

That is why sales executives also measure activity, or a salesperson's effort. Again, activities such as new business calls, demonstrations, and proposal presentations can be observed and compared with quotas.

## Measuring Productivity

When the measures of effort and output are combined, the sales executive can examine the efficiency of the salesperson or sales force. Combinations of activity and performance measures are productivity measures. We discussed these **conversion ratios** in Chapter 12 as they related to other marketing activities. For example, at Freeman Exhibit Company, the sales executive examines the ratio of sales to proposals. The question is how many proposals were actually closed. Other conversion ratios might be the number of new business calls that turn into appointments, the number of appointments that are converted to demonstrations, and then the number of demonstrations that became sales.

If a sales executive has a map of the sales process, then a conversion ratio can be calculated for each step of that process. An example is found in Exhibit 13–12, which illustrates the typical sales cycle for Konica Minolta copier salespeople. Measuring conversions at each step can enable the sales manager to pinpoint problems that sales people may encounter. These problems can then be rectified with training, changes in strategy, or marketing support.

## Balanced Performance

In addition to examining the productivity or output of individual reps, the sales executive must also examine the productivity of the overall sales force in order to make such decisions as quantity discounts and deleting products from the product line. Therefore, examining average order size, order mix (which products are purchased with other products), and sales by product is important factors to consider. Low sales of a particular product may signal low demand for the product, a need to train the sales force in how to sell that product, or a need to change compensation.

## Customer Satisfaction

An important component in building customer relationships is customer satisfaction. Many companies measure customer satisfaction regularly and set satisfaction objectives for their sales force. IBM measures customer satisfaction at both the executive and

**Exhibit 13–12**
Konica Minolta
Sales Cycle

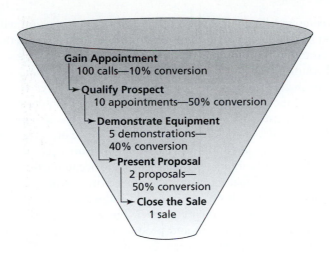

salesperson level. These satisfaction ratings are part of the salesperson's performance evaluation—40 percent of salesperson compensation is tied directly to the ratings.[8] We will discuss customer satisfaction measures in greater detail in Chapters 15 and 16, but for now, recognize that customer satisfaction is an important part of many companies' sales force performance evaluation and compensation programs.

## Other Measures

Salespeople have many nonselling activities to perform and also have to know a great deal about competitors, customers, and the industry. Sales managers often evaluate salespeople on their knowledge of the market, how well they work with others in the company, and other measures that are similar to those employed in the evaluation of any member of the organization. These measures are usually used only to evaluate individuals, but sometimes recognition of knowledge gaps or internal workplace problems across the sales force can trigger training or policy change.

Salespeople also have the responsibility for managing financial resources. If they travel, then travel expenses must be managed. Resources such as free samples, loaner equipment or products, trial units, and other costly resources are managed as well. Salespeople are evaluated on their ability to manage these resources within the budgets established by the sales executive.

## Summary

Sales differs from other forms of marketing communication because sales is person-to-person. Salespeople create value by adapting their products to fit customer needs. Salespeople have further responsibilities that involve managing the relationship between buyers and their organization. Salespeople not only have to close sales; they also provide customer service and coordinate company resources so that the customer is satisfied.

Business marketers can choose from a number of sales strategies; we discussed four as being representative of the wide array of possible strategies. The first is script-based selling, which is used when there is little variation among customers. A more sophisticated approach is needs satisfaction selling, which works best when there is variance in needs across buyers and an array of finished products from which to choose.

Consultative selling may appear similar to needs satisfaction selling, but in this case, the buyer has less information about what is needed and relies on the consultant's knowledge to custom-tailor a solution. Partnering, the fourth strategy, goes beyond consultative selling because of the long-term nature of partnerships. There are many sales strategies that can be used when partnering; these include cross selling and full-line selling.

The sales function can be organized in many ways, depending on the sales strategy. At the top of the structure is the sales executive, who has responsibility for deciding the size and type of sales force. Most sales organizations are organized geographically at some level. The most basic level is to assign each salesperson a geographic territory.

Other sales organizations assign salespeople to accounts, including key accounts, national accounts, or global accounts. Still other firms organize by product. In some situations, companies need both account and product representatives, so they create sales teams to meet the needs of their customer. The account manager coordinates activities and determines sales strategies, and product representatives and representatives from other areas of the organization carry out more specific objectives. Customer-focused teams are one type of team structure that includes representatives from manufacturing, billing, shipping, and other areas that serve the customer.

Sales force size is determined by the sales executive. One method of determining the appropriate number of salespeople is the workload approach, based on the expected number of sales calls that a salesperson can make. Of course, companies can, and do, outsource the selling effort. Some companies choose to use manufacturers' reps, or firms that represent a number of manufacturers. Telemarketing service firms are also available. Some companies even outsource selling temporarily, hiring temporary salespeople for special sales campaigns.

Once the sales force is in place, its activities must be directed. Quotas, or minimum levels of acceptable performance, are one control method. Quotas can be set for activities as well as outcomes. Compensation plans also direct sales activities. The sales executive can choose from salary, commission, and bonus, and may create a plan involving a combination of two plans or all three.

Sales performance is measured two ways: in outcomes and by activities. By combining outcomes and activities, conversion ratios can be calculated to measure salesperson efficiency. These three figures (outcomes, activities, and conversions) enable sales executives to compare salesperson performance. Salesperson performance measures also include data such as average order size and order mix so that decisions concerning pricing and product can be made.

Sales is the last element of the marketing communication mix that we examine. In the next chapter, we examine pricing strategies. Yet like the product itself, pricing must be consistent with the positioning strategy that we intend to communicate through advertising, trade shows, direct marketing, and our selling efforts. Position cannot be created through communication but must also be delivered.

# Key Terms

| | | |
|---|---|---|
| account salesperson | consultative selling | geographic |
| activity quota | conversion ratio | salesperson |
| bonus | cross selling | house account |
| cap | draw | inside salesperson |
| combination plan | field salesperson | key account |
| commission base | (outside salesperson) | line-and-staff |
| commission rate | full-line selling | organization |

matrix sales team

multilevel selling

needs satisfaction
    selling

performance quota
    (outcome quota)

preferred supplier
    status

quota

script-based selling

straight commission

straight salary

strategic account
    manager (SAM)

strategic partner selling

team selling

upgrading (upselling)

workload

# Discussion Questions

1. One of your best salespeople just announced that she is going to work for a company that sells different products but to the same customers. She's given you two weeks' notice. What concerns will your customers raise about this transition? What would your concerns be, as the chief sales executive? What would you do to make this a smooth transition? How would your answer differ if the salesperson was moving to a competitor?

2. Should the salesperson handle all customer complaints or should the customer be told to call the appropriate department? Why or why not? Would your answer change if the account were in the exploration stage versus the commitment stage? What other factors might influence your decision?

3. The sales executive notes that there is a 2-to-1 ratio of proposals, so an edict is published that requires all salespeople to double the number of proposals. What are the possible outcomes of such a command? (There are at least four.) In general, is such a requirement a good idea? How firm should the executive be on enforcing this policy?

4. Assume you are an SAM who must rely on geographic salespeople to service far-flung locations of your customer. They are paid 40 percent of their normal commission on every sale made to your account. (You get the rest.) The account, though, is complaining that service is really bad in certain parts of the country. What would you do and how would you do it? Why?

5. An experienced salesperson argues against salaries: "I don't like subsidizing poor performers. If you paid us straight commission, we'd know who could make it and who couldn't. Sure, it may take a while to get rid of the deadwood, but after that, sales would skyrocket!" Explain why you agree or disagree with this statement.

6. Describe how decile analysis could influence sales strategy. Organize a sales force using different types of salespeople for different accounts for the top decile, the two middle deciles, and the bottom decile.

7. Your company is planning to begin exporting to Mexico and wants to use local sales agents. What should you look for in a sales agent?

8. Conversion ratios tell us that sales is a numbers game. If it takes 10 calls to make a sale and you need 10 sales, you need to make 100 calls. In an audit of sales practices in one organization, managers were continually increasing the minimum number of calls that salespeople were supposed to make in order to continually increase sales. What are the negative consequences of such a strategy? What are the ethical implications?

9. Consider the influence of contests, salary and commission, and recognition in motivating salespeople. How would you create similar forms of motivational tools if you were the professor for this class? For example, how would you use contests, salary and commission or other incentive "pay," and recognition to get students to perform at higher levels? Would these work equally well with everyone? Why, or

why not? How much of a difference would it make if every professor had exactly the same combination of motivational tools?

**10.** Since buyers work from 8 to 5 in the United States, Monday through Friday, your company has started holding sales training all day every first Saturday of every month. This way, you can get training without impacting your sales productivity. Is this ethical? Does it matter if you are paid straight commission or straight salary?

# Cases

## Case 13.1 Contemporary Technologies

Contemporary Technologies (CT) has two primary offerings. The first is a series of products that are used to track inventories and involve handheld scanners, computer software, and the like. In addition, supplies such as bar code labels, tags, and other items that are stuck on or applied to products to track them are also sold by CT. The second offering is an inventory management service that helps organizations create supply chain management strategies.

The firm has two sales staffs. One sells the product and the other sells the service. The services sale is a longer-term sale and those salespeople have more education, call at a higher level of the buyer's organization, and are paid salary. The other salespeople may not have a college degree and certainly no master's, they are paid straight commission, and they make their money on the sale of the supplies rather than the hardware.

Sometimes, salespeople from both staffs make calls together and there can be some overlap in the buying centers. Usually, however, there isn't much overlap and even if there is, they refuse to work together. The services sales staff tends to patronize the hardware/supplies salespeople and the hardware/supplies salespeople mock the lack of "hard-sell" aggressiveness that characterizes the services reps' selling style.

Recently, Molly Molloy, the vice president for sales, noticed two trends. One is that the hardware/supplies reps were losing supply sales within a year of making the hardware sale. This loss occurred in about 15 percent of all accounts, enough to cause some concern. The second issue is that buyers seem to be centralizing a lot of purchasing. When they centralize, it means that the buying centers tend to converge and the same people are making the decisions. But she participated in several sales calls with members of both teams and thought these were disasters. The hostility was apparent even to the customer.

**1.** Should Molly reorganize the sales force to address these two trends? If so, how? If not, why not?

**2.** Assuming that she is not going to reorganize, what can she do to create more of a team spirit? How can she get the two sides to work together?

## Case 13.2   Jackson Timers & Controls

Jackson Timers & Controls has the following compensation program: Reps are paid a $1,500 draw per month, with straight commission paid on a point system, and a bonus depending on quota performance. Here is the point system:

| Product | Points/Sale | Quota |
|---|---|---|
| Digital wamometer | 50 | 4 units/month |
| Lambadameter | 40 | 5 |
| Origameter | 35 | 6 |
| Cyclometer | 25 | 8 |
| Universal tricometer | 5 | 45 |

Reps are paid $5 per point, or $5,175 plus a bonus of $500, if they sell quota for each product, for a total of $5,675. The total number of points to reach each month is 1,035, but they have to reach quota for each product to get the bonus. Here is the performance of the district:

| Product | District Quota | Number sold |
|---|---|---|
| Digital wamometer | 40 | 22 |
| Lambadameter | 50 | 78 |
| Origameter | 60 | 63 |
| Cyclometer | 80 | 82 |
| Universal tricometer | 450 | 479 |

| Salesperson | Dig. Wam. | Lambada. | Origameter | Cyclometer | U. Tricometer | Total Points |
|---|---|---|---|---|---|---|
| Chonko | 5 | 6 | 7 | 9 | 53 | 1,225 |
| Dunn | 1 | 7 | 5 | 8 | 45 | 930 |
| Easley | 0 | 6 | 5 | 8 | 44 | 835 |
| Cooper | 1 | 8 | 6 | 8 | 48 | 1,020 |
| Madden | 1 | 7 | 7 | 8 | 47 | 1,010 |
| Moore | 3 | 11 | 7 | 9 | 52 | 1,320 |
| Roberts | 2 | 9 | 7 | 11 | 46 | 1,210 |
| Weeks | 2 | 8 | 6 | 7 | 48 | 1,045 |
| Johnson | 3 | 8 | 7 | 6 | 48 | 1,105 |
| Davis | 4 | 8 | 6 | 8 | 48 | 1,170 |

| | Dig. Wam. | Lambada. | Origameter | Cyclometer | U. Tricometer | Total Sales Calls |
|---|---|---|---|---|---|---|
| Sales Call Quota | 20 | 20 | 10 | 10 | 10 | 70 |
| Roberts | 28 | 17 | 11 | 9 | 10 | 75 |
| Weeks | 24 | 24 | 8 | 8 | 7 | 71 |
| District | 27.2 | 18.6 | 9.5 | 10.4 | 9.7 | 75.4 |

1. Evaluate the district's sales performance. Draw conclusions just on where it is both doing well and doing poorly. (Don't fix anything yet.) Justify your conclusions.
2. Compare Roberts's and Weeks's performances. What are some possible explanations for the poor digital wamometer sales?
3. The VP of sales says the problem is a compensation plan problem. How would you fix it?
4. Design a contest to promote the sale of digital wamometers. Justify your choices.

# Additional Readings

The July/August 2006 issue of *Harvard Business Review* is devoted to sales and sales management topics.

Brashear, Thomas G., James S. Boles, Danny N. Bellenger, and Charles M. Brooks. "An Empirical Test of Trust-Building Processes and Outcomes in Sales Manager—Salesperson Relationships." *Journal of the Academy of Marketing Science* 31 (2003), pp. 189–200.

Darmon, René Y., Benny Rigaux-Briemont, and Pierre Ballofet. "Designing Sales Force Satisfying Selling Positions: A Conjoint Measurement Approach." *Industrial Marketing Management* 32 (2003), pp. 501–15.

Ferrell, O. C., Thomas N. Ingram, and Raymond W. Laforge. "Initiating Structure for Legal and Ethical Decisions in a Global Sales Organization." *Industrial Marketing Management* 29 (2000), pp. 555–64.

Harris, Eric G., John C. Mowen, and Tom J. Brown. "Re-Examining Salesperson Goal Orientations: Personality Influencers, Customer Orientation, and Work Satisfaction." *Journal of the Academy of Marketing Science* 33 (2005), pp. 19–35.

Homburg, Christian, and Ruth M. Stock. "The Link between Salespeople's Job Satisfaction and Customer Satisfaction in a Business-to-Business Context." *Journal of the Academy of Marketing Science* 32 (2004), pp. 144–58.

Hunter, Gary K., and William D. Perreault, Jr. "Making Sales Technology Effective." *Journal of Marketing* 71 (January 2007), pp. 16–34.

Johnson, Devon S., and Sundar Bharadwaj. "Digitization of Selling Activity and Sales Force Performance: An Empirical Investigation." *Journal of the Academy of Marketing Science* 33 (2005), pp. 3–18.

Lynch, Joanne, and Leslie de Chermatony. "Winning the Hearts and Minds: Business-to-Business Branding and the Role of the Salesperson." *Journal of Marketing Management* 23 (2007), pp. 123–34.

McFarland, Richard G., Goutam N. Challagalla, and Tasadduq A. Shervani. "Influence Tactics for Effective Adaptive Selling." *Journal of Marketing* 70 (October 2006), pp. 103–17.

Michailova, Snejina, and Verner Worm. "Personal Networking in Russia and China: Blat and Guanxi." *European Management Journal* 21, no. 4 (2003), pp. 509–19.

Murphy, William H., Peter A. Dacin, and Neil M. Ford. "Sales Contest Effectiveness: An Examination of Sales Contest Design Preferences of Field Sales Forces." *Journal of the Academy of Marketing Science* 32 (2004), pp. 127–41.

Schwepker, Charles H. Jr., and David J. Good. "Understanding Sales Quotas: An Exploratory Investigation of the Consequences of Failure." *Journal of Business & Industrial Marketing* 19, no. 1 (2004), pp. 39–48.

Stock, Ruth Maria, and Wayne D. Hoyer. "An Attitude-Behavior Model of Salespeople's Customer Orientation." *Journal of the Academy of Marketing Science* 33 (2005), pp. 536–52.

Venkatesan, Rajkumar, and V. Kumar. "A Customer Lifetime Value Framework for Customer Selection and Resource Allocation Strategy." *Journal of Marketing* 68 (October 2005), pp. 106–25.

Wilson, R. Dale. "Using Online Databases for Developing Prioritized Sales Leads." *Journal of Business & Industrial Marketing* 18, nos. 4/5 (2003), pp. 388–402.

# Chapter 14

## Pricing and Negotiating for Value

### DUPONT

From an antitrust trial involving DuPont de Nemours and Company we have extensive data on prices, costs, and sales of cellophane, the plastic wrap that continues to be used extensively today. This bit of time travel reveals much about prices through innovation, market adoption, line extensions, and competitive challenges.●

In 1923 the DuPont Cellophane Company was founded and cellophane was introduced at an average price that year of $2.51 per pound. Price reductions enabled and were enabled by production efficiencies over the next three years. At a price of $1.43 in 1927, volume increased substantially. The next year DuPont patented a process for moisture-proofing cellophane and the market potential jumped even more dramatically. In 1930 sales were 11.1 million pounds. Although about one-third more expensive than plain cellophane, prices on the moisture-proof product had dropped to $.38 by 1940, while the profit rate remained about the same.●

Mirroring the textbook product life cycle, in the 1940s cellophane was produced in many different forms: transparent plain and colored, moisture-proof heat-sealable transparent, heat-sealable colored, adhesive transparent, and so on. In 1945 prices ranged from $.33 to $.62 per pound. Volume was 95 million pounds.●

From its introduction, cellophane was never priced to match its substitutes: wax paper and glassine. It was always more expensive. But the steady decrease in prices "was intended to open up new uses for cellophane and to attract new customers." A bonus effect from expanding markets was a steady decrease in cost due to learned efficiency and scale economies.●

After World War II, DuPont and its competitor, American Viscose, faced rising material and labor costs. The accompanying table shows that in close harmony with Viscose, DuPont's prices rose across the product line in the postwar decade. In 1955 DuPont cellophane sales totaled 125 million pounds. Cellophane sales began their decline in the 1960s as new materials were developed, but its biodegradable quality has sparked a resurgence of late. The case is a fascinating preview of the determinants of price in business marketing: the benefits to customers and their price sensitivity, costs and experience, competitive pressures, the legal environment, and more.[1]●

Visit DuPont today at **www.dupont.com/index.html.**●

| Year | 300 PT | | 300 MT | | 300 MSAT | | 450 MSAT | |
|------|------|------|------|------|------|------|------|------|
| | dP | AV | dP | AV | dP | AV | dP | AV |
| 1945 | .33 | .33 | .41 | .41 | .57 | .57 | .46 | .46 |
| 1947 | .42 | .43 | .44 | .44 | .54 | .54 | .55 | .55 |
| 1950 | .49 | .53 | .51 | .55 | .59 | .64 | .59 | .64 |
| 1955 | .62 | .64 | .59 | .59 | .66 | .66 | .66 | .66 |

Key: dP = DuPont; AV = American Viscose; numbers 300 and 450 are thicknesses; PT = plain transparent; MT = Moisture-proof and transparent; MSAT = moisture-proof, sealed, adhesive, and transparent.

## LEARNING OBJECTIVES

The cellophane story hints at the connections between price and market penetration and experience, the interrelationships between products in a line, and the considerations of competitive behaviors. Indeed, it exemplifies the need to think about price comprehensively.

*After reading this chapter, you should be able to*

● Describe a comprehensive framework for pricing decisions.

● Identify some of today's pricing pitfalls in business-to-business marketing.

● List the key interest groups in the pricing decision.

● Appreciate price as a strategic variable at the intersection of many factors: costs, demand, competitors, channel coordination, and regulations.

● Recognize the tactical value of price for cash and production flow, inventory control, promotion, and more.

● Demonstrate facility with the financial rudiments of pricing: break-even analysis, channel margins, simple pro forma income statements, and margin analysis.

● Manage prices of related products in the line, evaluate bid pricing opportunities, and apply principles of conflict management to price negotiation including negotiations for global pricing contracts.

**Exhibit 14–1**
Pricing
Principles
in Practice

> You've got to have *X* percent margins; every product, every division has to have *X* percent margins. There's no way you can live without that margin.
>
> industrial marketing manager
>
> Prices decline 10 percent per year, so your costs must decline 15 percent per year.
>
> financial manager at high-technology firm
>
> If we don't get this deal they're gonna walk. We're going to lose their business. We potentially may jeopardize this business.
>
> sales managers at information service company
>
> Whatever you do, do not underprice and leave money on the table!
>
> pricing manager, computer systems business

SOURCE: Adapted from Gerald Smith, "Managerial Pricing Orientation: The Process of Making Pricing Decisions," *Pricing Strategy & Practice* 3, no. 3 (1995), pp. 28–39.

# THE PRINCIPLES AND PRINCIPALS OF PRICE

Prices are a source of frustration for many business professionals. Customers complain of rising prices, complicated discounts, and more. Within selling organizations, there is often a power struggle among people (the principals) over who sets price. This struggle often reflects an underlying conflict over the theories (principles) of price.

At an executive seminar some years ago, participants were asked to write the decision rules or "truisms" about price at their companies. Exhibit 14–1 summarizes some of the pricing principles that emerged from the exercise.[2] The exhibit illustrates the emphasis some companies place on margin maintenance, competitive pricing, and cost cutting, the importance of particular customers, and avoiding a price that is below the value of the product package. Although each principle has merit, we will want to find a proper balance of emphasis and fit within the marketing strategy of the firm.

"Too many cooks spoil the broth." When it comes to pricing business products, this saying points to a real risk. Cost accountants scrutinize buying, manufacturing, selling, and shipping. The financial managers know the target return rates for each arm of the enterprise. Marketing departments stay abreast of competitor prices and count the bids won and lost. The sales force knows the pressure on distributor margins. Every day they get asked for new discounts. And a growing number of end users compete in intense markets where cost containment has become a motto that is played out in supplier relationships. Meanwhile, the Environmental Protection Agency may demand new handling or disposal procedures, increasing costs of product inputs. Some ingredients may be specially taxed or have their availability and prices affected by import and export restrictions.

Each interest group has a tendency to emphasize a particular pricing principle in accordance with the criterion measures of its "turf." Thus, if we revisit Exhibit 14–1, note the origin of the different pricing principles. The marketing manager is evaluated each period on her operating margin. The financial manager frets about trimming costs ahead of prices. The sales manager considers price concessions in order to retain key accounts. Naturally, the pricing manager doesn't want tinkering with the "system" of prices resulting from careful value analysis. From the Field 14–1 reveals the many factors to be considered by a pricing manager.

---

**14–1**

# FROM THE FIELD

## Professional Pricing Career

My professional pricing career started after I received my MBA and was recruited on campus by NCR Corporation for their U.S. Data Processing Group. I was given pricing responsibility for several products within the company's portfolio. The 10-member Pricing Group was responsible for developing the U.S. pricing strategies for their respective products, as well as handling the financial analysis, for all large bids. This position gave me exposure to competitive analysis, financial analysis, product positioning, and the marketing challenges for each of my products. This was also my first experience seeing how a company's culture can influence its long-term growth and market share as a result of its willingness to take risks.

With that initial experience, I moved into the Federal Systems Division, which was responsible for selling all of the company's products to the federal government. Selling to any government entity is very challenging because it's one of the most competitive selling environments and you must understand how to win and make money in this type of environment. Let's just say that the reason you hear the media talking about $500 toilets being sold to the government is because there are other items on that contract that were sold at a loss by the winning supplier, and the loss items carried the most weight in the bid evaluation.

My career led to the management of pricing staffs, which is very interesting because you work cross-functionally with manufacturing, sales, and marketing as well as senior management. This is an exciting position because you focus on ways to improve corporate sales and profits and the work changes constantly as there are always areas for improvement. To do well in pricing, you need to be analytical, open-minded, and a strategic thinker. Pricing is not black and white; you need to be comfortable working with "gray." You also need to take a general management perspective since you need to balance the needs of sales, manufacturing, finance, marketing, and the customer. You should recognize that different pricing strategies (cost-based, value-based and market-based) are required for different situations. Multidimensional pricing strategies are better than one-dimensional ones!

Dan Ward, Pricing Manager, Reynolds and Reynolds, Dayton, OH.

---

# What Is Price?

Let's make it clear what we mean by price before we go any further. **Price** is the amount of money paid by a buyer to a seller for a particular product or service. Of course, the payment terms are a part of the price. Is payment due at delivery or at the end of the month? In what country's currency? Is freight included? How about service over the first 90 days? Buyers and sellers also know that price can be changed by adjustments in the financial terms or the product characteristics and its bundle of ancillary services. For example, adhesive prices can go from $60 a gallon to $66, or the price per can might remain at $60 while the can shrinks to 116.34 ounces.

Thus, a product can provide value in business markets not only when its invoice price is lower than the competitor's, but when its performance is superior. Performance includes quality, durability, and safety as well as energy efficiency, ease of operation, portability, and more. The fundamental job of the business marketing program is to establish and extend the sphere of benefits or value provided for a "price."

Second, we need to review the fact that no item is priced in isolation. Prices for countless items are connected in an exchange economy. With $40 in your pocket, you can take a friend to a movie and enjoy popcorn and a drink. But if your car won't start

**Exhibit 14–2**
A Model for
Managing Price

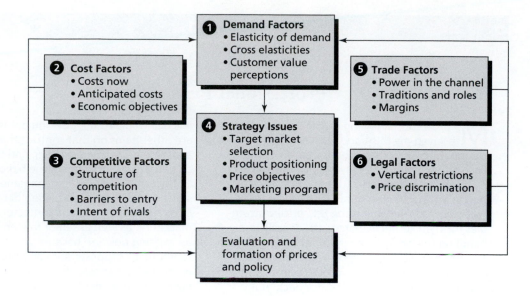

and you have to take a cab to the cinema, you may have to forgo the popcorn or your friend. The same is true in business markets. As the price of freon has increased, the price of installed refrigeration equipment has climbed, and the demand for substitutes has pushed their prices higher. As buyers pay more for these inputs, there is less money to distribute to stockholders or spend on other inputs.

## A Model for Price

Exhibit 14–2 maps the complex array of price determinants.[3] The model shows that prices are rightly determined by *demand factors*—price sensitivity, connectedness to other products, and customer perceptions—interacting with *cost factors* and *competitive factors* in the economic environment. At the same time, we must acknowledge the intersection of market factors with company *strategy issues*—targeting, positioning, programming, and goals—within a marketing environment that is circumscribed by *trade factors* and *legal factors*.

In the remainder of this chapter, we will examine the pricing impact of six major factors in two major sections. The first deals especially with boxes 1, 2, and 3 from Exhibit 14–2, in a brief refresher of microeconomics. A short review of financial basics at the end of this section serves as a bridge from the clarity and internal consistency of economic models to the financial objectives of price management. The second major section treats an array of managerial issues arising primarily from boxes 4 through 6. Major subsections will address channel pricing, product line pricing, bidding, and negotiation. Specific legal matters arise within the subsections.

## CUTTING TO THE QUICK: THE SCISSORS FACTORS OF PRICE

As a basic framework for pricing, recall the analysis you applied in your microeconomics class. Exhibit 14–3 shows the "scissors" of intersecting supply and demand functions in a market. The demand function is a downward-sloping line that represents the

**Exhibit 14–3**
Supply and
Demand

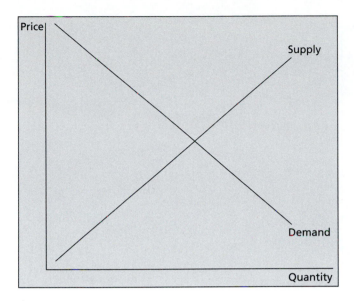

tendency of firms to purchase increasing amounts of our product—or additional firms to make purchases—as price declines.

The steepness of this slope is determined by the availability of substitutes for the product. A product providing unique benefits exhibits a steep slope; its demand is **inelastic,** or not very price sensitive. Products with lots of substitutes tend to be price **elastic,** meaning the quantity demanded is highly sensitive to changes in their price. An elastic demand function is flatter.

The product market demand picture can translate into firm-level demand curves in a number of ways. For example, the restaurant demand for salmon is downward-sloping—more chefs will feature salmon when they can buy the fish at low prices. Still, a specific Seattle fishing company or wholesaler has minimal pricing latitude. They sell at the market price because restaurants will go elsewhere if they try to price above the market. On the other hand, below-market prices are not apt to bring the supplier any more revenue than the market price. Essentially, any producer of a me-too product faces a flat demand function and has little pricing flexibility.

Only a firm providing unique value to customers enjoys a downward-sloping demand for its product and finds some pricing latitude. The amount of pricing discretion is rooted in the strategic advantages the firm uses to provide distinct benefits to customers. If a special lubricant can save a user $100 per machine in maintenance, it would be reasonable for a user to pay up to this level—whether the supplier's costs are $50 or $.50.

One company developed a new method of cleaning pipes in industrial furnaces. Using small propellants in a carrier gas to knock loose scale and coke deposits, this new process was called shotblasting. Compared to the traditional methods of cleaning, steam air decoking, or "turbining" (cutting or reaming out deposits), shotblasting was quicker, provided more energy efficiency for the system, and did minimal damage to pipes. The company used marketing research with prospective customers to find the priority and approximate dollar value of these advantages. It could then predict market share at different price and service configurations.[4]

Of course, the gently sloping downward demand curve we see in Exhibit 14–3 is an abstraction. In reality, the line may be more jagged or stair stepped as substantial gains

**Exhibit 14–4**
Often Supply and
Demand Show
Dramatic and
Discontinuous
Reactions to Price

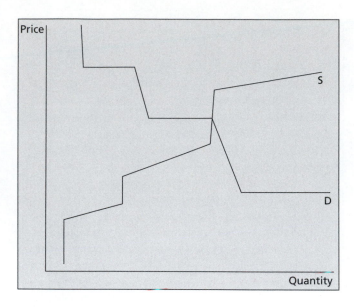

in purchases come at different price thresholds. Cellophane penetrated several successive applications as its price declined.

Meanwhile, back in Exhibit 14–3, the supply function is sloped upward. This represents suppliers' motivations to increase supply as prices increase. Higher prices prompt suppliers to hire additional shifts, use overtime, adjust capacity by subcontracting or retooling, and employ other measures to boost supply. This curve could actually be rather jagged, too. For example, adding a second shift may provide just a small increase in our output because it replaces a good deal of first-shift overtime. But when we open a large automated factory, supply surges at the current price; a rather flat sector of the supply function results. Furthermore, when *experience* can be expected to reduce costs—as in our cellophane vignette—we have suppliers driven to build cumulative volume and thereby secure a cost advantage. From the Field 14–2 profiles experience effects in both a labor-intensive and highly automated production setting.

The intersection of the two jagged functions, as shown in Exhibit 14–4, represents an abstract equilibrium price for our product. Practically, the "equilibrium" may be in a constant state of flux as needs change, technology advances, the costs of substitutes rise or fall, and supplies vary with weather, war, and whim. The simple model can nevertheless provide significant insights into the direction of future price pressures if we can develop tracking systems for the variables that affect supply and demand. Indeed, a classic study of a large petroleum company's pricing of gasoline in local markets, daily checking of market prices, internal product costs, and forecasts of overall market supply were key strategic variables.[5]

# THE NATURE OF COMPETITIVE MARKETS

As you know, economists have developed models of prices in several different market structures. Recapped in Exhibit 14–5, two of these—monopoly and pure competition—are rarely observed in practice. Most products have substitutes, so it is not particularly useful to discuss monopolistic pricing in a business marketing text. Likewise, except for some minerals, metals, and agricultural products—and perhaps even in these areas—it

## 14–2

# FROM THE FIELD

## The Learning Curve

Kathleen Haefner stumbled into commercial upholstery when a friend asked her to renew the seats on a raft of cafe chairs for a new restaurant. She began with careful attention to original design and construction. Measures were double-checked. Assembly was tested and retested in process. The first chair took an entire day.

Chair 2 was knocked out the next morning. Chairs 3 and 4 were completed that afternoon. Ms. Haefner's output continued to improve until about halfway through the job, when things leveled off at about an hour per chair.

This example of the **learning curve,** the tendency of costs to decline with repetition, has been observed in countless studies. It is a component of a more encompassing concept called the experience curve. The experience curve reflects declining cost as a function of accumulated experience or output. Efficiency comes not only from repetition, but also from production and distribution innovations as well as product design simplification.

The accompanying table shows the forecast of experience-based economies in CD-ROM manufacture. When such cumulative volume effects are anticipated, pricing strategy should aim to penetrate successive markets.

0.15 = Learning curve constant
$2.00 = Average variable cost during first period
2,000,000 = Average production per period

| Period | Cumulative Production | Variable Cost/Unit | Percent Reduction | % Reduct. as Prod. Doubles |
|--------|----------------------|--------------------|-------------------|----------------------------|
| 1 | 2,000,000 | $2.00 | 0.00 | |
| 2 | 4,000,000 | $1.80 | 9.87 | 9.87 |
| 3 | 6,000,000 | $1.70 | 5.90 | |
| 4 | 8,000,000 | $1.62 | 4.22 | 10.12 |
| 5 | 10,000,000 | $1.57 | 3.29 | |
| 6 | 12,000,000 | $1.53 | 2.70 | |
| 7 | 14,000,000 | $1.49 | 2.29 | |
| 8 | 16,000,000 | $1.46 | 1.98 | 10.26 |
| 9 | 18,000,000 | $1.44 | 1.75 | |
| 10 | 20,000,000 | $1.42 | 1.57 | |
| 11 | 22,000,000 | $1.40 | 1.42 | |
| 12 | 24,000,000 | $1.38 | 1.30 | |
| 13 | 26,000,000 | $1.36 | 1.19 | |
| 14 | 28,000,000 | $1.35 | 1.11 | |
| 15 | 30,000,000 | $1.33 | 1.03 | |
| 16 | 32,000,000 | $1.32 | 0.96 | 10.33 |

SOURCE: CD-ROM data courtesy of Michael V. Laric, Merrick School of Business, University of Baltimore, 1997.

**Exhibit 14–5**
Economic Models of Market Structure.

Most of the action in business marketing is in oligopoly and monopolistic competition.

SOURCE: *Reprinted from E. Jerome McCarthy and William D. Perreault,* Basic Marketing, *Burr Ridge, IL: Richard D. Irwin, 1987, p. 102. Used with permission of the McGraw-Hill Companies.*

| Important dimensions / Types of situations | Pure competition | Oligopoly | Monopolistic competition | Monopoly |
|---|---|---|---|---|
| Uniqueness of each firm's product | None | None | Some | Unique |
| Number of competitors | Many | Few | Few to many | None |
| Size of competitors (compared to size of market) | Small | Large | Large to small | None |
| Elasticity of demand facing firm | Completely elastic | Kinked demand curve (elastic and inelastic) | Either | Either |
| Elasticity of industry demand | Either | Inelastic | Either | Either |
| Control of price by firm | None | Some (with care) | Some | Complete |

is difficult to identify products that are undifferentiated across suppliers. Relationships supported by joint planning, delivery coordination, and an array of services can differentiate practically anything.[6] Thus, we won't discuss the price-taking situation of products in pure competition.

# Oligopolies

Many business markets are **oligopolies,** characterized by just a few sellers. Each offers a product that is quite similar to the others. Consider Oracle versus SAP in enterprise software or Owens Corning and Johns Manville in fiberglass insulation. Each firm may strive for a differential advantage in customer service, brand image, logistical excellence, or such. But any advantage tends to net only a narrow latitude for a price premium, and that advantage tends to be short lived. Like the classic story of cellophane, imitation is the rule, and pricing decisions of competitors are highly constrained and made with due consideration of the reaction by others.

As a result, firms see themselves competing in a market with a *kinked* demand, as shown in Exhibit 14–6. That is, at prices above the kink, demand is very elastic. Therefore, any attempt to raise prices above the current equilibrium zone will lead to sharp drops in volume. Going the other way, it is not likely that competitors will allow another's price cut to siphon their market share. Even not so radical price cuts stand to trigger a price war—a situation that certainly benefits customers in the short run, but which typically produces no winner on the supply side.

# Monopolistic Competition

Another realistic case in business markets is **monopolistic competition,** a large number of differentiated sellers—such as corporate training companies, custom marketing research firms, and industrial distributors. In these fields, the actions of one firm have a

**Exhibit 14–6**
An Oligopoly's Kinked Demand Curve Has Elastic and Inelastic Segments

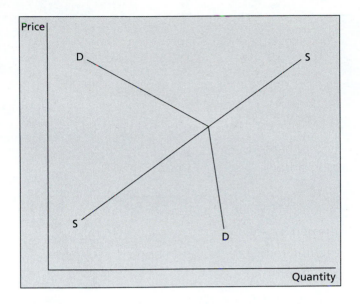

**Exhibit 14–7**
A Competitive Advantage in Monopolistic Competition

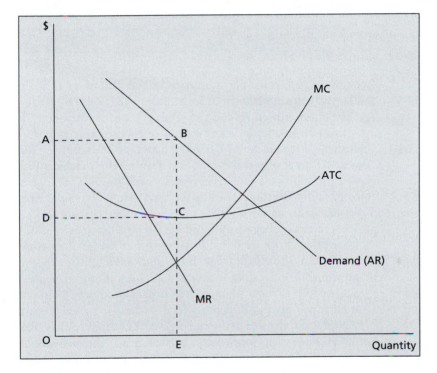

smaller effect on others. Each seller brings some unique competency to the market and offers distinctively valued services and products, but, in the eyes of buyers, some other makes are tolerable substitutes. As a result, each firm faces a downward-sloping demand curve.

This is a useful case for illustrating the profit maximization model. Exhibit 14–7 shows the product's demand curve. Because each point on the line represents the quantity sold at a given price, it also represents the average revenue (*AR*) or price per unit. The line labeled *MR* is the very important function showing marginal revenue. Thus, if

**Exhibit 14–8**
Unsustained Advantage in the Long Run in Monopolistic Competition: Average Total Costs Equal Average Revenue

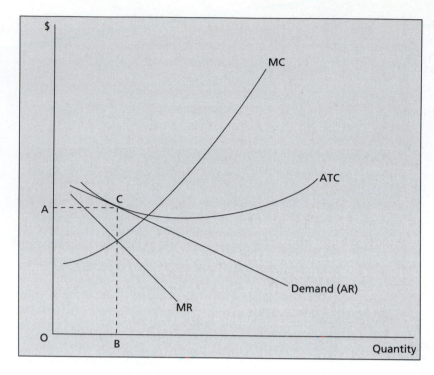

we can sell 200 units per month at $4 and 300 units at $3, the marginal revenue or additional sales is $100 [i.e., ($3 × 300) − ($4 × 200)].

The curve labeled *ATC* is the product's average total cost. This includes fixed costs that must be paid regardless of volume (managers' salaries, occupancy costs, advertising). Naturally, these produce high average costs at low volumes. But the *ATC* also includes the direct costs of producing and delivering the products (e.g., raw materials, direct labor, packaging). These costs start to swell the *ATC* at high volumes when crowded factory floors, overtime, stress, poor supervision, and the like begin to impair efficiency.

If managers at this firm could clearly measure costs and collect perfectly accurate market research, they would produce the quantity *E* per period. At this level of output, sold at price *A* per unit, the firm finds that marginal revenue equals marginal costs. Think about what this means. If the additional selling expenses are just a tiny bit less than the additional sales minus direct costs, profits increase. On the other hand, it would be folly to incur $101 in costs to gain another $100 in sales. Alas, profits are maximized at this price and quantity level—where marginal revenue equals marginal costs.

Graphically, the area of the rectangle ABEO depicts dollar sales, total revenue. The area of DCEO represents total costs. Their difference, shown by rectangle ABCD, is profit.

In monopolistic competition, firms have distinct skills, brands, and distribution advantages. They have no perfect substitutes. But firms making substantial profits tend to be emulated and draw competitive activity from rivals. This has the effect of reducing demand—moving the demand curve downward to the left—or making demand more price sensitive—flattening the demand curve. The result is to bring AR and ATC closer to tangential. Of course, this shrinks the once substantial profits, because when average revenue equals average total costs, as in Exhibit 14–8, there are no profits. Perhaps better than any other perspective, this framework underscores the importance of a market orientation, a focus on innovation, and constant striving to maintain and extend distinctive competencies in order to be able to price for profits.

---

**14–1**

# BUSINESS 2 BUSINESS
## Take Two Tablets . . .

The networks and virtual communities we've discussed in Chapters 2 and 12 support a variety of dynamic pricing mechanisms. This is a departure from administered prices, like those printed or posted in the catalog or formulated by the seller for each specific product model and quantity of purchase. We're talking about auctions—the "English" type like those used at estate sales where sales go to the top bidder, to "Dutch" auctions where asking prices move downward until a buyer comes forward, to sealed bids (time ordered), or to reverse auctions where one buyer invites qualified suppliers to bid down the price on a specified product or service.

Writing in 2003 about the tendency of the purchasing executives at American auto-making companies to emphasize price to the detriment of cost reduction and supplier collaboration, *Purchasing*'s editor-in-chief, Doug Smock, proposed the Ten Commandments of Reverse Auctions:

1. Mean it if you do it . . . award the business at the end.
2. No reconnaissance by auction . . . using auctions for intelligence insults supply partners.
3. No outside quotes. Play within the rules.
4. Keep out the shills . . . invite only those you'll do business with.

Try to provide a couple of candidates for inclusion among these commandments, and give a brief justification.

---

# Economic Theory and Financial Basics

These abstractions from economics underlie a number of tools used in marketing and financial management every day. The equality of average revenue and average cost in Exhibit 14–8 is the basis for break-even analysis. At the **break-even quantity,** we realize a sales level—at a specified price—at which total revenue equals total cost. Similarly, we can speak about a **break-even price,** the average revenue needed to cover costs, given a particular sales level.

Of course, most marketing decisions are not made with an aim to break even, but with a goal to improve from the current position. In this case when we speak of breaking even, we mean attaining a situation that does no harm to our current profit level. Marginal analysis is the name frequently given to this task of evaluating the incremental volume needed to cover incremental costs or the incremental loss of average revenue in the instance of price cuts. Exhibit 14–9 offers a series of examples of break-even and marginal analysis to reacquaint you with these essential financial basics of pricing.

# Some Final Words on Models of Competitive Environments

These models of competitive environments require ambitious assumptions about the completeness of information on costs and customer demand. The oligopoly model is not too clear about how the equilibrium at the kink is obtained. Both models also mask the countless means by which competitors can challenge one's profitable position.

But they effectively simplify a complex interaction between demand and supply factors. They provide a structure for thinking about changes from the status quo. And they identify some normative prescriptions for pricing.

**Exhibit 14–9**
Financial
Rudiments

At break-even, Total revenue = Total cost

Alternatively, Price × Q     = FC + VC = FC + (UVC × Q)

  Where   Q is quantity, FC is fixed costs, VC is variable costs, UVC is unit variable costs, and price is
       average revenue

We can solve for Q using algebra:

$$(\text{Price} \times Q) - (UVC \times Q) = FC$$
$$Q\,(\text{Price} - UVC) = FC$$
$$Q = FC/(\text{Price} - UVC) = FC/\text{Unit margin}$$

This is the infamous BEQ equation you've memorized for three classes already.
We can also solve for price, assuming a fixed Q

$$\text{Price} \times Q = FC + (UVC \times Q)$$
$$\text{Price} = [FC + (UVC \times Q)]/Q = \text{Average cost}$$

When selling a mix of products, break-even is usually considered as a dollars-in-sales figure. We have
unit costs typically expressed as a percentage of revenue. Thus, at break-even,

$TR = FC + (C\% \times TR)$

$(1 - C\%) \times TR = FC$ or $TR = FC/(1 - C\%)$

Thus, we break even if sales × margin equals fixed costs.

An income statement equivalent of break-even is: Gross profit = GS&A

| | | |
|---|---|---|
| Net sales | $60,000,000 | 100% |
| Cost of goods sold (COGS) | 45,000,000 | 75 |
| Gross profit | 15,000,000 | 25 |
| General, selling, administrative (GS&A) | 15,000,000 | 25 |
| Net profit before taxes | 0 | 0 |

Consider the case of profits:

| | | |
|---|---|---|
| Net sales | $60,000,000 | 100% |
| Cost of goods sold | 45,000,000 | 75 |
| Gross profit | 15,000,000 | 25 |
| General, selling, administrative | 12,000,000 | 20 |
| Net profit before taxes | 3,000,000 | 5% |

Marginal analysis scenario: What sales increase is needed to cover a $1.2 million increase in
marketing expenditures?

We "break-even" on the expenditure if new revenue (NR) covers $1.2 million and the new COGS

$NR = \$1.2\text{ million} + COGS$

$NR = \$1.2\text{ million} + .75NR$

$.25\,NR = \$1.2\text{ million}$

$NR = \$1.2\text{ million}/.25$  And doesn't this look like $BE\$ = FC/\text{margin}$?

$NR = \$4.8\text{ million}$

In the heat of battle, some managers have lost sight of these pricing fundamentals.
For example, under pressure from its regional distributor one cutting tool manufacturer
cut its prices by 10 percent. This effectively halved its gross profit margin. But there was
no way on earth to double sales volume in the market, the critical expansion rate needed
to avoid a profit decrease.

---

**14–3**

## FROM THE FIELD

### Pricing Process Brings Profits

Parker-Hannifin Corporation has been making valves, sensors, and compressors for nearly 90 years. Its $9 billion in sales in 2006 came from over nearly 800,000 products. But only recently has it forsaken a tired cost-plus approach to pricing—a method that usually aimed to add 35 percent for margin. The new approach groups products according to product market conditions reflecting pricing latitude. For example their commodity products in highly competitive markets were under price pressures and their prices were changed only a couple of percentage points up or down. In partially differentiated products serving niches with no close competitive options, prices were raised up to 9 percent. Highly differentiated products and systems featuring highly engineered solutions got bumped up to 25 percent. Custom-designed items might have even higher price hikes.

CEO Donald Washkewicz, who initiated the system in 2002, points to a $200 million gain in operating income since then. It's a little more sophisticated than cost-plus, but it has allowed Parker-Hannifin to claim more value.

Timothy Aeppel, "Seeking Perfect Prices, CEO Tears Up the Rules," *The Wall Street Journal* (March 27, 2007), pp. 1+; http://www.parker.com/; http://www.marketingmo.com/blog/template_permalink.asp?id=188.

---

Another company in the food service industry thought its selection and delivery service justified a 5 percent price premium with its institutional customers. Unfortunately, purchasers didn't place such a high regard for the service because they were measured on acquisition costs. The firm's market share and profits dropped through the floor. From the Field 14–3 outlines a much more successful approach at Parker-Hannifin.

## ISSUES IN PRICE MANAGEMENT

This section reviews a number of key concepts and tools for the effective management of price. We begin with a look at pricing objectives. Then we address pricing through the channel and the indirect means of channel margin management. We take up several issues involving pricing a line of products, including the knotty legal and tactical challenge of pricing for different market segments. The chapter offers a succinct discussion of bid pricing and negotiation, with related material on leasing. We conclude with an overview of the qualities and benefits of a pricing system.

## The Pricing Strategy

The formulation of a sound pricing strategy requires consideration of demand and cost factors in a competitive environment approximating one of these market structures. A price strategy consists of a specific approach to achieve the pricing objective. Pricing objectives might be

- To increase profitability by 12 percent over the next year
- To thwart the efforts by competitors to gain a foothold in the market
- To get competitors to accept us as a price leader
- To restore order in a chaotic market

- To increase market share to 17 percent
- To smooth the seasonality of purchases

To achieve these outcomes, a pricing strategy capitalizes on the unique strengths of the enterprise and the opportunities in the market. Here are examples of price strategies:

- To gain market share by concentrating on small users served by our full-line distributors
- To build customer trust by reducing prices on products having highly visible cost reductions
- To win customers from competitors by bundling items at a low total price, including items not carried by our rivals
- To reduce inventory of displaced and remanufactured products without damaging brand image or trade relations
- To capture a higher portion of customer value by pricing according to a new metric (e.g., a pharmaceutical gas sold to hospitals on the basis of clock time of use, rather than by volume)

Clearly, the execution of a sound price strategy involves effective product management, careful formulation of the communication mix, and apt collaboration with channel partners. As the program is formulated, it is important to subject it to various tests of financial soundness, such as those in the previous section. In order to be able to develop sound pricing strategies, let's explore some of the managerial issues to be handled.

# Channel Pricing

We explained in Chapter 9 that channel intermediaries should be compensated for the work they do. That requires that we incorporate channel intermediary prices, costs, and margins into our pricing strategy. In this section we describe how prices and costs ripple through the channel. We show how organizations are connected using sets of unit cost breakdowns. We apply the mechanism in a new product scenario.

We highlight the tendency to enlarge the set of functions expected from channel partners when new products are introduced. With this backdrop we explore avenues for managing price to ensure channel margins that match up to the functions needed to be performed by the channel. Importantly, reseller prices cannot be specified directly for legal reasons we will discuss shortly. We have to manage price *indirectly*.

## *Prices through the Channel*

Pro Spot is a California manufacturer of welding equipment especially useful for automotive body shops. Body shop owners and other buyers purchase Pro Spot equipment from distributors. Hence, Pro Spot's factory price is different from what Ray's Auto Body pays for a welder. Nevertheless, Pro Spot and Ray are connected in the unit cost breakdowns of the channel participants. When we analyze purchase volume on assorted products, we can follow the same procedures with simple pro forma income statements instead of unit costs.

Follow the example in Exhibit 14–10. The left-hand box shows the manufacturer's net sales to distributors, the direct costs involved, and resulting gross profit. Practically speaking, the factory price represents the distributor's cost of goods sold (COGS)—

**Exhibit 14–10**
Channel Margin Chain

When stated that margins in the channel are 15, 25, and 20 percent for manufacturers, wholesalers, and dealers, respectively, these are the product-level income statements implied.

| Manufacturer | | Wholesaler | | Dealer | |
|---|---|---|---|---|---|
| Net sales | 100% | Net sales | 100% | Net sales | 100% |
| COGS | 85 | COGS | 75 | COGS | 80 |
| Gross profit | 15 | Gross profit | 25 | Gross profit | 20 |

For managerial purposes it is useful to equate the net sales of the firm on the left to the COGS of its neighbor on the right. Below we do this for a single item, so think of net sales as price.

| Manufacturer | | Wholesaler | | Dealer | |
|---|---|---|---|---|---|
| Net sales | $100 | Net sales | $133 | Net sales | $167 |
| COGS | 85 | COGS | 100 | COGS | 133 |
| Gross profit | 15 | Gross profit | 33 | Gross profit | 34 |

Because gross profit and COGS are complements and we connect net sales to COGS on the right, any dollar figure known in the channel allows us to complete the chain. Use the same margin chain to complete the income statements below, where dealer COGS is $48 (and 80% of net sales).

| Manufacturer | | Wholesaler | | Dealer | |
|---|---|---|---|---|---|
| Net sales | | Net sales | | Net sales | |
| COGS | — | COGS | — | COGS | $48 |
| Gross profit | | Gross profit | | Gross profit | |

actually nearly all of its direct costs. If the distributor follows a discount structure that's negotiated with the manufacturer or that's simply typical of the product category, its price to dealers can be determined. The boxes above apply to unit prices and costs. We see the same connection between factory net sales and distributor costs of goods and gross profit; likewise for distributor sales and dealer costs of goods sold.

Finally, in the third set of boxes, we invite you to apply the percentage terms to complete the picture of connected prices, costs, and margins of channel partners. Unit profits or margins are often used in conversation that connects to income statement gross margins. When income statements are summarized line by line in percentages, the base is conventionally the net sales or net revenue line. That is, costs and gross profits are percentages of net sales. The same convention holds true at the unit level. Thus, *unless stated otherwise, gross profits or unit margins at any level of the channel are expressed as percentages of that organization's unit price or net sales.*

## Margin Chains

It is not uncommon for channel margins to be expressed as a string of percentages. For example, construction sealants are marked up 15 percent and 30 percent by wholesalers and dealers. Given factory or end user price, and using the framework from Exhibit 14–10,

**Exhibit 14–11**
Margin Chain
Solution

| Wholesaler | | Dealer | |
|---|---|---|---|
| Net sales | 100% | Net sales | 100% |
| COGS | 85 | COGS | 70 |
| Gross profit | 15 | Gross profit | 30 |
| Apply the chain to work from a $10 dealer price | | | |
| Net sales | $7.00 | Net sales | $10 |
| COGS | 5.95 | COGS | 7 |
| Gross profit | 1.05 | Gross profit | 3 |

**Exhibit 14–12**
New Product
Pricing
throughout
the Channel

Here we price a product through the channel that costs $4.50 to produce and a 25 percent factory margin is expected. First, $4.50 = .75 factory price. Therefore, factory price = $6.00.

| Wholesaler | | Dealer | |
|---|---|---|---|
| Net sales | $7.06 because 6.00 = .85 net sales | Net sales | $10.08 because 7.06 = .7 net sales |
| COGS | 6.00 | COGS | 7.06 |
| Gross profit | 1.06 | Gross profit | 3.02 |

we can easily determine prices and costs throughout the distribution channel. The algebra of channel pricing looks a bit tedious. But with regular involvement in a particular product setting, the mechanics become second nature.

Consider some of the pricing issues that involve the channel. Say marketing research has identified a new segment that would pay $9 to $11 for a sealant delivering certain new benefits. The pricing problem is What is the maximum factory price that will play out in the channel as a $10 price to users? Exhibit 14–11 works the numbers. The analysis could go the other way after the cost analysts reveal that it will cost $4.50 to make the product and a 25 percent gross profit is expected. Exhibit 14–12 works the numbers from the factory costs.

## Channel Margin Management

Especially with a new product, the promotional tasks of channel intermediaries may be quite significant. Manufacturers may advertise and cultivate leads in order to support their channel partners, but there remains an important role for resellers. They must stock sufficient levels of inventory of a product whose demand has not yet been proven. Also, the selling tasks may require extensive demonstration and contact with multiple parties in a customer organization.

What are the prospects of obtaining such important channel functions if reseller margins are inadequate? Right; the prospects are dim. Our channel intermediaries can cut back on the roles they perform for our product or reallocate their effort to products and activities that may be more profitable.

A key part of our pricing strategy will be to manage the margins of our intermediaries. This has to be done indirectly in the United States because the Supreme Court has not seen fit to distinguish between price fixing by competitors and "price fixing" between channel partners. (Thus, it is just as illegal for Monsanto to tell its wholesalers to sell its herbicides at no less than $X as it is for Monsanto and Scott to conspire to fix their factory prices at $Y.)[7]

Manufacturers can affect reseller margins by several indirect means: exclusivity, territories, location restrictions, customer assignments, and advertising. Each method aims to control the pressure on a reseller's price. Sheltered from price pressures, channel members will then have margins sufficient to compensate for intensive selling effort, stocking, or other channel services.

## Vertical Restrictions

When a manufacturer promises a reseller **exclusivity,** a pledge to supply no other resellers in the trade area, the supplier aims to bridle **intrabrand competition,** price pressure from sellers of the same brand. For example, ComputerEase has enjoyed success with its project management software for the construction industry as a result of two essential elements in their dealer incentive program: high margins and exclusive territories. High margins are needed to compensate dealers for the extent of their services in the value-added process—especially finding and educating prospects, demonstrating and selling, and providing post-sale service. High margins without exclusive territories are practically impotent. Exclusive territories protect the high margins; if rival ComputerEase dealers pursued the same accounts, discounting would erode the margins and eventually service would fade, too. Usually, this manufacturer pledge is reciprocated by the reseller, which promises not to carry directly competing products. As we have mentioned elsewhere, bilateral pledging provides a structure for refining and deepening a business relationship.

Another way to manage intrabrand competition is to judiciously space resellers or, more realistically, use resellers that serve different market areas. This can be done by **territorial restrictions,** confining the reseller's activities to a particular geographic zone, or by **location restrictions,** specifying the site or sites from which the product may be sold. Obviously, each approach brings a measure of exclusivity. The explicit territorial clause is more exclusive than the location clause because the former forbids activities outside one's territory, whereas the latter has a range limited only by the efficiency and inventiveness of the fixed-site reseller.

**Customer restrictions** specify the type of business the reseller may or may not serve. If distributors can resell to other distributors, all the above mechanisms for rationalizing the distribution network may be jeopardized. Therefore, it is common to prohibit wholesalers from selling to other types of wholesalers. In addition, a manufacturer may make certain large accounts explicitly off-limits to its resellers.

Of course, the Internet has the capacity to transcend spacial limitations. Unless carefully managed, a manufacturer's transactional Web site can radically magnify intrabrand competition, thwarting completely the purpose of its vertical restrictions in distribution. If distributors and the manufacturer's Web site can work effectively as a team to service, say, small or very large accounts, the potential for conflict can be minimized. Also, it is not unusual for distributors to receive a profit from sales to customers in their territory that are obtained through the manufacturer's Web site. This looks a little like an effort to "buy peace" in the channel, but is reasonable if the sale results—at least in part—from past local marketing efforts by the distributor or the distributor's available stock and potential to give other customer services.

## Advertising

What about advertising's effects on channel margins? In the evolution of markets it sometimes happens that the marketing channel is not the best way to differentiate the product. If buyer sophistication increases or new advertising can effectively communicate product benefits, why not use it to do so? The results may be a positive brand image and strong customer preferences. The secondary effect of highly effective advertising is to intensify price competition *among resellers*. Think about it. Imagine you're purchasing a large quantity of ink jet printers. You know the product performance advantages of Hewlett-Packard machines from reliable test issues in computer magazines, and HP advertising outlines benefits you appreciate in terms you can understand. You don't need a distributor salesperson to school you on how or what to purchase; you're looking for a good price. Distributors soon recognize this character of the marketplace and begin to discount the HP printers.

## Push versus Pull

If we take this idea a little bit further, we see that advertising and other promotions to differentiate the brand effectively among end users can essentially pull the product through the channel. This is the fundamental aim of the **pull strategy,** direct communication with end users to differentiate the product through the media. This contrasts with some of the ideas presented earlier in this section that preserved reseller margins and otherwise enabled their performance of key promotion activities. The **push strategy** is the label attached to the general approach to support and reward reseller activities to differentiate the brand among customers.

### To Classify Promotion Mixes

In some marketing texts, push and pull strategies are discussed as polar options that compete for resources in a firm's marketing communication efforts. True, these strategies do manifest themselves in the communication mix: push strategies reflecting trade promotions, selling aids for the channel, healthy margins, and low levels of advertising aimed principally at supporting the claims of salespeople; pull strategies showing high levels of advertising, a strong brand image, and broad distribution of 800 numbers for presale support from the manufacturer. In the field of abrasives, most of you know 3M because of its advertising, but you may not have heard of the world's leader, Norton, because it stresses a push strategy. We want you to see, however, that the two strategies are much more than a simple dichotomy of promotion emphasis.

### To Manage Channel Effectiveness—via Prices!

Recognize push and pull in Exhibit 14–13 for their roles in channel coordination and price management—and *recognize their roots in careful analysis of market behavior*. Can customers and prospects use media-provided information to form strong preferences? Or is product evaluation and use so difficult that it takes personal selling or a close look at an array of options or special help with installation and training, and so on, to differentiate?

   In the former case of media-provided data, a business marketer should develop a strong advertising campaign and commit to high spending to build and maintain the brand image. Sales gains and declining end user prices prove the aptness of the strategy. One business marketer described this situation as "heaven," noting that he was able to raise factory prices, though distributors continued to cut prices to end users—who touched a bit of heaven themselves. In essence, the manufacturer was able to use effective advertising to capture a larger share of total margin (value) in the channel. The advertising heightened reseller competition on price, increasing the quantity demanded—total channel throughput.

**Exhibit 14–13**
Push versus Pull
Strategies

**Push:** Product is differentiated by personal selling, channel service, and so on.

**Pull:** Product is differentiated through the media.

In the latter case, when customers depend on the channel to differentiate products, upstream business marketers must apply their resources to enable, support, and reward reseller activities. For example, the manufacturer's Web site would surely support the brand image, tout its blue ribbon dealers, and feature a dealer locator. It would probably not support online transactions. High reseller margins—thus protected from intrabrand competition—are the rule.

### Final Words on Channel Pricing

Business products sold through intermediaries must be priced to account for the margins earned by those intermediaries. This section demonstrated the connection of unit costs, margins, and prices in the channel. Clearly, if reseller margins—and therefore prices—are too high, users forgo the benefits of the product, and factory sales suffer. But if reseller margins are too low, grave consequences may occur also: Intermediary selling effort, service, stocking, and so on, may deteriorate, causing end user frustration and eventually a switch to products of another manufacturer. We identified exclusive territories, location clauses, and customer restrictions as means to limit intrabrand competition on price but encourage reseller service.

Finally we noted that markets evolve or creative breakthroughs occur in communications that result in viable alternatives to reliance on resellers to differentiate the brand. As reseller participation in promotion and other channel functions declines, intrabrand competition can greatly intensify, thereby reducing prices and reseller margins. A real key to the decision to push or pull is determining how customers in the segment process information. They call the shots: If differentiation can occur through media—including manufacturer Web sites—a pull strategy will squeeze reseller margins and users will benefit from low prices. When the preponderance of differentiation can only be performed by the channel, we opt for a push strategy that must support and rightly compensate the differentiation efforts of our channel partners. Users gain from fitting reseller services.

# Product Line Pricing

To this point in the chapter our discussion has presumed the price management of a single product. But many companies offer a line of products. To some extent the products may be substitutes. An example is the array of high-speed personal computers from Dell or the overnight and second-day delivery options from UPS. Or the products in the line may be complements: Loctite adhesives for Loctite applicator systems or books authored by a well-regarded seminar leader on setting priorities and achievement. This section briefly discusses some of the managerial issues involved in pricing related products.

## Pricing Substitute Products

When substitute products differ in size, the pricing task tends to be driven largely by cost factors. Following this line, a $6' \times 10'$ tarp carries a price twice as high in the $10' \times 12'$, and a $20' \times 20'$ goes for 6.67 times the price. There is something to be said for the simplicity of this approach, but it clearly neglects the demand side of the equation. Small-size buyers may be triers who might be induced in greater numbers with a discount price. Are $10' \times 12'$ tarp buyers looking for the same benefits as $20' \times 20'$ buyers? Do they have the same range of alternatives? Can the large size encourage use and repeat purchases?

Similarly, when products differ in quality, we find a tendency to use cost or input formulas too. This, of course, neglects to consider the value of the quality differences to customers. Often the cost associated with a quality-enhancing component, design, or ingredient is far less than the value it provides the user. An overpowered starter on trucks used in Manitoba is vital for machine performance in winter because the cost of downtime is so monumental. This can work the other way too: a large incremental cost for small gains in performance or value. Scrubbers that remove 90 percent of emissions may cost $\$X$ to produce; those that remove 95 percent may cost $\$2X$. Clearly, both cost and benefit sides must be examined in pricing any product. Some firms tend to forget the benefit side when cost differences in the line are so handy. The reason a firm carries multiple products in a line is to appeal to different market segments. Examine the price sensitivity of each segment—as well as the differences in production and selling costs to each.

## Pricing Complementary Products

We know that the demand for many business products is derived from demand for other goods and services. This section looks at the situation involving a single firm selling the products used in combination. For example, many commercial buildings feature washroom soap dispensers sold by firms that also supply soap. The sale of a materials testing system brings follow-up sales of replacement parts and service. Monthly expenditures on ink cartridges rival the cost of the printer used in many small and home offices.

The popular approach is to price the "driver" product relatively low in order to penetrate the market, and then make high margins on the follow-up business of parts, consumables, or service. But most buyers are weary of such "traps" and will try to evaluate alternative supply arrangements on a system basis. Indeed, they may avoid the driver product for fear of being locked into a vulnerable supply position. When the driver product represents a specific investment on the buyer's part, the seller may wish to provide some assurances to the buyer that it won't be "held up" by exploitative prices on complementary products or services over the life of the asset.

A relationship management approach to pricing would enable the parties to consider a structure for adjusting prices in a long-term supply contract. Current prices could be adjusted at a programmed annual rate to reflect the likelihood of changing input costs. Then we might add a clause that provided exceptions. A company in the Northwest pegged its price in a long-run supply contract to fluctuations in the market price of gold because gold was a costly material for one component. Costs were hard to forecast and a slight rise in the price of gold meant the supplier's profit margin evaporated, unless some price adjustment was made.

Recall from Chapter 2 that contracts represent just one set of ways that firms might organize for ongoing exchange. The selling firm could make matching investments to service the buyer's specific investments, perhaps locating a supply facility near the customer. Alternatively, the seller might license proprietary products to enable customers to purchase from another source in the event the seller ever gouged the customer on price—or shirked other obligations in the relationship.

## Segmentation Pricing

Throughout the chapter we have instructed you to price according to both supply and demand factors. We consider costs to the extent that they must be covered, but we attend to the value customers can expect from the product. Now, if different customer segments derive different value from the product, we should thoroughly explore the opportunity to charge them different prices. Indeed, the entire motivation for segmenting markets is to reap greater financial rewards by customizing a marketing mix for a group of customers.

It may or may not be easy to isolate different markets in order to charge different prices. When segments are defined geographically, it may be possible to charge different prices in different regions. When segments are accustomed to service by distinct channels (e.g., adhesives via catalog versus bearings distributor versus plastics wholesaler), different prices are possible. But it may take a great deal of creativity and remarkable integration with other elements of the marketing program—especially channels and advertising—when purchasing habits are fluid. Bootlegging and "gray markets" attest to the inevitability that buyers from one locale, channel, or industry find out when there are better deals given in another.

### Different Prices to Competitors

The **Robinson–Patman Act** (1936) prohibits some types of **price discrimination.** When sellers charge different prices on similar products to customers that are in competition—and the effect is likely to lessen competition substantially—they violate U.S. pricing statutes. Most litigation involves alleged price discrimination by sellers, but buyer initiatives for obtaining price advantages over their competitors buying the same product also are illegal.

Understand all key ingredients here. If a railroad charges one rate for 10 boxcars to a company shipping scrap metal and another rate to a company shipping air compressors, is that illegal? The answer is no because the scrap metal shipper does not compete with the air compressor shipper. And managerially, it makes good sense to charge different rates to groups of customers with different price sensitivities: Scrap metal could go by barge or truck, compressors realistically only by truck.

What if a company sells processed beer brewing by-products to a large pet food company in St. Louis for $X per ton and to a small pet food company in Rochester, New York, for $1.2X per ton? First off, it may be that the St. Louis market is more competitive than Rochester's. Thus, $X is what it takes to meet competition in St. Louis. If Rochester and other markets are not "subsidizing" predatory (below-market) prices in St. Louis, then there is no legal difficulty here.

Alternatively, the law allows for price differences based on quantity purchased, when the associated cost differences are evident. Compared to a small order, often a large purchase has more economical shipping and handling costs per unit, and equivalent administrative costs (e.g., order processing and billing) are distributed over more units.

Illegal price discrimination must be reasonably expected to have an adverse impact on competition. Adverse impact does not mean one of our competitors is unhappy or has slumping sales. We distinguish *injury to a competitor* from *injury to competition*. When competition suffers, we might see firms going out of business because of losses attributable to price discrimination or we could expect a small number of firms to increase their already high market shares. This tends toward a monopoly and restricted purchasing options for buyers.

Finally, we need to note that *price discrimination to resellers that participate in different channel functions appears to be legal.* In today's business environment we see all kinds of purchasing strategies by end users. Some buy direct and receive shipments centrally in order to route to the plants. Other users will rely on wholesalers to ship to plants and set up parts and materials for use on the shop floors. We see similar variation in functions performed by different wholesalers. For example, some will exclusively serve end users, others will do substantial business with another level in the channel: dealers or resellers. It seems silly in such an environment to apply a simplistic trade discount scheme such as end users pay list price, $Y$, wholesalers pay $.7Y$, and dealers $.8Y$.

Instead, manufacturers can charge different prices, based on customer performance of the different channel functions. The Supreme Court has stated that functional discounts do not violate the Robinson–Patman Act.

> *In general, a supplier's **functional discount** is said to be a discount given to a purchaser based on the purchaser's role in the supplier's distributive system, reflecting, at least in a generalized sense, the services performed by the purchaser for the supplier.*[8]

# Bidding and Negotiating

Up to now, our discussion of price has implicitly emphasized **administered prices:** that is, prices established by a seller as impersonal, take-it-or-leave-it offers to prospective buyers. This type of pricing dominates the consumer marketplace and is common in business markets. Nevertheless, many transactions between firms involve competitive bidding or negotiation.

## Bid Pricing

At the Web site for *Commerce Business Daily* (**http://cbd.savvy.com**), an undergraduate intern at PPG Industries might notice that the U.S. Department of Energy has asked for proposals to construct and evaluate a solar-powered post office in Utah. The city of Centerville advertises for bids from highway construction companies to repair a stretch of US 48. A metropolitan hospital asks three waste disposal companies to bid for the task of properly managing medical wastes.

As you can see from these examples, buyers take a proactive role in making market forces work to satisfy organizational needs. Competitive bidding is very common in government and quasi-public institutions (schools, hospitals, social service agencies) largely to satisfy external constituencies that otherwise have difficulty auditing performance.

Competitive bids provide some assurance of input efficiency. At Internet hubs where commercial buyers enter a request for quotes, product specifications are quite tight.

## Goals and Constraints

Not every bidding occasion is a business opportunity. The potential bidder must carefully examine the request for proposals or bids. A successful bid is one that meets the goals of both buyer and bidder. Begin by taking stock of your firm's mission and strategy. Do we have experience in this area? Do we want to build on this experience? If so, with this type of account? Will we have the capacity to complete the project if we get it? Is this a contract that can develop our company's reputation in a new field connected to important follow-on business? What level of effort is involved in preparing the proposal?

Next, and certainly as part of preparing a proposal, consider the buyer's objectives. Frequently price is not the ultimate criterion. For a Department of Defense communication system, the first criterion might be security; for aircraft landing gear, reliability; for highway repair, speed.

With an informed appreciation of your competitors' abilities, realistically assess your firm's capacity to measure up on buyer criteria. Not every competitor is in a position to bid. They may have capacity tied up in previously won jobs. They may have key personnel assigned elsewhere. They may have let it be known that they are no longer interested in a particular line of business.

We should bid for the job if we want the business and have a reasonable chance of competing favorably for the contract. The bid price should reflect consideration of costs and competitive action.

Many firms prepare bids according to a standard formula built from experience. A marketing consultant calculated a bid for one project by estimating the hours of telephone interviewing, analytical services, and report writing using standard rates of $24, $150, and $275, respectively. A building contractor summed 1.2 × materials cost + 1.5 estimated labor.

These standards are fine as starting points, but the final bid should reflect current operating realities. For example, why bid the telephone interviewing at $24 if the call center is already at full use? Why price to recoup $20,000 of warehouse rent if the space will be idle otherwise? And why bid $15,000 if you are confident that no competitor can deliver for under $20,000?

Exhibit 14–14 shows how decision theory can help in the evaluation of bid options in uncertain situations. In this example, IROD's knowledge of its rival's scant ability to prepare a low-price bid leads it to submit a high price, $12. Although there is a slight chance of losing the contract at the high price, the expected payoffs are superior to the expected profits from a bid that's sure to win.

## Protocol

Buyers opt for one of two general formats for soliciting proposals. **Open bidding** means that any organization can vie for the business. Open bids tend to be sought in two polar situations: (1) when needs are tightly defined for simple products or services—for example, 400 yards of pea gravel or printing political handbills—and (2) when needs are vaguely defined, perhaps only specifying a solution—for example, extinguish wellhead fires or transport earthmoving equipment from Peoria to Siberia. In the former case, open bidding energizes market pressures on commodity-like products. Price is the only criterion.

In the latter case, open bidding enables the broadest set of creative solutions to address the problem. The buyer may ask to negotiate price with the vendor whose proposal reflected the best thinking and promise.

**Exhibit 14–14**
Bidding:
Applied
Decision
Theory

In this simple illustration, IROD is considering two bid levels: one high and one low. If IROD wins at the high level, its profits will be about $150,000. If IROD wins at the low level, its profits will be around $100,000.

A rival firm, Doro, has a realistic chance of winning the contract too. Although it cannot match IROD's cost structure to prepare a bid better than IROD's low bid, Doro could edge IROD's higher bid level. Finally, with its current labor problems, Doro is far behind on three other projects. IROD executives think it is unlikely that Doro will pursue the job except at a high profit level.

The accompanying table summarizes the situation and the expected payoffs from each possible bid by IROD.

| IROD's Options | Possible Actions by Doro (probability) | | Expected Profits |
| | Bid $13/unit (.8) | Bid $10/unit (.2) | |
| --- | --- | --- | --- |
| Bid $12/unit | IROD wins, Profit = $150K | IROD loses, Profit = 0 | .8 * 150K = $120K |
| Bid $9/unit | IROD wins, Profit = $100K | IROD wins Profit = $100K | $100K |

**Closed bidding** features the solicitation of proposals from an exclusive set of potential suppliers. For example, American Express may ask three marketing research companies to submit proposals to conduct a concept evaluation for a new type of corporate credit card. Or General Motors will invite just five potential suppliers to a reverse online auction. The closed bidding format reflects the buyer's ability to identify capable suppliers. Closed bidding also recognizes the significant costs of bid preparation. Imagine five companies spending $5,000 each preparing bids on a research project that yields $20,000 in profit. The industry risks self-destruction if the costs of bids outrun the profits from projects.

## Negotiated Prices

Unlike the bidding process, in which the buyer essentially asks potential suppliers to "give us your best shot," **negotiation** involves two-way communication and problem solving to come to mutually agreeable terms. Recall our discussions of negotiation in Chapter 7 and conflict management in Chapter 9. Of course, the parties have conflicting interests: Seller wants a high price, buyer a low price. But seldom does the entire transaction pivot on the number to the right of the dollar sign.

Often negotiation over price spills over into other issues. The buyer makes a concession on price if buyer inventories are trimmed by JIT. The seller makes a concession on price if the buyer will agree to share production schedule information, enabling more efficient seller production and distribution. Sometimes payment timing solves what initially appeared to be a price issue.

### Negotiation Strategy

Business marketers cannot approach every business bargaining situation in the same way. Some exchange parties are long term, others are brand new. And haggling over a lease is apt to be more significant than customer late payment fees.

Two fundamental questions are key to selecting an initial negotiation strategy: (1) Is the relationship with the other party important? (2) Are the material outcomes important?[9]

**Avoidance** is a common course when the party doesn't really need the deal or the partner. A small supplier may find a potentially large account that fails to read proposals or even return phone calls. **Accommodation** is sacrifice to build or sustain a relationship. **Compromise** is a hybrid of competition and accommodation. It is often an easy solution, bringing a premature end to the negotiations. **Competitive negotiation** has a winner and a loser; it is the right course when it is critical to win *this* deal. Little regard is given to the prospects for subsequent exchange with the party. **Collaboration** is joint problem solving, searching for creative win–win solutions.

The real negotiation strategy options are then competition, collaboration, and accommodation.[10] The characteristics are summarized in Exhibit 14–15. Think carefully of the stakes of the issue and the relationship as you prepare to pursue one of these strategies.

Preparation for any negotiation process requires an opportunity to present the value proposition and quantify it. If you have done this, by all means have confidence in your package, but make sure you will be dealing with a person at the buying organization with the authority to negotiate. Patience and good listening will enhance trust and may uncover a win–win solution, so resolve to exhibit these virtues. During the negotiation itself, continue to seek understanding of the buyer's needs, probably emphasizing open-ended questions and confirmation of your restatement of their responses. Sometimes agreements on small items can build momentum for knottier issues. After the negotiation try to summarize the agreement in writing for all parties and take note of the factors that seemed to advance the process with this account. If no agreement was reached it may be wise to give the customer an out. If they decline after you've boxed them in, they may think they have lost face or trust, and may be hesitant to do business again.

## Global Pricing Contracts

The pricing framework from Exhibit 14–2 must be judiciously applied in global markets. Certainly, supply costs and channel structures can differ from one country to the next. Government regulations and trade environments impact prices, as does the competitive environment. Even within panregional markets such as the Andean Group in South America or the European Union, these factors can produce country-by-country variations. From the Field 14–4 offers a case in point with steel.

But what about global customers? An increasing number of multinational customers are asking suppliers for global pricing contracts. The pressure comes not so much from the decentralized, multidomestic enterprises with local purchasing autonomy, but especially from those with procurement functions run from international headquarters. In 1998 General Motors asked suppliers of components used in its engines and transmissions to charge the same price for parts in all parts of the world. HP Financial Services ensures worldwide consistency in financing terms and conditions, pricing methodology, structuring and deployment, and provides a consistent global template for lease pricing, no matter where the lease originates.

Customers stand to benefit from global pricing contracts in several ways. They expect efficiencies from standardization in logistics, inventories, new product development, and customer service. Of course, they expect aggregated purchases to result in lower prices. Suppliers stand to improve their international presence, grow sales, forge stronger relationships with key customers, and even showcase global partnerships for a competitive edge in market development. But a win–win relationship is hardly certain. Suppliers must do extensive research—on market variance in customer operations and profit-loss responsibility, country-by-country differences in customer prices, and legal and competitive

## Exhibit 14–15
## Characteristics of Different Negotiation Strategies

| Aspect | Competition (Distributive Bargaining) | Collaboration (Integrative Negotiation) | Accommodative Negotiation |
|---|---|---|---|
| Payoff structure | Usually a fixed amount of resources to be divided | Usually a variable amount of resources to be divided | Usually a fixed amount of resources to be divided |
| Goal pursuit | Pursuit of own goals at the expense of those of others | Pursuit of goals held jointly with others | Subordination of own goals in favor of those of others |
| Relationships | Short-term focus; parties do not expect to work together in the future | Long-term focus; parties expect to work together in the future | May be short term (let the others win to keep them happy) or long term (let the other win to encourage reciprocity in the future) |
| Primary motivation | Maximize own outcome | Maximize joint outcome | Maximize others' outcome or let them gain to enhance relationship |
| Trust and openness | Secrecy and defensiveness; high trust in self, low trust in others | Trust and openness, active listening, joint exploration of alternatives | One party relatively open, exposing own vulnerabilities to the other |
| Knowledge of needs | Parties know own needs, but conceal or misrepresent them; neither party lets the other know real needs | Parties know and convey real needs while seeking and responding to needs of the other | One party is overresponsive to other's needs so as to repress own needs |
| Predictability | Parties use unpredictability and surprise to confuse other side | Parties are predictable and flexible when appropriate, trying not to surprise | One party's actions totally predictable, always catering to other side |
| Aggressiveness | Parties use threats and bluffs, trying to keep the upper hand | Parties share information honestly, treat each other with understanding and respect | One party gives up on own position to mollify the other |
| Solution search behavior | Parties make effort to appear committed to position, using argumentation and manipulation of the other | Parties make effort to find mutually satisfying solutions, using logic, creativity, and constructiveness | One party makes effort to find ways to accommodate the other |
| Success measures | Success enhanced by creating bad image of the other; increased levels of hostility and strong in-group loyalty | Success demands abandonment of bad images and consideration of ideas on their merit | Success determined by minimizing or avoiding conflict and soothing all hostility; own feelings ignored in favor of harmony |
| Evidence of unhealthy extreme | Unhealthy extreme reached when one party assumes total–zero-sum game; defeating the other becomes a goal in itself | Unhealthy extreme reached when one subsumes all self-interest in the common good, losing self-identity and self-responsibility | Unhealthy extreme reached when abdication to other is complete, at expense of personal and/or constituent goals |
| Key attitude | Key attitude is "I win, you lose" | Key attitude is "What's the best way to address the needs of all parties?" | Key attitude is "You win, I lose" |
| Remedy for breakdown | If impasse occurs, mediator or arbitrator may be needed | If difficulties occur, a group dynamics facilitator may be needed | If behavior becomes chronic, party becomes negotiationally bankrupt |

SOURCE: Reprinted with permission from Roy Lewicki, David Saunders, and John Minton, *Essentials of Negotiation,* Burr Ridge, IL: Richard D. Irwin, 1997, pp. 96–97. Also reprinted by permission of the publisher from Robert Wayne Johnston, "Negotiation Strategies: Different Strokes for Different Folks," *Personnel* (March–April 1982). Copyright © Robert Wayne Johnston. Published by American Management Association, New York. www.amanet.org. All rights reserved.

---

**14–4**

# FROM THE FIELD

## Steel Drumming for Revenue . . . and Supply

The market for steel showed a few signs of chaos in 2004. World iron ore prices jumped in the spring, largely due to tight supplies and surging sales to China. A similar scarcity has developed for scrap metal. Shredded auto scrap in Chicago, for example, jumped over 40 percent in four months. At the same time, the supply of coke—metallurgical coal that has been baked in the absence of air and is used in blast furnaces as a source of carbon—has been stretched not only by China's demand, but by a fire at an important mine in Pineville, WV. Because some steelmakers have been canceling orders, many service centers and fabricators have been *double ordering*, thereby exacerbating perceptions of shortage by magnifying the true demand! The result has been increasing pressure on prices. Ipsco, Nucor, AK Steel, and others have issued news releases announcing cost-driven surcharges because material costs cannot be absorbed through "normal price changes."

Some buyers have said they will refuse to pay for some or all of the surcharges; distributors threaten to withhold delivery. Some large buyers have sought steel from Mexico and other foreign sources.

Clearly, price is a critical yet imperfect means of allocating supply in the cyclical market for steel.

See Tom Stundza, "Steel Mills Bombard Buyers with Cost-Driven Surcharges," *Purchasing*, February 5, 2004, p. 14; see one supplier's view of the situation at www.cisco-eagle.com/steel/; also see the congressional testimony of Robert J. Stevens, CEO, Impact Forge, Inc., Columbus, Indiana, and President, Emergency Steel Scrap Coalition, "Spike in Metal Prices: What Does It Mean for Small Manufacturers?" March 2004, www.wrf.com/publications/publication.asp?id=1334143102004.

---

environments. They must also weigh carefully the amount of dependence they want on the customer, what other business relationships it might foreclose or put in jeopardy, and the potential for long-run collaboration within the global pricing contract. Exhibit 14–16 summarizes the array of forces needed to make global pricing contracts effective.[11]

### Final Words on Bid Pricing and Negotiation

Many companies price their products and services by means other than a single administered schedule. Sales to government agencies often involve bid pricing. When proposals are complex, negotiation may occur after proposals are evaluated. And a variety of leasing options may be considered in light of the objectives of both buyer and seller.

Negotiation strategy is best determined by the importance of the outcome and the exchange relationship. In a partnership, the temptation to split the difference is the lazy way out. It forgoes the opportunity to look at price negotiation as a collaborative problem-solving process—a process that looks at the entire exchange and the roles performed by the partner. New roles—stocking, promoting, ordering, exchanging—and new means of coordination—forecasting, producing, shipping, holding—could emerge.

# A Pricing System

Price is a critical element of marketing strategy. It belongs under the purview of the marketing manager. But he or she must be equipped with the right tools. These pricing tools include information on costs, customers, and competitors as well as familiarity with channel policy and the law.

## Exhibit 14–16
### Leverage Needed for Successful Global Pricing Contract
SOURCE: *Adapted from Das Narayandas, John Quelch, and Gordon Swartz, "Prepare Your Company for Global Pricing," Sloan Management Review 42 (Fall 2000), pp. 61–70.*

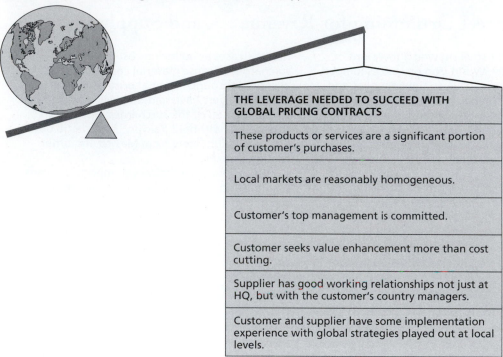

| THE LEVERAGE NEEDED TO SUCCEED WITH GLOBAL PRICING CONTRACTS |
|---|
| These products or services are a significant portion of customer's purchases. |
| Local markets are reasonably homogeneous. |
| Customer's top management is committed. |
| Customer seeks value enhancement more than cost cutting. |
| Supplier has good working relationships not just at HQ, but with the customer's country managers. |
| Customer and supplier have some implementation experience with global strategies played out at local levels. |

Accurate and timely information on internal operating costs and channel margins is critical. Supplier assistance in cost containment, design efficiency, and related facets of supply chain coordination should be reflected in the cost data as well. Finally, realistic cost forecasts should reflect consideration of experience effects, global supply factors, and government action.

Unless our products provide value to customers, we are out of business. Our capital goods must be reliable and durable, efficiently producing quality output and enabling customers to realize cash flows sufficient to pay the price (lease) on our equipment. Similarly, supplies and MRO items must provide value to the customer in excess of our price. We need careful analysis of customer requirements, supported by empathic dialogue and sound feedback from the sales force. We must train and reward the sales force for its critical role in this system.

Competitor price data are also needed in the pricing system. Again, we want to encourage our salespeople to bring good information to the process. Another component here is a bid tracking system that records the bids tendered, by account, and allows scorekeeping. Are we winning 25 percent of bids or 35 percent? How does this compare to year-ago rates? What are the batting averages of different managers making pricing decisions?

Can a pricing system pay off? Of course! Elliot Ross of the McKinsey Company tells of a firm that revised its accounting system to better sort fixed and variable costs by product and market. Then, with the help of its sales force, it compiled buying profiles and pricing histories for major customers by product type and key competitor. Finally,

---

**14–2**

# BUSINESS 2 BUSINESS
## The Importance of Price

Sales reps often press for lower prices or more pricing authority, thinking that their offerings are not competitive with their accounts. This bias for lower and lower prices is not simply a customer advocacy position. It might well reflect an incomplete understanding of buyer needs or their selling roles.

What do these data on the importance of different attributes in the customer–supplier relationship reveal about this phenomenon, and what do they suggest for sales force management and pricing?

| | Purchasing Managers | | Sales Reps | |
|---|---|---|---|---|
| | Rank | Mean | Rank | Mean |
| *Product Attributes* | | | | |
| Reliability | 1 | 1.31 | 1 | 1.36 |
| Quality | 2 | 1.37 | 2 | 1.42 |
| Durability | 3 | 1.39 | 8 | 2.03 |
| Engineering | 4 | 1.48 | 7 | 1.83 |
| Workmanship | 5 | 1.63 | 10 | 2.21 |
| *Service Attributes* | | | | |
| Delivery | 6 | 1.73 | 6 | 1.76 |
| Service | 7 | 1.80 | 5 | 1.53 |
| Reputation | 8 | 2.01 | 3 | 1.45 |
| Marketing | 9 | 2.17 | 11 | 2.44 |
| *Monetary Attributes* | | | | |
| Financial Terms | 10 | 2.25 | 9 | 2.18 |
| Price | 11 | 2.63 | 4 | 1.51 |

Source: Data used with permission from Ramon A. Avila, William B. Dodds, Joseph D. Chapman, O. Karl Mann, and Russell G. Wahlers, "Importance of Price in Industrial Buying: Sales versus Purchasing Perspectives," *Review of Business* 15 (Winter 1993), pp. 34–38.

it loaded the new cost, customer, and competitor databases on personal computers for each pricing manager, provided guidelines, and issued periodic feedback on personal performance. Margins improved in a slumping business cycle and profits increased $25 million in the first year.[12]

# Summary

Price is the dollar amount exchanged for a particular product-and-service configuration. It captures the focus of accountants, market managers, operations managers, sales staff, and pricing specialist on the seller side. It's the aim of buyers seeking value on the customer side.

The factors of supply and demand have been formally analyzed by economists. Their models of competitive structure give important insights into the dynamics of pricing in different competitive situations. We reviewed the fragile equilibrium status of prices in oligopolistic settings and reviewed the profit maximization axioms of monopolistic competition. The latter supported a refresher treatment of the financial rudiments of simple pro forma income statements as well as break-even and marginal analysis, enabling us to evaluate candidate pricing strategies.

The key managerial topics of pricing involve channel margin chains and margin management. Because reseller margins should generally compensate for performance of channel functions, it is vital to manage price in order to ensure adequate reseller rewards and fitting channel services to end users. Reseller prices can only be managed indirectly through vertical restrictions—territory, location, and customers—and advertising.

In a critical discussion of the strategies of push and pull marketing, we examined how they best fit customer buying processes and work to manage channel margins and functions. Essentially, if products can be differentiated via the media, we should follow a pull strategy and allow reseller margins to erode. If personal selling and logistical excellence are needed to differentiate the product, the supplier should push—that is, work to support the margins of channel partners who provide the key differentiating functions.

The chapter developed key ideas for managing prices of related products. Substitutes should be priced for different segments. Complements should be viewed as a system, recognizing the possibility of specific investments by buyers. When buyers seek to safeguard their specific investments, sellers should recognize their ability to make pledges or otherwise reduce buyer perceptions of vulnerability.

When companies charge different prices to customers in different market segments, they must pay careful attention to Robinson–Patman Act provisions against price discrimination. Violations occur when (1) different prices are charged to competitors, (2) the differences are not attributable to cost differences, (3) the product is essentially the same for each, and (4) the effects are damaging to competition. Fortunately, in the face of channel systems in flux, the Supreme Court has said that functional discounts appear to be contractually fitting and legal.

Before concluding the chapter with a brief discussion of a system for pricing, we covered the topics of bid pricing, negotiation, and success factors for global pricing contracts.

# Key Terms

| | | |
|---|---|---|
| accommodation | elastic demand | oligopoly |
| administered prices | exclusivity | open bidding |
| avoidance | functional discount | price |
| break-even price | inelastic demand | price discrimination |
| break-even quantity | intrabrand competition | pull strategy |
| closed bidding | learning curve | push strategy |
| collaboration | location restrictions | Robinson–Patman Act |
| competitive negotiation | monopolistic | territorial restriction |
| compromise | competition | |
| customer restrictions | negotiation | |

# Discussion Questions

1. Price is a means of allocating scarce resources in a society. Are there any other ways? Identify strengths and weaknesses of one or two other means of allocating scarce resources in a society. How about allocating generators following a severe hurricane?

2. As a budding business marketer you have been advised in this chapter to price products according to the value they provide customers. But customers seldom come right out and say, "If I could get a good custodial service (or MRO supplier or parts source or manufacturers' rep, etc.), I'd gladly pay $X." Identify two or three marketing research tools that could help define the dollar value of product benefits for a business customer.

3. Select members of the class to call at least four local businesses to obtain prices on the following specific items. (Try to find someone in the market to actually buy each of these products or services.) Record each quote and speculate about the aptness of a kinked demand curve in the product market.

   One hundred pounds of dry ice

   Close cracks and seal a specific blacktop parking lot

   Paint a specific building

   40  4′ × 16′ × 1/2″ sheets of drywall, delivered

   A copy machine that makes 35 to 45 copies per minute

4. For a copy machine that makes 35 to 44 copies per minute, identify one or two market segmentation bases that would capitalize on different price sensitivities among prospects.

5. Wexford Bearings sold casters and ball bearings through a network of industrial distributors throughout North America. Although margins could be as high as 35 percent on specialty bearings, most products were priced to afford distributors 25 percent margins. Recently Buskin, a distributor in Erie, Pennsylvania, gave a 5 percent discount to Midland Motors on a large order of standard bearings. Buskin took the order for the whole year's anticipated volume and promised up to three deliveries per month within 48 hours of reorder. What's Buskin's gross profit on the Midland account if its purchases run to $46,000?

6. Continuing from question 5, Gustav Himmelfarb, marketing vice president at Wexford, took a call from Hank Buskin, owner of Buskin Distributing. Hank asked for a price break on the volume he did with Wexford to service Midland. "Look, we've engineered a good supply contract and they've made a commitment to us. This is probably 20 percent of Wexford's volume in western Pennsylvania. And it's predictable! Steady! But I've got to let you know that it's really a stretch for me to make money on Midland. We've cut our margin 20 percent and have eaten what's left with the blue ribbon service Midland has come to expect. We need a 2.5 percent price break from Wexford on the Midland business if this thing is going to hold together." How should Himmelfarb respond?

7. The commercial painting business you set up last year has been a remarkable success. Now your company is one of four invited to submit proposals and prices for painting and glazing West Fork's community conservatory. What are the factors to be considered as you evaluate this opportunity and prepare a proposal?

8. The sales staff at Central Supply had known most of the electricians at Johnson Electric for nearly 25 years, but since old man Hank Johnson died last November,

things had become increasingly tense. Buck Johnson, eldest son, pressed billing clerk, Emma Spade, pretty hard about a recent invoice, but—since 99.9 percent of it is $230,000 per year in sales to Johnson Electric—it turned out to have no errors. Yesterday Buck and Timmy Johnson came by the Central Supply warehouse with about 10 pages of products—wire, boxes, conduit, and the like—printed off the Internet. They sort of ganged up on Rodney at the counter, who then called in owner, Burt Murray. The Johnsons wanted prices from Central to match the prices they found online. Even with shipping, many of the online items were at prices 20 percent below Central's. What should Burt Murray do?

9. Paul Winston runs the executive training program at a small private school in the Northeast. He schedules a slate of about 50 seminars that he aims to fill each year, using brochures, e-mail, and two seasonal catalogs to a database of about 10,000 managers at companies and nonprofit agencies within a 60-mile radius. The seminars are priced from $150 to $4,000, depending on content, location, and duration. As the summer began, Paul began to sketch the basis for a new way to market the courses. He was thinking that he would sell memberships on a Leadership Roundtable for $25,000 to up to 10 area companies, enlisting their input in program design and allowing up to 30 person-days of training for "free" to member firms. Evaluate the strengths and weaknesses of these two pricing methods.

10. Lockheed Martin is a $26 billion defense contractor. At the end of the last millennium, it was a loose coalition of business units that resulted from acquisitions, growth, and reorganization. Because the purchases across these units summed to over $10 billion, a move to centralize and reap companywide savings was initiated in 2001. Introducing the use of reverse auctions where appropriate and reducing the number of suppliers on machine parts brought savings of 25 to 40 percent. Similar approaches have been implemented on the $600 million annual spent on fasteners by aeronautics.[13]

   Are buyer initiatives such as Lockheed's apt to foster or impair business-to-business relationships?

## Cases

### Case 14.1   Paction

Paction (a large, multiproduct company) was analyzing pricing options for a new antistatic flooring. Market research had determined a potential of 1.5 million square yards per year in research and computer labs, even if priced at $80 per yard. Profit targets and fixed costs were $5.2 million per year. Direct costs per yard were hard to estimate. Estimators figured $28 per square yard at volumes less than 100,000 and $18 per square yard at greater volumes.

Develop a schedule for Paction showing break-even yardage and market share at prices of $40 to $80 per yard, in $5 increments.

### Case 14.2   Medicus

Medicus uses overseas manufacturers to supply small medical instruments and supplies. Among several channels to distribute its products, Medicus uses a national distributor, Axel, which does half its Medicus business selling directly to large hospitals and the other half to small local dealers that supply small hospitals and clinics. Margins are conveyed through a suggested discount off "list." Small hospitals and labs pay about list. Large hospitals typically buy at list less 10 percent. Wholesalers buy at list less 40 percent. Dealers pay, on average, list less 25 percent. What are the prices paid by all resellers and users for examination lenses sold by Medicus for $14? What is the average gross profit earned by the wholesaler on Medicus products? A small clinic pays the $42 list price on a water-activated fiberglass splint.

1. What are the prices paid by the dealer and Axel on the splint? Why should the intermediaries receive different discounts?

2. What increase in sales must Axel produce to cover the new debt service costs of $350,000 per year for its truck fleet expansion?

3. Clark is a little disappointed with the account coverage Axel has provided it in the South. One solution up for discussion is to try to line up Augusta Supply (a leading distributor in the South), which has made several acquisitions in the past two years in trying to establish a national presence. What are the possible consequences on prices, channel margins, and channel functions if Medicus adds Augusta to its distribution system?

## Additional Readings

Andrews, Whit. "The New Laws of Dynamic Pricing." *Internet World* (December 15, 1999), pp. 24–37.

Calantone, Roger J., and C. Anthony Di Benedetto. "Clustering Product Launches by Price and Launch Strategy." *Journal of Business & Industrial Marketing* 22, no. 1 (2007), pp. 4–19.

Daly, John D. *Pricing for Profitability: Activity Based Pricing for Competitive Advantage.* New York: John Wiley, 2002.

Dutta, Shananu, Mark E. Bergen, Daniel Levy, Mark Ritson, and Mark Zbaracki. "Pricing as a Strategic Capability." *Sloan Management Review* 43, no. 3 (2002), pp. 61–66.

Fisher, Roger, and Daniel Shapiro. *Beyond Reason: Using Emotions as You Negotiate.* New York: Viking, 2005.

Forman, Howard, and Richard Lancioni. "The Determinants of Pricing Strategies for Industrial Products in International Markets." *Journal of Business-to-Business Marketing* 9, no. 2 (2002), pp. 29–61.

Jap, Sandy. "The Impact of Online Reverse Auction Design on Buyer–Seller Relationships." *Journal of Marketing* 71 (January 2007), pp. 146–59.

*Journal of Business Research*, special issue on pricing, vol. 33 (July 1995).

Kaplan, A. D. H., Joel Dirlam, and Robert Lanzillotti. *Pricing in Big Business.* Washington, DC: The Brookings Institution, 1958.

Lee, Kun-Chang, and Soon-Jae Kwon. "The Use of Cognitive Maps and Case-Based Reasoning for B2B Negotiation." *Journal of Management Information Systems* 22 (Spring 2006), pp. 337–76.

Lewicki, Roy, David Saunders, and John Minton. *Essentials of Negotiation.* Burr Ridge, IL: Richard D. Irwin, 1997.

Monroe, Kent B. *Pricing: Making Profitable Decisions.* New York: McGraw-Hill, 2002.

Nagle, Thomas T., and Reed K. Holden. *Strategy and Tactics of Pricing: A Guide to Profitable Decision Making.* Upper Saddle River, NJ: Prentice Hall, 2002.

Phillips, Robert. *Pricing and Revenue Optimization.* Palo Alto, CA: Stanford University Press, 2005.

Schrader, Richard W., Julie Toner Schrader, and Eric P. Eller. "Strategic Implication of Reverse Auctions." *Journal of Business-to-Business Marketing* 11, nos. 1/2 (2004), pp. 61–80.

Stock, Ruth Maria. "Can Customer Satisfaction Decrease Price Sensitivity in Business-to-Business Markets?" *Journal of Business-to-Business Marketing* 12, no. 3 (2005), pp. 59–85.

Uslay, Can, Naresh K. Malhotra, and Fred C. Alvine. "Predatory Pricing and Marketing Theory: Applications in Business-to-Business Context." *Journal of Business-to-Business Marketing* 13, no. 3 (2006), pp. 65–113.

# Part 4

## Biological Resources and Ecology

# Managing Programs and Customers

L ike the finale to a week at summer camp, Part 4 aims to conclude the text with the boldest material for you to take away. We introduced Part I saying, "This is what business marketing is about." The same overture can play for Part 4. But now we're looking at the essentials of business marketing with a new level of sophistication. In fact, the term *sophistication* comes from the Greek word *sophist,* or "learned man." ●

Chapter 15 is all about control—gauging success or failure and making adjustments. Accountability impels this. The learning organization demands this. Throughout this text we've spotlighted innovation and touted the creative and quick-footed organization. You can soon join the game. But let's be ready to assess new systems and arenas with apt measures and models. ●

Looking at the table of contents for this book, a colleague told us that Chapter 16 seemed like Mom's departing admonition: "Don't forget your coat!" or "Be careful!" Granted, you've heard in marketing class that the customer is a firm's most important asset, but here we describe different types of customer relationships and vividly highlight the profit sensitivities to increasing retention rates. With a heightened motivation to retain customers, we examine some imperatives for managing relationships. ●

# Chapter 15

## Evaluating Marketing Efforts

### TEKTRONIX

Tektronix is a supplier of test, measurement, and monitoring devices for a number of different industries, so one might expect Tektronix to also lead in the development of measurement and monitoring systems for marketing activities and performance. In fact, the company is quite good at measuring marketing performance and monitoring sales and marketing progress, but it wasn't without some struggle.●

For example, has marketing done a good job if someone responds to an advertisement or trade show booth? Marketing people would call this "generating a lead," and feel that they had done something worthwhile. Salespeople, on the other hand, would toss that lead away, convinced that it would never lead to a sale. So where should money be spent—on generating more leads? Or on hiring more salespeople who can generate their own leads? And how would an executive know which decision was right?●

At Tektronix, the first challenge was simply to build a common language. Even defining the term "lead" required six months and the end result was a system of 19 possible versions of a lead. Once this language was developed, measurement systems could be put into place to identify effective sources of leads, as well as how well salespeople did once they were given the leads.●

Once the measurement systems are in place, monitoring systems are also required. Tektronix adopted a dashboard approach, or a system that provides executives five to seven key statistics every day. For example, the person in charge of trade shows could monitor the number of leads generated by trade shows on a daily basis by quality of lead, as well as how well the sales force was doing in closing those leads. A sales executive might keep track of other key performance metrics, such as conversion ratio for leads, average sales per salesperson, or other important measures. The chief marketing officer, though, may watch marketing cost per order, leads to sales, and headcount (number of staff) to operational dollars. ●

One result has been a shift in promotional activity. The company has moved toward public relations and Internet marketing and away from advertising. Shifting marketing dollars from one communication channel to another seems like a simple enough decision; the difference is knowing whether the shift worked. ●

Visit the Web site, **www.tektronix.com.** ●

Sources: Anonymous, "BtoB's Best: Martyn Etherington, VP–Worldwide Marketing, Tektronix," *BtoB* 91 (October 24, 2006), pp. 4–15; Kate, Maddox, "CMOs, CFOs Work on ROI, Relationships," *BtoB* 91 (August 14, 2006), pp. 1–2; Michele, Marchetti, "When Is a Lead Not a Lead?" www.salesandmarketing.com (December 1, 2006), accessed July 19, 2007.

## LEARNING OBJECTIVES

Throughout the book, we've discussed how to evaluate specific marketing actions, such as how to evaluate the success of a direct mail compaign. In this chapter, we'll tie those evaluations together into part of an overall marketing evaluation system.

*After reading this chapter, you should be able to*

● Describe the importance and dimensions of information and control systems.

● Select appropriate tools of control for specific situations.

● Calculate tolerance ranges for marketing performance.

● Describe how control processes contribute to other organizational processes such as reengineering and strategic planning.

For learning to occur from experience, there must be some judgment of success and failure. There must be some notion of what worked and what didn't; being able to identify what works and what doesn't is dependent on a system that spots success.

# THE IMPORTANCE OF EVALUATING MARKETING EFFORTS

Not too long ago, a company (one that asked to remain nameless) set a goal for a particular product of selling 100,000 units. It dropped two products that were similar and increased sales for the preferred product from 70,000 units to three times the goal, or 300,000 units. The sales force had their best year ever, making more money per rep than ever before. Yet every unit sold cost an average $2 in losses. How could this happen?

It happened because information concerning performance wasn't gathered and shared on a timely basis. Costs were higher than expected; prices were lower than expected as more buyers took advantage of quantity discounts, and, worse, the information didn't reach decision makers in time.

In this example, getting the right information to the right people was critical. Without that information, money was lost. In many cases, the issue is not quite so dramatic, but it is important nonetheless. Imagine what it is like to take a class with four exams, 10 assignments, and a term project, and the professor never returns any work at all. How would you know what to improve? Or what grade you were likely to get? You wouldn't know whether to drop the class or spend a little more time studying to boost your grade to an A. For most students, such a situation would cause anxiety and confusion. For most marketing executives, operating without any information would be similar, though probably worse because they would lose their jobs if they guessed wrong.

Such is the purpose of information and control systems—these systems provide the feedback needed to adjust marketing programs. Should we advertise more? Should we add a show to the trade show schedule? Should we invest in more online capability? The answers to those questions, and more, lie in the information we are able to collect and analyze.

This is a chapter about evaluation of performance, but it is also as much about the use of information as about the creation of information. An important element of successful learning in learning organizations is that information is shared and then acted on. Successful marketing requires understanding the impact of one's decisions on the organization's profit, which means recognizing costs as well as projecting revenue.

## Customer Equity

In previous chapters, we've discussed customer lifetime value, or the value of a single customer over time. One way to view that lifetime value is as an annuity, or a stream of revenue that, if accurately predicted, has a value today. In other words, that customer could be "sold" and that annuity transferred to another vendor. If a customer is like an annuity, then the customer is an asset.

Further, if a company sums up the value of all its customers' future purchases, discounted back into today's dollars, a new picture of the value of the firm emerges. This value of the firm is called **customer equity.** Telindus, a Belgian telecommunications supplier, calculates customer equity as one measure of performance. If customer equity is trending upward, then the firm should enjoy greater stock prices as that customer equity translates into actual sales.

# CONTROL SYSTEMS

Tektronix, using marketing research, identifies a segment of the market whose needs have not been well met and for whom competition is soft. It designs a product and strategy, launches the product, and then what? Does it turn its back in order to focus on the

**Exhibit 15–1**
Process of Control

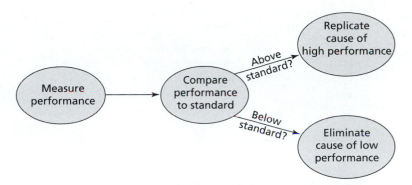

next product? Scan the research data looking for another market opportunity? Of course, someone at Tektronix does.

Someone else, though, is responsible for seeing that the first product is successful. As the strategy is implemented, the product manager must sift through the data from the field in order to learn what works and what doesn't. The **marketing control system** is the system that measures actual performance against planned performance; measures productivity and profit by types of products, customers, or territories; and measures other key marketing variables such as customer satisfaction. A sound marketing control system is not just an income statement, totaling revenue and subtracting costs. A sound marketing control system is balanced and includes—in addition to financial information—**operational measures,** measures of productivity, process (or operations) effectiveness, and other elements that impact customer satisfaction.

The process of control, illustrated in Exhibit 15–1, is measuring performance, comparing performance against a standard, and then examining why performance was either above or below standard. If performance was above standard, management would like to duplicate those circumstances that led to greater performance. If performance was below standard, then whatever barriers prevented standard performance should be identified and eliminated.

Two important elements of a control process are the **sensor,** or measuring tool, and the **standard,** or the goal against which performance is compared.[1] Standards can be absolute, such as a budget. Significant deviation under budget can be just as bad as deviation over budget if it means that opportunities are lost. For example, the marketing manager can decide to bring salary expenses well under budget by reducing everyone's pay, but if all the employees left, there would be trouble. Standards can also be a range of acceptable performance, called a **tolerance** range. For example, if management decides that no action will be taken against salespeople who achieve 95 percent of their quota, nor will significant bonuses be paid until reaching 150 percent, then 95 to 150 percent of quota is the tolerance range.

## Dimensions of Control

The processes of control are universal and can be applied to any level of marketing analysis. The marketing executive has to develop a strategy for the firm's marketing efforts and then analyze results and make the necessary changes; a salesperson has to develop a sales strategy for a territory and analyze results in order to adapt. There are, however, two dimensions of analysis and control that help us categorize and understand control processes. These dimensions are macro versus micro levels of control, and inputs versus outputs. Exhibit 15–2 illustrates the two dimensions of control systems.

**Exhibit 15–2**
Dimensions of
Control

|  | **Micro** | **Macro** |
|---|---|---|
| Input | Regional Sales Office Expense | Total Selling Expenses |
|  | Trade Show Budget | Promotion Budget |
|  | Product X Development Cost | Total R & D Budget |
| Output | Regional Sales Office Revenue | Total Revenue |
|  | Leads from Trade Shows | Corporate Position |
|  | Sales for Product X | Total Division Revenue |

## *Macro versus Micro Control*

The macro versus micro dimension of control is the level of the organization that is being evaluated. When the total organization is undergoing evaluation, the level of control is macro. For some organizations, a macro control system may include divisional control or strategic business unit (SBU) control if those operate as virtually stand-alone units; 3M, for example, operates its 40+ divisions as independent companies. Anything less than that would be micro control, including analysis of a product line, a market segment, or functional area such as sales or marcomm.

### Macro Control

Learning organizations are dynamic, meaning that their strategy is adjusted on the basis of the results as they go. Macro controls enable the chief marketing officer to evaluate the overall strategy as it is being executed. Dashboards, such as that designed by Martyn Etherington, worldwide marketing vice president at Tektronix, provide daily feedback at the macro level for strategy adjustment.

### Micro Control

Micro control involves monitoring the progress of a subset of the overall marketing strategy. Micro control processes can include evaluations of product lines, market segments, or functional areas like a sales office or the Internet marketing group. At this level of control, managers would compare monthly or even weekly performance of specific areas against goals or standards. Tracking salesperson performance against quota is an example of micro control.

From the Field 15–1 presents Bruce Culbert's perspective on metrics. Culbert is CEO of an information technology services company. Notice how his discussion of how metrics are created and used illustrates how control systems flow from the macro to the micro level.

## *Input-Output Analysis*

An income statement is probably the ultimate input-output analysis. The company puts money in (expenses) and hopes to take money out (revenue). What happens in between is the marketing program, as illustrated in Exhibit 15–3. In recent years, however, input–output analyses have gotten more sophisticated as business marketers have recognized that income statements do not measure all of the inputs that go into delivering value, nor does revenue provide adequate output analysis when examining the total marketing health of the organization.

**15–1**

# FROM THE FIELD

## Metrics and Marketing Management

### Metrics

During my 25-year career in sales and marketing in the IT services field I have had the great fortune to work with some of the finest high-performing companies in their industries, but at companies such as IBM, KPMG, BearingPoint, and Salesforce.com, success did not just happen by accident. Success was due to a commitment by the people in the company to execute a set of repeatable but dynamic business principles, practices, and processes which in essence becomes the culture and heart of a sustainable organization.

Now, as CEO of i-Symmetry, an information technology staffing company, we regularly set goals collaboratively with customers, partners, and employees, then measure our progress against those goals, share and discuss that progress, and make adjustments to the people, process, practice, or technology to continue to improve our chances of obtaining and overachieving our goal.

One of my five key business principles is "fail quickly." Since no decisions in business are 100 percent fool proof you want to know as quickly as possible what the incorrect or bad assumptions are so you can focus on getting it right. Create your hypothesis for success and prove or disprove it as quickly as possible. The quicker you do this the sooner you get it right.

So what are the critical success factors in establishing a successful measurement program for a business?

1. Establish effective performance measures and clear accountability for achieving results. If the business can make assumptions about process, personal, or business performance during the planning process then you should take the extra step to specifically define what to measure and how it will be done. A common approach is to map metrics to business process outputs and total cost of ownership, establishing both an outcome and cost for delivering that outcome.

2. Measure benefits through a consistent, disciplined, and structured approach. You don't want to have arguments over, or a misunderstanding of, what the measurements are telling you. When making business assumptions and identifying how progress will be measured, it is important that everyone involved understand what the goals are and how they will be measured.

3. Once the measures have been defined and agreed to, establish clear ownership at organizational and individual levels. Ask yourself these questions. What function or organization in the business is responsible for these results? Who in that function is responsible for these results? It may be that more than one function or one person is responsible as is many times the case. In these situations certain functions and people may share the same or similar measurements. You should establish program and project accountability through a transparent (visible and understood by all) and interlocked (shared) set of metrics.

And finally you should establish a feedback loop in the organization to analyze the measurements, understand what they are telling you about the current and projected future state of your business, and take corrective action if required or accelerate progress as appropriate. There should always be a plan to address issues and take advantage of success.

Bruce Culbert, CEO, i--Symmetry.

### Input Analysis

For a long time, business marketers were most concerned with managing costs as the key input variable. The reasoning for such concern goes something like this: There is a cost associated with every action; thus the best way to manage inputs (to control actions) is to manage costs.

**Exhibit 15–3**
Control of Input and Output Variables in Marketing

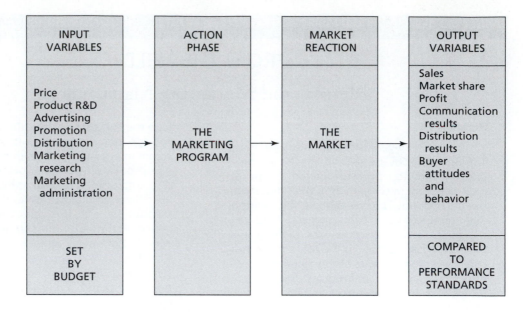

| INPUT VARIABLES | ACTION PHASE | MARKET REACTION | OUTPUT VARIABLES |
|---|---|---|---|
| Price<br>Product R&D<br>Advertising<br>Promotion<br>Distribution<br>Marketing research<br>Marketing administration | THE MARKETING PROGRAM | THE MARKET | Sales<br>Market share<br>Profit<br>Communication results<br>Distribution results<br>Buyer attitudes and behavior |
| SET BY BUDGET | | | COMPARED TO PERFORMANCE STANDARDS |

A value-based approach, though, challenges the fundamental assumption that costs represent the best way to manage inputs. At times, the best way to manage inputs may be to consider the value of the input rather than its cost. For example, **cycle time,** or the time it takes to complete an action such as to develop a product, is rapidly gaining recognition as having a value that cannot be adequately represented by cost. EIS, a company that prints pricing labels for grocery stores, has gained a significant competitive advantage by reducing cycle time. Grocery stores want to put new pricing labels on the shelves as soon as they make the decision to change a price; hence, the company like EIS that can most quickly print and ship these labels to all stores in a particular chain is most likely to get the business as long as costs are reasonable.

Cycle time is a core competency for Federal Express (which we profiled at the start of Chapter 5), as it has to get some packages to their destination by 9:30 the next morning. Mitsubishi gained a significant competitive advantage by reducing the cycle time associated with product development. JIT (just-in-time) delivery is another example of how cycle time is reduced. Cycle time is becoming a significant factor in success, and not just for companies like Federal Express.

Other inputs include price, marketing activities, and the costs associated with those activities. Price is considered an input variable because it is an input into the marketing process and must be managed, as discussed in Chapter 14. Budgets are a key element in the control of marketing activities; pricing plans operate much the same way in controlling pricing. We'll discuss these more later in the chapter when we address using control systems.

One input is satisfied employees. Typically we might think of employee satisfaction as an output, and it may be if we were examining management or human resource systems. But we're interested in marketing systems, and in service, an input into the service process is the person doing the service. At Rockwater, an underwater construction company, they found that satisfied employees do a better job of satisfying customers. They also found that satisfied customers pay their bills faster. There are two elements to recognize here: first, not all inputs are costs in the traditional sense (we've already mentioned cycle time, but here there is a different form of input, the satisfaction of the service employee); and second, one process's output is another process's input. The management system that produces satisfied employees as an output offers those same employees as an input to the customer service system.

## Output Analysis

In the previous few chapters, we've examined performance evaluations for marcomm activities, including performance evaluation for trade shows, the sales force, and other marketing areas. These are forms of output analysis. Output analysis, therefore, includes more than just revenue; for a particular marketing activity, output analysis can include the number of leads gathered, or the number of demonstrations, or the number of displays set up in distributors' locations. For example, Tektronix exhibit managers tally the number of leads generated at each trade show as a measure of the show's success.

The issue is, How effective is the marketing system? Effectiveness means performance, or the outcomes, and the manager seeks to answer the question, "How effective was the marketing system, or plan, at accomplishing desired outcomes?" Thus, important measures of effectiveness are usually those that measure revenue or intermediate steps that can predict revenue. For example, the number of leads generated through a Web site is a predictor of future success if we know how effective the selling process is. Leads would be a desired outcome (and recall from our earlier discussion, such leads would then be an input into the selling system).

Another important output of the marketing program should be customer satisfaction. We will discuss how to measure customer satisfaction when we discuss customer retention strategies in Chapter 16, but it is important to recognize here that customer satisfaction can be viewed as a surrogate for future sales. Although customer satisfaction cannot predict competitive action or leapfrogging technology that can hurt sales, without customer satisfaction, there can be no repeat sales. Hence, customer satisfaction is not only a measure of performance but also a measure of the market health of the organization.

## Efficiency Analysis

Combining input and output figures gives the marketing manager an indication of the efficiency with which those inputs were managed. For example, you may have learned about return on assets managed (ROAM = net income divided by assets) or return on investment (ROI = net income divided by investment) in an accounting class. While you may have thought you could leave ROI or ROAM as you left your accounting class, the reality is that business marketers are now talking about ROMI, or return on marketing investment. Marketing managers have to understand how efficiently they are managing the assets they have control over—in this case, marketing investments.

Efficiency means how well assets were used. Were they wasted, spent on activities that did not generate the appropriate return? For example, two companies each sell $100 million. The first company spent $100,000 on advertising whereas the second spent only $50,000. The second company was twice as efficient, meaning it spent less money to achieve the same result, whereas, on the face of things, the first company wasted $50,000. Thus, to figure a ratio where advertising was converted into sales, the managers would divide their advertising expenditures by their revenue. The first manager had a 1:10 conversion, meaning that $1 of advertising translated into $10 of revenue, whereas the second manager's conversion was 1:20.

Similar marketing combinations are conversion ratios (the input being the number of sales calls and output being the number of sales), return on advertising, and other measures that combine the cost of an input and the associated sales or output. Dividing outputs by inputs results in measures of how efficiently the marketing manager used those inputs to generate the outputs.

**Exhibit 15–4**
Examples of
Measures Used
in the
Balanced
Scorecard

| Financial | Customer |
|---|---|
| Net income | Revenue per customer |
| Profit margin | Account share |
| Return on investment | Customer satisfaction |
| Return on assets managed | Intent to repurchase |
| **Internal Processes** | **Learning and Growth** |
| Employee satisfaction | Completed training programs |
| Data availability | New patents obtained |
| New product development cycle | New products introduced |
| Credit approval cycle | |

ADP Lightspeed, a division of the payroll services company ADP, sells services to powersports dealers. When Scott Robinson, ADP Lightspeed marketing manager, launched a campaign targeting the 6,000 RV dealers across the United States, he tracked results daily, tinkering with the campaign to improve response. "In real time, I could go to my management team and say, 'As of right now, these are the results.' It gave me credibility . . . to show them what worked and what didn't." At the same time, he could see how efficiently his marketing investment was working.[2]

# The Balanced Scorecard

The Balanced Scorecard concept suggests that there are four key areas for input-output analysis. These are financial, customer, internal business processes, and learning and growth (see Exhibit 15–4, which includes some of the measures for each area).[3] Prior to the balanced scorecard, companies tended to focus only on financial returns, such as ROI, ROAM, and net profit. The outcome was a short-term perspective, because any particular financial results were often the outcome of decisions made many years before. For example, hiring policies have a very long-term effect because employees can stick around for a long time. Therefore, the balanced scorecard is an attempt to identify today's outputs that are inputs for tomorrow's outputs. Back to Rockwater—the company found that satisfied employees serve customers better. That means, for the manager of the human resource system, that it is important to hire employees who will fit well with the company culture.

Customer satisfaction is often considered by marketing executives to be an output of the customer service process. That same customer satisfaction, however, is an input into future revenue from that customer, as well as future share of that customer's business. Therefore, it is safe to say that output and efficiency analyses are examinations of what has happened, whereas input and efficiency analysis can help predict future outcomes. Such prediction is necessary to making the right marketing decisions.

# Control and the Nature of Data

Marketing control is the gathering, evaluation, and use of information regarding marketing processes. The first step is to gather information, or to collect data. As you may recall from a marketing research or statistics class, data have several important properties or characteristics. These characteristics are that data vary, and that the variance is likely to remain within a range. Understanding the causes of variance is important in order to know how to secure the desired results.

**Exhibit 15–5**
Variance in Sales
Performance

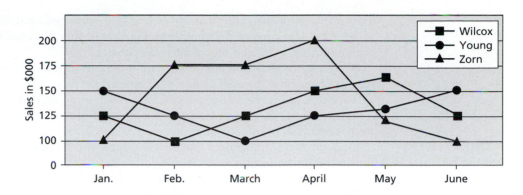

## Data Vary

First, performance data vary. For example, if we are examining the performance of a sales office with 10 salespeople, it is likely that we will find 10 different revenue figures, a different revenue figure for each salesperson. If we examine each salesperson, we will find that revenue will vary for that salesperson over time. In Exhibit 15–5, we have the performance of three salespeople plotted over time. As you can see, Young starts and ends with the best sales performance but is not the best rep for any other month. Zorn has three great months and three so-so months. Thus, sales performance varies both across reps and for any rep over time.

Sales, as with any marketing results, will vary for any combination of reasons. Zorn could have been sick in May and June or spent two weeks in a training seminar. Wilcox may have learned a new method of prospecting that accounts for the three-month rise. Or Wilcox's territory may have had several new businesses start operations. The process of selling is imperfect, and variance will result from month to month. Sales may also vary for no known reason. To expect that sales should always go up is unrealistic because variance can be positive or negative.

## Observations Fall within a Range

A second important characteristic is that the data will fall within a range. As long as the process is held steady, the outcome will vary but within a set of boundaries. If the observation is outside that boundary, then something is different with the system. In a well-understood system, this natural range of performance is the same as the tolerance. For example, a manufacturing system may allow a gap of .5 millicrons between two parts. From 0 to .5 is the tolerance, or allowed range of the gap. In sales, tolerance is usually described in terms of a minimum standard of performance, or quota. (Note, though, that quota can sometimes be set higher than tolerance. See Chapter 13 for quota-setting methods.) Going back to Exhibit 15–5, the observed tolerance would be $100,000 to $200,000, with $100,000 being quota.

Sales above the tolerance range (in this case, greater than $200,000) would certainly be accepted, but management would want to examine the situation closely. Is the territory too large? Does this salesperson use a strategy better than the company's suggested strategy?

At the same time, however, that plant management wants its manufacturing line to operate at capacity, sales management wants each salesperson to sell to the potential (or capacity) of the market. If 10 buying decisions are made in January in Zorn's territory, then capacity would be 10 sales (the equivalent of those 10 decisions). The control process should provide information regarding the salesperson's output relative to potential.

The challenge in marketing control is knowing what potential is, because potential varies. (It is a function of the number and type of buying decisions that could be made that month and is beyond the salesperson's control.)

Marketing control systems are not just interested in sales performance. Marketing managers must also consider a number of internal processes that support sales and marketing efforts and impact customer satisfaction. For example, how quickly the credit department assesses the creditworthiness of a potential customer impacts shipping because the product can't be shipped until the sale is accepted, and the sale can't be accepted until the account's credit has been qualified and approved. Management must control cycle time in the credit department.

AT&T, for example, significantly improved cash flow by redesigning a new sales installation process, reducing the number of steps from 12 to 3. The new system increased the number of invoices paid in the first 30 days from 31 to 71 percent. More importantly, customer readiness to repurchase increased from 53 to 82 percent.[4] Thus, internal systems, like how quickly products are delivered and installed, can impact customer satisfaction and sales performance.

# Four Causes of Variance

A marketing control system can identify variance, but more important than simply identifying variance is understanding the cause of variance so that something can be done about it. There are four causes of variance: tinkering, systematic, external, and random. Systematic and tinkering causes of variance occur because of changes to the process. For example, deciding to use a particular selling strategy over another strategy may represent a change to the selling process. Random and external causes of variance are not due to the process but due to other factors.

## Tinkering Variance

**Tinkering** is making changes within a process in order to make the process more productive, by either reducing defects or increasing volume. The purpose of tinkering is to narrow the range of variance. If the upper boundary of the tolerance range represents the system in perfect working condition, then tinkering should raise the bottom boundary. Referring back to Exhibit 15–5, tinkering may account for the overall rise from March through May. Note, though, that performance fell in June; tinkering does not always work to improve sales performance.

Tinkering might include such activities as reviewing objection-handling skills among the salespeople, changing the media schedule for advertising, changing the graphics in the booth for the next trade show, or adjusting the price. Tinkering is making minor adjustments within the marketing process that are intended to improve performance.

## Systematic Sources of Variance

**Systematic change** is changing systems and creating a new tolerance. If a new selling strategy is used, for example, then a new range of performance should be expected. The new strategy is successful if the new range is higher than the old range. Tinkering is changing within a system; systematic variance is change due to the implementation of a new system.

For example, in Exhibit 15–6, we see the effects of a new product introduction on sales. For the first six months of the year, sales performance stayed within $100,000 to $200,000

**Exhibit 15–6**

An Example of Systematic Variance

Each dot represents a salesperson's performance. With the introduction of a new product, a higher tolerance range is achieved.

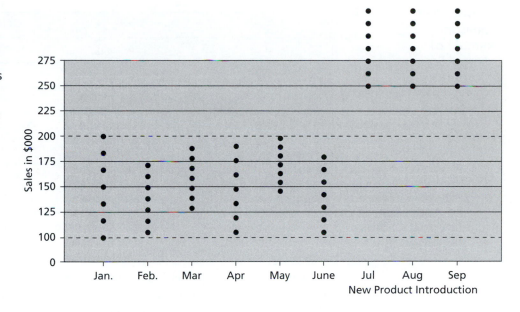

for each of the seven salespeople. With the introduction of the new product, however, sales were immediately no lower than $250,000. As the sales team gained experience and learned more about how to sell the new product, sales continued to climb. This climb will continue until a point at which the system is stable and a new tolerance is established.

## External Causes of Variance

The marketing system operates in an environment that has an impact on the system's effectiveness. For example, there may be seasonality in purchasing habits. There are also economic cycles that must be contended with. Like random variance, marketing managers do not have control over external causes. Marketing managers can react to those external causes (like offering off-season discounts) or seek to influence the external causes (such as furthering political agendas that impact the organization), but only when external causes and their impact are identified. Exhibit 15–7 illustrates the tolerance for a sales office with seasonal sales.

## Random Causes of Variance

**Random variance** is that variance caused by uncontrollable and unidentified causes. We must recognize a certain degree of randomness in every system. The important thing for managers is to be able to recognize random variance. Managers often try to fix random variance with tinkering. Because tinkering can't affect random variance, however, money and energy spent on such tinkering are wasted. Hence, recognizing random variance is important.

For example, suppose a salesperson's performance varies by 15 percent over time; one month she is 5 percent below quota, the next she is 10 percent over quota, and her performance is almost always within that range. After a year, she gets a new manager who doesn't understand the concept of random variance, so every time her performance is below quota, he makes her come straight into the office at 8:00 every morning and return

**Exhibit 15–7**
A Seasonal Example of External Source of Variance
Each dot represents a salesperson's performance. The range of performance across the sales team varies due to seasonality in purchasing.

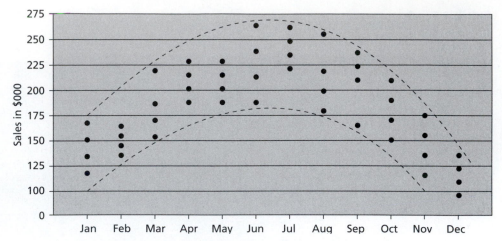

by 5:00 every night. Her territory being 30 minutes away from the office, she was in the habit of going straight from home to her first appointment and home after her last call, enabling her to begin with an appointment at 8:00. Thanks to this new manager's plan, she loses at least one sales call each day, or 20 per month. As a result, her sales fall further, she gets frustrated, and she considers quitting before she will get fired. Tinkering to fix random variance can be fatal.

In the chart showing systematic increase in performance, there is also variance within the first six months of performance. The key for the sales manager is to identify how much of that variance is random and how much is due to salesperson actions, or tinkering. Similarly, marcomm managers have to consider how much of the changes in advertising, direct mail, and trade show exhibit performance are due to random variance, just as pricing managers have to recognize random variance in response to price changes. The potential for tinkering inappropriately can be just as great and just as dangerous in all aspects of marketing as in sales.

Understanding the nature of data is important so that management can recognize controllable and uncontrollable sources of variance. Tinkering and systematic sources of variance are within the manager's control, whereas random and external sources are not. Management can, however, respond to external sources of variance, turning them into competitive advantage. For example, Rockwell has had to contend with the end of the Cold War, which reduced the need for military equipment by the United States. By anticipating the change and planning for it, Rockwell has been able to remain profitable.

# Tools of Control

Having the right tool for any job makes the job much easier. Whether you are working on your car, on a computer, or on the kitchen sink, knowing what needs to be done is not enough. Being able to finish the job requires the right tools.

The same is true in business. Getting the job done right requires both the knowledge of what should be done and the knowledge and tools to complete the job. Controlling marketing programs requires knowing what to do and choosing among an array of tools. There are three types of tools in control systems: standard setting processes, measurement tools, and tools used to search for causes of variance.

**Exhibit 15–8**
Tools of
Control

| Standard-Setting Processes | Pro | Con | Comment |
|---|---|---|---|
| Benchmarking | Can learn and improve | Hard to find someone willing to let you benchmark | Can use industry association measures |
| Quotas and Targets | Easy to establish | Can be difficult to account for variance | Consider sources of variance when setting |
| Budgets and Pricing Plans | Easy to establish | Lack of flexibility can lead to missed opportunities | Create systems for opportunity evaluation |

## Standard Setting Processes

The first type of tool used in any control process is the process for setting a standard of performance, listed in Exhibit 15–8. As mentioned earlier, the process of control begins with setting standards and then observing performance. In marketing, output standards are often goals for performance, such as desired market share, sales quota, delivery time, product development cycle time, and other marketing processes. Budgets are input standards.

### Benchmarking

One type of standard is a **benchmark,** or the performance level of the best organization for that particular task. For example, Conoco was concerned with meeting market needs for certain oil products. The company identified several companies in other industries that respond quickly to market needs and have to change manufacturing facilities to address those needs. One such company was an auto manufacturer that can change a plant over to new product production in less than two weeks. While two weeks may have been a new standard for Conoco, what was also important was understanding the processes that the benchmark company used to accomplish that feat. Did Conoco hit the two-week mark? Not the first time, but throughput did increase 15 percent as a result.

Benchmarking is most appropriate if a company has fallen behind its competitors in a given area, or if there is a process that is having a major impact on an industry. In both instances, the purpose is to learn about the process. In one survey, such benchmarking was found to result in financial gains nearly half the time and quality improvement about 75 percent of the time.[5]

A second point about benchmarking that the example illustrates is that a benchmark can come from any industry. What you are looking for is the best in the world at a particular function; in this case, an office equipment company examined the distribution systems of a mail order clothing merchant.

Benchmarks are just one type of standard; other standards are set by trade associations (such as quality standards) or reflect goals that management desires. Many industry associations are engaged in benchmarking studies to provide baseline comparisons for their industry. For example, European machine manufacturers engaged in a study of costs and processes in order to provide data to their industry. Such averages can then be compared by each company to determine if it is spending too much or too little in any given area.[6] Chances are your school is participating in such a study conducted by the AACSB, an association for business schools. Since 1998, the AACSB has been conducting benchmark studies of student satisfaction, faculty satisfaction, and other

---

### 15–1

## BUSINESS 2 BUSINESS

### Benchmarking Tektronix

Entire books have been written on the process of benchmarking. One problem is getting permission to benchmark a company. Why would Tektronix, for example, want to allow a company to benchmark against it? If you wanted to benchmark against a company like Tektronix, what would you offer in return?

---

important areas so each school's administration can evaluate the effectiveness of various programs.

### Quota and Target Setting

Quotas are minimum acceptable levels of performance, usually associated with sales performance. (See Chapter 13.) As minimum levels of performance, quotas can represent the bottom of the tolerance range in sales performance. Sales quotas are often determined by estimating market potential for a particular product and then estimating the market share or penetration for the product based on historical performance and estimated impact of marketing plans. For example, if Rockwell Engineering held 20 percent of the market for the previous year, all things being equal, the division should expect 20 percent next year. All things are rarely equal, however, and if the company expected a new product launch to significantly increase sales, estimated market share may rise to 24 percent. Applied to a market of $100 million, Rockwell Engineering's total sales quota would be $24 million. Individual salesperson quotas are then a function of the overall quota. One such method would be to divide total sales quota by the number of salespeople to determine individual quotas.

Quotas are also determined for each activity deemed important. (See Chapter 13.) If management wants to increase the amount of business coming from current customers, they may impose a customer call quota. The number of calls to be made on current customers would be determined by setting a customer sales target and then using conversion ratios to determine a call quota.

Performance targets can be set for all marketing activities, such as setting a new product development cycle target of 18 months, or a billing cycle time of three days. Quotas can also be set for the number of credit applications or orders processed by the credit or order entry department. Using past performance as a guide and accounting for future plans, quotas and performance targets can be used as standards for performance.

### Budgets and Pricing Plans

Budgets and pricing plans are tools of control systems that act as limits on marketing activities. For example, the pricing plan in the first example of this chapter did not limit discounts appropriately, and the company ended up losing money on each product it sold. A good pricing plan, as you know from Chapter 14, optimizes sales while also maximizing profit. A sound pricing plan also provides guidance for salespeople when responding to customer requests.

**Exhibit 15–9**
Summary of
Measurement
Tools

| Measurement Tools | Pro | Con | Comment | Sources of Data |
|---|---|---|---|---|
| Marketing Audits | Complete process review | Difficult and time consuming | Most beneficial when done regularly but not frequently | Observation and survey in the field by the auditors |
| Customer Satisfaction Measurement | Can be a predictor of future sales | Challenge to find what or who caused (dis)satisfaction | Used as a measure of performance | Surveys of customers, including decision makers and users |
| Accounting Systems | Enables allocation of fixed costs | Hard to apply to specific customers | Use a variety to understand customer and product profitability | Transaction systems such as accounts receivable, shipping, and manufacturing |

Budgets are like benchmarks and other standards, but in this case, budgets are used to provide limitations and guidance on what can be spent rather than a goal to be achieved. Budgets are determined for personnel (how many people and at what cost), equipment, advertising, trade show activity, and so forth. We've already discussed budgeting procedures for personnel decisions about sales (Chapter 13), advertising and other promotional activity (Chapter 10), and other marketing activities. These procedures for setting marketing budgets are important tools for controlling marketing decisions.

## Measurement Tools

Another set of important tools for controlling marketing decisions are measurement tools. Measurement tools used in marketing include marketing audits and customer satisfaction measures (see Exhibit 15–9). Accounting systems are also important marketing measurement tools, and marketing managers can choose from among several.

### Marketing Audits

Most students who think of audits first think of the IRS. An audit, however, can be any close examination of any part of the business. One particular type of audit that can be a useful control tool is the marketing audit.

A **marketing audit** is a comprehensive and systematic evaluation of the firm's marketing operation and the environment in which it operates. The audit gives marketing management the opportunity to step back and view the big picture, and then reexamine the details in order to make sure that all of the internal processes are contributing to strategic objectives. The audit also enables management to examine the environment to determine if the strategic objectives are most appropriate.

One question that many students have is how a marketing audit differs from the SWOT analysis discussed in Chapter 6. A SWOT analysis is necessarily a macroanalysis, and can contribute that big-picture view to the marketing audit. The marketing audit, however, will examine all of the internal processes that are part of the marketing function. For example, we discussed earlier how marketing control processes would monitor such elements as the cycle time of processing credit applications. The process of evaluating credit applications would be one of those internal processes that an audit would examine.

There are six areas audited as part of the marketing audit:

- *The environment:* customers and competitors, government regulations, and other macrolevel factors: This is similar to the opportunity–threat analysis of a SWOT.
- *Marketing strategy:* goals, strategy; this is similar to the strengths–weaknesses analysis of a SWOT.
- *Marketing orientation:* an examination of the marketing culture; determining the company's attitude toward the customer. Understanding the orientation is important, as it can be the basis for how processes are carried out and the resulting customer satisfaction.
- *Marketing systems:* an evaluation of the systems for marketing analysis, planning, and control; seeks answers to questions such as How does information flow from the market to decision makers? and Who is involved in planning for new products or new markets?
- *Marketing functions:* an examination of the marketing practices, such as product development, sales force management, bidding, invoicing, shipping, promotion, and others, on the basis of financial and customer performance.
- *Marketing productivity:* seeks to answer questions concerning how well each functional area uses resources, such as people, money, and facilities.

A periodic marketing audit is good practice, regardless of the degree of learning orientation. Some students (and some businesspeople) think that if a company has embraced and practices learning, with appropriate information-sharing mechanisms and empowered managers to act on information, then audits are not necessary. The thinking goes that what would be learned in an audit would already be known from the course of daily operations. The reality is, though, that even members of learning organizations need to step back and look at how each of the minute parts contributes to the overall organization's effectiveness. An audit may not be necessary annually, but regular audits do provide management an opportunity to examine how well each part fits into the overall scheme of the organization.

## Customer Satisfaction Measurement

An area of growing importance is the measurement of customer satisfaction. The area of customer satisfaction is so important that we've devoted an entire chapter to the retention of customers in which we discuss customer satisfaction measurement in detail.

At this point, though, remember that just as there are multiple determinants in choosing products, there are also multiple determinants of customer satisfaction and that these are not always the same. Peterbilt Trucks may choose Rockwell axles because of the ease in installing these axles, but poor delivery may cause dissatisfaction. Measuring satisfaction at the macrolevel can tell the company something about the overall marketing orientation of the firm and its performance relative to customer expectations. From a diagnostic perspective, though, management must find out what each of those determinants of satisfaction is and gather information about the company's performance so that they can manage the processes that result in satisfied customers.

Customer satisfaction can be measured by surveys. Some customers create their own satisfaction indices. Rockwell, for example, regularly reviews vendor performance, giving each vendor a grade as well as specific performance feedback. Vendors who are willing to participate in this process learn how to improve their service in ways that they can then translate to other customers, increasing overall business, not just business with

**Exhibit 15–10**
Income
Statement
Using Full Cost

| | |
|---|---:|
| Revenue (after returns) | $1,050 |
| Less cost of goods sold | 400 |
| Less selling expenses | 158 |
| Less administrative expenses | 285 |
| Less research & development | 110 |
| Income before taxes | $    97 |

Rockwell. At the same time, Rockwell asks these vendors to rate Rockwell as a customer. Rockwell learns important lessons on how to work with the vendors to improve their own operations, perhaps cutting Rockwell's cost but certainly increasing the vendors' commitment to the partnership.

## Accounting Systems

Accounting systems measure financial performance: costs and revenue. For a marketing manager, the key is to understand how costs are allocated so that the true profitability of any particular area, product, or market can be determined. The issue is how fixed costs and overhead are allocated. Any accounting system can take the direct cost of supplies and components and add those together to come up with the cost of a product. The challenge is adding into the cost of that product costs for management, office supplies, warehousing, and so forth. There are three approaches to cost allocation: full costing, contribution analysis, and activity-based costing (ABC). Choice of a costing approach is very important to marketing managers; products have been mistakenly eliminated, for example, because the accounting information used by managers didn't allocate costs appropriately.

*Full Costing*   Assume that a sales office sells two products. In the sales office are two sales teams: one responsible for selling product A and another that sells product B. In this example, we can directly allocate the cost of team A to the sales of product A to calculate the profit generated by product A. The challenge is what to do with overhead costs associated with running the sales office. Rent, for example, could be split between the two teams on the basis of space allocated to each team. The sales office would have to keep track of who made how many copies in order to allocate copying charges.

As much as possible, each cost would have to be directly related to one product or the other in order to truly understand the profitability of each product. Otherwise, fixed costs are allocated on the basis of the number of units sold, sales revenue, or other arbitrary amount. Unfortunately, costs are not always that easy to allocate accurately. At some point, a rule has to be established that allocates fixed costs to one product or the other. For example, assume one sales team sold both product A and product B and each represented 50 percent of the office's sales. To determine the profitability of each product, as illustrated in Exhibit 15–10, sales costs would be divided by two and then subtracted from the revenue of each product.

*Contribution Analysis*   Contribution analysis allocates costs based on incremental costs along each step of the marketing process. For example, the costs of a sales office are added to manufacturing and distribution costs in order to determine the profit, or contribution, of that sales office. Fixed costs associated with headquarters management are not added until it is time to calculate the overall profit. Contribution costing is a form of value added, in that costs are added as they occur along the supply chain and profit (or contribution) can be calculated at any given point in the supply chain, as illustrated

**Exhibit 15–11**
Income
Statement:
Contribution
Margins with
Three Sales
Offices

|  | Sales Office A | Sales Office B | Sales Office C | Total |
|---|---|---|---|---|
| Sales | $350 | $320 | $380 | $1,050 |
| Less variable costs | 170 | 160 | 175 | |
| Contribution margin | $180 | $160 | $205 | |
| Fixed costs controllable by sales manager | 53 | 52 | 54 | |
| Sales manager's contribution margin | $127 | $108 | $151 | |
| Fixed costs identified with but not controlled by sales manager | 19 | 19 | 19 | |
| Sales office contribution | $108 | $ 89 | $132 | $328 |
| Common costs | | | | $231 |
| Income before taxes | | | | $97 |

in Exhibit 15–11. Note that net income remains the same after all costs are accounted for, as we are simply allocating costs. The additional information learned is the profit for each sales office, which doesn't affect total profit.

Contribution costing works well in evaluating the overall cost containment practices and revenue generation of the sales office, but it does not allow management to examine issues within the office. For example, if several products are sold and the incremental costs associated with selling each product are not readily identifiable, contribution costing does not provide a mechanism for allocating the costs of running the sales office to each of the various products.

***Activity-Based Cost Accounting***   ABC allocates fixed costs to products or other units (such as a sales office) according to the activity that creates or drives the cost. For example, suppose a sales office is responsible for selling two products and has only one team of salespeople selling both products. Each product represents 50 percent of the office's sales. The important activity in this situation would be the number of sales calls per product. If digital wamometers (DWs) take three sales calls to close and tricometers take two sales calls to close, then the total calls to close two sales (one of each product) are five. The DW is allocated 60 percent of the office's costs because it is more difficult to sell, and the tricometer gets 40 percent. Contribution or full-costing approaches would allocate 50 percent of fixed costs to each product on the basis of sales volume as illustrated earlier. Note the difference in income in Exhibit 15–12. Would management decisions be the same using ABC versus contribution?

As another example, suppose 20 percent of leads generated from advertising are in the Atlanta region. If so, then 20 percent of the national advertising costs would be allocated to the Atlanta sales office. At the same time, however, we would like to allocate revenue to the advertising in order to determine the direct effectiveness of the advertising. In order to judge each method of lead generation fully, we must know both costs and revenue.

One method, if the company does not have the ability to track leads all the way to the sale, is to examine conversion ratios and then estimate revenues. For example, if marcomm could tell us how many hot leads were sent to the field, then we could forecast sales on the basis of the conversion ratio. We should know where a hot lead is in the buying cycle (if you remember from Chapter 10, a hot lead is defined as someone near a decision in the buying cycle), and the sales force should have the data that tell us the

**Exhibit 15–12**
Comparison of Contribution and ABC Methods

| | Digital Wamometer | | | Tricometer |
|---|---|---|---|---|
| Sales | $545 | | | $545 |
| Less variable costs[1] | 320 | | | 335 |
| Contribution margin | $225 | | | $210 |
| | | *Contribution Method* | | |
| Less fixed mfg. costs[2] | 85 | 50 | 50 | 15 |
| Less fixed selling costs[3] | 30 | 25 | 25 | 20 |
| Income using ABC | $110 | | | $185 |
| Income using contribution | | $150 | $135 | |

[1]Includes commission paid to salespeople as well as direct manufacturing and shipping costs.
[2]Total fixed mfg. costs = $100 but allocated based on complexity of setup and other activities in mfg. process in ABC.
[3]Total fixed selling costs (administrative overhead and sales office expenses) = $50, but allocated on the basis of digital wamometer requiring six calls to every four for the tricometer using ABC.

conversion ratio at that point in the buying cycle. If the conversion rate is 50 percent and average order size is $1,000, then for every 100 leads, we should generate $50,000 in revenue. Allocating revenue to the show program enables the manager to estimate the profit (or contribution) of the program, information needed to make decisions concerning future marketing activity investments.

**Which Accounting System Is Better?**   As usual, the answer to the question of which accounting system is better is "It depends." If the objective is to evaluate the overall sales office and treat that office as a profit center, then the contribution approach is appropriate. In that situation, an income statement is created that indicates how well the office manager did in generating revenue and controlling costs in order to contribute to the company's profitability. Contribution costing is also used to make decisions about adding, keeping, or eliminating products and works fine when costs are directly attributable to the entity (e.g., sales office or product) being examined. If there are shared resources that have to be allocated, ABC may be more useful. The final objective, though, is always to create an income statement that accurately reflects the use of resources (costs) in order to generate value (revenue).

One determining factor of which accounting system to use is who is using the information. A sales manager who has to allocate salesperson time between products is probably quite satisfied with contribution margin information. But once that salesperson time is spent, activity-based costing can help the product manager determine which products to keep and which to terminate. Accounting is a service function in the firm; it provides decision makers such as sales managers, product managers, and marcomm managers with the information they need to make marketing decisions.

## Search Tools

Search tools are those tools that management uses to search for variance and causes of variance. Reporting systems and information systems enable management to accumulate data in a way that can be used to search for variance. These tools provide mechanisms for data analysis.

Although these tools can be used to identify variance, they do not always identify the cause for the variance (see Exhibit 15–13). Other tools, such as case analysis and experimentation, are used to examine the data for causes of variance.

**Exhibit 15–13**
Types of Search Tools

| Search Tools | Pro | Con | Comment | Sources of Data |
|---|---|---|---|---|
| Reporting Systems | Method of information sharing across work groups | Can get tradition-bound | Companies are moving to real-time systems like dashboards | Salespeople, trade show managers, other marketing managers, as well as transaction systems |
| Information Systems | Self-serve reporting | Difficult to get data into a format everyone can use | Increasing use of data warehouses lets managers access data directly | Surveys, transaction systems, and third-party sources such as Dun & Bradstreet |
| Case Analysis | Method of organizational learning | Can be hard to apply learning to new situations | Look for underlying principles of success or failure | Interviews of people involved |
| Experimentation | Establishes cause and effect | Hard to control for all potential causes | Used more frequently with CRM systems | Marketing systems that track source of sale |
| Statistical Analysis | Can inform forecasts, as well as explain past success | Can lead to incremental, rather than innovative, thinking | Often combined with experimentation for more powerful decision making | All of the above |

## Reporting Systems

In marketing, as in many areas of business management, information flows in many directions. **Reporting systems** are formal mechanisms for creating and sharing information and generally involve the flow of information either up or down the organization. For example, each week each salesperson tallies the number of sales calls made for each type of account and about each type of product. Also tallied are the number of new prospects, the number and amount of new sales, customer service calls, total sales, and other sales information. This information is given to the sales manager, who tallies it for the sales team. The district manager sums it up for the district, and so forth. For example, Richard Langlotz, branch manager for Konica Minolta, has identified time with customers as a key variable. By tracking the amount of time his salespeople spend with customers, Langlotz can estimate sales for the next four weeks, make decisions regarding training needs, evaluate individual salesperson performance, and handle other marketing decisions.

One form of information system is the heads-up display or dashboard (see From the Field 15–2 for a short history of digital dashboards). Both of these terms are analogous to the dashboard of your car. You watch the speedometer to see how fast you are driving, and you can monitor oil pressure, water temperature, and other factors that relate to engine performance. If there is a problem, a warning light comes on to alert you.

Software companies like SAP and Oracle are designing similar types of monitoring systems for businesses that provide information in real time, meaning as business happens. For example, Royal Bank of Canada tracks its commercial customers' deposits. If a customer makes an unusually large deposit or withdrawal, the customer's account

---

**15–2**

## FROM THE FIELD
### The End of the Paper Chase?

GE has long been a leader in management practice, developing such tools as the GE product portfolio matrix. Credit another innovation to GE: the digital dashboard. Tired of waiting days, even weeks, for critical information, a GE vice chairman hatched the idea for a digital dashboard—an information system that provided real-time online display of critical company stats. Over 120 days and $1 million later, 300 GE managers now have access to essential data on their desktop PCs and even their Blackberry PDAs.

What to track? In marketing, analysts suggest identifying "needles of interest," a term Tom Lacki, senior director for Carlson Marketing Group, uses to describe those critical measures that relate to financial success. For example, the number of sales leads generated from a Web site can be tracked daily; a precipitous fall indicates that the Web site may need revising. The point is, though, to track the right needles of interest, factors that will vary from company to company.

Research suggests that the number of key performance indicators for any given executive be kept relatively small. As the number of measures increases, satisfaction with the measurement system decreases, as does the perceived value.

Of course, GE may have invented it, but other companies are cashing in on the idea. Oracle, SAP, and other software companies have developed products that create digital dashboards for companies, dashboards that can vary from manager to manager or by level in the organization. While these digital dashboards haven't completely eliminated paper reports, the days of chasing information manually in week-old reports may soon be over.

Bruco Clark, Andrews Abela, Tim Ambler, "An Information Processing Model of Marketing Performance," *Journal of Marketing Theory & Practice* 14 (summer 2006), pp. 191–206. Arundhati Parmar, "Barriers to Success," *Marketing News,* March 1, 2004, pp. 20–21; Bob Tedeschi, "End of the Paper Chase," *Business 2.0* (March 2003), p. 64.

---

officer calls to determine if there is a problem or an opportunity. A large deposit, for example, may be an opportunity to cross-sell one of the bank's services such as a money market account. A large withdrawal may be an opportunity to offer a loan. Prior to the installation of heads-up software that identified such transactions, the bank would not find out about them until it was too late.

One challenge with reporting systems is they become tradition-bound. Information is gathered and reported because it was once needed; but when the need no longer exists, sometimes the reporting system continues operating. Then people are engaged in creating wasted reports that no one uses.

Another challenge is collecting good information. Some of the data, for example, may come directly from salespeople, exhibit managers, marketing communication managers, and others who put the data into the system in a way that makes them look good. A similar problem is putting the right data into the system. For example, EDS wanted to track the languages spoken in the company's various call centers, so it surveyed the call center managers (EDS operates over 500 call centers for various clients). Some of the languages listed were Cobol, SQL, and other computer languages, when EDS wanted to know if anyone spoke French, German, Hindi, and so forth!

Reporting systems, when created and maintained properly, serve several functions: They provide information used in forecasting, performance evaluation, and problem identification. At the macrolevel, reporting systems enable management to spot general trends, potential threats, and opportunities whereas at the microlevel, reporting systems enable managers to identify and implement successful tactics and strategies or identify problem causes and eliminate them. Reporting systems are important for learning to occur because these are one set of mechanisms by which information is carried that enables such learning.

## Information Systems

A reporting system represents the creation of information by gathering data, assembling them in a meaningful way, and then sharing them. An **information system** is the mechanism for storing information, providing access to the information, and manipulating that information. Part of the access–manipulation function is the ability to aggregate data from various sources and combine them in meaningful ways. For example, suppose Rockwell decided to enter the forklift market. Would it be a profitable market? Forecasts would have to be generated concerning expected revenues and expected costs. Revenue information would have to come from external sources and would be a function of the number of warehouses in a geographic area, the number of forklifts used, the frequency of purchase, and so on. Costs, on the other hand, would have to be determined from a number of internal sources, such as procurement, manufacturing, and sales. An information system would enable the manager to pull this information together and create income statements representing net income under various market conditions.

As another example, we've discussed the use of decile analysis in Chapter 11 and other chapters. In the industrial paper–plastics industry, profitability is a function of account share, or the percentage of the customer's purchases that we sell. So if Johnson Packaging buys 30 percent of its paper from Mead, Mead has a 30 percent share of Johnson Packaging's business. By mining customer databases, management can identify customer share break-even points (what customer share do we need to break even?), identify profitable and unprofitable accounts, and then develop specific account strategies to turn unprofitable accounts into profitable ones. This type of analysis requires an information system that stores information in the form needed and then allows access to the appropriate manager, usually via data warehousing and data mining.

Let's take a global account example from Rockwell International. The minimum required annual revenue potential is $1 million, so we'll start with sales equal to that. (The average should be higher, as most global accounts will have greater potential.) Suppose that the salesperson's compensation is $100,000 per year, with a travel-and-entertainment budget of an additional $60,000. If the contribution margin is less than 16 percent (or $160,000), then Rockwell will lose money even when selling 100 percent of potential.

The example sounds easy and seems obvious. Yet that analysis requires an income statement for each account, plus an estimate of customer share. A financial statement is the responsibility of the accounting department; estimates of share come from the sales force. We have two very different functions in the organization that probably collects and stores information to meet their own needs. Accounting may not have the ability, for example, to create independent financial statements for each account, especially in situations where we may want to know profitability for smaller accounts. Creating a reporting system that feeds into an information system capable of providing this type of analysis is challenging.

One mechanism being established to improve information systems is the data warehouse. The data warehouse takes data from various sources and then puts it into one database. The goal is to make information more accessible to decision makers so that they can format it and combine it in a way that they need it. For example, a data warehouse may enable Rockwell decision makers to create that income statement by customer. In that instance, the data have to have information from transaction systems such as order entry and accounts receivable, as well as operational systems such as shipping and manufacturing. Other forms of data in the data warehouse may include financial data on customers from sources like Dun & Bradstreet or Standard & Poor. Companies can buy that information, put it into the data warehouse, and use it to model credit capability of customers, for example. The point is that with all of the data in one location, managers can access what they need and combine it in new ways to make decisions more effectively.

## Case Analysis

Probably every marketing major will conduct case analyses before graduation. Certainly, students using this book will engage in some case analysis. The question for consideration now is, when is case analysis used in business?

Case analysis is used as a method of explaining success or failure after the fact. When a new product is launched and is either successful beyond expectations or fails miserably, a case analysis should be conducted to examine potential causes. The hope is that successes can be replicated and failures avoided. Case analyses are also used by exhibit managers, advertising managers, and other marketing managers to understand performance. What these examples illustrate is that case analysis methods that you use to learn from cases in this book are appropriate for conducting an examination of marketing projects.

Case analysis can also be used as a method of stepping back and examining an ongoing marketing system. Sound case analysis involves the gathering of relevant facts, an examination of assumptions underlying decisions, identification of causes and possible solutions for problems, and making recommendations, just as a student does when writing up a case from this text. Such case analyses are used by learning organizations to further learning by having managers from other areas conduct case analyses on ongoing operations.

## Experimentation

Experimentation is one method used to identify causes of variance. An experiment is defined as research to measure causality by changing one or more variables in order to see the effects on another variable. Some experts consider tinkering, where the manager changes things such as prices until the desired results occur, as a form of experimentation. Experimentation, however, is properly used to isolate sources of variance.

Experimentation differs from tinkering in two important ways. First, the intention of experimentation is to determine the cause of an outcome and then affect the outcome by manipulating the cause. Of course, the ultimate desire of any manager is to manipulate causes in order to influence the outcome, but the initial intention of experimentation is to find the cause. The only goal when tinkering is to improve performance and the manager does not care how or why it works.

The second difference is that other causes are controlled for. In order to isolate a cause, other potential causes must be identified and ruled out or controlled for (meaning that we can identify how much variance is due to each cause, so that we can see just how much variance is due to the potential cause being examined). Tinkering does not contain any control for other possible causes, which can lead to imperfect understanding of cause and effect. Without controlling for competitive action, for example, a manager may think that a price reduction will always result in a gain in

**Exhibit 15–14**
Current Reality
Tree

*source: Adapted from
J. F. Tanner and E.
Honeycutt, "Re-
Engineering the Sales
Force Using the
Theory of Constraints,"
Industrial Marketing
Management 25
(1996), pp. 1–9.*

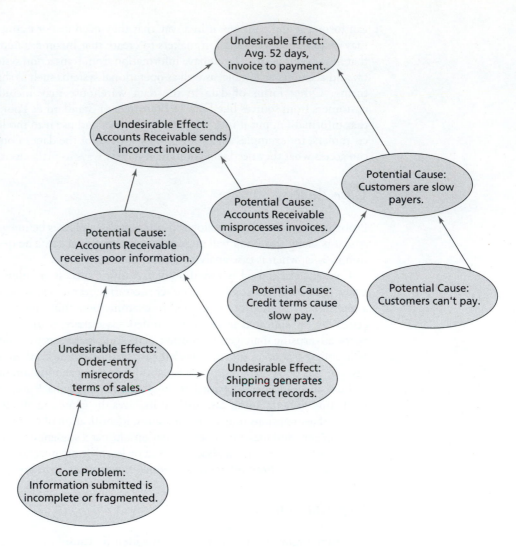

sales if a gain in sales is observed the first time the manager lowers prices. If the manager lowers prices again and competition does the same, the result is likely to be no change in sales, but a lower profit. Experimentation should control for the impact of competitive action.

Firms using experimentation often create a reality tree, an example of which can be found in Exhibit 15–14. A reality tree begins with an outcome, usually an undesired effect. (Although experimentation can be used to determine causes of positive variance, more often it is used to determine sources of negative variance.) All possible causes are hypothesized and other effects of each cause are also listed. For example, if low sales are hypothesized to be due to either low quality or poor sales effort, possible other outcomes of each potential cause would be listed. Low quality would also result in more complaints about product performance whereas poor sales effort would show up in conversion ratios and other sales factors. The list of possible causes can be narrowed down to one or a few by examining other outcomes of those causes. Then an experiment can be designed to isolate the impact of each cause. Exhibit 15–14 illustrates the reality tree that Moore-Wallace created concerning an invoicing problem.

### Statistical Analysis

As mentioned earlier in this chapter, data vary. Management uses a tolerance range when evaluating variance to determine if it is due to tinkering, random, systematic, or external sources of variance. Statistical analysis is being used at a greater rate in order to understand variance.

For example, a quota may be set that determines the bottom of the tolerance range. (Quota is usually set without thought given to tolerance range, but quota is the minimum accepted performance or, by definition, the bottom of the tolerance range. See Chapter 13 for more details on quota setting.) At the same time, however, management must identify at what point above quota is a salesperson's performance high enough to represent a systematic improvement in performance. Similarly, a marcomm manager may use statistical process control methods to examine advertising and trade show performance.

Variance is calculated by first calculating an average. If there were 10 salespeople who sold a total of $20 million, then the average would be $2 million. Then subtract the average from each individual observation and square the result. So if one salesperson sold $2.5 million and another sold $1.5 million, the squared difference in both cases would be .25 (i.e., $2.5 - 2 = .5; .5 \times .5 = .25; 1.5 - 2 = -.5; -.5 \times [-.5] = .25$). Then calculate the average squared difference. (Add all of the squared differences and divide by the number of observations, in this case salespeople.) The average squared difference is called the variance but is not the statistic we want to use. Take the square root of the average squared difference and you have the standard deviation, which is the statistic that is used to examine variance in performance.

Any performance greater than two standard deviations above or below the mean, or average, performance would be considered significantly different; causes of that performance should be explored. Thus, the usual performance range is two standard deviations in either direction from the mean. Anything more than that represents systems-level variance. If we are talking about salesperson performance, then anyone below the mean by more than two standard deviations may need significant training or the opportunity to look for another line of work, for example. On the other hand, check the salesperson more than two standard deviations above the mean and see if there is anything that can be copied by others.

### Predictive Modeling

Experimentation and statistical analysis go together, and in many instances, companies are using the two sets of techniques to determine what to do next. For example, LexisNexis uses direct mail to identify leads. Using a predictive modeling process involving SAS software, the marketing team pinpoints their mail to people more likely to respond. The results of one mailing are then input to help predict who will be likely to respond to the next one. Savings were over $1 million in the first year; plans are now to take the predictive modeling and apply it to other areas such as field sales and trade shows.[7]

# USING CONTROL SYSTEMS

Control systems allow for the control of daily activities and investment decisions. Control systems are an integral part of the business marketing manager's existence, but control systems also have roles in special situations.

---

**15–2**

## BUSINESS 2 BUSINESS

### Partnering within Rockwell

In Chapter 7, we discussed the importance of building internal partnerships. Rockwell International, with so many divisions spread out over the world, has as tough a challenge as any organization in creating internal partnerships. Think for a moment about just the need for partnerships within marketing. When Rockwell exhibits at a defense show, who is in charge: the division that sells planes, the division that sells military communications, the radar division, or someone else? And when advertising is created, how can Rockwell develop advertising across all of the various divisions that still has a Rockwell look? What processes have to be engineered to make sure that these internal partnerships develop?

---

For example, Tektronix manufactures and markets test and measurement equipment. Martyn Etherington, worldwide marketing vice president, uses the dashboard approach to track Tektronix's marketing performance. In addition, the rest of the marketing and sales management team track the control variables under their responsibility. The purpose is to determine what strategies are working among their wide variety of markets and offerings. Control systems are also important contributors to organizational learning and reengineering.

## Strategic Planning

Control at the macrolevel is an important element in the strategic planning process. A firm's control processes, as discussed earlier, should contribute information concerning the firm's performance in various areas in order to assist in making strategic decisions. Control tools, such as the marketing audit, can also contribute information to aid in the identification of opportunities and threats in the environment.

Companies tend to move into and out of markets as they perceive opportunities to either grow or shrink. Those companies that learn faster than others are quicker in their recognition of opportunities and threats. Since its founding in 1946, Tektronix has acquired and divested a number of companies, including acquiring Minacom in late 2006. These strategic decisions were made incorporating information from marketing audits, performance evaluations, financial analyses, customer satisfaction studies, and marketing research studies tracking expenditures and opportunities in specific markets.

## Reengineering and Process Design

In order to increase output, one of two things must occur. Either greater inputs must be placed into the process or the process must be made more efficient. For example, the number of salespeople could be considered an input into the selling process. In order to sell more, more salespeople could be hired or each salesperson could be asked to sell more. Just asking them to sell more, though, won't see that it happens. Neither will paying more per sale lead to the quantum levels of productivity improvement that firms seek. In many cases, the selling process itself will have to be improved in order to achieve greater sales. **Reengineering**—the designing of work processes in order to achieve objectives—reflects the fact that most processes have evolved over time, serving objectives that may no longer be considered relevant. Reengineering the sales process, in this example, is a viable alternative to simply hiring more salespeople.

## Summary

Marketing control systems are important elements in organizational learning. The control process consists of measuring performance, comparing performance against a standard, and then examining performance to determine causes of variance, or deviation from the standard. Learning occurs when the manager recognizes the cause of variance and then eliminates negative causes or repeats positive causes.

Control occurs at both the macro, or system, level and the micro, or subsystem, level. Control processes also exist for inputs and outputs. Combining input and output analysis is useful for examining efficiency.

The data used to evaluate performance vary from one observation to the next due to changes in the system, tinkering with the system, external causes, or random variance. The tolerance range is the amount that the measurements can vary without cause for alarm.

Tools for controlling marketing performance include the standards used to compare with performance. Types of standards include budgets and quotas, benchmarks, and pricing plans. Measurement tools include marketing audits, customer satisfaction measurement, and different types of accounting systems, such as cost accounting and activity-based costing. Causes of variance can be determined through experimentation, reporting and information systems, case analysis, and statistical analysis.

Control systems are used to support strategic planning, reengineering, and organizational learning. With proper control systems, organizations can learn to repeat successful performance and avoid the causes of poor performance.

## Key Terms

benchmark

customer equity

cycle time

information system

marketing audit

marketing control system

operational measure

random variance

reengineering

reporting system

sensor

standard

systematic change

tinkering

tolerance

## Discussion Questions

1. Each Wednesday, Jon Archer holds a meeting with his salespeople. Those who aren't reaching quota get yelled at; those who are get cheers. "We set our quotas a little high because it gives each person something to shoot for. Then, with encouragement or a kick in the pants, we motivate them to achieve it." Is Jon's plan a good one? Why or why not? Utilize the sources of variance information in your answer.

2. Classify the following sources of variance:
   a. An advertising manager observes that three new publications have been introduced in one industry, fragmenting readership of the magazines that have carried the company's advertising.
   b. A company trains every salesperson on partnering skills, changing the company's selling strategy from needs satisfaction to partnering.

    **c.** An exhibit manager observes downsizing in corporate purchasing departments, fewer visitors to the booth, and an increase in time spent by each visitor in the booth.

    **d.** A Webmaster observes more hits in the spring than in the fall.

    **e.** A call center manager tells a new rep to use the customer's name more often.

**3.** When is cycle time an important consideration? Explain the value created by a reduction in cycle time in the following instances:

    **a.** The sales cycle

    **b.** The product development process

    **c.** The process of creating and placing advertising

    **d.** The credit approval process

**4.** Is customer satisfaction measurement microanalysis or macroanalysis? Justify your choice.

**5.** Research shows that managers who evaluate their own company's performance tend to inflate their company's abilities. What methods of information gathering discussed in the chapter are more likely to allow for this tendency? How would you control for that tendency?

**6.** The Balanced Scorecard is said to have both current measures of financial performance as well as leading indicators of future financial performance. What are the leading indicators, and why are they leading indicators?

**7.** Can the contribution method be combined with the ABC method? If so, how? If not, why not?

**8.** Three different industries buy the same motor from Anderson Electric, using the motors for different applications. The same salespeople sell to all three industries, but because the applications are different, different advertising campaigns have to be created. The same booth is used for trade shows in each industry, with different graphics that illustrate the different applications. Advertising is designed to support both field sales and trade show efforts. The manager of marketing for Anderson's line of motors wants to evaluate the performance of the marketing program. What information is needed? Where would you go to find it? What analyses would you conduct with the information?

**9.** If customer equity is greater than market cap (the price per share of stock multiplied by the number of shares), should you invest in the company? Why or why not?

**10.** Will the utilization of a dashboard system lead to greater short-term emphasis, at the expense of long-term company health? In other words, will it cause managers to make decisions that might "move the needle" in the short run but damage the long-term viability of the firm? If so, what are the ethical implications? If not, what has to be in place to prevent such damage?

# Cases

## Case 15.1    Megalith Tool Company

Chelsea Swanson slammed the door to her office and reflected on the meeting with the new division president that had just concluded. "Either prove to me that your program is working or face the fact that you'll need another job," was how the president ended the conversation.

    Chelsea thought angrily, Prove it! I've never had to prove my performance before!

As exhibit manager for Megalith Tool Company, Chelsea is responsible for managing the trade show program that includes five national shows and 24 regional events. The company manufactures tools and controls, selling in three different industries. Chelsea's first thought, after she calmed down a little, was the budget for the program, which we see in Exhibit 1. Perhaps the president would be satisfied if I just cut the budget, she thought.

But she did ask for performance, Chelsea remembered. She pulled out a series of reports that she creates after each show and began compiling performance data. Selected results for show performance are in Exhibit 2. Additional sales and marketing data can be found in Exhibit 3.

Analyze the results. Create a tolerance range that she can use to predict future performance given current investment and strategy. Is the program profitable?

**Exhibit 1**
Exhibit Budget Data

| Salary | $42,000 |
|---|---|
| Benefits | 13,000 |
| Travel | 25,000 |
| Booth shipment/storage | 95,000 |
| Booth refurbishing/building | 200,000 |
| Direct mail pre- and postshow | 100,000 |
| Booth giveaways | 30,000 |
| Total | $505,000 |

## Case 15.2   TNT Manufacturing

TNT Manufacturing makes chemicals for contract manufacturers. Founded by two childhood friends, John Turner and Austin Taylor, the company sells three product lines: maintenance chemicals such as lubricants and cleansers; caustics, or chemicals that are used in etching processes; and plating chemicals, such as brass and chrome. Sold by the railroad tank car or by the 50-gallon drum, these chemicals are sold by three field and seven inside salespeople to distributors all across the eastern seaboard. The distributors then sell to contract manufacturers, job shops, and others.

After a decade of slow but steady growth, the company suddenly began to grow quickly. But something was wrong—sales increased by some 24 percent in the previous year but as Turner and Taylor looked at the data, they realized that the company had actually turned a profit of only a few hundred dollars, and that was before depreciation.

"Some of this has to reflect our investment in new equipment to handle the higher quantities," said Turner. "We need to ask our accountant about that."

"We need to hire a CFO," argued Taylor. "We can't wait until the end of the year to find out we're in the hole like this." Turner agreed, so they began to advertise for a CFO. Cathy Coker came recommended by their CPA, and turned out to be the sister of another high school classmate. With her experience in a larger manufacturing firm, they felt she had a lot to offer TNT.

At the end of her first week, Coker found Turner and Taylor in her office, where they both wiped sweat from their brows and gratefully took a seat. "So, what do you think?" queried Taylor. "You've had a week to watch the company—what's the first thing we need to do?"

She stared at him blankly, then shook her head. "First thing? Good grief, there are so many things that need to be done. This company's in horrible shape!" she exclaimed.

**Exhibit 2**
Hot Leads
from Trade
Shows

| | Last Year | Current Year |
|---|---|---|
| **National Shows** | | |
| NTC | 1,300 | 1,725 |
| ICC/Pro-Form | 1,870 | 1,480 |
| ToolCon | 1,525 | 1,775 |
| Con-Squared | 1,760 | 1,640 |
| Global Tool Expo | 1,820 | 1,890 |
| **Regional Shows** | | |
| Northwest region | 420 | 540 |
| | 380 | 460 |
| | 620 | 480 |
| | 320 | 330 |
| | 455 | 610 |
| Central region | 390 | 520 |
| | 545 | 415 |
| | 610 | 530 |
| | 480 | 760 |
| | 675 | 480 |
| | 370 | 520 |
| Southern region | 490 | 540 |
| | 510 | 580 |
| | 485 | 525 |
| | 395 | 490 |
| Southwest region | 495 | 475 |
| | 395 | 520 |
| | 510 | 425 |
| | 430 | 540 |
| Northeast region | 670 | 580 |
| | 630 | 655 |
| | 540 | 510 |
| | 470 | 545 |
| | 535 | 690 |

"Like what?" barked Turner. Realizing he might have overreacted, he said more calmly, "Look, we're doing pretty well. Revenue is up a lot; we just need help getting a handle on expenses."

"Oh, I know," replied Coker, hastily. "But guys, you don't have an accounting system any more sophisticated than a checkbook! We can't just cut *any* costs. We need to know what costs to cut. For example, you have seven inside salespeople who also handle customer service. Do you really need all of them?"

"Of course we do," replied Turner.

"Probably you do. But what I'm saying is it could be real easy to make cuts that look good now, but make it difficult to continue to grow. And there are other issues, too. For

**Exhibit 3**
Additional Marketing and Sales Information

| Regional Sales Office | Sales | |
| --- | --- | --- |
| | **Last Year** | **Current Year** |
| Northwest | $10.50 million | $10.75 million |
| Central | 12.20 | 13.45 |
| Southern | 9.25 | 10.70 |
| Southwest | 9.35 | 11.65 |
| Northeast | 10.60 | 12.10 |
| Average order size = $10,000 | | |
| Conversion ratio of hot leads = 10% | | |
| Contribution margins for each regional sales office | | |
| Northwest region | 20% | |
| Central | 22 | |
| Southern | 24 | |
| Southwest | 18 | |
| Northeast | 21 | |

example, you offer a 10 percent discount when someone buys a full tank car. But do you make any money on that sale?"

Turner shook his head yes. "Our gross margin is 30 percent, so a 10 percent discount still leaves us a positive gross."

"But you pay a 10 percent commission, and you haven't figured in fixed costs either. Not only that, but average number of days to get paid has increased from 22 to 37, and that is costing you money, too."

1.  Is all growth good growth? Of course not. But Turner and Taylor don't really have a system to know which is good and which is not. Construct a set of questions to ask Turner and Taylor to help them identify measures to select good growth opportunities. Would these questions and measures change if TNT sold directly to users, rather than through distributors? Why or why not?

2.  In the first column of a table, list a set of measures that Turner and Taylor should consider in order to create a Balanced Scorecard. Then in the second column, identify the source of information for each measure. Be sure to group measures by area of the Scorecard.

3.  If you were tasked to build a dashboard for Turner and Taylor, what are the five "needles of interest" or critical measures that they should watch every day?

4.  What is the relationship between the Balanced Scorecard and the dashboard you created?

# Additional Readings

Anderson, Eugene W., Claes Fornell, and Sanal K. Mazvancheryl. "Customer Satisfaction and Shareholder Value." *Journal of Marketing* 68 (October 2004), pp. 172–85.

Bolton, Ruth, Katherine N. Lemon, and Peter C. Verhoef. "The Theoretical Underpinnings of Customer Asset Management: A Framework and Propositions for Future Research." *Journal of the Academy of Marketing Science* 32 (2004), pp. 271–92.

Cooil, Bruce, Timothy L. Keiningham, Lerzan Aksoy, and Michael Hus. "A Longitudinal Analysis of Customer Satisfaction and Share of Wallet: Investigating the Moderating Effect of Customer Characteristics." *Journal of Marketing* 71 (January 2007), pp. 67–83.

Dickinson, Victoria, and John C. Lere. "Problems Evaluating Sales Representative Performance? Try Activity Based Costing." *Industrial Marketing Management* 4 (May 2003), pp. 301–8.

Du, Rex Yuxing, Wagner A. Kamakura, and Carl F. Mela. "Size and Share of Customer Wallet." *Journal of Marketing* 71 (April 2007), pp. 94–113.

Fang, Eric, Kenneth R. Evans, and Timothy D. Landry. "Control Systems' Effect on Attributional Processes and Sales Outcomes: A Cybernetic Information-Processing Perspective." *Journal of the Academy of Marketing Science* 33 (2005), pp. 553–74.

Haenlein, Michael, Andreas M. Kaplan, and Deter Schoder. "Valuing the Real Option of Abandoning Unprofitable Customers When Calculating Customer Lifetime Value." *Journal of Marketing* 70 (2006), pp. 5–20.

Lam, Shun Yin, Venkatesh Shankar, M. Krishna Erramilli, and Bysan Murthey. "Customer Value, Satisfaction, Loyalty, and Switching Costs: An Illustration from a Business-to-Business Service Context." *Journal of the Academy of Marketing Science* 32 (2004), pp. 293–313.

Lehman, Donald R. "Metrics for Making Marketing Matter." *Journal of Marketing* 68 (October 2004), pp. 73–77.

Lune, Nicholas H., and Charlotte H. Mason. "Visual Representation: Implications for Decision Making." *Journal of Marketing* 71 (January 2007), pp. 160–77.

Narayanan, Sridhar, Ramarao Desiraju, and Pradeep K. Chintagunta. "Return on Investment Implications Pharmaceutical Promotional Expenditures: The Role of Marketing-Mix Interactions." *Journal of Marketing* 68 (October 2004), pp. 90–105.

O'Sullivan, Don, and Andrew V. Abela. "Marketing Performance Measurement Ability and Firm Performance." *Journal of Marketing* 71 (April 2007), pp. 79–93.

Richardson, Robert J. "Marketing Resource Allocation Model." *Journal of Business and Economic Studies* 10 (Spring 2004), pp. 43–53.

Rust, Ronald T., Tim Ambler, Gregory S. Carpenter, V. Kumar, and Rajendra K. Srivastava. "Measuring Marketing Productivity: Current Knowledge, and Future Directions." *Journal of Marketing* 68 (2004), pp. 76–89.

Ryals, Lynette J., and Simon Knox. "Measuring Risk-Adjusted Customer Lifetime Value and Its Impact on Relationship Marketing Strategies and Shareholder Value." *European Journal of Marketing* 39 (2005), pp. 456–74.

Smith, J. Brock, and Mark Colgate. "Customer Value Creation: A Practical Framework." *Journal of Marketing Theory and Practice* 15 (Winter 2007), pp. 7–23.

# *Chapter 16*

## Customer Retention and Maximization

**PLUMTREE'S REAL PLUM**

It began with an unsolicited e-mail request for trial software. Now it's a partnership with remarkable qualities: Silicon Valley start-up Plumtree and its Fortune 25 new customer, Procter & Gamble.●

Plumtree has developed portal technology that supports business process management in a variety of ways. Akin to a typical consumer portal, Plumtree Corporate Portal provides links to Web pages, company documents and messages, sales and production reports, and e-commerce services where you would otherwise see a boxscore, stock report, or travel tip. In one simple Web environment, management can obtain a complete view of the business, drawing on resources from a wide range of operations and applications.●

The Procter & Gamble company markets over 300 brands and employs over 100,000 people worldwide. P&G has deployed the Plumtree Corporate Portal to give employees a single Web destination for the information, tools, and services they need to do their jobs. Its initial efforts to bring this kind of order to the enterprise used SAP to help the company define its operations, from sourcing ingredients to scheduling deliveries. But SAP was difficult for nontechnical employees to use, and it was never designed to be easily integrated into a company Web system. P&G contacted Plumtree looking for easy-to-use software that extracts data from the intimidating corporate systems, such as inventory management, and presents them in a browser format. Plumtree got the nod after days of meetings, presentations, and demonstrations that addressed P&G's 68-page requirements roster. After another two months of concept testing, over a salmon dinner in San Francisco, a deal was sketched on a napkin. ●

The Plumtree-powered portal aggregates content for more than one million Web pages and thousands of Lotus Notes databases. Applications such as SAP R/3 enterprise resource planning system, Oracle data warehousing and business intelligence applications, and E.piphany E4 customer relationship management system are integrated into the portal. Employee content and services correspond to their security profiles and roles in the company. ●

In this blossoming relationship worth approximately $5 million, P&G has since invested $2 million in Plumtree for a 2 percent stake, and its engineering personnel have learned to run faster. The mutual spirit of striving and teamwork was built over common workspace for Plumtree and Procter staff, plus shared time at brew pubs and chili parlors. Since implementation, P&G estimates that Plumtree's portal provides $2 million in annual cost savings at just one paper plant. Furthermore, P&G's credibility and experience have helped Plumtree land and manage other accounts. For example, Ford Motor Company has come aboard at twice the scale of Procter, and P&G executives moderated a dispute attributed to communication snags between Plumtree and Motorola. Plumtree was acquired by BEA in 2005.[1] ●

## LEARNING OBJECTIVES

In a number of ways, this chapter is a companion to Chapter 5's discussion of opportunity. That chapter began with attention to current customers as a basis for growth, new product ideas, and accesses to other markets. We think we've established the importance of keeping good customers in subsequent chapters on strategy, product development, communications, channels, and more. As one of our final lessons in business marketing, of course, we echo some of those key concepts. In a systematic and vivid fashion, Chapter 16 addresses the managerial challenge of retaining—that is, keeping—good customers. We can think of no more important topic for you to take away from the class.

We need to evaluate the makings of a good customer and sharpen attention to what it takes to satisfy customers. The financial implications of customer retention are detailed and complemented by emerging measures for tracking customer satisfaction. Imperatives for marketing strategy and action will be discussed.

*After reading this chapter, you should be able to*

- Classify different customer relationship as always-a-share or lost-for-good.
- Identify the structural characteristics of the transaction environment that make for the above classification.
- Graph the profit implications over a range of customer retention probabilities.
- Identify the points of emphasis for retention efforts—strong or marginal customers.
- Describe some of the key avenues for bonding exchange parties in a relationship.
- Apply a basic satisfaction measurement system in the management of relationships.
- Discuss three avenues for strengthening good relationships.

# CONQUEST AND AFTERMARKETING

Marketing strategy and action frequently pivot on military metaphors and jargon. Managers talk about battlefields, penetration, flanking, reinforced positions, combative advertising, retaliation, and more. Perhaps such activities reflect the warrior archetype that resides in the heart of many striving professionals.

But what happens after the victory? In the history of business and the history of nations, conquest is an enigma. Sometimes the machinery of conquest is reapplied in new territories. Alexander the Great moved his armies ever eastward. Hitler's machine ground up nations on every compass point. Indeed, the past two centuries are replete with now scorned expansion-minded dictators. Do we stretch the metaphor to note that many of 1970's Fortune 500 firms are no longer on the roster?

Frankly, as Wang found out in the field of office automation, conquest is a much smaller piece of marketing than the jargon and jingles convey. In military parlance, if one cannot hold and secure conquered territory, the conquest is for naught. Indeed, much as thousands of Napoleon's troops retreated from the Russian winter without coats or shoes, Wang lost account after account as its service deteriorated.

Good news! The lost art of customer retention has been rediscovered in business. In almost every sector of commerce we see a renewed interest in recognizing and keeping best customers and in improving the value of average and below-average accounts. Interestingly, these efforts are guided largely by another metaphor, marriage, and motivated by new market measures and financial tools.

In contrast to the military symbols, many observers see marketing in terms of courtship, betrothal, and permanent union. For example, Theodore Levitt notes that

*the sale merely consummates the courtship. Then the marriage begins. How well the marriage is depends on how well the relationship is managed by the seller.*[2]

Recall the relationship development model presented in Chapter 2. This model proposed a gradual deepening of dependence between buyer and seller, propelled by positive reinforcements of trusting behaviors.

In this chapter we want to build on the background of Chapters 2 and 5 to examine the financial impact of lasting customers. In order to do this, let's revisit and examine more closely the types of customer relationships we are apt to find in business markets.

# THE NATURE OF A CUSTOMER

The behaviors of buyers and sellers interact with fundamental characteristics of the exchange environment to define the nature of their relationship. This section will use some basic elements of each sphere to describe a continuum of trading relations.

## Always-a-Share Relationships

Almost every organization needs printing services. It might be menus, training manuals, product literature, catalogs, company newsletters, or newspaper inserts. Given the technical specifications of a printing job, usually a buyer can choose from several capable printers. Price and credible delivery date are prime selection criteria. The buyer can award a printer in the set of candidates almost any share of its printing business.

Furthermore, this share of business can fluctuate from year to year, largely depending on the competitive environment and the printer's aggressiveness in pricing and scheduling. Lone Star Web may do 40 percent of a customer's printing in one period, none in the next, and 60 percent in the period after that. Notice that even though the printing customer did not use Lone Star Web for a period, the buyer can and often will make purchases in subsequent periods. This type of account is called an **always-a-share** customer because the buyer can taper or augment purchases in increments, and multiple suppliers can have a share of a customer's business in either the current period or future periods.

Like printing services, other products frequently purchased on an always-a-share basis include standard trucking services, catering, consulting, supplies, basic chemicals, and materials. Multiple suppliers typically vie for an increasing percentage of the customer's business. And buyers can rely on a mix of suppliers without incurring significant additional variance that jeopardizes product performance.

The situation is very much akin to your use of several stores, catalogs, and garage sales for your wardrobe. Even if you buy almost all of your clothing from The Limited or L.L. Bean, it is always easy to spend a portion—always-a-share—of your budget at the Gap or the new consignment shop near campus.

# Lost-for-Good Customers

When Ford or Toyota selects a supplier of exterior mirrors for one or more of their models, the styling and assembly processes tend to cement this relationship for long periods. It will be difficult to switch from a metal mirror to an injection-molded plastic mirror except at model change periods.

Thus, **switching costs** are the forgone value of investments plus economic penalties and other expenses associated with finding, evaluating, and using a new supplier. To further illustrate, many toolmakers will rely on a JIT relationship with a regional metal service center. To switch to a new supplier means finding another well-qualified one, bringing it up to speed on the specialty metals and fabrications needed, and testing the Internet order system. There may be additional costs associated with learning the language of each other's firm and ironing out miscommunications. Sometimes legal costs are incurred for litigation or the voidance of contracts.

When a customer willingly incurs these costs to use a different supplier, it is because the incumbent is no longer regarded as viable. There's a better alternative out there that the customer, in essence, must pay to deal with. And is it likely that the customer would "pay" the switching costs again to return to the incumbent? Usually the answer is no. Relationships cemented by switching costs are called **lost-for-good relationships** because the prospects of a customer making a costly switch to a competitor followed by a costly return to the incumbent are remote—probably weaker than a cold call prospect.

The lost-for-good labels on these types of exchange motivate retention by accentuating the "dark side." That is, a customer is lost when it grows disenchanted with our performance and finds an alternative that promises sufficient advantages to overcome the associated switching costs. Reacquiring such a customer is practically hopeless. Apply the model in your own purchasing sphere. Will you return to a bank where you closed your accounts? Will you rejoin a Greek organization that you quit in protest last spring? Indeed, cold calls probably yield better prospects for these organizations than you yield.

Notice that these types of accounts can have excellent staying power. Because the customer incurs costs to switch suppliers, we might expect frequent communication, joint planning, and requests for adjustment in these durable associations. *Consistent, high performance* is required to retain these accounts. And structural features of the exchange support its continuity. Plumtree recognized P&G as a lost-for-good type of customer it did not want to lose.

## Implications of Exchange Type

Always-a-share and lost-for-good represent polar ends of a continuum of exchange situations. Sellers will retain customers by giving good service and responding to customer needs. Differentiating the offering on dimensions that forge structural ties and create exit barriers will tend to move the relationship toward the lost-for-good variety. For example, an always-a-share supplier might move from a fill-in role to become a major supplier by meeting customer criteria for becoming a preferred supplier. The standards for preferred supplier vary from firm to firm, but often include quality programs, employee safety and training efforts, and delivery specifications. Sellers can seek long-run supply contracts, build interpersonal linkages, and attempt to forge technical ties in an effort to move the account toward the lost-for-good type. We will develop these ideas next.

Of course, supplier action and market evolution can move the exchange the other way too. For example, plug compatibility and software standards have dramatically lowered exit barriers in the field of computers, moving the exchange from lost-for-good toward always-a-share.

Exhibit 16–1 summarizes the characteristics of each type of exchange. The classification is quite simple, but it puts a valuable focus on the nature of the customer relationship. The classification also illuminates the durability of any exchange and prompts management to consider the value of key accounts or customer groups.

# RETENTION PROBABILITY AND CUSTOMER VALUE

The marketing concept has always emphasized the satisfaction of customers to keep them coming back. But only in the past decade or two has information technology helped us put a dollar value on this highly strategic asset, the satisfied customer. Exhibit 16–2 depicts the expected food service purchases from a growing key institutional cafeteria account at a food wholesaler. The volume figures are rough forecasts, but represent the best estimates available, based on historical data, industry analysis, and revealed company strategy. If we also connect our expectations of slimming margins over the life of the account (reflecting shared economies in purchasing and servicing), we can forecast gross profits from the account.[3] These profit forecasts are discounted at 10 and 20 percent and summed to give the two NPV estimates at the bottom right.

Of course, we must not bank on these boxed NPV figures because *they are realized only if we retain the account.* Therefore, Exhibit 16–3 plots NPV against different retention rates. Understand what a retention rate is. With just a 20 percent chance of continuing a lost-for-good business relationship each year, the probability of holding the account through the sixth year is tiny ($.2^6 = .000064$). Even at .6 retention, the chance of serving the account in year 6 is less than 5 percent.

The story is different with an always-a-share account. In this analysis, retention probabilities equate to expected share of purchases. You may recall that in Chapter 5 we modeled customer lifetime value accounting for the probability of purchase as a function of recency, the time since their last purchase. Regardless of approach, purchase probabilities do not drop precipitously as in the lost-for-good situation. Thus,

**Exhibit 16–1**
Lost-for-Good
and Always-a-
Share Customers

Permaglide conveyance systems—
integrated materials handling products

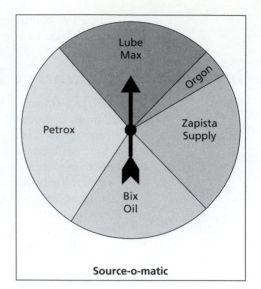

**Source-o-matic**

**Lost-for-Good**

Customers are tied to a system. They face significant switching costs. Switching costs may include

Specific investments
Cancelation penalties
Setup costs for a new supplier
Retraining
Finding and evaluating a new supplier

*Examples*
Telecommunications systems
Franchises
Warehouse rackings
Computer systems

**Always-a-Share**

Customers can allocate their purchases to several vendors. A period of no purchases can be followed by a period of high purchases.

Suppliers are largely interchangeable.

*Examples*
Lubricating oils
Printing services
Office supplies
Bulk chemicals

Exhibit 16–4 shows NPV as a function of retention rates, which remain at the same level in each buying period.

Compare the simple graphs in Exhibits 16–3 and 16–4. First note that a .8 retention rate with a lost-for-good customer brings less profit than a .4 retention (share-of-purchase) rate with an always-a-share customer. Although these simple models ignore the promotion and account service expenses, the retention imperative for lost-for-good customers comes through quite clearly. Do not doubt: What's lost is lost. A 20 percent defection rate is a serious problem.

Another insight from the graphs concerns the payoffs from efforts to improve retention. Exhibit 16–4 shows that with a linear relationship between retention and net present value, efforts to boost retention yield the same incremental profits at various

**Exhibit 16–2**
Food Service
Key Customer
Purchase
and Profit
Forecasts

| Year | Expected Purchases | Estimated Margin | Gross Profit | NPV @ 10% | NPV @ 20% |
|------|--------------------|------------------|--------------|-----------|-----------|
| 1 | $1,000,000 | 15.0% | $150,000 | $136,364 | $125,000 |
| 2 | 1,080,000 | 14.4 | 155,520 | 128,529 | 108,000 |
| 3 | 1,166,400 | 13.4 | 156,204 | 117,359 | 90,396 |
| 4 | 1,259,712 | 12.5 | 156,892 | 107,159 | 75,661 |
| 5 | 1,360,489 | 11.6 | 157,582 | 97,846 | 63,329 |
| 6 | 1,469,328 | 10.8 | 158,275 | 89,342 | 53,006 |
| | | | | $676,598 | $515,392 |

**Exhibit 16–3**
Customer NPV
as a Function of
Retention Rate:
Lost-for-Good
Customers

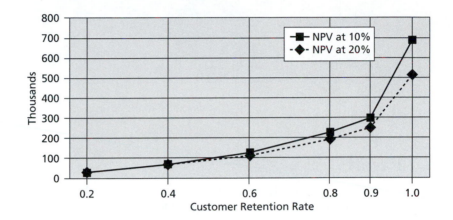

**Exhibit 16–4**
NPV as a Function
of Retention
Rate: Always-a-
Share Customers

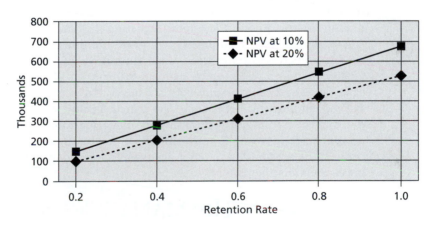

retention levels for always-a-share relationships. Thus, whether we boost retention (share-of-purchases) from .2 to .3 or .8 to .9, Exhibit 16–4 shows the same incremental profits. In contrast, at lost-for-good accounts, with the curvilinear relationship between retention and NPV, retention gains at the high end tend to dwarf gains obtained on the low end. For example, at the 10 percent discount rate, improving retention rates from .4 to .6 brings a $57,000 gain in profits. Meanwhile, moving from .8 to .9—half the other increment in retention—nets an additional $75,000! Therefore, marketing expenditures to cement business with an already good account will typically yield a better payoff than those same expenditures aimed at making a marginal customer an average customer.

**Exhibit 16–5**
Relationship
Benefits to Sellers
*SOURCE: Jon Anton,
Customer Relationship
Management: Making
Hard Decisions with
Soft Numbers, © 1996.
Reprinted by
permission of
Prentice Hall, Inc.,
Upper Saddle
River, NJ.*

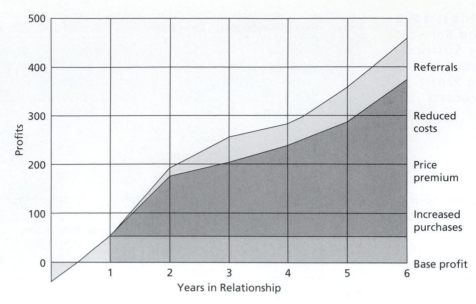

## Additional Payoffs

The simple models in the previous section don't tell the whole story. They show only mysteriously expanded purchases. They aptly demonstrate the payoffs of retention and the distinction between always-a-share and lost-for-good accounts. But they skirt the detail that can reveal the source of additional payoffs in long-term relationships. Exhibit 16–5 is a powerful graphic depicting the "stack" of benefits that can result. A good buyer–seller relationship will grow additional business opportunities: new products, increased purchases. When supported by first-rate service and product quality, premium prices can be charged. Selling costs can be better managed, and because of tighter coordination between buyer and seller, the benefits of production, staffing, and logistical efficiencies are shared. Finally, we should explicitly recognize the "spillover" from one relationship to others. Customer referrals, joint demonstrations at trade shows or at new prospective customers, and articles in the trade press connect the relationship to other business. Indeed, long-standing relations represent implicit endorsements.[4]

## CUSTOMER RELATIONSHIP MANAGEMENT

Now that we have underscored their financial impact and provided a scheme for classifying relations, it is time to address systematically the challenges of building, running, and strengthening relationships. The challenge of "building" will pivot on the relationship development process from Chapter 2 and emphasize the strategy of forging relational ties through role performance, social ties, technical linkages, investments, and contracts. Are there product positioning options, pricing mechanisms, and other strategic measures that can build relationships? We show that there are indeed.

"Running" a relationship involves the values, personnel, and systems dedicated to maintaining a high-performance relationship. The topical distinction is a bit artificial because some maintenance is needed in the building phase, and building or expansion may be a phenomenon in an established relation. Nevertheless, we use this organizational

## 16–1

## BUSINESS 2 BUSINESS

### Kendle Care for Customers

Kendle International Inc. is a contract research organization for the pharmaceutical industry, employing 3,000 people in 80 countries. As a nimble provider of Phase I drug testing ("first time in man") to postmarket evaluation, Kendle assists customers with clinical trial management, safety data management, medical writing, and statistical analysis.

Twenty major and 200 other pharmaceutical companies compete vigorously on many planes—innovativeness, effectiveness, and speed to market. It's not unusual for a pharmaceutical firm to test hundreds of compounds before a promising compound is discovered; then it may open up the door to even more compounds. Breakthroughs come unpredictably in this environment, so research must begin immediately to test the first promising compound even while scientists strive to improve it. Rather than keeping a bevy of specialists and project managers on staff, poised to take the baton at the cry of "Eureka!" from the lab, today's

lean-running pharmaceutical companies look to contract research organizations, like Kendle, to conduct the needed studies.

Kendle knows that quality in research design is essential but not sufficient in the contract research business. Frequent, detailed, and efficient communication is needed too. Because Kendle is organized both by location and function, it leans heavily on its proprietary information technology. Global Project Manager Denise Breiner explains that Kendle's systems such as TrialWatch Reg™ and TrialWare™ are used by project managers throughout the company to create "dashboard" reports that can be posted on TrialWeb, its Web-based forum for Kendle and customers that also provides security-scored access to corporate documents and data and training resources. Here Kendle and sponsors share ideas and information on a real-time basis. The result is a shorter time line in clinical development, plus closer collaboration with customers. Visit **www.kendle.com.**

device to focus on a fitting capstone set of concepts. For example, at Exhicon Endo-surgery commitment to customers is shaped by leadership and corporate culture. Customer service and product quality are not just marketing jobs. They require "all hands" working with empathy, efficiency, and empowerment toward the goal of customer satisfaction. Naturally, reward systems and information systems are needed to control the process.

Similarly, we carve out a separate discussion for "strengthening" relationships. "Strengthening" uses the themes introduced in the "building" phase to fortify and maximize the value of a strong buyer–seller relationship. The realm of possibilities for deepening dependence and expanding the scope of joint action in an established relationship is quite different from those we see in the fragile associations that promise someday to evolve into strong working partnerships.

# BUILDING RELATIONSHIPS

Companies remain in business relationships for two basic reasons: (1) because they have to and (2) because they want to. Firms have to stay in a relationship when there are no alternatives or when technical features of the exchange bind the parties for extended periods. Firms want to stay in relationships that are satisfying; they meet financial objectives, they evidence cooperation, and they can be projected into the future with confidence.

A happily married couple doesn't really care if their state's divorce laws are strict. Likewise, parties to a mutually satisfying business relationship are not apt to fret about switching costs. Thus, let's begin this section with a discussion of quality performance as a relational tie.

## Performance and Exclusivity

Time and again business buyers tell us they are looking for performance at a good price. They call this value. Value is often described as the ratio of quality and service to price. In many markets, however, customers respond to service improvements as if the value equation has an exponential function in the numerator. That is, instead of

$$V = Q/P \tag{1}$$

it seems more accurate to posit

$$V = Q^2/P \tag{2}$$

In Equation 1, a 9 percent price cut or a 10 percent quality boost yields the same impact on customer value:

$$V = Q/P \ldots 1.00/(1.00 - .09) = 1.1 \sim 1.10/1.00 = 1.1$$

In Equation 2, the impact of quality on value dwarfs the cut:

$$V = Q^2/P \ldots 1.10^2/1.00 = 1.21$$

Thus, a 10 percent increase in quality nets a 21 percent gain in value. The model formalizes what we see in the marketplace routinely: Superior performance, quality, and distinctive and reliable service are sources of competitive advantage that build customer loyalty. Customer retention is a logical and empirical reality for high-performance firms, organizations that do their job better than the rest.

Of course, quality and service expectations are shaped by the market. What begins as a unique service—a distinction that gains market share or enables a price premium—often becomes widely mimicked. In a short time it becomes the industry standard. The business travel industry is replete with examples of breakthroughs that are now common: frequent flier programs, express checkout, fax service, in-room high-speed Internet, and more.

So where is the glamour in business travel? Sadly, the promise of a service does not correspond to fulfillment. Exhibit 16–6 is a composite of some of the service breakdowns recounted by business travelers.[5]

The impact of quality and service in building a relationship comes from actually delivering it . . . every time. Consistent execution of what counts with the customer distinguishes your offering from the offering of your competitors. This gets you repeat business. This gets you requests to tackle special needs. This gets you invitations to propose new means of conducting business. This is the critical prerequisite for relationship development. From the Field 16–1 details the array of new services developed within business relationships in the electronics field.[6]

## Social Ties

The importance of social ties in business relationships is evident all around us. Business relationships are built on friendships, and friendships are built on a variety of social interactions. Consider these examples. The mayor and the school superintendent sit in the university president's box at Saturday night's basketball game. An account executive at a midsized ad agency heads the local direct marketing association. An air-conditioning

**Exhibit 16–6**
Service Quality
Breakdowns

Most of us encounter poor service with distressing regularity. On a typical business trip, the only thing worse than the service may be the response to your complaints.

| What You Experience | What the Service Provider Says |
|---|---|
| Your radio alarm fails. | We only sell it. Read your warranty. |
| The trunk of your airport limo is full of water and greasy tools, so your garment bag and its contents get soaked. | Did you buy our optional personal-property insurance? |
| You try to check in to claim your assigned seat on the plane. | Sorry, this line is closed. Please move on. |
| You pick up your rental car at your destination. | We're all out of compacts, but we can rent you a minivan once the mechanic is through with it. |
| You check into your hotel with a supposedly guaranteed reservation. | Sorry, but we have no record of your reservation, and we're full. |
| Breakfast is a half-hour late. | Sorry, it went to the wrong room. |
| Your secretary calls. Back at the office, the photocopier is down. | We'll need a few days to get it fixed. |
| The hotel telephone is making funny noises. | We'll have to schedule a service rep, but I can't say for sure when he'll be out. |
| Your answering service abruptly says, "Oops, hold on," and you get cut off from a long-distance call. | This happens all the time. It's nothing to worry about. |
| You order a hot sandwich for lunch, but it arrives cold and greasy. | Our chef is out sick today, so an assistant is cooking. |
| You check out of the hotel—or try to. Your bill is wrong; the breakfast charge was not included. | I'll fix it for you as soon as I track down my supervisor. |
| When you finally pick up your baggage after the flight home, it's torn and broken. | Fill out a claim form, but I'll warn you: Our liability limit is low. |

SOURCE: Robert Desatnick, and Denis Detzel, *Managing to Keep the Customer*, © 1993. Reprinted by permission of Jossey–Bass Publishers, San Francisco, CA.

manufacturer hosts heating, ventilating, and air-conditioning (HVAC) engineers for a Toronto harbor cruise and cocktails. The sales rep asks about the CFO's family and community chest activities before taking up the new leasing options. The hospital purchasing agent receives three hams, 22 greeting cards, and four cans of nuts at Christmastime.

Although we don't doubt that many gifts and outings are intended to bring quid pro quo, the "strings-attached" variety are apt to be resented and eschewed for the complexity they bring buyers. If 18 holes is intended to bribe, what purchasing agent can enjoy the round? And how can it weigh against the slightly lower bid from the supplier who hosted a small group at the symphony? Marketing professionals regard gifts and social affairs as a means of thanking customers and building personal relationships in a world of e-mail and faxes.[7] One purchasing expert summed up this tradition from the customer's vantage point:

> Business lunches—and other reasonable forms of entertainment—are old, pleasant, and respectable parts of buyer–seller relationships. . . . A good buyer knows, for example, that a supplier is not trying to subvert him by taking him out to lunch. But he also realizes that the supplier has sound business, as well as personal reasons, for his largesse.[8]

---

**16–1**

## FROM THE FIELD

### Board Stuffers Offering the Right Stuff

Computer and telecommunications firms have relied on electronics manufacturing subcontractors for decades. Dubbed "board stuffers" in the early days, they are now a $50 billion business, most often referred to as Electronics Manufacturing Services (EMS) firms. As many other OEMs in aerospace, military, automotive, and consumer fields continue to outsource, they look to EMS providers for a broader array of services.

To cement their relationships with OEMs, EMS majors such as Plexus and Sanmina-SCI have added design services. Indeed, Plexus has 350 people on its design team. Other EMS firms have looked to downstream services, too. For example, Flextronics, headquartered in Singapore, but with over 50 global locations, provides top-drawer logistics services, typically postponing product completion and final configuration until the customer is ready. The system yields low logistics service costs and rapid time to market.

Look for EMS players to continue their expansion of design, sourcing, manufacture, and fulfillment services to further penetrate medical and consumer sectors, and note the several EMS companies serving Visteon, Delphi, and first-tier suppliers to the automotive industry.

Visit Flextronics at www.flextronics.com/ and Plexus at www.plexus.com/cgi-bin/r.cgi/index1.html to see how strategic partnerships can result from a supplier's growing competencies and the buyer's need for an expanded array of services.

---

Exhibit 16–7 details how buyers and sales reps view luncheon meetings.[9]

Indeed, often (and more effectively than tacit bribery), these social exchanges occur to support the candid disclosures, frank feedback, and high-risk proposals inherent in problem solving as well as the inevitable requests for flexibility and adjustment that commercial trading involves. Considerable research shows how communication, concern for one's partner, fairness, honesty, and shared values enable trust, which fosters a long-term orientation and commitment to a relationship.[10] Exhibit 16–8 shows an empirically supported model of the precursors and consequences of trust and commitment. More recent research examining over 100 studies verifies the impact of trust and commitment on performance, but adds an important third mediating variable—relational investments.[11] We will look at these in the sections that follow.

In the evolution of business relationships it's common for parties to interact at equivalent organizational levels: sales rep to buyer, installer to user, engineer to general manager, director of purchasing to VP of marketing. But as a relationship matures, interactions cut across levels. Account managers and customer teams interface with cross-functional high-performance work teams on the buyer side. How effective can the partnership be without courtesy, professionalism, empathy, and justice? Do you think business friendships support or impair communication, shared visions, problem solving, and adjustment? Would a customer switch to another supplier without giving the people its managers like at the supplier organization a chance to amend service breakdowns or explore new means of working together? Indeed, it's hard to overemphasize the role of social ties and forthright behavior in business relationships.

## Exhibit 16–7
## Buyer's and Seller's Views of the Business Lunch

### Exhibit A

The objectives and reasons for business luncheon meetings, as perceived by buyers and sales representatives.

*Statement to Evaluate*

1. Buyer–seller business is the purpose of the business lunch.
2. The business lunch provides an opportunity for buyer and seller to get to know each other better.
3. A function of the business lunch is to "sell something."
4. The business lunch gives the buyer (seller) a chance to get away from the office and all its distractions to discuss buyer–seller business.
5. Business lunches help solve some kind of business problem.
6. Buyer–seller business talk on a business lunch is valuable.
7. Personal talk on a business lunch is valuable.
8. Buyers expect to be taken out to lunch.

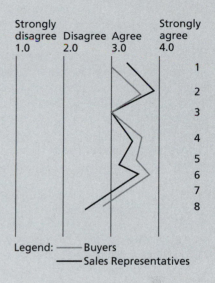

### Exhibit B

Appropriate topics for discussion at business luncheon meetings and effects on personal relationships and order placement, as seen by buyers and sales representatives.

1. Conversations on the business lunch are typically buyer–seller business oriented.
2. Price negotiation occurs on the business lunch.
3. Delivery problems are discussed on the business lunch.
4. Quality issues arise and are discussed on business lunches.
5. Personal relationships do develop between buyer and seller as a result of the business lunch.
6. The personal relationships that do develop help the buyer (seller) get his job done more efficiently.
7. The more a buyer gets taken out to lunch by a particular supplier, the more likely it is that supplier will receive orders from that buyer.
8. Salespeople who develop personal relationships with buyers get more orders, assuming *all* other things are equal, than those salespeople who don't develop personal relationships.
9. Very few orders are ever given (or received) as a result of the business lunch.

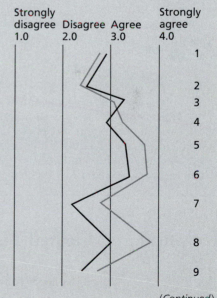

*(Continued)*

## Exhibit 16–7
(*continued*)

### Exhibit C

Reactions of buyers and sales representatives to various suggestions for making business luncheon meetings more effective.

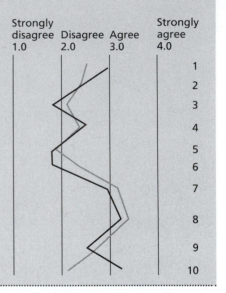

|  | Strongly disagree 1.0 | Disagree 2.0 | Agree 3.0 | Strongly agree 4.0 |
|---|---|---|---|---|

1. There should be more buyer–seller business discussed on the business lunch.
2. There should be more personal talk on the business lunch.
3. The business lunch should follow prearranged lines of discussion.
4. There should be more prelunch preparation by both buyer and seller on business topics that are going to be discussed on the business lunch.
5. The amount of time allowed for the business lunch should be decreased.
6. Alcohol should be forbidden on the business lunch.
7. The best business lunch results when just buyer and seller go out to lunch together.
8. The best business lunch results when buyer and seller and a person from a support group (engineering, quality control, etc.) go out to lunch together.
9. The best business lunch results when an additional buyer or seller—besides the original one buyer and one seller—go out to lunch together.
10. Managers (or principals) should participate in the business lunch often.

SOURCE: Adapted from Paul Halvorson and William Rudelius, "Is There a Free Lunch?" Reprinted with permission from *Journal of Marketing* 41 (January 1977), pp. 44–49, published by the American Marketing Association.

---

### 16–2

## BUSINESS 2 BUSINESS
### The Fairway

You have landed a part-time job in the county purchasing department. After looking at proposals from three suppliers, you recommended purchasing all the golf course herbicides from GreenBlade. It's been six weeks since your recommendation went forward. Now you receive a small package with a note from Bernie Tassmer at GreenBlade: "Thanks for picking a winner, GreenBlade. And next time we go out, I get two strokes a side. Best regards, Bern." The package contains four all-week passes to the PGA tournament upstate next month and two dozen tour-quality golf balls. What should you do?

## Technical and Formal Ties

We can sometimes get caught up in the feel-good aspects of buyer–seller relationships to the neglect of critical structural ties. An aluminum casting company that locates in proximity of the aluminum supplier, so that molten aluminum can be conveyed by pipeline, is structurally committed to the supplier. A telemarketing agency that uses

**Exhibit 16–8**
The Foundation and Payoffs of Trust and Commitment in Business Relationships

SOURCE: *Adapted from Robert Morgan and Shelby Hunt, "The Commitment–Trust Theory of Relationship Marketing," Reprinted with permission from* Journal of Marketing *58 (July 1994), pp. 20–38, published by the American Marketing Association.*

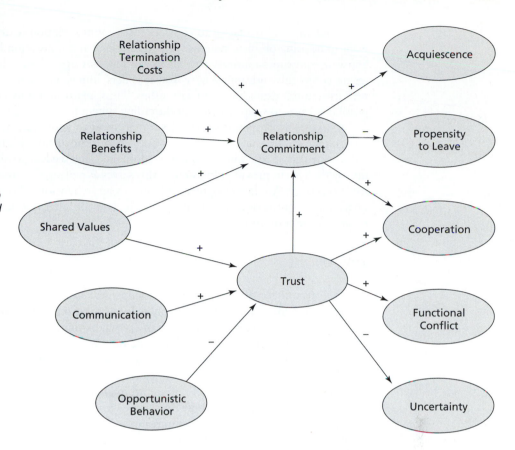

IBM computers and call distributors is technically tied to that operating system. Likewise, a supermarket chain that adopts NCR's point-of-purchase scanners cannot easily change systems or suppliers.

Selling a "system"—whether offering computational power, medical and disability insurance, telecommunications, MRO supplies, or food service—is a double-edged sword. On the one hand, by coupling formerly separable elements, it increases the complexity of changing any element. A switch to another system or product configuration means a high dollar outlay, new learning, ensuring compatibility, and sustaining efficient work flow. These are switching costs that tend to move the exchange toward the lost-for-good variety. On the other hand, the lack of system divisibility can be an impediment to trial, making new account acquisition difficult.

## Systems and Modules

Thus, a customer adopting our system becomes locked in to a degree. But the system itself can be an impediment to adoption. This double-edged character of systems demands that firms give careful attention to the modularity of their system. **Modularity** means the system is composed of distinct subsystems or components. If a module can be tested to "sample" the performance of the full system, market penetration possibilities are enhanced. For example, a dockable laptop computer can lead a user to purchase an entire workstation. A keyless door lock may lead a hotel to adopt the supplier's complete security system.

Modularity is also a factor to consider for account retention. Current customers don't want to be using obsolete systems when technology and innovation bring improvements. Software companies routinely provide free or low-cost upgrades to current users. This can regain competitive advantage over rival suppliers' innovations and nip sources of current user frustration, extending the relationship. Thus, many accounts can be retained if the possibility exists to swap elements of the fading system for new and improved modules.

Of course, if competitors' modules can connect to your system, the relationship begins to take on the character of always-a-share. But the upside risk is that such openness reduces perceived risk among potential adopters. They see less possibility of being "held up" by the system provider. In essence, this serves as a pledge to provide exemplary quality and service. A seller recognizes the buyer's apprehensions about being locked in to one supplier, but is so confident it can do the best job, that it welcomes the presence of rivals to keep it on its toes.

## Investments

Another avenue for establishing relationships that last involves **specific investments,** the dedication of assets that have sharply reduced value outside the relationship. Think of the scope of investments that companies make—in people, locations, procedures, equipment, and more—that have real value only within a relationship. For example, an industrial distributor may send its people to a weeklong seminar to learn how 3M wants distributors to connect to its new order systems and conform to new standards of reporting distributor activities, performance, and quality control. Little of this investment in man-hours, talent, and know-how carries over to relationships with other suppliers. The distributor stays in the relationship to reap the return on the training investment.

Similar effects result from investments in specific locations (a steel mill locates near a coal depot), specific supplier qualification standards (ISO 9000), or specific equipment (a customer designs an assembly process utilizing a supplier's proprietary technology built into unique components). These are technical and structural commitments that bind the parties.

You probably have enough relational scar tissue to recognize the instability of one-way commitments. (But you don't have to tell us you forked out $220 for the security guard uniform in the job you kept one week, or took a French course to talk to the cute exchange student across the hall.) A relationship is apt to last when both parties commit. Indeed, many business relationships are supported by *mutual* investments or pledges. This has the effect of building exit barriers or switching costs for both parties, motivating the parties to resolve differences.

Consider how suppliers may pledge or signal their commitment to the relationship by making reciprocal investments. For the shipper who locates at the railroad spur, the carrier designs a railroad car for the special transport of its industrial valves and controls. Distributors who attend manufacturer training may receive special displays and promotion assistance from their supplier and know that the training costs often exceed the small fees—if any—charged by the manufacturer.

## Contracts

We would be remiss in our discussion of customer retention if we neglected the topic of contracts. A **contract** is a promise to perform some act in exchange for a payment or some other consideration. A contract has the force of law, but when used to cement a relationship, a contract typically specifies means of adjustment other than litigation. Indeed, in classical contracting, the parties try to foresee every contingency and specify adjustments and outcomes.[12] Of course, when the contract is for 3, 5, or 10 years or more, the relevant future is quite cloudy. Uncertainty pervades. Hurricanes, strikes, wars, power failures, acquisitions, supply shortages, technology, new regulations, adverse publicity, bridge collapse, and other calamities may impact the exchange. It is impossible to anticipate every event.

The parties try to forge contractual terms that preserve the relationship in the face of these and other unknown contingencies. An account can be retained through even the worst circumstances if the contract gives guidelines for joint action and adjustment. Better yet are mechanisms that look forward in the relationship. These involve information sharing for *structural planning*.

To illustrate, consider Beta, a company shipping automobile parts with carrier Gamma. Beta holds very low inventories at its different assembly plants, so it is vital that Gamma provide reliable, on-time delivery. Accordingly, Beta and Gamma hold formal meetings to discuss the most troublesome routes and set goals for service improvement. After 30 days if targets are still being missed on a significant percentage of shipments, other routes might be tested.

A Beta representative summed up, "We will make every effort to help them correct their problems. Usually the problem is legitimate and usually they fix it. If they can't, I want them to know that I don't like having to switch [carriers] on them, but that I have to. We can't afford to have a plant close down."[13]

## The Mix of Relationship Ties

We have discussed five basic means of cementing relationships: superior performance, social ties, systems, specific investments, and contracts. Our treating each bond in a separate subsection should not suggest that the bonds are used on an either–or basis. They interact with each other—sometimes positively, but also sometimes negatively.[14]

For example, firms making specific investments in people, sites, or equipment need to protect the value of those assets. Although we talked about reciprocated investments serving as pledges of continuity, contractual provisions or social ties may also provide assurances. This is a positive interaction.

On the negative side, detailed contractual elements can blemish a relationship. Imagine, over lunch and a handshake, a vendor says, "We'll send a testing truck right away if ever the boiler shows signs of stress." How many billable hours can the customer's attorney rack up defining the "signs of stress," specifying what testing truck and the qualifications of the testing crew, and pinpointing the clock time equivalent of "right away"? Most professionals recognize the risks to a relationship from such legalism and know that because the vendor's reputation is on the line, an earnest effort at performance is apt to result.

# RUNNING RELATIONSHIPS

Recently at a beautiful wedding before a standing-room-only congregation of family and friends, the presider told the bride and groom that the strength of their marriage would depend on three things: accepting each other as they are, communication, and help from Above. We needn't stretch the metaphor: These success factors hold for buyer–seller relationships too.

**Exhibit 16–9**
Communication
Channels and
Objectives

| | |
|---|---|
| Telephone | Confirm appointment. |
| | Answer a question about delivery. |
| Fax | Summarize yesterday's meeting. |
| | FYI: an article in a trade magazine. |
| E-mail | Request the name of a former consultant. |
| | Give congratulations on a story in the press. |
| | Request easy-to-find data in a planning document. |
| Business letter | Formally introduce a new account representative. |
| | Summarize reasons for next quarter's price increase. |
| | Thank you for the order. |
| Face-to-face | Negotiate production commitments. |
| | Resolve dispute about marketing effort. |

# Organizational Character

It is folly to plan to remake a business partner into the organization yours wants to deal with. Certainly it is fitting to consider the prospects for mutual learning and skill development. And over the long run, trading is a means to effect change. We expect trading partners to discover new means of doing business and become more efficient as a result. But don't pretend that you can make a strong working relationship with a late-paying customer with corruption in its purchasing department. Chances are very slim that the customer can be straightened out by your culture of integrity at the supply firm. The same goes for buyers: Don't believe your zeal in a relationship is enough to reform a low-price supplier with delivery and quality problems.

# Communication

Communication has been called the "glue that holds together" a relationship.[15] Between buyer and seller in a durable association, communication includes meetings between top executives (e.g., director of purchasing and VP of marketing) to forge the goals and principles of the relationship, as well as the interactions over transactions and operations between sales and purchasing reps. Furthermore, when buyer and seller partner, interfirm contact occurs in many positions: between engineers, among financial and production planners, between operators and delivery and service personnel, and so on.

Managerial attention is given to a number of aspects of these communications. Recalling concepts from Chapters 9 through 12, communication objectives and message requirements will determine the channels used and formality. Exhibit 16–9 summarizes the options and gives illustrative examples of objectives. From the Field 16–2 gives hints about how much work communication can entail.

### Formal Structures

Efficiency considerations must be weighed, not only in each discrete communication episode, but also in the establishment of a system for coordinating the relationship. Electronic data interchange (EDI) mechanizes ordering and information sharing on inventories and deliveries. Biweekly vendor review meetings formalize a process for identifying snags in current operations, detailing plans that might indirectly affect the partner, introducing new systems and products, and spotting new opportunities in markets and technologies. These are just a few of the possibilities for structuring communication opportunities.

---

**16–2**

# FROM THE FIELD

## 100 Breakfasts?

Put yourself in Dorothy Coleman's shoes. You move to Cincinnati as the newly appointed CEO of UnitedHealthcare Southwest Ohio/Indiana. Your aim is to make UHC a company known for its service to clients and forge strong working relationships with the provider community. But UHC has developed a reputation for nonresponsiveness to client concerns. Indeed, two large orthopedic groups left the UHC network following a breakdown in contract negotiations.

Coleman's tackled the challenge by meeting 100 leaders in 100 days. Large receptions and conferences didn't count. She booked one-on-one breakfast, lunch, and dinner meetings with physicians, practice managers, and hospital administrators. Some were ornery and some had gripes going way back, but Coleman wanted a "healthy dose of listening" and a chance to start building relationships.

The personal meetings gave Coleman a cross section of opinions and ideas about the needs and issues of the region. They also gave members of the provider community a glimpse of her energy, enthusiasm, and essential interest in the facts and data about health care. For ongoing input she's establishing an advisory board of doctors, hospital administrators, other health professionals, and employers.

Is all this time at Starbucks truly a productive use of CEO—and provider—time, and how can other communication channels be employed to the same end?

Andrea Tortora, "A Meeting Marathon," *Business Courier* 21, June 11, 2004, pp. 1, 9.

---

### Specialists

Successful companies apply creative means to get customers to talk. Consultant Carla Furlong tells of an external contractor hired by the U.S. Department of Defense to work with an in-house technical expert to develop a series of training modules on the safe operation of agency motor vehicles. After a long period of no progress, a new team of customer contact specialists was assigned and the first module was delivered in just three months. In the next two years another 17 rolled off the presses.

Why the great turnaround? One visit by the new team uncovered the initial snag. It turned out the contractor was keen on in-depth training, but the customer wanted less. "Operating a nuclear-powered airship might need that kind of detail," laughs program manager Bernard Lukco. "But we were looking at a pallet jack. You weren't going to fly it, just push it across the floor." Looking back, the customer let things drag with the contractor because dealing with an array of experts intimidated client people and tied their tongues. They simply couldn't articulate concerns properly. The relationship support team solved a key linkage breakdown.[16]

### Forums

Sometimes it can be quite productive to monitor chat rooms and bulletin boards or to bring customers together to interact. Together they just might disclose how you might be able to serve them better. For example, Service Master invited CEOs from the health care industry to attend a seminar featuring famed management consultant Peter Drucker. Service Master President Chuck Stair explained: "This was another way to listen to [our] customers as they interacted with a respected source of leadership [Drucker]."[17]

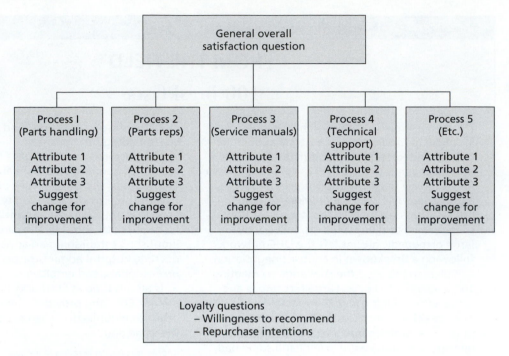

**Exhibit 16–10**
Satisfaction
Survey Design
SOURCE: *Jon Anton,
Customer Relationship
Management: Making
Hard Decisions with
Soft Numbers, © 1996.
Reprinted by
permission of Prentice
Hall, Inc., Upper
Saddle River, NJ.*

# Customer Satisfaction Surveys

Many companies have instituted customer satisfaction measures, a distinct communication tool with remarkable potential to decrease price sensitivity and impact retention. Satisfaction surveys assess performance on many elements from many levels in the customer organization and even other downstream customers. To presume that no news from customers is good news puts the firm in a precarious position. Proactive satisfaction measures are necessary because many customers don't take the time to register complaints with a supplier and allow problems to be addressed; *they simply switch suppliers.*

## Types of Information

Satisfaction studies can be done by Web, telephone, or mail, but the typical high level of detail favors mail. Summarized in Exhibit 16–10, there are four major types of information to capture in a satisfaction study.[18]

1. Ascertain satisfaction with the overall relationship. These relationship-defining questions include

   a. Overall satisfaction: "Overall, we are very satisfied with our relationship with the Sigma Company." (Customer personnel indicate their degree of agreement or disagreement with the statement.)

   b. Intention to repurchase: "My company is very likely to make additional purchases from Sigma."

   c. Willingness to recommend: "I would certainly recommend the Sigma Company to a friend at another firm."

   d. Likelihood of a sustained relationship: "We expect to be doing business with Sigma for the next three years or more."

Willingness to recommend has been a good predictor of the durability of relationships. The other overall satisfaction measures work well as criterion variables in models that statistically estimate the factors that best explain variation in customer satisfaction.

2. Measure satisfaction with specific aspects of the relationship using a battery of questions. For example, a parts supplier might be evaluated on several key facets or processes of the relationship (its sales representative, its product manuals, its order process, product performances, technical support, etc.). A company that performs several very different functions for its customers—say, parts supply, applications engineering, and product reconditioning—will need to evaluate facets in each arena. Parts supply, for example, might be evaluated on facets unlike the facets of product reconditioning. Each facet is reflected on several attributes. Thus, satisfaction with the sales rep is gauged in terms of customer reports of rep knowledge, courtesy, follow-through, availability, and so on.

3. Use open-ended questions to invite customers to express issues not covered in the structured portion of the survey. Many times, we can find out the number one source of frustration in a relationship by asking the customer to identify "the one thing our company could do to improve XXX."

4. Finally, the survey will need to ask for important classification data: customer firm characteristics, product types, complaint experience, and so on.

## Analysis and Meaning

What would you do with performance ratings for eight relationship processes on a total of 61 product and service attributes from informants at 450 customer organizations? Indeed, take shelter when you see an avalanche coming. If you can overcome the anxiety and trepidation, there's a good chance you'll see beyond the avalanche to the gold mine of customer retention avenues.

A good starting place with the data is a look at the overall satisfaction scores. Note the percentage of customers rating your company in the top one or two categories on the scale. Compare these "top-box" scores to previous measures, perhaps graph-ing the history of quarterly top-box scores over the past several years, as in Exhibit 16–11.

Whether the overall score is stable or trending up or down, to manage customer relationships it is vital to understand how different facets of the relationship affect the level of satisfaction. Remember that each facet (e.g., sales reps, warranty claims, product literature, technical support, logistical services) is measured on several attributes. By calculating an average performance score for the attributes of each facet, we obtain a relationship facet performance score (RFP score).

The RFP scores can then be used as independent variables in a regression analysis of overall satisfaction. That is, we suspect that

Overall satisfaction = f(customer reports of sales reps, warranty claims, product literature, and other facets)

Statistical output from a regression analysis might read like this:

$$\text{Overall satisfaction} = 3.2 + .82\ (\text{RFP}_{\text{warranty}}) + .53\ (\text{RFP}_{\text{rep}})$$
$$+ .12\ (\text{RFP}_{\text{technical support}}) + .06\ (\text{RFP}_{\text{product literature}}) + e$$

If we have taken care to standardize the RFP scores, the regression coefficients on each score indicate the relative importance of each facet in "explaining" variation in overall

**Exhibit 16–11**
History of
Top-Box
Satisfaction
Scores

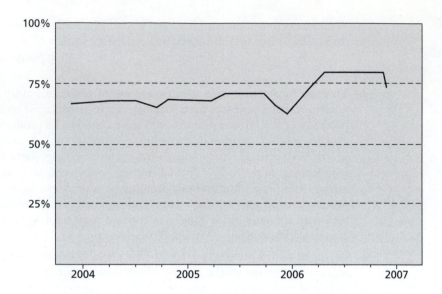

satisfaction. In this situation, based on the highest regression coefficient, how the supplier handles warranty claims is the key determinant of overall satisfaction, followed by sales rep performance. Supplier performance on technical support and product literature plays a relatively minor role in overall satisfaction. Exhibit 16–12 shows the strong and weak statistical associations graphically.

## A Closer Look

Now that we know that handling warranty claims and sales rep behaviors dramatically impact overall satisfaction, we can more closely examine the effect of specific attributes of these two facets. Again, regression analysis helps us in this regard.

This time we suspect that

Overall satisfaction = f(attributes of the facet warranty claims service) and
Overall satisfaction = f(attributes of the facet sales rep behaviors)

Illustrative statistical output shows that some attributes of warranty claims handling have large effects on satisfaction while other attributes have minimal impact:

Overall satisfaction = 2.9 + .73 (helpful operators) + .46 (fairness)
+ .28 (minimal paperwork) + .09 (prompt payment)

These statistical estimates help us to work on the most important attributes to provide good warranty service. Streamlining paperwork, the subject of much company attention of late, builds customer satisfaction in the preceding example. But take a look at the regression weights. Having operators who can solve customer problems has nearly three times the impact as paperwork reduction. Another key attribute is fairness. Perhaps our customers need some clarification on warranty service standards. If we can properly manage their expectations so that we can match their standards of fairness, we stand to improve customer satisfaction.

In summary, customer satisfaction measurement has exploded as a commercial activity in parallel with the dissemination of relationship marketing and the harder data showing the costs of winning versus keeping customers. Satisfaction surveys have become standard means of tracking and tuning business relationships.

**Exhibit 16–12**
Strong and Weak Statistical Models of Customer Satisfaction

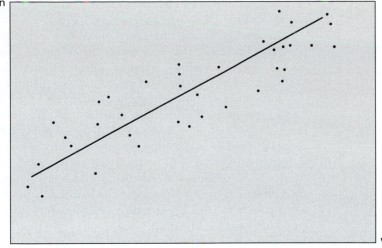

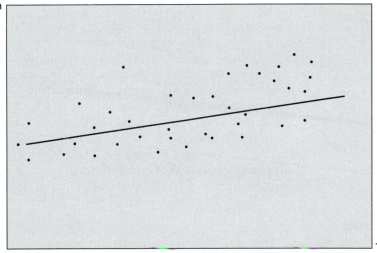

No doubt there are many companies offering a plethora of statistical and graphical models. Most work on this basic premise that one or more key criterion variables (overall satisfaction, willingness to recommend, intention to continue buying) can be statistically "explained" by specific seller activities arranged in a hierarchy of facets and processes. When used in concert with customer correspondence, hot line calls, e-mails, person-to-person, group-to-group, and other less-structured means of customer interaction, the satisfaction survey is part of a valuable system of relationship communication. It helps to keep relationships running.

# Forces from Beyond

This final subsection on running relationships matches the final element in the wedding sermon. Despite standard insurance provisions, managers seldom are allowed "act of God" alibis in business. On the other hand, good strategy is often the preferred label for good fortune.

Our message here is that no relationship is entirely governable by the parties. Key personnel get reassigned. New ownership brings an array of new expectations and supply connections. And key accounts relocate to other lands. Let's not even pretend that every facet of relationship management can be planned and controlled.

Consolation derives from periodic attention to the upside—some of the fortuitous breakthroughs in one's business relationships. We have seen partnerships born out of calamities—a cash flow crisis staved off by a supplier willing to share risk, a plant safety concern solved by engineering expertise met on the touchline, and more. One of the authors invited a panel of professionals to his class. Two of the panelists—who were total strangers beforehand—forged a strong working relationship. In the months following their classroom presentations, they orchestrated a partnership between their respective firms to serve a large client with a complicated marketing program that neither firm could have executed by itself.

# STRENGTHENING GOOD RELATIONSHIPS

It could well be argued that effectively managing a good relationship implicitly consists of strengthening it—*Nolo contendere*.

This section gives explicit and separate attention to the task of strengthening good relationships. We can regard the previous section as presenting the fundamental building blocks for relationships—they are akin to the security, nutrition, and physical and mental exercise we need to be healthy. But one does not live to be healthy. One maintains a healthy lifestyle as a means to higher things: intellectual accomplishment; service to family, business, and community; artistic expression; and aesthetic enrichment of the culture.

Along these lines, we want to borrow the school motto, *Semper altius* (always higher), from Gateway Academy in St. Louis. It is a powerful theme for the challenge of strengthening business relationships. There is no pinnacle in a business relationship. Complacency can spoil the best relationships—it must be fought at every level. Effective management is ever striving, as we see in From the Field 16–3.

## Supragoals

Relationships last to the extent that they satisfy the goals of the partners. When joint stakes are high, we expect close collaboration and durability. To strengthen relationships, one or both of the partners may need to work hard to keep these shared goals in focus.

Research in countless different settings has shown that members of a group tend to put aside differences and work intensively and cooperatively in the face of a threat from outside the group. Although the impact of a potential calamity is stronger than the impact of potential gain, a good relationship manager can rightly cast the prospect of a missed opportunity as a calamity or threat.

When companies attend to the entire value-added chain, it becomes a bit easier to perceive opportunities and threats to relationships with their immediate or primary exchange partners. For example, Chrysler engages its suppliers in a cost-cutting program called SCORE (Supplier COst and Reduction Effort). Geiger Technic (Kalamazoo, Michigan) suggested changes to the engine cooling system in the 1998 Intrepid and Concord. By combining coolant pressure bottle, overflow bottle, and bottle bracket into a single injection-molded part, Geiger reduced cost, weight, and space—an eventual savings of nearly $1 million.[19] Similarly, in upstream partnerships, Microsoft rallied its

## 16–3

# FROM THE FIELD

## Serving Customers in a Direct Marketing Career

I've been blessed with an exciting and successful direct marketing career that has spanned two and half decades, five companies, hundreds of clients, and thousands of profitable campaigns. Over the years I've learned that, although the secret to direct marketing success may sound increasingly complicated and technical, it's really not.  It's simply this: Know your customer.

My first job, for example, as marketing director for Latonia Race Course, a thoroughbred racetrack in Northern Kentucky, afforded me a direct marketing laboratory of sorts, where I developed a successful database marketing program, slicing and dicing the preferences of 40,000 loyal fans, and executing data-driven, targeted mail programs that consistently generated outstanding response rates and ROI and helped set attendance records year after year.

From the racetrack I joined Yeck Brothers in Dayton, Ohio, a top-notch creative agency known for their award-winning work. For Yeck, I managed key accounts and campaigns (FedEx, IAMS, 3M, Schering-Plough) and was highly involved in the creative process, with sometimes sole responsibility to conceive, develop, and present complete themes and programs. During these years I developed a strong understanding of segmentation marketing principles (strategic and creative) and how success is the result of bringing together what a buyer values and the benefits a product or service delivers.

In 1991 I accepted a ground floor opportunity to create and manage a new direct marketing operation for a Cincinnati-based general advertising agency, Martiny & Company. Through 1997, I established and led this new effort, helping customers like Cintas, Heinz Pet Products, and Ross Laboratories launch and sustain integrated marketing programs across multiple channels, e.g., advertising (general and direct-response), public relations, yellow pages, telemarketing, direct-to-customer and emerging Web marketing. Profitability is driven by efficient access which requires leveraging a consumer's preferred means of communication.

In 1998, I became an independent consultant selling, producing, and managing profitable campaigns and programs for a variety of clients. It was during this time that the dot.com revolution was at its height, transforming marketing almost overnight to 360° customer relationship marketing. That's when I decided that Harte-Hanks was an excellent career choice—a leading global direct and interactive firm ($1 billion sales, 7,000 employees, global footprint), progressive and financially stable, with an entrepreneurial environment that provides excellent ongoing resources and education into the rapidly emerging customer optimization era.

Fact is, whether you call it database marketing, **segmentation marketing**, integrated marketing, 360° customer relationship marketing, or customer optimization marketing, businesses will continue to redesign and improve information and direct marketing processes for one simple reason: to better know their customers.

Bernie Joyce, Vice President of Business Development, Major Brands, Harte-Hanks.

suppliers and reemphasized its commitment to PC workstations when the prospects of simpler, network-linked machines started to glimmer.

## Needs Anticipation

Although superordinate goals typically derive from forces outside the relationship, ongoing vigilance and creativity must be applied to the internal workings of the relationship itself. A supplier who notes high turnover among customer personnel can count on some role in retraining each newcomer on its equipment. Perhaps the supplier's ad agency can redesign manuals and operating instructions to include better graphics and make them easier to follow.

Another alternative for the supplier is to detail tactfully to the customer the costs of turnover in terms such as reduced productivity, training costs, and machine repair attributed to inexperienced operators. With a good understanding of the impact, some strategic joint action can be undertaken to develop a better recruiting and hiring policy, design a career path or a job rotation plan, or establish an apprentice program for high schoolers.

Does the supplier usually know a better way to run its customer's business? We doubt it. But the supplier who knows the customer well and examines the root causes of operational inefficiencies and opportunities can be an important resource of ideas, skills, and linkages to other resources.

When a Ground Heaters customer wanted to imbed its network of thermal hoses in a slab of concrete upon which it planned to pour 300 concrete panels for tilt-up construction in a New Hampshire winter, it represented a new application with huge potential. Ground Heaters personnel were on-site at various stages lending expertise. After all went well, the construction customer went on the trade show circuit detailing their success with their approach and Ground Heaters system. Business expanded significantly as the "revolution in construction" was warmly received by contractors in frigid climates, which so often thwarted their winter productivity.[20]

# Lagniappe

Pronounced lan-yapp and rooted in Louisiana's Creole dialect, this word **lagniappe** means anything given beyond strict obligation, a surprise or surplus benefit from an exchange. We think you have seen the power of lagniappe in personal or family relations. Recall your sweetheart's reaction to the card or flowers you sent on "no special occasion." Maybe predawn on the day of the big game, your dad knocked off the mud and polished your soccer shoes. The grins and gratitude from these simple actions can take a relationship to a higher plane.

Business marketing relationships work similarly. Hugh Hart Pollard, who heads a consulting firm in Little Rock, Arkansas, sends a handwritten, personal note to his clients at their homes, thanking them for their business. Moreover, with each note he sends a book matching the personal interests of the client: sports, history, travel, gardening. Pollard says his letters and books are intended to say, "You are very important to me, not only professionally, but personally." In the short run, customers typically call Pollard to thank him. But in the longer run, Pollard believes the "higher plane" his relationships attain makes it more likely his clients will approach him with problems. The relationship becomes more robust to inevitable and unnoticed slipups. Pollard gets an extra chance to make things right.[21]

In another instance, a travel agent ordered too many theater tickets for a summertime tour group. By the terms of sale, the theater company did not have to reimburse the agent. But with empathy for what the agent was trying to set up and with an eye toward future business, the theater waived all charges but a $25 cancellation fee.

In a corporation with many employees, this orientation toward the customer must pervade. Furthermore, it must be matched with empowerment. A Marriott bellman called a cab for a departing guest and casually asked about the man's stay. When he grunted that his breakfast was a little late and cold, the bellman confidently stated, "I don't think you should pay for that." He took the man to the front desk and quickly voided the breakfast charges.[22]

Had the bellman gotten any static from the desk manager or the cashier, or if he had needed a manager to sign off, none of the hotel's empowerment seminars would have been worth the scratch pads provided. We are reminded of a quip from Lou Holtz, football coach: "When all is said and done, a lot more is said than done." It's not the *polemics* of service in excess of expectations, but the *practice* that produces payoffs.

# Summary

Despite a tradition and vocabulary of conquest, marketing has embraced the renewed priority of customer retention. Newly assembled data at many firms have shocked managers by detailing the astronomical cost of acquiring one customer. At the same time, fresh looks at the lifetime value of a customer's purchases reveal the huge opportunity loss when a customer "defects."

Our analysis of this marketing challenge profiled two basic types of business relationships: (1) lost-for-good and (2) always-a-share. Lost-for-good could be dubbed stuck-for-a-while because they are cemented by significant switching costs. The buyer cannot easily switch to another supplier because personnel might have to be retrained, product designs would need reworking, downstream customers would be let down, or some aspect of setup would be costly.

Always-a-share customers can taper and restart their purchases. They may be responsive to promotions or price incentives, but lost-for-good customers are cemented by quality service and reliability. Simple NPV models of each type of customer dramatize the retention imperatives of lost-for-good accounts. Furthermore, they point to an emphasis on best customers. If a supplier's retention efforts can realize a 10 percent gain in retention probability, the efforts have a much higher payoff on accounts with a .8 retention likelihood than on accounts with a .5 retention rate.

Beyond the NPV models, lasting customer relationships can provide additional business opportunities through new products, increased purchases, premium prices, and selling efficiency. We can also expect positive reputational spillover from relationships that last.

The overall challenge of customer relationship management was broken down into three processes: building, running, and strengthening. The process of building relationships consists of several interacting devices for bonding. First is the bond attained by superior performance. Customers might ask their best supplier for a price break, but they will seldom ask a cut-rate supplier for blue-ribbon service. The latter just can't do it. Plain and simple, superior performance is a powerful means of securing repeat business.

Social ties also play a key role in business relationships. To cooperate in commercial exchange, parties must comfortably disclose needs and dissatisfaction. A common language, some shared expectations, and reciprocated confidence in each other's abilities and motives are critical to a productive exchange relationship. Thus, social affairs, gifts, and personal interaction can strengthen relational bonds.

We must also consider technical and formal ties between trading parties. If XYZ's video and graphics editing system is built around an Apple computer, Apple and XYZ are cemented by the technical design of the system. Similarly, where I choose to locate my factory to process bauxite into aluminum fairly well settles my limited slate of potential suppliers of electricity.

Finally, contracts can be forged on mutual pledges that bind the trading parties for long-run exchange. The contracting parties know they cannot specify every contingency held in the future. So they establish mechanisms for joint planning and flexibility. They aim to allow dispute resolution and adjustment to occur within the relationship.

The process of running relationships pivots on the presumption of good partner selection, effective communication, and outside help. Trading partners should not expect their counterpart to change. Effective communication includes formal structures for interaction, such as EDI and regularly scheduled meetings; specialists, such as relationship support teams; and professional forums, such as user groups and conferences.

Customer satisfaction surveys have emerged as a widely used tool of customer retention. Typically, criterion measures such as satisfaction and intention to repurchase are modeled statistically as a function of a hierarchy of service attributes, facets, and roles.

Relationships should never be taken for granted. To avoid complacency we proposed business marketers adopt the motto "always higher." Attention to external opportunities and threats as well as to the root cause of internal inefficiencies and underachievements can uncover new avenues for bonding. Furthermore, companywide commitment to and empowerment for delivering lagniappe is a true manifestation of a customer retention priority.

# Key Terms

| | | |
|---|---|---|
| always-a-share relationship | lost-for-good relationship | segmentation marketing specific investments |
| contract | modularity | switching costs |
| lagniappe | | |

# Discussion Questions

1. In March 2007, *BusinessWeek* listed the top 25 firms on customer service, using its own indexing formula. Several B2B firms made the list—UPS, FedEx, Apple, Enterprise Rent-A-Car. And after badly treating customers in the havoc of a snowstorm, JetBlue was stripped from the list just before press time. Noticeably absent is Microsoft. Perhaps its decision to spend $1.2 billion to fix the "red ring of death" for Xbox 360 consumers reflects an aim to make the next *BW* list. What customer service facets should Microsoft measure for Office 2007?

2. For many years the Chicago Marriott Hotel has been a site of the American Marketing Association's Summer Educators' Conference. The AMA conference locale follows a three-year cycle: East Coast, West Coast, Chicago (headquarters of the AMA). Is this an always-a-share or lost-for-good relationship? What sort of ties do you think bond the AMA and the Marriott? How can the Marriott maintain those ties?

3. The Market Rex consulting firm hosted a brunch for several of its key clients at the Tavern on the Green in Manhattan when the major trade show was held at the New York Hilton. Outline three reasons why such an apparent extravagance might be good business practice. Describe three special cautions or hazards in this type of hospitality. Would your answers be the same if it were Pharma Rex hosting physicians at a medical conference in Manhattan?

4. Examine two or three suppliers to your college or university, perhaps a food service, a forms supplier, engineering, or maintenance. What are the bonds in the relationship? How secure is the university or college account?

**5.** List the switching costs for the following situations:

    **a.** A large insurance brokerage moves from its downtown high-rise office to an office in the suburbs.

    **b.** A computer manufacturer switches from Intel to AMD microprocessors.

    **c.** A commercial interior design firm must fire its award-winning, but obnoxious, designer.

    **d.** A small motor manufacturer will terminate its offshore telemarketing operation to bring the operation in house.

**6.** Outline a customer satisfaction survey for your college. First, who are the customers? What arenas and facets will be measured? What are three to five attributes of two of these facets?

**7.** Outline a customer satisfaction survey for a copier company. Now consider the following: 18 percent of customers are dissatisfied, a third of which complain to the company and receive redress such that the company retains 75 percent as customers. Of the dissatisfied customers who do not complain, only 40 percent are retained. From the CRM system at the company, we estimate that retained customers provide $150 in gross profit per year and the average customer acquisition cost runs about $250. Name three points for management attention to improve customer retention. Prepare a model showing potential profit gains from one of these actions, assuming a customer base of 1,000.

**8.** Computer chip manufacturers strive to get computer companies to design machines around their chips. But to get adopted into a design, the chip must typically be licensed to other chip makers. Computer makers are afraid of "holdup" by the chip supplier. How does licensing solve this problem? What can the chip maker do to cement a relationship in the absence of a strict technical tie?

**9.** Professor Gary Frazier at the University of Southern California is one of the world's experts on relationships between firms. Time and again he has shown that a company's track record of performing key functions in a superior fashion is a source of power or bargaining leverage. For example, key roles for cutting tool manufacturers selling through industrial distributors in India are (1) product quality, (2) allocation and delivery of goods, (3) reimbursement for damaged products, (4) distributor assistances (training programs, operation manuals), and (5) a cooperative representative. A manufacturer doing these things well is less likely to coerce its distributors or disagree over key issues than a similar manufacturer doing its job poorly. Indeed, superior role performance correlates very highly with distributor satisfaction with the supplier relationship.

    What are the key roles for a bank, marketing research firm, rental car company, or commercial laundry? Ask two or three professionals who purchase such products to rate the suppliers on these roles and describe how they allocate their purchases to the possible suppliers in one of these areas.

**10.** Lagniappe means exceeding expectations. But what are the origins of customer expectations? Are expectations an important facet of relationship management?

**11.** A guest speaker concluded his presentation to the B2B class with the following: "Customer satisfaction studies are borrowed from consumer marketing. They may be fine for businesses that serve many atomistic customers, such as hotels, overnight couriers, MRO, and cell phone service. But that's not the way to go with large customers. They won't admit to being satisfied because it opens the door to higher supplier prices. They want superior economic value." Do you agree or disagree?

# Cases

## Case 16.1   Has the Fat Lady Sung?

You know that when your *Consumer Reports* subscription is about to expire, the publisher sends appeal after appeal—even beyond expiration—to get your renewal. Such behaviors beg the question, When is a lost customer lost?

Ben Barclay, owner of Barclay Business Products, follows a five-step process that many companies in business markets have employed:

1. *Spot the flagging account.* Key accounts are fairly easy to track through personnel changes and restructuring. But smaller customers may fall through the cracks if not routinely tracked in the customer database.

2. *Find out why the account left.* This may take some digging. Talk to associates with recent or frequent contact with the customer. A face-to-face meeting is a chance to uncover difficulties and missteps. Sometimes a solution can be found.

3. *Request another chance.* An apology and request for another try gets a better response than not asking.

4. *Offer an inducement.* Sometimes the seller needs to buy back the account with a special deal—a customized service or discount.

5. *Mechanize follow-up.* When the face-to-face contact fails, continue goodwill communications and assign the account to a telemarketer to call the account periodically.

At a business where you've worked or by conducting a convenience interview with a friend or family member, describe the particular steps taken with "lost" accounts.

## Case 16.2   Centerberg Courier Strives for Relevance

Rocky's World of Soccer is Centerberg's top retailer of soccer gear and fashions. Rocky Cantino has used a variety of data capture techniques—a newsletter, clinics, and events—to build a file of 15,000 soccer players, parents, and coaches in Centerberg. He bought a 65 PageMaker and in the past three months has run two very successful mail promotions. He spent about $9,000 on each of these mailings and "found" the money for this venture by reducing his newspaper ad budget.

Ron Wilson is advertising rep for the *Centerberg Courier.* He learned of Rocky's newfound interest in direct mail in a recent call to pick up an ad if it was ready. Indeed, noting that Rocky's spending with the paper was running about $16,000 behind last year's pace, Ron took Rocky to breakfast last Friday. Before they went out, Rocky took Ron to the back to show him his Mac and laser printer. Copies of the last letter and minicatalog were on the desk. Ron was surprised and impressed by the quality of work and marketing savvy of Centerberg's former soccer all-star.

At breakfast Wilson praised Rocky's efforts to stay in closer touch with his customers by mail, but underscored the potential to leverage their responses by using multiple media. Indeed, Ron reviewed recent multimedia programs the *Courier* had run with Rotundo's (suits for large men), and the Countryside Jeep Dealership.

Rocky expressed interest in testing a similar program. Ron—with the help of Randall Matrix, the database marketing staff person at the *Courier*—put together a quasi experiment for the next promotion period. Rocky had some great ideas for capturing the identities of purchasers and disclosed that his gross profits averaged 40 percent, including featured merchandise. The key elements and results of this test are outlined below. Your assignment is to interpret the results for decision making and indicate what they mean for the relationship between Rocky's and the *Courier.* Oh, the *Courier* also seemed to bring in 104 new customers to Rocky's.

| Test Group: | 1 | 2 | 3 | Totals |
|---|---|---|---|---|
| Sample size: | 3,000 | 3,000 | 4,000 | 10,000 |
| **Results** | | | | |
| No. transactions | 280 | 220 | 525 | 1,025 |
| $ sales | 12,000 | 8,000 | 20,000 | $40,000 |
| Newspaper advertising costs | | | | $8,000 |
| Minicatalog printing | | | | 3,520 |
| Bulk rate postage and labels | | | | 850 |
| Total costs | | | | $12,370 |

**Group Descriptions**

| Group 1 | These are Rocky's customers who do not subscribe to the *Courier.* They receive only Rocky's minicatalog by mail in this program. |
|---|---|
| Group 2 | These are Rocky's customers who subscribe to the *Courier.* They receive only Rocky's ads in the *Courier.* Rocky does not mail the minicatalog to them in this program. |
| Group 3 | These are Rocky's customers who also subscribe to the *Courier.* They receive both the minicatalog and Rocky's ads in the *Courier.* |

## Case 16.3   Your Serve!

You probably know this firsthand. What a headache when one's computer crashes! The need for Excedrin might be twice that if one's locomotive won't run or crane won't pivot. It's hard to imagine a product that doesn't require service because of damage, malfunction, or need to upgrade. One bit of a surprise from recent CRM applications is the profit potential in aftersale service. Think about a PC. From network administration and tech support to system administration and file management, many experts see service revenue opportunities at about five times the revenue from desktop hardware. And margins on this revenue-favored service beat product margins by 2:1 or better. For locomotives, the service-to-product revenue opportunities are estimated at 20:1.

Until recently manufacturers have neglected these aftersale revenue opportunities because demand for spare parts was unpredictable, failures were nonroutine, parts inventories were extensive, service requirements varied, and service capabilities needed to be locally distributed—and were difficult to control for consistent quality. Those days are fading.

Business marketers can now anticipate customer service requirements. They can offer service contracts and warranties, provide repurchase and upgrade policies, design the product with sensors, and involve the customer in problem diagnosis. Otis Elevator relies on a database to forecast repair needs and stock appropriate parts. Using data on parts' mean time between failure, the size of the installed product base, and product use at the customer level, and the potential for upgrades and adaptations, software vendors such as Servigistics can provide spare parts optimization, identifying needed parts and locations for different service (e.g., fill rate) levels. These tools can aid the tasks of "reverse logistics" for product disposal and recycling, also. Finally, information systems and collaborative strategies allow business marketers to partner with specialists in the provision of after-sale services.[23]

Map the after-sale service opportunities at your school for the air-conditioning equipment, the faculty or student computer workstations, or classroom audiovisual equipment. Evaluate who does what today against what could be obtained with more involvement by the firm whose name is on the equipment.

## Additional Readings

Anton, Jon. *Customer Relationship Management: Making Hard Decisions with Soft Numbers.* Upper Saddle River, NJ: Prentice Hall, 1996, p. 12.

Berry, Michael J. A., and Gordon S. Linoff. *Data Mining Techniques: For Marketing, Sales, and Customer Relationship Management.* Indianapolis, IN: Wiley, 2004.

Bradach, Jeffrey, and Robert Eccles. "Price, Authority and Trust: From Ideal Types to Plural Forms." *Annual Review of Sociology* 15 (1989), pp. 97–118.

Day, George. *The Market Driven Organization: Understanding, Attracting, and Keeping Valuable Customers.* New York: The Free Press, 1999.

Dunfee, Thomas W., N. Craig Smith, and William T. Ross, Jr. "Social Contracts and Marketing Ethics." *Journal of Marketing* 63 (July 1999), pp. 14–32.

Ghosh, Mrinal, Shantanu Dutta, and Sefan Stremersch. "Customizing Complex Products: When Should the Vendor Take Control?" *Journal of Marketing Research* 43 (November 2006), pp. 664–79.

Gupta, Sunil, and Donald R. Lehman. *Managing Customers as Investments.* Upper Saddle River, NJ: Wharton School Publishing (2005).

Jackson, Barbara B. *Winning and Keeping Industrial Customers.* Lexington, MA: Lexington Books, 1985.

Knox, Simon, Stan Maklan, Adrian Payne, Joe Peppard, and Lynette Ryals. *Customer Relationship Management: Perspectives from the Marketplace.* Oxford: Butterworth Heinemann (2003).

Levitt, Theodore. *The Marketing Imagination.* New York: The Free Press, 1983.

McDonald, Malcolm, Beth Rogers, and Diana Woodburn. *Key Customers: How to Manage Them Profitably.* Amsterdam: Elsevier Butterworth Heinemann (2000).

Narayandas, Das, and V. Kasturi Rangan. "Building and Sustaining Buyer-Seller Relationships in Mature Industrial Markets." *Journal of Marketing* 68 (July 2004), pp. 63–77.

Palmatier, Robert W., Lisa Scheer, and Jan-Benedict E. M. Steenkamp. "Customer Loyalty to Whom? Managing the Benefits and Risks of Salesperson-Owned Loyalty." *Journal of Marketing Research* 44 (May 2007), pp. 185–99.

Rust, Roland, Valarie Ziethaml, and Katherine Lemon. *Driving Customer Equity: How Customer Lifetime Value Is Reshaping Corporate Strategy.* New York: The Free Press, 2000.

"Special Section on Customer Relationship Management." *Journal of Marketing* 69 (October 2005), pp. 155–263.

Vavra, Terry G. *Improving Your Measurement of Customer Satisfaction: A Guide to Creating, Conducting, Analyzing, and Reporting Customer Satisfaction Measurement Program.* New York: Marketing Metrics, 1997.

Zeithaml, Valerie, A. Parusuraman, and Leonard Berry. *Delivering Quality Service.* New York: The Free Press, 1995.

# Cases

| Case title & summary | Setting | 1 | 2 | 3 | 4 | 5 | 6 | 7 | 8 | 9 | 10 | 11 | 12 | 13 | 14 | 15 | 16 |
|---|---|---|---|---|---|---|---|---|---|---|---|---|---|---|---|---|---|
| | | | | | | | | | Chapter correspondence (*cont.*) | | | | | | | | |
| 15. **Strategic Marketing Insights.** Marketing research company evaluates customer groups with different relational orientations. | | x | x | x | x | X | X | x | X | | x | | | | x | X | X |
| 16. **SPC Products.** Software engineering subcontractor for a large, well-known firm must cope with uncertainty and tough performance standards. | India & Japan | X | X | X | X | X | X | X | X | X | X | | | X | X | X | X |
| 17. **Three Rivers Optical.** A growing family business with proprietary optical lenses for specific markets must develop a plan for winning new accounts. | U.S.A. | X | X | X | X | X | x | x | x | x | X | X | x | x | | x | x |
| 18. **Whole Tree Energy.™** Entrepreneur's vision and R&D projects show the viability of generating electric power by growing and burning whole trees. Communication planning and scenario forecasting. | U.S.A. | x | x | x | x | X | X | x | | | X | x | x | x | | x | x |

# Blue Track Sourcing

## Introduction

The lobby of the Hyatt Hotel was as good a place as any to kill time waiting for clients to arrive. It was a cool and comfortable place to escape the elements of the summer heat and humidity. And best of all, it was only moments away from the airport where the clients would shortly disembark after a long flight.

Mr. Peter Drechsler was all too familiar with the sequence of events that was about to unfold over the next few hours and into the next few days. Drechsler had arrived in Mumbai, India, a few days earlier. He had finished organizing the program for his clients Mr. Jim Wendle and Mr. Joe Hoffman, who were due to arrive on 11:00 p.m. flight from Milan, and he could relax for a brief moment. The tension returning, Drechsler glanced down at this watch, packed up his laptop, and headed to the main entrance of the hotel to catch a taxi to the airport. As he left the hotel, a slight sprinkle dropped from the dark, dense night sky and the bell hop commented that the monsoon season was, "so close to finally starting again to provide some relief from the long, hot dry spell." Drechsler hoped that he was wrong and that the rains would hold off at least until his clients had completed their trip to India and the audit of his company: Blue Track Sourcing. The monsoon rains are notorious for causing traffic snarls and excruciating travel times between the different meeting locations across Mumbai. The Mumbai trans-portation system didn't need additional challenges to complicate an already overloaded network of streets and highways that typically operated in constant gridlock.

## Background

Drechsler's first visit to India was in 1998 when he was asked to conduct a training seminar on equipment qualification and validation for the Indian team in charge of constructing a new pharmaceutical plant. He was living in Germany at the time and had conducted similar training sessions throughout Europe. He vividly remembered the first time he landed in Mumbai on a similar dark night eight years earlier. An Indian businessman sitting across from him on the plane could sense his apprehension after the plane landed and felt compelled to dole out some wisdom as he collected his carry-on bag and prepared to disembark from the plane. "Is this your first trip to India?' the man asked. "Yes," Drechsler quickly replied. The man looked him straight in the eyes and said, "Well, you are not going to like this place until your third trip." Having shrugged it off as friendly small talk from a stranger on an airplane, he later understood the truth of the message behind the man's words. After the initial trip, Drechsler returned to India five times over the next year. Only after the third trip did he finally begin to understand and enjoy India.

Drechsler's first few trips were filled with constant frustration from expecting Western standards in the rapidly developing country. But, after the third trip, he learned to accept the current level of standards

Peter Drechsler prepared this for the purposes of class discussion. Used with permission.

and stopped searching for the things he took for granted while living in the West. Instead, he focused his energy on enjoying the differences in culture, food, and business and took the time to learn and understand the people. That effort paid off years later when he started his company called Blue Track Sourcing to provide engineering and architectural services to clients from the United States via a technical center in Mumbai. Drechsler had first-hand experience working with technical resources in India on numerous projects and was convinced that their level of competency was equivalent to his colleagues' in the West. The business model for Blue Track Sourcing was to offshore work associated with well-defined portions of technical projects to a team in India. The lower labor rates in India provided cost savings opportunities for Western companies even after management and overhead costs were factored into the equation.

## The Key Component

The cost savings opportunities always attracted the attention of perspective new clients upon whom Drechsler called. But the initial euphoria was always checked with the same series of questions: "What about quality?" "What about confidentiality and intellectual property protection?" "Do they speak English?" Concerns about quality, data security, and communication skills were the main reasons Wendle and Hoffman made the trip from Cincinnati, Ohio, to Mumbai. They needed to experience it personally and be convinced Blue Track Sourcing was capable of handling the project they planned to award.

Drechsler had been working with Wendle and Hoffman for over a year, trying to convince them to use the services of Blue Track Sourcing. Finally, Wendle told Drechsler, "In order to persuade my clients that it is the right thing to do, I need to better understand the risks involved with outsourcing." With that, Drechsler offered to host them on a trip to India to "see for themselves" and then make a decision. Wendle accepted the offer and Drechsler organized an agenda designed to audit and "thoroughly check out the capabilities of Blue Track Sourcing."

The commitment was a good sign that future business was possible, but the visit by Wendle and Hoffman had to be completed without any problems. Drechsler drew upon his years of experience of working in India and knew every last detail that needed to be addressed to pull off a successful visit. The mission was simple—to demonstrate that the Blue Track Sourcing operation was a competent and secure organization capable of handling a technical project from the West. The travel plans included a comfortable hotel for the clients to rest after a 22 hour journey, along with a detailed plan even covering where each meal was to be consumed. Drechsler knew that keeping the clients healthy was just as important as showing them technical competency.

## Plan Execution

It was no surprise when Drechsler arrived at the airport that the client's plane was slightly delayed, but it wasn't long before the two travel-weary clients emerged into the sea of people gathered outside the International terminal. Drechsler had assured them that he would be there to meet them and escort them back to the hotel. A former British boss of Drechsler once told him that "Darkness is very kind to India." This basically translates that tremendous ugliness can be covered up by nightfall. The two clients had no idea what life was like past the lights outside the airport terminal or what lay beyond the headlights of the taxi en route to the hotel. Only in the morning, drawing back the curtains of their hotel room windows, they would understand the real India they had gotten themselves into. But for now, the landscape and bustling city streets appeared normal as viewed during the taxi ride between the airport and the hotel. The hotel check-in went smoothly. After the clients had their room keys, Drechsler informed them he would meet them in the lobby at 9:00 a.m. for breakfast. The additional challenge of this visit was to factor in the 9½ hour time difference between Cincinnati and Mumbai. Assuring that the clients stayed awake and alert was essential for success.

Breakfast turned out to be the kickoff for a three-day meeting that rolled along without a hitch. Wendle and Hoffman started slowly each morning, but gathered steam as the day went on and provided feedback that the meetings were going well. They were increasingly convinced that they could accept the risk of outsourcing a project to India. The agenda was full of meetings with both Blue Track Sourcing personnel and pre-selected subcontractors that Blue Track Sourcing planned to use to supplement the internal team. Drechsler had coached everyone before the meeting to relax and be natural, knowing that it was technical expertise that Wendle and Hoffman were really looking for. All the engineers chosen to meet the clients were seasoned veterans in the field of engineering, and graduates of some of the top technical universities in India. All were capable of going toe-to-toe with any engineer in the clients' Cincinnati office.

The wrap-up meeting on the final day was rather anti-climatic due to the constant feedback provided throughout the visit. The clients commented on how smoothly everything went and appreciated that all the details, down to knowing which location in the hotel lobby would have the best wireless connection for them to check e-mail, had been anticipated and provided.

The only thing left on the agenda was a final dinner before Wendle and Hoffman left for the airport later in the evening. Drechsler carefully selected some of the top people with whom Wendle and Hoffman had met during the visit to attend this wrap-up dinner. The plan was to provide one last opportunity to sell the competence of Blue Track Sourcing. However, at that point in the visit, Wendle and Hoffman were already convinced and were more interested in learning about the human side of India. The dinner conversation even drifted into the dangerous topics of politics and religion before it was time to head for the airport. A short, uneventful taxi ride between the hotel restaurant and airport concluded a flawless visit. Drechsler was scheduled to remain in Mumbai a few more days and wished his clients a safe trip back to Cincinnati. Drechsler let out a sigh of relief after the clients proceeded to the check-in terminals, knowing that the trip was a success. He was already looking forward to a follow-up meeting in Cincinnati to address the few easy-to-solve outstanding issues noted during the visit.

## The Current Situation

The Blue Track Sourcing Company successfully delivered a significant project for Wendle and Hoffman and used it as a case study to convince other clients of their capabilities. Drechsler understood the importance of a successful client visit and knew the potential outcome if they were able to secure and complete a large project. The project proved pivotal to the start-up of Blue Track Sourcing Company and helped it to become established as a legitimate contender among those offering outsourcing services.

## Discussion

Blue Track Sourcing's Business Model depends on its ability first to convince new clients that Outsourcing work is a good idea and then that Offshoring that Outsourced work makes sense. What factors are critical to the success of the Business Model?

> What are the threats to the long-term success of Blue Track Sourcing?
> What is the importance of trust in the client relationship and how can it be measured and tracked?

# Calox Machinery Corporation (A)

Mike Brown, international sales manager, tapped his pencil on the notepad and contemplated his upcoming discussion with Calox's executive committee concerning the distributor situation in New Zealand. The Labor Day weekend break had not been especially conducive to his sorting out the conflicting information and varied opinions concerning the New Zealand predicament. After only three months on the job Mike had not expected to be involved in a decision that would have such far-reaching consequences.

On paper the decision looked simple: whether or not to adhere to his earlier decision to replace the original New Zealand distributor, Glade Industries, with a newly formed company, Calox New Zealand, Ltd. Despite his newness to the company, Mike was confident that Calox's executive committee would agree with whatever recommendations he made in this situation, because he had been charged with "solidifying" the International Sales Division. If he decided to reverse his decision to terminate Glade Industries, could he "undo" any damage done so far?

By Lester A. Neidell of the University of Tulsa. This case was written with the cooperation of management, solely for the purpose of stimulating student discussion. Data are based on field research in the organization. All events and individuals are real, but names have been disguised at the company's request. Faculty members in nonprofit institutions are encouraged to reproduce this case for distribution to their own students without charge or written permission. All other rights reserved jointly to the author and the North American Case Research Association (NACRA). Copyright © 1993 by the *Case Research Journal* and Lester A. Neidell.

Three previous faxes were spread on his desk along with the brief notes that he had jotted down during Thursday's conference call between Calox's executives and the company's legal counsel. Mike swung back to the PC behind his desk and began to draft what he hoped would be the definitive Calox policy for New Zealand.

## The Company

Calox Machinery Company began in 1946 as a partnership between John Caliguri and William Oxley. The two engineers met during World War II and discovered mutual interests in mechanical engineering and construction. Both were natives of Kansas City, and at the end of the war they established a partnership with the expressed purpose of developing high-quality excavation equipment and accessories. Their first product was an innovative hydraulically operated replacement blade for a light-duty scraper.

Calox's principal customers were independent contractors engaged in excavation of building sites and airport and highway construction and maintenance. Calox's products were primarily replacement items for OEM (original equipment manufacturer) parts and accessories. Some OEM sales were achieved; that is, contractors could order new equipment from OEMs with Calox blades and accessories already installed. Growth over the years was slow, but steady.

The product line expanded to include payloader buckets, a number of dozer and scraper blades, and parts for aerial equipment including construction forklifts and snorkels. A key to the company's success was their specialty status; their products were used to enhance the performance of expensive equipment produced by Caterpillar, Eaton, International Harvester, Case, and other OEMs. Calox's strategy was simply to provide a better part, often at a premium price, and to have it readily available in the field through a network of strong distributors. Direct competitors in the United States included small specialty producers such as Bobcat, Dresser, and Gradall, as well as the parts divisions of the large OEM manufacturers. Primary competitors in international markets included Terex, Deutsch, Takeuchi, and Hitachi. William Oxley compared Calox to the Cummins Engine Company, which had achieved a superior position in the diesel engine market through a similar strategy.

The partnership was replaced by an incorporated structure in 1970, when Bill Oxley, Jr., became CEO. Despite slow growth of the U.S. economy, both 1990 and 1991 were very good years for Calox; annual sales increases of 12 percent were achieved, and the company set profit records each year. Sales for the 1991 fiscal year broke the $70 million barrier for the first time in the company's history. That year, approximately 280 people were employed at the single location in Kansas City, of whom three-fourths were hourly workers engaged in fabrication.

## International Sales

Calox's first international sale occurred in 1971, when the company responded to an unsolicited inquiry and shipped a small order to Canada. International sales languished throughout the 1970s, when a great deal of construction was put on hold due to the "energy crisis." Channels of distribution for international sales were much the same as for domestic sales. Independent distributors were given nonexclusive rights, although in practice most countries had only one distributor. Forty of Calox's 110 distributors were located outside the United States. In 1991 almost 25 percent of Calox's sales were generated internationally. In the 1988 to 1991 period, aided by the relative decline of the U.S. dollar against most other currencies, international sales grew at an annual rate of 16 percent.

Prior to Mike's arrival, there was no uniform procedure by which Calox investigated foreign markets and appointed distributors outside the United States. Bill Lawrence, Mike Brown's predecessor, essentially ran export sales as a one-man operation. Because Calox had very limited international experience, and most international markets were relatively small compared to the United States, primary market research was considered to be an unnecessary expense. In those countries guesstimated to have large enough markets, Bill obtained a list of potential distributors by advertising in that country's construction journal(s) (if available) and principal newspapers. He then made a personal visit to interview and select distributors. In smaller markets, distributors were appointed through one of two methods. Most commonly, Bill appointed a distributor after receiving an unsolicited request. In a very few cases, distributor applications were solicited via advertisements as in "large" markets, which were then reviewed in Kansas City. In all cases in which personal visits were not made, distributor applicants had to submit financial statements. Efforts to interview distributor applicants by telephone were not always successful, due to time constraints and the lack of a suitable translation service.

### The New Zealand Distributorship

In 1986 Calox appointed G.W. Diggers, Ltd., as its agent for New Zealand. This arrangement was a novel one, for G.W. Diggers was also a producer of excavating equipment. Because of some earlier poor experiences in certain foreign markets, Calox had instituted a policy of not distributing through any company that also manufactured excavating equipment. This policy was not followed in New Zealand because of the limited distributorship options available. At the time of the appointment, the owner of G.W. Diggers, Geoffrey Wiggins, assured Calox that the two lines were complementary rather than competitive, and that he intended to keep it that way. During 1989, G.W. Diggers purchased $800,000 of equipment and supplies from Calox.

In 1990 an abrupt change occurred in what had been a very successful, if short, relationship. G.W. Diggers was purchased by a large New Zealand conglomerate, Excel Ltd., which gave a new name, Glade Industries, to its excavating facility. The former owner of G.W. Diggers, Geoff Wiggins, was not associated with Glade Industries.

**Exhibit 1**
Annual Sales to
G.W. Diggers
and Glade
Industries
(in thousands of U.S.
dollars)

| | Sales to G.W. Diggers | | | | Sales to Glade | | |
| --- | --- | --- | --- | --- | --- | --- | --- |
| | **1986** | **1987** | **1988** | **1989** | **1990** | **1991** | **1992 (6 months)** |
| | 21 | 310 | 535 | 801 | 105 | 70 | 10 |

Mike Brown's predecessor felt that the acquisition by Glade could only help Calox's position in New Zealand, because the resources available through Excel, Glade's parent company, were so much greater than what had been available to G.W. Diggers.

However, it soon became apparent that working with Glade was going to be very challenging. Glade raised prices on all Calox products in stock. Then they complained that Calox products were not selling well and that a "rebate" was needed to make Calox's products competitive in the New Zealand market. Simultaneously, Glade began production of a line of products competitive with Calox, but of a substantially poorer quality. During 1991 sales to Glade were virtually zero, and market information obtained by Calox indicated that Calox's former position in the New Zealand market was being occupied by Wescot Industries, with products imported from Great Britain. Exhibit 1 gives annual sales of Calox products to G.W. Diggers and to its successor, Glade Industries.

Mike Brown began his new job as international sales manager for Calox in June 1992. A few weeks after arriving at Calox, Mike received a long letter from Geoff Wiggins. Geoff suggested that the situation in New Zealand was critical, and that he would be willing and able to establish a new distributorship, Calox New Zealand, Ltd., to the exclusive distributors of the Calox product line. Mike then invited Geoff to come to Kansas City the last week of July to discuss the proposal. Mike found Geoff to be very affable, technically knowledgeable, and an excellent marketing person. In the time period since selling his business to Excel Ltd. Geoff had been working as a general contractor. The 24-month "no-compete" clause Geoff had signed when he sold G.W. Diggers had expired. Geoff provided figures that indicated New Zealand's 1991 imports of excavating equipment were roughly NZ$2 million, out of a total domestic market of nearly NZ$3 million. (In 1991, US$1 equaled NZ$0.62.) He claimed that G.W. Diggers had achieved, at the height of its success, almost a 50 percent share of the New Zealand market. Geoff argued persuasively that with his personal knowledge of New Zealand's needs, Calox could once again achieve a dominant market position. With the blessing of the vice president of marketing, Mike and Geoff shook hands on a deal, with the exact details to be worked out by mail and faxed over the next few weeks. Geoff urged that time was of the essence if Wescot's market advances were to be slowed, and left a $100,000 order for 75 units to be shipped in 120 days, but not later than November 15, 1992.

## Communications with Glade

Mike began to prepare a letter of termination to Glade. However, before this was completed, Calox received three mailed orders from Glade, totaling $81,000. This was the first contact Mike had with Glade and the first order received from Glade in 5 months. Because the standard distributor's agreement required a 60-day termination notice, Mike felt the Glade orders had to be honored.

A short time later Calox received a letter in the mail from Glade stating that they had heard rumors that another company was going to supply Calox products to Glade's customers and that delivery had been promised within 150 days. The letter continued by saying that this information could not possibly be true because Glade had an exclusive distributor agreement. This was news to Mike as well as to others at Calox headquarters because it was against company policy to grant exclusive distributorships. A search of Bill Lawrence's files turned up a copy of the initial correspondence to Geoff Wiggins, in which Geoff was thanked for his hospitality and a sole distributorship arrangement was mentioned. However, the distributorship agreement signed with Wiggins was the standard one, giving either party the ability to cancel the agreement with 60 days' notice.

Mike and the other senior Calox executives assessed the situation at length. The letter mentioning the "sole distributor agreement" was in a file separate from all other New Zealand correspondence. It was nothing more than a statement of intent and probably not legally binding in the United States. However, New Zealand courts might not agree. Further, the distributorship agreement should have been renegotiated when Excel purchased G.W. Diggers, but this had not happened. Glade could make a case that the distributorship had endured for two years under the existing agreements, which included the letter in which exclusivity was mentioned.

Mike determined that the "sole distributorship" letter also contained "extenuating circumstances" language that Calox could use to justify supplying the new New Zealand distributorship:

> [T]here may be occasions in the future, when, due to unforeseen circumstances, some entity in your nation refuses to purchase any other way than direct from our factory. We do not want to lose any potential sales; however we pledge our best efforts to cooperate with you for any such possible sales should they present themselves and provided there is a reasonable profit to be made on such sales by us and cooperation can be worked out.

The letter also specifically stated that all agreements between Calox and G.W. Diggers were subject to the laws of Missouri. Furthermore, Mike felt that Glade had not lived up to the actual signed distributorship agreement in that Glade had not promoted Calox products, had not maintained adequate inventory, and had engaged in activities and trade practices that were injurious to Calox's good name.

Armed with this information, Mike sought legal counsel, both in the United States and New Zealand. After a week, Calox's U.S. attorney, based on their own investigations and those of a law firm in Christchurch, New Zealand, offered four "unofficial" observations:

1. New Zealand is a "common law" nation, whose commercial law is similar to that of the United States.

2. It was possible to argue that because G.W. Diggers had changed ownership, previous agreements might not be binding. However, the most likely court finding would be that there was an implied contract between Calox and Glade on the same terms as with G.W. Diggers, because numerous business dealings between Calox and Glade had occurred after the takeover.

3. Calox was required to give Glade 60 days' termination notice.

4. There was a possibility that a New Zealand court would agree to assume jurisdiction of the case.

After reviewing the above issues Mike suggested to Calox senior management that Glade be terminated. Mike reasoned that Glade would react in one of two ways. One possibility was that they would accept termination, perhaps suggesting some minor compensation. A second scenario was that Glade would attempt to renegotiate the distributorship agreement. Mike was instructed to draft and fax a termination letter to Glade. This letter, sent by fax on August 20, is reproduced in Exhibit 2. The next day the first order for the new distributorship was shipped; the expected arrival date in New Zealand was October 10, 1992.

Glade's faxed reply, dated August 24, was not encouraging (see Exhibit 3). It appeared that Mike and the rest of the Calox management team had miscalculated. Despite the tone of the Glade letter, and the expressed request to ship order #52557, Mike suggested to the executive committee that no additional product be shipped to Glade.

While Mike and the rest of Calox management was deciding how to respond to Glade's initial rejection of the termination letter, a longer fax, one with a more conciliatory tone, dated August 31, was received from Glade (see Exhibit 4). In this letter Glade argued that Calox's best interests were served by working with Glade and mentioned an order for approximately 10 times the "normal" amount of product. However, the order was not transmitted with the fax letter. Glade offered (for the first time) to come to Kansas City for a visit.

Glade's conciliatory letter created a great deal of consternation at Calox headquarters. Its arrival the week before Labor Day meant that holiday plans would have to be placed on the back burner while a

**Exhibit 2**
Fax from Calox to Glade, August 20, 1992

Calox Company, Inc.                                      August 20, 1992
P.O. Box 21110
Kansas City, MO 64002
U.S.A.

Mr. Ian Wells
Group General Manager
Glade Industries
39 Ames Road
Christchurch, New Zealand 2221

Dear Mr. Wells:

This letter is to inform you that Calox Company terminates any International Distributor's Sales Agreement or other Distribution Agreement that you may have or be a party to as Distributor expressly or impliedly with Calox Co. as Manufacturer. Said termination is effective 60 days from the date of this letter.

During the past year the following have gravely concerned us and effectively shut off our sales to the New Zealand market.

Reorganization of G.W. Diggers under Glade leading to continuous loss of personnel knowledgeable of the excavation business and difficulty for Calox's understanding with whom we are doing business. In June 1990, we were advised by telex that we were dealing with Excel Ltd., not G.W. Diggers or Glade.

Only $10,000 purchases for an eight-month long period from us, which we clearly found led to major loss of Calox sales to the marketplace and a complete domination of the excavation business by Wescot Industries, a major competitor.

Lack of effort on the part of Glade in promoting our product and maintaining effective selling facilities.

Numerous complaints to us from Customers in New Zealand about Glade continually changing policies, lack of stock, and wildly increasing prices have clearly pointed out that our reputation, as well as G.W. Diggers', has been badly hurt and will impair sales for some time to come.

No progress has been made in introducing our heavy industrial line to the New Zealand market despite assurances from Glade personnel that progress would be made.

We have thoroughly investigated the New Zealand Market and now have firmly decided that it is time for Calox to make a change in its distribution of products.

For the long term, this will allow us to best carve out a full niche in a market we and you have allowed competitors to dominate for too long. We must guarantee ourselves a consistent, aggressive sales effort in the market, which will not be subject to the effects of major policy changes such as those we have seen from Glade.

While two shipments are already en route to you, order number 52557 has not yet been completed for shipment. Since it will be ready imminently, please let us know immediately whether you wish, under the circumstances, to receive shipment or to cancel this order.

Sincerely,

Michael Brown
International Sales Manager

**Exhibit 3**
Fax from
Glade to
Calox, August
24, 1992

Glade Industries                                              24 August 1992
39 Ames Road
Christchurch, New Zealand 2221

Mr. Michael Brown
International Sales Manager
Calox Company, Inc.
P.O. Box 21110
Kansas City, MO 64002
U.S.A.

Dear Sir:

We acknowledge receipt of your letter dated 20 August 1992.

We are currently discussing its contents with our solicitors. They are also reviewing the distribution agreement.

Please proceed with the shipment of order #52557.

Yours faithfully,

GLADE INDUSTRIES LTD.
Ian Wells
Group General Manager

suitable response was formulated. Two distinct camps developed within Calox.

One set of managers, whose position was supported by Mike Brown, felt strongly that despite potential legal risks, retaining Glade as a distributor would be a bad business decision. Although Glade had made promises and was offering to renegotiate, it was still producing a competitive line. Also, Glade's historical performance did not augur well for Calox's long-term competitive situation in New Zealand. The "extraordinary" order was viewed as a ploy to entice Calox into continuing the relationship. It was likely to take upwards of two years for all that machinery to clear the New Zealand market. Cognizant of Glade's earlier price manipulations, many of this group felt that Glade might resort to "fire sale" prices when confronted with a large inventory, further damaging Calox's reputation as a premier supplier.

This camp considered that Calox's long-term interests would best be served by terminating the Glade distributorship and completing a formal agreement with Geoff Wiggins. However, there was concern that outright rejection of the Glade order would add to potential legal problems.

These managers also suggested that any further correspondence with Glade should emphasize that Calox could and would exercise a unique product repurchase option on termination of the distributorship. This provision in the distributorship contract provided that Calox, on proper termination of the distributorship by either party, could repurchase all remaining Calox inventory from the distributor at 80 percent of its net sales price to the distributor. Thus, if Calox did produce and ship the large Glade order, Calox would, if the order were shipped normally via sea freight, be able to buy it back for 80 percent of the price paid by Glade before it ever reached New Zealand.

The alternative camp wanted to forestall any legal battles. Headed by the U.S. sales manager and the comptroller, they argued that Glade had finally "gotten its act together" and that the new Glade team of three sales executives would provide greater market coverage than Geoff Wiggins's "one-man show." This group introduced the possibility of re-opening negotiations with Glade, supplying Glade by diverting the order already shipped to Geoff Wiggins, and producing the (yet unreceived) large Glade order.

By Wednesday, September 2, the two sides had hardened their positions. Mike was determined to break with Glade and begin anew in New Zealand. However, he was concerned about legal

**Exhibit 4**
Fax from
Glade to
Calox, August
31, 1992

Glade Industries                                    31 August 1992
39 Ames Road
Christchurch, New Zealand 2221

Mr. Michael Brown
International Sales Manager
Calox Company, Inc.
P.O.Box 21110
Kansas City, MO 64002
U.S.A.

Dear Sir:

I refer to your letter dated 20 August 1992, terminating our agreement which was executed on 28 February 1986.

In accordance with this agreement and attached to this letter is our order #A1036, for 600 products and parts. We would be pleased if you would confirm this order in due course.

We respectfully ask that you reconsider your termination decision as we believe that it is not in your best interests for the following reasons:

1. G.W. Diggers/Glade were not achieving an adequate return on investment until June 1991. An unprofitable distributor certainly is not in your best interests as principal.

2. The individuals that contributed to that unprofitable performance are no longer working for our company. Incidentally I understand that you have appointed Mr. Geoffrey Wiggins to a position as distributor in New Zealand. How can you justify appointing the person responsible for your market share decline over the past three years?

3. Our purchases certainly have been reduced the last nine months due to our need to get inventory down to lift overall return on investment. That situation has now been corrected with the order attached to this letter.

4. We now have a young aggressive marketing team, all highly experienced in marketing products of a similar nature to yours. When Bill Lawrence was in New Zealand, I advised him that I was restructuring our marketing group. A resume on our three senior marketing men is attached. These men have all commenced in the last four months. I am confident that this team will achieve market leadership in New Zealand and selected export markets with or without Calox's involvement. We have already commenced targeting Wescot's customers. Our recommendation is that you renegotiate your distribution agreement with us, with the inclusion of mutually agreed performance targets which will satisfy your objectives in terms of profitability and market share from the New Zealand market. I would like you to advise me a time which is convenient to you, for me to meet with you in Kansas City to commence negotiation of this distributor agreement.

Yours faithfully,

GLADE INDUSTRIES LTD
Ian Wells
Group General Manager

These are the three new men who have commenced to work for us:

Sean Cox, Sales Manager
35 years old. Formerly CEO of Sean Cox Industries of Christchurch. SCI was the chief contractor for the Auckland airport, but sold its business to Midland Industries. Mr. Cox has fifteen years' experience in the construction industry.

Joshua Dunn, Sales Representative, North Island
46 years old. Formerly an independent sales representative for various equipment manufacturers, including Hitachi and Ford New Holland.

Brian Muldoon, Sales Representative, South Island
23 years old. Construction engineering degree from New South Wales Institute of Technology (Sydney, Australia). Formerly a management trainee with our parent company, Excel Ltd.

ramifications, and, on Thursday, September 3, Calox's executive committee and Mike conferred with their Kansas City attorneys via a conference call.

The lawyers agreed that any further business conducted with Glade would be detrimental to a termination decision. They warned that despite the termination letter (Exhibit 2) any further shipments to Glade would likely yield a court ruling that the distributorship was still in effect and, furthermore, that the buyback provision could not be enacted. They also said that if all business with Glade were terminated, and Glade did come to the United States to file, the most they would be likely to receive if they won the court case were the profits on the new sales to Geoff Wiggins, which amounted to $10,000. This sum was probably not large enough to warrant legal action by Glade, especially considering the apparently poor financial situation at Glade and the expense of initiating legal action in the United States.

At the end of this conference call, which lasted about 30 minutes, Bill Oxley, Jr., turned to Mike and said, "Mike, I'm off to the lake now for the holiday. I'd like your recommendation Tuesday morning on this Glade thing."

# Calox Machinery Corporation (B)

Mike Brown decided that, despite the potential legal risks, sound business practice dictated that he follow through with the termination of Glade's distributorship, and his recommendation to that effect was accepted by the Calox executive committee. Mike's letter fax of September 9 (Exhibit 1) was very specific. First, he restated that it was in the best interests of both parties to terminate the distributorship. Second, because there was no prospect that the Glade order could be completed and delivered prior to the termination date of October 20, 1992 (60 days from the first letter; see Case A, Exhibit 2), he made it known that Calox would exercise its buyback option if Glade did indeed forward the missing order. Following legal advice, Mike added the caveat, "We are open to your comments, of course." The legal reasoning behind this was that if Calox did begin producing the large Glade order, and then bought it back while it was on the open seas, it could be interpreted by the courts that Calox was deliberately attempting to damage Glade financially.

Glade's "hardball" reply (Exhibit 2) was discouraging. In it Glade requested an accounting of sales to other distributors, claiming that they (Glade) were legally entitled to recover all Calox profits from these sales. Several Calox executives began to waffle, and proposed again the solution of diverting the order already shipped to Geoff Wiggins, producing the (still unreceived) large Glade order, and renegotiating with Glade (see Case A).

Before an acceptable response could be agreed upon, another fax (Exhibit 3) was received from Glade. In this conciliatory letter, Glade offered to forgo any claims if their large order was completed and if Calox agreed not to exercise their buyback right.

Calox management breathed a huge sigh of relief and instructed Mike to inquire about the specifics of the order, complete it, ship it to Glade, and be done with them! Mike, however, felt it was necessary to obtain additional legal counsel before doing this.

The lawyers were emphatically negative. They felt quite strongly that if Calox shipped the large order, the courts would rule the original agreement binding, despite all the communication about termination. The courts would interpret the correspondence as a ploy by Calox designed to coerce Glade into placing a large order. They reiterated their previous advice that at the current time, Glade could only obtain minimal damages in U.S. courts; it would hardly be worth Glade's time and energy.

Mike and the company's legal counsel agreed that a final letter had to be written to Glade that would summarize the communications between Calox and Glade and make perfectly clear Calox's position. This letter had to clearly impart that Calox, with the

By Lester A. Neidell. This case was written with the cooperation of management, solely for the purpose of stimulating student discussion. Data are based on field research in the organization. All events and individuals are real, but names have been disguised at the company's request. Faculty members in nonprofit institutions are encouraged to reproduce this case for distribution to their own students without charge or written permission. All other rights reserved jointly to the author and the North American Case Research Association (NACRA). Copyright © 1993 by the *Case Research Journal* and Lester A. Neidell.

**Exhibit 1**
Fax from Calox
to Glade,
September
9, 1992

Calox Company, Inc.                                      September 9, 1992
P.O. 21110
Kansas City, MO 64002
U.S.A.

Mr. Ian Wells
Group General Manager
Glade Industries
39 Ames Road
Christchurch, New Zealand 2221

Dear Mr. Wells:

Reference your 31 August letter, we must regretfully advise that we feel it is in our best interest to continue with our termination of sales to Glade Ltd. as we explained. We appreciate the points you made in your letter, but nevertheless remain convinced that working with Glade Industries Ltd. is not the best way for Calox to achieve its goals in New Zealand.

While we have not yet received your order number A1036 for 600 items referenced in your letter, I should point out that first, Calox is not able to complete an order for all 600 items prior to the termination date, and second, we would want to exercise our option to purchase back all good outstanding products at 80% of our net selling price.

In consideration of these factors, we do not believe it advisable to accept your offer. We feel that this would only affect your situation and we do not seek to take advantage of you in this regard. We are open to your comments, of course.

Sincerely,

Michael Brown
International Sales Manager

**Exhibit 2**
Fax from
Glade to
Calox,
September
14, 1992

Glade Industries                                         14 September 1992
39 Ames Road
Christchurch, New Zealand 2221

Mr. Michael Brown
International Sales Manager
Calox Company, Inc.
P.O. Box 21110
Kansas City, MO 64002
U.S.A.

Dear Sir:

I acknowledge receipt of your letter of 9 September 1992.

I am very concerned at the position in which Calox Co. has been selling direct into New Zealand to Glade's customers. This is in direct contravention of your obligations and undertakings under the Distributor Agreement between us and in particular in breach of the undertaking contained in your letter of 27th January 1986.

We have clearly suffered loss and damage as a result of these actions on your part in breach of the Distributor Agreement which we would be entitled to recover in legal proceedings.

We therefore seek from you a full account of all sales made by you direct into New Zealand in breach of the agreement and payment to us of all profits made by you in respect of those sales.

Yours faithfully,

Glade Industries, Ltd.
Ian Wells
Group General Manager

**Exhibit 3**
Fax from
Glade to
Calox,
September
17, 1992

Glade Industries                                          17 September, 1992
39 Ames Road
Christchurch, New Zealand 2221

Mr. Michael Brown
International Sales Manager
Calox Company, Inc.
P.O. Box 21110
Kansas City, MO 64002
U.S.A.

Dear Sir:

I refer to my open letter of 14 September 1992.

As indicated in that letter we are most concerned at the loss and damage we have suffered by your acting contrary to the terms of the existing Distributor Agreement.

We are, however, prepared to forgo our rights in relation to those breaches in return for your agreeing to supply the 600 items referred to in our order #A1036 and not to seek to exercise any rights of repurchase in relation to those items upon termination of the agreement.

Yours faithfully,

Glade Industries Ltd.
Ian Wells
Group General Manager

advice of legal counsel, did not recognize as valid Glade's claim that any agreement had been breached. Glade, in fact, had violated the previous distributorship agreement by failing to market Calox's products. Due to Glade's negligence, Calox had sustained damage to their reputation and good name, so that any legal recompense would be forthcoming to Calox. Calox's intent in the New Zealand market was to repair the damage that Glade had done to Calox's reputation by forging ahead with an aggressive new distributor.

# Daynor Chemical Company

Daynor Chemical Company is finalizing four years of development efforts on a new agricultural chemical formulation (mixture of active ingredient and other materials that enable the product to be diluted with water so it can be sprayed on crops) of a product called MDA. This new dry formulation may potentially replace a long-standing, well-established current liquid formulation. The primary reason for this new product was to develop a formulation that can be packaged in water-soluble bags, thereby eliminating a container disposal problem that existed with liquid formulations.

Modern agriculture depends heavily on pesticides. Estimated usage in one recent year, according to the USDA, exceeded 330,000 tons. Even in very small quantities, some of these pesticides can have substantial impact on the environment. As a result, there has been a growing concern in recent years for protecting the environment from undue pesticide contamination. Empty pesticide containers may create serious hazards for farm families, farm workers, animals, and the environment, so disposal of the empty cans, barrels, bags, bottles, and plastic containers accumulated in the course of using pesticides is becoming a serious issue.

Pesticide labels require that empty containers be rinsed at least three times (triple rinsing). This triple-rinse procedure should be done immediately after the container is emptied according to the following procedure:

- Empty all concentrate in the container into the mix/spray tank, letting it drain thoroughly (at least 30 seconds).
- Fill the container one-fourth full of water if it is designed to hold less than five gallons, one-fifth full if it holds five gallons or more.
- Replace the closure; then agitate the container so that the rinse contacts all of the interior surfaces.
- Pour rinse into the mix/spray tank, allowing the container to drain for 30 seconds after emptying.
- Repeat the rinsing procedure at least two more times.
- Puncture, crush, and dispose of the empty, rinsed containers at approved landfills or recycling facilities.

Despite these regulations, the federal government and several states were concerned about the residues left in pesticide containers and the disposal problems associated with plastic containers. Plastic containers have the further disadvantage of not being biodegradable. Some states had even begun to require that manufacturers accept the empty containers back from users, and others were considering imposing taxes or fees to cover disposal costs. Although no states are currently charging farmers for container disposal, there have been proposals that indicate that a surcharge of up to $1.00/one-gallon plastic container might become a possibility in the near future, especially if comparable products are available in water-soluble packaging. These container disposal problems

This case was prepared by Michael T. Smith, Christian Brothers University, Memphis, Tennessee, for discussion purposes only; the company described and data presented have been disguised. Used with permission of the author.

were only expected to become more widespread and severe in the future. A further advantage of the water-soluble bags would be the elimination of any possible human contact with the product because the farm workers will simply toss the entire bag into the spray tank for mixing with water prior to application to the crop. Although MDA is considered relatively non-toxic, anything that reduces potential exposure to pesticides is desirable.

Daynor is a major supplier of MDA to market, controlling about a 35 to 40 percent market share. Daynor faces two competitors in this market, Multi-Chemical and Seacoast Products. Multi-Chemical has about the same market share as Daynor, and Seacoast has the remainder. Neither competitor has a commercially available dry product, although Multi-Chemical had marketed a dry formulation for the potato market segment in the past with relatively poor results due to difficulties in mixing caused by an inferior formulation and manufacturing process. This product had never been offered to the larger to-bacco segment and although it is technically still available, it is not being actively promoted in the potato market.

MDA can be considered a commodity product with no real marketable differences in the liquid for-mulation products available from the three suppliers. Like virtually all agricultural chemicals, sales are made to independent distributors who then sell to retail dealers or directly to farmers. Competition at all levels of the distribution channel is intense and farmers have been known to travel 20 to 30 miles to save $0.25/gallon of their desired brand of MDA. Brand image and reputation are extremely important, especially in the tobacco market because of the high per-acre crop value and the relatively small per-farm acreage. Changes in this market therefore come slowly. In addition to price competition, all produc-ers also mount advertising and promotion cam-paigns and occasionally incentive programs, especially at the distributor level.

Agricultural chemicals are applied on the basis of a specific amount of active ingredient (ai) that is to be used per acre of the specific crop. These chemicals are generally mixed with water prior to application to dilute the active ingredient to a level that can ade-quately cover the crop to be treated. Convenience and simplicity of mixing are important considera-tions in determining appropriate package sizes. Cost is another significant consideration. When using water-soluble packaging, smaller packages generally cost more on a per pound of ai (active ingredient) basis. The cost of the water-soluble packaging film is relatively constant on a per pound of finished product basis. Labor costs, however, are primarily a function of the number of packages produced in a given period of time rather than the number of pounds in each pack-age because output on a package per-minute basis is not significantly different over a reasonable weight range. This means that fewer pounds will be packaged in the same length of time with smaller packages.

There are two major markets for MDA that Daynor had to consider in determining the appro-priate package size. These markets are tobacco and potatoes. Tobacco represents the largest market seg-ment, accounting for over 60 percent of total sales. Ideally, one package size can be used for both mar-kets to avoid duplicating inventories of both packag-ing materials and finished product as well as to minimize tooling costs for the new packaging equip-ment. Each different package size would represent an incremental capital investment of about $25,000 for filling equipment tooling.

Because tobacco farms are so much smaller than potato farms, this group of customers, which also represents the largest total volume for Daynor, prefers smaller-sized packages that are easier to handle, store, and use. Tobacco farms may be as small as 0.5 acre and typically do not exceed 20 acres. Their applica-tion equipment is consequently quite varied; small farms may have handheld equipment that only has the capacity to treat less than one acre, whereas larger farms typically have larger equipment that may be able to treat up to five acres before the farmer has to mix another batch of the pesticide and water. Most of these customers have been using the liquid MDA product packaged in one-gallon polyethylene bottles.

Potato farms, on the other hand, are much larger, and application of MDA is often done by contract aerial applicators who prefer large package sizes that can be quickly and easily mixed with water in large mixing tanks prior to filling the airplanes for appli-cation. From 20 to 40 acres can be treated with each mixing tank. These customers have typically used liquid MDA packaged in 2.5-gallon plastic bottles or 30-gallon plastic drums.

The maximum weight that can be packaged in the water-soluble bags is 2.5 pounds. Beyond this, the bags will break when handled because of the inherent strength limitations of the water-soluble film.

Heavier-gauge film will not properly dissolve when placed in water. Package size was not such a critical issue with the old liquid formulation because liquids can be easily stored in bulk and then packaged on demand to meet orders for the specific markets. In the field, liquids are easy to measure to adjust for various application rates and pieces of application equipment. Further, material not used could be simply stored in the plastic jug for the next season. Packaging to meet orders is not possible with the dry product because of the highly seasonal nature of the markets. Packaging equipment that is economically practical simply will not have the capacity to fill all orders as they are received. Field measurement is not practical because of both dry measurement problems and the fact that the entire water-soluble bag is supposed to be placed in the mix/spray tank to avoid contaminated containers and worker exposure. This further means that there would be no material from opened containers to be stored for the next year. The dry formulation in water-soluble bags has at least a three-year shelf life, provided the bags are not exposed to moisture.

Application rates for the liquid product ranged from four to eight quarts per acre for tobacco (depending on crop type and number of plants per acre) and from four to six quarts per acre for potatoes (depending on variety and growing conditions). The liquid product contains 2.25 lbs. of active ingredient per gallon and is typically packaged in 1-gallon and 2.5-gallon plastic bottles and 30-gallon plastic drums. The new dry formulation contains 60 percent by weight active ingredient MDA.

In addition to size of the individual water-soluble bags of MDA, Daynor also has to determine how many of these bags should be placed in each overpack bag. This overpack contains a moisture barrier to prevent moisture from attacking and dissolving the water-soluble packaging during shipment and storage from the time the product is manufactured until it is used by the farmers. It is highly desirable to place multiple water-soluble bags in each overpack bag to reduce costs of these overpack bags, as they cost more on a per-bag basis than the individual water-soluble bags. Although these overpack bags can be resealed and stored if all the water-soluble bags were not used at one time, Daynor is concerned that all farmers will not follow proper storage instructions on carryover stocks and allow the water-soluble bags to be exposed to moisture, after which whey will dissolve and release the product. Farmer application convenience

and handling considerations are the primary limiting factors as to how many water-soluble bags can be placed in each overpack. These overpack bags will then be placed in a fiberboard carton and palletized for shipment to Daynor's customers.

For purposes of determining the price for the new dry MDA, it can be assumed that both the new dry formulation and the older liquid formulation will be applied to crops at exactly the same rate of active ingredient per acre, which is nominally 2.25 lbs./acre.

Daynor knows that their manufacturing costs for the new dry formulation will be somewhat higher than for the current liquid formulations. New facilities will have to be built to produce and package the dry formulation. An investment of about $500,000 will be required to build enough capacity to completely satisfy Daynor's market share needs. Capacity to supply about 30 percent of their demand can be put in place for about $250,000, with future expansions possible at about $150,000 for each additional 30 percent capacity increase. There will be some savings in freight costs from the manufacturing plant to distributors, however, because the liquid product weighs 10 lbs./gallon (2.25 lbs. active ingredient with the remaining weight being water and other materials) and the dry product will contain 60 percent active ingredient (0.6 lbs. ai/1 lb. of product). Freight costs average approximately $0.02/lb. The current average distributor price for MDA is $6.25/gallon with FOB Delivered and Freight Prepaid terms.

Direct costs for the current liquid product and the new dry formulation are shown on the next page:

Walter Sedgwick is a new marketing assistant and was asked by the product manager to help determine the optimum individual water-soluble and overpack package sizes for the new dry product and to recommend a price for the new dry product.

# Questions

1. On what basis should Walter make his recommendation for the size of the water-soluble package?

2. What is your recommendation for the size of the water-soluble package?

3. How many of these water-soluble bags should be placed in each overpack bag?

4. How should Daynor define "value" for the new dry product? How will Daynor's ultimate customers (the farmers) define value?

**5.** How should the costs for the two products be compared, considering that one is a liquid and the other a powder?

**6.** What price should Daynor charge for the new product if they want to:

   **a.** Maintain the same dollar profit per pound of active ingredient?

   **b.** Maintain the same gross profit percentage?

   **c.** Maintain the same cost per acre for the farmer?

   **d.** Receive full value for the improved product features?

**7.** What other factors, if any, should Daynor consider in establishing their price for the new product?

| | Liquid Product (2.25 lbs. ai/gal) Cost/gallon | Dry Product (60% ai) Cost/lb. |
|---|---|---|
| Materials Cost | $3.420 | $1.020 |
| Container Cost | 0.558 | 0.085 |
| Labor Costs | 0.048 | 0.026 |
| Total Direct Cost at Plant | 4.026 | 1.131 |

# ExhibitsPlus: A Change in a Customer's Paradigm for Buying

ExhibitsPlus is a supplier of custom-built exhibit booths for companies to exhibit their products and services at trade shows. Pat Nelson, senior account executive, is working with Data Telecom (DT), a company whose North American operations are based in Toronto but that has significant operations located across the United States and Mexico. Data Telecom's primary business is selling telephone switching systems to companies for internal phone systems. The switches range in cost from $500,000 to $5 million.

## Data Telecom

Data Telecom is a well-established company, having been in business for over 70 years. Conservative, the company entered the U.S. and Mexican markets only 20 years ago and is often referred to as the IBM of telecommunications for its blue-suits–and–white-shirts image. This carefully cultivated image is believed to lower the perceived risk among buyers when choosing Data Telecom. On the other hand, the company has experienced severe competition over the last 10 years and actually lost money in domestic (Canadian) operations last year. The U.S. business barely breaks even, and the Mexican operations carry the profit ball for DT.

At the end of last year, the company announced a 10 percent reduction in workforce, along with a significant restructuring. One area that has been restructured is corporate marketing, and the company, which was known as a leader in manufacturing quality, is now applying TQM principles to marketing.

Jack Truitt is the marcom director for DT. His job is to manage all marketing communication in North America, so he manages advertising, trade shows, sales collateral (brochures, pamphlets, etc.), direct mail, Web sites, and public relations. He told Pat that he is the strategist; his primary job is to work with sales and upper management to determine marketing strategy, and then oversee the groups who carry out the strategy in the specific areas just mentioned. Pat has labeled Jack as a driver, and he has been the subject of a lot of press in the trade show industry as a maverick who likes to be innovative for the sake of being innovative. Jack came to DT's North American Operations from Europe, where he headed marketing and was very successful. Company pundits predict he will be the next VP of marketing and sales.

Jack wants to own no booths, which is opposite of the DT policy in the past. DT has always purchased custom-built booths, usually one per year at a price of about $150,000 to $175,000. Each booth has a life of about five years, and because the company does about 150 shows each year (each show equates to about one week of booth use), the booths rotate from show to show. Each old booth also has to be refurbished whenever corporate marketing strategy dictates, usually about every other year at a cost of about $50,000 per booth. Now Jack wants his exhibit vendor to buy the existing booths back at book value (except for the one that needs replacing, which

This case was prepared by J. F. Tanner Jr. for the purposes of class discussion, based on general industry information and trends. Data Telecom and ExhibitsPlus have been disguised.

will be trashed) and then rent them to him when he wants them. ExhibitsPlus would have to cover any refurb costs, but could rent the booths to companies that do not compete with DT. Custom graphics and other adaptations could be made for any customer who wanted to use the booths at a price of about $25,000—a one-time-per-booth charge. His belief is that this will lower his costs substantially. DT pays ExhibitsPlus about $100,000 to store exhibits between shows plus costs to ship the exhibits to various destinations. The storage fees would no longer be applicable because DT would not own the booths. Shipping would still be a separate item and not included in the rent. Truitt expects the rent to be about 40 percent of current costs of building, refurbing, and storing.

Betty Franklin is the trade shows manager. She has worked her way up to the North American Corporate office over a 20-year career, in which she began as a secretary while in her midthirties and a single mom. She earned her college degree while with DT, and Pat classifies her as an expressive. Pat has sensed some tension between Betty and Jack, which she has put down to the fact that Betty may feel passed over by Jack's promotion. Betty has very strong relations with the field sales force, which has always made booth design very effective. She can express the company's communication strategy in the same terms as the customer and the salesperson, which is useful when creating a new booth look, graphics, a show theme, etc. Jack, being new to NA Ops, doesn't have the same type of relationship with sales.

Jack reports to the VP of sales and marketing, a man who is nearing retirement. The VP came out of sales, so he focuses more time on sales than on marketing. He is entirely responsible for the allocation of budget to the various marketing areas, including new product development, customer service, and marcom. All marketing research is outsourced. Pat has met this man several times and feels that he is very conservative, particularly in terms of graphic design. Pat also feels that he patronizes women, and a quick glance at the management of the sales force would indicate that women have a tough time getting promoted at DT.

There are four exhibit managers (EMs) who each manage one of the displays. They are responsible for shipping the booth to the next show and making sure it is set up properly and then taken down at the end of the show. They are also responsible for coordinating all aspects of each show they manage. They work closely with the sales force to plan the right atmosphere for each show, targeting the right types of accounts, and saying the right things so that many leads can be generated. Each EM also manages the follow-up to each lead, tracking what each salesperson does with leads and if they close. This is so DT will know if the show was worthwhile.

Bill Bradley is the most senior of the EMs. He is also expressive, and has been with DT for about 12 years. His background is advertising, and he is very strong with graphics. He is the least detail-oriented person, which always causes Betty problems because he'll forget stuff at shows and depend on Betty to take care of him.

Toniqua Davis has been with DT for eight years, beginning right out of college. She has a bachelor's degree in marketing and wants to move into sales. Pat figures Toniqua is a driver, but she hasn't worked much with her.

Shawn Gale is the youngest of the exhibit managers, at 27, and has been with DT five years. Shawn is an analytical, has the firmest grasp on how to evaluate a show's success, and probably has the dullest eye for graphics. Senior management always likes the results of Shawn's shows because it is so obvious if the show was successful, and Shawn never needs to be bailed out at a show by Betty, but the salespeople don't think much of her.

Gerry MacDonald is the newest member of the DT show staff, having joined the company from Giltspur, a competitor of ExhibitsPlus. She has been with DT for about six months and has been in the show industry for over 10 years. Pat hasn't classified Gerry's personality yet. Gerry doesn't have a college degree, but seems to make up for it with her experience.

## The RFP

Each year, DT puts out an RFP (request for proposals). In this RFP, the needs for a new booth and any refurbishing of old booths are spelled out. Companies such as ExhibitsPlus are expected to create speculative designs (called spec designs for short), building scale models of their designs. These are then presented to DT, which selects a supplier. Pat has argued that this drives up DT's costs because spec designs are very expensive (a company may have as much as

$20,000 invested), and the costs have to be covered for designs that are bid and lost. DT hasn't paid any attention to that argument in the past, but then again, most buyers in the industry request spec designs.

For a spec design, Pat schedules meetings with the buyer and her design staff. The design staff includes architects and graphic designers. Sometimes, she includes the buyer's advertising agency if they aren't also bidding on the job. Sometimes, the buyer's sales department is involved, and in some organizations, trade shows are managed by a sales manager or director of sales. These meetings are designed to give the staff the greatest amount of information possible, but some companies don't allow these meetings. Some buyers also cherry-pick, taking the best ideas out of each spec design and including them in the final design. DT has been known to do that.

Jack has mentioned to Pat that this year's RFP will be for a custom-designed booth with modular design so that the booth can function as a $10' \times 10'$ up to a $40' \times 40'$. If purchased, it would be about a $200,000 sale. Jack also expects the RFP to require the winning company to buy the four old booths and refurbish them to fit the same specifications. Length of the rental agreement has not been determined. The RFP, though, will be sent to several advertising firms who are encouraged to bid in the hopes of winning other advertising business. They would then subcontract the building of the booth to someone else.

## ExhibitsPlus

Pat managed to win the DT business two out of the last three years, but two years ago, it was won by Freeman Exhibit Company out of Dallas. Before that, the business was held exclusively by Southern Designs, a company that is no longer in business.

ExhibitsPlus has two sister companies: a shipping company that ships the booths (all competitors except Freeman have to ship using a major carrier like Mayflower or Allied, which have special trade show divisions) and a drayage company (*drayage* is the term used to describe unloading the booth at the shipping dock of a convention center, then moving it to the appropriate point on the exhibit floor, then moving it out, and loading it up at the end of the show). Drayage, though, is usually sold to the show organizer, who then requires all exhibitors to use the same drayage company. The only advantage to ExhibitsPlus's customers is that for those shows where ExhibitsPlus is the drayage provider, the unloading and loading process is much smoother and faster. This is, however, a significant advantage because it means more time for installing and dismantling the booth. Saving time is a critical advantage in the eyes of most exhibit managers, because it means more time to fix any problems (and there are always problems) and greater likelihood of getting the exhibit installed on time.

ExhibitsPlus also has its own install-and-dismantle (I&D) team to set up and take down the booth if the customer wants. Only Freeman has this complete set of offerings. The RFP is really cloudy on who will provide these services and Pat, in talking with Jack, believes that it is because Jack hasn't really thought these things through. The contract with ExhibitsPlus expires in four months, and the new RFP will probably be issued in one month to six weeks.

ExhibitsPlus is a family-owned business founded in 1920 by a young WWI veteran, Ted Ruch (pronounced *roosh*). Ted's daughter, Sally R. Massy, took the company over in 1960 and is about to retire, passing the reins on to her two children: Gil, who runs the transportation side, and Nancy, who runs the exhibit building and I&D business.

The transportation business was acquired in 1948. Most custom booths are built of plywood and laminate materials; therefore, they can be quite heavy. The life of the booth is also a function of how well the booth is cared for when it is shipped and stored. For those reasons, Sally Massy realized that she could save her customers money and provide better service by doing the shipping, so she bought a struggling home-moving company and turned it into an exhibit-shipping company. Then she purchased an Army surplus warehouse and used it to store exhibits.

The business, though, has changed. Companies like Nimlok provide lower-cost and shorter-life booths by using newer materials, fabrics, and special structural and fastening technologies. These technologies make it easier to snap pieces together to create a nice look with materials that are lighter (and therefore less expensive to ship and store). Shorter booth life is not a problem when a company wants to change the look year after year. For that reason, ExhibitsPlus also developed its own line of low-cost customizable but standard booth designs, called the

# Fleury Equipment de Batiment

The rate of change in the market never failed to astound Jacques Fleury, he thought, as he opened up his office after a week's trade fair in Paris. Just when he thought he understood the market, along came another competitor, a new technology, a new government regulation, or something else to rewrite the rules of the game.

This time, it was Yenja, a Turkish company that entered France in a big way. The Turkish company was preparing itself for the eventual admission of Turkey to the European Union (EU) by entering the market beforehand, and with prices at least 15% below those of EU manufacturers.

Fleury momentarily looked out of his office in Caen, overlooking the castle of William the Conqueror. Once again, his eyes took in the pockmarks on the castle walls where a few stray American bullets had landed during the Normandy Invasion. The Americans had decided not to bomb the castle or the two monasteries that William had built early during the eleventh century in this little Norman town near the English Channel coast, even if any Germans had hid in them. After all, what was a small castle against such an overwhelming force? Almost all of the rest of Caen, though, was razed. Fleury wondered sometimes if his little company was not unlike those few Germans hiding in the castle—the war swirled past and left them behind, able only to surrender.

Gathering his resolve, he punched a button on his phone, turning it into an intercom. "Marie!" he cried.

"Oui, monsieur."

"Call a meeting of the executive committee for tomorrow morning, first thing. We've got to discuss the results of the trade fair."

At the meeting the next day were Jean Montier, director of manufacturing; Christian Deleuze, director of marketing; Nadege David, director of accounting; and Jacques. He quickly called the meeting to order, and asked Mr. Deleuze for a report on sales from the fair.

"We finished slightly under our expectations, closing business for 94% of plan," reported Deleuze. He passed around copies of a single sheet with figures on it (see Table 1). "As you can see, average discount was 8%, somewhat above our normal average of 5%. Further 34% of orders are open, which means these are options, not firm orders." He ignored David's rolling of her eyes, indicating that he had stated the obvious. "This is up from 28% at last year's fair."

"All in all, I would say this indicates a pretty significant softening of the market," said David. "Either that, or our sales guys have let us down, and I know we don't believe that." Yet her smile said just the opposite.

Deleuze grew red in the face. "Look," he said, pointing for emphasis, "it has been over a year since we've had a new product. Our sales representatives understand the need for selling at or near book. But the choice was either discount or don't sell, and I chose to discount."

"Let's not fight amongst ourselves," ordered Fleury, raising his hand to give a stop sign. "We need all of our creativity to figure out what to do. Not only do we have increasing competition from the Belgians and the Russians on top of the Germans; now we have this Turkish company in our market. Let's focus on what we need to do." With that, a

ExhibitPro line. These sell for about half the price of a custom booth, and are customized through the use of special graphics. In addition, ExhibitPro booths don't necessarily require special I&D, so the exhibit manager can save money by installing and dismantling the booth personally. In terms of units sold, ExhibitsPlus sells twice the number of ExhibitPro booths as it does custom booths, but revenue is about equal and profits are greater on the custom booth sales. Currently, ExhibitsPlus does not rent any booths.

## Competition

As mentioned earlier, Freeman Exhibit Co. is the only competitor that offers comparable services. Freeman, based in Dallas, offers one advantage that ExhibitsPlus does not—it also provides show services to the show organizer. (Show services include carpeting the exhibit hall, setting up the drapes that separate the booths, putting up signs, providing cleaning services, and offering other services to exhibitors sold through the show organizer.) That results in about a 2:1 market share advantage for drayage between Freeman and ExhibitsPlus. Freeman also has a reputation as an industry leader because of the Freeman family's participation in many of the industry associations and its donations to industry causes. Freeman is the industry's largest exhibit builder.

Most exhibit builders are small, serving a limited geographic area, meaning that although they may ship exhibits anywhere in the world, their customers come from a limited area. It is unlikely that Data Telecom will send the RFP to any of these companies, but Pat does know that DT's advertising agency is planning to bid on the job. Usually an advertising agency will farm the work out to one of the small exhibit builders. Ad agencies also usually cost 5 to 10 percent more than ExhibitsPlus because they add their profit to all charges. In addition, ad agencies have to find shippers and storage facilities.

Champion Communications is a rapidly growing competitor that has acquired a number of the smaller custom shops around the country. Its strategy has been to go into a large city like Atlanta or Dallas and buy two exhibit builders: one known for creativity and one with an established customer base. The company is run by Marjorie McGaslin, who left ExhibitsPlus because she wasn't one of the family and couldn't expect to be CEO. She has partnered with a financier in Denver. The firm is expected to continue to grow through acquisition until she has locations in 10 cities; currently Champion covers six cities and is already probably one of the top five companies in terms of annual revenue. Champion does offer storage but contracts all shipping through Mayflower.

Giltspur, in the process of changing the name to GES, is another large competitor, but does little exhibit building. It specializes in providing show services, I&D, shipping, drayage, and everything but exhibit building, but it does a little of that when needed. Pat believes that Gerry will get GES an invitation to bid, and if GES does, it will sub the building of the booth out and try to make its money on the other aspects of the deal (shipping, storage, etc.).

Develop an account plan for Data Telecom. In your plan, you need to consider issues such as the stage of the relationship between DT and ExhibitsPlus, the risks associated with this change in buying strategy for both sides, and relative merits of the various vendors.

**Table 1**
Paris Fair Results (sales figures in millions of Euros)

| Product | Actual | Percentage Open | Average Discount | Budget | Last Year Actual | Percentage Open | Average Discount |
|---|---|---|---|---|---|---|---|
| Earthmovers | 7.2€ | 28% | 7.4% | 7.7€ | 7.4€ | 28% | 6.8% |
| Lifts | 12.3€ | 40% | 8.2% | 13.2€ | 12.8€ | 29% | 6.4% |
| Materials Handling | 1.2€ | 1% | 6.2% | 1.1€ | 1.0€ | 1% | 6.0% |
| Total | 20.7€ | 34% | 8.1% | 22.0€ | 21.2€ | 28% | 6.5% |

babble of each person's pet agenda broke out, as they rehashed old battles and repeated old points. Fleury felt sick to his stomach. With this kind of fighting, they would get nowhere.

## Background

Jacques Fleury was the son of the man who was mayor of Caen during the German occupation and Allied liberation. Fleury's father had owned a small machine shop prior to the war, and when the Germans occupied Normandy and began building the Atlantic Wall, the defensive fortifications along the English Channel, the Fleury machine shop was turned into a manufacturer of construction hand tools. In the post-war years, the American government and other Allies had helped French companies re-establish and re-build France. This rebuilding period meant that con-struction tools were in high demand, and Fleury flourished. He expanded, rebuilding Allied and German diesel engines and other instruments of war into instruments of construction. As Europe moved into the fifties, the Fleury name became known for high-quality, long-lasting construction equipment. Unfortunately, Fleury began resting on that name, and while quality did not decline, competitors managed to match, then surpass Fleury for quality. Fortunately, trade barriers kept foreign competition from being price competitive.

When the European Union was created, trade barriers were removed. For the first time, Fleury had to compete on an equal playing field with German companies. The German engineering was superior, for Fleury had lost its edge by this time. By the end of the twentieth century, even the Russian compa-nies (whose record of quality was suspect) were com-peting on equal footing, and Fleury was known for lower-end equipment. Further, the company special-ized in smaller equipment—the smaller bulldozers,

lifts, cranes, and other pieces of equipment particu-larly well suited to the smaller work areas of Europe. As economic growth continued in Europe, the need for larger equipment was growing.

The trade fair in Paris is an annual event, at which Fleury typically completes about 40% of its annual sales contracts. The remaining 60% are sold at either the construction fair in Hanover, Germany, or indi-vidual sales. Salespeople contact accounts during the year, making sure that they are satisfied and getting some idea of their needs prior to the fairs. Only 15% of Fleury sales are made outside of the trade fairs. These sales occur when equipment breaks down and becomes irreparable or if the needs of a specific proj-ect overwhelm a customer's resources.

Fleury offered three primary product lines: earth-movers of various types, such as small bulldozers and trenchers, as well as attachments that could be used in conjunction with small tractors; lifts, or hydraulic machines that could lift a person 11 meters into the air (called cherry pickers in the U.S.); and specialized materials handling equipment. These latter machines were used to move construction materials around a job site, similar to fork lifts but adapted for use out of doors over rough terrain. Further, these products were integrated with the lifts, so that materials could be positioned onto lifts for installation on second stories or onto roofs, for example. The lifts that Fleury specializes in are scissor-type lifts. These lifts use a hydraulic system to expand the scissor beams and lift a platform of about 1.5 meters by 1.5 meters. Each lift has its own motor for moving about the job site and uses standard truck wheels. Earthmovers accounted for about 35% of Fleury's sales and accounted for 25% of gross profit. Lifts were nearly 60% of sales and generated 55% of gross profit. The materials handling equipment were almost a side-line and, while highly profitable, rarely pushed. There just simply wasn't a large market for it.

Fleury equipment market share varied by product category. Their earthmoving equipment sales accounted for less than 2% of the European market. Their lift sales were 8% and materials handling, 3%. Fleury's shares of the French market were significantly higher than the above figures, but all shares had been declining for the past decade.

The Fleury name was stronger in lifts than earthmovers. Ditch Witch, Deere, and Caterpillar all had European distributors though EU trade restrictions made these products particularly expensive. Deere and Caterpillar focused more on the higher end earthmoving products, while Ditch Witch sold specialized products like trenchers for which it has a significant engineering advantage. The leader in the earthmover market was a former division of Mercedes Benz, Allied Benz, but other players included the Belgian company Poirot, several small Russian companies each of whom had less market share than Fleury, and now Yenja.

These other companies not only had earthmovers, but many also had paving equipment, something that Fleury never offered. These machines included hot asphalt layers (machines that heat asphalt and lay it on a rock surface or roadbed), cold asphalt layers, asphalt removers, cement pouring equipment, and others. The addition of these types of products sometimes gave Allied or Poirot an advantage, as it allowed road construction companies to single source. But most of Fleury's business was in residential and small commercial building construction, not roads. For that reason, when ScanRode, a Swedish company with additional manufacturing facilities in the U.S., approached Fleury with an offer to distribute ScanRode asphalt laying equipment in France, Fleury declined. To Jacques' knowledge, ScanRode had not entered the French market, even though it had success in Asia and the Americas.

## The Current Situation

Paris trade fair sales typically accounted for 25% of total European Union construction equipment sales, while the Hanover fair accounted for 45%. Smaller regional fairs in Great Britain, Belgium, and Italy accounted for the remainder of European "trade fair" sales. Because construction equipment needs were fairly predictable, trade fairs accounted for 90% of construction equipment sales in Europe.

Some two months after the Paris fair, and at least a month before Hanover, Fleury sat in his office, sweating in quiet desperation. Half of the open orders from Paris had already cancelled, and nearly 20% of the firm orders were delayed. Manufacturing capacity was being utilized at just below 65% for earthmovers, slightly more than 80% for lifts, and almost 70% for materials handling. Currently, he had on hand enough finished goods to ship 2 month's worth of business. If he didn't turn some of that finished goods into cash quickly, he was going to default on his line of credit with Credit Lyonnaise. Something had to be done, and it had to be done before Hanover.

Nadege David suggested shutting down the earthmover assembly line, perhaps for good. French law required such a long notification period and payment of workers that Jacques wondered if it was worth it. She had already met with the appropriate government officials, as well as with the Credit Lyonnaise, and was prepared to do that, even though it meant carrying the costs of the line for six months past its shut-down period if liquidated. The firm was not obligated if the shutdown was temporary, though Montier indicated that all of the workers were likely to strike if the plant were shut down even temporarily. David argued that the lift plant was still profitable, and her long-term projections showed the company returning a profit if sales held firm for lifts after a period of two and a half years. Jacques thought a strike might not be a bad thing, because at least then, the plant was closed and he wouldn't have to pay wages.

Montier argued that there were fixed costs that couldn't be fully accounted for, and that David's argument was based on selling the manufacturing equipment. He said that her estimates of the market value of equipment were overly generous, as there were no ready buyers for the outdated manufacturing facility. He argued for cheaper materials so that he could drive the manufacturing cost down, which would then enable the company to earn a profit at the price they were now able to charge.

Deleuze's typical argument was that the company needed to consider tying up with another manufacturer, preferably Asian, which could provide some products at a lower cost. At the Paris fair, he had taken Montier and Jacques around and shown them products that were manufactured in Asia and sold in France for about what it cost Fleury to manufacture them. While these were primarily products that were not Fleury's bread and butter, the thought of these Asian companies moving into the heart of Fleury's business frightened Jacques. When they entered the Yenja stand and saw the Turkish earthmoving product prices, Jacques' stomach dropped. These products were directly aimed at Fleury, priced 15% below his. On closer examination, though, he relaxed as he realized that the engineering was at least a decade behind. Still, he knew that price was a trade-off some buyers would make—after all, the stuff just moved dirt.

Deleuze and Jacques met to discuss the upcoming Hanover Fair. "I've got something I want you to look at," said Deleuze, a sly grin on his face. "I've been talking with an Israeli engineering firm; they've got a new hydraulic system that should make a tremendous improvement on our lifts. First, it can increase the carrying capacity of our typical lift by 30%." Jacques nearly gasped, as he thought of the benefits of being able to lift additional building materials each time and the time and money it could save his customers. "Second, it can do so and cut the lift time by 20%. Third, we can increase our lift size by 4 meters." Deleuze nearly hugged himself with delight. "And, get this; they've approached only us so far about a joint manufacturing arrangement!"

Jacques was astounded. "This is amazing. How did this come about?"

"My sister. You remember, she married that American fellow who sponsors new companies, finds them capital, and so forth. Well, he helped this engineering firm get started. What they do is take existing products, try to find ways to make them better, then sell the idea to a manufacturer, like us. They share the risk, meaning that they get some money up front, but take most of their profits from the ongoing sale of the product. And, if it proves successful, the idea is that they continue to engineer improvements."

"This is like the answer to a prayer!" exclaimed Jacques. "So how long have they done this?"

Deleuze hemmed and hawed, "Well, um, actually, we would be their first customer." Picking up speed, he continued, "But it is the answer to a prayer. We've got enough time to get a prototype developed for Hanover. They've already been working on it and they are nearly ready. If we take our 4000 product, and provide them with what they need, we can introduce the Fleury 5000, a 15-meter lift with 30% more power and 20% less lift time at the Hanover Fair!"

Jacques thought for a moment. "How much money do they need up front?"

Deleuze beamed again. "Because we are their first customer, the American, my brother-in-law, will take care of that. You will have to work out the situation with Credit Lyonnaise and so forth. But he understands the need to avoid having to ask for additional credit with the bank."

Jacques continued to think, ideas swirling in his head. He wondered how many lift sales they could recapture with this product. "I think, actually, the bank might be quite happy about this turn of events. Let's bring in Nadege and Jean and see what they have to say."

"Before you do, there is one bad thing about it."

Jacques looked up, as his hopes fell. Too good to be true, he knew. "Oh? And what's that?"

"Well, it is more reliable, so it only needs preventive maintenance twice a year instead of three times. So that will cut into our service revenue by about 300€ per unit. But on the positive side, the useful life is still going to be eight years, or at least that's what they expect."

Typically, lifts require maintenance three times per year. This is preventive maintenance because should a lift fail, it could prove fatal if someone was in it and it was at its highest point. The maintenance includes changing seals and hydraulic fluid. Occasionally a switch will need replacing, but nonroutine maintenance tends to be rare for the first five years. Most equipment is turned over, either sold off as used or junked, after eight years, because at that point the scissor beams begin to need replacing, and that cost is substantial.

Nadege David and Jean Montier were summoned to Jacques' office. Once the initial idea was proposed, both immediately saw the benefit. Montier was sent off to talk with the Israelis and determine the manufacturing costs. Meanwhile, Deleuze was ordered to gather competitive pricing information and prepare a report on the pricing options for the new product. Once both costs and market realities were accounted for, David and Jacques would set the final price, though at this point, little in the way of new manufacturing facilities would be needed. The engineers believed that Fleury could manufacture the new lifts using the equipment they already owned.

Table 2 summarizes Christian Deleuze's report. Table 3 provides the manufacturing costs identified

**Table 2**
Comparison of
List Prices

| Manufacturer | 5 meter | 9 meter | 11 meter |
|---|---|---|---|
| Fleury | 18,000€ | 25,000€ | 32,000€ |
| Allied Benz | 21,000€ | 28,000€ | 34,000€ |
| Skyjack | 17,000€ | 23,500€ | 29,950€ |
| Poirot* | 16,000€ | 22,000€ | 28,000€ |

NOTE, actual prices paid are discounted off of list price. Industry estimates are that the average discount for lifts is currently somewhere between 7.5 and 8%, although it can vary from year to year depending on demand and capacity.
*Poirot offers a 6-meter, 8-meter, and 12-meter lift, rather than 5, 9 and 11 meters.
There are additional vendors in the market; these were selected to be representative of the range of prices that are available.

**Table 3**
Manufacturing
Costs

| Product | Labor | Common Parts & Controls | Hydraulics | Total |
|---|---|---|---|---|
| 5 meter | 6,940€ | 2,960€ | 2,450€ | 12,350€ |
| 9 meter | 7,360€ | 4,120€ | 2,600€ | 14,080€ |
| 11 meter | 7,955€ | 5,340€ | 2,895€ | 16,190€ |
| 15 meter estimate | 8,600€ | 6,520€ | 3,300€ | 18,420€ |

Montier's estimate is based on the cost of parts that are common across the lifts, additional labor to assemble the 15-meter lift relative to the cost of assembling the smaller lifts, and the cost estimates of the new hydraulics provided by Steinmetz Engineering, the Israeli company that designed the new system. Costs are variable only. Allocation of fixed costs is not included. The estimate for new plant requirements is not included at this point.

by Jean Montier. Jacques, upon receiving the information, asked these questions:

What price should we set for the 5,000?

What does this mean for pricing the remaining lift products? What should we say about the remaining lift products and their future?

What do we say about the earthmover products?

How can we generate the appropriate level of cash, not only to satisfy the bank, but also to promote the new lifts and add the needed equipment to manufacture the new lifts?

Will the market believe this new level of quality and productivity?

# JC Decaux

## Corporate Overview

In 1964, Jean-Claude Decaux invented the concept of "street furniture" around a simple but pioneering idea: to provide well-maintained street furniture free of charge to cities and towns in exchange for the right

This case was written by Emilie Dupré, Denis Empereur, Jean-Benoît Gareau, Julien Gledel, and Francis Godard for the purpose of class discussion, and not to illustrate effective or ineffective marketing strategies. Data are based on JC Decaux's corporate reports and personal research of the authors.

to place advertising on such structures. From the beginning, street furniture became a very attractive communication medium for advertisers, because it gave them access to advertising space in city centers, in areas where advertising was generally very limited.

JC Decaux is the only global "pure play" outdoor advertising company with a leading position in the sector's three core areas:

- *Street Furniture:* This is the youngest and fastest growing sector of the outdoor advertising market,

JC Decaux's Business Repartition by Product

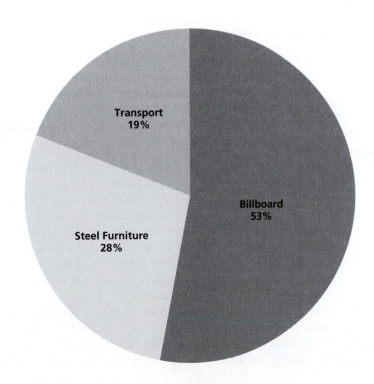

Transport 19%

Billboard 53%

Steel Furniture 28%

with an estimated 60% increase in global expenditures from 1995 to 2000. JC Decaux is number one worldwide in street furniture with 290,000 panels in 37 countries.

- *Billboards:* The traditional outdoor products represent the greatest portion of outdoor expenditures worldwide. JC Decaux is number one in Europe and operates 192,000 billboard panels in 28 countries.
- *Transport Advertising:* This is advertising panels installed in areas with significant passenger traffic. JC Decaux is number one worldwide in airport advertising with 145,000 panels in 147 airports and 150 rail transit systems in 19 countries.

Today, JC Decaux is the world's leading street furniture company, based both on the number of advertising faces and on revenues. The group is currently present in 43 countries around the world: The company has concessions in 34 of the 50 largest cities in Europe and also has street furniture operations in shopping malls in the United States, Europe, Japan, and Latin America. In 2002, the firm achieved a turnover of €1.578 billion and street furniture accounted for 53.3% of JC Decaux's sales.

A key aspect of JC Decaux's street furniture business is its maintenance service, which it typically provides as part of its street furniture contracts. (In December 31, 2002, two-thirds of its street furniture employees were responsible for cleaning and maintenance.)

## Geographic Coverage

As of December 31, 2002, JC Decaux had street furniture concessions in approximately 1,400 cities of more than 10,000 people, totaling more than 285,000 advertising faces in 34 countries. A majority of its street furniture activities are in Europe, and in particular in France.

A key strength of JC Decaux's Group is its extensive presence in major cities in Europe. Currently, the company has street furniture concessions in 34 of the 50 largest cities in Europe by population. JC Decaux believes that having street furniture concessions in key cities is essential to its ability to offer attractive national advertising networks to advertisers. The company's top management also believes that its network of major European city concessions will enable it to offer attractive pan-European

advertising networks to advertisers, which are becoming increasingly sought after by large multinational advertisers.

One of JC Decaux's main focuses for future growth is the North American market. Having won significant Street Furniture contracts in San Francisco and Chicago, the firm won, together with Viacom, a contract with the City of Los Angeles in 2002. JC Decaux also won its first street furniture contract in Canada in 2002, with the City of Vancouver, Canada's third largest city. There the company will succeed Patterson Outdoor, which had held the concession for 26 years.

Providing street furniture to shopping malls is also a key part of JC Decaux's expanding activities in the United States, and a business that grew significantly in 2002. Top management views shopping malls as the "downtown" of many cities in the United States, offering similar opportunities for street furniture as traditional city centers in Europe. In addition to offering a large audience, shopping malls have a commercial purpose, providing advertisers with an opportunity to advertise close to points of sale. JC Decaux's shopping mall contracts include some of the most prestigious malls in the United States, including Roosevelt Field (New York), The Mall at Short Hills (New Jersey), Water Tower Place in Chicago (Illinois), and Century City and Beverly Center in Los Angeles (California). As of December 31, 2002, JC Decaux had installed street furniture in 99 shopping malls in the United States.

## The Operations in North America

In the United States, Viacom Decaux, a joint venture with Viacom Outdoor (a subsidiary of Viacom Inc.) and JC Decaux North America, entered into a street furniture contract with the city of Los Angeles. With a population of 3.7 million, Los Angeles is the largest outdoor advertising market in the U.S. This 20-year agreement provides for the installation of 2,500 bus shelters, 700 kiosks and columns, and 150 public toilets, and represents estimated revenues of €900 million. The company also entered into a street furniture contract with the city of Chicago, the third largest city in the U.S. with 3 million inhabitants. This 20-year agreement provides for the installation of more than 2,000 bus shelters and more than 200 other pieces of street furniture and represents estimated revenues of €850 million.

Repartition by
Geography

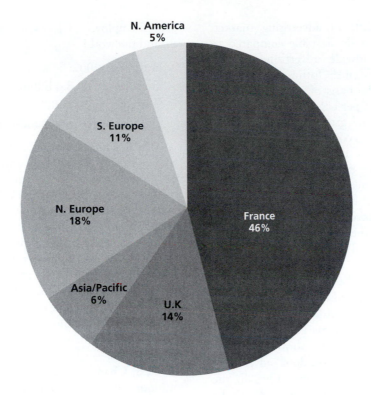

In Canada, teaming up with Viacom Outdoor, JC Decaux won the street furniture tender with the city of Vancouver, Canada's third largest city. This 20-year agreement, which was signed in December 2002, provides for the installation of 900 bus shelters, 235 bicycle racks, 100 newspaper distributors, 210 city map distributors, and more than 1,400 waste bins; it should represent estimated revenues of €150 million.

## The Outdoor Advertising Market

### A Rapidly Growing Market

### Three Main Segments
Outdoor advertising consists of three principal types of activities:

- Advertising on billboards ("Billboard")
- Advertising on and in public transportation vehicles and stations ("Transport")
- Advertising on street furniture ("Street Furniture")

Billboard is the most traditional and continues to be the most utilized form of outdoor advertising. Transport consists of advertising in or on buses or subway cars; inside buses, subways, and train stations; and inside airports and ferry terminals. Advertising on street furniture (bus shelters, free-standing information panels, and multiservice columns) is the newest activity. It is also the fastest growing segment. Other outdoor advertising activities, such as advertising on shopping trolleys, are grouped together as "ambient media."

Based on its knowledge of the market, JC Decaux estimates that, in 2002, Billboard accounted for more than 48 percent of worldwide outdoor advertising expenditures, Transport accounted for approximately 26 percent, Street Furniture accounted for approximately 18 percent, and ambient media accounted for the remaining 8 percent (source: JC Decaux).

### Growth
After a period when outdoor advertising growth outperformed that of the overall media market, outdoor advertising strengthened its position in the advertising market, which includes other media such as broadcast and cable television, radio, newspapers, magazines, cinema, and the Internet. In 2002, outdoor advertising expenditures worldwide were approximately €17 billion, representing 5.3% of worldwide advertising expenditures estimated at

€325 billion. In a difficult advertising market, outdoor advertising remained stable compared to 2001, while the worldwide advertising market grew by 0.2% (source: ZenithOptimedia estimates, December 2002, on the basis of an average 2002 exchange rate of €1.061 per U.S. dollar). According to ZenithOptimedia, the growth rate of outdoor advertising suffered, when compared to other media, from the strength of the dollar against the Euro, since outdoor advertising expenditures were proportionally more significant in countries outside the United States compared to other media. Expressed in local currency, the growth rate of outdoor advertising in countries outside the United States was slightly greater than that indicated by the ZenithOptimedia data.

JC Decaux believes that the 2002 ZenithOptimedia estimates are optimistic, based on their market experience. In 2002, growth in outdoor advertising was particularly strong in certain markets, such as the United Kingdom where, in the third quarter of 2002, the market share of outdoor advertising exceeded 9% for the first time ever. Overall, the outdoor advertising market share grew by 2% in the UK in 2002, compared to 2001.

**Competitive Environment**

The outdoor advertising market is highly competitive, with several major international companies operating in all three principal market segments and in multiple countries. There are also a variety of local and niche players, particularly in the Billboard activity. In 2002, JC Decaux estimates that the top three outdoor advertising companies accounted for 30% of the market and that these companies continue to increase their market share. The firm's principal competitors in substantially all of its activities and regions are Clear Channel and Viacom and their respective affiliates.

## Clear Channel

Clear Channel is a collection of media and entertainment companies: Clear Channel Radio, Clear Channel Television, Clear Channel Entertainment, and Clear Channel Outdoor. The company is led by Lowry Mays. The company was founded in 1972 by Lowry Mays and B.J. "Red" McCombs with the purchase of KEEZ-FM (currently KJ97-FM) in San Antonio, Texas. The firm has approximately 55,000 employees. Clear Channel is in 65 countries around the world.

In the year 2002:
Turnover: USD 8.4 billion
Personnel: over 50,000
Outdoor advertising panels: over 800,000

Clear Channel Radio is the largest operator of radio stations in the United States and provides advertisers with a coast-to-coast platform of more than 1,200 stations. Broadcasting across all 50 states and the District of Columbia, Clear Channel programming reaches more than 110 million listeners every week.

Clear Channel Entertainment is the world's leading producer and marketer of live entertainment events. Each year, more than 66 million people attend approximately 26,000 events staged by the company, including live concerts, Broadway productions, West End and touring Broadway shows, family entertainment shows, and sports and motor sports events.

Clear Channel Outdoor is one of the largest outdoor advertising companies in the world. The outdoor products vary from traditional highway billboards to Times Square Spectacolor, taxi tops, shopping malls, mobile truck panels, buses, and train station and airport advertising.

Clear Channel Outdoor is present in France through:

Dauphin Affichage: France's # 1 in outdoor advertising panels
Turnover in 2002: €205 million
Dauphin Adshel: France's # 2 in street furniture
Turnover in 2002: €62 million

## Viacom Inc.

Viacom is a leading global media company, with preeminent positions in broadcast and cable television, radio, outdoor advertising, and online. With programming that appeals to audiences in every demographic category across virtually all media, the company is a leader in the creation, promotion, and distribution of entertainment, news, sports, music, and comedy. Viacom's well-known brands include CBS, MTV, Nickelodeon, VH1, BET, Paramount Pictures, Viacom Outdoor, Infinity, UPN, Spike TV, TV Land, CMT (Country Music Television), Comedy Central, Showtime, Blockbuster, and Simon & Schuster.

In the year 2002:

Turnover: USD 25 billion

Outdoor advertising panels: over 1 million

Viacom Outdoor is the world's largest out-of-home media company with a major North American presence throughout the United States, Canada and Mexico; and across Europe in the United Kingdom, Ireland, Finland, France, Italy, the Netherlands, and Spain.

Viacom Outdoor is the largest outdoor advertising company in the world. It is present in 550 towns and cities.

Viacom Outdoor France turnover in 2002: €192 million

Personnel: 934 employees

## JC Decaux's Business

### Street Furniture

#### Street Furniture Contracts

Street furniture is installed primarily in city center locations and along major commuting routes where road traffic is the most significant. JC Decaux receives, by means of concessions from landowners, the right to display advertising on these street furniture structures. The street furniture contracts have a duration of 8 to 25 years. In France, a majority of JC Decaux's street furniture contracts are 10 to 15 years long. Approximately 29% of JC Decaux's street furniture contracts (based on 2002 revenues, excluding shopping malls) also required the firm to pay a fee, calculated as a percentage of its gross advertising revenues, of 5% or more of the gross advertising revenues generated by the contract to the concession grantor.

Over the past several years, JC Decaux has expanded its street furniture business to include shopping malls in several countries, including United States, Japan, and Singapore. Shopping mall contracts typically require JC Decaux to pay performance-based fees calculated as a percentage of its net contract revenues. (In a minority of cases, these contracts also include a minimum rental payment.)

As of December 31, 2002, JC Decaux's street furniture contracts had an average remaining term of 9 years and 9 months (weighted by 2002 revenues, adjusted to account for projected revenues from newly won street furniture contracts and concessions in shopping malls in the United States). In France, the average remaining term of street furniture contracts is approximately five years and four months (weighted by 2002 revenues). Between January 1, 2003, and December 31, 2005, approximately 13.3% of its street furniture contracts (weighted by 2002 street furniture revenues) will come up for renewal.

The company continues to successfully renew its existing contracts through competitive bids and wins a majority of the new contracts that it competes for. In France in 2002, JC Decaux successfully renewed 83% of its existing contracts that came up for bid and won approximately 86% of the public bids for new contracts that the firm competed for. Overall, in 2002, JC Decaux won 85% of the street furniture bids (renewals and new contracts) in which it participated. As of January 1, 2003, approximately 64% of its global street furniture revenues (based on 2002 revenues) were contractually secured until 2010, including Paris.

#### Growth

The company believes that Street Furniture is the fastest growing segment of the outdoor advertising market, as shown in particular by the strong growth of street furniture advertising in the United Kingdom, Europe's second largest advertising market. Street Furniture is most highly developed in Europe, where JC Decaux estimates that street furniture advertising expenditures currently constitute approximately 30% of the total outdoor advertising expenditures. Street Furniture is also becoming an increasingly popular advertising medium in the United States, particularly in major urban areas and in shopping malls, which JC Decaux views as the "downtown" of many cities in the United States. Following the recent public tenders for street furniture contracts made by the cities of Chicago and Los Angeles, JC Decaux believes that concessions with other large American cities could be put out for bid in the near future, especially in New York. In the Asia-Pacific region and Latin America, where street furniture remains a relatively new concept, street furniture concessions have been put out to tender in the last few years in major cities such as Sydney, Singapore, Seoul, Bangkok, Montevideo, and Salvador de Bahia.

#### Marketing and Sales

JC Decaux markets its street furniture as a premium quality advertising medium. The firm has a sophisticated database that enables it to analyze the social and demographic characteristics of the areas where it positions its street furniture products. These tools enable JC Decaux to offer advertisers both "mass media" coverage as well as access to targeted audiences.

JC Decaux has pioneered major innovations that are now being implemented in several countries to improve audience measurement for outdoor advertising. Using this technology, organizations like POSTAR in the United Kingdom, SUMMO in the Netherlands, AFFIMETRIE in France, and GEOMEX in Spain have recently completed innovative studies that provide both quantitative and qualitative information about advertising audiences. Improvements in audience measurement should enable outdoor advertising to enhance its competitiveness compared to other media, in attracting advertising expenditures from advertisers.

In 2002, the overall occupancy rate on JC Decaux's street furniture networks was 76%, and 80% in networks of countries where street furniture is a well-established advertising medium (excluding shopping malls in the United States and Japan, and new contracts in Korea and South America). This latter occupancy rate was 85% in 2001. The drop in occupancy rate reflects the company's decision to pursue its firm pricing strategy in 2002, in spite of a difficult advertising market for the second year in a row. JC Decaux commercializes all of its own advertising space to advertising agencies or media buyers. Generally, its contracts with advertisers are irrevocable and are made four to six months before the start of the campaign (particularly in France and Germany). JC Decaux's rates are specified on standard rate cards, and it is its policy not to offer discounts, other than volume discounts. Rates across the company's network may vary in its main markets according to the size and the commercial attractiveness of the city, the season, or the occurrence of special events, such as the Olympic Games or the World Cup in soccer.

## Billboard

JC Decaux is the number-one billboard advertising company in Europe in terms of sales. In 2002, the number of faces remained stable, compared to 2001, due to its ongoing strategy to dismantle panels of lesser quality and, at the best locations, to replace some of these panels with modern, high-quality displays. In 2002, Billboard accounted for 28% of the firm's consolidated revenues.

### JC Decaux's Product Offering

Its billboard network enables JC Decaux to offer a broad range of products to its advertisers. The size and dimension of JC Decaux's billboards vary across its networks, due primarily to local regulations. The firm's premium billboards are also illuminated, which according to JC Decaux estimates, increases their audience size by up to 40%. The use of scrolling panels increases the number of faces that can be marketed per display and creates new marketing opportunities, such as time-sharing.

### Land Rental

JC Decaux leases the sites of its billboards principally from private landowners and, to a lesser extent, from city and railway authorities. Contract lengths vary greatly throughout the firm's network, often as a result of local regulation, but generally do not exceed 5 to 6 years and provide for automatic renewal.

### Geographic Coverage

JC Decaux has over 192,000 display faces in 23 European countries and two countries in Asia. The majority of these panels are located along the principal commuter routes that run within and around the major cities in each country. JC Decaux's most significant city, in terms of business, is Paris where the firm has 1,762 display faces, representing approximately one-third of the total market share in that city.

### Marketing and Sales

JC Decaux accommodates the needs of its diverse clientele by offering high-quality advertising packages in prime locations that enable them to reach a wide audience or to target a specific audience. The firm's clients are both national and local advertisers. JC Decaux also has a strong relationship with media buyers and advertising agencies, which typically serve as intermediaries between its advertisers and the company.

A large proportion of JC Decaux's business comes from short-term, 7- to 15-day advertising campaigns, although in some countries, such as France, long-term packages averaging from one to three years also contribute significantly to the firm's revenues. Long-term packages tend to be purchased in order to provide directions to the location of a particular advertiser or to promote its corporate image. JC Decaux is able to post a nationwide campaign in France within 24 hours.

Unlike Street Furniture advertising, prices may be discounted from JC Decaux's standard rate cards, consistent with market practice. With this practice in mind, the firm has developed a system that allows the company's sales force to optimize billboard sales. This "yield management" system allows JC Decaux to follow the evolution of offer and demand for its advertising networks in real time, and permits to offer discounts to advertisers in order to sell each billboard network at the highest possible price.

Each of its advertising packages is assembled in conjunction with audience measurement techniques that the firm has helped to develop. Based on its market research regarding the audiences that come into contact with its billboards, JC Decaux offers a variety of short-term advertising packages aimed at meeting its advertisers' various needs and objectives. For example, advertisers can buy display faces that provide them with homogenous national or regional coverage, focused coverage in a key city, or a location near stores, movie theaters, or metro stations.

Time-sharing is the latest example of how JC Decaux's geo-marketing expertise and state-of-the-art network of billboards can work together to serve its advertisers best. With the advent of scrolling billboards and remote control technology, JC Decaux is now able to manage in a very precise manner the display face that appears on a billboard at a given time.

Finally, in the United Kingdom, the company has developed a new billboard technology called "Chameleon," which makes it possible to put up two completely different displays, night and day, on a single back illuminated structure. JC Decaux financed the development of this new technology and owns the exclusive marketing rights to use it for its clients.

## Transport

JC Decaux's Transport advertising business includes the world's leading airport advertising businesses, advertising concessions in metros, trains, buses, trams, and other mass transit systems, as well as the express train terminals serving large international airports around the world. These contracts cover 190 cities in Europe, South America, and Asia-Pacific. A significant number of these contracts are in Italy, where the company offers advertisers a national coverage for advertising in buses.

In 2002, the firm's Transport revenues represented 18.7% of its consolidated revenues. Airport advertising accounted for 63% of its Transport revenues, with advertising in other transport systems accounting for 32% of the remaining revenues. Marginal operations conducted by subsidiaries in its Transport business, like billboard or cinema advertisements, represented the remaining 5%.

### Airport Advertising

Although it is difficult to obtain reliable industry performance sources for airport advertising, JC Decaux estimates that it has increased its worldwide airport advertising market share to over 35% in 2002, based on its performance in the key British international airports where the company holds concessions, and that JC Decaux is the leading airport advertising company in the world.

### Geographic Coverage

Under a single trade name, "JC Decaux Airport," the firm reaches 30% of worldwide airport traffic with a presence:

- In Europe, with 90 airports, three of which are the largest in Europe: London, Frankfurt, and Paris
- In Asia, with the concession for the Hong Kong airport (Chek Lap Kok), the major entry point into the region
- In the United States, with concessions in 47 airports (subsequent to a decision not to renew concessions for some unprofitable regional airports)
- In Mexico, where the firm won the advertising concession for the 9 airports in southeastern Mexico

### Airport Advertising Contracts

Most of the authorities that operate the airports are government or quasi-government authorities. Concessions are typically granted through competitive bids, for a term that typically ranges between 5 and 10 years.

JC Decaux pays a percentage of its advertising revenues to airport authorities under its concession agreements (varying between 50 and 70%, on average). However, JC Decaux's initial capital investment, which is often shared by the airport, as well as ongoing maintenance expenses, is typically much less than that for its open-air street furniture contracts.

## Audience and Traffic

Audience in international airports is particularly sought after by advertisers because it typically includes a high percentage of business travelers, who are difficult to reach by another medium, who spend a considerable amount of time waiting for flights and luggage, and who are relatively open to receive an advertiser's message. Between 1995 and 2001, the volume of passengers in airports grew by an average annual rate of 5.5% (source: ACI). Although the terrorist attacks of September 11, 2001, in the United States have had a negative impact on air passenger traffic growth, the company believes that this impact is temporary and that the growth of passenger traffic will resume once the geopolitical climate improves.

## Marketing and Sales

JC Decaux designs and positions its airport advertising structures to blend in with the overall design of airport terminals and to provide its advertisers with the best possible exposure and impact upon its target audience. The panels are placed where passengers tend to congregate, such as check-in areas, passenger lounges, gate areas, passenger corridors, and baggage carousel areas, offering advertisers the opportunity to interact with its target audience close to points of sale and to the commercial areas of the airport.

JC Decaux also builds custom-made structures for its advertisers, such as oversized models of their products, which the firm designs and locates so as to have a maximum impact on incoming and outgoing road traffic.

The firm was the first airport advertising company to develop a transport audience measurement system, called RADAR, which JC Decaux uses to map the location of its advertising panels by retail proximity and to determine the sociodemographic characteristics of their potential audience.

## Metro and Other Transport Advertising

As of December 31, 2002, JC Decaux had 150 transport advertising contracts with major metro, train, bus, and tramway systems. Metro audiences are similar to Billboard and Street Furniture audiences. The firm uses similar geomarketing techniques (time-sharing, networks tailored to specific audiences) to maximize the audience of each network and the impact of its advertisers' campaigns.

The term of JC Decaux's metro contracts is typically between 3 and 10 years. The initial investment and ongoing maintenance expenses required in metro concessions are typically lower than those required in Street Furniture contracts; the company pays the concession grantors a percentage of its revenues.

# Existing Risks for JC Decaux

### Risks Related to the Strategy and the Company

Regarding the growth strategy of JC Decaux, we can distinguish different types of risks, which could affect the business of the French company. First, JC Decaux has many current contracts that will expire in the next two years. That is why the firm will have to compete for many bids. For example, from 2003 to 2005, 13.3% of its Street Furniture contracts will expire as well as 35.1% of its Transport advertising concessions. Indeed, JC Decaux intends to bid for the renewal of the existing contracts; this represents a main problem since the company will probably have to invest a lot in the making of its offers. The extra costs will be added in its advertising prices. However, if JC Decaux does not succeed in making up these increased costs for its customers, its earnings could be affected.

### Risks Related to Key Accounts

JC Decaux attracts a lot of famous advertisers in each country in which the company has an advertising network because it owns many concessions in the key cities. However the company is concerned about these strategic concessions since it will not be able to satisfy its large advertisers if the company loses these concessions. In this case, JC Decaux will probably not attract the same quality of advertisers that are ready to pay a high price for the premium quality products delivered by the company.

### Risks Related to Contracts with Governmental Bodies

JC Decaux faces legal problems concerning its contracts with local governments, more particularly in France. The procedures which are linked with the public bid process in France are complex: The contracts are renewed by local state representatives in accordance with French administrative law. Some competitors of JC Decaux have proved that all the procedures have not been always followed. For this reason, they challenge the validity of the contracts based on defects in the public bid process. According to French law, penalties for failure to comply with the public tender requirements include cancellation of the underlying contract and suspension of the breaching party from participating in public tender offers for a minimum of three years.

In the same way, the street furniture (such as public automatic toilets or electronic bulletin boards) that JC Decaux rents to cities for a fixed annual fee does not comply with a public bidding process. The validity of such contracts could be soon called into question.

Another risk related to contracts with local governments lies in the fact that the authorities can terminate the current contacts for public interest reasons. JC Decaux would receive in such a case a compensation for early termination but this compensation will not cover the investments of JC Decaux or its loss of future profits.

## Risk Related to Regulation of Competition

An important element of JC Decaux's growth strategy involves the acquisition of additional outdoor advertising companies and properties, many of which are likely to require pre-approval of national and European competition authorities. Antitrust authorities in the UK have already acted to prevent JC Decaux from completing acquisitions. In addition, the Minister of Economy in France has, in the past, imposed restrictions upon the firm's external growth. Although the entrance into the outdoor advertising market of Viacom and Clear Channel in the past few years has lessened the firm's leading position in several areas of activity, it is still possible that the European Commission or national antitrust authorities might seek to bar JC Decaux from acquiring additional outdoor advertising operations or to limit some of its business activities.

## Risks Related to Economic Conditions

Advertising spending is highly dependent on the general condition of the economy. In 2001 and 2002 many customers of JC Decaux cut their advertising budgets. Since most of the costs of JC Decaux are fixed, the operating profit and the net income are seriously affected by a decrease in its revenues. However, the company has no interest in emerging market countries, which reduces the country risk.

## Risks Related to Applicable Regulations

Outdoor advertising is subject to significant governmental regulations at the national and local level in Europe and the United States. These regulations include limits on the density, size, and location of billboards and other types of signage in urban and other areas. There are more and more changes in laws and regulations affecting outdoor advertising, but JC Decaux cannot predict what additional regulations may be imposed. Therefore, the business is vulnerable on this point.

More generally, JC Decaux has to face problems concerning directives, which are taken by the EU-Commission. One of the most dangerous for JC Decaux is the directive regarding the termination of restrictions on television advertising by large retailers. It means that the directive "Cross-Border Television" broadcasts will allow the large European retailers to advertise on television. The adoption of this new rule will have a negative impact on the Business of JC Decaux, since 4.1% of its consolidated revenues come from advertising on billboards for large retailers. Besides, two others directives concerning the Tobacco Advertising and the Alcoholic Beverage Advertising represent an obstacle for JC Decaux. These directives stay relatively flexible and vary considerably from country to country. However, measures involving the total prohibition of this type of advertising could have a negative impact on the business of JC Decaux.

# JEWELMART.COM

Axel Quist, the marketing manager of JEWELMART. COM, an electronic market for trading jewels and related products, was perplexed with the large numbers of firms that joined JEWELMART.COM and left the market within a year. The market offered jewelry buyers, sellers, retailers, pawnbrokers, and appraisers access to potential business partners from across the world. In a fragmented jewelry industry, this meant that these small firms were no longer hostages to a few (if not one) business partners and could have access to more suppliers and buyers. Quist believed the attractiveness of a market depended on firms participating in the market. If there are a large number of firms participating in a market (i.e., a market has a *critical mass* of firms), it is attractive for other firms to join the market, as these other firms have the higher likelihood of trading in the market. With this *network externality* argument as a basis, Quist had focused all resources at his disposal to build the membership of JEWELMART.COM. With more than 2,000 enrolled members, Quist believed that the market was attractive for new members and was puzzled by the large number of new members leaving the JEWELMART.COM market. Quist decided to hire Capuro and Associates, a leading consulting firm, to help understand the reason for the departure of new members.

This case was written by Professor Rajdeep Grewal at Washington State University and Professors Raj Mehta and James M. Comer at the University of Cincinnati for discussion purposes. It does not illustrate the effective or ineffective marketing strategies. Used with permission.

## Background

JEWELMART.COM was established in 1983 primarily to provide an electronic market for jewelry pawnbrokers, appraisers, manufacturers, wholesalers, retailers, buyers, and sellers. It is a subscription-based service where members pay a monthly access fee, which enables the members to buy and/or sell such jewelry items as cut diamonds, watches, and rings, as well as acquire other benefits such as gemological and related technical information. For example, a member in Iowa might be interested in acquiring several diamonds of a specific carat, cut, and color. The member would simply "Broadcast" (send a general message to all members) describing that interest. Other subscribers (anywhere in the United States or around the world) can read the "Broadcast" and send a "Direct" (private) message to that potential buyer describing and perhaps showing a picture of the diamonds they have available. The potential buyer might winnow the suppliers down to a few and conduct negotiations with sellers either by telephone or over the secure Trading Network.

JEWELMART.COM migrated in the late 1980s to an "exchange hub." Because the market facilitated interfirm transactions in days prior to the Internet, it relied on user firms to call the New York server to retrieve (1) their e-mail and (2) information from the buyer-seller bulletin board. The firms on the system conducted business by exchanging information through the use of e-mail and postings on the bulletin board. In the late 1990s and more specifically in late 1997, JEWELMART.COM acquired a domain name and started to move its operations to

**Exhibit 1**
Market Adoption Process

*This figure is derived from: Rajdeep Grewal, James M. Comer, and Raj Mehta. "An Investigation into the Antecedents of Organizational Participation in Business to Business Electronic Markets,"* Journal of Marketing, Vol. 65 (July 2001), p.20

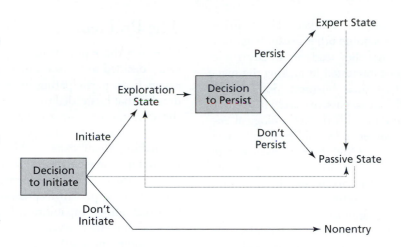

Intenet-based platforms. During late 1997 and early 1998, JEWELMART.COM migrated completely to the Web. Although the transition to the Web has eased access for user firms, as they do not have to make calls to New York any more, the nature of the information exchange has remained the same. The "Trading Network" on the JEWELMART.COM website allows access to bulletin boards, e-mail, and buyer-seller discussion boards. JEWELMART.COM still remains a subscription-based electronic market; that is, the participants have to pay a monthly fee to get access to the site. In fact, just recently the subscription rates were increased to $200 per month. Further, the site is only open to established companies in the jewelry industry (any firm in the trade association can become a member), but is not open to an average individual consumer.

This access to a worldwide base of sellers and buyers increases a subscriber's sales, lowers transaction costs, and saves considerable time. These advantages exist for low-priced commodities (e.g., diamonds) and high-priced differentiated products (e.g., wedding rings). As these advantages have become known in the industry and the industry members more comfortable with Internet security, sales growth has been spectacular with membership increasing by six times since 1994. This growth has paralleled the recent explosive growth experienced in similar environments known as "Business Bots." Clearly, this electronic market represents an "open bazaar" where buyers and sellers meet in an electronic environment. In fact, JEWELMART.COM makes it efficient for firms to exchange information related to price, product specifications, and terms of

trade. Although JEWELMART.COM does not make it possible for participating firms to make payments electronically, it does provide a rating for all participating firms, which is based on their payment history.

# Network Externality: A Redefinition

Capuro and Associates conducted in-depth interviews and focus groups with existing members and with firms that had decided to leave JEWELMART. COM. They found that participating firms could be in one of three possible states: (1) exploration state, (2) expert state, and (3) passive state.

Firms in the *exploration state* did not know how to conduct operations in the market, but were willing to spend effort to learn how to do business in the marketplace. Firms in the *expert state* had made the market a regular part of their operations and believed that they knew their way around the marketplace. Firms in the *passive state* carried out virtually no business in the market, but continued to maintain a presence, perhaps for some other motivation.

Research also showed that firms that joined JEWELMART.COM initially moved to the exploration state (Exhibit 1). If these firms decided to persist with their operations in the market, they moved to the expert state; otherwise they moved to the passive state. Besides this main adoption cycle of firms in JEWELMART.COM, alternative paths existed (shown by dotted arrows in Exhibit 1). A few firms moved straight to the passive state at the time of their adoption of the market. These firms adopted the market for some other reason (e.g., just to tell their clients that they trade in an electronic market) and were not interested in making the market a regular part of their business. Some firms moved from expert state to passive state. These firms did not keep up to date with the technological enhancements in the market and would eventually skittle into the passive state. Often firms in passive state decided to spend more effort in the electronic market and make it a regular part of their business and moved to the exploration state.

The crux of the research of Capuro and Associates was that the network externality of JEWELMART.COM did not depend on number of firms adopting the market, but instead was a function of number of expert firms in the market. Eventually, if a firm decided to adopt JEWELMART.COM, it would trade with expert firms in the market, as passive firms do not trade in the market, whereas exploration firms do not know how to trade in the market.

## The Problem

Digesting the report from Capuro and Associates, Quist decided to focus on increasing the number of expert firms participating in Jewelry Exchange. He decided that he needed to move the firms faster from the exploratory state to the expert state, and he needed to awaken the passive firms with hope of making them experts. He asked his assistant marketing manager, Patrick Behan, to find out how expert firms become experts. Behan's research showed that expert firms possessed greater information technology capabilities, laid heavier emphasis on attaining efficiency, and expended more effort to learn about the market. In addition, the longer a firm stayed on with JEWELMART.COM, the more likely it was to eventually become an expert firm. Armed with these facts, Quist sat down to devise a new marketing strategy with the objective of creating a greater number of expert firms.

# Lafarge - Aget Heracles

## Company Background

Aget cement (written "aget" but pronounced "ayet"), a major Greek company, was formed in 1911. In 1992 it sold its 50.5% shares to the Italian Calcestruzzi, SpA., currently in the Italcementi group.

In 1996, Aget acquired Halkis Cement Group, reducing the number of domestic players in the Greek market. In 2000, 54.48% of its shares was sold to the English Group Blue Circle Industries, plc. In 2001, Blue Circle Industries, plc was acquired by the French Group Lafarge, a global building materials producer.

Aget, a national company, has major regional operations throughout the prosperous market of the Middle East and periphery with terminals and bulk cement storage and concrete/aggregate facilities in Egypt, Saudi Arabia, Nigeria, and Algeria. It presently contemplates expanding into Lebanon, Kuwait, and UAE. Aget is regionally famous for having a top quality product and in the Greek market enjoys a large market share, about 50% in the cement/concrete (beton) business.

It has a large share of the public works and other institutional markets. Its major competitors are Titan cement and Halyps cement, currently a subsidiary of the Italcementi group, whose combined share almost equals the other 50% of the market. Aget's presence in the Middle East is threatened by the conglomerate Italcementi's aggressive entry into the above market. The Italcementi group is a vertically integrated company, owning limestone gypsum and rock quarries, processing plants and distribution facilities in more than ten countries.

Aget has a collective production capacity of 11.2 million tons, but achieves about 8.5 million tons in annual sales,[1] indicating a utilization rate of about 76%. Its cement is distributed and delivered by sea-vessels and trucks.

## The Product

Cement may be used, in combination with other ingredients, to produce *concrete* for a variety of construction needs. The product may be delivered for mixing at the building site or already mixed and delivered for immediate use upon arrival at the site.

Cement is a solid gray powder manufactured using pyroprocessing in kilns from limestone, silica sand, clay, slate, and other additives using a chemical process and a great amount of heat. The resulting compound, known as clinker, is ground into powder and blended with gypsum which controls the setting of concrete. The powder is so fine that one kilogram of cement contains more than 300 billion grain-particles.

*Professor Constantine G. Polychroniou developed this case for class discussion. The discussion on the various topics in this case is meant to have pedagogical impact and does not intend to indicate effectiveness or ineffectiveness of managerial action. The author brings into the case information that he had gained when he was in an advisory capacity with Aget Heracles in the early 80s. Other data have been pulled in from public sources. Certain company information or data have been subtly disguised so as to enhance or conversely not affect the instructive effect of the case.*

[1] 2004 Sales: 390,215 + 45.91 = 8.49 mmt. (see P&L statement, exhibit I).

**Exhibit A**
Portland
Cement
Specification—
Purchase Order

---

*Technical Specification of Portland*

Portland cement bs12/196 grade # 42.5r "British standard".

Chemical analysis $SiO_2$: 19.62%, $Al_2O_3$: 5.18%, $Fe_2O_3$: 3.89%, CaO: 61.62%, MgO: 2.44%, $Na_2O$: 0.46%, $K_2O$: 0.27%, Cl: 0.07%, $SO_3$: 2.71%, I.O. I: 2.15%. Undetermined: 0.37%.

Total: 100%.

C3A 7.15% max 3.5.

Physical & mechanical:

Standard consistency: 25.5%

Packaging: in 50 kgs pp bags

Quantity: min 12.500 metric tons (+/− 5 %)

Price: contact us

Size of shipment: min 12.500/mt

Loading rate per day: 2000 tons a day

Discharge rate per day: min 2000 tons a day

Inspection: SGS certificate is required as a supporting documentation for product quality

Delivery time: within 30–45 day after confirmed L/C

Origin: Supplier's plant origin

Payment term: DL/C at sight, irrevocable, non transferable, confirmed and payable at sight by a prime first class bank

Shipment: first shipment will commence (30–45 days) after receipt and acceptance of designated buyer's payment instrument L/C

Documents: full set of international accepted standard

---

Cement quality, strongly guided by technical specs, is viewed as extremely important by cement or concrete users. The product seems to be viewed as a commodity product given its broad use and the lack of distinctive branding. *Portland cement,* invented in 1824, is not a brand name but the generic term, just as sterling is a type of silver, and represents several types of cement made predominantly of calcium silicates and manufactured from limestone, shale, clay, and iron ore. Its important ingredient is cement clinker which is a granulated product produced under temperatures in excess of 1500 $^{\circ}$C. Portland cement accounts for more than 95% of all cement produced.

The number and amount of compounds in a cement, when converted into concrete, determine the cement's engineering performance vis-a-vis its durability and resistance to decay. So *Portland cement* may be specified in types I, II, III, IV, and V. Each of these types has a different chemical composition. For instance, the type IV *Portland cement,* a "low heat" cement, is deemed appropriate for use in extensive concrete structures such as the Hoover Dam. The type V is a "sulfate-resistant" cement and it is deemed appropriate for use in areas that have sulfate-rich soils or waters, whereas, the type II is both a "moderate heat" and "moderate in sulfate-resistance" cement. See Exhibit A.

Portland cement is a cost-effective material used practically in all forms of construction, either in precast or ready-mix concrete. The concrete is a mixture composed of 11% percent cement, 41% gravel, 26% sand, 16% water, and 6% air. The quantity of water helps determine the strength of the concrete. That is, more water makes the concrete weak, while adding more cement increases its strength.

*Blended cements* represent a wide range of products with which to prepare concrete with specific applications. These cements are ideal for specific environments, to counteract chemical reactivity, for particular projects such as roads, bridges, etc.

*Specialty cements,* such hydraulic cements are excellent binders for soil stabilization and act as retardant to fluid accumulation.

*Masonry/mortar cement* used for concrete bricks, stucco products and tile-joint applications.

*White cement* used in special architectural designs that require a colored surface finish.

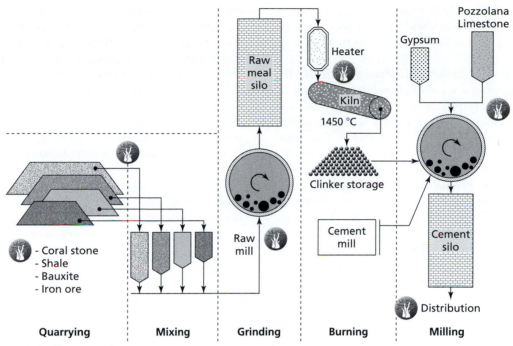

Raw
meal
silo

Heater

Pozzolana
Limestone

Gypsum

Kiln

1450 °C

Clinker storage

- Coral stone
- Shale
- Bauxite
- Iron ore

Raw
mill

Cement
mill

Cement
silo

Distribution

| Quarrying | Mixing | Grinding | Burning | Milling |

SOURCE: http//www.abmburicement.com/make.htm.

## Exhibit B
### Global Market Structure*

| Company | Global Market Share |
| --- | --- |
| CRH | 4.10% |
| Holcim | 4.00% |
| Lafarge | 3.50% |
| Taiheiyo | 1.20% |
| Other | 87.20% |

*DATAMONITOR; Global Construction Materials; Industry Profile; Reference Code: 0199–2030. Publication date: May 2004.

Cements may also be identified using numbers. For instance, #325 is a lower-grade cement, whereas #525 is a high-grade cement.

## The Industry

The global cement industry is driving toward oligopoly through mergers and acquisitions resulting in capacity concentration and potential cartelization through the dominance of a few transnational players. However, the industry remains largely fragmented, where no one player has a double-digit market share, and lacks the capacity to exercise price discipline, being plagued by excess capacity, rising operating costs, and depressed margins. It has been growing at a rate of about 4% annually over the past 20 years showing an aggregate production, in 2003, of about 1.82 billion metric tons of cement with an annual turnover[2] of about $100 billion. It is a highly fragmented industry with a few players controlling a disproportionally high market share (Exhibit B).

Industry capacity utilization is around 71% signifying likely downward pressure on prices. Increasing capacity utilization, given an increase in the demand for cement, would mean greater pricing leverage and profitability for the producer. It is a capital intensive industry making change-introduction less desirable and less likely. The capital investment per worker in the cement industry is among the highest in all industries.

The global industry operates plant and processing facilities in some 150 countries worldwide. It is projected that the industry will enjoy continuing growth

[2] Annual turnover is the value of all supplies made or to be made in the current year.

on expectations of high cement consumption. It is noteworthy that worldwide the import duty on cement and clinker has been reduced by an average of 30%.

As mentioned earlier, the industry worldwide has been witnessing a wave of consolidation driven by acquisitions, strategic alliances and partnerships as dominant, more efficient players focus on adding synergistic value[3] to their organizations. This trend has been the result of the need to increase cost efficiencies by investing in new precalciner kilns that would increase production capacity and cut costs, exploiting economies of scale, enhance market presence and beef up market share in an increasingly competitive and mature industry.

The players' market dominance and strength of competitive positioning is manifest by means of point of manufacture and point of distribution. This is the case because proximity of plant to market is an enhancer to cost efficiencies and distribution proximity is a catalyst to achieving market power which is exceedingly important as market networking becomes increasingly critical. Also, manufacturing costs are rising, requiring a greater focus on cost control and increasing efficiency levels. In response to that, the cement industry has enhanced efficiency by directing new capital investment in plants that replace the wet-process with the dry-process of cement manufacture. The latter technology is less energy intensive and thus more cost efficient.

As global competition heats up international cement producers find that positioning may render a competitive advantage, given that market presence plays a decisive role in influencing capacity utilization deemed particularly significant in a commodity market. Furthermore, global operations have also brought about added pressure for focusing on industrial ecology and carbon dioxide emission management, an orientation that is deemed to be a strategic policy for establishing trust and community relationships, a concern that is juxtaposed to industry standards and specifications that address issues of product performance vis-a-vis safety and structural integrity. Nevertheless, it should be pointed out that the cement business is largely a local business, in that, for most projects product availability and delivery are both decisively pivotal.

The industry is in a long maturity and, given its nature of capital intensity, players in it frown upon change. However, the industry must balance endogenous concerns and exogenous challenges. Endogenous concerns would include: commoditization, capital and resource intensity, market pressures, product maturity, etc. Exogenous challenges would include: customer needs, innovation in technologies, global consolidation, regional integration, environmental sensitivities,[4] energy prices, regulatory interference, etc.

## Market—Competition

In 2003 the global construction materials market grew by 4.2% reaching a value of $249.9 billion. The forecast for 2008 is that the global market will reach a revenue level of $306.4 billion, representing an increase of 22.6% within the 5-year period. Cement is the leading source of revenue for the market generating 49.9% of the market's total revenue or $124.7 billion valued at manufacturers' selling price.[5]

Cement customers that are able to consolidate into becoming major customers exert decisive pressure upon suppliers. Under these circumstances, and feeling the need to increase market share, suppliers succumb to pressure to lower prices adversely affecting industry profitability.

Cement or concrete customers being guaranteed low prices, by virtue of competition and the commodity character of the product, look to identify differential niches such as "trusting a supplier." This reality constitutes a potential base for developing effective anti-commoditization strategies.

Also, as customer needs evolve the pressure for product development increases. For instance, certain customers such as governments, hospitals, or other institutions are showing interest in specialty cements and cement mixtures that have been produced with environmentally appropriate products or products whose use would not deplete natural resources. Also, emerging needs for special designs that call for extra durability of structures require the development of such specialty cements or cement products. For instance, the Middle East market seems to exceedingly value concrete structures and concrete-based

---

[3]Synergistic value would also include "strategic enterprise value" which is value measurable in nonfinancial terms, i.e. image.

[4]It is reported that the cement industry contributes about 3% of the total greenhouse gas emissions. (Pressures of the Kyoto protocol may intensify investment in cement production technology.)

[5]DATAMONITOR; Global Construction Materials; Industry Profile; Reference Code: 0199-2030. Publication date: May 2004.

**Exhibit C**
Total Regional Market Sales Allocation per Segment— 2004

| *2004 Regional Sales by Market Segment* | | |
|---|---|---|
| **Building Segment** | | **Non-Building Segment** |
| A.  Residential: 11.89 mmt. | | Heavy construction |
| B.  Non-residential: 39.26 mmt. | | (industrial & non-industrial): 22.09 mmt. |
| Total sales: A + B + C = 73.4 mmt. | | |

**Exhibit D**
Anticipated 5-year Segmental Regional Growth in Cement Consumption

| Segment | *Years* | | | | |
|---|---|---|---|---|---|
| | **2005** | **2006** | **2007** | **2008** | **2009** |
| (Growth rate) | 3.9% | 3.8% | 4.1% | 4.3% | 4.0% |
| Non-residential | 40.79 | 42.34 | 44.07 | 45.97 | 47.81 |
| (Growth rate) | 4.0% | 4.1% | 3.8% | 4.7% | 6.1% |
| Non-building | 22.97% | 23.91% | 24.82% | 25.99% | 27.57 |

construction. This may incentivize cement producers to make long-term investments in new cement-compositions even though they have resigned to the fact that cement is strictly a commodity whose price is uniform in a given market.

Market demand for cement is normally elastic (elasticity is around 1.5) given its low value commodity character. However, demand for cement is local, and price inelasticities may be observed especially among grades of cement.

Furthermore, the market demand for cement worldwide keeps growing, and, as the standard of living keeps increasing, the opportunity for continued cement sales and specialty cements is likely to grow, as well.

Innovation in technology is likely to beef up the gamut of construction materials and intensify competition among them. Portland cement, despite its high popularity, may lose its differential edge if substitutes that render a greater net value can be produced.

Volatility in energy prices will likely enhance uncertainty and be counterproductive to achieving desired cost efficiencies. Such reality may give impetus to global or regional players to seek out alternative energy sources or proceed with investments in production technologies or processes that effectively answer the call of higher energy prices. Nevertheless, diesel prices are critical to improving operating costs and transport costs considering that about 60–70% of the cement is transported by road.

Competition is likely to intensify as consolidation increases and product differentiation remains re-mote. The transnational model of global reach and local responsiveness is the field in which the drama of competitive action will unfold.

Competitive sustainability pivots on the player's ability to control costs, increase operational efficiencies, reduce uncertainty by effectively managing risk, establish a better distribution system, and last and most importantly to differentiate.

The markets for cement are identified as *building* and *non-building* construction. The building construction market has two distinct segments: the *residential* and *non-residential,* with the latter being the largest. The non-building construction[6] is heavy construction and addresses areas such as: *highways, power plants, pipelines,* and *heavy industrial structures* (chemical facilities, petroleum refineries, nuclear structures, etc.). The non-building market is the fastest growing market given the developmental needs of infrastructure.

Market segments that Aget wants to focus on are: *non-residential,* and the *non-building* market. Regionally, Aget has a market share of 11.6% of 73.4 million metric tons (mmt) or 8.5 mmt. (2004 sales). Total regional market sales for 2004, allocated on a per segment basis, are shown in Exhibit C.

Of the 8.5 mmt of Aget's total annual sales the non-residential segment accounts for 58% or 4.93 mmt, the non-building segment accounts for 36% or 3.06 mmt, and the remaining 6% or 0.51 mmt is residential. Anticipated regional growth in cement consumption, per segment of interest, is indicated in Exhibit D.

---

[6] http://www.census.gov/epcd/naics/NDEF234.HTM.

**Exhibit E**
Aget's 5-Year
Projected Sales
Growth*

| Segment | Years | | | | |
| --- | --- | --- | --- | --- | --- |
| | 2005 | 2006 | 2007 | 2008 | 2009 |
| (Growth rate) Non-residential | 3.9% × 4.93 = 5.12 | 3.8% × 5.12 = 5.31 | 4.1% × 5.31 = 5.53 | 4.3% × 5.53 = 5.77 | 4.0% × 5.77 = 6 |
| (Growth rate) Non-building | 4.0% × 3.06 = 3.18 | 4.1% × 3.18 = 3.31 | 3.8% × 3.31 = 3.43 | 4.7% × 3.43 = 3.6 | 6.1% × 3.6 = 3.82 |

*Assuming maintenance of current share levels.

If current share levels are maintained Aget's sales for the next 5 years are depicted in Exhibit E. The collective market potential of the markets of Lebanon, Kuwait, and UAE is estimated to be 9.7 mmt. Preliminary estimates of required investment and expected sales have been $6.3 million and 1.94 mmt., or about 20% market share, respectively.

## Pricing

Demand is locationally differentiated, i.e., it varies from location-to-location depending largely on population density, but highly undifferentiated in terms of quality, i.e., cement standards are usually common across borders because cement is an experience or performance good. The demand for cement depends on macroeconomic factors such as population growth, GDP growth, interest rates, economic policies formulated that, for instance, affect infrastructure development, etc.

Cement is a homogeneous product with a low price elasticity due to lack of substitute materials. Specialty cements, used for their strength in specific applications such as pavement restoration, special architecture, and other projects, as a differentiated line are priced higher and demand for them seems to be even more inelastic. However, a material known as "fly ash," chemically reinforced, may replace even 100% of that cement.[7] In 2002, as the price of specialty cement increased 12% there was an increase in its demand of about 4%. However, in 2004 the specialty cement's price increased further by 9% effecting a 17% increase in sales of fly ash.

High production and transportation costs and a sizeable incipient investment constitute formidable entry barriers to local firms. Under such conditions cost efficient firms are able to engage in selling on the basis of marginal costs. Economies of scale beefed up by operational flexibility are at the forefront of effective competition making price the competitive variable in the cement industry, further indicating the criticality of cost efficiencies. Despite an increase in the price of materials, there is downward pressure on cement market prices due to the gap between production capacity and utilization, on the one hand, and competition on the other.

Although operational costs in the cement industry are subject to the industry's dependence on production factors, with prices largely administered, cement pricing is guided by market commoditization. So, if volume growth continues, as expected, cement prices will depend on whether and/or to what extent capacity increases or remains unchanged. That is, a decrease in the gap between demand and supply is deemed to enhance the suppliers' pricing power. Therefore, increases in the prices of raw materials or production factors do not automatically get passed onto the customer. Passing such price increases on to the customer depends on excess capacity or rate of utilization. On the other hand, when competitors cut prices, players that do not follow suit run the risk of market share loss while collectively they suffer a net loss in profitability.

Despite such realities Aget is contemplating to further cut its price by 12% in order to increase capacity utilization, resulting in an increase in market share and a reduction in unit costs. Moreover, Aget is pondering that its regional competitors will not match its price cuts as they operate at capacities close to 95%. Specifically, in an internal survey Aget's executives

[7]http://www.civil.columbia.edu/meyer/publications/2002_04_ShahPaper.pdf. Concrete and Sustainable Development (C. Meyer).

## Exhibit F
## Average Cost Structure (as % of cost of sales)*

| | |
|---|---|
| Power & fuel | 32.8% |
| Material cost | 12.4% |
| Freight (outward) | 19.7% |
| Admin. & overhead | 19.8% |
| Employee cost | 8.0% |
| Selling expenses | 4.2% |
| Repair & mainten. | 3.1% |

*Averages cover the period of 1995 through 2004.

believed that the probability of any one competitor cutting prices was no more than 25%. They all agreed that if a price cut was to occur it would not be more than 70% of Aget's contemplated price cut. Aget expected to achieve a 20% increase in market share, if the price cut was not matched and an 8% market share if the price cut was matched to the level of 70%.

Aget's largest competitors had a lower cost structure than Aget because they offered fewer support services and they employed a transactional approach. As a result they were better positioned to compete on price. However, Aget was poised to increase its profitability if it could bundle its offering and maintain its niche on customer relationships.

In terms of production operations, energy and power inputs account for about ¾ of the cost of production. Freight cost is the single largest cost element for any cement company (see Exhibit F). Competitive pricing that may lead to greater market concentration is discouraged due to the industry's high and rising energy and transportation costs. Tariffs that range from 10% to 40% continue to be an impediment to effective or "value-oriented" pricing for both the customer and the supplier. These tariffs are gradually being eliminated as WTO regulations take hold. Such pending reality is expected to enhance both demand and the cement industry's profitability. In 2004, however, prices increased by 2.8% over those of 2003, from $58.5 to $60 pmt.[8] This may have been the result, among others, of a brisk increase of 10.1% in construction spending over that of 2003.[9]

---

[8] In euros (€) this would be equivalent to 45.91€, at an exchange rate of 1 USD = 0.765286 EUR.

[9] U.S. Department of Commerce's report for August 2004.

# Company Operations

The company operates multiple quarries from which it extracts the raw materials of limestone, clay, and marl. The method for material extraction used is blasting and breaking up stone deposits with heavy machinery. The raw (rock) material is then transported to special installations in which the rock is further broken down to small size roadbed-surfacing stones (metalling). In turn, this crushed material is transported into a storage area, using conveyor-belts, railways, or even trucks, in which it is blended and homogenized. At this stage, the combining of the raw mix with silica sand, iron oxides, alumina deposits, shell, and other organic materials is decided upon and machine-executed on the basis of the type of cement the production schedule calls for. That mixture enters a processing mill in which it is ground to a fine powder. This raw meal is then transferred to a silo in which it is further homogenized. Following the homogenization process the raw meal enters the kiln in which it is burned at 1,450°C. The extreme heat helps the raw meal to chemically convert into a new product, known as *clinker.* The clinker is then cooled down and taken to special ball mills where it is ground to a powdery dust and with gypsum and other polymers it comes out as cement. The amount of gypsum and other additives used is dictated by the type of cement to be produced, or the need for which it is produced. At this point the cement is stored in silos from which it is distributed for use, either in bulk or packaged in bags by special rotary packers and automatically palletized. At this juncture, the production process is complete and it is traditionally monitored by production controllers. Aget wants to computerize the entire production process, thus minimizing errors and increasing efficiencies. The ratio of raw material requirements to cement production is 1.6:1: That is, for 1 ton of clinker produced 1.6 tons of raw material are required. This means that it is imperative for the cement producer to have access to ample quarry material. Access to quarries is deemed essential not only in terms of raw material availability but also for controlling costs, such as, royalty payments, etc.

Aget's platform product line is *Portland cement.* The company also produces *hydraulic cement* which is capable of hardening under water and which is unique for constructing water tanks, sewer pipes, tunnels, dams, etc.; *specialty cement,* such as white cement for architectural applications, is a low-alkali cement used in special construction requiring slow strength gain; *aggregates and concrete,* such as sand, gravel, cracked rock, and precast or ready-mix concrete; *roofing,* which is tiles in concrete; and, *gypsum,* which is plasterboard for walls and ceilings.

From the above product lines *Portland cement* is by far the most dominant in terms of sales and operational impact. Aget products are used in residential, industrial, commercial, and infrastructure applications. Operations mainly focus on selling cement or formulating, preparing, and delivering ready-mixed concrete at customer's designated job sites. Aget's operational objective is to offer services that reduce its customers' overall construction costs and increase net value.

Revenues from operations may be allocated as follows: cement trading 26%; ready-mix concrete 68%; other operations 6%. About 95% of revenues are from direct sales and the remaining 5% are generated using agents and dealers who sell a broad array of building products sourced from several suppliers. Such intermediary relationship is of a transactional character with no exclusivity on purchasing or selling. Trade margins range from 8% to 12%. Fifty-five percent (55%) of the cement traded is sold in bulk form and the other 45% is packaged in 50-kgr. bags.

Aget's manufacturing operations improvement plan calls for adding two new dry-process kilns totaling an investment of 10.7 million €. The aforesaid improvement is estimated to help increase current capacity by 18% over current levels and raise energy efficiency and productivity. Such kiln technology is said to have synergistic effects in that it allows the utilization of organic waste for fuel. The over 2000° C heat is considered by technicians an ideal process for consuming waste such as chlorinated organic compounds considered persistent organic pollutants, such as used tires, solvents, paint-wastes, used oil, and petroleum residues to name a few. This model of environmentally friendly production is considered advisable also from the standpoint of adherence to environmental regulations despite their relatively high costs.[10]

The cement kiln's great appetite for energy is typically satisfied using coal. Because energy costs can account for up to 40 percent of the total cost of cement manufacturing, the use of efficient energy is considered critical. Conversion to coal was started in the 1970s. Currently, more than 90% of production is achieved using relatively low-priced high-sulfur coals as primary fuel. In addition, recently Aget has introduced internal changes such as operator training, improving work procedures and maintenance scheduling, training on material handling, optimizing production schedules, etc. Above changes are expected to incrementally improve operating efficiencies[11] resulting in a further decrease of operating costs.

## International Expansion

Collectively, the market of the Middle East is a high growth market as demand exceeds available supply. For instance, Syria[12] has beefed up its production to 96% of capacity (4.8 mmt of 5 mmt) and is planning to increase capacity by 3 mmt or 60% in the next 4 years. At the same time, OMRAN—a state-owned company—is increasing its imports from the peripheral countries.

The demand for cement in Saudi Arabia has been growing in response to sustained population growth and continued development of infrastructure. It is projected that the annual growth in demand consumption will be around 5%. Recently, the domestic production has been sold in advance to domestic users, reducing exports and catapulting producers into increasing capacity. In the Gulf States demand exceeds supply due to feverish construction and development of major projects such as airports, island development, railways, waterfront building, etc. Such demand has accelerated cement production and overall capacity is expected to increase by 60% (from 36 mmt to 60 mmt) over the next 3 years. Growth in demand is expected to be an average of 12% a year.

In such an environment, Aget expects a push for industry consolidation as a drive for market share will increase the pressure for cost reduction.

---

[10]It is estimated that about 25% of the capital costs of building new plants and major modernizations go to meeting environmental regulations.

[11]Operating efficiencies address overall productivity. They include: labor improvement, effective use of financial resources, enhanced production capabilities, effective materials management, and generally the functioning of the internal organization.

[12]http://www.ameinfo.com/news/Detailed/43865.html.

In Jordan, cement monopolies that have resulted in distribution overpricing and supply discontinuities have been countered by government measures to increase cement availability in the Jordanian market, indicating the need for imports. In addition, Iraq's pending reconstruction is estimated to add to an already healthy Middle East cement market.

Aget's bid for a stronger presence into the Middle East market is a test to its management international know-how as the region presents special challenges across several functional areas. First and foremost, Aget's cultural orientation is deemed essential in adjusting its efforts to the demands of Middle East business culture. Aget realizes that although business solutions across cultures may be similar those solutions are arrived at in unique ways because of business customs and practices. In foreign markets, a new entrant may experience the need to lubricate and at times even to suborn. This is all in the name of facilitating doing business in the foreign market, from getting a license to passing a ministerial decree.

Second, Aget faces the challenge of developing and motivating a local sales force in the Middle East market. It has decided that incipiently it should establish a sales office in each of the three countries, Lebanon, Kuwait, and UAE, and staff each of those offices with a sales manager and two salespeople.

Third, in addition to the pricing inflexibilities inherent in the cement market, due mainly to the commodity character of the product, Aget must contend with the prospect of price escalation and the possible creation of parallel markets. Appropriate action is being planned to ward off such a possibility. (The incidence of a parallel market was manifest as recently as 2003 in Syria where the demand for cement kept rising while OMRAN, the state-owned company, limited supplies by restricting imports. Such disequilibrium created a black market for cement.)

Fourth, the cement industry's economies of scale in production and marketing, the cement's uniform global image, and Aget's ability to transfer expertise and know-how are all vital to the success of its global strategy. Aget recognized that in order to be competitive in a global business market it must meet the challenge of creating collaborative relationships that are guided by unique local marketing idiosyncrasies, essentially upgrading it to a transnational enterprise.

## Customers—Distribution

Aget's types of customers include: contractors, builders, ready-mix producers, concrete product manufacturers, and masons.

Aget's channels of distribution and product/sales allocation encompass the following:

*Cement (bagged or bulk),* normally sold directly to small customers for sacking it or indirectly through retailers such as lumberyards, accounts for about 26% of total sales. Of that, 55% is bulk-cement and 45% is bagged. An average of 80% of the above is direct sales; the remaining 20% is transacted through brokers or dealers.

*Ready-mix concrete,* sold directly to customers that require a ready-application product and which is customarily dispensed using leased special cement trucks, also accounts for about 68% of aggregate sales.

*Precast concrete products,* sold directly to a range of customers and which account for about 6% of all activity.

The top 15% of customers account for 75% of total sales. These customers are, by and large, concentrated in the "ready-mix concrete" segment and are involved with major project construction such as road and massive structures.

Cement products are stored in silos to which bulk cement trucks have access via dispatch points. This network of cement storage and distribution terminals helps create a unique advantage as these silos or terminals are located in proximity to high growth areas and close to potential customer activity. In addition, they offer customers the opportunity to select from a wide range of cement blends to suit their particular needs.

About 90% of the production output is distributed from the plant to selling points, using sea-vessels or trucks. The rest, 10%, is picked up by the buyers using their own transport means. As indicated in Exhibit F, freight accounts for 19.7% of CoGS. Recently, Aget has been contemplating acquiring and operating its own transport. Specifically, it plans to purchase maritime vessels and land trucks that, it is estimated, would transport up to 75% of the remaining (2004) production of 90%. The investment required is 14.5m €. This undertaking is expected to render an estimated 24% in transport net savings after recouping the incipient investment.

Aget has established regional sales offices through which it coordinates sales and delivery. The company has organized customer-teams made up of civil engineers, chemical engineers, and production specialists. These teams' primary goal is to help the customer achieve optimum use of the product, be it cement or concrete mix. By "optimum" we mean to use the right product for the right project or structure. This may best be accomplished using a proactive approach to the customer's contemplated needs; that is, in the design phase of the project the customer works in tandem with Aget's customer-team to identify product requirements and decide on an optimum product spec. This is an overall win–win exchange as both parties to the exchange are better able to implement and communicate joint value-added efforts leading to synergistic benefits. The customer decides on the right product and is assured availability and prompt delivery, avoiding construction delays, etc. The supplier is alerted to the type of product needed, ensuring timely production and product-project compatibility. Both customer and Aget get a chance to test the advisability of developing a relationship.

Transportation is a very critical element for the cement industry, given its cost impact of almost 20% (Exhibit F). The modes of transportation used are generally *road, rail,* or *sea.* Transport proliferation enhances the commoditization of cement, as a larger number of competitors have greater access to a given market/location.

The high costs of transportation in the cement industry help transform an otherwise transnational enterprise into a locally responsive and physically present operation.

Cement/concrete customers, in particular the larger ones, operate a decision-making unit (DMU) also known as buying center (BU) which plays a pivotal role in the interworkings of the cement/concrete construction market. The buying center of the larger customer could be stratified into two groups, on the basis of orientation. The group whose orientation was deemed to be strategic was made up of executives whose interests converged at achieving targeted business results, such as project profitability and long-term market posturing. The other group had a more tactical orientation and its direct goal was the successful functioning of the buying project. The latter group was largely made up of hands-on staff and their influence was expertise-related. Aget had realized that its approach to its customer's buying center should be bipolar, entertaining the concerns and interests of both groups by defining each group's particular real or perceived trade-offs between *product value* and *product cost.* The second group usually had a civil engineer as a team leader whose role was to integrate intragroup actions and to be the liaison between the two groups. This team leader was the incipient most important link to seeing the eventual success of a transaction. Aget executives thought that an effective approach to developing a project with a customer would pivot on how strong a relationship Aget sales people could develop with, and how they can empower, the team leader in the buying center's further proceedings.

As demand for cement/concrete-based construction increases and the competitive environment changes customers adapt to the new dynamics by changing their expectations. When customers lack prior experience in, or with, a given project they tend to take whatever steps necessary to see their first experience successful. To that effect, they are quality and service-oriented and are willing to pay the asking price. As those customers acquire experience with the product and process-relevant services they migrate to a different market position which prescribes a set of different expectations. For instance, when customers start to first use fly ash in the concrete mix they need the advice of a specialist in determining the ratio of fly ash to cement that would prospectively produce the desired durability. But as the customers acquire that expertise their needs change compelling them to migrate to a different product/customer relationship. This is further enhanced by a gradual change in the purchasing strategy of the buying center in which procurement seems to gradually dominate the engineering and other quality-oriented influences. That new relationship seems to beef up the customer's negotiating leverage with the cement supplier for added services and lower prices, resulting in eroding the supplier's profitability. This may be, at least to some degree, countervailed by focusing on a bundled offering.

Product policy may be used as a strategic tool to broaden the influence of Aget on the customer simply because the product affects the entire organization. Consequently, Aget should use its product offering in a way that positively affects the customer's product/output, its engineering challenges, financial considerations, etc. Aget salespeople have, up to this point, concentrated on selling cement or concrete mix, the actual product. This type of selling is strictly transactional and does not seem to be cultivating a relationship, which in the longer term may produce loyalty. This approach called for dealing with the procurement/purchasing agent of the buying center, who is mostly interested in getting the lowest possible price, and not with other influentials such as engineers and project managers whose interest goes beyond that of a low price. If Aget wanted to change its customer policy it would have to revise its salespeople's current approach, i.e., whom they called on, how, etc.

Changes in the scope and approach of Aget's sales force would require that they be an integral part of a change in the structure of its sales organization. This would mean devising a sales architecture whose pivotal drivers would be customer profitability resulting from the greatest possible opportunity for Aget.

## Marketing Strategy—Issues

The idiosyncrasy of the industry and its uniquely defined structure set the parameters for formulating growth strategies for those cement players that strive for market share and dominant local market presence. Forward thinking cement producers are planning on how to increase their customer-base, how to get closer to their market activity, how to enhance cost efficiencies, and last and most importantly, how to differentiate their position vis-a-vis that of their competitors. Advances in chemical engineering and production-process technologies are expected to have an impact on product development and profitability. The ability to differentiate on the product offering, be it either bundled or unbundled, is a strategic advantage to gaining growth, sustaining market dominance, and to safeguarding and in fact increasing profitability.

Aget, having a viable market position and a strong financial structure, is poised to achieve future growth through market penetration and market development. In accomplishing the above the company has decided to implement a three-prong strategy goal:

- To expand into new markets
- To consolidate, defend, or enhance existing market shares and,
- To offer a core product that the customer perceives to have superior value to that of the competitors

Aget should capitalize on its distinctive competencies and its expertise that has developed in the Middle East market. Understanding the business culture and practices, unique to the Middle East market, constitutes an edge that Aget can and should exploit in entering into, and developing, the markets of Lebanon, Kuwait, and UAE. Aget's good image has already penetrated into the regional Middle East market and it is considered pivotal to establishing the links and networks necessary to enjoy an early and sustainable growth in market share.

Aget executives have been perplexed as they seek out additional ways to differentiate in such as generic commodity. They thought that an effective way to seek out sustainable "differentiators" might be to use segmentation to better understand customers. They had observed that customer decision making was affected by previous experience, or lack thereof, with the seller and was guided by the type of purchasing strategies selected. In addition, they recognized that customers differed in terms of their buying objectives and expectations. That is, there were customers who required a full service transaction and customers who were in search of a low cost supplier. Moreover, product pricing and services rendered defined behavioral attitudes that were deemed to strongly influence decision making as their fluctuating values affected relevant demand. Also, the customer's likelihood or capability to switch supplier directly depended on the extent of the relationship with that supplier, given the product's relative price uniformity and commodity character. Therefore, it became obvious to Aget executives that a well-defined marketing strategy to address the issue of customer relationship would be advisable and that it should be formulated on the basis of the key roles in the buying center, who performs those roles, the organizational structure, both formal and informal, as well as conceiving of guidelines by which to effectively manage those relationships. Furthermore, such marketing strategy's core value would pivot around the cement/concrete offering, customer management, and pricing issues. Revamping Aget's marketing strategy should be done against desired trade-offs between profitability and market share. These are the elements that such a revised marketing strategy should be fine tuning.

Cement is sold using specifications that establish the properties needed in the cement, depending on the project for which it is destined. This means that

**Exhibit G**
Average
Returns on
Capital
Employed*

| | 1994 | 1995 | 1996 | 1997 | 1998 | 1999 |
|---|---|---|---|---|---|---|
| Pure Cement Companies | 15.8% | 22.9% | 28.8% | 13.9% | 4.8% | 4.0% |
| Diversified Cement Cos. | 16.4% | 17.5% | 14.3% | 10.7% | 7.7% | 6.7% |

*Source: INDIAN Cement industry; http://www.icraindia.com/biz-arch/u2000ceaexecutive.pdf.

differentiating on cement properties is not viable unless the cement producer has some distinctive proprietary advantage vis-a-vis product development. Aget would have to look elsewhere for achieving differential market position. Developing relationships using incremental value-added services would seem to offer a sustainable competitive advantage. Thus, Aget considers customer development a critical issue and one which requires a strategic focus. Specifically, it must identify its customer's needs/problems/opportunities current and future, pragmatic and perceived, prioritize them, determining how its customer assesses value, and develop programs/product offerings that would be appropriate. To that effect, it contemplates developing customer-support teams which will aid the customer starting with the project design and materials specification through to the maintenance phase. The use of such prior and posterior support is thought to help differentiate Aget from other competitors by delivering differentiable value and create or enhance working relationships with customers. The value delivered will be further increased by transforming a sales-oriented sales force into a management information and advisory team at the disposal of the customer. These evolving networks are deemed to not only help in the growth of market share but also to solidify market position, increase customer satisfaction, fend off competition, and enhance incremental profitability.

Aget executives have reasoned that the product offering must go beyond customer's expectations as such expectations, when met, can only deliver threshold-level satisfaction. On the other hand, when such expectations are not met their absence produces intense dissatisfaction and increases the likelihood of supplier-switching. By achieving beyond customer expectations, Aget will eliminate the risk of not meeting such expectations and its potential consequences and, simultaneously, achieve viable customer satisfaction levels. Such product augmentation will be conducive to developing customer relationships but also, through conditioning, it would help upgrade current customer expectations resulting in intensifying future competition among cement producers.

**Exhibit H**
Balance Sheet

**AGET GROUP OF COMPANIES**
**BALANCE SHEET**
**AS OF 30.9.2004**
**(In 000s EURO €)**

| ASSETS | | 2004 | | 2003 | |
|---|---|---|---|---|---|
| B. FORMATION EXPENSES | | 1,778 | | 2,829 | |
| C. FIXED ASSETS | | | | | |
| I. II. Intangible, Tangible assets | | 651,349 | | 642,284 | |
| Less: Acc. Depreciation | | 440,016 | 211,333 | 413,426 | 228,858 |
| III. Investments & other long-term Assets | | 15,260 | | 15,256 | |
| TOTAL FIXED ASSETS | | 226,593 | | 244,114 | |
| D. CURRENT ASSETS | | | | | |
| I. Inventories | | 58,393 | | 63,538 | |
| II. Receivables | | | | | |
| 1. Trade debtors | | 158,746 | | 183,516 | |
| 2. Sundry debtors | | 44,458 | 203,204 | 38,584 | 222,100 |
| III. Cash at bank and in hand | | 40,786 | | 17,932 | |
| TOTAL CURRENT ASSETS | | 302,383 | | 303,570 | |
| E. ACCRUALS & PREPAYMENTS | | 1,343 | | 1,626 | |
| TOTAL ASSETS (B + C + D + E) | | 532,097 | | 552,139 | |
| MEMO ACCOUNTS | | 174,050 | | 74,769 | |
| LIABILITIES | | | | | |
| A. SHAREHOLDERS' EQUITY | | | | | |
| I. Issued Share Capital | | 109,467 | | 109,467 | |
| II. Share premium | | 1,279 | | 1,279 | |
| III. Revaluation reserves | | 9,028 | | 9,362 | |
| IV. Reserves | | 153,771 | | 137.309 | |
| Consolidation difference | | (1,523) | | (1,523) | |
| V. Retained earnings | | | | | |
| Retained earnings brought forward | (22,079) | | (39,765) | | |
| Profit for the period | 86,185 | | 83,023 | | |
| Less: Other taxes | (586) | 63,520 | (8,739) | 34,519 | |
| TOTAL SHAREHOLDERS' EQUITY | | 335,542 | | 290,413 | |
| B. PROVISION FOR RISK & CHARGES | | 80,490 | | 75,013 | |
| C. LIABILITIES | | | | | |
| I. Long-term | | 1,249 | | 28,545 | |
| II. Short-term | 71,490 | | 64,432 | | |
| III. Bank overdrafts | 30,160 | 101,650 | 82,039 | 146,471 | |
| TOTAL LIABILITIES | | 102,899 | | 175,016 | |
| D. ACCRUALS & DEFERRED INCOME | | 13,166 | | 11,697 | |
| TOTAL LIABILITIES (A + B + C + D) | | 532,097 | | 552,139 | |
| MEMO ACCOUNTS | | 174,050 | | 74,769 | |

**Exhibit I**
Income
Statement

## AGET GROUP OF COMPANIES
## PROFIT AND LOSS STATEMENT
### AS OF 30.9.2004
### (In 000s EURO €)

| Operating Results | | 2004 | | 2003 |
|---|---|---|---|---|
| Turnover (Sales) | | 390.215 | | 393.559 |
| Less: Cost of sales | | 281.405 | | 285.805 |
| | | 108.810 | | 107.754 |
| Add: Other operating income | | 5 | | 1 |
| **Gross operating results** | | 108.815 | | 107.755 |
| Less: Administration expenses | 19.808 | | 19.497 | |
| Research & development expenses | 183 | | 178 | |
| Selling & distribution expenses | 4.842 | 24.833 | 5.559 | 25.234 |
| Oper. Income before investing & financial activities | | 83,982 | | 82,521 |
| Less: Interest expense and financial charges | | 543 | | 2.898 |
| **Total operating income** | | 83.439 | | 79.623 |
| Plus : Extraordinary & non-operating income | 1.677 | | 2.598 | |
| Less : Extraordinary & non-operating expenses | 2.357 | (680) | 3.163 | (565) |
| | | 82,759 | | 79,058 |
| Less : Total depreciation | 20.577 | | 18.507 | |
| Less : Charged to the operating cost | 20.577 | — | 18.507 | — |
| **Net income before tax** | | 82,759 | | 79,058 |

# Li & Fung Limited

Li & Fung Limited is a global trading group. It manages the supply chain for high-volume, time-sensitive consumer goods, delivering the right product at the right price at the right time to the right location. As a supply chain manager for many producers located in many countries, it focuses on providing a one-stop shop service through a network of 69 sourcing offices in 40 countries. Provided services range from product design and development, through raw material and factory sourcing, production planning and management, quality assurance, and on to export documentation and shipping consolidation.

For example, if The Limited is looking for a new line of trendy shirts, a team from Li & Fung would customize a plan to meet their needs. They would design the shirt line, source the best yarn for the product—perhaps in Italy—and ship it to a factory in China for knitting and dyeing. Then the work-in-process might be shipped to Bangladesh for assembly before the newly finished shirt line is delivered to Los Angeles, California, in the United States (U.S.) ready for The Limited to offer to the final consumer at its stores.

In the time-sensitive world of fashions, execution is key. At this writing, Li & Fung is currently negotiating and finalizing a new licensing agreement with Levi Strauss & Company. The plan is for Li & Fung to design, source, and distribute men's, women's, boys', and girls' tops under the Levi Strauss

This case was researched and written by Yu Ha Cheung, Department of Management at the University of Missouri—Columbia, for classroom discussion rather than to illustrate either effective or ineffective handling of an administrative situation.

"Signature" label for sale to Wal-Mart, Target, and other major mass market value retailers. When the deal is completed, Li & Fung will be required without fail to deliver the line to stores in time for the Fall 2004 season.

## Operations and Organization

Li & Fung does not own any production facilities so as to promote its constant search for cost-effective, quality-conscious manufacturers that can operate within a deadline. It does manage a number of cost-effective, quality-conscious manufacturers mainly concentrated in Asia that can deliver products on a deadline to customers. A large part of the business involves garments, sometimes referred to as "soft goods." They also source hard goods, including fashion accessories, gifts, handicrafts, home products, promotional merchandise, toys, sporting goods, footwear, and travel goods.

While Li & Fung does have some retailing joint ventures, it generates its profits mainly by earning commissions on its facilitating activities. A product may cost US$1 when it leaves the factory in Asia and sell for US$4 to the final consumer in the retail store in the U.S. The Li & Fung strategy is to earn a bigger share of the 4:1 markup. They do that by being involved in both the "front end" and the "back end" of the production process. At the front end they do the marketing, designing, and engineering. At the back end they do the testing, packaging, and shipping (see table). In a sense they pull apart the value chain and attempt to optimize each step on a global basis with the idea of customizing the value chain to best meet customer needs. Overall, Li & Fung will earn about 7% to 12% commission on the value of each hard goods order that it fills and 5% to 8% commission on apparel orders.

Customers are willing to pay these fees to Li & Fung in return for its services because the reduction in production cycle time and lower costs resulting from outsourcing enable Li & Fung's customers to enjoy substantial savings both in terms of cost of goods and administrative expenses. And the uncertainty involved in the transfer of raw materials and work-in-process between supply chain members at different production stages is also reduced. Therefore, through outsourcing their supply chain management functions, Li & Fung's customers can enjoy cost savings, reduced risks, and higher efficiency because it is generally easier to deal with one party at one relatively convenient location than to deal with multiple parties potentially located in several countries situated on different continents.

Headquartered in Hong Kong, Li & Fung employs about 5,300 people worldwide who generate an annual turnover of about US$4.8 billion. The company is organized around 60 divisions which can be set up or closed down very quickly in response to changing market demand. Each division does about US$20 million to US$50 million in business annually. Headed by an entrepreneurial division manager with a high degree of autonomy whose pay is tied to division profits with no cap on the bonus that can be earned, these divisions work with 7,500 suppliers in some 25 countries. The main suppliers depend on Li & Fung for 30% to 70% of their business, effectively reserving priority production resources to meet Li & Fung's customers' needs and giving Li & Fung increased bargaining power over these suppliers.

To provide customized service, each division serves one customer or a group of smaller customers with similar needs. All divisions operate as small business units and are composed of specialized teams, such as technical support, merchandising, raw material purchasing, quality assurance, and shipping. Also, each division may have its own dedicated sourcing teams in different branch offices to serve the division. That suggests that the whole organization is built upon a somewhat mutually supporting operational structure.

The division-based operations mode, as noted earlier, provides considerable organizational flexibility as the addition and termination of individual divisions can be arranged quickly, allowing Li & Fung to be more responsive to rapidly changing market conditions. Not owning production facilities adds to this organizational flexibility since no fixed assets are tied to a single customer, product line, product type, or physical plant (which itself would be tied to a specific country location with all of the potential risks this entails).

While the divisions are operating with great autonomy, the corporate headquarters in Hong Kong has centralized and tight control over financial resources and operating procedures. All divisions use one standardized, fully computerized operating system for executing and tracking orders. By employing centralized financial management and standardized operating procedures, Li & Fung is able to maintain sufficient supervision and coordination of the management of each division to ensure that goals and objectives are properly met without taking away entrepreneurial operational advantages from the division managers.

Despite its size and the range of services it provides, Li & Fung—like its main competitors APL Logistics, Exel, and Tibbett & Britten—is almost invisible to final consumers. But its role is indispensable in getting many products that they desire into their hands.

## History

Current Chairman Victor Fung and his brother, Managing Director William Fung, who are the third generation of the Fung family, own about 50% of Li & Fung, which is part of a family business founded in 1906. Li & Fung began operating at Canton—now Guangzhou—in southern China about 100 miles northwest of Hong Kong, evolving from a small Chinese export trader into a multinational trading company. It was probably the first Chinese-owned company to export from China at a time when foreign businesses controlled the exporting of Chinese products from China. In its early days it traded in porcelain and silk, then diversified into bamboo, rattan ware, jade, ivory, handicrafts, and Chinese fireworks.

Since Canton's port was located on the Pearl River some distance inland from the sea, it was too shallow to handle visits from ocean-going clipper ships. Hong Kong's South China Sea location and natural harbor provided the deep water port these ships needed. So Li & Fung's first branch was established there in 1937 under the name Li & Fung Limited (which today is the holding company for the Group), making it one of the oldest trading companies in Hong Kong.

Following the revolution that established the People's Republic of China in 1949 and again during the famine of 1958 to 1961 and the Cultural Revolution of 1966 to about 1971, the influx of refugees into Hong Kong provided large quantities of relatively inexpensive labor to help Hong Kong develop its economy exporting labor-intensive consumer products. Li & Fung expanded its export activities to include garments, toys, electronics, and plastic flowers, making it one of Hong Kong's biggest exporters in terms of the value of goods exported.

As China slowly opened its borders to international trading beginning about 1979, many Hong Kong manufacturers relocated their factories to southern China, not far from Li & Fung's offices located there. With this opening came business opportunities, so Li & Fung extended their sourcing business to China and to southeast Asian countries. The rapid pace of industrialization going on in less-developed Asian nations also provided Li & Fung with additional sources of supply through its own developing network of regional offices. This effectively transformed the company from a Hong Kong–based exporter to a Hong Kong–based regional trading company.

This network and these relationships developed over the years were to become a key to the company's success as a supply chain manager. From 1995, Li & Fung positioned itself as a multinational trading company through several acquisitions and as a supply chain manager that differentiates itself from other trading companies.

## Supply Chain Management

Li & Fung strategically positions itself as one of the premier global consumer products trading companies and as a supply chain manager for high-volume, time-sensitive consumer products. A supply chain involves a series of activities that leads to the transformation of raw materials into a final product that is purchased by a customer. Supply chain management is the systematic effort to provide integrated management to the supply chain in order to meet customer needs and expectations, from suppliers of raw material through manufacturing and on to the end-customers.

Supply chain managers coordinate activities within and between vertically linked firms. These managers can capitalize on the competitive advantages of their sourcing network, their knowledge, social capital, experience, and goodwill. Competitive advantage based on these sorts of factors is usually referred to as "sustainable" competitive advantage because it is very difficult for a potential competitor to duplicate them successfully at a competitive cost level in the short run.

Companies themselves may not have the expertise and the resources to do their own supply chain management. They often cannot afford the time, cost, and risk to develop advanced supply chain and information technology (IT) capabilities. This leads them to consider outsourcing possibilities in a "make or buy" decision framework. In essence, they may lack the core competencies to fully vertically integrate backwards toward their suppliers or forwards toward their customers, these moves being among the most difficult growth options to execute successfully. This provides an incentive for companies facing these constraints to outsource their supply chain management function, a role Li & Fung is well equipped to fill.

It appears that firms practicing supply chain management could achieve supply chain cost improvements of 10% to 50% and functional improvements of 10% to 80%. But there seems to be little difference in the performance of internal purchasing and third-party purchasers for nonstrategic items. Third-party purchasers like Li & Fung may actually do a better job of tracking supply market trends and coordinating electronic linkages with multiple suppliers for some types of goods.

## Going Global Adds New Problems for the Supply Chain

Global sourcing is an important part of supply chain management activities. Effective execution of global outsourcing strategies involves top management commitment, international language capabilities, global sourcing structures and processes, and global sourcing business capabilities overlaid with cultural and social factors that influence how business is done in a given country. The problems associated with supply chain management are very likely to increase when firms extend their supply chain management activities to overseas suppliers. Performance problems with overseas suppliers that do not meet delivery deadlines and quality requirements and that possess limited technical capabilities are frequently encountered. It appears that increased switching costs, lost control over inventory and transportation, and limited flexibility are major potential problem areas for buyers.

U.S. firms doing business in China frequently note local suppliers' lack of responsiveness to their needs in purchasing and local carriers' lack of delivery dependability in transportation services as being extremely severe barriers to successful business operations in their host environment. What these U.S. firms need wherever they do business in the world is a synergy of transportation services, import/export services, and purchasing-related services as these are critical to the successful development of an international logistics system to support international operations.

The structural problems in the supply chains and individual firms' global sourcing provide opportunities for certain channel intermediaries, such as Li & Fung, to add value to these activities as supply chain managers. In addition, Li & Fung's global sourcing and manufacturing network gives it the ability to maneuver around certain import quotas imposed by the U.S. and the European Union, among others.

## Growing through Acquisitions

Li & Fung quickly realized that it needed to be close to both potential clients seeking a supply chain manager and its network of suppliers. It found that it could rapidly expand its global sourcing network through acquisitions since developing networks from the ground up tends to take a long time and to be relatively expensive.

Li & Fung acquired Inchcape Buying Services in 1995, which doubled the size of the company and expanded the company's customer base in Europe. To strengthen its position in the U.S. and European markets, Li & Fung acquired Swire & Maclaine Ltd. and Camberley Enterprises Ltd. in 1999.[1] In 2000, Li & Fung acquired Colby Group Holdings Ltd., a

buying agent for the sourcing of consumer goods with a 35-office network. In just the three-year period beginning in 1999, these acquisitions increased the size of Li & Fung's sourcing network from 48 offices in 32 countries in 1999 to 68 offices in 40 countries in 2001.

*Colby Group Holdings Ltd.* Headquartered in Hong Kong, Colby Group Holdings Ltd. was founded in 1975. Colby Group is a buying agent for consumer goods with a turnover of US$451 million and an after-tax profit of US$8.7 million in 1999. It has a global network of 35 offices with 626 full-time employees and over 4,200 suppliers in 59 countries.

The products sourced include ladies', men's, and children's clothing and fashion accessories, household products (including electrical and electronic appliances), gift items, footwear, travel goods, handbags, and furniture and furnishings. Apparel accounts for about 80% and hard goods accounts for about 20% of its business.

The client base is prominent department stores, specialty chain stores, mail order houses, brand name importers, and other retailers. Approximately 83% of the Colby Group's clients were based in the U.S., with the remainder based in South America, Australia, Europe, and Canada.

In addition to providing sourcing services for its clients, Colby Group provides onsite quality control, factory evaluation, and compliance inspection services as well. It also advises on product development and assists in investigating the financial standing of suppliers for clients.

*Swire & Maclaine Ltd.* Established in 1946, Swire & Maclaine primarily provides product sourcing and quality assurance services. It had 12 offices in Asia, a service center in the U.S., and 11 quality control hubs covering about 31 production markets. Turnover in 1998 was US$302 million and after-tax-profit was US$1.6 million.

Approximately 65% of the company's turnover was derived from apparel products and the remainder from nonapparel products, including toys, furniture, gifts, cookware, and cutlery. About 80% of Swire & Maclaine's sales are derived from clients in the U.S. and the remaining 20% from the United Kingdom, other European countries, Canada, and Japan.

*Camberley Enterprises Ltd.* Camberley is an apparel company established in 1979. By 1998 it boasted a turnover of US$63.5 million and after-tax profit of US$4.9 million. It focuses on high-quality ladies sportswear, ready-to-wear fashion, and home

---

[1]Later financial information does not appear to be available for these acquisitions individually since Li & Fung consolidates subsidiary financial information on its balance sheets.

accessories for retailers, brands, and designer labels. Camberley designs, produces patterns, and makes samples of apparel in-house. The manufacturing process is then subcontracted to factories in Shenzhen, China, where Camberley has a quality assurance laboratory. Customers in the United Kingdom and the U.S. accounted for approximately 70% and 27% of sales, respectively, with the remainder from Japan and other countries.

## Product Diversification

The majority of the business at Li & Fung is generated from the soft goods market with only 28% of the business derived from the hard goods market. To avoid something of an overdependence on the soft goods market, Li & Fung increased its stake in the hard goods market through the acquisition of Colby Group Holdings Ltd. and Swire & Maclaine Ltd. This move, in addition to further expanding Li & Fung's global network, increased the contribution of hard goods from 22% of total turnover in 2000 to 28% in 2001. In 2002, Li & Fung acquired Janco Overseas Ltd. to further develop its hard goods market. Li & Fung ended 2002 with 32% of its turnover in hard goods, but senior management would still like to decrease their reliance on the soft goods business even more.

*Janco Overseas Ltd.* A wholly owned subsidiary of a U.S. private company, JII Capital, Janco Overseas Ltd. had a turnover of US$316.1 million and after-tax profit of US$4.1 million in 2001. With offices in Hong Kong, Taiwan, Korea, Thailand, Indonesia, Singapore, and the Philippines, Janco's 218 staff members allow Janco to serve as a buying agent for consumer goods. The major customers of Janco are supermarket and hypermarket chains based in North America that mainly use Janco to source hard goods for them. Its particular strength is supplying the supermarket and hypermarket nonfood sector. Janco operates on a much lower margin than the rest of the Li & Fung Group, given that its target customers are in the value sector.

## Stumbling toward Business-to-Business E-commerce

Li & Fung's customers are typically a group of relatively few but very large corporations requiring Li & Fung's supply chain management skills to obtain large volumes of goods. In order to capture economies of scale, large customers are required. Li & Fung usually only wants customers with annual sales of at least US$100 million. However, Li & Fung senior management noticed that there is an even larger number of small to medium-size businesses that would benefit from the services they could provide. This market segment is characterized by small order size and shorter delivery time requirements since these smaller businesses cannot afford to tie up large sums of money in inventory. The problem was how to service their needs profitably. The Internet suggested itself as a solution. An online business outlet could allow Li & Fung to consolidate small orders for mass production by the existing supplier network.

Li & Fung's approach would, in essence, allow these smaller businesses to have their own private label. There would be different styles with limited customization using American yarn knitted in China and assembled in Bangladesh, for example. While sizes and styles would be fixed, choices available online would allow a product to have the small business's own distinctive label attached, with choices of embroidery, colors, and packaging. Li & Fung would still be able to obtain the benefits of mass production, but with perhaps enough limited customization to meet the needs of the smaller business. And cannibalization did not seem to be a problem since its large customers would not likely be satisfied with the limited services provided on the Web when they typically needed and expected to have full service provided by "their" division.

Li & Fung entered a joint venture with a U.S. online business consulting firm, Castling Group, to launch the Internet-based StudioDirect online retail venture in February 2001 with the notion that it would drastically expand Li & Fung's traditional business. Brokerage house HSBC Securities said that within five years this new business would produce US$2 billion in sales each year, a sum equal to the total revenues of Li & Fung in 1999.

*StudioDirect* The potential market that Studio-Direct is targeting consists of some 20,000 retailers and 2,800 wholesalers that are largely left out of the US$50 billion private-label business because they lack the purchasing power of their larger competitors. It appears to be the first company to target this huge business-to-business market (B2B). StudioDirect will be able to draw on Li & Fung's network of some

6,000 factories in 100 countries to meet the needs of their smaller customers. The new San Francisco, California–based company is backed by capital of US$250 million which represents Li & Fung's single largest investment.

StudioDirect business activities will not be conducted exactly like those of its parent, although there are similarities. Li & Fung creates a special customer group for each customer wishing to source polo shirts from them. If 50 customers order polo shirts, there would be 50 separate teams sourcing the order. But StudioDirect would essentially market the product once on the Web to thousands of customers. However, taking a page from Li & Fung's playbook, Studio-Direct representatives will meet with customers before placing their order on the Web, in part to help build personal relationships. The key business idea here is that StudioDirect will combine its expertise in sourcing and merchandising of apparel with supply chain efficiencies it will derive from its Web-based trading.

A small retailer with order sizes of 1,000 polo shirts, for example, could now receive almost the same services that large clients expected from Li & Fung. A Web page at *www.studiodirect.com* with a three-dimensional illustration of the basic shirt would allow the buyer to choose online from among 14 colors, with many pocket, button, and collar options. The retailer's own logo could also be embroidered on the shirt for an additional fee. Retailers ordering this small volume of polo shirts through traditional channels might expect only one or two color choices and little in the way of customization, so they are likely to be delighted at this new level of service available to them.

To take advantage of additional efficiencies to help support this level of service for the relatively small volumes expected on a per-order basis, StudioDirect has outsourced every aspect of delivery from pick-and-pack, shipping, and customs clearances to final store distribution to Danzas AEI Intercontinental based in Darien, Connecticut. Despite the rosy forecasts from financial markets and Li & Fung senior management, some observers wonder if this Internet business model can produce the economies of scale necessary for StudioDirect to earn a profit.

# Questions for Discussion

1. Why would a company want to use the supply chain management services of Li & Fung rather than simply organizing an in-house department or appointing a senior manager to handle these activities?

2. Much of Li & Fung's growth is through acquisitions. Why would it spend the money to buy other companies' networks rather than just creating its own?

3. How will Li & Fung use the Internet to capture additional business? What will it need to do in order to make this additional business profitable?

## References

David Woodruff (2003), "Li & Fung Limited," *Hoover's Online,* http://www.hoovers.com, last accessed November 28, 2003; Anonymous (2003), "Li & Fung (Trading) Limited," Hong Kong General Chamber of Commerce, http://www.chamber.org.hk, last accessed October 27, 2003; Anonymous (2003), "Li & Fung (Trading) Limited," *Hong Kong Business Directory,* Hong Kong General Chamber of Commerce, http://www.chamber.org.hk, last accessed October 27, 2003; Anonymous (2002), "Li & Fung Limited Annual Report 2002," http://www.lifung.com, last accessed November 29, 2003; Anonymous (2003), "Li & Fung Limited Interim Report 2003," http://www.lifung.com, last accessed November 29, 2003; Anonymous (2003), "History," http://www.lifung.com, last accessed November 29, 2003; Anonymous (2000), "The New Global Blue Chips—Li & Fung Hong Kong," *money.com,* http://www.money.com, last accessed November 20, 2000; Leslie P. Norton (2003), "Sizing Up Li & Fung," *Barron's,* August 18, Market Week Section, 10; Winston Yau (2003), "Li & Fung Deal Crowns Leap in Profit," *South China Morning Post,* August 14, Business Section, http://biz.scmp.com, last accessed August 14, 2003; James Leung (1996), "Fung & Fung Pioneer New Trade Era," *Asian Business,* March, 26–32; Frederick Balfour (1992), "Stick to Knitting," *Far Eastern Economic Review,* June 18, 80–81; Joanna Slater and Eriko Amaha (1999), "Masters of the Trade," *Far Eastern Economic Review,* July 22, 10–13; Joanna Slater (1999), "Corporate Culture," *Far Eastern Economic Review,* July 22, 12; Joanna Slater (1999), "One-Stop Shop," *Far Eastern Economic Review,* July 22, 14; Joan Magretta (1998), "Fast, Global, and Entrepreneurial: Supply Chain Management Hong Kong Style," *Harvard Business Review,* 76 (5),

102–114; Andrew Tanzer (1999), "Stitches in Time," *Forbes,* September 6, 118–121; John Gittings (1999), *China through the Sliding Door,* London, England: Simon and Schuster; Nicholas D. Kristof and Sheryl Wudunn (1994), *China Wakes,* New York, New York: Vintage Books; Chris Zook and James Allen (2003), "Growth Outside the Core," *Harvard Business Review,* 81 (12), 66–73; Reuven R. Levary (2000), "Better Supply Chains through Information Technology," *Industrial Management,* 42 (May–June), 24–30; Martin Stein and Frank Voehl (1998), *Macrologistics Management: A Catalyst for Organizational Change,* Boca Raton, Florida: St. Lucia Press, 263; William C. Copacino (2000), "The Supply Chain's Driving the New Economy," *Logistics Management and Distribution Report,* 39 (November), 32; Gary J. Cross (2000), "How e-business Is Transforming Supply Chain Management," *Journal of Business Strategy,* 21 (March/April), 36–39; Arnold Maltz and Lisa Ellram (1999), "Outsourcing Supply Management," *The Journal of Supply Chain Management,* 35 (Spring), 4–17; Carl R. Frear, Lynn E. Metcalf, and Mary S. Alguire (1992), "Offshore Sourcing: Its Nature and Scope," *International Journal of Purchasing and Materials Management,* 28 (Summer), 2–11; Lisa M. Ellram and M. Cooper (1990), "Supply Chain Management, Partnerships, and the Shipper—Third Party Relationship," *International Journal of Logistics Management,* 1 (Summer), 1–10; John N. Pearson, Joseph Carter, and Li Peng (1998), "Alliances, Logistics Barriers, and Strategic Actions in the People's Republic of China," *International Journal of Purchasing and Materials Management,* 34 (Summer), 27–36; Kenneth J. Petersen, David J. Frayer, and Thomas V. Scannell (2000), "An Empirical Investigation of Global Sourcing Strategy Effectiveness," *The Journal of Supply Chain Management,* 36 (Spring), 29–38; Anonymous (2000), "Li & Fung to Acquire Colby—Acquisition Further Cements Its Leadership Position in Global Supply Chain Management," and "Major Transaction Relating to the Acquisition of Colby Group Holdings Limited," November 9, http://lifung.com, last accessed November 30, 2003; Anonymous (2000), "Discloseable Transaction Relating to the Acquisitions of Swire & Maclaine Limited and Camberley Enterprises Limited," January 17, http://www.lifung.com, last accessed November 30, 2003; Anonymous (2002), "Li & Fung Acquires Hong Kong–Based Buying Agent Janco—Acquisition in Line with Strategy of Expanding Hardgoods Lines," July 9, http://lifung.com, last accessed November 30, 2003; Rahul Jacob (2000), "Inside Track: Traditional Values at the Click of a Mouse," *Financial Times,* August 1, http://www.ft.com, last accessed December 15, 2000; Bruce Einhorn (2000), "A Different Kind of B2B Play in China?" *BusinessWeek Online,* May 8, http://www.businessweek.com, last accessed November 20, 2000; Louis Kraar (2000), "Hong Kong Is Buzzing with Risky Dot-Com Startups That May—or May Not—Turn into Great Companies," *Fortune,* May 15, 324; Dan Biers (2000), "Trading Up," *Far Eastern Economic Review,* August 10, http://www.feer.com, last accessed November 20, 2000; Anonymous (2001), "Business: Link in the Global Chain," *Economist,* June 2, 62; William J. Holstein (2002), "Middleman Becomes Master," *CEO Magazine,* October, 53–56; Jon Rhine (2001), "Asian Cash Fuels Online Retail Venture," *San Francisco Business Times,* February 16, 1; Anonymous (2001), "StudioDirect," *Austin Business Journal,* February 23, 8; Ken Cottrill (2001), "Old-Fashion Dot-Com," *Traffic World,* March 26, 17.

**Supply Chain Management Activities Performed by Li & Fung**

| Production Stage | Supply Chain Management Activities |
| --- | --- |
| Product Design | • Production program design |
| | • Product design |
| | • Prototype development |
| Production Planning | • Production scheduling |
| | • Contracting production |
| Procurement | • Sourcing raw materials |
| Production | • Product testing |
| | • Conducting quality assurance |
| | • Packaging |
| Delivery | • Export documentation |
| | • Shipping |
| | • Warehousing |
| Other Support Services | • Inspecting factories for production quality and capacity |
| | • Inspecting factories in developing countries to ensure that they comply with the regulations in importing countries on environmental standards, child labor, and prison labor |
| | • Handling import quotas |

# Little Tikes Commercial Play Systems

## History

In the early 1990s Rubbermaid, Inc. (Wooster, OH) identified an opportunity to leverage the powerful Little Tikes brand in the commercial playground market. Rubbermaid, long considered one of the most-admired companies in America, had a reputation for brand dominance, innovation, and "speed to market." This extension of the Little Tikes name appeared to be the latest in a series of solid, strategic moves.

Rubbermaid worldwide sales eclipsed $2 billion in the early 90s. The great majority of these revenues were credited to the Home Products and Seasonal Goods divisions. Although the company allocated over 90 percent of its human and economic resources to its position in the consumer market (Rubbermaid, Little Tikes, and Graco), the company was quickly establishing a position in the commercial market.

Rubbermaid was attracted to the commercial play equipment market for a number of reasons. First, the company possessed the economic resources to acquire a handful of privately held companies and quickly become the world leader in the market. Second, many of the product components used in the industry were rotationally molded plastics—a core competency for Rubbermaid. Third, market research suggested a strong desire among day care and children's service providers to use equipment bearing the trusted Little Tikes brand name. Finally, Rubbermaid was convinced that by standardizing product lines, integrating manufacturing resources, and slashing non-value-added (or redundant) processes, the company could return strong profits along with bullish (20 percent + per year) sales growth.

In 1992, Rubbermaid entered the market acquiring Iron Mountain Forge in Farmington, Missouri. Iron Mountain's 1990 revenues equaled nearly $55 million. Iron Mountain's product line contained traditional, outdoor play equipment and park service products, such as picnic tables, grills, and basketball goals. Traditional play equipment is used in parks and on school playgrounds. The materials most common to the product line are steel, plastic, and wood. Later that same year, Rubbermaid acquired Ausplay in Victoria, Australia. Ausplay enjoyed the reputation as market leader for outdoor playground equipment in Australia, Asia, and the Pacific Rim. 1990 sales were over $40 million.

Rubbermaid extended the buying spree into 1993 with the acquisition of Paris Playgrounds in Paris, Ontario. This Canadian firm offered Rubbermaid a solid entry opportunity into the Canadian market along with powder coating expertise and design and production capability for soft-modular play—the fastest-growing segment of the commercial play market. Soft-modular play equipment, typically used indoor in fast-food restaurants (e.g., McDonald's PlayPlaces) and family entertainment centers (e.g., Discovery Zone), is designed using steel, plastic, foam, and netting. Rubbermaid's final acquisition took place in early 1994. Interested in establishing a

This case was prepared by William E. Carigan, III, MBA student at the University of Cincinnati, under the supervision of F. Robert Dwyer, Joseph S. Stern, Professor, University of Cincinnati, as the basis for class discussion rather than to illustrate effective or ineffective handling of a managerial situation. © 1999.

dominant position in the soft-modular play segment, the company acquired the industry leader, Los Angeles–based Omni.

Rubbermaid's leaders realized that it would take time to integrate the units. Therefore, the 1993 strategy for the new division, Little Tikes Commercial Play Systems, was to allow the units to operate independently while Little Tikes analyzed the strengths and weaknesses of the newly acquired companies as well as the opportunities for consolidation. Little Tikes appointed General Managers for the units, each reporting directly to Little Tikes President—Gerry Kemper. Exhibit 1 shows the organizational chart for Little Tikes Commercial Play Systems (LTCPS) in December 1994.

### Market Opportunities

When Nick Smyth, Vice President of Business Development for Little Tikes, studied the commercial playground market in 1991, he fell in love with the opportunity. Rubbermaid's mission statement calls for the company to be the leader in each and every market served. The company's plan to acquire four major market players allowed Rubbermaid to satisfy this mission requirement with four bold strokes. Rubbermaid estimated the worldwide potential in the commercial playground market to be around $2 billion. About 90 percent of the total potential was in the traditional playground market.

Nick Smyth realized the power of the Little Tikes brand name. In numerous surveys and focus groups, mothers of young children associated the brand with words that all marketers adore—*trusted, quality, durability, innovative, fun, safe, colorful, developmental,* and *high end.* Certainly, the company could leverage the brand in the traditional play segment. But the real opportunity for leverage existed in the fast-growing contained play (soft-modular) segment.

## Soft-Modular Play

In the early 1980s, Jack Pentes built the first soft-modular playground in Charlotte, North Carolina. Pentes, a design engineer, responded to a need in the day care industry. For years, day care and children's service providers complained of the inadequacies in traditional play design for indoor applications. Traditional playgrounds require large, open areas (floor space) and 6′ tall zones of rubberized safety surfacing around structures. Moreover, the components used are manufactured of hard substances such as steel, wood, and plastic. Spills and falls usually resulted in bumps, bruises, and breaks.

Pentes invented a better way to play. Responding to the need for improved indoor equipment, Pentes built a line of play structures designed to minimize necessary floor space, maximize vertical space, and dramatically reduce injuries. Pentes used a traditional steel framework to support his structure. However, Pentes wrapped the frame with soft foam while enclosing landings and play events with netting. The result was a cost-effective, exciting brand of supersafe, easy-to-supervise play equipment.

Two years after Pentes built his first "soft" playground, a local Hardee's franchisee asked Pentes to build a unit for his restaurant in Charlotte. The response to the first soft playground in a fast-food restaurant was amazing. Local kids urged their parents to bypass McDonald's and Burger King for a chance to play at Hardee's. Sales at the store jumped 50 percent.

McDonald's quickly took notice of the Pentes playground. The company had always designed advertising and menu items to appeal to children. Now, they would take their strategy to a new level. McDonald's approached Pentes and a number of traditional playground providers to manufacture "soft" playgrounds for indoor and outdoor applications at their restaurants.

In the early 1990s, 20 or more companies began manufacturing the new, soft-style playground equipment. In 1993, McDonald's built nearly 700 soft-modular playgrounds worldwide. And there were new applications for the equipment. Chicago-based Discovery Zone attacked the family entertainment market by launching an indoor amusement concept centered around a herculean 60′ × 40′ × 20′ soft-modular playground. Food service, private party facilities, and arcade games were considered ancillary and alternative sources of revenue supporting the "main event." Eventually, soft-modular play crept its way into casual dining, airports, shopping malls, car washes, laundromats, car dealerships, movie theatres, video stores, zoos, museums, stadiums, fitness clubs, retail stores, hotels, and all other sorts of family destinations.

**Exhibit 1**
Little Tikes Commercial Play Systems—1994

Organizational Chart

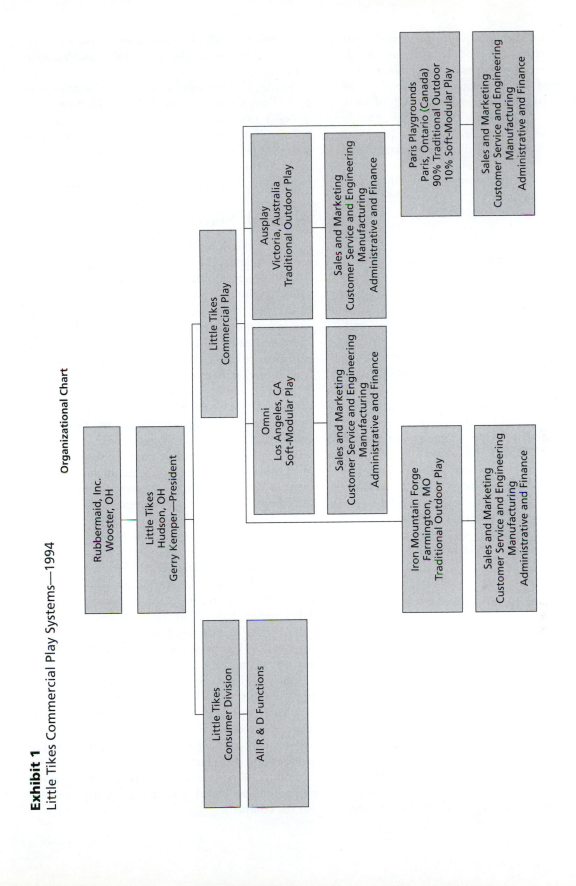

Unlike traditional play equipment in parks and on school properties, soft-modular play was considered an up-scale play experience for children. One operator termed the attraction "pay for play," as parents would pay $5.00 or more for each of their children to play on the equipment in some venues. It was in this market for upscale, high-end equipment that Nick Smyth and Rubbermaid management envisioned Little Tikes brand dominance. The acquisition of Omni was Rubbermaid's entry into this dynamic market segment.

## Distribution

In the traditional play market, manufacturers including Iron Mountain Forge, Paris, and Ausplay employed independent representatives, with protected geographic markets, to sell their products to landscape architects, school boards, day cares, and municipalities. These recreation industry specialists carried ancillary lines including outdoor seating, bleachers, baseball backstops, canopies, grills, safety surfacing, and water park products.

In the soft-modular play market, distribution strategies varied. Many companies used direct employees to sell to many market segments within geographic regions. Others relied on independent representatives. Omni employed a direct sales force to sell soft-modular playgrounds as well as restaurant seating products from sister company, Décor Concepts. By providing both products and maintaining a tight alliance with a supplier of kitchen equipment, Omni offered fast-food restaurateurs a "one-stop shop."

## Early LTCPS Initiatives

Although multiple market opportunities existed for the new division, Rubbermaid focused on the following 1995 priorities: Kemper's first initiative was the standardization of accounting and manufacturing software with the rollout of SAP for all units. Rubbermaid focused first on the Iron Mountain Forge facility targeting Missouri as the global headquarters for LTCPS.

The second key initiative was the streamlining and consolidation of product lines for the traditional outdoor product. Kemper envisioned standardization across the units, with Farmington

delivering the bulk of all roto-molded parts to staging depots in Los Angeles, Paris (ON), and Victoria, Australia.

Finally, Kemper sought to leverage the strength of Little Tikes Consumer R&D Group (Hudson, OH) to polish the "look" and the design of the commercial play line. Kleinjen felt that LTCPS customers around the world would respond favorably to a sleeker, more-attractive line of equipment designed to resemble the popular Little Tikes toy offering.

## A Rough Start

On paper, the three 1995 LTCPS initiatives seemed reasonable given the respective market positions of the component units. However, these moves served mainly to cloud and delay more pressing issues in the market and in the minds of new, LTCPS employees and independent representatives around the world. Moreover, each initiative failed to address critical performance factors at the unit level and within the various market segments.

In delegating responsibility for the successful integration of LTCPS to Kemper, Rubbermaid effectively separated top management from the commercial play market. In essence, Kemper and his team in Hudson presented a general strategy and list of priorities (initiatives) to Rubbermaid's management in Wooster. Once the strategy met approval at the corporate level, Kemper delegated the execution of the initiatives to the unit level.

The greatest challenge to LTCPS may well have been the struggles of Little Tikes consumer line. Although Kemper openly touted the potential of the commerical market, he spent the majority of his time attempting to correct a downhill slide of Little Tikes market share on the consumer side of the business. During this period, Little Tikes witnessed the defection of key personnel to Mattel, Fisher-Price, and other rival firms.

The sluggish response to the commercial market from the corporate level worried managers at the unit level. Moreover, every move that Kemper made seemed to confuse employees and suggest that jobs may be in jeopardy. Specifically, the consolidation of accounting, manufacturing, and R&D functions without clear explanation from corporate regarding these initiatives fueled "watercooler" gossip throughout the company.

From the outset, communication was the greatest challenge for LTCPS and Rubbermaid. As Kemper worked to correct problems with the consumer division, his involvement with LTCPS became limited to biweekly, status update meetings between the unit GMs and Kemper. These 30-minute discussions usually occurred via telephone and facsimile. Realizing that he lacked the time and focus to lead the fledgling division, Kemper appointed Nick Smyth as president of LTCPS in January 1996. Smyth moved from Hudson to Farmington to establish Missouri as worldwide headquarters for LTCPS. Exhibit 2 shows the organizational structure for LTCPS.

## Trouble in Playland

The appointment of Nick Smyth was generally considered a positive move throughout LTCPS. Smyth would give LTCPS the leadership of a seasoned Rubbermaid executive and a stronger voice in both Wooster and Hudson. However, Smyth's first months in Farmington were anything but positive.

First, Smyth struggled to execute the three 1995 initiatives he inherited from Kemper. The SAP software implementation nearly crippled Ausplay and Omni. Both companies offered a high degree of customization to key customers. The play units manufactured in these locations featured standard play events in custom configurations to meet specific site requirements. To use SAP, design and manufacturing engineers created hundreds of new part numbers per job just to ship a job and "flush" an order. Lead times doubled as a result.

Second, the attempts of Smyth and the management team in Farmington to standardize the product line were a disaster. Without clear understanding of international markets (Iron Mountain Forge's sales overseas were less than 5 percent of all revenue) engineers eliminated many popular play structures and overengineered others. Moreover, the new equipment failed to address the design opportunities created by limited safety regulations in many foreign markets. In short, LTCPS attempted to sell its high-end, supersafe, ADA-accessible line of equipment to a skeptical audience abroad.

Third, the decision to move R&D to Hudson put many important projects behind more important needs in the consumer line. Nimble competitors in the traditional market and the soft-modular segment introduced innovations at an increasing rate, further increasing the mounting frustration in the field. In April 1996, Smyth officially moved R&D back to Farmington.

In less than two years, revenues declined over 15 percent and profits slipped nearly 20 percent. Sales of the soft-modular play line (Omni) fell nearly 40 percent. Top management at Rubbermaid began to apply pressure to speed consolidation efforts as an attempt to preserve the bottom line. As pressure mounted in Farmington, the urgent message to "execute at all costs" resonated at the unit level. Smyth replaced each of the three GMs in Paris, Los Angeles, and Victoria. Throughout 1996, sales and profit numbers plummeted. In January 1997, Nick Smyth and Gerry Kemper were reassigned. Rubbermaid corporate controller, Lou Blackwell, was named president of LTCPS.

## The Beginning of the End

In June of 1997, Lou Blackwell announced the immediate closing of the Omni facility in Los Angeles and the sale of the Paris unit to the former management group of Paris Playgrounds. In November, the company announced the closing of the Ausplay plant in Victoria, Australia.

A former LTCPS-Omni manager summed up the feeling in Los Angeles: "10 years of record sales and profits simply vanished overnight. I have no idea what those guys in Wooster were thinking. At the end of the day, it's the customer that decides what is and what is not important. We didn't listen to a damn thing they had to say. We paid for that mistake with our jobs."

Employees in Australia echoed the sentiment: "Why didn't we just plaster the *Tikes* name all over our stuff? We knew what the customers wanted and we sure knew how to get it to them. The strength of all these companies was their ability to serve the customer within their own markets. We had the best sales forces in the industry and everyone, except Rubbermaid, knew it."

In October 1998, the LTCPS manufacturing facility caught fire. Over half of the production area was destroyed. Rubbermaid decided to rebuild in Farmington. It was an opportunity to rethink the organization structure and marketing program for LTCPS.

**Exhibit 2**
Little Tikes Commercial Play Systems—1996

Organizational Chart

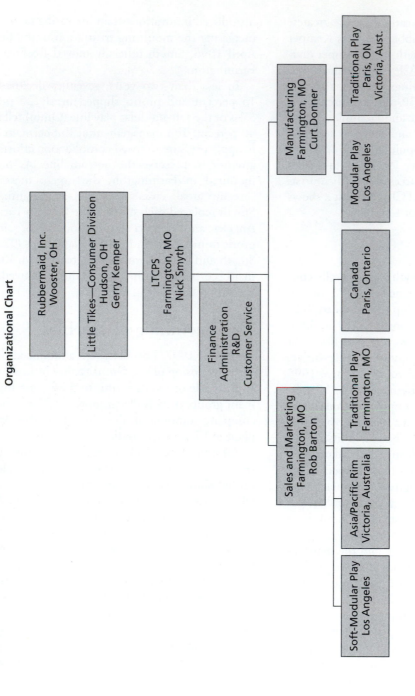

# Questions

1. In early 1994, what were the strengths of LTCPS? What opportunities existed?

2. Consider the decision to delegate the operation of the Commercial Play Division to the Consumer Division of Little Tikes. Was this the right move?

3. Assume that the number-one critical success factor for LTCPS is the communication between Rubbermaid Corporate and the four commercial play units. What type of organization would you create to maximize communication? What elements of the horizontal organization and the network organization would you employ?

4. Take the organization into the future. Assume one manufacturing facility and all administrative and support functions in Farmington, Missouri. Also assume a worldwide network of independent sales reps for the traditional and soft-modular play lines. Draw an organizational chart to include sales, marketing, R&D, and any necessary administrative functions.

# Materials Engineering and Testing Laboratories

Materials Engineering and Testing Laboratories (METL) is a sole proprietorship business, with Raymond Orban, P.E. as principal. The firm began operations in May of 1992. METL is a full service construction materials engineering and testing firm located in Round Rock, Texas. They are equipped to perform various asphaltic, portland cement concrete, and soils tests, both in the laboratory and in the field. They are also equipped to perform complete geotechnical investigations and can provide construction inspection services.

## Beliefs and Quality of Work

METL is one of the few commercial laboratories in Texas that is AASHTO accredited in asphalt and asphaltic concrete, soils, aggregate, and portland cement concrete testing. The American Association of State Highway and Transportation Officials (AASHTO) is a national entity which advocates transportation related policies and supports the efforts of states to efficiently transport goods and people.[1]

By providing accreditation services to businesses across the nation, AASHTO is trying to set a standard in the construction of structures used in the transportation industry. This certification is an important asset to METL since most of the services they perform are related to testing materials utilized in the construction of roads and bridges.

METL also participates in both the AMRL and CCRL sample proficiency test program for these materials. AMRL and CCRL are programs within the construction materials industry which strive for quality testing through laboratory assessments, proficiency samples, instruction, and guidance. Participation in these programs ensures that METL is providing quality services and is an indication to present and future clients of their commitment to provide quality work. They are also pre-certified by The Texas Department of Transportation (TxDOT) to perform work in these areas and also to perform certification of other laboratories and their personnel for testing on certain Texas construction projects. METL believes that one of the most important reasons for their success is their commitment to provide and continue providing quality service to their clients.

Mr. Orban is dedicated to ensuring that his company's reputation for quality work is maintained even at the cost of losing money on certain jobs.

## Background

Mr. Orban graduated from college with a B.S. in Civil Engineering. He obtained his professional engineering license while working in the materials division at TxDOT as a regional manager. After leaving TxDOT,

---

This case was prepared by Raul Benavidez for the purpose of class discussion. Materials Engineering and Testing Laboratories has been disguised.

[1]http://www.transportation.org/.

Mr. Orban proceeded to establish his own engineering laboratory along with a secretary and one other employee. Through his contacts at his previous job, Mr. Orban was able to obtain several small contracts to provide asphalt and concrete testing to various TxDOT clients.

## Business Growth

Initially, METL's focus was on asphalt and concrete testing. After several months of testing asphalt and concrete from the construction of local roads and bridges, Mr. Orban identified the need of his clients for soils testing. He realized that the soils testing could go hand in hand with the tests which he already performed, and several of his clients were willing to offer him an opportunity to provide these services under a single contract. Since most construction projects for roads and bridges take several years, the majority of METL jobs are based on contracts which provide from 1 to 3 years of services to its clients. Most of the longer 3 year contracts are for providing services to city and state entities. This type of work as well as the majority of the company's workload is based on time and material, meaning that the work being performed is charged as it is done.

The company has offered their services in lump sum contracts, but avoids them in favor of the more profitable time and material basis. METL offers individual testing to clients as well, charging a premium for their services. Some of the smaller contracts range from 2 to 6 months depending on the location and type of project. Much of the work performed on these shorter contracts is from repeat clients who like the quality of work done by the company.

After several years of long work hours Mr. Orban saw the need to expand his business into a bigger building to accommodate the additional services including soils testing. Through word of mouth and client contacts, METL grew to 36 employees in 1999. Mr. Orban was always looking for opportunities to expand his business and provide additional services to clients. The first opportunity he got was from providing geotechnical drilling. Initially METL would receive soil samples from clients for testing purposes. Now, METL was able to provide drilling and testing which would expedite the reporting of results to the client. Their strategy in the soils division is to provide inexpensive prices for drilling to

the client and make up the cost in the testing of the soil samples. This proved to be effective since other drilling companies in their industry were not able to provide such prices without losing money. The drill rigs initially used by METL were smaller, inexpensive trailer mounted rigs. Most of the jobs contracted to METL were for the construction of roads, thus only needing shallow geotechnical work with maximum depths of about 10 to 20 ft. This type of shallow drilling did not strain the drill rigs, and by providing routine maintenance, they were able to maximize their life expectancy and use.

In 2001, METL got a second opportunity to expand their services. Because of the quality work provided, a present client proposed to METL that they submit a contract for providing inspecting and testing services for the expansion and repair of existing small airport runways. Many of these airports are located in small towns and generally accommodate single and double propeller private airplanes. After completing the first part of this job, Mr. Orban noticed that the inspecting aspect of the contract proved to be the most profitable. This did not require equipment or testing, just overseeing the proper construction of the airport based on existing guidelines.

After talking with previous clients and contacts in the aviation industry, Mr. Orban identified the need many of these small airports had. With the increasing population in big cities such as Houston, Texas, many of the airports in the surrounding smaller cities saw an increase in traffic and use. Cities such as Sugarland and Pearland suddenly saw the need to repair their existing runways or expand them to accommodate slightly bigger airplanes such as private jets. They noticed that people flying in from closer distances preferred to land in the smaller airports and avoid the traffic found within the metropolitan area of these larger cities.

In the following years METL was able to acquire various contracts across the state for inspection work on such airport projects. Currently METL has 5 large contracts ranging from 1 to 3 years of service and approximately 20 smaller contracts of several months.

## Future Potential

METL, currently has three satellite offices and approximately 62 employees across the state of Texas. It consists of three professional engineers including

**Exhibit 1**

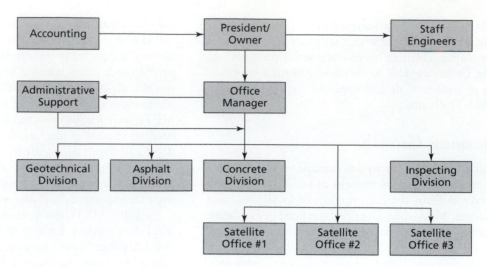

Mr. Orban, one of whom followed Mr. Orban upon retiring from his previous employment and brings to the company over 50 years of experience. These engineers work out of the main office and are each designated with overseeing the daily work done in their division. One oversees the asphalt and concrete divisions and the other oversees the geotechnical and inspecting divisions. However, since most projects encompass several divisions, the engineers work together more than they do individually. The office is run by an office manager who dictates work to the rest of the employees based on the work needing to be completed. She is joined by three additional employees, who serve as administrative support, and together they are in charge of scheduling activities, phone answering, and other office duties for the company.

As you have seen in Exhibit 1 on the previous page, Mr. Orban serves as the main person in charge. The bulk of the work force at METL is composed of engineering, inspecting, and geotechnical technicians. Several of METL's employees have followed Mr. Orban upon retiring from their previous jobs at TxDOT seeking an additional source of income while utilizing the skills they already have. Others just need something to keep them busy. Employees are required to be certified by the state of Texas prior to doing any form of geotechnical, asphalt, and concrete testing. METL has a training period in which the company personally trains their employees prior to taking the state certification exam. Employees are encouraged to do their best and perform at their fullest potential in these tests, and are rewarded if they get a perfect score. METL has a tradition of

rewarding each employee with a bonus of $100 if they successfully pass an individual certification with a score of 100%. In order to maximize the use of his employees, Mr. Orban certifies employees to do testing in several divisions. The structure of METL is such that employees are used in the division in which they are needed the most. Given that they have the proper certifications, employees may be testing asphalt on Monday, soils on Tuesday, and might be headed for a concrete pour on Wednesday. Many times an employee may work in opposite sides of the state in a given week. In some instances work may slow down in one project due to bad weather and may pick up in another due to favorable work conditions. Because much of the work is dependent on the weather conditions, the heaviest work for the company is at times surrounding the summer months with a steady decrease in the winter months and a steady increase in the spring.

After a day of work at the office while Mr. Orban was on his way out, he overheard the following conversation between Robert and George.

Robert: "Alright George, I'll see you tomorrow. Don't forget; Fridays we go to happy hour after work."

George: "Sorry man. I have to be in Dallas at 8:00 AM for a concrete pour at the airport, and then I have to swing by Waco to pick up some concrete cylinders which need to be tested on Saturday. I probably won't make it in until late at night."

Robert: "I know how it is. I was in Nacogdoches yesterday, because they were repaving the existing taxiway at the airport."

**Exhibit 2**

| Year | Revenue | %Increase | Employees | %Increase |
|------|---------|-----------|-----------|-----------|
| 2004 | $4.5 million | | 40 | |
| 2006 | $6.3 million | 40% | 62 | 55% |

George: "Yeah, I can't wait until December, when things begin to slow down a bit, and I don't have to work on Saturdays."

Robert: "You say that now, but when you're looking for things to do in December, don't be complaining that you need more work."

George: "You're right, and besides I was able to get Monday off to take my son fishing and to a baseball game for his birthday."

Robert: "Alright, have a good weekend."

George: "Thanks, you too."

Some employees may work longer hours than others due to the amount of work necessary. Mr. Orban has two part time employees which work the night shift when work is very busy and the client needs results over night. The employees fill out time sheets and the work that they do is supervised by the office manager who then reports all the work completed and pending to Mr. Orban.

Because it is a sole proprietorship, METL has only one person responsible for marketing the business and obtaining new work. They do not have a formal marketing department and do not use any form of advertisements for their business. Mr. Orban gives authorization to the office manager to purchase generally small equipment usually less than $500, but any larger equipment or items need prior authorization from Mr. Orban.

The majority of their growth has come about through Mr. Orban chasing potential contracts and meeting with potential clients across the state. METL does attend at least two conferences each year and they set up a booth to explain their services. Much of METL's success is in part due to Mr. Orban's determination to provide quality work. However, in recent times Mr. Orban has been concerned about the future of his business and its future growth. As you can see in Exhibit 2, in recent years the company has experienced tremendous growth both in the amount of services provided and in the amount of employees working for the company. This growth came about due to a large contract being awarded to a bid in which METL was involved for the construction of a toll road in the Central Texas area.

Mr. Orban does not see himself leaving his business any time soon, but he does want to eventually separate himself from the business and retire to spend more time with his family. Mr. Orban's main job is to continue to find work for his employees and to do problem solving when something goes wrong during a job. The majority of the work obtained by METL is because of the quality of work which Mr. Orban represents. More recently, a problem faced by METL is that the large contract which METL obtained had a life span of two years, and upon completion of the project Mr. Orban saw himself with additional employees which he had to find work for. This type of situation forces Mr. Orban into a difficult situation. Several employees found new jobs, and some were only working for the duration of the contract, but approximately 25 employees would remain working with the company. He is forced to continue as the sole person in charge of finding work.

Mr. Orban fears that if something was to happen and he would be forced to be away from work for a long period of time, the business would greatly suffer and some of his employees would end up with no work. He would like to see his investment continue to grow and wants to take the steps necessary to ensure that his business thrives even in his absence. Out of the two engineers, one is older and might not be working with the company much longer. The other is younger and will remain loyal with the company, but lacks the skills necessary to find more jobs. His technicians are relatively young and willing to work if given the opportunity.

# Outdoor Sporting Products, Inc.

The annual sales volume of Outdoor Sporting Products, Inc., for the past six years had ranged between $6.2 million and $6.8 million. Although profits continued to be satisfactory, Mr. Hudson McDonald, president and chief operating officer, was concerned because sales had not increased appreciably from year to year. Consequently, he asked a consultant in New York City and the officers of the company to submit proposals for improving the salespeople's compensation plan, which he believed was the basic weakness in the firm's marketing operations.

Outdoor's factory and warehouse were located in Albany, New York, where the company manufactured and distributed sporting equipment, clothing, and accessories. Mr. Hudson McDonald, who managed the company, organized it in 1956 when he envisioned a growing market for sporting goods resulting from the predicted increase in leisure time and the rising levels of income in the United States.

Products of the company, numbering approximately 700 items, were grouped into three lines: (1) fishing supplies, (2) hunting supplies, and (3) accessories. The fishing supplies line, which accounted for approximately 40 percent of the company's annual sales, included nearly every item a fisherman would need such as fishing jackets, vests, caps, rods and reels of all types, lines, flies, lures, landing nets, and creels. Thirty percent of annual sales were in the hunting supplies line, which consisted of hunting clothing of all types including insulated and thermal underwear, safety garments, shell holders, whistles, calls, and gun cases. The accessories line, which made up the balance of the company's annual sales volume, included items such as compasses, cooking kits, lanterns, hunting and fishing knives, hand warmers, and novelty gifts.

Although the sales of the hunting and fishing lines were very seasonal, they tended to complement one another. The January–April period accounted for the bulk of the company's annual volume in fishing items, and most sales of hunting supplies were made during the months of May through August. Typically, the company's sales of all products reached their lows for the year during the month of December.

Outdoor's sales volume was $6.57 million in the current year with self-manufactured products accounting for 35 percent of this total. Fifty percent of the company's volume consisted of imported products, which came principally from Japan. Items manufactured by other domestic producers and distributed by Outdoor accounted for the remaining 15 percent of total sales.

Mr. McDonald reported that wholesale prices to retailers were established by adding a markup of 50 to 100 percent to Outdoor's cost for the item. This rule was followed on self-manufactured products as well as for items purchased from other manufacturers. The resulting average markup across all products was 70 percent on cost.

Outdoor's market area consisted of the New England states, New York, Pennsylvania, Ohio, Michigan, Wisconsin, Indiana, Illinois, Kentucky, Tennessee, West Virginia, Virginia, Maryland,

Adapted from a case written by Zarrel V. Lambert, Auburn University, and Fred W. Kniffin, University of Connecticut, Stamford. Used with permission.

Delaware, and New Jersey. The area over which Outdoor could effectively compete was limited to some extent by shipping costs, as all orders were shipped from the factory and warehouse in Albany.

Outdoor's salespeople sold to approximately 6,000 retail stores in small and medium-sized cities in its market area. Analysis of sales records showed that the firm's customer coverage was very poor in the large metropolitan areas. Typically, each account was a one- or two-store operation. Mr. McDonald stated that he knew for a fact that Outdoor's share of the market was very low, perhaps 2 to 3 percent; and for all practical purposes, he felt the company's sales potential was unlimited.

Mr. McDonald believed that with few exceptions, Outdoor's customers had little or no brand preference and in the vast majority of cases they bought hunting and fishing supplies from several suppliers.

It was McDonald's opinion that the pattern of retail distribution for hunting and fishing products had been changing during the past 10 years as a result of the growth of discount stores. He thought that the proportion of retail sales for hunting and fishing supplies made by small and medium-sized sporting goods outlets had been declining compared to the percent sold by discounters and chain stores. An analysis of company records revealed Outdoor had not developed business among the discounters with the exception of a few small discount stores. Some of Outdoor's executives felt that the lack of business with discounters might have been due in part to the company's pricing policy and in part to the pressures that current customers had exerted on company salespeople to keep them from calling on the discounters.

## Outdoor's Sales Force

The company's sales force played the major role in its marketing efforts since Outdoor did not use magazine, newspaper, or radio advertising to reach either the retail trade or consumers. One advertising piece that supplemented the work of the salespeople was Outdoor's merchandise catalog. It contained a complete listing of all the company's products and was mailed to all retailers who were either current accounts or prospective accounts. Typically, store buyers used the catalog for purposes of reordering.

Most accounts were contacted by a salesperson two or three times a year. The salespeople planned

their activities so that each store would be called on at the beginning of the fishing season and again prior to the hunting season. Certain key accounts of some salespeople were contacted more often than two or three times a year.

Management believed that product knowledge was the major ingredient of a successful sales call. Consequently, Mr. McDonald had developed a "selling formula," which each salesperson was required to learn before taking over a territory. The "formula" contained five parts: (1) the name and catalog number of each item sold by the company; (2) the sizes and colors in which each item was available; (3) the wholesale price of each item; (4) the suggested retail price of each item; and (5) the primary selling features of each item. After a new salesperson had mastered the product knowledge specified by this "formula" he or she began working in the assigned territory and was usually accompanied by Mr. McDonald for several weeks.

Managing the sales force consumed approximately one-third of Mr. McDonald's efforts. The remaining two-thirds of his time was spent purchasing products for resale and in general administrative duties as the company's chief operating officer.

Mr. McDonald held semiannual sales meetings, had weekly telephone conversations with each salesperson, and had mimeographed bulletins containing information on products, prices, and special promotional deals mailed to all salespeople each week. Daily call reports and attendance at the semiannual sales meetings were required of all salespeople. One meeting was held the first week in January to introduce the spring line of fishing supplies. The hunting line was presented at the second meeting, which was scheduled in May. Each of these sales meetings spanned four to five days so the salespeople were able to study the new products being introduced and any changes in sales and company policies. The production manager and comptroller attended these sales meetings to answer questions and to discuss problems that the salespeople might have concerning deliveries and credit.

On a predetermined schedule each salesperson telephoned Mr. McDonald every Monday morning to learn of changes in prices, special promotional offers, and delivery schedules of unshipped orders. At this time the salesperson's activities for the week were discussed, and sometimes the salesperson was asked by Mr. McDonald to collect past due accounts

**Exhibit 1**
Salespeople:
Age, Years
of Service,
Territory, and
Sales

| Salespeople | Age | Years of Service | Territory | Sales Previous Year | Sales Current Year |
|---|---|---|---|---|---|
| Allen | 45 | 2 | Illinois and Indiana | $330,264 | $329,216 |
| Campbell | 62 | 10 | Pennsylvania | 1,192,192 | 1,380,240 |
| Duvall | 23 | 1 | New England | — | 414,656 |
| Edwards | 39 | 1 | Michigan | — | 419,416 |
| Gatewood | 63 | 5 | West Virginia | 358,528 | 358,552 |
| Hammond | 54 | 2 | Virginia | 414,936 | 414,728 |
| Logan | 37 | 1 | Kentucky and Tennessee | — | 447,720 |
| Mason | 57 | 2 | Delaware and Maryland | 645,032 | 825,088 |
| O'Bryan | 59 | 4 | Ohio | 343,928 | 372,392 |
| Samuels | 42 | 3 | New York and New Jersey | 737,024 | 824,472 |
| Wates | 67 | 5 | Wisconsin | 370,712 | 342,200 |
| Salespeople terminated in previous year | | | | 1,828,816 | — |
| House account | | | | 257,384 | 244,480 |
| Total | | | | $6,478,816 | $6,374,816 |

in the territory. In addition, the salespeople submitted daily call reports, which listed the name of each account contacted and the results of the call. Generally, the salespeople planned their own itineraries in terms of the accounts and prospects that were to be contacted and the amount of time to be spent on each call.

Outdoor's sales force during the current year totaled 11 full-time employees. Their ages ranged from 23 to 67 years, and their tenure with the company ranged from 1 to 10 years. Salespeople, territories, and sales volumes for the previous year and the current year are shown in Exhibit 1.

## Compensation of Salespeople

The salespeople were paid straight commissions on their dollar sales volume for the calendar year. The commission rate was 5 percent on the first $300,000, 6 percent on the next $200,000 in volume, and 7 percent on all sales over $500,000 for the year. Each week a salesperson could draw all or a portion of his or her accumulated commissions. McDonald encouraged the salespeople to draw commissions as

they accumulated, as he felt that they were motivated to work harder when they had a very small or zero balance in their commission accounts. These accounts were closed at the end of the year so each salesperson began the new year with nothing in the account.

The salespeople provided their own automobiles and paid their traveling expenses, of which all or a portion were reimbursed by per diem. Under the per diem plan, each salesperson received $70 per day for Monday through Thursday and $42 for Friday, or a total of $322 for the normal workweek. No per diem was paid for Saturday, but a salesperson received an additional $70 if he or she spent Saturday and Sunday nights in the territory.

In addition to the commission and per diem, a salesperson could earn cash awards under two sales incentive plans that were installed two years ago. Under the Annual Sales Increase Awards Plan, a total of $10,400 was paid to the five salespeople having the largest percentage increase in dollar sales volume over the previous year. To be eligible for these awards, a salesperson had to show a sales increase over the previous year. These awards were

**Exhibit 2**
Salespeople's
Earnings and
Incentive
Awards in the
Current Year

| Salespeople | Sales | | Annual Sales Increase Awards | | Weekly Sales Increase Awards (Total Accrued) | Earnings* |
| --- | --- | --- | --- | --- | --- | --- |
| | Previous Year | Current Year | Increase in Sales (Percent) | Award | | |
| Allen | $330,264 | $329,216 | (0.3%) | — | $1,012 | $30,000† |
| Campbell | 1,192,192 | 1,380,240 | 15.8 | $3,000 (2d) | 2,244 | 88,617 |
| Duvall | — | 414,656 | — | — | — | 30,000† |
| Edwards | — | 419,416 | — | — | — | 30,000† |
| Gatewood | 358,528 | 358,552 | (0.1) | 400 (5th) | 1,104 | 18,513 |
| Hammond | 414,936 | 414,728 | — | — | 420 | 30,000† |
| Logan | — | 447,720 | — | — | — | 30,000† |
| Mason | 645,032 | 825,088 | 27.9 | 4,000 (1st) | 3,444 | 49,756 |
| O'Bryan | 343,928 | 372,392 | 8.3 | 1,000 (4th) | 1,512 | 19,344 |
| Samuels | 737,024 | 824,472 | 11.9 | 2,000 (3d) | 1,300 | 49,713 |
| Wates | 370,712 | 342,200 | (7.7) | — | 612 | 17,532 |

*Exclusive of incentive awards and per diem.
†Guarantee of $600 per week or $30,000 per year.

made at the January sales meeting, and the winners were determined by dividing the dollar amount of each salesperson's increase by his or her volume for the previous year with the percentage increases ranked in descending order. The salespeople's earnings under this plan for the current year are shown in Exhibit 2.

Under the second incentive plan, each salesperson could win a Weekly Sales Increase Award for each week in which his or her dollar volume in the current year exceeded sales for the corresponding week in the previous year. Beginning with an award of $4 for the first week, the amount of the award increased by $4 for each week in which the salesperson surpassed his or her sales for the comparable week in the previous year. If a salesperson produced higher sales during each of the 50 weeks in the current year, he or she received $4 for the 1st week, $8 for the 2nd week, and $200 for the 50th week, or a total of $4,100 for the year. The salesperson had to be employed by the company during the previous year to be eligible for these awards. A check for the total amount of the awards accrued during the year was presented to the salesperson at the sales meeting held in January. Earnings of the salespeople under this plan for the current year are shown in Exhibit 2.

The company frequently used "spiffs" to promote the sales of special items. The salesperson was paid a spiff, which usually was $4, for each order obtained for the designated items in the promotion.

For the past three years in recruiting salespeople, Mr. McDonald had guaranteed the more qualified applicants a weekly income while they learned the business and developed their respective territories. During the current year five salespeople, Allen, Duvall, Edwards, Hammond, and Logan, had a guarantee of $600 a week, which they drew against their commissions. If the year's cumulative commissions for any of these salespeople were less than their cumulative weekly drawing accounts, they received no commissions. The commission and drawing accounts were closed on December 31 so each salesperson began the new year with a zero balance in each account.

The company did not have a stated or written policy specifying the maximum length of time a salesperson could receive a guarantee if commissions continued to be less than his or her draw. Mr. McDonald held the opinion that the five salespeople who currently had guarantees would quit if these guarantees were withdrawn before their commissions reached $30,000 per year.

Mr. McDonald stated that he was convinced the annual earnings of Outdoor's salespeople had

**Exhibit 3**

Comparison of Earnings in Current Year under Existing Guarantee Plan with Earnings under the Comptroller's Plan*

| Salespeople | Existing Plan | | | | Comptroller's Plan | | |
|---|---|---|---|---|---|---|---|
| | Sales | Commissions | Guarantee | Earnings | Commissions | Guarantee | Earnings |
| Allen | $329,216 | $16,753 | $30,000 | $30,000 | $16,753 | $12,500 | $29,253 |
| Duvall | 414,656 | 21,879 | 30,000 | 30,000 | 21,879 | 12,500 | 34,379 |
| Edwards | 419,416 | 22,165 | 30,000 | 30,000 | 22,165 | 12,500 | 34,665 |
| Hammond | 358,552 | 18,513 | 30,000 | 30,000 | 18,513 | 12,500 | 31,013 |
| Logan | 447,720 | 23,863 | 30,000 | 30,000 | 23,863 | 12,500 | 36,363 |

*Exclusive of incentive awards and per diem.

fallen behind earnings for comparable selling positions, particularly in the past six years. As a result, he felt that the company's ability to attract and hold high-caliber professional salespeople was being adversely affected. He strongly expressed the opinion that each salesperson should be earning $50,000 annually.

## Compensation Plan Proposals

In December of the current year, Mr. McDonald met with his comptroller and production manager, who were the only other executives of the company, and solicited their ideas concerning changes in the company's compensation plan for salespeople.

The comptroller pointed out that the salespeople having guarantees were not producing the sales that had been expected from their territories. He was concerned that the annual commissions earned by four of the five salespeople on guarantees were approximately half or less than their drawing accounts.

Furthermore, according to the comptroller, several of the salespeople who did not have guarantees were producing a relatively low volume of sales year after year. For example, annual sales remained at relatively low levels for Gatewood, O'Bryan, and Wates, who had been working four to five years in their respective territories.

The comptroller proposed that guarantees be reduced to $250 per week plus commissions at the regular rate on all sales. The $250 would not be drawn against commissions as was the case under the existing plan but would be in addition to any

commissions earned. In the comptroller's opinion, this plan would motivate the salespeople to increase sales rapidly, as their incomes would rise directly with their sales. The comptroller presented Exhibit 3, which showed the incomes of the five salespeople having guarantees in the current year as compared with the incomes they would have received under his plan.

From a sample check of recent shipments, the production manager had concluded that the salespeople tended to overwork accounts located within a 50-mile radius of their homes. Sales coverage was extremely light in a 60- to 100-mile radius of the salespeople's homes with somewhat better coverage beyond 100 miles. He argued that this pattern of sales coverage seemed to result from a desire by the salespeople to spend most evenings during the week at home with their families.

He proposed that the per diem be increased from $70 to $90 per day for Monday through Thursday, $42 for Friday, and $90 for Sunday if the salesperson spent Sunday evening away from home. He reasoned that the per diem of $90 for Sunday would act as a strong incentive for the salespeople to drive to the perimeters of their territories on Sunday evenings rather than use Monday morning for traveling. Further, he believed that the increase in per diem would encourage the salespeople to spend more evenings away from their homes, which would result in a more uniform coverage of the sales territories and an overall increase in sales volume.

The consultant from New York City recommended that the guarantees and per diem be retained on the present basis and proposed that

Outdoor adopt what he called a "Ten Percent Self-Improvement Plan." Under the consultant's plan each salesperson would be paid, in addition to the regular commission, a monthly bonus commission of 10 percent on all dollar volume over his or her sales in the comparable month of the previous year. For example, if a salesperson sold $40,000 worth of merchandise in January of the current year and $36,000 in January of the previous year, he or she would receive a $400 bonus check in February. For salespeople on guarantees, bonuses would be in addition to earnings. The consultant reasoned that the bonus commission would motivate the salespeople, both those with and without guarantees, to increase their sales.

He further recommended the discontinuation of the two sales incentive plans currently in effect. He felt the savings from these plans would nearly cover the costs of his proposal.

Following a discussion of these proposals with the management group, Mr. McDonald was undecided on which proposal to adopt, if any. Further, he wondered if any change in the compensation of salespeople would alleviate all of the present problems.

# Pfizer Inc. Animal Health Products (A) Market Segmentation and Industry Changes

Kipp Kreutzberg was just putting the finishing touches on his marketing plan for the coming year. As the senior marketing manager of Pfizer's Cow/Calf Marketing Team, he recognized that the industry was facing some daunting challenges that would result in significant changes. As consumer demand for beef products had declined over the years, the industry had faced a situation of overcapacity, which depressed prices. A flood of imports resulting from the NAFTA regulations further worsened the situation, as did high prices for feed. Most industry analysts were predicting a period of consolidation and alliances. Furthermore, many industry experts expected that beef quality would have to improve and be better marketed and packaged to meet consumers' changing lifestyles. Kipp wondered how the ranchers, who were the lifeblood of his division's sales, would handle the changes. In reports from the sales representatives out in the field, he knew that the situation was dire for many ranchers.

In light of these significant challenges, Kipp wondered whether his team's approach to the marketplace was still a useful one. The Cow/Calf Division had been segmenting the market of ranchers on the basis of herd size for at least 15 years. He wondered whether a different approach to segmenting the market might allow his division to develop more effective marketing strategies, in light of the changes looming on the horizon.

His division offered a full range of products to cattle ranchers, including vaccines for both newborn calves and their mothers, medications (for example, dewormers, antidiarrheals), and antibiotics (for pneumonia and other diseases). Pfizer positioned its products on the combination of superior science (resulting from its significant R&D efforts) and high-quality production/quality control techniques. Pfizer's pride in its sophisticated research-and-development was shown in its new and useful products for the market. The company invests more in research and development than any other animal health company.

## Industry Challenges and Change

The market share of beef products had declined from 44 percent in 1970 to 32 percent in 1997, whereas pork and poultry had gained share. The decline in beef consumption was due in part to well-known concerns about cholesterol and fat; in addition, preparation issues also affected the demand for beef. For example, two-thirds of all dinner decisions are made by a consumer on the same day. Of these same-day decisions, three-quarters of the consumers still don't know what they are going to make as late as 4:30 PM. Obviously, many beef products require cooking and preparation time, which limits consumer selection.

By Jakki Mohr of the University of Montana and Sara Streeter of the University of Montana. Some of the information in this case has been modified to protect the proprietary nature of firms' marketing strategies. The case is intended to be used as a basis for class discussion rather than to illustrate either effective or ineffective marketing strategies. © Copyright by Jakki J. Mohr, 1999, All Rights Reserved. Support from The Institute for the Study of Business Markets, Pennsylvania State University, is greatly appreciated.

**Exhibit 1**
Pfizer
Marketing
Segmentation,
1998

| Segment | # of Cattle | # of Operations | % of National Cattle Inventory |
|---|---|---|---|
| Hobbyist | <100 | 808,000 | 50% |
| Traditionalist | 100–499 | 69,000 | 36% |
| Business | 500+ | 5,900 | 14% |

Consumers were also being bombarded with new products from the poultry and pork industries. For example, in 1997 Tyson Foods introduced stuffed chicken entrees, roasted chicken dinners, and Southwest-style blackened fajitas, among a host of other creative products. The names "Tyson" or "Perdue" are well recognized by the public, unlike most beef products.

Some of the changes that had occurred in the poultry and pork industries were expected to diffuse into the cattle industry. Industry analysts believed that the beef industry would need to develop products that could be more easily prepared and to develop branded products that consumers could recognize and rely on for quality and convenience.

In addition, industry analysts believed that the beef industry would need to improve the quality of its products (in terms of more consistent taste and tenderness). Beef quality is assessed based on U.S. production targets for tenderness, juiciness, flavoring, and marbling (fat) of the cuts of beef. The targets are based on two dimensions. The first dimension is based on taste quality (tenderness, juiciness) and specifies that 70 percent of beef production should be rated high quality (choice or prime). The second dimension is based on yield, and specifies that 70 percent of beef cattle should be rated grade 1 and 2 (implying a good amount of beef for the carcass size), with 0 percent poor yield (meaning that the carcass did not yield much meat). Currently, only 25 percent of beef cattle meet these criteria. The Beef Quality Assurance program run through the federal government is a voluntary quality control program based on the education, awareness, and training of cattle producers to influence safety, quality, and wholesomeness of beef products. It specifies injection sites (neck versus rump) for shots, a seven-step quality check for cows, method and location of branding, and so forth. Forty percent of ranchers say they have participated in this program in the past two years, of which 67 percent have changed the way they manage their cattle.

## Segmentation Practices

As shown in Exhibit 1, Pfizer had traditionally segmented ranchers in the cow/calf business on the basis of herd size:

"Hobbyists" are so-called because, in many cases, these ranchers run their cattle as a side line to some other job held. For example, a schoolteacher might keep a herd of cattle simply because he grew up on a ranch and couldn't imagine not doing so. In many cases, the hobbyists' ranch income is a minor percentage of their overall income. The average age of hobbyists is 50 years old, and 15 percent hold a college degree. They have been in the cattle business for 26 years and spend 51 percent of their time with their cattle business.

"Traditionalists'" main livelihood is their cattle operation. The average traditionalist is 51 years old, and 26 percent hold a college degree. They have been in the cattle business for 30 years and spend 70 percent of their time with their cattle operation.

The "Business" segment operations are headed by ranchers who average 53 years of age, 22 percent with a college degree, and 33 years in the business. They spend 80 percent of their time with their cattle. These large ranch businesses are owned either by a family or a corporation.

Pfizer had an extensive network of field sales representatives that visited the ranchers to inform them of products, to offer seminars on herd health, and to sponsor industry activities (such as stock shows, 4-H, and so forth). Time spent with accounts is typically allocated on the basis of volume of product purchased. Ranchers then buy the animal health products they need from either a veterinarian or a distributor/dealer (typically, animal feed stores and so forth). The field sales reps also call on the vets and distributors/dealers to help them manage inventory and to inform them of new products and merchandising programs.

**Exhibit 2**
Summary of
Types of
Ranchers
Interviewed

| | Hobbyist | Traditionalist | Business |
|---|---|---|---|
| **Number of Interviews** | 3 | 6 | 3 |
| **Size of Herd** | | | |
| <100 | 3 | | |
| 100–250 | | 2 | |
| 251–500 | | 4 | |
| 501–1000 | | | 2 |
| >1000 | | | 1 |
| **% of Time Spent with Cattle** | | | |
| <80% | 2 | | 1 |
| 81–90% | | | |
| 91–99% | | 1 | |
| 100% | 1 | 5 | 2 |
| **% of Income from Cattle** | | | |
| <80% | 3 | | 1 |
| 81–90% | | 1 | 1 |
| 91–99% | | 1 | 1 |
| 100% | | 1 | |
| **Type of Operation*** | | | |
| Seed-stock | 2 | 2 | |
| Commercial | 1 | 4 | 3 |

*Seed-stock operators* focus on breeding high-quality bulls for use by commercial producers. The bulls are measured by the quality of their offspring. Desirable characteristics include low birth weight, rapid growth, high carcass yield, and grading of choice or better quality meat.

*Commercial producers* are those who raise calves to sell to feedlots. The feedlots fatten the calves, which are then sold to the packing houses, and on to the retail distribution channel for consumers. In some cases, commercial producers might *retain ownership* of their calves, where the rancher pays the feedlot to feed out the calves, but the rancher himself still owns them. Then, the rancher sells the calves to the packing houses.

# Research

In order to provide some insight into the continued viability of segmenting the market on the basis of herd size, Kipp asked Joan Kuzmack, the Manager of Marketing Research for the Livestock Division, to conduct a series of in-depth interviews with cattle ranchers in the Rocky Mountain/Midwest Region. In-depth interviews can offer qualitative insights into behavioral and attitudinal differences among cow/calf ranchers. More specifically, the objectives of the research were to:

- Identify the inputs driving ranchers' success as cow/calf producers
- Determine what motivates cow/calf producers in selecting products

- Identify whether ranchers' values and beliefs about herd management differed by herd size
- Examine ranchers' views about the future

A stratified random sample was used to select ranchers for interviews. Rocky mountain and upper midwest ranchers in each of the three groups (hobbyist, traditionalist, and business) were identified and randomly selected from within those strata. Exhibit 2 provides descriptive statistics on the types and numbers of ranchers interviewed.

Ranchers were asked a variety of questions, using a semistructured questionnaire, that focused on their herd management activities; attitudes, values, and beliefs about herd management; and views of the future trends in their industry.

## Research Findings

The result from the interviews suggested that commercial producers across all three herd size categories look for maximum output (weight gain, number of calves) with the minimum inputs. They attempt to improve the quality of their calves through health and nutrition programs, genetics, and herd culling. Activities used to manage the herd included vaccinations, nutrition, and breeding programs. Ranchers also strove for uniformity in the calves, typically based on size. These goals in managing the herd are traded off against the cost to do so. As one respondent stated:

> *"We strive for the largest amount of production with the least amount of input going in. That's really the only thing we can control at this point with the economy the way it is. We can't control the price that we get for our product, so the only way we can make ends meet is to control the input cost."—Traditionalist*

Some ranchers also focused on range management of their grasslands as another objective in managing their operations:

> *"Basically I think of us as ranchers, we're in the business of grass managers. We grow grass, and if we don't manage our lands to grow a lot of grass, the right kind of grass, we can't run the cows properly. All the genetics in the world won't be of use without the right grass."—Traditionalist*

The degree to which ranchers felt that health management was critical to their herds' success varied greatly. Some valued herd health as one of the most important concerns:

> *"You start off with the best breeding that you think you can do through bull selection. From there, it goes on with nutrition and herd health. You're expecting more from the cows. You have to put more into them with nutrition and herd health. You can't cut corners on either one of those. Some feeds will be cheaper some years than others, but we stay with the same drugs."—Traditionalist*

Others tended to put in the bare minimum on herd health, sometimes because ranchers were uncertain what results the health management programs yielded:

> *"We only do the bare minimum on health care. We do more of a preventative maintenance than*

*anything else. We don't do any more than we have to because you can vaccinate for so many things. Our philosophy has been, if you don't need it, don't do it. You can get an awful lot of money in your cows giving them shots of stuff I don't know if you need."—Traditionalist*

> *"I try to keep them healthy with shots and nutrition. I don't want to skimp on the health of a cow, but if I can save some money by supplementing different things in the ration or with vaccinations. . . . "—Hobbyist*

Seed-stock producers were seeking "best genetics," a loosely defined goal that commonly focused on breeding bulls that would maximize weight gain in commercial calves. Seed-stock producers consistently used artificial insemination on their cows and kept computer records to track information on their herd. They used software programs provided through the breed association to record animal registry and performance information.

To aid in herd management, most of the ranchers in the Hobbyist and Traditionalist categories collected information on their cows and calves. Information collected on calves included birth date, birth weight, sex, and weaning weight. Information collected on the cows included calving history, mothering ability (temperament and/or milk production), calving ease, and which cows birthed the replacement heifers. This information was typically handwritten in a book of some type. The ranchers maintained an intimate familiarity with their cattle and saw them as individuals.

> *"We knew everything there was to know about our cattle. . . . We knew more about our cattle than we did about our family. We could tell you every calf a cow had, pretty much the exact minute she had it every year. I've got little books here that I wrote everything down exactly."—Traditionalist*

> *"To us, the cows are individuals. They stand out, you notice them when you go out to the field. You notice their good and bad qualities, both stay in your mind."—Traditionalist*

In the Business category, ranchers collected some information on their crows and calves. This information might be collected on an exception basis, because of the number of head that the ranchers were working with. The ranchers were familiar with their cattle, but not to the same degree demonstrated by the owners of smaller herds.

Some ranchers used a very sophisticated approach to gathering information in order to refine their herd management practices. For example, one purebred operation sent some of its calves to a test station where all the calves from various ranches were fed and cared for similarly. This control allowed the rancher to show how well his bulls stacked up to other ranches in a controlled experiment. Another rancher stated:

*"We've performed quite a few experiments of our own over the years, and still do. I have a fair sense of what a true experiment is with controls and so forth. We get a lot of cooperation from the pharmaceutical industry. We've tested new products such as ear tags. We get a lot of things free as long as we're willing to put in some controls and report on the results. I enjoy that sort of thing. We've had some experiments going for a couple of years on range management. The opportunities are out there if you're cooperative. I think I probably have an advantage because I know how to conduct an experiment. We can get information firsthand from experiments we conduct ourselves. . . . We've changed our method of supplementing cattle in the winter. We're using more expensive supplements that don't rely on salt. We seem to distribute cattle better. I think it worked. It's cheaper in the long run because you have more grass."—Business*

Changes made on the basis of the information ranchers collected varied in their sophistication. Some made changes based primarily on judgment and intuition.

*"It's the everyday observing of what's going on where we can make our decisions."—Business*
*"It's done by eye and is not as scientific as it could be."—Business*
*"A lot of times you know in the back of your mind what you want to do with a cow. It's sure nice to have the records, because you go back and refer to it."—Hobbyist*

Many of the ranchers did attempt to get information back from the feedlot on their calves in order to assess how well they did after leaving the ranch. In some cases, they also received carcass data, which allowed them to assess weight gain, quality of the meat, and so forth.

There were isolated, but notable, exceptions to gathering and using information about the herd.

One rancher kept no information on his herd, did not attempt to gain new information on herd management practices, and relied strictly on the information "in his head" based on his cumulative years of experience. Another said:

*"It was just a matter of whatever the good Lord gives them when they come out, that's what they are. I can't change that very much."—Hobbyist*

The information ranchers gathered was used primarily as a tool in culling the herd. Culling of open cows (not pregnant) or those that were "unsatisfactory producers" usually occurred in the fall. In general, it seemed that changes to herd management were highly judgment based. Cause-and-effect links for possible problems were hard to establish. For the larger herds, information was not collected on a detailed enough level to analyze and draw specific conclusions.

*"Where I've got a thousand head, and we've got one full-time employee, we don't track detailed information on a cow-by-cow basis. I've always got a book with me, so when we're working them, I put things down in the book. That information will be put on the computer. After a while you kind of know your cows. It's visual, when you see things you don't like."—Business*

Of all the information ranchers collected on their herds, only vaccination records seemed to be valued by cattle buyers. Even ranchers with complete histories of their cattle were selling their calves at the same price as ranchers without the information. Hence, the information was not viewed as a way to command a premium for the calves.

*"For many years, it seemed like having good health records on the calves didn't matter. One herd would keep excellent records and be real progressive, and the next-door neighbor was the exact opposite, and it was the exact same price for both. The local cattle buyers didn't give a premium to keep the records, give the vaccines. . . . There were green tag programs in the 80s (we followed one) where the vet certified you used them (preconditioning records). But the cattle buyers didn't pay a premium for them. They as much as said 'We don't care.' Today, 10 years later, cattle buyers are starting to ask, will you precondition your calves? Will they be 'bunkbroke' (so when they get to the feedlot, the*

*calves will be trained to go to a feedbunk to eat)? Will they be weaned? There's a stress period associated with weaning. So there's more of a focus on those questions now than there has been. But there's still no rule, it's not a given. It's still ambiguous when it comes to marketing the cattle whether it matters or not [gets a better price for the cattle]."—Traditionalist*

Ranchers as a whole were interested in gaining additional information on how to better manage their operations. They read industry trade publications, attended seminars, and talked to neighbors. They were most likely to view information as credible if it came from a local source that was more familiar with specific local conditions. As a whole, it was clear that the person the ranchers trusted most was their veterinarian. The ranchers also found the animal health product firm reps to be a good source of information, but not as credible as the veterinarian.

*"On a drug situation, I wouldn't necessarily trust one person over another, but I would certainly pay attention to my veterinarian. He knows my area and my situation better than the drug rep from the company does. Even though I know the drug rep from that company is going to represent the drugs he sells, I don't necessarily not trust what he says. I just like to have more information about what works in my environment."—Traditionalist*

Ranchers bought their animal health products from both veterinarians and supply houses. Price was an important consideration, but not an overwhelming concern.

The ranchers all expressed concerns about the future. The number one concern among the commercial Hobbyists and Traditionalists was the low prices on their calves. Although Business producers, too, were concerned about price for their "outputs" (cattle), they were also concerned about the input side of the equation (expenses). All ranchers noted that with the low prices they were getting for their calves, they couldn't afford to maintain and replace old, dilapidated equipment they were using.

*"It takes a lot of calves to buy a new pickup, when they want about $30K or something."—Hobbyist*
*"My number one concern is] pricing, and not just the price of the product, but the price of what it costs to produce that product. Compare the price of beef with the price of machinery. Calves are*

*bringing what they brought in the '60s, but a tractor costs three times as much."—Traditionalist*

In addition, they noted the high price of land. One rancher stated, "the land around here grows houses better than cattle."

*Ranchers spoke vehemently against NAFTA, and the influx of cheaper imports.*
*"Well, the biggest issue we have right now is NAFTA. NAFTA is probably the worst thing they've come up with. It has lowered our cattle market so bad, it's put a lot of people out of business, driving the prices down so low. It is not fair trade from the standpoint of shipping Australian cattle into Mexico, they become Mexican cattle and come right into the United States. They can get our top dollar (whatever we're getting here—say 60 cents), but were brought in through Mexico at 30 cents. They flooded the market. They didn't have to make as much, they don't have as much in their cattle. With this R-Calf thing, they're investigating Canada. Let's face it: They're overrunning our market. It takes away the supply and demand. It's not just affecting us, it's affecting everybody—for example, the beef business, the car business, the timber industry."—Traditionalist*

Vertical integration by the packers was viewed with fear and trepidation and also with a sense of increasing helplessness. Ranchers sold their calves to the feedlots, who in turn sold to the meatpackers. Packer concentration (four packers controlled 80 percent of the market) and the packers' perceived ability to set prices (the implication is "collusively") for the industry was a recurring theme.

*"We have no market for our agriculture products. To back that up, when you've got packers controlling 80 percent of the cattle and they'll buy cattle for a half-hour in the middle of the week, you either take the offer or you leave it. If you turn them down, pretty soon they won't come back and look at your cattle or price your cattle. This is where we're going to have to have more players in our market or we're going to have to become one of the major players against the packer in supplying food to the consumer. We cannot compete with packers that own their own cattle and slaughter their own cattle instead of paying the market value for cattle they don't own. So that's why I say we have no market. The grain is the same way, because basically,*

*the same companies that control the grain control the cattle, Cargill, ConAgra, ADM. You just look through the hall of mergers. One of these days, if things don't change, we will know the true value of our food when the corporations get it and we're all working for those people. The consumer will find out what the value of it is."—Business*

Tightening environmental regulations (Endangered Species Act, pesticides, water quality, etc.) also made an impact on the economics of ranching operations. In general, the view among the commercial producers was one of extreme pessimism. They saw a lot of other ranchers going broke (but usually not themselves).

*"I think it's all offset by the good things, but sometimes you wonder. You have to wonder about your mentality. You work and you work and you work and you work and you work and then you sell your cows at a loss, and you think 'Why am I doing this?' Either I'm really stupid, or really stubborn."—Traditionalist*

*"I think the day that the old rancher that gets on his horse at daybreak and gets off his horse at sunset and never sees another human being, and everybody is knocking on his door to buy his calves—those days are through. I hate to admit it, but everywhere you turn, somebody is trying to put you out of business. If it isn't the Bambi-huggers, then it's the prices, and if it isn't that, then somebody's coming along with those brainy ideas. The small producer is really going to have to work at it to stay in business."—Traditionalist*

*"I don't know if any kind of marketing at this point is going to get us where we need to be without a change in the price structure of cattle."—Traditionalist*

Ranchers were asked about possible solutions to the depressed prices they were facing. Possible solutions discussed in industry publications included value-added marketing, or marketing strategies designed to increase the value and quality customers receive from beef purchases, and a branded beef model. The development of branded beef would require a tracking system from "birth-to-beef" in the supply chain. Such tracking would allow standardized health, quality, and management protocols, as well as improved feedback through the entire production model. This change would also necessitate

the producers being more closely linked to the feedlots to improve the quality of the beef. Branded beef production would move the industry from a cost-based (production) model to a value-added model. Better coordination along the supply chain would ensure an increased flow of information from the consumer to the producer. Alliances between the cow/calf producer and the feedlots would allow ranchers to better track the success of their calves (based on health and weight gain). Such data could allow the ranchers to further improve the genetics of their herd by tracking which cow/bull combinations had delivered the higher-yield calves. As part of these trends, some degree of integration or vertical coordination would occur in the beef industry. Ranchers would need to participate in order to ensure market access for their product. Ranchers would have to think beyond the boundaries of their own ranches.

Most ranchers were familiar with the concepts of value-added marketing and a branded beef model. However, most were dubious about their viability and impact on ranchers' independence.

*"If there is a demand for high-quality beef, then the market should show it, and the packers will start bidding more for a piece of that quality. There may be some niches somewhere that people can fall into, but it's not going to be the salvation of many ranches. What we need is a mass market. Whatever niche there is is going to be saturated very quickly, and the price will come down. I think the solution is cutting costs. People are eating a tremendous amount of beef, but the production is enormous as well. Numbers are down, but tons are up. The amount of beef being eaten is still quite high. I just think that some people have got to quit producing beef."—Business*

*"They're trying to come at that through the packer end of it, what they called added value. By you retaining ownership on your calves, you can lock 'em in at a certain price at the end. I guess it will work, I don't know. I'm skeptical because there's only three packing plants."—Traditionalist*

*"We are concerned about the vertical marketing approach big companies are introducing into the system. Ranchers are very independent-minded people. We are fearful about the control that companies will be able to exert on us."—Traditionalist*

Skepticism about value-added marketing is also derived from history: Other programs used in the past to provide a more consistent product to the feedlots, with supporting documentation, had not resulted in noticeable price differences. The feeling was that price premiums, if any, would accrue to others in the supply chain (e.g., the packers, retailers, and so forth). Despite that, some with more progressive views noted the need to have more of a consumer focus in their efforts:

*"We need better beef quality if we're going to increase consumption. A lot of the breed associations are concentrating on carcass quality right now. There's measurement, there's selection for marbling and yield on cattle. I think as long as there is a possibility there might be some added value, a person should start working on it a little bit, along with the other production traits. I think it's something to pay attention to."—Traditionalist*

*"I think in the future, all ranchers are going to have to retain ownership of their cattle more and follow them closer to the consumer. I think that's part of our problem right now with our packer concentration. The producer's going to have to be a meat producer, and not just sell calves. I think some of our long-range goals are going to have to be to get closer to the consumer with our product and know what he wants instead of listening to the packer tell us what he wants."—Business*

*"The money in agriculture is not in producing it. It's in processing it. This is where more ranchers and farmers have to realize that you can't produce the raw product anymore; you've got to follow it on through."—Business*

Ranchers also noted that the idea of consistent quality beef was important.

*"I'm expecting to see a change to where quality is more important. I think, down the road, that it's going to be mandatory that you know exactly what your cattle are doing. Those that aren't producing well at the kill floors are going to come back to haunt you."—Business*

Interestingly, each of the respondents with whom we spoke felt that the quality of their beef was above average. However, there was some doubt about whether consistent quality would be easily achieved with range cattle.

*"That's going to be pretty tough with cattle. With chickens and hogs, you can throw up a confinement building. One person can control x amount of hogs and turkeys and chickens. But how do you do that with cattle? You can only have so many cattle in one spot because they're bigger and they need more feed. You're going to have to have pasture. It's going to be pretty tough to get everything uniform. There are a lot of small producers with just a few cows around."—Hobbyist*

*"I'm not convinced that branded products are going to magically save the beef industry. I think we're in competition on a world scale, and we're going to have to cut our costs of production. I think we could get our costs down to about 45 cents per pound of critter sold if we had to. Our total production would go down, but I think our costs would go down more."—Business*

Because of the doubts about the viability of moving to a branded beef model, ranchers tended to focus more on controlling the cost of inputs, and weathering the current downturn in the production cycle. One respondent cited earlier summed this up as "striving for the largest amount of production with the least amount of input."

Despite these hardships and concerns, the ranchers were passionate about their love for their lifestyle, feeling that the benefits of living a life on the land outweighed the drawbacks.

*"You get up in the morning and go out there, and everything's bright and fresh. We're fortunate in this part of the world that we don't have a lot of noise from cars and trains. It's gratifying to see what happens when spring turns around, new things start to grow, new animals come into the world. It's pretty special, something that you can't explain to a lot of people because they don't understand what you're talking about. . . . It isn't the highest paying job in the world, but it's got a lot of happenings that money can't buy."—Traditionalist*

They expressed pride in their work and a sense of ownership for feeding the country's people.

As Joan perused the findings from the qualitative interviews, she wondered what she would report to Kipp about possible changes in their approach to market segmentation. There was a lack of understanding of the various segments of beef consumers and their needs, how brand marketing could affect consumer demand, and how alliances within the supply chain could affect the ranchers' situations.

Unfortunately, the fragmented nature of the cow/calf producers, combined with their focus on production rather than marketing, meant that the beef industry was not very consumer focused. Joan wondered about their approach to segmenting the market based on herd size. As she pondered how all these pieces fit together, she began to brainstorm new ways to look at the market. She wanted to work with Kipp in developing a plan to maintain Pfizer's market position in light of the changes in the industry.

# Questions

1. Based on the research findings, evaluate Pfizer's Cow/Calf Team's herd-size segmentation approach.

2. If it doesn't make sense to continue segmenting on the basis of herd size, what variables can be used to segment that more accurately capture differences in the market? What would the resulting segments look like? What segments are most viable for Pfizer?

3. How does the suggested segmentation approach capitalize on changes in the cattle industry? What implications do the industry changes have for Pfizer?

4. How good is the research for drawing conclusions about market segmentation of beef producers?

5. Assuming that support is found for the recommended segmentation approach, how can it be implemented as a marketing strategy?

# Pfizer Inc. Animal Health Products (B) Industry Downturns and Marketing Strategy

Gail Oss, Territory Manager of Pfizer Inc. Animal Health Group in western Montana and southeastern Idaho, was driving back to her home office after a day of visiting cattle ranchers in her territory. The combination of the spring sunshine warming the air and the snow-capped peaks of the Bitterroot Mountains provided a stunningly beautiful backdrop for her drive. But the majestic beauty provided little relief to her troubled thoughts.

The NAFTA agreement with Canada and Mexico had hit local ranchers particularly hard. The influx of beef cattle into the U.S. market from these countries, as well as beef from other countries (e.g., Australia) that entered the United States via more lenient import restrictions in Mexico, had wreaked havoc over the past year. Prices of beef had declined precipitously from the prior year. Ranchers in the past had retained sufficient reserves to come back from a bad year, but this year, things were particularly bad. The prices being offered for the calves by the feedlot operators were, in many cases, less than the costs of raising those calves. Ranchers' objectives had changed from making some modest income off their cattle operations to minimizing their losses.

In this environment, ranchers were actively seeking ways to cut costs. Gail sold high-quality animal health products, oftentimes at a premium price. One way in which ranchers could cut costs was either to skimp on animal health care products, such as vaccines and antibiotics, or to switch to a lower-cost alternative. The current environment posed a particularly severe threat, not only to Gail's company, but also to her very livelihood. Gail had spent a substantial amount of time and effort cultivating long-term relationships with many of these ranchers—many of whom she had to convince of her credibility, given her gender. Given the time and effort she had spent cultivating these relationships, as well as the camaraderie she felt with her customers, she did not want to see the ranchers in her territory go under. Ranching was an important part of the history of Montana; many ranchers had ties to the land going back generations. They took pride in producing the food for many tables in the United States and other areas of the world. Gail felt that Pfizer could use its fairly significant resources in a very influential manner to help these ranchers. Simply lowering the price on her products (if that was even possible) was merely a Band-Aid solution to the problem.

As part of Gail's weekly responsibilities, she communicated via an automated computer system to her sales manager, Tom Brooks (also in Montana), and to the marketing managers at headquarters (in Exton, Pennsylvania). She knew she needed to report the severity of the situation, but more importantly, she wanted to encourage headquarters to take the bull by the horns, so to speak. So she was pondering the message she would write that evening from her kitchen table.

By Jakki Mohr and Sara Streeter of the University of Montana. Some of the information in this case has been modified to protect the proprietary nature of firms' marketing strategies. The case is intended to be used as a basis for class discussion rather than to illustrate either effective or ineffective marketing strategies. © Copyright Jakki J. Mohr, 1999, All Rights Reserved. Support from The Institute for the Study of Business Markets, Pennsylvania State University, is greatly appreciated.

**Exhibit 1**
Supply Chain
for Beef

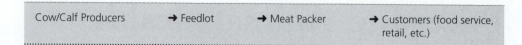

Cow/Calf Producers  →  Feedlot  →  Meat Packer  →  Customers (food service, retail, etc.)

**Exhibit 2**
Per Capita Meat
Consumption %
Market Share
(Retail Weight)
SOURCE: USDA & NCBA.

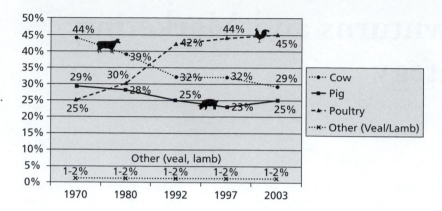

## Industry Background

The supply chain (Exhibit 1) for beef begins with the cow/calf producer (the commercial rancher). Commercial ranchers are in the business of breeding and raising cattle for the purpose of selling them to feedlots. Ranchers keep a herd of cows that are bred yearly. The calves are generally born in the early spring, weaned in October, and shipped to feedlots generally in late October/early November. The ranchers' objectives are to minimize death loss in their herd and to breed cows that give birth to low birth weight calves (for calving ease), produce beef that will grade low choice by having a good amount of marbling, and produce calves that gain weight quickly. Success measures include: conception rate of cows exposed to bulls; live birth rates, birth weights, weaning weights, death loss, and profitability. By the time a rancher sells calves to the feedlot, the name of the game is pounds. The rancher generally wants the biggest calves possible by that time.

Within a commodity market, basic laws of supply and demand are influenced by those in a position to control access to the markets. Four meatpackers controlled roughly 80 percent of the industry. Meatpackers have acted as an intermediary between the meat consumer and the meat producer. This situation has not facilitated a free flow of information throughout the supply chain, and therefore, the industry has not been strongly consumer focused.

Exhibit 2 traces the market share for beef, pork, and poultry from 1970 to 1997 and projects changes in the market through 2003. The market share for beef fell from 44 percent in 1970 to 32 percent in 1997, a 27 percent drop.

Some of the reasons for the decline included:

- Changes in consumer lifestyles (less time spent in preparing home-cooked meals); an interesting statistic is that two-thirds of all dinner decisions are made on the same day; of those, three-quarters don't know what they're going to make at 4:30 PM.
- Health/nutritional issues (dietary considerations involving cholesterol, fat content, foodborne diseases, etc.)
- Switching to alternative meat products

In addition, the pork and poultry industries had done a better job of marketing their products. During 1997, the number of new poultry products (for example, stuffed chicken entrees, gourmet home meal replacements) introduced to the market increased 13 percent from the prior year, compared to an increase of only 3.5 percent for new beef products. And retail pricing for beef remained stubbornly high (although this high price did not translate into higher prices of the calves in a per-weight basis to the ranchers, as discussed subsequently).

**Exhibit 3**
Beef Production
and Price

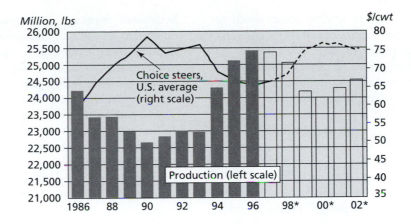

**Exhibit 4**
Total U.S.
Inventory Cattle
and Calves,
January 1 (million
head)

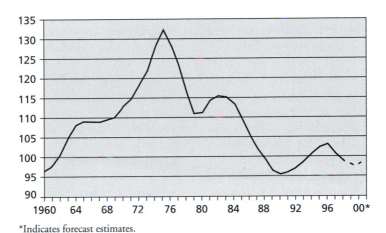

*Indicates forecast estimates.

Based on historical data, shown in Exhibit 3, the beef production cycle spans a 12-year period in which production levels expand and contract. As Exhibit 3 shows, the amount of beef produced (bars in the chart, millions of pounds on the left-hand scale) increased through the mid-90s—despite the declining beef consumption in the United States shown on Exhibit 2. This relationship between production and consumption is consistent with other commodity markets, where there exists an inverse relationship between supply and demand.

Some of the reasons for increased beef production in the mid-90s included:

- Herd liquidation: low cattle prices, coupled with the high cost of feed drove some producers out of business.
- Improved genetics and animal health/nutrition increased production yields; indeed, although cow numbers had decreased by 10 percent since

1985 (as noted by Exhibit 4) productivity per cow increased by 29 percent.

- Export of beef increased seven-fold since 1985 (to 2 billion pounds); key markets include Japan (54 percent of export volume); Canada (16 percent); Korea (11 percent), and Mexico (9 percent).

Exhibit 3 also shows that the price the ranchers received for their beef cattle varied inversely with production (right-hand scale). Although calf prices were expected to rise slightly through the late 90s/early 2000s, the prices paid were still far below the relatively high prices consumers paid at retail. One of the reasons given for the relatively low prices paid to ranchers on a per-pound basis for their calves was the high degree of concentration at the meat-packer level of the supply chain. As noted previously, four packing houses controlled access to the market. Some ranchers believed this gave the packing houses near-monopoly power in setting prices (both for what they would pay feedlot operators for the calves and in charging prices to their downstream customers, e.g., the grocery store chains). Although the U.S. government had investigated the possibility of collusion among packers, the evidence was not sufficient to draw any firm conclusions.

To further complicate matters, the NAFTA agreement passed in 1989 had given open access to the United States markets from Mexican and Canadian ranchers. The lowering of trade barriers, coupled with weakness in the Canadian dollar and the Mexican peso, made imported livestock cheap, compared to U.S.-grown animals. As a result, thousands of head of cattle came streaming across the borders. The flow was heaviest from Canada.

During the summer of 1998, ranchers had been quite vocal in drawing attention to the influx of cattle from Canada. Local governments were somewhat responsive to their concerns. Indeed, trucks carrying Canadian cattle had been turned back at the U.S.–Canadian border for minor infractions such as licensing. In addition, the trucks were consistently pulled over for inspections. A private coalition of ranchers, calling itself the Ranchers-Cattlemen Action Legal Foundation (R-CALF), filed three separate petitions with the U.S. International Trade Commission (ITC) on October 1, 1998, two against Canada and one against Mexico, asking for U.S. government trade investigations. The group requested that antidumping duties be levied on meat or livestock imports from the two countries. The Montana Stockgrowers Association had been an early and steadfast supporter of R-CALF.

The ITC determined that there was evidence to support the charge the Canadian cattle imports are causing material injury to U.S. domestic cattle producers. The Department of Commerce began to collect information on Canadian subsidies and prices at which Canadian cattle are sold in Canada and in the United States. In the case against Mexico, the ITC determined that there was no indication that imports of live cattle from Mexico were causing "material injury" to the domestic industry in the United States. Dissatisfied with the response, R-CALF decided to appeal the case to the Court of International Trade.

Ranchers were doing what they could to minimize the impact of the NAFTA agreement on their livelihoods; however, some could not sustain their operations in light of the lower cattle prices. The number of cattle operations was declining. In many cases, smaller ranchers were selling out to their larger neighbors. This reality was reflected in the cattle inventory statistics, shown in Exhibit 4.

The number of cattle kept by U.S. ranchers had declined from a high of approximately 132 million head in 1975 to just under 100 million head in 1998. As noted previously, improvements in genetics and animal health and nutrition allowed ranchers to increase production yields, even with fewer head.

## Additional Industry Changes

Some of the changes that had occurred in the poultry and pork industries, including more ready-to-eat products and branded products, were expected to diffuse into the cattle industry. Industry analysts believed that the beef industry would need to develop products that could be more easily prepared and to develop branded products that consumers could recognize and rely on for quality and convenience. In addition, industry analysts believed that the beef industry would need to improve the quality of its products (in terms of more consistent taste and tenderness), as currently only 25 percent of the beef produced met quality targets.

The development of branded beef would require a tracking system from "birth-to-beef" in the supply chain. Such tracking would allow standardized health, quality, and management protocols, as well as improved feedback through the entire production model. This change would also necessitate the producers being more closely linked to the feedlots to improve the quality of the beef. Branded beef production would move the industry from a cost-based (production) model to a value-added model. Better coordination along the supply chain would ensure an increased flow of information from the consumer to the producers. Alliances between the cow/calf producer and the feedlots would allow ranchers to better track the success of their calves (based on health and weight gain). Such data could allow the ranchers to further improve the genetics of their herd by tracking which cow/bull combinations had delivered the higher-yield calves. As part of these trends, some degree of integration or vertical coordination will occur in the beef industry. Ranchers will need to participate in order to

**Exhibit 5**
Pfizer Animal Health Organization

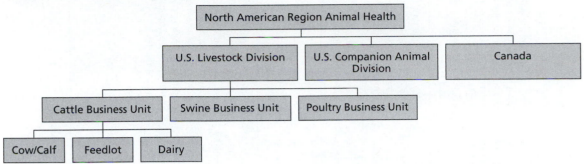

ensure market access for their product. Ranchers will have to think beyond the boundaries of their own ranches.

## Pfizer Animal Health Group

Pfizer Inc. is a research-based, diversified health care company with global operations. Pfizer Animal Health is one of the corporation's three major business groups (the other two being the Consumer Health Care Group, and U.S. Pharmaceuticals). The Animal Health Products Group accounted for roughly 12 percent of the company's revenues in 1998 (Pfizer Annual Report).

Pfizer Animal Health products are sold to veterinarians and animal health distributors in more than 140 countries around the world for use by livestock producers and horse and pet owners; the products are used in more than 30 animal species. Pfizer Animal Health is committed to providing high-quality, research-based health products for livestock and companion animals. The company continues to invest significant dollars for research and development. As a result, Pfizer has many new animal health products in its research pipeline, a number of which have already been introduced in some international markets and will become available in the United States in the next several years.

As Exhibit 5 shows, the Animal Health Group is divided into a North America Region with a U.S. Livestock Division, a U.S. Companion Animal Division (cats, dogs, etc.), and Canada. The Cow/Calf Division falls under the Cattle Business Unit within the Livestock Division. That division is organized further by product type (Wood Mackenzie Report).

The marketing managers for each cattle market segment work closely with product managers and sales managers to ensure timely, accurate information back from the field. Territory managers responsible for all sales activities report to an area sales manager, who in turn reports to the national sales and marketing manager. Territory managers are typically compensated on a roughly 80 percent salary/20 percent commission basis. This percentage would vary by salesperson by year; in a good year the commission might be a much higher percentage of overall earnings, whereas in a bad year, the salary component might be a greater percentage of the salesperson's overall earnings.

## Marketing Strategy

Pfizer's Cow/Calf Division offers a full range of products to cattle ranchers, including vaccines for both newborn calves and their mothers, medications (for example, dewormers, antidiarrheals), and antibiotics (for pneumonia and other diseases). Pfizer's sophisticated research-and-development system resulted in a number of new and useful products for the market. For example, Pfizer developed a long-lasting dewormer that was simply poured along the cow's back. This technology was a significant time-saver to the rancher, eliminating the need to administer either an oral medication or an injection. Moreover, Pfizer had been the first company to come up with a modified-live and killed virus vaccine, a significant technological breakthrough that provided safety in pregnant animals and the efficacy of a modified-live virus.

Pfizer offered a diverse product line to cow/calf ranchers. Some of Pfizer's key product lines are compared to competitors in Exhibit 6.

# Exhibit 6
## Comparison of Product Lines*

| | Pfizer | American Home Products (Fort Dodge) | Bayer | Merial | Boehringer Ingelheim |
|---|---|---|---|---|---|
| **Sales and Profitability** | 10-year average annual sales growth increase of 3.8%; average for global veterinary market is 6.9%. Profit rate in 1997 was 8.4%. Market share in 1997 was 15.3%. | 10-year average annual sales growth increase of 7.8%; average for global veterinary market is 6.9%. Profit rate in 1997 was 11.0%; market share was 9.0%. | 10-year average annual sales growth increase of 10.2%; average for global veterinary market is 6.9%. Profit rate in 1997 was 16.8%; market share was 10.9%. | 10-year average annual sales growth increase of 11.9%; average for global veterinary market is 6.9%. Profit rate in 1997 was 22.8%; market share was 16.4%. | 10-year average annual sales growth increase of 6.0%; average for global veterinary market is 6.9%. Profit rate in 1997 was 12.3%; market share was 3%. |
| **Bovine Diseases Covered by Product Range** | IBR; P1-3; BVD; BRSV; eptospira; rotavirus; coronavirus; campylobacter; clostridia; E.Coli; pasteurellosis; haemophilus | Pasteurellosis; enterotoxaemia; chlamydia; salmonella; IBR; P1-3; brucellosis; rabies; E.Coli; anaplasmosis; tetanus; BVD; BRSV; leptospirosis; trichomonas; campylobacter; papilloma; haemophilus | IBR; FMD; IPV; P1-3; balanoposthitis; clostridia; haemophilus; BRSV; BVD; leptospira; E.Coli; rhinotracheitis; campylobacter | Foot and mouth; rabies; brucellosis; paratuberculosis; rhinotracheitis; rotavirus; coronavirus; colibacillosis; parainfluenza; BVD; agalactia; foot rot; black leg; IBR; leptospira; clostridia; pasteurella; BRSV; E.Coli | BRSV; campylobacter enterotoxaemia; tetanus; pasteurella haemolytica; haemophilus somnus; leptospirosis; staphylococcus aureus; clostridia; respiratory synctial virus; E coli-K99; viral diarrhea; moraxella bovis; parainfluenza; rhinotracheitis; pateurella multocida |
| **Significant Products for Cattle** | Comprehensive product line; anti-infectives have formed basis of product line for many years; vaccine businesses also very important; also sells a performance enhancer, virginiamycin; parasiticides, led by Dectomax, starting to make significant impact on sales; Valbazen anthelmintic; broad range of general pharmaceuticals. | Predominantly a vaccine company; antibiotics centered on antimastitis products; anti-infectives based on penicillins, tetracyclines, sulphonamides and quinolones; parasiticides led by Cydectin; main products in general; pharmaceuticals are anabolic implants for muscle growth. | Product range biased towards parasiticides, particularly ectoparasiticides and antibiotics; overall product range is diverse; some mastitis antimicrobials; wide range of pharmaceuticals, but sales value of each product is limited; focus is more toward companion animal market. | Most-important product sector is parasiticides, with product range dominated by Ivermectin, which was the first endectocide to reach the market; success of Ivermectic has drawn strong competition; remainder of product range made up primarily of anthelmintics and a range of general pharmaceuticals and vaccines. | Products focused on specialist veterinary pharmaceuticals for respiratory disorders (Bisolvon), corticosteroid preparations (Voren), spasmolytics (Buscopan), and parasiticides. |

*This information is taken from the Wood MacKenzie Animal Health Market Review and its Veterinary Company Profiles, both done on a worldwide basis.

| | Pfizer | American Home Products (Fort Dodge) | Bayer | Merial | Boehringer Ingelheim |
|---|---|---|---|---|---|
| **Strengths** | Strong manufacturing capabilities based on fermentation expertise and capacity; global marketing coverage supported by strategic local manufacture; strong range of new products in early commercialization; broad product range with strength in companion animals. | Leading global vaccine business; good international exposure; comprehensive vaccine product range; potential for growth through Cydectin. | Growing market in expanding companion animal sector; solid in-house manufacturing supported by global distribution capability; business focused on key market areas. | Leading veterinary vaccine company with broad product portfolio; strong line of new product introductions; good companion animal business; global distribution network; strength in parasiticides and vaccines sectors. | Specialist veterinary pharmaceuticals, especially for respiratory disorders; good distribution capabilities; good strength in swine market; specialty products targeted to particular niches. |
| **Weaknesses** | North America still dominates turnover; high proportion of sales due to off-patent products; heavily dependent on performance of livestock markets. | Business with disparate parts requiring strong central focus; except for vaccines, product range is dominated by commodity products; R&D likely to be reduced. | Underweight in U.S.A; lack of critical mass in biologicals; no blockbuster product in North American market; narrow anti-infectives product portfolio; current R&D emphasis away from new product discovery. | Specialist pharmaceutical product line, not significantly involved in livestock sectors; aging anti-infectives portfolio; Ivermectin subject to intense competition. | Anti-infective product range dominated by commodity products, limited parasiticide product range, turnover dominated by the U.S. market. |
| **% of R&D to Sales*** | 5 | 3 | 3 | 2 | 1 |
| **Position on Quality vs Price**** | 5 | 3.5 | 3 | 3 | 1 |
| **Price Support of Distribution Channel**** | 2 | 4 | 3 | 3 | 5 |

*Specific ratios are considered proprietary. Hence, a general rating scale is used, where 5 means a higher percentage of R&D/Sales, and 1 is a lower percentage.

**5 = Focus on quality only; 1 = Focus on low price only.

***5 = strong emphasis on SPIFs (Special Promotional Incentive Funds) and price-related trade promotions, 1 = low emphasis.

**Exhibit 7**
Pfizer
Marketing
Segmentation,
1998

| Segment | # of Cattle | # of Operations | % of National Cattle Inventory |
|---------|-------------|-----------------|--------------------------------|
| Hobbyist | <100 | 808,000 | 50% |
| Traditionalist | 100–499 | 69,000 | 36% |
| Business | 500+ | 5,900 | 14% |

Pfizer segmented ranchers in the cow/calf business on the basis of herd size, as shown in Exhibit 7.

"Hobbyists" are so-called because in many cases these ranchers run their cattle as a sideline to some other job held. "Traditionalists," main livelihood is their cattle operation. The "Business" segment operations are large ranches, owned either by a family or a corporation.

Pfizer's extensive network of field sales representatives visits the ranchers to inform them about new and existing products. Time spent with accounts was typically allocated on the basis of volume of product purchased.

Pfizer positioned its products on the combination of superior science (resulting from its significant R&D efforts) and high-quality production/quality control techniques. For example, although other companies in the market (particularly generics) used similar formulations in their products, on occasion they did not have good quality control in the production line, resulting in batches of ineffective vaccines and recalls. Pfizer backed its products completely, with a Technical Services Department. If ranchers had any kind of health or nutritional problem with their herds, they could call on a team of Pfizer technical specialists who would work with the local veterinarian, utilizing blood and other diagnostics to identify the problem and suggest a solution.

Pfizer also was very involved in the cattle industry itself. Each territory manager was given an annual budget that included discretionary funds to be spent in his/her territory to sponsor industry activities such as seminars on herd health, stock shows, 4-H, and so forth. Gail Oss, for example, chose to spend a significant portion of her discretionary funds sponsoring meetings and conferences for the Montana Stockgrower's Association, which might include a veterinarian or a professor from the Extension Office of a state university speaking on issues pertinent to ranchers.

The majority of Pfizer's trade advertising was focused on specific products and appeared in cattle industry publications, such as *Beef Magazine* and *Bovine Veterinarian*. One ad read, "More veterinarians are satisfied with [Pfizer's] Dectomax Pour-On," and went on to describe veterinarians' superior satisfaction and greater likelihood of recommending Dectomax compared to a key competitor, Ivomec.

> *"Eighty-four percent of veterinarians who recommended Dectomax Pour-On said they were satisfied or very satisfied with its performance—compared to only 51 percent who were satisfied or very satisfied with Ivomec Eprinex Pour-On. . . . If choosing only between Dectomax and Ivomec, over three out of four veterinarians would choose to recommend Dectomax Pour-On."*

Another ad read, "Calf Health Program Boosts Prices by Up to $21 More per Head." The data in the copy-intensive ad highlighted that "cow-calf producers enrolled in value-added programs like Pfizer Select Vaccine programs are being rewarded for their efforts with top-of-the-market prices." Such programs are based on a consistent program of vaccinating animals with specific products that provide optimal disease protection. The programs result in cattle that perform more consistently and predictably in terms of weight gain and beef quality—resulting in higher prices at sale time.

Although the territory managers called on ranchers (as well as the veterinarians, distributors, and dealers) in their territories, they sold no product directly to ranchers. Ranchers could buy their animal health products from either a local veterinarian, a distributor, or a dealer (such as a feed-and-seed store). The percentage of product flowing through vets, distributors, or dealers varied significantly by region. In areas where feedlots (vs. cow/calf ranchers) were the predominant customers, 95 percent of the product might flow through distributors. In areas where ranchers are the predominant customers, vets might sell 50 percent of the product, depending on customer preferences.

Vets were particularly important, given that the overwhelming majority of ranchers said that the person they trusted the most when it came to managing the health of their herd was their veterinarian. Pfizer capitalizes on this trust in the vet in its marketing program. When the vet consults and recommends a Pfizer product to a rancher, the vet gives the rancher a coded coupon that may be redeemed at either a vet clinic or supply house. When the coupon is sent back to Pfizer for reimbursement, the vet is credited for servicing that product, regardless of where the product is purchased.

Pfizer offers some trade promotions to vets and distributors, including volume rebate programs, price promotions on certain products during busy seasonal periods, and so forth. However, Pfizer's competitors oftentimes gave much more significant discounts and SPIFs to distributors. As a result, when a rancher went to a distributor to buy a product that the vet had recommended, the distributor might switch the rancher to a similar product for which the distributor was making more profit. If it was a Pfizer product that the vet had recommended, the distributor might switch the rancher to a competitors' product. Pfizer had historically avoided competing on the basis of such promotional tactics, feeling instead that redirecting such funds back into R&D resulted in better long-term benefits for its customers.

So, as Gail pondered these various facets of the company's market position and strategies, she decided to take a strong stance in her weekly memo. It was time to cut the bull.

## Questions

1. Evaluate the trends affecting the cattle ranching industry.

2. To what degree is a high-quality/premium-price position a strength or a liability during an industry downturn? What are the various ways Pfizer could handle this situation?

3. Evaluate the various dimensions of Pfizer's marketing strategy: market segmentation and positioning; product/price; distribution; trade advertising and trade promotion; personal selling; and public relations and sponsorships. What makes sense and what doesn't? Why or why not?

4. Would Pfizer benefit from a relationship-marketing focus? How would their marketing strategy need to be modified to take such a focus?

5. When an industry is in decline, to what extent should a supplier be involved in ensuring its customers' livelihoods?

# Planktos Inc.

In recent years, several environmental concerns have caused discussion and disputes to arise between environmentalists and governments. One of the most publicized is the increase in earth's average temperatures due to global warming. Recently, many companies have begun to research the possibilities of reducing what is believed to be the main cause of global warming, carbon dioxide ($CO_2$). Due to the increase in environmental concern from the public, both industries and governments around the world have been trying to reduce as much $CO_2$ emissions as economically possible. While it is still in dispute as to whether human impacts have drastically affected the amounts of naturally occurring $CO_2$, it remains a fact that its concentration continues to increase in our atmosphere. One company among many, Planktos Inc., is trying to establish a business out of reducing the amount of $CO_2$ found in our atmosphere. Planktos Inc. will aim to stimulate the growth of $CO_2$-reducing phytoplankton in the world's oceans.

Recently, Planktos Inc. has received much opposition from environmentalist who oppose this process because of the potential environmental concerns which they believe may arise through their process. The company's growth has been attributed to the recent concerns of global climate changes. Planktos wishes to establish a marketing strategy which will allow them to continue to grow and expand in the global market.

## Global Warming

Global warming is an issue which has received much attention by scientist, industrialists, and governments. Global warming refers to the increase of temperatures around the world due to several factors including the increase of greenhouse gases such as $CO_2$. Some consequences of global warming include the melting of ice sheets, rise in sea levels, and the increase of severe weather worldwide which can have harsh effects on economies and can hinder the potential growth of developing countries.

The argument about the human effects on the increase of $CO_2$ in the atmosphere is still under debate by scientists around the world. Several things that are agreed upon are the facts that $CO_2$ gases have an impact on the climate changes on our planet, and that they continue to rise as the years progress. The projected rise in $CO_2$ is visually explained in Exhibit 1.[1]

## Company Background

Planktos Inc. is a for-profit company whose main purpose is to restore damaged habitats around the world. The company hopes to accomplish this by two means, by restoring the declining forests on land and by stimulating the growth of phytoplankton in the worlds oceans.

Through its subsidiary, KlimaFa Ltd., the company is currently seeking to restore thousands of acres of declining forests in European nations. However, Plankto's main efforts in restoration lie in its desires to stimulate growth of $CO_2$-reducing

---

[1] This case was prepared by Raul Benavidez for the purpose of class discussion. There is no association between Mr. Benavidez and Planktos, Inc. Values used in this case are estimates and should not be regarded as official.

**Exhibit 1**

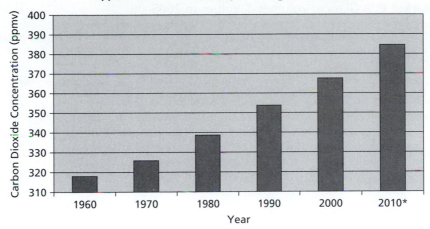

Approximate Global Atmospheric $CO_2$ Concentrations

* Value is a projected estimate
ppmv = parts per million by volume

phytoplankton in the ocean. The process begins by having a ship sprinkle iron shavings on the ocean surface. These iron particles will stimulate the growth of rapidly growing plankton. Through photosynthesis, the plankton will soak up atmospheric $CO_2$ and store it in its tissue and when the algae die, they decompose and sink deep into the ocean. Russ George, CEO of Planktos, claims that the plankton sucks up $CO_2$ more efficiently than any other process. All of the $CO_2$ which is absorbed by the plankton does not end up in the ocean floor. Some of the plankton is eaten by other organisms such as krill, which is then eaten by other fish. Although the amounts that do sink to the bottom of the ocean are sufficient enough to be measured by modern day equipment, Plankto's solution does not eliminate carbon dioxide; instead it only sequesters it at the ocean bottom. Plankto's estimates that the algae needs to sink to a depth of about 1,000 feet before long-term storage occurs. The company says that at 1,000 feet the $CO_2$ will remain stored for decades. At 1,500 feet, centuries, and at 3,000 feet they estimate it will remain stored for a millennium.

Since Plankto's main focus is environmental restoration, they only seek to restore the ocean's plankton population to normal levels which have fallen approximately 10% over the past 37 years. The company estimates that every ton of carbon sequestered will equal approximately 3 tons of $CO_2$ removed from the atmosphere. Planktos earns credits

from reducing $CO_2$ from the atmosphere. The company then sells these credits to other companies in the global carbon market.

The carbon market can be divided into several segments in which participating governments or companies are allowed to trade allocated carbon credits. These segments include, among others, the EU ETS market (European Union Emissions Trading Scheme) in Europe, the NWS market (New South Wales) in Australia, and the CCX (Chicago Climate Exchange) in the U.S. As you can see in Exhibit 2,[2] the carbon trading market has increased over the past two years beginning in 2005. It is estimated that approximately $30 billion worth of carbon credits were traded in 2006, with trades doubling in 2007.

Some of these segments are voluntary (CCX) and others, such as the EU ETS, came about due to agreements, such as the Kyoto Protocol, which were formed by several countries around the world. The Kyoto Protocol is an agreement which was established in Kyoto, Japan, on December 11, 1997. Its purpose is to stabilize greenhouse gases around the world to a level which would not interfere with the worldwide climate system. This works by allocating a set amount of $CO_2$ which can be emitted by participating countries. As of December 2006, 169 countries have voluntarily signed and ratified the agreement. This agreement allows companies in those countries to produce a set amount of $CO_2$ designated as "credits."

## Exhibit 2
Carbon Market at a Glance, Volumes & Values in 2005–06

| | Allowances | | | | | Project-Based Transactions | | | |
| | 2005 | | 2006 | | | 2005 | | 2006 | |
| | Volume (MtCO$_2$e) | Value (MUS$) | Volume (MtCO$_2$e) | Value (MUS$) | | Volume (MtCO$_2$e) | Value (MUS$) | Volume (MtCO$_2$e) | Value (MUS$) |
|---|---|---|---|---|---|---|---|---|---|
| EU ETS | 321 | 7908 | 1101 | 24357 | Primary CDM | 341 | 2417 | 450 | 4813 |
| NSW | 6 | 59 | 20 | 225 | Secondary CDM | 10 | 221 | 25 | 444 |
| CCX | 1 | 3 | 10 | 38 | JI | 11 | 68 | 16 | 141 |
| UK ETS | 0 | 1 | na | na | Other | 20 | 187 | 17 | 79 |
| **Subtotal** | **328** | **7971** | **1131** | **24620** | **Subtotal** | **382** | **2893** | **508** | **5477** |

| | 2005 | | | 2006 |
| | Volume (MtCO$_2$e) | Value (MUS$) | Volume (MtCO$_2$e) | Value (MUS$) |
|---|---|---|---|---|
| **Total** | **710** | **10864** | **1639** | **30097** |

MtCO$_2$e—Million Ton Carbon Dioxide Equivalent.
MUS$—Million U.S. Dollars.

CDM, JI—Clean Development Mechanism, Joint Implementation.

CDM and JI are mechanisms which allow companies to earn additional credits.

When companies such as electricity-producing coal plants have used up the amount of credits which have been allocated to them, they can purchase all additional credits from companies such as Planktos, which earns these credits.

Currently, most of the credits being traded are in overseas markets such as Europe and Australia. While the United States has been slow to catch up on the carbon trading market, some states such as California are trying to establish the necessary certifications so that they may trade carbon credits in the latter part of 2007. This will be done by setting a cap on state emissions.

## Factors Affecting Growth

Planktos is facing competition from several up and coming companies looking to cash in on plankton restoration. Two companies in particular are Climos and GreenSea Ventures. Climos is younger than Planktos and has yet to establish the presence held by Planktos in the plankton restoration business. GreenSea is expected to begin business within the next year. Planktos currently has the advantage over the two companies in experience, but GreenSea Venture has a patented method to control the iron fertilization which may prove to be a more efficient process than that of Planktos.

Ocean fertilization on a large scale has a possibility of causing some problems as well. The iron's potential side effects include the depletion of oxygen, overproduction of nitrogen, and the production of carbonic acid. However, since Planktos only looks to restore the iron concentrations to their previous levels, Planktos claims that there is no threat.

Recently, Planktos has received criticism from the World Wildlife Fund (WWF) for its plans to dump iron in the oceans near the Galapagos in its first demonstration project.

Scientists are concerned about the effects that dumping iron will have on the balance of abundant life forms surrounding the islands, specifically the 400 species of fish that swim the coast. Planktos argues that the reason for the vast number of species in the area is because of the iron being released by the island into the ocean.

Furthermore, according to Mr. William Coleman, COO at Planktos, the project is not planned for "The Galapagos"; instead it is planned for the Equatorial Pacific, some 500 miles west of The Galapagos.

With environmental concerns rising, it is possible that Planktos will face issues such as this in other parts of the world on their quest to reduce the amount of carbon dioxide in the ocean.

Regardless of all of the environmental concerns which Planktos may face, it is undeniable that $CO_2$ emissions will continue to rise in the future. This rise in emissions will continue to spur the growth of Planktos's credit selling power. According to

## Exhibit 3

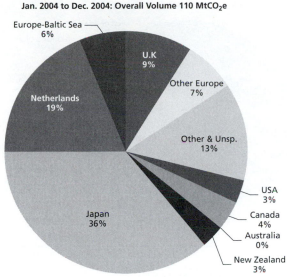

Jan. 2004 to Dec. 2004: Overall Volume 110 MtCO₂e

Europe-Baltic Sea 6%
U.K 9%
Other Europe 7%
Netherlands 19%
Other & Unsp. 13%
USA 3%
Canada 4%
Japan 36%
Australia 0%
New Zealand 3%

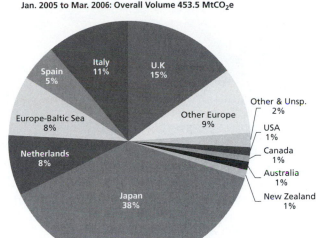

Jan. 2005 to Mar. 2006: Overall Volume 453.5 MtCO₂e

Spain 5%
Italy 11%
U.K 15%
Other Europe 9%
Other & Unsp. 2%
Europe-Baltic Sea 8%
USA 1%
Canada 1%
Netherlands 8%
Australia 1%
New Zealand 1%
Japan 38%

Mr. Coleman, there are two major market categories: the voluntary market, motivated by individual or institutional interest in "Going Green," and the regulated market motivated by policies that are in place now or soon to emerge. Planktos plans to cater to both markets.

There are several ways in which a company can obtain credits. Credits can be initially earned by being allocated to a company through an agreement such as the Kyoto protocol. They can then be traded between companies in the market, or they can be earned in a couple of ways. A Clean Development Mechanism (CDM) and Joint Implementation (JI) were set in place by the Kyoto protocol, and they allow industrialized countries to earn additional credits when they help other developing or industrial countries reduce their emissions.

Exhibit 3[3] illustrates the percentage of the top market buyers of carbon credits around the globe. As shown in the exhibit, the major buyers and traders lie in the western part of the world. North and South America have slowly begun to enter the market and have yet to become major players. Japan seems to be the overall market leader. But as you can see, countries such as Spain and Italy continue to join the market as the years progress. The carbon market is still in its infancy and remains very fragmented throughout the globe, and since much of it is de-

pendent on government policy it is hard to accurately determine its potential. The company's major selling competition around the globe, by country, can be identified in Exhibit 4[4] on the following page. Planktos has various possible companies to which they can sell credits. Among them, the most prominent client could be electricity producing coal power plants. Professor Gary Rochelle of the University of Texas estimates that by 2030, approximately two-thirds of $CO_2$ emissions will be produced by coal fueled power plants[5]. According to the Joint Report for Natural Resources Council, $CO_2$ emissions from power plants have risen approximately 25% since 1990 and will continue to rise. Planktos also has various industries within the U.S. which the company can possibly sell credits to. Exhibit 5[6] on the following page demonstrates the increase in emissions of major U.S. sources. However, potential companies must be participating in the credit exchange market to be beneficial.

However prominent the emergence of coal plants in the future, their construction faces opposition by the general public on a daily basis. In 2006 and 2007, Texas faced this dilemma when a large energy provider planned to build 18 new coal fueled power plants in the state. Opposition by environmental groups quickly escalated in the state level and got national attention. As published by the Associate Press:

## Exhibit 4

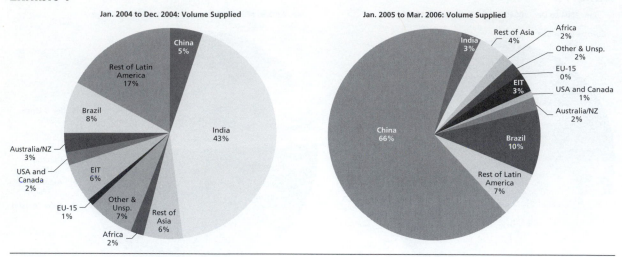

Jan. 2004 to Dec. 2004: Volume Supplied

China 5%
Rest of Latin America 17%
Brazil 8%
Australia/NZ 3%
USA and Canada 2%
EU-15 1%
EIT 6%
Other & Unsp. 7%
Rest of Asia 6%
Africa 2%
India 43%

Jan. 2005 to Mar. 2006: Volume Supplied

India 3%
Rest of Asia 4%
Africa 2%
Other & Unsp. 2%
EU-15 0%
EIT 3%
USA and Canada 1%
Australia/NZ 2%
China 66%
Brazil 10%
Rest of Latin America 7%

## Exhibit 5
### U.S. Greenhouse Gas Emissions and Sinks (Tg $CO_2$ Equivalents)

| U.S. Greenhouse Gas Emissions and Sinks (Tg $CO_2$ Equivalents) | | | | Change from 1995–2005 | |
| --- | --- | --- | --- | --- | --- |
| $CO_2$ Gas Source | 1995 | 2000 | 2005 | Value | Percent |
| Fossil Fuel Combustion | 5030.0 | 5584.9 | 5751.2 | 721.2 | 14.34 % |
| Non-Energy Use of Fuels | 133.2 | 141 | 142.4 | 9.2 | 6.91 % |
| Cement Manufacture | 36.8 | 41.2 | 45.9 | 9.1 | 24.73 % |
| Iron and Steel Production | 73.3 | 65.1 | 45.2 | (28.1) | (38.34) % |
| Natural Gas Systems | 33.8 | 29.4 | 28.2 | (5.6) | (16.57) % |
| Municipal Solid Waste Combustion | 15.7 | 17.9 | 20.9 | 5.2 | 33.12 % |
| Ammonia Manufacture and Urea Application | 20.5 | 19.6 | 16.3 | (4.2) | (20.49) % |
| Lime Manufacture | 12.8 | 13.3 | 13.7 | 0.9 | 7.03 % |
| Limestone and Dolomite Use | 7.4 | 6 | 7.4 | 0 | 0 % |
| Soda Ash Manufacture and Consumption | 4.3 | 4.2 | 4.2 | (0.1) | (2.33) % |
| Aluminum Production | 5.7 | 6.1 | 4.2 | (1.5) | (26.32) % |
| Petrochemical Production | 2.8 | 3 | 2.9 | 0.1 | 3.57 % |
| Titanium Dioxide Production | 1.7 | 1.9 | 1.9 | 0.2 | 11.76 % |

$TgCO_2$ —Teragrams of carbon dioxide equivalents. Tg = $10^9$ kg = $10^6$ metric tons = 1 million metric tons.

"Carrying signs with slogans of "Stop the Coal Rush" and "Shame on Texas," about 1,000 people rallied at the state Capitol to persuade lawmakers to abandon a plan to build up to 18 new coal-fired power plants."[7]

Currently, Planktos mainly serves the voluntary market composed of environmentally aware individuals and companies, such as those mentioned, who understand the concerns associated with the increase of $CO_2$ in the atmosphere. With more and more environmental concerns arising, Planktos's market continues to grow. Credits obtained can be treated as commodities. This means that they can be sold, banked, traded, and resold. People can purchase carbon credits to offset their individual carbon footprints. However, with the establishment of new environmental policies in the nation and around the world, the regulated market might begin to emerge as the leading contender for the carbon trading business. If the United Sates were to begin regulating the amount of $CO_2$ allowed to be produced, Planktos might find more benefit from selling to energy providers or other industrial entities.

*References:*

1. National Oceanic and Atmospheric Administration (NOAA ), Exhibit 1 adapted from a figure created by Robert A. Rhode, based on data obtained by NOAA, Earth System Research Laboratory, Global Monitoring Division, http://en.wikipedia.org/wiki/Image:Mauna_Loa_Carbon_Dioxide.png.

2. The Associated Press, "Texans Rally against New Coal Plants," published: Monday, February 12, 2007, http://www.commondreams.org/headlines07/0212-01.htm.

3. The World Bank in cooperation with the International Emissions Trading Association, State and Trends of the Carbon Market 2007, Washington D.C., May 2007, www.carbonfinance.org.

4. The World Bank in cooperation with the International Emissions Trading Association, State and Trends of the Carbon Market 2006, Washington D.C. , May 2007, www.carbonfinance.org.

5. Science Daily, Lower Carbon Dioxide Emissions from Coal-Fueled Power Plants Possible with Technology Developments, March 21, 2007, www.sciencedaily.com/releases/2007/03/070319175954.htm. (Note: Story adapted from a news release issued by The University of Texas at Austin)

6. United States Environmental Protection Agency, http://www.epa.gov.

7. The Associated Press, "Texans Rally."

# Strategic Marketing Insights

On "holiday" in Australia Nicole Burwell laughed as the Australian newscaster talked about "thinking outside the square." It was funny how expressions were translated! Having never traveled internationally, in taking a vacation to Australia she had clearly moved "out of her square" and maybe she should start thinking that way as well! A holiday always provided time to think. Invariably, "thinking" included her work, which was very important to her.

As the senior customer relationship manager for SMI, an international marketing research firm, Nicole was looking for new insights into their customers and ultimately engagement and retention. In the marketing research industry most sales are "project oriented." They arise out of the need to solve a problem or test a specific commercial, etc. As such, customers often select suppliers based on request for proposals (RFPs). While this is common among some organizations, others tend to use the same research organization on a routine basis, establishing more of a "relationship" with the research supplier. As Nicole thought about increasing SMI's business, she was concerned with satisfying her customers' need for information while at the same time making the best use of her time and effort.

Two strategic issues continued to plague her:

1. Attracting customers
   a. Was SMI doing the right things to attract new customers?

2. Keeping customers
   a. What is different about selling to "relationship customers"?
   b. Was she doing a good job of handling relationship customers?

## Background

Strategic Marketing Insights (SMI) has been in the marketing research business for over 50 years and has established a solid reputation of excellence. In that time, they have evolved into an international marketing research firm and are one of the largest research firms in the United States. SMI has developed a full array of marketing research and industry expertise. Many of the largest organizations have come to rely on their relationship with SMI as they make strategic market, product, and business decisions.

As a "customer-centric" organization, SMI has participated in strategic alliances, engaged in joint initiatives, developed and delivered custom education programs and developed new and cutting edge techniques. SMI has always regarded the customer relationship as an integral component of their service offering, long before relationship marketing became a mantra.

Key to SMI's success is first and foremost its people whom they refer to as associates, not employees. They support their associates with a strong investment in state of the art tools and technology. They develop their people and give them the leverage and leeway to act on behalf of the customer. Associates at all levels are empowered to serve the customer and customer management is structured to facilitate excellent service delivery. Team work is essential and ingrained in company culture.

This case was prepared by Susan M.B. Schertzer, Ohio Northern University, and Clint Schertzer, Xavier University, for purposes of class discussion. Company names and data have been disguised. Used with permission.

Customer relationship managers (CRMs) have full responsibility for managing the customers they develop. Relationship responsibility includes the sales process as well as oversight of all projects. In this customer-centric organization, managers are not evaluated on short-term profitability alone. Building customer trust and loyalty that lead to overall satisfaction and an eventual "relationship" with customers is as, if not more, important to SMI top management. Consistent with this philosophy, many CRMs have elected to set up their office in a geographic location that is most convenient for serving their customers.

SMI assigns teams of associates to work with the CRMs. SMI's research teams are led by seasoned professional project managers (PMs). The CRMs and PMs generally develop strong relationships and will work together for years. The PMs lead the teams and also develop strong working relationships with the customers while executing the research plan.

SMI develops associate teams around industry and customer expertise and believes that education and training of associates is critical to effective teams. This team approach translates into a deep level of company and industry expertise as well as interpersonal working relationships. To be successful, marketing research suppliers must not only have technical and marketing expertise, but they must also gain rapport with the customer. The relationship with the customer is important to understand the problems, the political environment at the organization, and the customer's specific market characteristics in order to devise an appropriate research plan and effectively communicate the solution. This requires working deftly with the customer company as the quality of the interactions and communication can directly affect both the ease with which the work is conducted and the quality of the project outcome. Thus, all aspects of the relationship—the interactions, the joint efforts, and the bonds that develop between the customer and the supplier firm are important elements required for successful completion of the project. The goal is to have relationships with customers really at several levels: with the firm, with the CRM, and with the PMs, and with the project teams. The customer has the benefit of the researcher's deeper knowledge of their company, industry, and organizational challenges that go into the solution.

All of SMI's customers conduct marketing research regularly as a key decision tool in their business strategy. Organizations embark on a marketing research project (e.g., new product development, customer satisfaction, sales promotion, corporate strategy) because they are looking for an answer, solution, or direction related to a specific problem or initiative. Projects are usually awarded on a project-by-project basis. There is generally no long-term contract so reputation, relevant experience, and previous relationship may be important assets in acquiring additional projects. It is critical that SMI be one of the first research firms that the customer calls.

Over the past decade, many customers have undergone rounds of "rightsizing" and streamlining personnel and systematizing and automating many of their business processes. SMI as a company and each of the CRMs worked to stay in touch with customers on both a business and personal level through all these changes. This has been accomplished with traditional promotional activities and personal selling activities.

Nicole pondered the changes in the business landscape, she looked at the portfolio of customers and projects over the last few years. Clearly, not all customers evolve into real relationships. Some customers seemed to really value the relationship and insights that the SMI teams bring to projects and others seem to seek the lowest price. She decided that this dichotomy might be useful to understand her business. Current and potential customers could really be separated into two groups: those that are interested in long-term relationships and price-driven customers. The question she wrestled with now was whether SMI's current promotional activities were targeting and meeting the needs of both types of customers. Additionally, she wondered whether the "price" driven customers were really worth the effort to SMI and whether they should target them at all, or focus all of their effort on "relationship" oriented customers.

As part of the formalizing and automating of processes, many companies have started purchasing professional services through their procurement departments—not directly by the user. Taking more of a buying center approach, procurement departments often use the same exacting procedures to purchase both goods and services. Many procurement departments require that suppliers submit to an annual vetting process and comply with specific invoicing and payment procedures to get on the "Approved Vendor List." Information commonly requested includes things like financial statements, financial references, customer references and company policies. This can be a long and arduous process, and while some of the information is the same, the format and exact process to comply is unique to each customer. In such an environment, being an approved vendor only *allows* SMI to be considered for projects. This adds additional complexity to the sales process. In some cases, after weighing the time and energy involved in the vetting process against the amount of business they have been awarded by this customer and the time and energy this may drain from customers with projects in process, the CRMs had declined the opportunity to be an "approved vendor." Is this a good long-term decision?

The actual first step in a potential engagement is a "request for proposal" (RFP). Responding to an RFP requires that the CRM must work closely with the potential customer to understand the problem and objectives and to prepare a proposal detailing the research plan. Significant effort can be expended as this is a very important part of the research planning process.

Up until now, the CRM, as relationship manager, was responsible for completing and complying with all aspects of each customer's process. To keep CRMs focused on fully supporting their customers and the relationships, should SMI, as a company, absorb some of this burden? Is this interference or assistance? Nicole wondered what else SMI could do, centrally, as an organization to support our CRMs' efforts to sell, service, and build customer relationships. Net, are current promotional efforts effective?

As a company, SMI has a three-pronged approach to promotional activities aimed at reaching a broad audience. Over the years the three most important efforts have been trade show sponsorship and participation, trade publications, and customer recognition events. Attendance and sponsorship at industry trade shows provide face-to-face exposure with current as well as potential customers, suppliers, and competitors. They are attended by many levels of the constituent organizations and SMI feels they have both long-and short-term returns. Small, useful gifts such as pens, flashlights, and key

chains keep the name of SMI in front of attendees long after the trade shows. Additionally, SMI spends a tidy sum to take ads in three trade journals. These journals reach much of the same audience but get the SMI name in front of them 12–20 times a year. In the most prestigious and widely subscribed trade journal, they pay a premium to be in the optimal and most visible location. Finally, to recognize and set up a forum to really listen to customer needs, they sponsor several annual dinners for key customers. These dinners include the users, management, and, if at all possible, the procurement contact at these organizations. Over the years, these have been very instrumental in staying in the loop with the customer's long-term strategic plans and thinking and have enabled SMI to proactively address emerging trends and needs.

As a research company, one thing SMI knows how to do is listen to customers. One critical method is to listen to actual customers in post-project surveys. SMI has maintained a practice of surveying all customers after projects are completed to assess the project and the likelihood that they will reengage the firm. The survey measures:

1. Loyalty—both the intention to return and the willingness to recommend to an associate (5 point scale—5 equals highest likelihood)
2. Satisfaction with the project (5 point scale—5 equals highest degree of project satisfaction
3. Value of the project (5 point scale—5 equals highest perception of value)
4. Overall image of the firm and its capabilities (9 point scale—9 equals most positive image)

These surveys are used for immediate feedback and the identification and correction of any problems that may have occurred. Over the years, this tool also helped them to not only correct any problems but to identify traits and practices that customers really appreciated and to integrate them into their practices wherever possible and appropriate. They are especially useful in customizing the service offering to specific customers and in training new team members about the customers.

What occurred to Nicole is that the SMI had never really taken a look at the long-term trend inherent in these data. In a project-oriented professional services business, if customers are not satisfied and do not see value in your services they will not re-engage you, but could some other information be gleaned from this data? The more she thought about it, the more interested she became in the analysis. Customer project survey results are readily available for the fiscal years 2000–2007. With that many years of data, she realized that she really could look at what actually

returning customers had to say and whether it differed significantly from what non-returning or more transactional customers had to say. To get a quick picture of what was going on, she asked Megan, her IT associate, to pull some annual data and run some simple analyse's. Table 1 shows the results of the preliminary analysis.

### Table 1
### Mean Difference in Customer Evaluation

|  |  | 2000 | 2001 | 2002 | 2003 | 2004 | 2005 | 2006 | 2007 |
|---|---|---|---|---|---|---|---|---|---|
| **Loyalty** |  |  |  |  |  |  |  |  |  |
|  | Relationship customer | 4.70 | 4.73 | 4.76 | 4.85 | 4.75 | 4.90 | 4.95 | 4.80 |
|  | Non-relationship | 4.65 | 4.64 | 4.54 | 4.71 | 4.59 | 4.68 | 4.77 | 4.65 |
|  | Difference: sig @ .95 |  |  |  |  |  |  |  |  |
| **Satisfaction** |  |  |  |  |  |  |  |  |  |
|  | Relationship customer | 4.85 | 4.83 | 4.79 | 4.69 | 4.86 | 4.85 | 4.92 | 4.85 |
|  | Non-relationship | 4.76 | 4.71 | 4.71 | 4.80 | 4.74 | 4.76 | 4.82 | 4.76 |
|  | Difference: ns |  |  |  |  |  |  |  |  |
| **Value** |  |  |  |  |  |  |  |  |  |
|  | Relationship customer | 4.45 | 4.45 | 4.59 | 4.53 | 4.76 | 4.60 | 4.63 | 4.45 |
|  | Non-relationship | 4.29 | 4.42 | 4.39 | 4.45 | 4.43 | 4.43 | 4.47 | 4.29 |
|  | Difference: ns |  |  |  |  |  |  |  |  |
| **Corporate Image / Reputation** |  |  |  |  |  |  |  |  |  |
|  | Relationship customer | 8.17 | 8.30 | 8.39 | 8.47 | 8.38 | 8.55 | 8.51 | 8.59 |
|  | Non-relationship | 8.08 | 8.13 | 8.15 | 8.21 | 8.16 | 8.21 | 8.28 | 8.08 |
|  | Difference: sig @ .95 |  |  |  |  |  |  |  |  |

### Table 2
### Annual Revenue and Gross Margin ($million)

|  |  | 2000 | 2001 | 2002 | 2003 | 2004 | 2005 | 2006 | 2007 |
|---|---|---|---|---|---|---|---|---|---|
| **Total** |  |  |  |  |  |  |  |  |  |
|  | Revenue | 48.3 | 42.5 | 37.9 | 39.0 | 44.1 | 39.8 | 30.6 | 48.3 |
|  | Gross margin | 20.6 | 16.5 | 14.7 | 15.7 | 18.8 | 17.1 | 13.4 | 20.6 |
| **Relationship Customers** |  |  |  |  |  |  |  |  |  |
|  | Revenue | 22.2 | 22.6 | 19.1 | 20.0 | 22.7 | 20.7 | 15.1 | 22.2 |
|  | Gross margin | 8.2 | 6.9 | 5.6 | 6.8 | 8.6 | 8.0 | 6.1 | 8.2 |
| **Non-Relationship Customers** |  |  |  |  |  |  |  |  |  |
|  | Revenue | 21.8 | 19.1 | 18.2 | 18.6 | 21.1 | 17.7 | 13.4 | 21.8 |
|  | Gross margin | 7.7 | 5.9 | 5.6 | 6.3 | 8.1 | 6.9 | 5.4 | 7.7 |

# SPC Products Company— Project Pops

## Lakshmi Software

In the lead-up to the new millennium, an industry emerged that sought to protect companies against computer failures due to clock settings in software. One of the companies that benefited the most from the Y2K industry was Lakshmi Software, a company with headquarters in Chennai, India. The company is named after the Hindu goddess of wealth, Lakshmi, and wealth was what they enjoyed as companies around the globe turned to Lakshmi and its low-cost software engineering.

Even before Y2K passed, however, the company realized that new markets would be needed. One such market was enterprise resource management, with SAP and PeopleSoft leading the way. Many companies implementing such software often needed help, particularly as they needed to integrate their current systems into the new software. Lakshmi found that to be a good, but uneven, market.

For that reason, the company began to seek opportunities in product development, or software that is integrated into products such as video games, telephones, and other electronics. The greatest opportunities for Lakshmi were in manufacturing automation, specialized automation in insurance and finance, and other areas that enabled the company to make use of the same talents that supported SAP of PeopleSoft integration.

This case was written by Dr. John F. Tanner Jr. and Brian Kiedan, for the purposes of class discussion rather than to illustrate effective or ineffective decision making. Some data are disguised.

The company was reasonably successful in working with European (particularly German) and U.S.-based companies. Part of the company's success with such clients is that many of the managers at Lakshmi had experience working in either Germany or the United States. But the second-largest software market in the world is Japan, where the company had only limited success. Because of the importance of the Japanese market and its influence on the rest of the world, Lakshmi management had targeted Japan as an important objective. One of the company's largest Japanese customers was Sonpan, and it was critical to Lakshmi's marketing objectives that it be able to use Sonpan as a successful case study when selling to other Japanese companies.

## Customer Background

Sonpan Products Company (SPC) is a leading Japanese company specializing in providing automating solutions for financial, insurance, and manufacturing applications. It also produces PCs, midrange computers, and peripherals for the Japanese market. Some of these are manufactured under license from world-known companies like HP. SPC is well known in the Japanese market as a software producer of very high quality. Due to its wide range of hardware, software, and networking solutions, it is also one of the largest system integrators in Japan.

With the economic recession in the country during the last five years, SPC is under increasing pressure to cut down costs. The software division has been looking outside Japan to outsource software development at lesser prices. It has evaluated and chosen a handful of Indian software companies including Lakshmi.

Japan is the second-largest software market in the world and is a focus market for Lakshmi. So far, the company has been doing business through a Japanese business associate. To show its commitment to the market, Lakshmi has recently invested in setting up Lakshmi-Japan at an upmarket location in Tokyo.

## The India Project Team (IPT)

In order to streamline the outsourcing procedure, SPC has set up the India Project Team (IPT). It is expected to champion the outsourcing concept with all SPC's divisions. Its performance is measured by the volume (yens) of outsourcing done to Indian companies. In the past few years, through IPT, SPC has outsourced more than 50 projects to Lakshmi. The projects were mainly in the R&D and embedded systems area. Projects in these areas tend to be of small size (completed by an engineering team size of five or six and short duration, four to six months). With an increasing recession in the Japanese economy, the R&D budgets are dwindling. Consequently, IPT has been looking for a large end-user project (where the user is a customer of SPC) to be outsourced to Lakshmi.

The end-user projects tend to be larger in size and duration. However, they are "known technology" projects and do not require the higher value-added engineering of projects using new technologies. Most of these have Japanese screens and Japanese reports, meaning that if the engineering is done in English, translations are required.

IPT also helps Lakshmi in understanding the business practices and culture of Japanese companies. Unlike western customers, Japanese companies give very vague specifications and give deadlines that cannot be changed. The Japanese consider their customers as god and agree to required schedules, even when the specifications are not ready. They generally work around a given budget and expect that their suppliers provide software required within the budgets available and within the schedule specified.

## The Relationship

SPC has been giving business worth a few million dollars every year to Lakshmi on an assured basis. Lakshmi saves on marketing costs and has a guaranteed loading factor from SPC. A loading factor is a profit percentage that Lakshmi is guaranteed. The other major advantage Lakshmi derives from the relationship is that it gets to work on state-of-the-art technology that will give it an edge when it goes to newer markets and other potential customers (especially other Japanese companies). SPC's data-driven project management strengths are well known, and Lakshmi expects to understand these techniques to help better manage its other projects.

SPC is the largest customer for the SBU that handles the account and is the biggest customer for Lakshmi in Japan, so the customer is important for both the SBU and the company. In addition, word of mouth is a powerful tool in Japan. Lakshmi has to ensure customer delight and show ability to successfully manage large projects if it wants to expand business in Japan. It is currently looking for a major success story to help it approach large Japanese corporations.

Realizing that language is a major issue in dealing with Japanese businesses, Lakshmi has invested in forming a Japan desk that takes care of language translation and interpretation requirements. It has also invested in Japanese language computers and software. Because the translation volumes are small, Lakshmi has agreed not to pass the cost of Japan desk services to SPC.

Lakshmi has a standing agreement with the customer on the rates to be used for its project proposals. The prices are negotiated and agreed upon during March for the coming financial year. The rates for on-site services have not been increased for the past three years, as most projects are executed predominantly offshore (in India) and the on-site component is very low.

## The Current Scenario

It has taken time for Lakshmi to get used to the Japanese way of working, and the SBU is just about getting a handle on what the Japanese customers look for. Due to estimation and project management issues in the previous years, Lakshmi and the SPC have recently agreed on guidelines for estimation of project size and quality for all projects. SPC has informed Lakshmi that it will not be able to give projects unless Lakshmi's productivity matches its own. This has been brought in as a standard for all subcontractors (Indian, Japanese, and Chinese) of SPC. Lakshmi has agreed to do estimation based on these productivity figures. Typically, these indicate 40 to 60 percent better productivity than Lakshmi's baseline. This means that SPC can typically complete a project in half of the person-hours it takes Lakshmi, so Lakshmi's costs have to be less than half of SPC's in order to make any profit and in order to make using Lakshmi worthwhile.

At the end of May, Lakshmi's top management met with IPT. IPT stated that to improve the relationship, Lakshmi has to work in a model similar to that of a Japanese subcontractor; in other words, there must be no difference to the division of SPC between Lakshmi and any Japanese subcontractor.

Lakshmi committed to working in the Japanese subcontractor model. The implications of that were that Lakshmi will be like any other Japanese subcontractor—they will take specifications in Japanese, conduct business in Japanese, and have management available during Japanese business hours (even though the management will be in India). By committing to this model, Lakshmi hopes that will help IPT to project Lakshmi as another Japanese subcontractor, resulting in additional business from other SPC business units.

SPC has been talking with other suppliers because some divisions have raised concerns about the quality of code delivered by Lakshmi. SPC expects bug-free code, whereas Lakshmi has been delivering code with a defect density of about 0.1 per thousand lines of code (KLOC), which is much better than what Lakshmi typically delivers.

Given all these factors, the relationship with the customer is "delicate" at this juncture. KOS, a division of SPC dealing with end-customer projects, is in the process of bidding for POPS—a large system development and system integration project. IPT has been speaking to KOS for outsourcing this to Lakshmi. KOS has never worked with a non-Japanese subcontractor before and is reluctant to do so now. However, IPT is outlining the cost advantages to KOS to change their mind. It also tells them that Lakshmi would be willing to work like any other Japanese subcontractor so that KOS can feel comfortable.

KOS is almost sure of winning the POPS project and has already started discussions with Lakshmi and other subcontractors to prepare them.

## The Preproposal Phase

At the end of May, the order plan sent by IPT for the POPS project shows that the person-hours for the project is expected to be 17,000 hours. It is not fixed. About 233 applications need to be developed. IPT has indicated that a large number of programmers will be required. There is a larger Japanese language component, so it is necessary to include Japanese staff. The approximate volume of documents for translation was given as:

| | |
|---|---|
| User Requirement Specification | 1700 pages |
| Software Specification | 3400 pages |
| Functional Specification (Basic Edition) | 200 pages |
| Other documents | 500+ pages |

All these documents will be in Japanese and will have to be translated for use in the project. No specifications are available at this stage. Lakshmi is asked to start preparing for the project.

Lakshmi operates by appointing a project manager who then assembles the staff. Each project manager has a group of programmers, and they are divided into teams based on the actual projects they are working on. In June, the project manager assigned to POPS arranged for relevant training for the team members who are likely to work on this project. Lakshmi Japan arranges for two Japanese staff to help in translation and for attending meetings. It later appoints one more program manager–type person (Japanese) for interfacing with the customer. It is expected that this person will represent the interests of Lakshmi and also help with the project management techniques used by the Japanese.

On June 3 IPT informs that project size (Lakshmi's portion) has gone up by three to four times, the schedule is unchanged, and details are still not known. The customer says that up to 60 engineers may be required to execute the project. IPT also says that if Lakshmi does not want to take up the project, SPC will never give another project to Lakshmi.

Lakshmi agrees to execute the project and asks for more details, skill sets, and numbers required. It requests for information on how the 60 engineers requirement was arrived at. IPT later informs that 60 was arrived at based on budget available.

Lakshmi says that for a project of this size, the customer must plan for sending three or four of its engineers from Japan to Bangalore (India) for the duration of project to sort out clarifications and technical issues that may come up. It also suggests that one Lakshmi senior person should be available on-site. These are costs that SPC would have to cover.

Lakshmi's business partner in Japan meets with IPT on the 4th of June. IPT emphasizes the importance of the project and that it would like to deal with Lakshmi just as it would deal with any other Japanese subcontractor. IPT requests that one PM and one engineer (both Japanese) should be placed in Japan for the duration of the project, at Lakshmi's cost, to which Lakshmi agrees.

On June 5, IPT sends a sample specification document in Japanese. They state that the whole document may undergo change later.

On June 7, Lakshmi receives an e-mail from IPT indicating that the project size may not be that big, but KOS (the division of SPC that has the POPS project) has to make the decision. KOS may feel it is not possible to order offshore.

On June 8, Lakshmi informs KOS that in the absence of details of skill required, Lakshmi will assume the following manpower requirements:

10 associates at the PM, PLs, MI, and DBA levels

30 associates with COBOL/Oracle and Tuxedo skills

20 associates with VB skills

On June 9th, IPT thinks it requires 30 to 40 people for three months. Lakshmi suggests gradual ramp-up for better control and states the start date as July 1st.

IPT informs SPC that specification for 45 functions must come by the end of June, the rest by mid-July. They expect to be able to explain the sample program by mid-July. Specification for common components will be provided by July and the associated stubs (software components that simulate functions with which Lakshmi software has to interact) will be provided by the end of July. IPT informs that the system test should happen in the beginning of October.

IPT provides the expected COBOL productivity figures for the Coding and Testing phases as 45 hours/KLOC, which translates to approximately 180 lines of code per day. IPT also informs that most programs are the same, and only 20 percent will be different in each program. The productivity expected by IPT is about 60 percent better than Lakshmi's baseline.

On June 8th, Lakshmi informs that given the "template" nature of programs, it may be possible to achieve the productivity. Lakshmi suggests development of sample functions to check environment, complexity of development, and validate the estimate. Also, since one of the major risk factors was the Japanese language screens and reports, Lakshmi suggests on-site screen design.

On June 11th, IPT sends an e-mail saying that their previous communication stating that if Lakshmi does not accept this project, no future projects would be given to Lakshmi, was a miscommunication. It was the individual opinion of only one member of IPT.

Lakshmi requests KOS not to commit dates to the end customer unless Lakshmi has had a chance to review specification, make an estimate, and review schedule.

While this was going on, the project manager began building a team. Associates from other SBUs were being interviewed, shortlisted, trained, and transferred. The SBU receiving the project picked up the costs of training and transfer.

IPT, by mid-June, still cannot confirm scope and schedule. They inform that internal design progress is slow; specifications are going to have many changes. They also communicate that the Functional Specification is being made by a third party, another subcontractor.

On June 15, Lakshmi informs IPT that the team ramp-up plan has been put on hold based on IPT's inputs, and that instead of 60, Lakshmi was now planning only for 25 programmers. Lakshmi further explains that if the number needs to be increased to 60, four weeks lead time is required. Similar lead time is required for other resources like workstations, space, Japanese software, etc.

IPT comes back saying delivery is pushed by two months and asks Lakshmi to wait until June 18th before proceeding. It says sample program development is postponed to mid-July.

Design progress is slow, and schedule will be decided shortly. It also says that it is not required to translate all pages, but only about 150 to 200 relevant pages.

IPT says that in line with the Japanese sub-contractor model, all communication will be in Japanese. This increases Lakshmi's dependency on the on-site Japanese PM, as all meetings will be held in Japanese.

IPT confirms the project size on June 22nd. They say that there are 360 software components. The estimated scope of translation is 850 pages. At this juncture, IPT shifts the total responsibility of the project to Lakshmi and Lakshmi Japan. Lakshmi asks for more details before commitment.

On June 28th, customer specifies part of the schedule, with delivery required by October. No specifications have been received so far.

Based on the suggested platform (hardware and software) by the customer, the software costs were calculated and communicated to SPC. This software is software needed to write and evaluate the programs. SPC says software is not their responsibility. However, a few days later, they agree to share costs.

On July 1st, IPT sends an e-mail saying that they feel the project size is 106 person months (18,600 hours) and gives the calculation based on their productivity figures. This estimate is significantly less than half of Lakshmi's own baseline and calculations.

On July 2nd, another IPT person estimates the same scope at 16,000 hours, justifying the reduction in time as attributed to even higher productivity. Later the same day, IPT says there was a mistake in productivity figures used. The new IPT estimate is now 11,600 hours.

Lakshmi's PM points out his fears on estimation—the productivity figures were not realistic, translation effort not added, and some software components not considered at all.

On July 7th, the project start is officially postponed to July 15th.

# The Proposal

The formal request for proposal (RFP) was received by Lakshmi in September after the project was in full swing. The RFP contained details of each function, and the PM estimated that as per Lakshmi standards, the project size would be about 25,000 hours.

Lakshmi's senior management opines that given the new subcontractor model and risks associated with such a large project, Lakshmi should use slightly discounted Japanese rates for the quotation. Based on several considerations, Lakshmi finally decides to quote USD 600,000.

KOS and IPT are shocked beyond words.

## Postproposal

IPT asks for details on how the price was arrived at. Lakshmi explains the fixed bid subcontractor model and details the on-site Japanese costs, idle time cost of engineers, offshore translation costs (Japanese into English and back), infrastructure costs, and software development costs. IPT is very unhappy with the costs and says that it expects Lakshmi to use KOS's productivity figures, use agreed off-shore rates, and refuses to pay separate rates for Japanese on-site resources. It says rates can be negotiated only in March. It refuses to recognize translation costs, as no Japanese subcontractor charges this cost. Lakshmi pleads that the on-site Japanese managers cost a lot of money and their services cannot be given at earlier agreed costs, which represented only expenses for Indian engineer coming to Japan. IPT requests Lakshmi to take those managers away and that IPT will help in interfacing.

# The Project Execution

The project starts with a 25-engineer team. KOS and IPT send one engineer each to help the team in India. IPT engineer decides which pages need to be translated. Due to the dynamic nature of clarifications, plans are changing on a daily basis, as work cannot stop while clarifications are awaited from Japan. Schedule has to be met. Programmers have to switch from one unfinished program to another while awaiting clarifications. They have to work on unfamiliar screens and reports, which are in Japanese.

The Lakshmi project manager is comfortable that the KOS representative is providing clarifications and that IPT is helping mark out the pages for translation, which is reducing the workload for the Japan desk. He is grateful to IPT and KOS for all the cooperation in the process of translation and technical clarifications.

The project manager submitted regular project reports in KOS format, which showed that the project was on schedule. All relevant data like lines of code completed, to be completed, number of unit test cases, and so forth were collected. All the test cases and errors reported met SPC's quality criteria. The project itself was completed with about a week's delay, which was considered acceptable by SPC.

# Questions

1. Was SPC the right customer for Lakshmi's growth plans in Japan?
2. Did IPT help or hamper Lakshmi's growth within SPC?
3. From the customer relationship viewpoint what things should Lakshmi have done and at what points? Where did the major challenges occur?
4. In such a changing scenario, what should have been Lakshmi's customer communication strategy?
5. What are the customer's responsibilities in building and maintaining a relationship?
6. Was Lakshmi justified in its costing strategy for the project? What assumptions did it start with and what was in the customer's mind?

# Three Rivers Optical

## Introduction

Spring is trade show time with two important events for Three Rivers Optical (TRO): SECO and International Vision Expo East. TRO is a family-owned business. Steve Siebert (CEO and head of marketing) had just returned from the International Vision Expo East, when his sister, Mary Ann (CFO), greeted him at the coffee pot in the employee lounge.

"How was the show, Steve?" she asked, smiling. "Another great party?"

"Not exactly," he replied with a frown. She looked at him quizzically. "We just didn't get the leads," he explained. "Although SECO was well worth it, we may need to re-think what we're doing with our trade show budget."

"Well, it's not like it's a cheap way to market," she said. "Wasn't Vision Expo over $50,000?"

He shook his head yes, adding, "Plus our travel expenses." Results were so bad, in fact, that he was really wondering what impact the poor showing would have on his marketing, sales, and growth plans for the next few years.

He knew that including trade shows in his marketing plan was worthwhile, especially since SECO and the show he did the year before in Arizona really paid off. He looked Mary Ann in the eye: "I've just got to allocate our budget to the correct shows. The problem is figuring out which ones those are, how big a space we should have, how many people to take, and what promotions will generate the best return on the budget you give me."

This case was written by Margit B. Weisgal and Dennis Pitta as a basis for class discussion. Certain data and names are disguised. Used with permission.

Mary Ann grinned back at her brother. "If you can justify what you're doing, I'll work with you on budget."

Steve, along with his brother, Joe, and his sister, Mary Ann, managed the company their parents founded. They divided the work responsibilities so that each managed a specific area. His sister was in charge of finance; his brother was responsible for managing the lab. Steve headed marketing and sales and was responsible for generating enough orders to keep the lab busy.

Three Rivers Optical is a lab supplying prescription lenses for opticians, optometrists, and ophthalmologists. It has a proprietary products used as a differentiator in the market along with standard materials available from its competitors. The company has been named as one of the top 25 largest optical laboratories in the country a number of times over the past several years, offering high-quality mass-customized products at competitive prices.

Exhibiting at trade shows had the potential to fuel the company expansion along with the ability to add salespeople. TRO only sells to independents and small chains of up to 10 stores, not large chain optical shops like Sears and Wal-Mart because the buying decision for these national companies is purely based on price, not service or the ability to provide specialized products.

Currently, TRO has salespeople in nine territories, all east of the Mississippi River.

1. Western Pennsylvania Central Pennsylvania; Northeastern Ohio
2. West Virginia, Northwestern Virginia, Northern Virginia and part of eastern Ohio
3. The rest of Ohio

4. Northern Wisconsin; Upper Peninsula Michigan
5. North and South Carolina
6. Alabama, Eastern Mississippi, South Georgia
7. Maryland, District of Columbia, Eastern Virginia
8. East Pennsylvania, New Jersey, Northern Delaware
9. New England

For TRO, growing the business is a "chicken and the egg" problem. Sometimes, to grow the business, a salesperson is needed but TRO can't afford to hire the salesperson until there is more business. Exhibiting at trade shows, though, often proved the solution. Exhibiting provided leads and, many times, new accounts. With sufficient accounts in a given area, he could justify hiring a salesperson to manage those accounts.

Steve is a firm believer in controlled growth, only opening new territories and hiring new salespeople when there is ample business to support them. "I want to 'own' my salespeople, giving them a car and enough salary to live so they're not dependent on just commissions," he explained. "They have to do their jobs without fear, which is usually the case with commission- only salespeople. They end up owing money to the company from their draw. Doing it my way, they'll go out, call on more people, and survive any rejection." TRO's commission structure for sales gives his people a very comfortable living when they achieve their goals.

Steve predicts the growth of the company over the next five years to be in western Ohio, Indiana, and south and central Michigan. From there, because of existing accounts, he'll move into the Denver area and then California. He will only hire salespeople when the existing accounts can support, at minimum, the base salary and also have room for considerable growth. Trade shows, as one of his marketing strategies, will be a large facet of making this happen.

# Background

## Target Audiences

TRO has three very specific target audiences:

- Ophthalmologists (Doctors of Ophthalmology— MDs)
- Optometrists (Doctors of Optometry—ODs)
- Opticians

### Doctors of Ophthalmology

Ophthalmologists are medical doctors who specialize in the medical and surgical treatment of eye disorders, vision measurements for glasses (refraction), eye muscle exercises (orthoptics), and the prevention of blindness and care of the blind. Some common diseases they treat include blindness, cataracts, glaucoma, diabetic retinopathy, senile macular degeneration, retinal detachment, and opacities of the cornea.

### Doctors of Optometry

Optometry is a specialty requiring a four-year postgraduate professional degree, hence the title "doctor." Optometrists cannot do surgery and, in some states, cannot write medical prescriptions. They provide eye examinations, determination of visual abilities, diagnosis of eye diseases and conditions, and the prescription of lenses and other corrective measures. The principal concern of early optometrists was the prescription of corrective lenses for defects of vision due to refractive error. Modern optometry also includes the fitting of contact lenses and of telescopic eyeglasses as an aid to the near-blind, as well as the field of orthoptics, i.e., the practice of strengthening the eye muscles and improving their coordination by eye exercises. Prescriptions for corrective lenses provided by an optometrist are often brought to an *optician,* who grinds and fits the lenses.

The word *optometry* came into use in 1904 with the organization of the American Optometric Association. Until this time people bought eyeglasses from traveling vendors whose activities were not supervised. With the passage of optometry laws, this method of dispensing glasses was prohibited. Optometrists must now fulfill certain educational requirements and be examined and licensed by the state. Some of the schools of optometry in the United States are affiliated with colleges or universities. (See also ophthalmology.)

### Opticians

Opticians fill prescriptions for and dispense corrective lenses. An optician may grind lenses as instructed by the prescription of an optometrist or ophthalmologist or transcribe the instructions for laboratory mechanics. The optician also fits and adjusts the lenses to the client and makes suggestions as to the selection of frames. Increasingly, opticians have taken over the task of fitting contact lenses as well as eyeglasses. Some states require that lab technicians and retail merchandisers be licensed opticians. Requirements may be met through academic training or through a laboratory apprenticeship.

## Situational Analysis

The optical industry has a long and glorious history. Spectacles, vision correcting lenses, were first invented around 1300 AD.[1] Unfortunately opticians, as a separate and distinct category in optometric services, are a dying breed. Called retail or dispensing opticians, they could fit customers with eyeglasses and contact lenses but could not prescribe corrective lenses or do vision exams. During the first half of the 20th century opticians were not regulated by any body or association. Then licensing exams became the norm. In 2007, although some states have an optician's licensing exam, a comparable number don't, so in those states anyone with some experience can fit spectacles. Opticians also used to own stores where people could buy lenses and frames but today most shops are owned by optometrists who do eye exams and, in turn, employ opticians to just do fittings.

In the category of opticians, there are two groups: Independents and Chains. Chain optical shops include stores such as Pearl Vision, Sears, and Wal-Mart. It's difficult to turn on the television and not be bombarded by advertisements for these shops. Chains are also the driving force behind eye-wear as a fashion statement and are great at selling multiple pairs of glasses to patients: sunglasses, different colored frames, contact lenses, etc. Successful stores sell customers/patients more than one pair at a time. Individual practices, on the other hand, aren't as productive and don't sell multiple pairs as often. If they do, it's usually limited to a pair of regular glasses and a pair of sunglasses as opposed to sufficient pairs to match clothing colors.

Over the last five years ophthalmologists have looked at dispensing eyeglasses as a way to regenerate their practices. Because Medicare payments have lowered the income for surgeries and the like of many of these doctors, some are looking at eyeglasses as a way to enhance the profitability of their practices.

[1]http://www.drjankowski.com/history.htm.

Schools and hospitals are also capturing more business. Optical shops are wholly owned by university medical schools and/or the hospital/medical centers under the aegis of medical schools. These become profit centers whose revenues offset losses or pro bono work. They view internal optical stores as opportunities for income rather than generating rent from an contractor who takes advantage of on-site patients. For instance, a patient is seen at an eye and ear hospital or clinic and is given a prescription for glasses. The patient then goes to the on-site shop to fill the prescription.

The University of Pittsburgh's Eye and Ear Hospital, part of the UP Medical Center, fired the person who had been there for 15 years and put in a shop that the hospital owned, a revenue producer that contributed to its profits. The store went from a small space carrying a few hundred eyeglass frames to big business, generating high revenues.

## About Three Rivers Optical

Three Rivers Optical (TRO) is a privately owned company based in a suburb of Pittsburgh, Pennsylvania, with revenues over US$17 million. It manufactures all types of optical lenses and ophthalmic products including frame bases and glass, plastic, polycarbonate, and hi-index lenses.

When the company was started in 1969, it had three sales territories: Western Pennsylvania and Western New York; West Virginia and Ohio; and Eastern Pennsylvania, Delaware, and New Jersey. Its manufacturing facility has grown from 250 square feet in 1969 to a 30,000 square foot, state-of-the-art manufacturing facility in suburban Pittsburgh, and there is an additional 25,000 square feet plumbed and wired and ready for expansion in the near future.

The salespeople are a vital link to ophthalmologists, optometrists, and opticians providing detailed product information, technical and customer service training for professionals' staff members, and even comprehensive seminars which satisfied the American Board of Opticians (ABO) requirements for on-going professional and staff qualification and development courses.

It has over 70 employees and every member of the customer service staff has passed all 80 hours of ABO training for certified opticians. Professional development specialists produce major seminars for hundreds of practitioners promoting and expanding expertise in the marketplace.

## History

Since its beginning in 1969, Three Rivers Optical has been, first and foremost, a family business. The first manufacturing complex was a 250-square foot storeroom in McKees Rocks. It started out grinding only wholesale uncut glass lenses, which meant customers had to have their own edging and finishing equipment. Obviously this was not consistent with the vision of a full-service optical lab.

TRO began manufacturing uncut plastic lenses and quickly grew to 700-square feet and then to 7,000. In 1979, it added finishing equipment giving it the capability to edge and finish ground lenses. Next came polycarbonate lens equipment and the first coating line. From there, it was a natural progression to Transitions® light-sensitive cosmetic lenses and eventually to the full gamut of progressive lens products, frames, cases, and sundries. Finally, the company made huge commitments to the optical coatings business with state-of-the-art equipment from Zeiss and SOLA.

The company is a recognized leader in the industry and has a national scope with accounts from Maine to California. It has been selected as the Transitions® Lab of the Year and honored by the Optical Lab Association as one of the top 25 labs in the country.

In 2003, Bill Seibert and his wife Madeline, the founders of the company, retired and turned the business over to their three children: Steve Seibert—Sales and Marketing (President); Joe Seibert—Director of Operations (Vice President); Mary Ann Seibert Zappas—Controller (Secretary/Treasurer).

As Steve put it, "The management is split equally. Each of us is responsible for our own specific areas as our titles indicate, but major decisions are done together. It's always 'we.' Because we're three people, not one, we can focus on areas at which we excel rather than one person trying to do everything, as it was when my dad ran the business."

He then described how the three of them worked: "We are successful because of how we run the business. Everything is a 'we' and that's how we feel about it. There is no superstar. I'm the face of the company, the public relations person, but I don't take credit for the success of the business. Nothing happens that the three of us don't share. It's why we're successful."

Within four months of taking over, Joe, who manages the laboratory and is responsible for manufacturing all the lenses, doubled the capacity without increasing costs by simply streamlining the existing processes so Steve was free to grow the business as much as he wanted. Within 18 months, the total revenues doubled.

When TRO moved out of the first facility in McKees Rock, the company outgrew its 13,000 square feet in 10 years—it literally ran out of space. When Bill Seibert bought the property for the current lab, he looked at everything they could possibly need in the future and doubled it. Bill bought nine acres in the industrial park where TRO is now located. It could quadruple the facility—build out as much as 85,000 additional square feet with the property the company owns in the industrial park, add parking and whatever else is required—and still be in compliance with local ordinances that require one-third of the property be green. As Steve stated, "Our future is really secure."

As for a next generation, there are eight grandchildren of the founders, but only one is currently working in the business. Five are too young to know what they want, and two are definitely not interested. "Family businesses are a special situation and passing along ownership can be really difficult. The three of us are lucky. We really like each other and work great together. We respect each other's abilities and don't step on toes. We also cover for each other when we go on vacation so we really know all the jobs in the business."

## Proprietary Product Information

TRO has proprietary products that can be a great door-opener for new accounts: The TRO Seg and the blended TRO Seg; and Discovery lenses (see Exhibits 1 and 2). These are patented bifocals available in all resin materials, expanding the availability for lined and non-lined bifocals. The aging baby-boomer population doesn't feel old or, more importantly, doesn't want to be perceived as old, and wearing lined bifocals is, to them, not acceptable. Unfortunately, a percentage of people cannot adapt to non-lined bifocals (progressive lenses) because

**Exhibit 1**
Three Rivers
Optical
Proprietary
Products

---

**TRO DISCOVERY Progressive Lenses Dispensing Guide**

What is Discovery?

Discovery is a fourth generation progressive with a minimum fitting height of 171/2 mm.

What is the benefit of the reduced fitting height?

Frame selection is made easier for both the patient and the eyecare professional. Today's fashion frames are smaller making them less than ideal for Presbyopic customers. Discovery will function normally for virtually all small frames.

What is the benefit of a short corridor?

By shortening the corridor the wearer will enter the near zone more quickly thus reducing the likelihood of having the wearers hold their heads in an unnatural position when viewing through the near zone.

What are the lens specifications of discovery?

Discovery will satisfy a prescription range of +6.00 to -8.00 out to 4 diopters of cylinder and adds from +1.00 to +3.00 available in CR-39 and transitions III grey materials

Do I measure discovery just like other progressives?

Yes

If a customer is already wearing another brand of progressive, will they have trouble wearing discovery?

Discovery lenses are designed to be compatible with other progressive lens designs. Each of the distinguishing design characteristics of the most popular selling progressives have been considered in the "Discovery." Discovery gives a large clear distance, fully usable intermediate zone, and a large near zone.

---

**Fitting Guide for the Lens That "Fits All"**

- Choosing a frame:

  The Discovery progressive lens's short corridor (minimum fitting height of 17.5 mm) allows the use of virtually any frame shape or size!

  - Select a quality frame and adjust form minimum vertex distance. This will afford the wearer the maximum field of vision.
- Measuring:
  - Dot the patient's pupil position on the frame lens or pupil position gauges for frames without sample lenses. Use the diameter cut-out diagram to confirm cut-out.
  - Fitting height: Measure from the deepest portion of the frame to the center of the patient's pupil.
  - Take a distance PD. A monocular PD is best, but not critical with Discovery.
- Verification:

  When Discovery lenses come from our Laboratory, they will be marked with an ink layout.

  - Check the PD and fitting height by placing pupil position dots on the fitting cross on the lens cut-out chart.
  - Check the distance Rx by taking a reading through the near reference circle.
  - This reading should be the total of the distance reference and add designation.
  - Check the distance optical center at the MRP. Disregard distance power when measuring prism.
- Restoring lens markings:
  - You can restore lens marking at any time to re-check measurements if necessary. Simply use the hidden engraved relocators. Line up the Discovery re-identification decal with the hidden circles and restore the points using a marker pen.

**Exhibit 2**
For Immediate
Release

CONTACT: Steve Seibert
Three Rivers Optical
(800) 555-5555
threeriversoptical@prodigy.net
TRO BLENDED SEG

PITTSBURGH, April 5, 2006—Three Rivers Optical laboratory has risen to achieve what the eyecare professional has requested. An innovative new patented milling process makes it possible for Three Rivers Optical to offer eyecare professionals this unprecedented flexibility in lens design combined with premium lens materials.

"We recognized a gap in the availability of Transitions Lenses, and released the TRO SEG last year. We were able to create a customized process to meet our customers' needs, allowing them to give their patients the best photochromic technology in the material and design right for them."

After the release of the TRO SEG last year eyecare professionals have recognized the value in some of the lens styles from yesterday. Patients still want them but because of availability issues dispensers had to turn patients away. We are answering needs from our customers. "If you can dream it we will do our best to make it for you," says Seibert.

Combining equipment and specialized programming, Three Rivers Optical is able to modify patented design characteristics to grind a blended segment bifocal. The design is available in three varying-sized segments to match today's frame sizes.

For complete details or to order TRO BLENDED SEG, call Three Rivers Optical at (800) 555-5555.

**About Three Rivers Optical**

Founded in 1969 by the Seibert family, Three Rivers Optical remains a family-owned and operated laboratory, though now it has grown into a 30,000 square foot, full-service, state-of-the-art manufacturing facility located in suburban Pittsburgh. With accounts that extend from Maine to California, it primarily serves the central and eastern U.S. regions.

A recognized leader in the industry, Three Rivers Optical has consistently embraced new technologies and has partnered with the optical community on many important education and professional development initiatives. Their pioneering marketing efforts have included a mix of consumer and trade advertising focusing on premium products and a "1-800 number" it has been honored by the Optical Lab Association as one of the top 25 labs in the country.

For more information, visit Three Rivers Optical online at www.3riversoptical.com or call (800) 555-5555.

there is actually a third power correction between the regular and bifocal prescription. In the optometric industry, these are known as progressive non-adapts.

The other primary audience for this is children who need bifocals. Wearing glasses, for them, is bad enough but add a lined bifocal and they are usually embarrassed. The line on the TRO Seg can be virtually invisible in the as-worn position. The visibility of the line varies by power.

Because of these audiences, TRO concentrates its marketing efforts at trade shows on optometrists and ophthalmologists with pediatric practices and those who have a large number of progressive non-adapts.

### Future Marketing

Future trade shows will draw their target audiences from territories that Steve wants to develop plus

nationwide shows that are target specific such as Optometry's Meeting™ produced by the American Optometric Association (AOA) and the American Academy of Ophthalmology's (AAO) Annual Meeting. Seibert evaluates regional events individually. "Some want too much money for four hours of time with attendees; others are reasonable and are worth doing," he said.

A good example was the show he did in Arizona in 2006 with the College of Optometrists in Vision Development (COVD). Although there were only 300 attendees, he opened between 40–50 accounts there.

## Trade Show Experience

TRO has only been doing trade shows since Steve and his siblings took over from their parents. The first year the company exhibited was 2005; it had a booth at SECO and International Vision Expo East. The SECO booth has always been TRO's alone. At Vision Expo, in 2005 and 2006, TRO shared space with I-Concepts, a company with which TRO has a strategic alliance. I-Concepts makes eyeglass frames that TRO's salespeople also sell. The booth was in I-Concepts' name. In 2007, the booth was in TRO's name.

Seibert plans to keep the space for his company although he hasn't excluded the option of inviting I-Concepts to come in with him. The owner of that firm, Brad Conrey, is great with visitors and it expands TRO's product offerings at the show. Before the show, Steve planned to expand his space at Vision Expo from a 300 square foot in-line exhibit to a 20' × 20' island space. After he got the results, though, he decided he had to rethink this.

At SECO 2007, TRO did a pre-show mailing created by one of his salespeople. It included a coupon for a free TRO Seg or Blended TRO Seg. The staff opened three new accounts before the show opened and, by the end of the three-day event, signed up 23 new accounts. One recipient of the mailer used the coupon and came to the booth to tell the staff how delighted he was with the product. He then roped in friends of his which contributed to sales at the show.

Accounts average $1,500–$2,500 per month in sales revenues so the return on investment for this event was just under $700,000. Cost of the show: $10,000–$12,000.

Vision Expo 2007, though, cost well over $50,000 and the results were identical to those from SECO for more than three times the investment. After taking a close look at the attendee breakdowns provided the by show sponsor, Vision Council of America, he discovered that fewer than half the attendees were potential prospects.

His strategy at Vision Expo was to have a scratch-off game distributed to attendees at the door by a temporary worker. Transitions® lenses (photochromic lenses; they are clear indoors and go to sunglass-dark outdoors) provided some of the prizes for the game. The temp worker didn't pay attention to the different colors on the badges, which defines buying roles at the show, so she distributed the game cards to anyone and everyone, most of whom were not part of TRO's target audience. So, although the booth was flooded with traffic, most weren't people with whom the staff wanted to speak.

In 2006 and 2007, he hired a trade show consultant and worked with her to train his staff on trade show skills and develop some of the strategies that were effective. She also provided him with an outline of upcoming trade shows (see Exhibit 3). In addition to the training and consulting, she defined for him how trade shows differ from direct sales.

"Trade shows are like business-to-business shopping malls and your company has just opened a retail store in the mall. The behaviors you hate with retail clerks are the same behaviors that will turn trade show visitors off," she told him. "You have four

**Exhibit 3**
**Trade Show Profiles**

| SECO Data: |  |
|---|---|
| SHOW HOURS—15 hours |  |
| Thursday, February 22 |  |
| 3:00 PM–6:00 PM |  |
| Friday, February 23 |  |
| 11:00 AM–5:00 PM |  |
| Saturday, February 24 |  |
| 10:00 AM–4:00 PM |  |
| Booth space: $25 per sq. ft. |  |
| **Category** | **Count** |
| Education Program Attendees (AOP, OD, and Students) | 3,257 |
| Exhibit Only | 2,366 |
| Guests | 569 |
| **Total Verified Attendance** | **6,192** |
| Exhibitors | 1,792 |
| **Grand Total** | **7,984** |

(*Continued*)

**International Vision Expo East 2007 data:**

Price per sq. ft: $34.00/sq. ft.

$250 per corner charge applies.

Minimum booth size—10 feet × 10 feet

VCA Full Members are eligible for a pricing discount.

Exhibits:

Friday, April 11—9:30 AM–6:00 PM

Saturday, April 12—9:30 AM–6:00 PM

Sunday, April 13—9:30 AM–5:00 PM

### *INTERNATIONAL VISION EXPO EAST REGISTRATION LIST (2006)*

Eyewear and eyecare products and services for the ophthalmic profession.

**22,104 Total Registrants**

Highlighted information represents TRO's prospective audience.

| Type of Organization | Number of Registrants |
|---|---|
| Chain/Superstore Corp. Management | 815 |
| Independent Ophthalmological Practice | 2100 |
| Independent Opticianry Chain, 1–5 locations | 2917 |
| Independent Opticianry Chain, 6–10 locations | 258 |
| Independent Opticianry Chain, 10+ locations | 229 |
| Independent Optometric Practice | 6793 |
| Laboratory | 745 |
| Manufacturer | 1647 |
| Multidisciplinary Practice | 622 |
| Retail Optical Chain, 1–5 locations | 1714 |
| Retail Optical Chain, 6–10 locations | 4 |
| Retail Optical Chain, 10+ locations | 549 |
| Superstore Outlet | 82 |
| Wholesaler/Distributer | 1872 |

| Title or Position | Number of Registrants |
|---|---|
| Buyer | 4063 |
| Laboratory Manager | 556 |
| Laboratory Technician | 347 |
| Manufacturer's Representative | 1020 |
| Optician, Licensed or Certified | 3648 |
| Optician, Non-Certified | 885 |
| Opticianry Assistant | 770 |
| Ophthalmologist | 376 |
| Ophthalmic Medical Personnel—COA | 106 |
| Ophthalmic Medical Personnel—COT | 25 |
| Ophthalmic Medical Personnel—COMT | 39 |
| Ophthalmological Assistant (non-certified) | 211 |
| Opthalmological Resident | 16 |
| Optometrist | 3383 |

*(Continued)*

| | |
|---|---|
| Optometric Technician | 509 |
| Optometric Resident | 23 |
| Optometric Student | 643 |
| Practice/Business Manager | 1838 |
| Other | 3481 |

*SECO*

**SECO International 2006 Attendance Analysis**
**Category Count**
Education Program Attendees (AOP, OD, and Students) 3,257
Exhibit Only 2,366
Guests 569
**Total Verified Attendance 6,192**
Exhibitors 1,792
**Grand Total 7,984**

*American Optometry Association*

Optometry's Meeting™ is the premier event of the optometric profession. Every summer, thousands of ophthalmic professionals gather at Optometry's Meeting™ to network, learn, and have fun. Optometry's Meeting™ attracts thousands of

- Optometrists
- Paraoptometrics
- Optometric Students
- Optometric Educators
- Ophthalmic Industry leaders

Optometry's Meeting™ is a combined meeting, bringing together the annual meetings of several optometric professional groups including:

- The Annual AOA Congress
- The Annual AOSA Conference
- Many others

$29 a square foot. An additional charge of $250 per corner applies for island and peninsula booths only.

*Continuing Education*

Optometry's Meeting™ supplies over 200 hours of <u>top-quality continuing education.</u> Courses take place Wednesday through Sunday for Optometrists, Paraoptometrics and Students. Most Optometrist courses are COPE-approved, and several are Transcript Quality courses. Many Paraoptometric courses are approved for ABO, NCLE, or JCAHPO. Student education includes NBEO preparation courses.

*Exhibits*

The <u>Optometry's Meeting™ Exhibit Hall</u> is a spectacle for any optometric professional. Packed with the latest ophthalmic technologies from industry leaders, Exhibit Hall attendees can receive hands-on demonstrations of new products and services and make business contacts to help their practices grow. The Exhibit Hall offers many opportunities to win prizes including cash, plasma TVs, and much more. The Exhibit Hall also hosts fun events, like Friday's Buck-a-Beer Night.

*Events*

Attendees of Optometry's Meeting™ are treated annually to entertaining, and sometimes historical, keynote events. Included in registration is admission to the <u>AOA Opening General Session,</u> sponsored by Essilor. Recent speakers at this special event include Scott Adams, creator of the

*(Continued)*

Dilbert cartoon series; political commentators James Carville and Mary Matalin; and Former President Jimmy Carter.

### Locations

Optometry's Meeting™ travels around the United States offering attendees the opportunity to travel to many of America's great cities. Attendees and their guests often take advantage of the recreational highlights of the year's location. Recent locations of Optometry's Meeting™ include New Orleans, LA; San Diego, CA; Orlando, FL; Dallas, TX; and Las Vegas, NV. Future locations include Seattle, WA, in 2008, Washington, D.C., in 2009, Orlando, FL, in 2010, Salt Lake City, UT, in 2011, and Chicago, IL, in 2012.

### Exhibitor Information

The 110th Annual AOA Congress & 37th Annual AOSA Conference: Optometry's Meeting™ will be held June 27–July 1, 2007, in Boston, Massachusetts, at the Hynes Convention Center. The exhibit hall will be located at the Hynes Convention Center in Level 2—Halls C and D and Auditorium.

Optometry's Meeting™ has always found great success in Boston and is a favorite destination for many! If your business needs ophthalmic professionals to succeed, then you've picked the right show to attend.

The AOA has over 34,000 members, which are easy to reach through such outlets as the _AOA News and Optometry,_ two of the AOA's publications. The AOA also produces a Registration Brochure for Optometry's Meeting™ that is mailed to every member and an Onsite Book which is handed out to all ophthalmic professionals attending Optometry's Meeting™ and used as a quick reference guide. If that isn't enough, there is always the Web site, www.optometrysmeeting.org. If you are interested in any of these avenues please call 800-365-2219 and ask to speak to Kellie Rodrigue for more information.

### Exhibit Hall Hours
Thursday, June 28, 4:00 PM–7:30 PM
- Exhibit Hall Ribbon Cutting Ceremony Thursday at 4:00 PM
- International Wine & Cheese Reception (Courtesy of HOYA)

Friday, June 29, 10:00 AM–6:00 PM
- 4:30 PM–6:00 PM Buck-a-Beer Night (Courtesy of AOA)

Saturday, June 30, 9:00 AM–2:00 PM
- 11:00 AM–1:00 PM Designated Assistant/Tech and Student Hours

***Times and Events are Subject to Change***

### Why Should I Exhibit at Optometry's Meeting?
- Healthy Eyes, Healthy People™, AOA's full-scope public health message, provides direct opportunities for you to align your products and services, which will help ODs enhance their practice and promote for visual well-being.
- More decision makers (specifically more practicing ODs) attend Optometry's Meeting™ than any other optometric meeting worldwide.
- This is optometry's fastest-growing meeting. We have the education, the locations, and the programs that have now made Optometry's Meeting™ the largest in the country.
- Optometry's Meeting™ offers exhibitors and attendees alike more non-compete hours for the exhibit hall than any other show.
- Optometry's Meeting™ offers the best value for your exhibitor dollar. With the incorporation of the AOSA's meeting into our Congress, we deliver the highest touch rate with both the decision makers of today and tomorrow.
- We can accommodate/facilitate your every need, for both first-time exhibitors and for those returning exhibitors who are upgrading their booth in size and features, to maximize your exposure and deliver your message.
- This is "Optometry's Meeting." Optometry's Meeting™ is unparalleled in its uniqueness, imagination, and national exposure!

*(Continued)*

*According to a Survey from the 2006 Optometry's Meeting™ in Las Vegas, NV:*
- 81% of attendees made purchases or planned to.
- 91% of exhibiting companies surveyed rated the overall value of exhibiting at Optometry's Meeting™ compared to other industry meetings as Excellent/Good.
- 61% of attendees made three or more visits to the exhibit hall during their stay.

### International Vision Expo West Oct 03, 2007–Oct 06, 2007 Sands Expo & Convention Center
No. of Exhibitors: 522
Exhibition Floor Size: 160,641
No. of Attendees: 12,520

**Venue Address:**
201 E. Sands Avenue
Las Vegas, NV 89109

**Event Description:**
West Coast edition of the leading optical event in the U.S. bringing together all eyecare professionals under one roof. See your future: then make it real, at International Vision Expo, the United States' most comprehensive optical trade show and conference! We've brought together all the products, solutions, connections, and professional education you need to transform your business and supercharge your career. It's the future of eyecare, in America's fun capital—Las Vegas!

**Exhibitor Information:**
Eyewear and eyecare products and services for the ophthalmic industry, including: frames, lenses, contact lenses, diagnostic equipment, dispensing and examination equipment, pharmaceuticals, sunglasses, and more.

**Attendee Information:**
The entire ophthalmic community, including: optometrists, opticians, ophthalmologists, retailers, laboratory technicians, practice managers, and assistants.

### American Academy of Optometry—Academy 2007 Oct. 24, 2007–Oct. 27, 2007 Tampa Convention Center

**Venue Address:**
333 South Franklin Street
Tampa, FL 33602

**Event Description:**
American Academy of Optometry—Academy 2007

**Exhibitor Information:**
Don't miss out on the opportunity to have your product(s) introduced to potentially 4,500 ODs, vision scientists, lecturers, and other optometric professionals!

### OptoWest 2008 March 13, 2008–March 16, 2008 Long Beach Convention and Entertainment Center

**Venue Address:**
300 E. Ocean Boulevard
Long Beach, CA 90802

**Event Description:**
OptoWest will offer continuing education for doctors of optometry, paraoptometrics and opticians, and will feature nationally renowned speakers who offer fresh topics and approaches; a two-day exhibit hall; and special events like a Gala Party.

*(Continued)*

*Midwest Vision Conference & Expo May 10, 2007–May 12, 2007 The Donald E Stephens Convention Center Information * Insight * Inspiration*

*Midwest Vision Congress is a joint effort produced by the North Central States Optometric Council (NCSOC), Vision Council of America (VCA), and Association Expositions & Services (AE&S) to present the premier event for the Midwest ophthalmic community. Midwest Vision Congress covers an extensive continuing education program and a comprehensive exhibit hall. The convention will be held at the Donald E. Stephens Convention Center Rosemont, Illinois.*

### Midwest Optical Market Strong, and Growing Stronger

As the fourth largest market in the optical industry, the Midwest is responsible for over $1.3 billion of the total optical sales in the nation. The ABO/NCLE counts 7,290 certified opticians and the AOA estimates over 5,075 ODs to be in private practice in the Midwest region.

According to Jobson's Top 25 markets, the top five markets in this region (Chicago, Detroit, Minneapolis/St. Paul and Cleveland) are responsible for 22 percent of the $6 billion in total retail sales of eyewear in the Top 25 U.S. Metro Markets in 2001, with Chicago holding onto the ranking as the number 2 metro market overall. Independents hold on to 47 percent of total retail sales in this region.

### Space Rental Options

$24 per square foot standard rate

$22 per square foot VCA Full Member rate

$200 per corner

No. of Exhibitors: Approx. 100

Exhibition Floor Size: 30,000

No. of Attendees: Approx. 3,000

**Venue Address:**
5555 N. River Rd.
Rosemont, IL 60018

**Event Description:**
The Midwest Vision Congress is the leading regional ophthalmic conference and trade show in the USA, with professionals coming from the North Central States Optometric Council (comprised of Illinois, Iowa, Kansas, Michigan, Minnesota, Missouri, Nebraska, North Dakota, South Dakota and Wisconsin). Midwest Vision Congress was established in 2003 as the new combined event of the former EyeQuest and Eyecare events.

**Exhibitor Information:**
Manufacturers of eyeglass frames, lenses, contact lenses, pharmaceuticals, solutions, diagnostic equipment, instruments, lens processing equipment, accessories, sunglasses, etc.

**Attendee Information:**
Optometrists, opticians, ophthalmologists, laboratory managers and technicians, retail executives, wholesalers, distributors, importers and exporters

**Future Dates:**
May, 2008

*International Vision Expo East March 23, 2007–March 25, 2007 Jacob K. Javits Convention Center The Place to Be*

No. of Exhibitors: 600

Exhibition Floor Size: 243,000

No. of Attendees: 15,000 (est.)

**Venue Address:**
Jacob K. Javits
New York, NY 10001

*(Continued)*

**Event Description:**
East Coast edition of the leading optical event in the U.S., bringing together all eyecare professionals under one roof. The New York show, held annually in March, is the first major optical show in which companies are able to launch their new products and services. It is estimated that more than 100 products are introduced. Don't be left behind—International Vision Expo draws optical professionals from all career paths.

**Exhibitor Information:**
Manufacturers and suppliers of all facets of the optical industry, including: frames, lenses, contact lenses, dispensing equipment, diagnostic equipment, instruments, pharmaceuticals, and sunglasses/sports glasses.

**Attendee Information:**
Ophthalmologists, Optometrists, Opticians, Lab Personnel, Practice Managers, Ophthalmic Medical Personnel, Retailers, Manufacturing Executives, Import/Export Buyers, Ophthalmic Assistants, Optical Interns, and more!

***American Academy of Ophthalmology Annual Meeting Nov. 10, 2007–Nov. 13, 2007 Ernest Morial Convention Centre***
No. of Exhibitors: 480
No. of Attendees: 15,000

**Venue Address:**
900 Convention Center Blvd.
New Orleans, LA 70130

**Event Description:**
American Academy of Ophthalmology Annual Meeting

**Exhibitor Information:**
Academy members and independent consultants offered user-friendly instruction on all things high-tech for business, clinical and academic applications, including: The latest in hardware, from PDAs to wireless computing Internet, e-mail and mobile communications topics, Software for medical records, presentations, image manipulations and more Free Internet stations, Meeting E-Abstracts and Meeting E-Guide, to download to your Palm OS and Pocket PC handheld.

seconds to lure a delegate into your booth. And once there, by your asking good questions, they'll tell you everything you need to turn them into customers. After all," she continued, "we all love to talk about our favorite subject: ourselves!"

She also explained that setting trade show goals was as important as setting corporate marketing goals. In 2006, TRO used contact goals as a baseline. This was calculated by multiplying the number of show hours times the number of staff (per shift) times five. Of this number, about 10% should become customers. In 2007, goals were based on the past year's actual results.

Now he's wondering what his strategy should be for 2008. Steve knows that the shows are working for him because in each of the last two years he's exceeded the goals he set. He wants to expand the business and use trade shows as the means to get

there, but after examining the list of attendees for Vision Expo, he's not sure what makes the most sense. Should he increase or decrease the space he rents? How many staff people are needed? How much money needs to be allocated? The buying centers are there (buyer, user, purchaser, decider, and gatekeeper); the question is how to reach them effectively.

His other problem is in which shows he should exhibit. Trade magazines usually provide a breakdown of readership, but not all trade shows provide audited data on attendees and their job titles. How can he find those shows with attendees who have pediatric practices who would be interested in his proprietary products?

Another objective is to expand the number of sales territories. If he can attract buyers interested in his proprietary products, he and his people can form

**Exhibit 4**
NAICS
Ophthalmic
Goods
Manufacturing

These manufacturers are competitors to TRO

**2002 Economic Census Industry Series Report**

Industry Series data are preliminary and are subject to change; they will be superseded by data released in later reports.

| 2002 NAICS | Report Title | Report Number | Release Date (PDF) | Full Report Link to PDF | Size in kb | Tables Only Link to PDF | Size in kb |
|---|---|---|---|---|---|---|---|
| 339115 | Ophthalmic Goods Manufacturing | EC02-31I-339115 | 09/01/2004 | | 443 | | 206 |

**NAICS Hierarchy: 1997**

| Industry Detail | NAICS Code | NAICS Title (and link to definition) | Establishments | Value of Shipments ($1,000) | Annual Payroll ($1,000) | Paid Employees |
|---|---|---|---|---|---|---|
| | 31–33 | Manufacturing | 362,829 | 3,834,700,920 | 569,808,845 | 16,805,127 |
| | 339 | Miscellaneous mfg. | 31,476 | 99,729,798 | 21,618,204 | 725,396 |
| | 3391 | Medical equipment & supplies mfg. | 12,675 | 44,893,840 | 10,008,144 | 291,522 |
| | 33911 | Medical equipment & supplies mfg. | 12,675 | 44,893,840 | 10,008,144 | 291,522 |
| | **339115** | **Ophthalmic goods mfg.** | **573** | **3,497,595** | **770,994** | **25,274** |

Table includes only establishments with payroll.

**NAICS 339115: Ophthalmic Goods Manufacturing**

This U.S. industry comprises establishments primarily engaged in manufacturing ophthalmic goods. Examples of products made by these establishments are prescription eyeglasses (except manufactured in a retail setting), contact lenses, sunglasses, eyeglass frames, and reading glasses made to standard powers.

Historical Comparability—Bridge between NAICS and SIC

| NAICS | SIC | Description | Establishments | Value of Shipments ($1,000) | Paid Employees | Annual Payroll ($1,000) |
|---|---|---|---|---|---|---|
| 339115 | | Ophthalmic goods mfg | 575 | 3,607,813 | 26,366 | 814,242 |
| | 3851 | Ophthalmic goods | 575 | 3,607,813 | 26,366 | 814,242 |

(*Continued*)

*Comparative Statistics for 4-digit SICs: 1997 and 1992*

Data are in current dollars and have not been adjusted for inflation. Introductory text includes methodology. Comparative statistics are also available for other industries. For descriptions of column headings and rows (SIC industries), click on the appropriate underlined element in the table.

| SIC | 1987 SIC Description | Year | Establishments | Value of shipments ($1,000) | Annual Payroll ($1,000) | Paid Employees |
|---|---|---|---|---|---|---|
| | | 1997 | 575 | 3,607,813 | 814,242 | 26,366 |
| 3851 | Ophthalmic goods | 1992 | 568 | 2,675,254 | 714,022 | 29,432 |
| | | % chg. | 1.2 | 34.9 | 14.0 | −10.4 |

**Exhibit 5**

NAICS 446130 Optical Goods Stores

Optical goods stores are prospective customers for TRO

*2002 Economic Census Industry Series Report*

| 2002 NAICS | Report Title | Report Number | Release Date (PDF) | Full Report Link to PDF | Size in kb | Tables Only Link to PDF | Size in kb |
|---|---|---|---|---|---|---|---|
| 446 | Health and Personal Care Stores | EC02-44I–06 | 09/30/2004 | | 457 | | 274 |

*NAICS Hierarchy: 1997*

Introductory text includes scope and methodology. For descriptions of column headings and rows (industries), click on the appropriate underlined element in the table.

| Industry Detail | NAICS Code | NAICS Title (and link to definition) | Establish-ments | Sales ($1,000) | Annual Payroll ($1,000) | Paid Employees |
|---|---|---|---|---|---|---|
| | 44–45 | Retail trade | 1,118,447 | 2,460,886,012 | 237,195,503 | 13,991,103 |
| | 446 | Health & personal care stores | 82,941 | 117,700,863 | 15,190,635 | 903,694 |
| | 4461 | Health & personal care stores | 82,941 | 117,700,863 | 15,190,635 | 903,694 |
| | 44613 | Optical goods stores | 15,192 | 6,432,078 | 1,401,239 | 73,049 |
| | **446130** | **Optical goods stores** | **15,192** | **6,432,078** | **1,401,239** | **73,049** |

Table includes only establishments with payroll.

**NAICS 446130: Optical Goods Stores.**

This U.S. industry comprises establishments primarily engaged in one or more of the following: (1) retailing and fitting prescription eyeglasses and contact lenses; (2) retailing prescription eyeglasses in combination with the grinding of lenses to order on the premises; and (3) selling nonprescription eyeglasses.

*(Continued)*

*Historical Comparability—Bridge between NAICS and SIC*

| NAICS | SIC | Description | Establishments | Sales ($1,000) | Paid Employees | Annual Payroll ($1,000) |
|---|---|---|---|---|---|---|
| 446130 | | Optical goods stores | 15,192 | 6,432,078 | 73,049 | 1,401,239 |
| | 5995 | Optical goods stores | 15,192 | 6,432,078 | 73,049 | 1,401,239 |

## Comparative Statistics for 4-digit SICs: 1997 and 1992

Data are in current dollars and have not been adjusted for inflation. Introductory text includes methodology. Comparative statistics are also available for other industries. For descriptions of column headings and rows (SIC industries), click on the appropriate underlined element in the table.

| SIC | 1987 SIC Description | Year | Establishments | Sales ($1,000) | Annual Payroll ($1,000) | Paid Employees |
|---|---|---|---|---|---|---|
| | | 1997 | 15,192 | 6,432,078 | 1,401,239 | 73,049 |
| 5995 | Optical goods stores | 1992 | 14,160 | 4,806,183 | 1,114,180 | 64,986 |
| | | % chg. | 7.3 | 33.8 | 25.8 | 12.4 |

$$ 1992 sales data include sales from catalog order desks. 1997 sales data exclude sales from catalog order desks.

## Geographic Distribution — Optical Goods Stores: 1997

Data for the Retail trade sector are published for the U.S., states, metropolitan areas, counties, places, and ZIP Codes.

For descriptions of column headings and rows (industries), click on the appropriate underlined element in the table.

| Other Industries | State | Establish-ments | Sales | Sales% of U.S. ($1,000) | Annual Payroll ($1,000) | Paid Employees |
|---|---|---|---|---|---|---|
| | United States | 15,192 | 6,432,078 | 100.00 | 1,401,239 | 73,049 |
| | New York | 1,323 | 630,751 | 9.81 | 156,211 | 6,777 |
| | California | 1,289 | 602,033 | 9.36 | 109,283 | 6,197 |
| | Florida | 1,187 | 480,772 | 7.47 | 106,033 | 5,721 |
| | Texas | 1,077 | 455,818 | 7.09 | 92,493 | 5,091 |
| | Illinois | 636 | 308,777 | 4.80 | 70,584 | 3,715 |
| | Pennsylvania | 755 | 297,678 | 4.63 | 63,728 | 3,576 |
| | Michigan | 570 | 275,435 | 4.28 | 68,342 | 2,949 |
| | Ohio | 707 | 259,524 | 4.03 | 56,277 | 2,961 |
| | New Jersey | 546 | 239,258 | 3.72 | 51,434 | 2,383 |
| | Georgia | 383 | 193,517 | 3.01 | 39,042 | 2,319 |
| | Virginia | 422 | 186,876 | 2.91 | 41,342 | 1,855 |
| | Maryland | 390 | 154,023 | 2.39 | 36,497 | 1,712 |
| | Massachusetts | 361 | 152,817 | 2.38 | 31,914 | 1,583 |
| | Missouri | 303 | 143,222 | 2.23 | 30,760 | 1,757 |
| | Minnesota | 341 | 135,539 | 2.11 | 28,970 | 1,727 |

*(Continued)*

| | | | | |
|---|---|---|---|---|
| Colorado | 332 | 130,229 | 2.02 | 25,309 | 1,337 |
| North Carolina | 313 | 129,013 | 2.01 | 27,094 | 1,495 |
| Arizona | 273 | 126,125 | 1.96 | 25,737 | 1,366 |
| Indiana | 279 | 123,182 | 1.92 | 27,600 | 1,634 |
| Washington | 341 | 118,881 | 1.85 | 24,029 | 1,308 |
| Connecticut | 220 | 110,009 | 1.71 | 28,321 | 1,148 |
| Wisconsin | 277 | 109,865 | 1.71 | 25,222 | 1,359 |
| Tennessee | 247 | 106,413 | 1.65 | 25,261 | 1,278 |
| Louisiana | 205 | 79,658 | 1.24 | 17,301 | 1,048 |
| South Carolina | 204 | 76,911 | 1.20 | 16,454 | 1,000 |
| Alabama | 192 | 67,949 | 1.06 | 16,054 | 907 |
| Oregon | 165 | 64,887 | 1.01 | 14,182 | 697 |
| Kentucky | 141 | 63,154 | 0.98 | 15,150 | 749 |
| Iowa | 166 | 56,462 | 0.88 | 11,822 | 769 |
| Oklahoma | 144 | 52,843 | 0.82 | 10,896 | 622 |
| Nevada | 79 | 44,310 | 0.69 | 8,594 | 413 |
| Kansas | 126 | 42,851 | 0.67 | 8,528 | 497 |
| Utah | 118 | 41,363 | 0.64 | 9,057 | 553 |
| Hawaii | 82 | 36,272 | 0.56 | 6,889 | 431 |
| New Mexico | 107 | 34,321 | 0.53 | 6,569 | 425 |
| Nebraska | 95 | 31,651 | 0.49 | 6,958 | 414 |
| West Virginia | 93 | 30,378 | 0.47 | 6,325 | 411 |
| New Hampshire | 75 | 30,149 | 0.47 | 6,802 | 344 |
| Mississippi | 92 | 29,413 | 0.46 | 7,324 | 382 |
| Arkansas | 73 | 24,385 | 0.38 | 5,403 | 322 |
| District of Columbia | 49 | 23,318 | 0.36 | 6,683 | 219 |
| Delaware | 53 | 20,561 | 0.32 | 4,594 | 234 |
| Idaho | 53 | 18,159 | 0.28 | 3,224 | 228 |
| Maine | 49 | 15,523 | 0.24 | 3,528 | 188 |
| Alaska | 43 | 13,867 | 0.22 | 2,959 | 123 |
| Rhode Island | 43 | 12,476 | 0.19 | 2,752 | 138 |
| South Dakota | 40 | 12,443 | 0.19 | 2,588 | 167 |
| North Dakota | 41 | 11,697 | 0.18 | 2,543 | 176 |
| Vermont | 32 | 11,343 | 0.18 | 2,912 | 130 |
| Montana | 38 | 11,185 | 0.17 | 2,656 | 138 |
| Wyoming | 22 | 4,792 | 0.07 | 1,009 | 76 |

relationships that will then produce sales of the company's standard products for which there are many competitors.

A study done by the Center for Exhibition Industry Research (CEIR) says that exhibitors at trade shows often find hidden buyers. For TRO, this includes optometrists and ophthalmologists from areas where he has no sales representation.

### Exhibit Marketing Plan

Steve believed he was ready to take the next steps to really grow his business. His task was to write an effective exhibit marketing plan along with a budget to present to his siblings at their next quarterly meet-

ing. He knew he could effectively grow the business using trade shows; he just needed to show Mary Ann and Joe that his plan made sense.

## Questions

1. Based on the geographic distribution of optical goods stores, do Steve's plans for growth make sense?

2. Are trade shows a viable option to generate sales, sales leads, and new customer accounts? If so, in which shows should he invest?

3. For the shows TRO already does, what should the strategic plan be? What tactics should be included?

# Whole Tree Energy™

"I can see the whole project goin' south when we meet with the community groups," contended Jeb Boskirk, director of licensing and environmental affairs at a Midwest power utility. "These are school teachers, students, bankers, hunters, shopkeepers, machinists, and housewives. Very few economists or tech heads are gonna be there, Dave. And we'll be lucky if there's no orchestrated counterpoint by some citizen group—it could be tree huggers, no-growth reverts, or just a well-oiled NIMBY.[1] We've got to do our homework, sure. But we're going to need lots of help from you to make this fly."

David Ostlie, founder and president of Energy Performance Systems, Inc., knew that Jeb Boskirk was right. Jeb was skilled in the vital process of securing land, working with state licensing agencies and EPA approval boards, as well as surviving the local hearings and town meetings, all prerequisites to bringing a new power plant into being. Ostlie believed in the promise of electricity from burning

This case was prepared by F. Robert Dwyer (University of Cincinnati) for the purposes of class discussion. Input from William Rudelius (professor of marketing at the University of Minnesota and a member of the board of directors at EPS, Inc.) and Thomas Osterhus (doctoral candidate at the University of Cincinnati and staff consultant at Cynergy) is gratefully acknowledged. Some of the case facts come from EPS literature and the case "Energy Performance Systems, Inc." in Eric Berkowitz, Roger Kerin, Steven Hartley, and William Rudelius *Marketing* (Burr Ridge, IL: Irwin, 1997), pp. 119–21.

[1]NIMBY stands for "not in my back yard." It is a crude label for groups that might agree on the need for, say, a new power plant or jail or bus depot, but not be willing to accept it in their neighborhood.

wood, and more than two decades of tests and research had supported his theory. But now he was close to bringing his patented Whole Tree Energy (WTE) system on line in a real 100-megawatt (MW) power plant—power for nearly 100,000 people. He needed to review again the role he and his tiny company would have to play in this complex marketing environment to make WTE happen.

## Background

Since Thomas Edison found carbon to be a suitable filament and invented the first practical lightbulb, civilization's appetite for electric power has expanded relentlessly. Most of this demand has been answered by power plants that burn coal, oil, or natural gas. Although research continues to show advances, currently very little electric power is generated from solar, wind, and geothermal energy. The construction of nuclear power facilities in the United States has virtually ground to a halt.

> *Biomass fuels are immense, ubiquitous, clean, and, in most cases, cost-effective sources of energy. Utilities have substantial and—with further R&D—growing opportunities to exploit this resource.[2]*

Biomass fuels are the energy resources in living things and their waste products. The greatest supply

[2]EPRI (Electric Power Research Institute), "Biomass State-of-the-Art Assessment," 1991. Abstract at **www.epriweb.com.**

of biomass energy lies in natural forests. Other sources include wood residue and agricultural by-products. For example, wood chips are frequently burned at small power plants owned by paper companies and sawmills. Ethanol is economically produced from corn. The energy from animal waste and grasses has also been studied.

What we call fossil fuels—coal, oil, and natural gas—are in essence prehistoric biomass. The difference is fossil fuel deposits are *depleted* by extraction; biomass fuels are *renewable*. In addition, biomass fuels yield fewer emissions. Burning trees, for example, emits carbon dioxide ($CO_2$), but no more than what the trees have absorbed from the environment during their growth. Fossil fuels emit $CO_2$ that hasn't been in the atmosphere for eons. Furthermore, although many coal-fired power plants require expensive equipment to control emissions of sulfur dioxide ($SO_2$), wood and grasses release very low levels of $SO_2$ that are sometimes barely measurable. Wood also has an advantage over coal in the release of very low levels of nitrogen oxides ($NO_x$).

Despite the promise of biomass fuels, many obstacles currently limit their viability. Power plants are constrained to small-scale operations, thermal efficiencies need to be improved, fuel delivery systems need to be developed, overall economic viability needs to demonstrated, and the public needs significantly more education about both the promise and limits.

## Whole-Tree Energy™

David Ostlie's inspiration for the WTE concept began in 1978 when he built his house in a new woodland development in central Minnesota. On cold winter mornings the smoke from each new home's fireplace or wood-burning stove was sometimes enough to make one choke. Ostlie set out to build a high-energy, smokeless woodburner. A former iron worker then employed by Northern States Power (NSP), Oslie built a chest freezer-sized unit that he installed and tested in a storage area beneath his garage. He used the same wood cleared for the driveways throughout his neighborhood, but dried it more thoroughly than his neighbors' woodpiles. As a result, Ostlie's device generated such high temperatures that the wood burned completely and gave off a clear, virtually sootless exhaust.

In a 1993 interview, Ostlie recalled his thinking that led him to start a company and begin the long road of concept drawings, slide presentations, and component testing: "Having some knowledge of the electric power industry, I knew that the few existing wood-burning power plants used chipped or shredded wood. I was also aware that the process of breaking wood down to this size is expensive. Being able to avoid these costs would be a great advantage."[3]

The key elements of the WTE concept are summarized below:

1. Tree plantations of fast-growing hybrid hardwoods provide a harvest in seven years. A 400-MW plant serving a 50-mile radius would require about 3 percent of this acreage for plantations—most likely marginal farmland, with some receiving subsidies to be taken from the production of food crops.

2. Trees are efficiently cut and transported to the plant site.

3. Within a large fiberglass dome whole trees are stacked in cross-hatch fashion upwards of 100 feet (30m) by a large crane.

4. Waste heat from the plant is piped into the dome to dry the stack for 30 days, removing over 65 percent of the trees' moisture and allowing a cleaner, more efficient burn.

5. Trees are conveyed from the dome to the nearby boiler wall, where they are cut to fit, approximately 28 feet (8.5m).

6. A ram pushes the pile of trees 12 to 16 feet high into a charge pit; then another ram pushes it into the furnace.

7. The slightly oversized boiler promotes high heat release and complete combustion.

The time line in Exhibit 1 summarizes the research that has gone into the WTE system. Ostlie sometimes wonders just how much more has to be demonstrated before a power utility will commence to build a commercial plant, and he wonders at what stage of the purchase process and what constituency he should direct his limited marketing resources.

At most power companies, the decision process to bring a new plant on line is lengthy and complex. Capacity planners play a key initiating role in the

[3]Leslie Lamarre, "Electricity from Trees," *Electric Power Research Institute EPRI Journal* (January/February 1994), p. 19.

**Exhibit 1**
WTE Time Line

| | |
|---|---|
| Early 1980s | Ostlie tests a clean wood-burning unit beneath his garage. It leaves no cinders and provides a clear exhaust. Ostlie convinces NSP to scale up the design to explore its commercial viability. |
| 1984 | Osltie works in cooperation with St. John's University in Collegeville, MN. Using St. John's' 1.6-MW boiler and 4-foot-long sections of dried trees, Ostlie reaches 2,400° F, besting the temperatures typical of the superheat cycles at the largest coal-fired plants. |
| 1986 | Converting one of its coal-fired boilers for 10 MW, NSP tests the WTE output capacity and emissions over a 100-hour period. Output efficiency of 30 percent of capacity is the criterion for success at utility scale. Ostlie achieves a rate of 90 percent and maintains an average output of 6–7 MW over the test. EPA reports the lowest measures of NOx emissions of any solid fuel in the United States. $SO_2$ and particulate emissions are also very low—even without the removal systems common at coal-burning plants. |
| 1988 | NSP puts the WTE project on hold. Ostlie leaves the company, takes his patent, and forms a new company called Energy Performance Systems, Inc. (EPS). |
| 1991 | EPRI releases its own study of biomass fuel, which shows the attractiveness of combustion of fast-growing tree crops. In Aurora, MN (pop. 3,000), EPS and EPRI join in a demonstration project to harvest, transport, stack, dry, and combust 3,000 tons of whole trees. Standard logging trucks each bring about 25 tons to the site. A tower crane and remote control grapple pile the trees more than 100 feet high on a base 30 feet square. The pile is stable, and the 30-day drying period reduces moisture content to 20 percent. Combustion tests are favorable, with one experiment producing a wood-burning world record of 4.2 million Btu per hour per square foot. (Compare to a coal-fired boiler's heat release rate of about 2 million Btu per hour per square foot.) |
| 1992 | NSP and Wisconsin Power & Light approach EPRI and EPS to explore the feasibility of building a WTE plant. |
| 1995 | EPRI releases computer models for evaluating biomass power technologies, saying WTE shows "the potential for improved cost and performance relative to the existing technologies." Cost and thermal efficiency estimates are provided, but the report states, "Since neither the advanced wood gasification nor the WTE technologies have reached maturity nor been commercialized, utilities should use the estimates for these advanced systems with caution." |
| 1997 | The Minnesota Department of Natural Resources continues to monitor a 1995 planting of 1,000 acres of fast-growing, hybrid poplar trees. |

process. Their job is to forecast energy demand for the market served and check the adequacy of current plant capacity. Demand is analyzed for base demand as well as peak demands, such as when air conditioners run flat out to cope with stifling summer temperatures. In these two areas, WTE is relatively attractive for base load service; natural gas plants serve peak loads.

Capacity planners typically evaluate the options by first specifying the resources for each alternative site, technology, and array of base loaders and peakers by calculating equivalent costs (e.g., dollars per kilowatt-hour). Optimization programs support the process of structuring the problem and allow sensitivity analysis on the sequencing of options, the impact of delays, input costs, and more.

An executive committee reviews the recommendations from capacity planning. Financial criteria and market service standards are tightly applied, and the environmental and political dimensions of the recommendation are fully considered. The utility's Licensing and Environmental Affairs staff will then seek to obtain EPA and state licensing agency approval, acquire the needed property, and interface with local governments and community groups.

# Glossary

## a

**accessibility** means that members of a market can be reached or impacted by some directed marketing activity, a criterion of a good market segmentation approach

**accessory equipment** hand tools, such as sanders, routers, portable saws, and other light tools, that are used in the manufacture of products

**accommodation** a negotiation strategy of sacrifice to build or sustain a relationship

**account retention** the percentage of accounts that continue doing business with the seller each year

**account salesperson** a salesperson who has responsibility for specified accounts

**action** the final stage of the hierarchy-of-effects model; the desired behavior that we want the audience of our marketing communications to do

**action goals** goals that are intended to cause or bring about a desired response on the part of the receiver

**activity quota** a type of quota that specifies the number and type of tasks or activities that salespeople should do; for example, a new business call quota would specify the number of noncustomers representing potential new business that should be visited in a period of time

**adaptive learning** learning that occurs within a set of constraints or learning boundaries

**administered channels** a form of channel relationship in which members recognize their participation in a larger system, but they interact without a formal chain of command or a set of rules. Coordination results from ad hoc division of labor and informal leadership

**administered prices** prices established by a seller as impersonal, take-it-or-leave-it offers to prospective buyers

**advantages** reasons for having features of a product or service

**adversarial purchasing philosophy** to have several vendors for each product

**advocate** users encouraged by premier salespeople to try and get decisions in their favor

**agent** a marketing intermediary engaged in prospecting, selling, and other functions but *does not take title* to the goods exchanged

**agent software** or **bots** terms used to describe programs that collect data on products preferences, purchase history, firmographics, and demographics in order to automatically profile customers and call up custom pages, tailored to the interests and needs of the customer

**aggression** a response to conflict that includes open or covert actions intended to injure the conflict party

**always-a-share** a purchasing situation that allows the buyer to taper or augment purchases in increments, while multiple suppliers can have a share of a customer's business in either the current period or future periods

**analyzer** an organization classified as a combination prospector–defender; less aggressive with innovation and change than a prospector, but not so attached to stability and efficiency as a defender; very selective in developing products and pursuing opportunities; seldom a first mover, but often a strong second or third, offering high quality and service

**attraction** the degree to which the interaction between buyer and seller yields them net payoffs in excess of some minimum level. The payoffs are tangible and intangible rewards from the association, less economic and social costs

**attraction efficiency**   a measure of trade show marketing efficiency, it compares the number of leads gathered at the booth with the number of prospects in the total show audience

**augmented product**   that part of the offering that is somewhat customized for each particular customer

**autonomous**   when a person makes a purchase decision alone for an organization

**avoidance**   a common negotiation strategy when one party doesn't really need the deal or the partner

**awareness**   a stage of the hierarchy-of-effects model, created when potential buyers become acquainted with the product or brand

**awareness stage** (of a developing relationship)   buyer and seller independently consider the other as an exchange partner

**b**

**barriers to entry**   obstacles potential entrant must overcome in order to compete in a market

**behavior choice theory**   states that buyers go through a choice process to arrive at decisions of *how* they will buy, as opposed to the choice process of *what* will be bought modeled as part of the buy-grid

**benchmark**   the performance level of the best organization for a particular task

**benefit**   how a product or service satisfies a need

**beta testing** (also called **field testing**)   testing the product by letting customers use it in real-world conditions

**bonus**   a lump sum payment for meeting a minimum standard of performance within a given period of time

**bots**   also called **agent software** are terms used to describe programs that collect data on product preferences, purchase history, firmographics in order to automatically profile customers and call up custom pages, tailored to the interests and needs of the customer

**breakdown budgeting**   methods of budgeting that begin with the manager setting a total budget, then allocating (breaking down) the budget to the various areas or functions, such as various forms of communication

**break-even price**   the average revenue needed to cover costs, given a specific sales level

**break-even quantity**   a sales level—at a specified price—at which total revenue equals total cost

**brokers**   businesses that do not hold title, but bring buyers and sellers together, typically in environments where buyers and sellers lack the information needed to connect with one another

**budget buildup** (also called **objective and task**)   a method of creating budgets that requires the decision maker to set the budget after determining the strategy and tasks; often used in creating communication budgets

**buildup approach** (to market size estimation)   estimates come from calculating the value of various materials or parts units needed (building up) in a specific application or from specific accounts. Also called **factoring**

**business marketing**   marketing products or services to other companies, government bodies, institutions (such as hospitals), and other organizations

**business strength**   the strength of a company's offering relative to other companies' products

**buy-class**   a type of buying decision, based on the experience of the buyer with a purchase of a particular product or service

**buy-grid model**   describes how purchasing practices vary along a continuum representing the buyer's experience in buying that particular product or service

**buy-phase model**   suggests that people go through a series of steps (or phases) when making a decision, beginning with problem recognition

**buying center** or **decision-making unit (DMU)**   when more than one person is involved, the group of participants in the company

**cap**   a limit to how much a salesperson can make, no matter the amount of sales, even under a straight commission plan

**capital equipment** (also called **installations**)   large equipment used in the production process that requires significant financial investment

**cash-and-carry distributors**   channel intermediaries that hold title but provide no buyer financing or delivery

**cash cows**   products that have high market share and strength in a steady market (no growth or shrinkage) and that, therefore, should contribute the most to the company's profit

**catalog wholesaler**   a channel intermediary that holds title and relies exclusively on mail, phone, and fax orders from its catalog and does not have a field sales force

**centralizing**  the concentration of an activity within company headquarters; a trend in purchasing

**champions** or **advocates**  of a vendor; that is, someone who influences the decision in favor of a particular vendor

**channel intermediaries**  organizations that facilitate the transfer of title between the producer and user of a product

**circulation audit**  a study of the readers who get a particular magazine; used by marketers to determine if their ads are reaching the right buyers

**closed bidding**  the solicitation of proposals from an exclusive set of potential suppliers

**coercive power**  the ability of one channel member to mediate punishments to get another to do what it otherwise would not do

**cognitive mapping**  a learning tool that is used to explore mental structures of beliefs and assumptions

**collaboration**  a negotiation strategy characterized by joint problem solving, searching for creative win–win solutions

**combination plan**  a sales force compensation plan that pays some combination of commission and/or bonus and a salary

**commission base**  the item from which the commission is determined—usually unit sales, dollar sales, or gross margin

**commission rate**  the amount paid per base item sold—usually a percentage

**commitment stage** (of a buyer–seller relationship)  a lasting desire to maintain or preserve a valuable relationship. Thus, this commitment phase is characterized by the parties exchanging significant resources. When the parties share a common belief in the effectiveness of future exchange, they dedicate resources to maintaining the relationship

**company orientation**  the degree to which the individual works to achieve benefit for the company

**competency trap**  any skill or technology that a company sticks with due to comfort with the familiar, in spite of evidence that better alternatives may exist

**competitive advantage**  something that provides incremental value when compared to other offerings

**competitive negotiation**  a negotiation strategy that has a winner and a loser; it is the right course when it is critical to win *this* deal but shows little regard to the prospects for subsequent exchange with the party

**compiled lists**  database of names, addresses, and classification information assembled by companies that comb directories and public records and even make physical observations

**complexity management**  the process of identifying links among components that raise costs if any changes are made

**compliance programs**  programs in which purchasers must be in compliance with federal guidelines in order to be eligible to supply the government

**component parts** or **OEM parts**  parts assembled into the final product without further transformation

**compromise**  a hybrid of competition and accommodation strategies of negotiation; often an easy solution that brings an end to negotiations before creative solutions delivering win–win outcomes can be explored

**conceptual map**  a picture of abstract ideas, options, persons, or companies based on two or three key variables

**concurrent manufacturing**  a system in which suppliers schedule their own manufacturing based on the shipment needs of their customers

**conflict**  felt or enacted tension between parties—in this situation, channel members

**consultative selling**  a form of selling in which the seller brings specialized expertise into a complex problem in order to create a somewhat customized solution

**contract**  a promise to perform some act in exchange for a payment or some other consideration

**contractual channels**  channel relationship form in which members are tightly coordinated by formal procedures and pledges of ongoing exchange. Nonrefundable fees and 5- to 10-year agreements are common devices to ensure longevity

**controlled circulation**  distribution of a magazine to only qualified readers; qualifications are usually based on the readers' influence over certain classes of purchases

**controller**  person who controls or sets the budget for the purchase

**conversion ratio**  a productivity index calculated by dividing outputs by specific antecedent efforts; for example, appointments booked/prospects contacted or sales made/appointments kept

**corporate channels**  a relationship structure in which we see the integration of most channel functions (delivery, selling, promoting, customer feedback, inventory, ordering, service, etc.). What we tend to see are degrees of vertical integration in marketing channels. A firm that uses its own sales force and its own fleet of trucks from its own distribution centers is highly integrated

**corporate relationship**  exchange safeguarded by ownership or vertical integration; represents the extreme of the contractual dimension

**cost per thousand (CPM)**  a critical variable in selecting trade publications; can be calculated by dividing the cost of an ad's space by the number of readers (in thousands)

**cost-plus contract**   the purchaser will reimburse the supplier for all of its costs, plus a certain percentage of those costs for profit

**creative plan**   an element of advertising strategy which involves determining what the content of the message will be (encoding)

**cross-functional sourcing teams**   purchasing teams that include members of various functional areas within the firm, and sometimes include personnel from suppliers and customers

**cross selling**   selling additional products after the first sale, but these products may not be related to the original sale

**customer lifetime value (CLV)**   an estimate of the net present value of the stream of benefits from a customer, less the burdens of servicing the account or managing the relationship

**customer relationship management (CRM)**   a business strategy or philosophy based on gathering data about individual customers and using that information to create individualized offers in order to optimize long-run (or customer life-cycle) profitability; suites of software that assist marketer efforts to (1) collect and store accessible data on each account, i.e., the name and position of key personnel, purchase history, delivery specifications, sales calls, trade show interactions, e-mails, and other contacts, (2) evaluate customer, program, and product performance, and (3) support the development of customized services, communications, and more in order to maximize the long-run profitability of each account

**customer restrictions**   contractual agreements in distribution that specify the type of business the reseller may or may not serve

**cycle time**   the time it takes to complete an action such as developing a product

*d*

**data mining**   describes the process of using numerous query tools and exploratory techniques to extract information from a database or data warehouse

**data warehousing**   uses centrally managed data from all functional areas of the organization (sales, purchasing, human resources, finance, accounts payable, etc.)—formatted to company standards—so

that it may be accessed by authorized users through their personal computers for queries, custom reports, and analysis

**decile report**   a method of customer analysis that orders the firm's customers from best to smallest, on the basis of purchase volume for the period, summarized by *tenths*

**decision maker**   the person who makes the final decision

**decline stage**   that stage of the product life cycle when sales decline and products are removed from the market

**defender**   an organization classified as one that aims to find and secure stable product market positions, offers a limited range of products, avoids the forefront of technology, ignores dynamic events on the outside of its core area of operation, and defends market position with low price, quality, and service

**defensive strategies**   strategies designed to minimize loss

**demand elasticity**   the percentage change in sales relative to the percentage change in price

**demand planning**   a strategy of attempting to influence demand for products and services made by your company so that the supply chain can be managed most efficiently

**dependence balancing**   a means of safeguarding a relationship by which one party reduces its dependence on the exchange partner by cultivating relationships with other exchange partners, perhaps making itself less replaceable in the exchange or giving itself new options to the current exchange relationship

**dependent variables**   the effects or outcomes of an experiment or statistical model

**derived demand**   situation in which demand for a firm's products and services is derived from the demand for its customers' products and services (whose demand may also be derived)

**desire**   the third stage of the hierarchy-of-effects model; the recognition by the buyer that when the needs occur, the advertised brand is the brand or product to buy (or the company to visit at the trade show, or the home page to visit, etc.)

**desk jobber**   a channel intermediary that takes title, buying products from a supplier, but never taking physical possession; instead products are delivered directly to the user. Also called a **drop shipper**

**development stage**   that stage in the product's life when it is being designed and readied for market

**direct influence**   the application of a social influence tactic that seeks certain behaviors without first changing attitudes toward the product or company. It relies on human tendencies to respond almost "automatically" to influence attempts based on scarcity ("while supplies last"), reciprocity ("order today and we'll also provide the travel alarm and free shipping"), and authority ("3 out of 4 doctors recommend"), among others. For harried buyers in a message-cluttered environment the marcomm manager applies these tactics believing that buyer action (e.g., trial) can be an effective precursor to attitudes and the attainment of positioning goals (liking and loyalty)

**direct marketing**   an interactive form of marketing using one or more advertising media to effect a measurable response and/or transaction at any location, with this activity stored on database

**dissolution**   termination of an advanced relationship

**diversification**   a growth strategy by which a firm aims to serve new markets with new products

**dogs**   products with low share in a poor market

**dormant accounts**   accounts that have stopped buying

**downsize**   to lower the number of employees through early retirement and layoffs

**draw**   a loan paid to the salesperson to provide him with stable cash flow; it is repaid from the salesperson's commission

**drop shipper**   a channel intermediary that takes title, buying products from a supplier, but never taking physical possession; instead products are delivered directly to the user. Also called a **desk jobber**

**dyadic relationships**   a concept of business relationships in which there are only two parties: one buyer and one seller

# e

**early supplier involvement (ESI)**   an outsourcing strategy whereby companies use suppliers to help design new products or processes

**economic order quantity (EOQ)**   the quantity that minimizes both ordering and storing costs

**elastic demand**   situation in which the quantity demanded of a product is highly sensitive to changes in its price

**electronic data interchange (EDI)**   the use of electronic transmission of data between buyer and seller to order and maintain product inventory

**empathic dialogue**   active listening and identification with customer concerns, resulting in customer-centered communication and problem solving

**engineer to order**   complete customization, with the product designed from scratch to meet the customer's needs

**environmental factors**   those characteristics of the world beyond the market level; includes the economy, technology, political factors, and social factors

**ethics**   moral codes of conduct; rules for how someone should operate that can be utilized as situations demand

**evoked set**   the products of which the buyer is aware

**exclusivity** (e.g., distribution or territory exclusivity)   a pledge to supply no other resellers in the trade area

**exit**   a means of managing conflict by leaving a relationship

**expansion stage** (of a developing relationship)   stage characterized by the association progressing from one of testing and probing to one of enlarging rewards and the scope of exchange

**experiments**   the systematic manipulation of variables to allow the detection of cause-and-effect relationships

**expert power**   the ability to gain a target firm's compliance based on that target's belief that the source is knowledgeable

**exploration stage** (of a developing relationship)   we find the parties probing and testing each other. Initial purchases can take place in this stage, but they are part of a trial process. The relationship is very fragile. The parties have not significantly invested in the exchange. Neither party depends highly on the other. The association is easily terminated

**extrinsic rewards**   rewards given by the organization

# f

**facilitating supplies** or **facilitating services**   support company efforts but are not part of the final product

**factoring**   approach to market size estimation in which estimates come from calculating the value of various materials or parts units needed (factors) in a specific application or from specific accounts. Also called **buildup approach**

**features**   physical characteristics of the tangible item or service

**field salespeople** (also called **outside salespeople**) salespeople who visit accounts at the accounts' locations

**field testing**    see **beta testing**

**financial risk** (also called **economic risk**)    risk associated with the cost of the new product and with the potential for lost revenue if the product breaks down or doesn't perform as advertised

**first-mover advantage**    a significant competitive advantage gained by being the first in the market

**five forces of competition**    industry rivals, powerful suppliers, powerful customers, threat of potential entrants, and substitutes

**fixed-price**    agreement that means that if it costs more to build an item than thought, the supplier has to cover the higher costs

**focus groups**    a method of qualitative marketing research that brings a small group of customers together to discuss a specific topic or issue, under the direction of a professional moderator

**formalization**    the degree to which purchasing tasks and roles are defined by written documents describing procedures and policies

**forward buying**    buying in larger quantities than are currently needed because the discount is greater than the carrying costs

**frequency**    the number of times a potential buyer is exposed to an ad

**full-function wholesalers**    intermediaries that hold title and provide a broad array of services for their suppliers and customers

**full-line selling**    selling the entire line of associated products

**functional discount**    a discount given to a purchaser based on the purchaser's role in the supplier's distributive system, reflecting, at least in a generalized sense, the services performed by the purchaser for the supplier

**functional structure**    organization by marketing function

**gap analysis**    a set of tools for comparing performance outcomes or expectations on specific criteria

**gatekeepers**    control information into and out of the buying group, or between members of the group

**generative, or double loop, learning**    the creation of knowledge that occurs when changing assumptions and beliefs

**geographic salesperson**    the most basic sales force structure, giving each salesperson all accounts within a specified geographic area

**global account manager (GAM)**    a salesperson who calls on the headquarters of an account that buys centrally for implementation or delivery globally; the salesperson is responsible for developing account strategy for the entire account although local salespeople may call on offices around the world. See also **national account manager**

**growth stage**    that part of the product life cycle when sales and profits grow at a fast rate, following the introduction stage

**hierarchy of effects**    a model used by many companies when planning communication campaigns because it describes the successive stages through which the audience progresses when interacting with marketing communications

**horizontal dimension**    a dimension of the buying center or how many departments are involved

**horizontal shows**    trade shows that include many industries and professions

**house account**    an account handled by a sales executive in which the company does not pay anyone commission on sales from the account

**identifiable**    a criterion for a good segmentation approach; it means that members of market segments can be enumerated and evaluated

**import quotas**    limits on the amount of a product that may be imported

**inbound telemarketing**    calls initiated by the customer or potential customer (compare with **outbound telemarketing**)

**independent variables**    the factors we manipulate in an experiment (price, headlines, telephone script, copy strategy, etc.) or control by selection in our marketing program (size of firms targeted, list source, time since last purchase, etc.)

**individual factors** demographic and psychographic factors, or psychological factors that influence an individual's buying behavior

**industrial distributors** merchant wholesalers, including a number of subtypes that differ in the functions they perform

**inelastic demand** situation in which the quantity demanded is not very price sensitive

**influencers** individuals who seek to affect the decision maker's final decision through recommendations of which vendors to include or which products are best suited to solve the organization's needs

**information power** a source of potential influence residing in a channel member's reliance on facts and figures, models, and insights from its partner

**information system** the mechanism for storing information, providing access to the information, and manipulating that information

**initiator** starts the purchase process by recognizing the need

**inside salespeople** salespeople who sell at their company's location

**instrumentality** the likelihood that if they successfully engage in certain actions, those actions will yield the rewards they want

**in-suppliers** suppliers whose products are ordered automatically in a straight rebuy

**integrated marketing communications (IMC)** strategic, two-way communication targeted to specific customers and their needs coordinated through a variety of media

**interest** the second step of the hierarchy-of-effects model; reflects the buyer's desire to learn more about what (e.g. product, brand, company) is being discussed in the marketing communication

**internal partnering** creating partnering relationships with other functional areas (customers and suppliers within the firm)

**intrabrand competition** price pressure from sellers of the same brand

**intrinsic rewards** rewards people give themselves (feelings of satisfaction, for example)

**introduction stage** the second stage of the product life cycle; here the product is first introduced to the market and potential customers are learning what the product is and does

**investment risk** the risk that is present when a company decides to go ahead with the product and, should it fail, the company would lose some or all of the investment

**JIT relationship** a form of buyer–seller partnership that requires the supplier to produce and deliver to the OEM precisely the necessary quantities at the necessary time, with the objective that products produced by the supplier conform to performance specification every time

**just-in-time (JIT)** the concept of shipping products such that they arrive at the customer's location exactly when needed

**justice** rendering what is merited or due

*keiretsu* in Japan, a family of companies (literally) in which members of companies sit on the boards of directors of their customers or suppliers

**key account** a large or high-volume customer, often assigned a specific sales representative

**known requisites** requirements for success that have been identified by the firm

**lagniappe** anything given beyond strict obligation; a surprise or surplus benefit from an exchange

**lead users** buyers or users who face needs that will be general in the marketplace, but they recognize these needs months or years before the market is aware, and/or they are able to generate solutions to needs independently of manufacturers or suppliers

**leapfrog** to introduce a product that is at least one step better technologically than other products already available

**learning** the connection of new information to what we already know

**learning boundaries**   an organization's assumptions and beliefs that limit learning

**learning curve**   the tendency of costs to decline with repetition or cumulative experience

**learning laboratories**   environments set aside for learning

**learning organization**   one that consistently creates and refines its capabilities by connecting new information and skills to known and remembered requisites for future success

**legal legitimate power**   explicit authority over certain behaviors granted to the source in a sales agreement or contract

**lifetime value (LTV)**   an estimate of the net present value of the stream of benefits from a customer, less the burdens of servicing the account or managing the relationship

**limited-function wholesalers**   channel intermediaries that take title but don't provide the full spectrum of services, perhaps stocking just a single line of products or extending no credit or no delivery

**line and staff organization**   an organizational structure in which those who conduct the primary tasks of the department are part of the line—their managers are called line managers—and all support personnel are staff

**lobbying**   any attempt to persuade a government official or governing body to adopt policies, procedures, or legislation in favor of the lobbying group or organization

**location restrictions**   contractual agreements in distribution channels specifying the site or sites from which the product may be sold by intermediaries

**loose lead strategies**   attempt to generate as many leads as possible, relying on a qualifying process to sort out good leads from bad

**lost-for-good**   a classification of customer relationships characterized by the prospects of a customer making a costly switch to a competitor followed by a costly return to the incumbent being remote—probably weaker prospects than a cold call prospect

**loyalty**   steadfast perseverance in the face of conflict's felt tension or abuse

**make-or-buy**   a comparison of the value of a product or service created internally versus if created by someone else

**make to order**   manufacturing or production begins making the product after receiving an order

**make to stock**   marketing supplies forecasts of demand, and manufacturing makes enough to handle that demand

**manufactured material**   material that has been transformed from raw material and requires further processing before the user can use it

**manufacturers' agents**   agents who do not take title but sell the lines of noncompeting principals for a commission

**manufacturers' sales branches and offices**   wholesaling operations that a manufacturer owns and operates

**market attractiveness**   a composite measure of the potential for sales and profits in a particular market segment for a particular company's portfolio of products

**market development**   a growth strategy in which a firm markets its current products to new markets

**market factors**   characteristics of the market that influence buyer behavior

**market orientation**   superior skills of understanding and satisfying customers via (1) the systematic gathering of information on customers and competitors, both present and potential, (2) the systematic analysis of the information for the purpose of developing market knowledge, and (3) the systematic use of such knowledge to guide strategy recognition, understanding, creation, selection, implementation, and modification

**market penetration**   an endeavor to gain a larger share of the market in which a firm currently competes using its existing products

**market position**   the strength of the company relative to competitors; can be measured by market share, but should also reflect forecasts of future share; used in the sales resource allocation grid to determine sales force allocation

**market sensing**   anticipating market requirements ahead of competition

**marketing audit**   a comprehensive and systematic evaluation of the firm's marketing operation and the environment in which it operates

**marketing channels**   systems organized to deliver products and related services

**marketing control system**   the system that measures actual performance against planned performance, measures productivity and profit by types of products, customers, or territories, and measures other key marketing variables such as customer satisfaction

**matrix sales team**   a form of team selling in which several product specialists work with several account managers

**maturity stage**   the third stage of the product life cycle, when sales level off

**media kit**   material to support staged events; contains information about the event and key information for publication in news stories; usually given to members of the press

**media plan**   an element of advertising strategy which involves choosing the channel of communication

**merchant wholesalers**   channel intermediaries that take title to the merchandise

**minority subcontracting**   programs that require general contractors and other major suppliers to allocate a certain percentage of the total contract to minority-owned subcontractors

**mission statement**   a formal expression of why the organization exists

**modified rebuys**   the process would include most or perhaps all of the steps in a new buy

**modularity**   a system composed of distinct subsystems or components

**monochronic time**   a linear perspective of time that is part of the culture of Americans (and Swiss, Germans, and Scandinavians) in which they divide time into small units, with only one activity per unit, and are obsessed with promptness

**monopolistic competition**   a market in which there are a large number of differentiated sellers, such as corporate training companies, custom marketing research firms, and industrial distributors. The actions of one firm have effects on others, but each seller brings some unique competency to the market and offers distinctively valued services and products. Each firm faces a downward-sloping demand curve

**motivation**   the amount of effort that the buyer is willing to expend to engage in that set of tasks

**MRO or maintenance, repair, and operations products**   products sold to users for use in the company's operations are often labeled MRO items

**multiattribute model**   model based on the idea that people view products as a collection of attributes or "bundle of benefits"; provides a picture of how alternatives are evaluated

**multilevel selling**   where members of a selling organization at various levels call on their counterparts in the buying organization; a form of team selling

**NAICS** (pronounced "knacks")   North American Industrial Classification System establishes a common code between the United States, Canada, and Mexico that is compatible with the United Nations' two-digit system of industry classification, ISIC

**national account manager (NAM)**   a salesperson who calls on the headquarters of an account who buys centrally for implementation or delivery nationwide; the salesperson is responsible for developing account strategy for the entire nation. See also **global account manager**

**needs satisfaction selling**   a process of selling that involves identifying the buyer's needs and tailoring the sales pitch to fit those needs

**neglect**   to leave the conflict untreated, perhaps allowing the relationship to atrophy or fade in significance

**negotiation**   method of decision making by give-and-take bargaining that is used to resolve conflicts

**net buying influences**   the percentage of a trade show audience that has influence in the buying process for the specific product exhibited

**network**   a web of companies sharing relationships with many other companies; these relationships are governed by reciprocity of ties, dependencies, and shared values

**new buys**   products or services never purchased before

**news release** (or **press release**)   a brief memo or report containing news information, such as the announcement of a new product, an award, or changes in management

**nondisclosure agreement**   an agreement that the parties involved will not share any information about the new products with anyone who has not also signed that agreement

**norms**   standards of behavior for the parties in a relationship; the guidelines by which the parties interact

**North American Industrial Classification System**   see **NAICS**

**objective and task**   see **budget buildup**

**offensive strategies**   strategies designed to maximize gain

**offering**   the complete package or bundle of benefits that includes how easy the product is to buy, how it has to be paid for, services that help the buyer get full value from the product's use, and sometimes assistance in disposing of the residual product when finished with it

**oligopolies**   markets characterized by just a few sellers, each offering a product that is quite similar to the others. Entry barriers tend to be high and pricing latitude very limited

**open bidding**   where any organization can submit a bid to vie for the business a buyer promises

**operational measures** measures of productivity, process (or operations) effectiveness, and other elements that impact customer satisfaction

**opportunity risk** the risk that occurs when a company decides to kill a product and thereby lose all of the revenue that could have been gained if it had been a success

**organizational buying behavior** how purchases are made within organizations

**organizational culture** the collectively held values, ideology, and social processes embedded in a firm

**organizational factors** characteristics of the organization that influence buying behavior; includes the size of the company, profitability, corporate culture, distribution of power, organizational policy, and other factors

**organizational learning** the process of developing new knowledge with the potential to influence behavior (or decisions) within an organization

**original equipment manufacturer (OEM)** a company that purchases a product or service to be included in its own final product

**outbound telemarketing** selling via telephone with the call made by the marketer (compare with **inbound telemarketing**)

**outside salespeople** see **field salespeople**

**outsourcing** the process of finding another organization to supply the buying organization with a product or service, usually one that was previously created in-house

**out-suppliers** suppliers whose products are not considered in a straight rebuy

**partnership** a relationship characterized by mutual commitment, high trust, and common goals

**partnership purchasing** or **preferred supplier system** system that seeks to maximize the benefits of collaboration between the buyer and a few suppliers

**payback** the amount of time needed for savings or revenues to equal costs or investments

**performance quota** a quota that specifies levels of outcomes, or performance, such as revenue, gross margin, or unit sales in a period of time

**performance risk** the risk that the product will not perform as intended

**personal selling** interpersonal communication in which one person attempts to secure a purchase from another person

**polychronic time** a perspective in non-U.S. and non-European cultures in which time is viewed in terms of the simultaneous occurrence of many things and with more involvement with people

**position** a product's place in the mind of the buyer

**positioning** a loosely used term that generally refers to marketing efforts to secure a valued categorization in the mind of a customer

**power** an ability of one organization, Alpha, to get another organization, Beta, to do what it would not do otherwise; it derives from Beta's dependence on Alpha for valued resources that are not easily obtained elsewhere

**preferred supplier** a status conferred by a buyer that grants a supplier an assured (usually large) percentage of the buyer's business and first opportunity to earn any new business

**press agentry** the planning and staging of an event in order to generate publicity

**press kit** (or **media kit**) material to support staged events; contains information about the event and key information for publication in news stories; given to writers for trade and general business publications

**price** the amount of money paid by a buyer to a seller for a particular product or service

**price discrimination** sellers charge different prices on similar products

**primary demand** buyer demand for a type of product, rather than for a specific company's product

**principal** the manufacturer or other person or firm who contracts for the services of the agent in its own behalf

**product** a bundle of benefits; a collection of solutions to needs and wants

**product development** an effort to serve customers in markets where a firm already has a presence using a new array of products

**product life cycle (PLC)** a cycle of stages that a product, technology platform, or product category goes through, from development, introduction, growth, and maturity to decline

**product line** a group of products that share a technology platform

**product portfolio management** methods of managing all products simultaneously as you would a financial portfolio, balancing risk and return among all product investments

**prospect** someone for whom we know of their needs, budget, and time frame for purchase

**prospector** an organization classified as likely to be a first mover, to detect early signals of opportunity and move on them, to compete in new markets or with new marketing methods, and to operate in many product markets

**prospector** (telemarketing position) the telemarketer supports the efforts of one or several field reps in finding and qualifying prospective customers

**public affairs** the part of PR that deals with community groups; there are two types of public affairs: lobbying and community involvement

**public relations (PR)** the management function that focuses on the relationships and communications with individuals and groups in order to create mutual goodwill

**publicity** the generation of news about a person, product, or organization; appears in broadcast or electronic media

**pull strategy** direct communication with end users to differentiate the product through the media

**purchasing agent** the person who actually makes the purchase

**push strategy** the general approach of supporting and rewarding reseller activities to differentiate the brand among customers

**Quality Function Deployment (QFD)** a process of linking customer needs to product attributes during the design process

**question marks** products in high growth markets that currently have low market share

**quota** a useful control mechanism for sales force management that represents a quantitative minimum level of acceptable performance for a specific time period

**random variance** that variance caused by uncontrollable and unidentified causes

**raw materials** materials processed only to the point required for economic handling and distribution

**reach** the total number of buyers that see an ad

**reactor** an organization classified as one that lacks a well-defined strategy, has an inconsistent product mix; is not a risk taker, and is not aggressive; generally takes action under environmental pressures

**reciprocation** a similar action returned by the other—for example, a seller's price concession in response to purchaser's commitment to an annual level of total purchases

**reengineering** the process of designing work processes in order to achieve objectives; reengineering reflects the fact that most processes have evolved over time, serving objectives that may no longer be considered relevant

**referent power** the potential to influence another based on the other's desire to identify with or be like the source firm

**relational contracts** contracts that don't try to bring every future contingency up for consideration in the present, but establish means of continuous planning, adjusting, and resolving conflicts; relational contracts can specify decision-making authority by issue (material standards, shutdowns, training, and maintenance) and establish procedures or structures for planning to ensure ongoing effective exchange

**reporting systems** formal mechanisms for creating and sharing information, generally involving the flow of information either up or down the organization

**response lists** the house files (direct order customers and inquirers) of other companies

**reward power** the ability to provide payoffs to a party for specified behaviors or outcomes

**risk** usually thought of in terms of the probability of an outcome and the importance or cost associated with the outcome

**Robinson–Patman Act (1936)** prohibits price discrimination when sellers charge different prices on like products to customers who are in competition and the effect is likely to lessen competition substantially

**role theory** suggests that people behave within a set of norms or expectations of others due to the role in which they have been placed

**rolling launch** to launch a new product in certain areas, rolling to (launching in) new areas as support personnel are trained and ready

**safeguarded relationships** relationships that are protected through contracts

**sales potential**   the total forecasted sales for a product category in a single account or sales territory

**sales resource allocation grid**   a method to determine workload that focuses on sales potential and market position to determine which accounts should be the focus of sales resources

**sample survey**   a questionnaire administered to a representative group of a particular population

**scenario**   a focused description of different futures presented in a coherent manner; a forecasting technique that requires managers to write explicit anticipated futures and articulate the chains of events that would need to occur to make the future happen; a method used for organizational learning

**script-based selling**   using scripts or memorized sales pitches from which the salesperson does not deviate

**search engine marketing (SEM)**   the marketer may bid on key search terms and thereby have its firm name appear when a potential customer searches using that term. The bid level is what the marketer offers to pay per click on its site when sought this way

**search engine optimization (SEO)**   an effort by organizations to manage the key word content of their Web pages and the number of external links to their site on other sites in order to come up on the first page of searches. Leading agencies have staff specialists who strive to be abreast of the latest criteria and algorithms used by the major search engines. They can then help their clients design their Web sites and suggest bloggers and other sites in the market space from whom it would be advantageous to be linked

**secondary demand**   demand for a particular vendor's offering or product

**self-efficacy**   a perception by a person in which she considers her own ability to carry out the tasks

**self-orientation**   the degree to which the individual works to achieve personal benefit

**sensor**   any measuring tool used in observing marketing performance

**services**   the application of specialized competences (skills and knowledge) through acts or processes for the benefit of another

**SIC**   Standard Industrial Classification codes were developed by the U.S. government to collect and disseminate meaningful information on different sectors of the economy

**single-line wholesalers**   limited-function wholesalers that don't carry a full assortment of items

**single sourcing**   occurs when a company selects one supplier to satisfy all needs in a given area

**social relationship**   a trading association supported principally by social bonds and habit; this organic dimension is the degree to which social bonds are part of the business relationship

**social risk** (also called **ego risk**)   risk that the purchase will not meet the approval of an important reference group

**spanning processes**   processes that link internal processes with the customer

**specialty advertising**   the use of products to advertise another product or company; for example, putting a company's name on pens and pencils, and then giving them away

**specialty wholesaler**   firm carrying a vary narrow line and supporting it with technical expertise and consultative selling

**specific investments**   the dedication of assets that have sharply reduced value outside the relationship, including investments in people, locations, procedures, equipment, and more that have real value only within a particular relationship

**split premiums**   a form of specialty advertising in which half of the freebie is mailed to the prospect; the other half is given to the prospect after he listens to a sales pitch at a trade show booth or after a visit by a salesperson

**spot exchanges**   money traded for easily measured commodities. Communication content is quite narrow between transacting parties and their identity is hardly relevant. Trading terms are simple and clear. Performance is practically immediate

**standard**   the goal against which marketing performance is compared in a marketing performance evaluation system

**Standard Industrial Classification codes**   see **SIC**

**stars**   products whose market growth is high in a market in which the products also have high market share

**statistical series**   an estimation technique that uses the correlation between demand and some other set of economic activities to yield a forecast

**straight commission**   a compensation plan that pays a certain amount for each sale, but there is no salary; see **commission base** and **commission rate**

**straight rebuy**   a purchase made with the vendor of the previous purchase, without any shopping or examining of other vendors

**straight salary**   a compensation plan in which a salesperson is paid a fixed amount of money for work during a specified time

**strategic sourcing**   the process of designing and managing supply networks networks to optimize operational and organization

**strategic goals**   what a company wants an overall strategy to accomplish

**strategic partner selling**   a sales strategy in which both parties share expertise and resources to create customized solutions, and there is a commitment to joint planning for mutual benefit

**strategic partnership**   results when both parties have keen interests in maintaining an ongoing exchange relationship. The strategic essence of the partnership rests on the significance of the resources and long-run consequences of the efforts

**strategic sourcing**   the process of designing and managing supply networks to optimize operational and organization performance

**strategy**   the science and art of conducting a campaign—achieving some end—on a broad scale, involving significant resources and long-run implications

**subsidies**   payments by a government that lower operating costs in order to make the country's companies more competitive

**substantial**   a market segment promises sufficient business to justify the efforts to serve it, a criterion of a good segmentation approach

**sugging**   the unethical practice of using marketing research as a guise for selling

**sunk cost**   an irretrievable cost or investment

**supplier relationship management (SRM)**   using computer models to identify the most valuable suppliers and to identify purchasing opportunities

**supplier verification**   formal efforts to obtain evidence of supplier capabilities and commitment

**supply chain management**   is proactively planning and coordinating the flow of products, services, and information among connected firms focusing on creating and delivering value to end users

**supragoal**   a goal against which other goals are aligned

**switching costs**   the forgone value of investments, the economic penalties, and the other expenses associated with finding, evaluating, and replacing a current supplier with a new one

**SWOT analysis**   a self-assessment framework for examining a firm's **S**trengths and **W**eaknesses, and **O**pportunities and **T**hreats

**synergy**   a situation in which the whole is greater than the sum of its parts

**systematic variance**   a change in performance outcomes due to changing systems and creating a new tolerance

**tactic**   decisions that have a narrow scope, involve limited resources, and have only short-run consequences, in contrast to **strategy**

**tactical goals**   desired outcomes for specific actions

**tariffs**   taxes on imported goods

**team selling**   the term for when a group of salespeople handle a single account and each salesperson brings a different area of expertise or handles different responsibilities

**technology platform**   the core technology that is often the basis for a product line or group of products

**telemarketing**   the systematic and continuous program of personally communicating with (potential) customers via telephone and/or other electronic media

**telequalify**   the telephonic process by which a list owner or compiler periodically verifies names, titles, addresses, and other data in the list, improving the quality of the list for direct marketers

**territorial restriction**   a contractual provision between supplier and reseller confining the reseller's activities to a particular geographic zone

**tight lead strategies**   direct marketing efforts seeking responses (especially inquiries) from individuals who are already highly qualified as potential customers

**time fragmentation**   one characteristic of buying centers, which is that members come and go

**tinkering**   making changes within a process in order to make the process more productive, by either reducing defects or increasing volume

**tolerance**   a range of acceptable performance, used when applying statistical process control to any work process, including marketing processes

**total buying plans**   the percentage of the audience planning to buy exhibited products within the next 12 months

**total cost of ownership**   the total amount expended in order to own a product or use a service

**touchpoint**   point in time or place where a customer interacts with the company

**trade publications**   magazines written for a specific profession, industry, or trade

**trade shows**   temporary exhibitions of products and services, somewhat like shopping malls for industrial products

**traditional legitimate power**   the ability of the source firm to influence the behavior of the target firm because cultural norms support the right of the source

**transactional relationships**   situations in which buyers and sellers interact with only selfish consideration, without thought of the possibility of future interaction

**truck jobber**   a wholesaler that carries all its inventory on a truck and services customers on a frequent basis or a route

**trust**   the belief that a party's work or promise is reliable and a party will fulfill his or her obligations in an exchange relationship

**upgrading (upselling)**   convincing the buyer to use a higher-quality product or newer product

**user**   the business equivalent of the final consumer

**user**   part of the buying center that tries to influence the decision; sometimes, other influencers will represent the users' perspective

**valence**   the degree of importance or value attached to a reward

**value**   the buyer's perception of benefit beyond the cost; the buyer's version of profit from a purchase

**value analysis**   a thorough review of the costs and value associated with a component part

**value chain**   system of value creation (each organization adds its value to whatever it is that the system is creating)

**vertical dimension**   a dimension of the buying center or how many layers of management are involved

**vertical integration**   bringing a function or technology within the boundary of the firm; ensures continuity in the relationship because suppliers are now hierarchically connected employees. That is, employees work in an environment of formal rules, authority, reporting structures, and special responsibilities. Goals tend to be shared and, overall, control of activities is enhanced

**vertical show**   a trade show that focuses on one industry or profession

**voice**   a response to conflict that involves articulating the perceived state or source of conflict

**volatility**   wide swings in demand that are caused by derived demand

**workload**   all of the activities that a salesperson must do to cover a territory

# Endnotes

## Chapter 1

1. Salt Institute, 1995 statistics provided by McLean, VA.

2. Philip Buskens, "The Four Pillars of BASF in One Project," My BASF Story, **http://www.my-basf-story.basf.com,** accessed June 4, 2007.

## Chapter 2

1. James P. Morgan, "Cessna Charts a Supply Chain Flight Strategy," *Purchasing* 129 (September 7, 2000), pp. 42–61.

2. *On Liberty,* People's ed. (London: Longmans, Green & Co. 1865), summarized in Milton Friedman and Rose Friedman, *Free to Choose* (New York: Harcourt, Brace, Jovanovich, 1980).

3. See Thomas V. Scannell, Shawnee K. Vickery, and Cornelia L. Droge, "Upstream Supply Chain Management and Competitive Performance in the Automotive Supply Industry," *Journal of Business Logistics* 21, no. 1 (2000), pp. 23–48.

4. Elana Epatko Murphy and Clarissa Cruz, "Real Payoffs Result when Suppliers Join in VA Effort," *Purchasing* (November 23, 1995), pp. 22–23.

5. F. Robert Dwyer, Paul H. Schurr, and Sejo Oh, "Developing Buyer-Seller Relationships," *Journal of Marketing* 52 (April 1987), pp. 11–27.

6. Katheryn Belyea, "Career Development Q & A. Gene Richter: How to Be a Leader," *Purchasing* (September 7, 2000), pp. 92–93.

7. Gary Frazier, Robert Spekman, and Charles R. O'Neal, "Just-in-Time Exchange Relationships in Industrial Markets," *Journal of Marketing* 52 (October 1983), pp. 52–67.

8. Susan Helper, "How Much Has Really Changed between U.S. Automakers and Their Suppliers?" *Sloan Management Review* 32 (Summer 1991), pp. 15–28. Anil Kumar and Graham Sharman, "We Love Your Product, But Where Is It?" *Sloan Management Review* 33 (Winter 1992), pp. 93–99.

9. See also Elizabeth J. Wilson and Richard P. Vlosky, "Partnering Relationship Activities: Building Theory from Case Study Research," *Journal of Business Research* 31 (May 1997), pp. 59–64.

10. Theodore Levitt, "After the Sale Is Over . . . ," *Harvard Business Review* 61 (September–October 1983), pp. 87–93.

11. James Comer and B. J. Zirger, "Building a Supplier-Customer Relationship Using Joint New Product Development," paper presented at the World Marketing Conference, 1995, Sydney, Australia.

12. J. Scanzoni, "Social Exchange and Behavioral Interdependence," in *Social Exchange in Developing Relationships,* eds. R. L. Burgess and T. L. Huston (New York: Academic Press, 1979), p. 72.

13. Thomas Leigh and Arno Rethans, "A Script-Theoretic Analysis of Industrial Purchasing Behavior," *Journal of Marketing* 48 (Fall 1984), pp. 22–32.

14. Paul Schurr and Julie Ozanne, "Influences on Exchange Processes: Buyers' Preconceptions of a Seller's Trustworthiness and Bargaining Toughness," *Journal of Consumer Research* 11 (March 1985), pp. 939–53.

15. Sandy D. Jap and Erin Anderson, "Testing a Life-Cycle Theory of Cooperative Interorganizational Relationships: Movement across Stages and Performance," *Management Science* 53 (February 2007), pp. 260–75.

16. Robert Ping and F. Robert Dwyer, "A Preliminary Model of Relationship Termination in Marketing Channels," in *Advances in Distribution Channels Research,* ed. Gary Frazier (Greeenwich, CT: JAI Press, Inc., 1992), pp. 215–34.

17. For a good overview, see Robert M. March, "Managing Business Relationships with East Asia: Building and Pilot Testing a Model of Long-Term Asian/Western Business Relationships," Working paper 3/1997, University of Western Sidney, Nepean, 1997.

18. Lance Dixon, "JIT II at Intel," *Purchasing* (May 19, 1994), p. 19.

19. Jan B. Heide and George John, "The Role of Dependence Balancing in Safeguarding Transaction-Specific Assets in Conventional Channels," *Journal of Marketing* 52 (January 1988), pp. 20–37.

20. Erin Anderson and Barton Weitz, "The Use of Pledges to Build and Sustain Commitment in Distribution Channels," *Journal of Marketing Research* 29 (February 1992), pp. 18–34. Sandy D. Jap and Erin Anderson, "Safeguarding Interorganizational Performance and Continuity under Ex Post Opportunism," *Management Science* 49 (December 2003), pp. 1684–1701.

21. Paul H. Rubin, *Managing Business Transactions: Controlling the Cost of Coordinationg, Communicating, and Decision Making* (New York: The Free Press, 1990).

22. Ian Macneil, "Economic Analysis of Contractual Relations: Its Shortfalls and the Need for a 'Rich Classificatory Apparatus,' " *Northwestern University Law Review* 75 (February 1981), pp. 1018–63; Thomas Palay, "Comparative Institutional Economics: The Governance of Rail Freight Contracting," *Journal of Legal Studies* 13 (June 1984), pp. 265–87.

23. Dale Buss, "Growing More by Doing Less," *Nation's Business* (December 1995), pp. 18–21.

24. Rebecca Morales, "Product Development and Production Networks: The Case of the Mexican Automotive Industry," *Journal of Industry Studies* 1 (October 1993), pp. 30–42.

25. "Best Practices: Dunnhumby Shops for Marketing Insight," **http://wwwoptimisemag.com/article/showArticle.jhtml? articleID=19700211&pg no=3** (viewed June 7, 2007); **http:// www.dunrmumby.com/relevance/case_kroger.htm** (viewed June 7, 2007); "Data-mining Central to Kroger Rebound Strategy," **http://www.swlearnin.com/marketing/marketing_ news/research_1106_001.html** (viewed June 7, 2007).

26. Jim Tompkins, "Beyond Supply Chain Management," *Supply Chain Management Review* (March–April 2000), pp. 77–82.

27. **www.verticalnet.com/about.**

28. Kristian Moller and David Wilson, eds. *Business Marketing: An Interaction and Network Perspective* (Boston: Kluwer Academic Publisher, 1995), pp. 10–11.

## Chapter 3

1. Paul E. Teague, "How to Select a Sourcing Strategy," *Purchasing* 136 (May 2007), p. 51.

2. M. G. Anderson and P. B. Katz, "Strategic Sourcing," *International Journal of Logistics Management* 9 (1998) pp. 1–14; S. M. Wagner, "A Strategic Approach to Professional Supplier Management," *National Productivity Review* (2000), pp. 21–29.

3. Thomas E. Hendrick and William A. Ruch, "Determining Performance Appraisal Criteria for Buyers," *Journal of Purchasing and Materials Management* (Summer 1988), pp. 18–26.

4. Paul E. Teague, "Change the Way You Source," *Purchasing* 136 (May 2007), p. 49.

5. "Adopting Suppliers," *Purchasing Executive Bulletin* (May 25, 1994), pp. 1–3.

6. Tomi Ventovyori, "Elements of Sourcing Strategies in FM Services—A Multiple Case Study," *International Journal of Strategic Property Management* 10, no. 4, 2006, 249–68.

7. A. Akacum and B. G. Dale, "Supplier Partnering: Case Study Experiences," *International Journal of Purchasing and Materials Management* (January 1995), pp. 38–44. Lingyun Wang and Pekka Kess "Partnering Motives and Partner Selection: Case Studies of Finnish Distributor Relationships in China," *International Journal of Physical Distribution & Logistics Management* 36, no. 6, 2006, 466–82.

8. Rodney L. Stump, "Antecedents of Purchasing Concentration: A Transaction Cost Explanation," *Journal of Business Research* 34 (1995), pp. 145–57.

9. Klotz and Chatterjee, "Dual Sourcing."

10. Morry Ghingold and David Wilson, "Buying Center Research and Business Marketing Practice: Meeting the Challenge of Dynamic Marketing," *Journal of Business and Industrial Marketing* 13 (1998), pp. 96–108.

11. Barton A. Weitz, Stephen B. Castleberry, and John F. Tanner, Jr., *Selling: Building Partnerships* 6e, Burr Ridge IL: McGraw-Hill.

12. Ram Narasimhan and Ajay Das, "An Empirical Investigation of the Contribution of Strategic Sourcing to Manufacturing Flexibilities and Performance," *Decision Science*s 30, no. 3 (1999), 683–718.

13. Sidney Hill, Jr., "The New Rules for Global Supply Chain Management," Manufacturing Business Technology 25, no. 4 (2007), 22; Kenneth B. Kahn, Elliot Maltz, and John T. Mentzer, "Demand Collaboration: Effects on Knowledge Creation, Relationships, And Supply Chain Performance," *Journal of Business Logistics* 27, no. 2, 191–222.

14. Hitachi Consulting, "Six Key Trends Changing Supply Chain Management Today," Hitachi Consulting Corporation White Paper, 2005; Tim A. Minahan, "5 Strategies for High-Performance Procurement," *Supply Chain Management Review* 9, no. 6 (2006), 46–54.

15. Cemal Zehir, A. Zafer Acar, and Haluk Tanriverdi, "Identifying Organizational Capabilities as Predictors of Growth and Business Performance," *The Business Review* 5, no. 2 (2006), 109–16.

16. Tanuja Singh Geoffrey Gordon, and Sharon Purchase, "B2B E-Marketing Strategies of Multinational Corporations: Empirical Evidence from the United States and Australia," *Mid-American Journal of Business* 22, no. 1 (2007), 31–44.

17. Chris Fill and Elke Visser, "The Outsourcing Dilemma: A Composite Approach to the Make or Buy Decision," *Management Decision* 38 (2000), pp. 43–50.

18. "Adopting Suppliers," *Purchasing Executive Bulletin* (May 25, 1994), pp. 1–3.

19. Jeffrey A. Ogden, "Supply Base Reduction: An Empirical Study of Critical Success Factors," *Journal of Supply Chain Management* 42, no. 4 (2006), pp. 29–39.

20. Matt Barnason, "Keeping Suppliers Competitive," *SAS.com Magazine* (third quarter, 2003), pp. 15–16.

21. Martha Cooper, Douglas Lambert, and James Pagh, "Supply Chai Management: More Than a New Name for Logistics," *International Journal of Logistics Management* 8 (Winter 1997), p. 1.

22. James Carbone, "Time-to-Market Is Key," *Purchasing* 136, no. 4 (2007), p. 30.

23. Charles Dominick, "The 2005 Purchasing Skills Report," white paper published by Next Level Purchasing Inc., Moon Township PA, 2005.

24. S. Martin, Kenneth Hartley, and A. Cox, "Public Procurement Directives in the European Union: A Study of Local Authority Purchasing," *Public Administration* 7 (1999), pp. 387–407.

25. Robert L. Janson, *Purchasing Ethical Practices* (Tempe AZ: National Association of Purchasing Management, 1988).

26. "GSA Participatory Contract," *Security Distributing & Marketing* 30 (March 2000).

27. Janson, *Purchising Ethical Practices.*

28. Michael J. Dorsch and Scott W. Kelley, "An Investigation into the Intentions of Purchasing Executives to Reciprocate Vendor Gifts," *Journal of the Academy of Marketing Science* 22 (Fall 1994), pp. 315–27.

## Chapter 4

1. Earl Honeycutt and Lew Kurtzman, *Selling Outside Your Culture Zone* (Dallas: Behavioral Sciences Research Press Inc.).

2. Morry Ghingold and David Wilson, "Buying Center Research and Business Marketing Practice," *Journal of Business Marketing* 13 (1998), pp. 96–108.

3. Margaret Bruce, Lucy Daly, and Neil Towers, "Lean or Agile: A Solution for Supply Chain Management in the Textiles and Clothing Industry?" *International Journal of Operations & Production Management* 24, nos. 1/2 (2004), pp. 151–70.

4. Charles Dominick, "The 2005 Purchasing Skills Report," white paper published by Next Level Purchasing Inc., Moon Township PA, 2005.

5. Catherine N. Axinn, Dawn Deeter-Schmelz, Brian T. Straley, and Earnest J. Zavoral, "How Do the Internet and Internationalization Affect the Buying Center? An Exploratory Case Study," *Advances in International Marketing* 17 (2006), pp. 347–51.

6. Paul Howard and Declan Doyle, "An Examination of Buying Centres in Irish Biotechnology Companies and Its Marketing Implications," *Journal of Business & Industrial Marketing* 21, no. 5 (2006), pp. 266–90.

7. Geok Theng Lau, Mohammed A. Razzaque, and Angeline Ong, "Gatekeeping in Organizational Purchasing: An Empirical Investigation," *Journal of Business & Industrial Marketing* 18, no. 1 (2003), pp. 82–104.

8. Andrew Pettigrew, "The Industrial Purchasing Process as a Political Process," *European Journal of Marketing* 9, no. 1 (1975), pp. 4–19.

9. Howard and Doyle, "An Examination of Buying Centres."

10. Donald W. Barclay and Michele D. Bunn, "Process Heuristics in Organizational Buying: Starting to Fill a Gap," *Journal of Business Research* 59, no. 2 (2006), pp. 186–204.

11. John Wood, "Organizational Configuration as an Antecedent to Buying Centers' Size and Structure," *Journal of Business & Industrial Marketing* 20, no. 6 (2005), pp. 263–75.

12. Das Naryandas, "Tool Kit: Building Loyalty in Business Markets," *Harvard Business Review* (September 2005), pp. 131–39.

13. Robert J. Thomas, "Industrial Market Segmentation on Buying Center Purchase Responsibilities," *Journal of the Academy of Marketing Science* 17, no. 3 (1989), pp. 243–52.

14. Howard and Doyle, "An Examination of Buying Centres."

15. Jeanne Rossomme, "Customer Satisfaction Measurement in a Business-to-Business Context: A Conceptual Framework," *Journal of Business & Industrial Marketing* 18, no. 2 (2003), pp. 179–96.

16. M. Jose Garrido-Samaniego and Jesus Gutierrez-Cillan, "Determinants of Influence and Participation in the Buying Center: An Analysis of Spanish Industrial Companies," *Journal of Business & Industrial Marketing* 19, nos. 4/5 (2004), pp. 320–32.

17. Stefania Borghini, Francesco Golfetto, and Diego Rinallo, "Ongoing Search among Industrial Buyers," *Journal of Business Research* 59, nos. 10/11 (2006), pp. 1151–69.

18. David Tucker and Laurie Jones, "Leveraging the Power of the Internet for Optimal Sourcing," *International Journal of Physical Distribution and Logistics Management* 30 (2000), pp. 255–67.

19. Marjorie Cooper, John F. Tanner, Jr., and Kirk Wakefield, "Industrial Buyers' Risk Aversion and Channel Selection," *Journal of Business Research* 59, no. 6 (2006), pp. 653–61.

20. Ray Hackney, Steve Jones, Andrea Lösch, "Towards an E-Government Efficiency Agenda: The Impact of Information and Communication Behaviour on E-Reverse Auctions in Public Sector Procurement," *European Journal of Information systems* 16 (2007), pp. 178–92.

21. Frank Jacob and Michael Ehret, "Self-Protection vs. Opportunity Seeking in Business Buying Behavior: An Experimental Study," *Journal of Business & Industrial Marketing* 21, no. 2 (2006), pp. 106–23.

## Chapter 5

1. A good summary of Frederick Smith's breakthrough with Federal Express can be heard in George Smith, *Giants of Political Thought: The Audio Classics Series: Joseph Schumpeter and Dynamic Economic Change* (Nashville, TN: Knowledge Products, 1985).

2. "RealDanmark makes real gains with VisualAge Generator,"**www2. software.ibm.com/casestudies/swcs.nsf/customername.**

3. James P. Morgan, "Cessna Charts a Supply Chain Flight Strategy," *Purchasing* 129 (September 7, 2000), pp. 42–61.

4. Katheryn Belyea, "Career Development Q & A. Gene Richter: How to Be a Leader," *Purchasing* (September 7, 2000), pp. 92–93.

5. Francis J. Guillart and Frederick D. Sturdivant, "Spend a Day in the Life of Your Customer," *Harvard Business Review* 72 (January–February, 1994), pp. 116–25. Edward F. McQuarrie, "Taking a Road Trip: Customer Visits Help Companies Recharge Relationships and Pass Competitors," *Marketing Management* 3 (April 1995), pp. 8–21.

6. Ken Main, "Case Studies in Implementation," in *Manufacturer and Automation Protocol/ Technical and Office Protocol: Users Group Summary* (Dearborn, MI: MAPTOP Users Group of Society of Manufacturing Engineers (SME)) 2, no. 3 (1987), pp. 141–47.

7. Identified in Carolyn F. Siegel, "Introducing Marketing Students to Business Intelligence Using Project-Based Learning on the World Wide Web," *Journal of Marketing Education* 22 (August 2000), pp. 90–97.

8. Simon Majaro, *International Marketing: A Strategic Approach to World Markets* (London: George Allen and Unwin, 1982), p. 42, cited in William Shanklin and John Ryans *Essentials of Marketing High Technology* (Lexington, MA: Lexington Books, 1987), p. 154.

9. Robert Bly, *Business to Business Direct Marketing* (Lincolnwood, IL: NTC Business Books, 1994).

10. Dennis H. Gensch, "Targeting the Switchable Industrial Customer," *Marketing Science* 3 (Winter 1984), pp. 41–54.

11. Adrian Slywotzky, *Value Migration* (Boston: Harvard Business School Press, 1996).

12. Jim Laiderman, "A Structured Approach to B2B Segmentation," *Database Marketing and Customer Strategy Management* 13, no. 1 (December 2005), pp. 64–75.

13. Roger Best, *Market-Based Management: Strategies for Growing Customer Value and Profitability* (Upper Saddle River, NJ: Prentice Hall, 2004).

## Chapter 6

1. Michael Dell, quoted in "CEO Says Dell Now Mixes Direct Sales, Retail Focus," *InformationWeek* (May 30, 2007); **http://www.informationweek.com/showArticle.jhtml:jsessionid=RBHG1EJVGYEZIOSNDLPCKHSCJUNN2JVN?articleID=199703645&queryText=dell+corporate.** Other sources include Nanette Byrnes and Peter Burrows, "Where Dell Went Wrong," *BusinessWeek* (February 19, 2007), pp. 62–63; Nanette Byrnes, Peter Burrows, and Louise Lee, "Dark Days at Dell." *BusinessWeek* (September 4, 2006), pp. 26–29; **www.Dell.com;** Michael Dell and C. Friedman, *Direct from Dell* (New York: Harper Collins, 1999).

2. David Aaker, *Strategic Market Management* (New York: John Wiley & Sons, 1992).

3. Frederick Webster, "The Changing Role of Marketing in the Corporation," *Journal of Marketing* 56 (October 1992), pp. 1–17.

4. "HP, Intel Form Broad Alliance on Computers," *The Wall Street Journal* ( June 9, 1994), p. 3.

5. Charles Waltner, "Computer Makers Shift Strategy: Growth of Networks Heightens Reseller Role," *Business Marketing* (June 1996), pp. 1+.

6. Gary Hamel and C. K. Prahalad, *Competing for the Future* (Boston, MA: Harvard Business School Press, 1994).

7. **http://www.hotel-online.com/News/PressReleases1999_4th/Nov99_OmniNewLook.html.**

8. Stephen R. Covey, A. Roger Merrill, and Rebecca R. Merrill, *First Things First* (New York: Simon & Schuster, 1994).

9. Adrian J. Slywotzky, *Value Migration* (Boston: Harvard Business School Press, 1996), p. 73.

10. Michael Porter, "How Competitive Forces Shape Strategy," *Harvard Business Review* 57 (March–April 1979), pp. 137–45; George S. Day, "Assessing Competitive Arenas: Who Are Your Competitors?" in Wharton on Dynamic Competitive Strategy, eds. George S. Day and David J. Reibstein (New York: John Wiley & Sons, 1997); D. Sudharshan, *Marketing Strategy: Relationships, Offerings, Timing & Resource Allocation* (Upper Saddle River NJ: Prentice Hall, Inc., 1995).

11. Cliff Edwards and Spencer Ante, "How Intel Ruined AMD's Happy New Year," *BusinessWeek* (January 24, 2005), p. 35.

12. Richard D'Aveni, *Hypercompetition: Managing the Dynamics of Strategic Maneuvering* (New York: The Free Press, 1994), p. 13.

13. Ibid.

14. Shelby Hunt and Robert Morgan, "The Comparative Advantage Theory of Competition," *Journal of Marketing* 59 (April 1995), p. 11.

15. Stephen L. Vargo and Robert F. Lusch, "Evolving to a New Dominant Logic for Marketing," *Journal of Marketing* 68 (January 2004), p. 1–17.

16. Theodore Levitt, "Marketing Myopia," *Harvard Business Review.* 38 (July–August, 1960), pp. 173–81.

17. Tim McGee, "How to Become a SuperStar Student," video course no. 140, Springfield VA: The Teaching Company.

18. Richard Luecke, *Scuttle Your Ships before Advancing* (New York: Oxford University Press, 1994), pp. 13–33.

19. Calhoun Wick and Lu Stanton Leon, "From Ideas to Action: Creating a Learning Organization," *Human Resource Management* 34, no. 2 (1995), p. 302.

20. "The Ethics Program: 1986–1986," General Dynamics Corporation, Sterling Heights, MI, 1986, quoted in Robert W. Rasberry, "The Conscience of an Organization: The Ethics Office," *Strategy and Leadership* 28 (May–June 2000), p. 18.

21. Robert W. Rasberry, "The Conscience of an Organization: The Ethics Office," *Strategy and Leadership* 28 (May–June 2000), p. 19.

22. "Opportunity and Challenge," Cintas—The Uniform People, Mason, OH 45040. See also: **www.cintas-corp.com/.**

23. Nanette Byrnes, Peter Burrows, and Louise Lee, "Dark Days at Dell," *BusinessWeek* (September 4, 2006), pp. 26–29.

24. Susan Jones, *Creative Strategies in Direct Marketing* (Lincolnwood, IL: NTC Business Books, 1991), p. 22.

25. See Richard Karpinski, "Heavyweights Show Off: Ariba, Commerce One Conferences Highlight Rivals' Aggressive Plans," *B2B* (September 25, 2000), pp. 3, 38. Also see "B2B Marketplaces in the New Economy," *Ariba White Paper* at **www.ariba.com.**

26. Wick and Leon, "From Ideas to Action," pp. 299–311.

27. D'Aveni, *Hyper Competition,* p. 351.

28. Luecke, *Scuttle Your Ships,* p. 103.

## Chapter 7

1. Daniel R. Denison, "What Is the Difference between Organizational Culture and Organizational Climate? A Native's Point of View on a Decade of Paradigm Wars," *Academy of Management Review* 21, no. 3 (1996), pp. 619–54.

2. George S. Day, "The Capabilities of Market-Driven Organizations," *Journal of Marketing* 58 (October 1994), pp. 37–52.

3. Hiu-Kan Wong and Paul D. Ellis, "Is Market Orientation Affected by the Product Life Cycle?" *Journal of World Business* 42 (June 2007), pp. 145–60; Zhen Zhu and Cheryl Nakata, "Reexamining the Link between Customer Orientation and Business Performance: The Role of Information Systems," "*Journal of Marketing Theory and Practice* 15 (Summer 2007), pp. 187–204.

4. Stanley Slater and John C. Narver, "Market Orientation and the Learning Organization," *Journal of Marketing* 59 (July 1995), pp. 63–74.

5. Woody Driggs, "Making the Pivot," *Customer Relationship Management* 11 (June 2007), p. 48.

6. Wong and Ellis, "Is Market Orientation Affected?"

7. Bulent Menguc, Seigyoung Auh, and Eric Shih, "Transformational Leadership and Market Orientation: Implications for the Implementation of Competitive Strategies and Business Unit Performance," *Journal of Business Research* 60 (April 2007) p. 314–30.

8. Olimpia C. Racela, Chawit Chaikittisilpa, and Amonrat Thoumrungroje, "Market Orientation, International Business Relationships and Perceived Export Performance," *International Marketing Review* 24 (2007), pp. 144–59; Kevin Zheng Zhou, James R Brown, Chekitan S. Dev, and Sanjeev Agarwal, "The

Effects of Customer and Competitor Orientations on Performance in Global Markets: A Contingency Analysis," *Journal of International Business Studies* 38 (March 2007), pp. 303–19.

9. Elliot Maltz, William E. Souder, and Ajith Kumar, "Influencing R&D/Marketing Integration and the Use of Information by R&D Managers: Intended and Unintended Effects of Managerial Actions," *Journal of Business Research* 52 (2001), pp. 69–82.

10. Michael D. Hutt, "Cross-Functional Relationships in Marketing," *Journal of the Academy of Marketing Science* 23, no. 4 (1995), pp. 351–57.

11. Mark Ingebretsen, "Mass Appeal: Ross Controls Builds Customers for Life with Mass Customization," *Business Marketing* (March 1997), pp. 1, 14, and 52; "Over 80 Years of Leadership: Ross" (2005), **http://www.rosscontrols.com/PDFliterature/ROSS_history_book.pdf.**

12. Paul Konignendijk "Dependence and Conflict between Production and Sales," *Industrial Marketing Management* 22 (1993), pp. 161–67.

13. Christopher Hosford, "Curing the Sales-Marketing Disconnect," *Sales & Marketing management* (June 2006), pp. 38–41.

14. William Strahle, Rosann L. Spiro, and Frank Acito, "Marketing and Sales: Strategic Alignment and Functional Implementation," *Journal of Personal Selling and Sales Management* XVI (Winter, 1996), pp. 1–20.

15. Hutt, "Cross-Functional Relationships." Hosford

16. Kristian Moller and Arto Rahala, "Organizing Marketing in Industrial High-Tech Firms," *Industrial Marketing Management* 28 (1999), pp. 521–35.

17. Paul Matthyssens and Wesley J. Johnston, "Marketing and Sales: Optimization of a Neglected Relationship," *Journal of Business & Industrial Marketing* 21 (2006), pp. 338–49.

18. George Huber, "Organizational Learning: The Contributing Processes and the Literatures," *Organizational Science* 2 (February 1991), pp. 88–115.

19. William Bakers and James Sinkula, "The Synergistic Effect of Market Orientation and Learning Orientation on Organizational Performance," *Journal of the Academy of Marketing Science* 27 (Fall 1999), pp. 411–27; Paul D Ellis, "Distance, Dependence and Diversity of Markets: Effects on Market Orientation," *Journal of International Business Studies* 38 (May 2007), pp. 374–86.

20. "The Innovator's Advantage," White paper published by Accenture, 2004.

21. Edwin A. Locke and Vinod K. Jain, "Organizational Learning and Continuous Improvement," *International Journal of Organizational Analysis* 3 (January 1995), pp. 45–68; Graham Leask and David Parker, "Strategic Group Theory: Review, Examination and Application in the UK Pharmaceutical Industry," *Journal of Management Development* 25 (2006), pp. 386–408; Martin J. Eppler, "A Comparison between Concept Maps, Mind Maps, Conceptual Diagrams, and Visual Metaphors as Complementary Tools for Knowledge Construction and Sharing," *Information Visualization* 5 (Autumn 2006), pp. 202–19.

22. Ian Clarke, Masahide Horita, and William Mackaness (2000), "The Spatial Knowledge of Decision Makers: Capturing and Interpreting Group Insight Using a Composite Cognitive Map,"

23. John Humble, David Jackson, and Alan Thomson, "The Strategic Power of Corporate Values," *Long Range Planning* 24, no. 6 (1994), pp. 28–42.

24. Lanyin Zhang and Malcolm Smith, "Customer Profitability Analysis," *Financial Management* (May 2006), pp. 30–1.

25. Anonymous, "Marketers' Skills Lag Behind Organizations' Needs," **www.marketingpower.com/content-printer-friendly.php?&Item_ID=143133,** accessed January 14, 2007.

## Chapter 8

International Review of Retail, Distribution, and Consumer Research* 10, no. 3 pp. 265–285.

1. Stephen L. Vargo and Robert F. Lusch, "The Four Service Marketing Myths: Remnants of a Goods-Based, Manufacturing Model," *Journal of Service Research* 6 (May 2004), pp. 324–35.

2. Saara Brax, "A Manufacturer Becoming Service Provider—Challenges and a Paradox," *Managing Service Quality* 15 (2005), pp. 142–55.

3. Wilfred Amaldoss and Amnon Rapoport, "Collaborative Product and Market Development: Theoretical Implications and Experimental Evidence," *Marketing Science* 24 (Summer 2005) pp. 396–414.

4. J. F. Tanner, Jr., and L. B. Chonko, "Using Trade Shows throughout the Product Life Cycle," Center for Exhibition Industry Research Report, 1996; Ari Buchalter and Humam Sakhnini, "Fighting Cannibalization," *The McKinsey Quarterly* (2006) pp. 12–24.

5. S. Edgett, D. Shipley, and G. Forbes, "Japanese and British Companies Compared: Contributing Factors to Success in NPD," *Journal of Product Innovation Management* (1992), pp. 3–10.

6. R. Phillips, K. Neaile, and T. Broughton, "A Comparative Study of Six Stage-Gate Approaches to Product Development," *Integrated Manufacturing Systems* (1999), pp. 289–297.

7. This section is based on J. H. Flournoy, "Organizing and Getting New Product Ideas," in *Product Planning,* ed. A. E. Spitz (Princeton, NJ: Auerbach Publishers, 1972).

8. B. Donath, "Beyond the 'Same Old, Same Old,'" *ISBM Insights,* no. 8 (1998).

9. Eric von Hipple, *The Sources of Innovation* (New York: Oxford University Press, 1988).

10. Stephanie Overby, "The Little Banks That Could; Faced with growing competition from the big guys, the little engine that could-in this case, small and midsize banks-are using CRM to make it over the mountain." *CIO* 15, no. 16 (2002), p. 1.

11. M. J. Liberatore and A. C. Stylianou, "Expert Support Systems for New Product Development Decision Making: A Modeling Framework and Applications," *Management Science* 41 (1995), pp. 1296–1314.

12. M. Montoya-Weiss and T. M. Driscoll, "From Experience: Applying Performance Support Technoloy in the Fuzzy Front End, "*Journal of Product Innovation Management* (March 2000), pp. 143–162.

14. Anthony W. Ulwick, "Turn Customer Input into Innovation," *Harvard Business Review* (January 2002), pp. 91–97.

15. R. Mukherjee, "Driving to Please," *The Economic Times* (July 2000), p. CD2.

16. K. Atuahene-Gima, "Market Orientation and Innovation," *Journal of Business Research* 35 (1996), pp. 93–103.

17. A. Gupta, K. Brockhoff, and U. Weisenfeld, "Making Trade-Offs in the New Product Development Process: A German/US Comparison," *Journal of Product Innovation Management* 9 (1992), pp. 11–18.

18. Roger A. Kerin, P. Rajan Varadarajan, and R. A. Peterson, "First-Mover Advantage: A Synthesis, Conceptual Framework, and Research Propositions," *Journal of Marketing* 56 no. 4 (1992), pp. 33–52; P. VanderWerf and J. F. Mahon, "Meta-Analysis of the Impact of Research Methods on Findings of First-Mover Advantage," *Management Science* 43 (November 1997), pp. 1510–19.

19. A. J. Campbell and R. G. Cooper, "Do Customer Partnerships Improve New Product Success Rates?" *Industrial Marketing Management* 28 (1999), pp. 507–19.

20. Lisa Gschwandtner, "The Remarkability Factor." *Selling Power* (November/December 2006), p. 61.

21. R. G. Cooper and E. J. Kleinschmidt, "Success Factors in Product Innovation," *Industrial Marketing Management* 16, (1987), pp. 215–23.

22. William E. Baker and James M. Sinkula, "Does Market Orientation Facilitate Balanced Innovation Programs? An Organizational Learning Perspective," *Journal of Product Innovation Management* 24 (July 2007), pp. 316–34.

23. This section is based primarily on S. J. Towner, "Four Ways to Accelerate New Product Development," *Long Range Planning* 27, no. 2 (1994), pp. 57–65.

24. W. He, X. G. Ming, Q. F. Ni, W. F. Lu, and B. H. Lee, "A Unified Product Structure Management for Enterprise Business Process Integration throughout the Product Lifecycle," *International Journal of Production Research* 44 (May 1,2006) pp. 1757–74.

25. Bo Glasgow, "PLM Software Vendors Formulate Strategies for Process Industries," *Chemical Market Reporter* (September 15, 2003), pp. 20–22.

26. M. Swink, C. Sandvig, and V. Mabert, "Customizing Concurrent Engineering Processes: Five Case Studies," *Journal of Product Innovation Management* 13 (1996), pp. 229–44.

27. S. Kitchell, "Corporate Culture, Environmental Adaptation, and Innovation Adoption: A Qualitative/Quantitative Approach," *Journal of the Academy of Marketing Science* 23 (summer 1995), pp. 159–205; Rajeev K Tyagi, "New Product Introductions and Failures under Uncertainty," *International Journal of Research in Marketing* 23 (June 2006), pp. 199–212.

28. G. Lynn, K. Abel, W. Valentine, and R. Wright, "Key Factors in Increasing Speed to Market and Improving New Product Success Rates," *Industrial Marketing Management* 28 (1999), pp. 319–26; Gary S. Lynn and Alie E. Akgun, "Launch Your New Products/Services Better, Faster," *Research Technology Management* 46 (May/June 2003) pp. 21–26.

29. P. F. Drucker, "The Discipline of Innovation," *Harvard Business Review* (September–October 1985), pp. 67–72.

30. Remco Prins and Peter C. Verhoef, "Marketing Communication Drivers of Adoption Timing of a New E-Service among Existing Customers," *Journal of Marketing* 71 (April 2007), pp. 169–83.

31. P. L. Link, "Keys to New Product Success and Failure," *Industrial Marketing Management* 16 (1987), pp. 109–18.

32. M. Barrier, "Customers Need Training, Too," *Nation's Business* (December 1995), pp. 74R–75R.

## Chapter 9

1. Background from Hochwald Lambeth, "Tuning In to the Right Channel," *Sales and Marketing Management* (March 2000), pp. 67–74. Quotation from p. 70. See also **http://biz.yahoo.com/p/n/neb.html; http://www.nebs.com/nebsEcat/about/index.jsp; http://www.deluxe.com/dlxab/deluxe-business-units.jsp.**

2. Louis P. Bucklin, *A Theory of Distribution Channel Structure* (Berkeley, CA: IBER Special Publications, 1996).

3. "Outsourcing's Rising Tide," *Chemical Engineering* (April 1997), pp. 28–31.

4. James Hlavacek and Tommy McCuistion, "Industrial Distributors: When, Who, and How?" *Harvard Business Review* 61 (March–April 1983), pp. 96–101.

5. Shantanu Dutta, Mark Bergen, Jan Heide, and George John, Understanding Dual Distribution: The Case of Reps and House Accounts," *Journal of Law, Economics, & Organization* 11 (April 1995), pp. 189–204.

6. Erin Anderson and Barton Weitz, "Determinants of Continuity in Conventional Industrial Channel Dyads," *Marketing Science* 8 (Fall 1989), pp. 310–23; Jan Heide and George John, "The Role of Dependence Balancing in Safeguarding Transaction-Specific Assets in Conventional Channels," *Journal of Marketing* 52 (January 1988), pp. 20–37.

7. Lou E. Pelton, David Strutton, and James R. Lumpkin, *Marketing Channels* (Boston: McGraw-Hill Irwin, 2002).

8. The MAC Group, now known as Gemeni Consulting, Inc., *The Planning Forum: Differentiation through Channel Strategy: Concepts and Practice* (May 1, 1990).

9. Adam J. Fein and Erin Anderson, "Patterns of Credible Commitments: Territory and Brand Selectivity in Industrial Distribution Channels," *Journal of Marketing* 61 (April 1997), pp. 19–35.

10. See Peter Pazmany, "Sun's Virtual Network," *Supply Chain Management Review* (November–December 2000), pp. 56–61; **http://www.sun.com/service/serviceplans/sunspectrum/; http://www.prognostics.com/.**

11. Mark Bergen, Shantanu Dutta, and Orville Walker, "Agency Relationships in Marketing: A Review of the Implications and Applications of Agency and Related Theories," *Journal of Marketing* 56 (July 1992), pp. 1–24.

12. Robert Ping, "The Effects of Satisfaction and Structural Constraints on Retailer Exiting, Voice, Loyalty, Opportunism, and Neglect," *Journal of Retailing* 69 (Fall 1993), pp. 320–52.

13. John Graham, "The Problem-Solving Approach to Negotiations in Industrial, Marketing," *Journal of Business Research* 14, (1986), pp. 549–66, Harold H. Kelley, "A Classroom Study of the Dilemmas in Interpersonal Negotiations," in *Strategic Interaction and Conflict,* ed. K. Archibald (Berkeley: Berkeley Institute of International Studies, University of California, 1966).

14. "Looking Back—1996 Was an Unusual Year: 1997 Doesn't Seem to Be Much Different," *Agency Sales Magazine* (May 1997), pp. 22–23.

15. James Anderson and James Narus, "Turn Your Distributors into Partners, *Harvard Business Review* 64 (March–April 1986), pp. 66–71.

16. Louis Stern, Adel El-Ansary, and Anne Caughlin, *Marketing Channels* (Upper Saddle River, NJ: Prentice Hall, 1996), p. 318.

17. Ibid., p. 252.

18. Brett Boyle, F. Robert Dwyer, Robert Bobicheaux, and James Simpson, "Influence Strategies in Marketing Channels: Measures and Use in Different Relationship Structures," *Journal of Marketing Research* 29 (November 1992), pp. 462–71.

19. Tom Stundza, "Service Centers Eye Processing Upgrades," *Purchasing* (May 1, 1997), pp. 32B1–B3.

## Chapter 10

1. K. Cleland, "A Lot of Talk, Little Action on IMC," *Business Marketing,* 1, no. 30 (March 1995); T. Duncan, "Is Your Marketing Communications Integrated?" *Advertising Age* 65, no. 4 (January 1997), p. 26; L. Eagle and P. Kitchen, "IMC, Brand Communications, and Corporate Culture," *European Journal of Marketing* 34 (2000), pp. 667–86.

2. Arens and Boveé (1994).

3. Center for Exhibition Industry Research, *The Power of Exhibitions,* Center for Exhibition Industry Research Report, 1996.

4. J. F. Tanner Jr., L. B. Chonko, and J. McKee, "Behind the Booth," *Marketing Management,* 3, no. 1 (1994), pp. 40–43.

5. R. Srivastava, T. Shervani, and L. Fahey, "Marketing, Business Processes and Shareholder Value: An Organizationally Embedded View of Marketing and the Discipline of Marketing," *Journal of Marketing* (Special Issue) (1999) pp. 168–179.

6. R. Chitwood, "Keeping Customers at Any Cost?" *Track Selling Times* (November 2000), p. 1.

7. George E. Belch and Michael A. Belch. *Advertising and Promotion: An Integrated Marketing Communications Perspective* (Boston: McGraw Hill/Irwin, 2004), pp. 219–20.

## Chapter 11

1. Mike Bradbury and Neal Kissel, "Investment in Marketing: The Allocation Conundrum," *The Journal of Business Strategy* 27 (2006) pp. 17–27; Rex Briggs, "Marketers Who Measure the Wrong Thing Get Faulty Answers," *Journal of Advertising Research* 46 (December 2006), pp. 462–74.

2. Shintaro Okazaki, Charles R Taylor, and Shaoming Zou, "Advertising Standardization's Positive Impact on the Bottom Line: A Model of When and How Standardization Improves Financial and Strategic Performance," *Journal of Advertising* 35 (Fall 2006), pp. 17–33.

3. J. David Lichtenthal, Vivek Yadav, and Naveen Donthu, "Outdoor Advertising for Business Markets," *Industrial Marketing Management* 35 (2006), pp. 236–47.

4. J. F. Tanner, Jr., T. Ponzurick, and L. B. Chonko, "Promotional Activities as Learning Activities: An Analysis of Trade Show Attendees," Research Monograph, Exhibit Management Educational Foundation of the Trade Show Exhibitors' Association, 1997.

5. DeLoitte & Touche Consulting Group, *The Role of Exhibitions in the Marketing Mix.* Available from the Center for Exhibition Industry Research (see the note above).

6. S. Gopalakrishna, G. L. Lilien, J. D. Williams, and I. K. Sequeira, "Do Trade Shows Pay Off?" *Journal of Marketing* 59, (1995), pp. 75–83.

7. E. Harris, "The Monitor," *Sales & Marketing Management* (2000), pp. 32–33.

8. Francis Farrelly, Pascale Quester, and Stephen A Greyser, "Defending the Co-Branding Benefits of Sponsorship B2B Partnerships: The Case of Ambush Marketing," *Journal of Advertising Research* 45 (2005), pp. 339–62.

## Chapter 12

1. Roger, Slavens, "E-mail 'Clown'-ing Nets Response from HR," *B to B's Vertical Insight: A Guide to Marketing in Vertical Industries* (June 25, 2007), p. 25.

2. "Direct Marketing Flow Chart," *Direct Marketing* (May 1997), p. 3.

3. F. Robert Dwyer, "Direct Marketing in the Quest for Competitive Advantage," *Journal of Direct Marketing* 1 (Winter 1987), pp. 15–22.

4. Rose Harper, *Mailing List Strategies: A Guide to Mail Success* (New York: McGraw-Hill Book Company, 1986).

5. Both figures reported in the *Marketing News 2007 Marketing Fact Book,* American Marketing Association (July 15, 2007), p. 32.

6. Bernard Joyce, "Direct Marketing to Business," Presentation at the University of Cincinnati, 1996.

7. Roger Slavens, "Marketing to Foodservice," *B to B's Vertical Insight: A Guide to Marketing in Vertical Industries* (June 25, 2007), p. 18.

8. Debra Ray, "1996 Caples Award Winners," *Direct Marketing* (March 1997), pp. 13–17.

9. Bob Stone and John Wyman, *Successful Telemarketing* (Lincolnwood, IL: NTC Business Books, 1992), p. 183.

10. See **http://www.youtube.com/watch?v=_EAVf3exA_0.**

11. Ernan Roman, *Integrated Direct Marketing* (Lincolnwood, IL: NTC Business Books, 1995), pp. 46–47.

12. Price Waterhouse, *Best Practices in Interactive Marketing: A DMA Management Guide* (New York: Direct Marketing Association, 1997).

13. Quinn, "How Leading Edge Companies Are Marketing," p. 44; John Hagel, "Marketplace: Net Gain: Expanding Markets through Virtual Communities," *Journal of Interactive Marketing* 13 (Winter 1999), p. 59; See www.agriculture.com. Also see John Hagel, "Marketplace: Net Gain: Expanding Markets through Virtual Communities," *Journal of Interactive Marketing* 13 (Winter 1999), pp. 55–65.

14. See Tode Chantal, "Blogging Boosts Product Sales for Steve Spangler Science," *DM News* (June 18, 2007), p. 4; Paul Gillin, "Looking at the Best of Breed Blogs," *B to B* (June 4, 2007), p. 11.

## Chapter 13

1. "Confronting the Talent Crunch," A Manpower White Paper (2007), Milwaukee WI: Manpower Inc.

2. J. B. DeConninck and D. J. Good, "Perceptual Differences of Sales Practitioners and Students Concerning Ethical Behavior," *Journal of Business Ethics* (Fall 1989), pp. 667–86.

3. Much of this section is based on B. A. Weitz, S. B. Castleberry, and J. F. Tanner, Jr., *Selling: Building Partnerships* 6th ed. (Burr Ridge, IL: McGraw-Hill Irwin 2007), Chapters 13 and 17.

4. T. Vavra, *Aftermarketing* (Homewood, IL: BusinessOne Irwin, 1992).

5. J. P. Morgan and S. Cayer, "Working with World Class Suppliers: True Believers," *Purchasing* (August 1992), pp. 50–52.

6. Ben Shaw-Ching Liu, Nicholas C. Petruzzi, and D. Sudharsan, "A Service Effort Allocation Model for Assessing Customer Lifetime Value in Service Marketing," *Journal of Services Marketing* 21 (2007), pp. 24–35; René Y. Darmon, "A Joint Assessment of Optimal Sales Force Sizes and Sales Call Guidelines: A Management-Oriented Tool," *Canadian Journal of Administrative Sciences* 22 (September 2005), pp. 206–19.

7. R. Carey, "Help-Wanted—Now!" *Sales & Marketing Management* (March 1997), pp. 30–31.

8. S. Sager, G. McWilliams, and R. Hof, "IBM Leans on Its Sale Force," *BusinessWeek* (February 7, 1994), p. 110.

## Chapter 14

1. A. D. H. Kaplan, Joel Dirlam, and Robert Lanzillotti, *Pricing in Big Business* (Washington, DC: The Brookings Institution, 1958).

2. Gerald Smith, "Managerial Pricing Orientation: The Process of Making Pricing Decisions," *Pricing Strategy & Practice* 3, no. 3 (1995), pp. 28–39.

3. Our model draws on Kent Monroe and Tridib Mazumdar, "Pricing Decision Models: Recent Developments and Research Opportunities," in *Issues in Pricing Theory and Research,* ed. Timothy Devinney (Lexington, MA: Lexington Books, 1988), pp. 361–88.

4. Arch Woodside, "Making Better Pricing Decisions in Business Marketing," in *Advances in Business Marketing and Purchasing,* ed. Arch Woodside (Greenwich, CT: JAI Press, 1994), pp. 139–83.

5. J. A. Howard and W. M. Morganroth, "Information Processing Model of Executive Decisions, *Management Science* 14, (1992) 416–28.

6. Theodore Levitt, *The Marketing Imagination* (New York: The Free Press, 1983).

7. *Monsanto Co. v. Spray-Rite Service Corp.,* 104 U.S. 1464 (1984).

8. *Texaco, Inc v. Ricky Hasbrouck, dba Rick's Texaco, et al.* 946 US 942 (1990), quoted in Louis Stern, Adel El-Ansary, and Anne Coughlan, *Marketing Channels* (Upper Saddle River, NJ: Prentice Hall, 1996), p. 363.

9. G. T. Savage, J. D. Blair, and R. J. Sorenson, "Consider Both Relationship and Substance when Negotiating Strategically," *Academy of Management Executive* 3 (1989), pp. 37–48.

10. Roy Lewicki, David Saunders, and John Minton, *Essentials of Negotiation* (Burr Ridge, IL: Irwin, 1997).

11. Das Narayandas, John Quelch, and Gordon Swartz, "Prepare Your Company for Global Pricing," *Sloan Management Review* 42 (Fall 2000), pp. 61–70.

12. Elliot Ross, "Making Money with Proactive Pricing," *Harvard Business Review* 62 (November–December 1984), pp. 145–55.

13. David Hanno, "Locklheed Martin: Negotiators Inc.," *Purchasing* (February 5, 2004), pp. 27–30.

## Chapter 15

1. Eric Fang, Kenneth R. Evans, and Timothy D. Landry, "Control Systems' Effect on Attributional Processes and Sales Outcomes: A Cybernetic Information-Processing Perspective," *Journal of the Academy of Marketing Science* 33 (2005), pp. 553–74.

2. Allison Enright, "Real-Time Analytics Boost ROI, Accountability," *Marketing News* (October 1,2006), pp. 20, 24; Diana Woodburn, "Marketing Measurement Action Research Model," *Measuring Business Excellence* 10 (2006), pp. 50–71.

3. P. Hepworth, "Weighing It Up—A Literature Review for the Balanced Scorecard," *Journal of Management Development* 17, no. 8 (1998), pp. 559–63.

4. R. W. Keidel, "Rethinking Organizational Design," *Academy of Management Executive* 8, no. 4 (1994), pp. 12–30.

5. B. Anderson, T. Fagerhaug, S. Randmael, J. Schuldmaier, and J. Prenninger, "Benchmarking Supply Chain Management: Finding Best Practices," *Journal of Business and Industrial Marketing* 14 (1999), pp. 378–89.

6. Carl McDaniel and Roger Gates, *Contemporary Marketing Research* 7th ed. (Hoboken NJ: John Wiley, 2007).

7. F. Luthans, M. J. Rubach, and P. Marsnik, "Going beyond Total Quality: The Characteristics, Techniques, and Measures of Learning Organizations," *International Journal of Organizational Analysis* 3 (January 1995), pp. 24–44.

## Chapter 16

1. See Jim Kerstetter, "A Fruitful Relationship," *BusinessWeek,* "E.BIZ" (November 20, 2000), pp. EB93-96; **http://en.wikipedia.org/wiki/BEA_Systems;** Eric Knorr, "BEA's Plumtree Buy Adds Missing Piece to SOA Plan," *InfoWorld* (August 29, 2005), **http://www.infoworld.com/article/05/08/29/35NNbeaplum_1.html.**

2. T. Levitt, *The Marketing Imagination* (New York: The Free Press), p. 111.

3. B. B. Jackson, *Winning and Keeping Industrial Customers* (Lexington, MA: Lexington Books, 1985).

4. J. Anton, *Customer Relationship Management: Making Hard Decisions with Soft Numbers* (Upper Saddle River, NJ: Prentice-Hall, 1996), p. 12.

5. R. Desatnick and D. Detzel, *Managing to Keep the Customer* (San Francisco, CA: Jossey-Bass Publishers, 1993).

6. James Carbone, "EMS Providers Expand Menu," *Purchasing* (May 20, 2004), pp. 37–42.

7. C. Kaydo, "Making an Impact," *Sales and Marketing Management* (September 1996), pp. 89–94.

8. P. Ferrell, "Eats, Ethics and Economics," *Purchasing* (December 1965), p. 5.

9. P. Halvorson and W. Rudelius, "Is There a Free Lunch," *Journal of Marketing,* 41 (January 1977), pp. 44–49.

10. R. Morgan and S. Hunt, "The Commitment-Trust Theory of Relationship Marketing," *Journal of Marketing* 58 (July 1994), pp. 20–38.

11. Robert W. Palmatier, Rajiv P. Dant, Dhruv Grewal, and Kenneth R. Evans, "Factors Influencing the Effectiveness of Relationship Marketing: A Meta-Analysis," *Journal of Marketing* 70 (October 2006), pp. 136–153.

12. G. Gundlach and P. Murphy, "Ethical and Legal Foundations of Relational Marketing Exchanges," *Journal of Marketing* 57 (October 1993), pp. 35–46.

13. T. Palay, "Comparative Institutional Economics: The Governance of Rail Freight Contracting," *Journal of Legal Studies* 13 (June 1984), pp. 265–287.

14. J. Bradach and R. Eccles, "Price, Authority and Trust: From Ideal Types to Plural Forms," *Annual Review of Sociology* 15 (1989), pp. 97–118.

15. J. Mohr and J. R. Nevin, "Communication Strategies in Marketing Channels: A Theoretical Perspective," *Journal of Marketing* 54 (October 1990), pp. 36–51.

16. C. Furlong, *Marketing for Keeps* (New York: John Wiley & Sons, Inc., 1993).

17. Ibid., p. 51.

18. J. Anton, *Customer Relationship Management: Making Hard Decisions with Soft Numbers* (Upper Saddle River, NJ: Prentice Hall, 1996), p. 12.

19. R. Kisel, "Chrysler: Suppliers Hit Savings Goal Early," *Automotive News* (May 1997), p. 6.

20. See **http://www.groundheaters.com/job_studies/tilt_up_wall_curing.**

21. C. Kaydo, "Making an Impact," *Sales and Marketing Management* (September 1996), pp. 89–94.

22. C. Furlong, *Marketing for Keeps* (New York: John Wiley & Sons, Inc., 1993), p. 90.

23. Adapted from H. Scott, "Winning Back a Lost Account," *Nation's Business* (July 1996), p. 31R.

24. Michael J. Dennis and Ajit Kambil, "Service Management: Building Profits after the Sale," *Supply Chain Management Review* 7 (January–February 2003), pp. 42–48.

# Index

Note: Page numbers in *italics* denote figures and exhibits.